A Comprehensive Introduction to SolidWorks 2013

Godfrey Onwubolu, Ph.D.

ISBN: 978-1-58503-809-1

Publications

SDC Publications

P.O. Box 1334
Mission KS 66222
(913) 262-2664
www.SDCpublications.com

Publisher: Stephen Schroff

The author and publisher of this book have used their best efforts in preparing this book. These efforts include the development, research and testing of the material presented. The author and publisher shall not be liable in any event for incidental or consequential damages with, or arising out of, the furnishing, performance, or use of the material.

Printed and bound in the United States of America.

A Comprehensive Introduction to SolidWorks 2013

Godfrey C. Onwubolu, Ph.D.

Preface

This textbook, **A Comprehensive Introduction to SolidWorks** is written to assist students in colleges and universities, designers, engineers and professionals interested in using SolidWorks for practical applications. This textbook pitches at an intermediate level for SolidWorks users, although it has been so organized in such a way that earlier chapters meet the needs of newcomers.

The textbook is divided into three parts. Part I covers the introductory principles of SolidWorks: simple and advanced-part modeling, assembly modeling, drawing, configuration and design tables, and part modeling with equation driven curves. Part II covers the intermediate principles of SolidWorks: reverse engineering, top-down design, surface modeling, toolboxes and design libraries, animation, and rendering. Part III covers the practice of SolidWorks. Applications are in the areas of manufacturing processes, mechanical systems, electro-mechanical systems, and engineering analysis. The sections on manufacturing processes include the design of molds, sheet metal parts, dies, and weldments. The sections on mechanical systems include aspects of routing such as piping and tubing, power transmission systems, and mechanism design. The section on engineering analysis covers finite element analysis, FEA.

Newcomers to SolidWorks should concentrate on Part I of this textbook. Intermediate users of SolidWorks should move on to Part II of this textbook. Part III is the meeting point for putting the principles learnt from the previous Parts into practice, in dealing with specific industry-based applications. Organizing the textbook in this way helps students, designers, engineers and professionals to decide how to optimize their strategy in covering the contents of the textbook; this is also useful to instructors in planning their delivery strategy depending on their course outlines. The ANSI and ISO standards have been used in this textbook.

This textbook is written using a hands-on approach in which students can follow the steps described in each chapter to model parts, assemble parts, and produce drawings. They create applications on their own with little assistance from their instructors during each teaching session or in the computer laboratory. This textbook has a significant number of pictorial descriptions of the steps that a student should follow. This approach makes it easy for users of the textbook to work on their own as they use the steps described as guides. Instructional support is also provided, including SolidWorks files for all models, drawings, applications, and answers to end-of-chapter questions.

The principles and exercises presented in Parts I & II have been tested in the SolidWorks courses that the author taught in Ontario institutions, Canada. All the examples in this textbook have been solved by the author. Several practical exercises are included at the end of chapters.

The 2013 version of this textbook has two new chapters included, with their highlights being:
- Geometric Dimensioning & Tolerancing (GD&T)—Chapter 32
- Evaluating the Cost of Machined Parts—Chapter 33

Another enhancement of the 2013 version of this textbook is the inclusion of the following additional features of sectional views in the second half of Chapter 9—Part and Assembly Drawings-CSWA Preparation:
- Full Section View
- Half Section View
- Notched Offset Section View
- Aligned Section View

SolidWorks 2013 now addresses customers' need to include sectional views other than only full section which it has supported previously. This means that the enhanced SolidWorks 2013 and later will compete with other CAD packages that support other options of section views other than the full section.

Other enhancements include additional end-of-chapter problems. It is hoped that students and instructors will find this current edition more useful than the earlier one.

Acknowledgements

For this edition, valuable feedbacks from professors who adopted the 2012 version of this textbook for their courses especially in USA have helped to enhance the current 2013 version. These feedbacks are greatly appreciated. This book is now in its third release as it keeps pace with the SolidWorks software. I would especially like to thank Stephen Schroff and Mary Schmidt of SDC Press for their helpful suggestions and assistance throughout this book project, especially with their motivation and publishing style, as well as assisting me with the contact with SolidWorks for additional resources. Special thanks to SolidWorks Inc. for providing the resources that enabled me to get this version of the textbook earlier than planned to the readers. Dr Ron Binda continued to support the second release of this textbook; his role is greatly appreciated. Some academic colleagues at different institutions who evaluated this textbook have given me valuable and encouraging feedbacks, and their efforts are greatly appreciated. My wife, Ngozi, and our children are greatly appreciated. My wife, Ngozi, shared some very challenging times with me during the early stage of my learning SolidWorks and when I contemplated writing the first version of this textbook as well as during the current revision. Without the role that members of my family played, this textbook project would not have succeeded.

About the Author

Dr. Godfrey Onwubolu teaches **computer-aided design (CAD)** and **engineering analysis using SolidWorks** as well as *Applied Mechanics* and *Engineering Mechanics* where he currently applies SolidWorks very extensively. He holds a BEng degree in mechanical engineering, and both an MSc and PhD from Aston University, Birmingham, England, where he first developed a geometric modeling system for his graduate studies. He worked in a number of manufacturing companies in the West Midlands, England, and he was a professor of manufacturing engineering, having taught courses in engineering design and manufacturing for several years. He has published several books with international publishing companies, such as Imperial College Press, Elsevier, and Springer-Verlag, and has published over 130 articles in international journals and refereed international conferences. His most recent application of SolidWorks to Mechanical Engineering Sciences is through his accepted book, titled *"Applied Mechanics with SolidWorks"* published by Imperial College Press, due in 2013. He is an active Senior Member of both the American Society of Manufacturing Engineers (ASMfgE) and the American Institute of Industrial Engineers (IIE).

Godfrey Onwubolu
Toronto, Canada
Spring 2013

Dedication

This book is dedicated entirely to God who did *solid works* in creation of everyone and everything in existence and in sustaining life. I owe Him all that I have because all that I have comes from Him.

References

[1] Planchard, D. C., and M. P. Planchard, Engineering Design with SolidWorks 2010, Schroff Development Corporation, 2010.
[2] Planchard, D. C., and M. P. Planchard, A Commands Guide for SolidWorks 2009, Thomson/Delmar Learning, 2009.
[3] Tickoo, S., and Sandeep, D., SolidWorks 2009 for Designers, CADCIM Technologies, 2009.
[4] Lombard, M., SolidWorks 2009, Wiley Publishing Inc, 2009.
[5] Howard, W. E., and Musto, J. C, Solid Modeling Using SolidWorks 2008, McGraw-Hill Ryerson, 2008.
[6] Engineering Design and Graphics with SolidWorks, Bethune, J. D. Prentice-Hall, 2009
[7] Applied Mechanics with SolidWorks, Onwubolu, G. C., Imperial College Press, Due 2013

Table of Contents

PART II: Intermediate Engineering Design Principles with SolidWorks

Chapter 1
Introduction

Objectives:

In this chapter you will learn:

- The Computer-Aided Engineering (CAE) framework
- The role of SolidWorks within the context of the CAE framework
- The background of SolidWorks
- How to start a SolidWorks session
- The SolidWorks User Interface
- How to set the Document Options
- How to set up a good File Management
- How to start a New Document in SolidWorks
- How to model your first Part
- About useful SolidWorks Resources

SOLIDWORKS WITHIN THE CONTEXT OF COMPUTER-AIDED ENGINEERING FRAMEWORK

Computer-Aided Engineering (CAE), which is the performance of engineering tasks or functions with the aid of a computer, has experienced rapid changes over the years. Engineering is a wide-ranging multi-disciplinary subject area and, consequently, so is the subject of computer-aided engineering. In order for us to cover the area in its entirety, we must examine the ways in which a computer can assist the mechanical, manufacturing, electrical, electronics, chemical, aeronautical and civil engineer. In this book, we concentrate on those areas of mechanical- and manufacturing-engineering, which can benefit from computer-aided engineering functions (Figure 1-1). Recent advances have resulted in concurrent engineering (CE) in which it is no longer necessary to go in a sequential manner from one step to the other within the product development cycle; thereby resulting in shortening the time from design conceptualization to production and shipping to the customer.

The first generation CAD packages were simply 2D computer-aided drafting programs which simply mimicked drafting boards. Several views had to be created as they would be on the drafting boards. Designers had to think in terms of 2D models, while having 3D models in mind. During my graduate studies at Aston University, the commonly available CAD packages were of 2D-type. Then, I was involved in developing an *Engineering Drawing Interpreter*; what that simply means, is a program that takes multiple 2D views of an object and interpret them to realize a 3D model as it would appear in reality. First, these 2D CAD packages were very limited in what they could do, and tedious to use. There was therefore, an obvious need for the development of 3D geometric modelers. The development of early 3D geometric modelers will now be briefly reviewed.

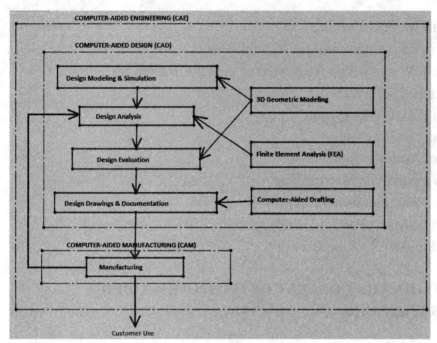

Figure 1-1 Computer-Aided Engineering Framework

Three-dimensional (3D) Wireframes

The development of early 3D geometric modelers commenced with 3D Wireframes, which are models made up of points and edges in form of straight lines connecting between appropriate points. There were no well-organized faces until the edges were interpreted to form closed-loop faces, which in turn defined enclosed volumes. Again at Aston University, I was involved in developing a *General Surface Geometric Modeler*; the surfaces were simply defined by mesh of edges which had to be interpreted to form closed loops. Computation of the overall surface areas and inertial properties of simple/complex general surfaces depended on the interpretation of the meshes describing the surfaces.

Constructive Solid Geometry (CSG)

In this representation, an object is described in terms of elementary shapes, or primitives. The CGS representation is based on a two-level scheme. On the second level, bounded primitive volumes are combined by Boolean set operations. The leaf nodes are either primitive leaves which represent subsets of three-dimensional Euclidean spaces (solid primitive shapes sized and positioned in space), or transformation leaves which contain the defining arguments of rigid motions. The branch nodes are operators, which may be either regularized union, intersection, or difference or may be rigid motions (Figure 1-2). The solid scheme is the most compact of all known representations, at least for the class of commonly machined parts. The most advantage of CSG is that it guarantees the validity of uniqueness of the model: a boundary representation can always be derived in a unique way.

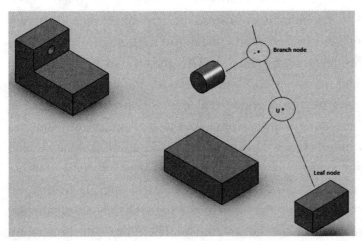

Figure 1-2 Constructive solid geometry (CSG)

Boundary Representation (B-Rep) Scheme

In this representation, a solid is defined by its boundaries. Each surface is *planar* or *sculptured* and bounded by edges of an adjacent boundary. Boundaries of a solid usually are represented as union of faces, with each face represented in terms of its boundary (union of edges), together with data which define the surface in which the face lies (Figure 1-3).

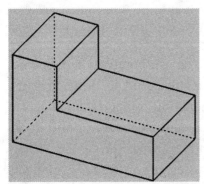   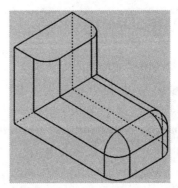

(a) Planar face boundary-rep   (b) Curved face boundary-rep
Figure 1-3 Boundary Representation (B-Rep) Scheme

Feature-based Parametric Modeling

By the 1980's, a new paradigm called *concurrent engineering* had emerged. With reference to Figure 1-1, it was no longer necessary for the sequential tasks of the left-hand side to be done in that manner. Instead, designers, design engineers, analysts, process planners, manufacturing engineers, and industrial engineers all work together closely right from the start of the product conception until production and shipping to customers. Personnel from different departments could work on their tasks concurrently; thereby supporting teamwork. Any problem encountered at any stage is collectively resolved, resulting in shortening of time from design conception to product manufacture. This concept is shown on the right-hand side Figure 1-1. This meant that a more reliable geometric modeling technique had to be used. Feature-based Parametric Modeling technique was developed to play its role in a concurrent engineering environment. In parametric modeling, shapes are driven by dimensions. At the leaf-nodes are sketches which are fully constrained (fully dimensioned). Features are made up of sketches which are acted upon by some operations such as *Extrude (Add)*, *Cut (Subtract)*, *Sweep*, *Revolve*, *Loft*, etc. Changing the dimensions of the sketches changes the 3D feature. In parametric modeling environment, changing the dimension of a sketch automatically changes the shape of the feature as well as the assembly. Therefore, the bottom-up hierarchy is defined as Sketches-Features (Solid Parts)-Assembly. Another interesting observation is that the Part, Assembly, and Drawings are all connected parametrically. If any change is made at the Part-level, the change cascades to the Assembly and Drawing documents. Different designs can be obtained and evaluated very quickly. Existing design data can be reused to create new designs. Geometric relations, dimensional constraints, and relational parametric equations can be used to capture deign intent. Design tables and configurations are easily generated to realize different design variations. All these advantages make Feature-based Parametric Modeling technique the choice for *concurrent engineering* environment.

BACKGROUND OF SOLIDWORKS

SolidWorks, registered trademark of the Dassault Systems Corporation in Concord, Massachusetts, USA is a design automation software package used to produce parts, assemblies and drawings. It is Windows native 3D solid modeling computer-aided design (CAD) program based on **parametric modeling**. This particular attribute of SolidWorks means that the dimensions of the parts, assemblies and drawings drive the shapes produced. SolidWorks provides easy-to-use, highest quality design software for engineers and designers for creating 3D parts, assemblies and 2D drawings which are all related. This means that changes made in part document will affect the assembly and 2D drawing documents. The advantages of parametric modeling are numerous, but some distinct ones include the face that when a designer realizes that changes need to be made in dimensions in an assembly document, making such changes in the part document automatically updates the assembly and 2D drawing documents. There is no need to start all over. Parametric modeling is not rigid; it is flexible and makes designing extremely flexible. This attribute of SolidWorks makes it extremely flexible when compared to some other CAD programs.

STARTING A SOLIDWORKS SESSION

There is more than one way to start a SolidWorks session. To start a SolidWorks session, choose **Start** > **All Programs** > **SolidWorks** from the **Start** menu or double-click on the SolidWorks icon on the desktop of your computer. When SolidWorks program is first accessed, the window that is displayed is the one shown in Figure 1-4. It is more or less a blank page from which the designer then decides what document to open: part, assembly or drawing.

Figure 1-4 Opening SolidWorks screen

SOLIDWORKS USER INTERFACE

There are basically four menus that are first seen when a new SolidWorks session commences: Menu bar menu, Menu bar toolbar, SolidWorks Help, and SolidWorks Resources. The menus are visible when you move the mouse over or click the SolidWorks logo. You can pin the menus to keep them visible at all times. In order to create a part, assembly, or drawing, click **File**, **New** from the *Menu bar menu* or click

New 📄 or click **Open** 📂 (Standard toolbar) from the *Menu bar toolbar*. The Menu Bar contains the following.

Menu Bar Toolbar

This is a set of the most frequently used tool buttons from the Standard toolbar as shown in Figure 1-5. By clicking the down arrow next to a tool button, you can expand it to display a flyout menu with additional functions. When the cursor is moved across the SolidWorks logo, the menu-bar-toolbar switches over to the menu bar menu. The toolbar moves to the right when the menus are pinned.

Figure 1-5 Menu toolbar

The available tools are:

New 📄 —Creates a new document.

Open 📂 —Opens and existing document.

Save 💾 —Saves an active document. This lets you access most of File menu commands from the toolbar. For example, the **Save** flyout menu includes **Save**, **Save As**, and **Save All**.

Print 🖨 —Prints an active document.

Undo ↩ —Reverses the last action taken.

Rebuild 🔴 —Rebuilds the active part, assembly or drawing.

Options ▤ —Changes system options and Add-Ins for SolidWorks.

Menu Bar Menu

The SolidWorks menus are visible when you move the mouse over or click the SolidWorks logo. You can pin the menus to keep them visible at all times. The default menu items for an active document are: *File, Edit, View, Insert, Tools, Window, Help*, and *Pin* (see Figure 1-6). However, the menu items change depending on which type of document is active.

Figure 1-6 Menu bar menu

Task Pane

The Task Pane is displayed when the SolidWorks session commences. The Task Pane contains the following default tabs: SolidWorks Resources 🏠, Design Library, File Explorer, SolidWorks Search, View Palette, Appearances/Scenes, and Custom Properties.

SolidWorks Resources

The SolidWorks Resources 🏠 tab in the Task Pane includes commands, links, and information.

Design Library

The Design Library 📊 tab in the Task Pane provides a central location for reusable elements such as parts, assemblies and sketches; but not for non-reusable elements such as SolidWorks drawings, text files, etc. It is the gateway to **3D Content Central** website. The Design Library abounds with resources for design and designers should take time to be familiar with these resources.

SolidWorks Explorer

SolidWorks Explorer 📁 is a file management tool designed to help you perform such tasks as renaming, replacing, and copying SolidWorks files. You can show a document's references, search for documents using a variety of criteria, and list all the places where a document is used. Renamed files are still available to those documents that reference them.

SolidWorks Search

SolidWorks Search 🔍 is used to search key words. The ten recent searches may be found by clicking the pull-down arrow.

View Palette

The View Palette 🔲 provides the ability to drag and drop drawing views of an active document, or click the Browse button to locate the desired document.

Appearances/Scene

Appearances/Scene 🅴 is a useful and easy-to-use way of providing photo-realistic rendering of models.

Help options

SolidWorks flyout menu of Help options 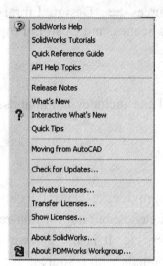 are used to access *Help*, *Tutorials*, **Reference Guide**, and other functionalities as shown in Figure 1-7. Another route for the Help options is through the SolidWorks menu.

Figure 1-7 Help options

So far, what we have considered are the menus that are displayed when a new session of SolidWorks is started. Once a task begins (part modeling, assembly modeling, or drawing), three more menus appear: CommandManager, FeatureManager Design Tree, and Head-up View toolbar. These are now briefly discussed.

CommandManager

The CommandManager, which is document dependent, contains most of the tools that you will need to create parts, assemblies or drawings. The CommandManager is a context-sensitive toolbar that dynamically updates based on the toolbar you want to access. By default, it has toolbars embedded in it based on the document type. For example, the default Part tabs are *Features*, *Sketch*, *Evaluate*, *DimXpert*, and *Office Products*. These tabs are illustrated hereafter. The two most widely used categories of tools for part modeling are features tools used to create and modify 3-D features and sketch tools used in creating 2-D sketches.

The main **Features tools** used to create and modify 3-D features are **extruded** boss/base, **revolved** boss/base, **swept** boss/base, **lofted** boss/base, **boundary** boss/base, for adding materials to a part; **extruded** cut, **revolved** cut, **swept** cut, **lofted** cut, **boundary** cut, for removing materials from a part; **fillet**, **linear pattern**, **mirror** for operations; specific features such as **rib**, **draft**, **shell**, **wrap**, **dome**; **reference geometry** and **curves**, as well as **instant3D** tool (see Figure 1-8).

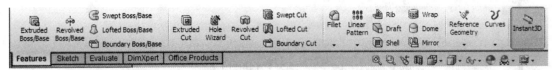

Figure 1-8 Feature tools

The Sketch tools used in creating 2-D sketches are sketch, smart dimension, line, rectangle, slot, circle, arc, polygon, spline, ellipse, fillet, plane, text, point, convert entities, offset, mirror, linear pattern, move, display/delete relations, repair sketch, quick snaps, and rapid sketch (see Figure 1-9).

Figure 1-9 Sketch tools

The **Evaluate tools** are mainly for **analysis** such as measuring distances between points on features, mass properties, section properties, etc. SimulationXpress, FloXpress, DFMXpress, DriveWorksXpress Wizards are also accessible through the evaluate tools (see Figure 1-10).

Figure 1-10 Evaluate tools

The **DimXpert tools** are mainly for **dimensions** and **tolerance** (see Figure 1-11).

Figure 1-11 DimXpert tools

The **Office products toolbar** allows you to activate any add-in application included in the SolidWorks Professional or Premium package. **eDrawings** and **Animate** are available using this toolbar as shown in Figure 1-12.

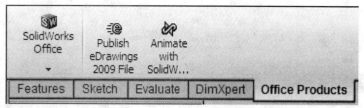

Figure 1-12 Office product tools

FeatureManager Design Tree

The FeatureManager Design Tree which is located on the left side of the SolidWorks Graphics window summarizes how the part, assembly or drawing is created. It is necessary to understand the FeatureManager Design Tree in order to be able to troubleshoot a model having some problems. The default tabs of the FeatureManager are: FeatureManager Design Tree, PropertyManager, ConfigurationManager, and DimXertManager. For example in the FeatureManager Design Tree shown in Figure 1-13, the standard planes are shown, and the first activity is shown to be *Extrude1* (extruded boss/base). A sketch (or sketches), which defines the extruded part would normally appear when the *Extrude1* is expanded. All the details for designing a part are summarized and stored in the FeatureManager Design Tree. It is the design information store-house, which fully describe a designed part, assembly or drawing. It is a design tree showing the relationship between *parents* and *children* in a design context. When information relating to a parent is changed, it automatically affects the *children*. Every designer using SolidWorks should be very familiar with the semantics and syntax of the FeatureManager Design Tree.

Figure 1-13 FeatureManager Design Tree

Head-up View Toolbar

The Head-up View toolbar (see Figure 1-14) is a useful tool for the user to have view options during modeling of parts, assemblies or drawing. The following views are available: *zoom to fit, zoom to area, previous view, section view, view orientation, display style, hide/show items, edit appearance, apply scene,* and *view setting.*

Figure 1-14 Head-up View toolbar

The **view orientation** (*top, front, bottom, left, right,* and *back; isometric, trimetric,* and *diametric; normal; single view, two view horizontal, two view vertical,* four view), and **display style** (*shaded with edge, shaded, hidden lines removed, hidden lines visible,* and *wireframe*) are illustrated in Figure 1-15.

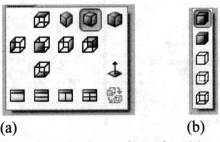

(a)   (b)

Figure 1-15 View orientation (a) and Display style (b)

Drop-down Menu

SolidWorks shares the familiar Microsoft® Windows user interface. Users communicate with SolidWorks through drop-down menus (see Figure 1-16), Context sensitive toolbars, Consolidated toolbars or the CommandManager tabs. As the name implies, a drop-down menu drops down other lower level menus which give more information in terms of design tool bars. A drop-down menu has a black triangular shaped symbol, which when clicked drops other menus. For example in Figure 1-16, choosing the Features option, drops another menu showing the features available: fillet/round, chamfer, hole, draft, shell, rib, scale, dome, freeform, shape, deform, indent, flex, wrap, etc.

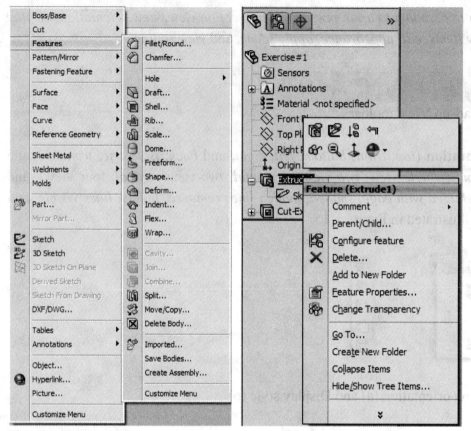

Figure 1-16 Drop-down menus   Figure 1-17 Right-clicking options

Right-click

Right-clicking in the Graphics window on a *model* or in the FeatureManager on a *feature* or *sketch* results in the display of a Context sensitive toolbar as shown in Figure 1-17.

Consolidated Toolbar

In the CommandManager, similar commands (instructions that inform SolidWorks to perform a task) are grouped together. For examples, a family of the Slot sketch tool is grouped together in a singly fly-out button as illustrated in Figure 1-18.

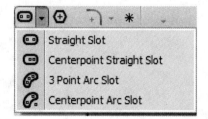

Figure 1-18 Group of the slot sketch

System Feedback

SolidWorks provides system feedback by attaching a symbol to the mouse pointer cursor which indicates what you are selecting or what the system is expecting you to select. Placing your cursor pointer across a model, results in system feedback being displayed in the form of a symbol next to the cursor as illustrated.

SETTING THE DOCUMENT OPTIONS

As has been already mentioned, the **Options** tool changes system options and Add-Ins for SolidWorks. There are two components of Options: System Options and Document Properties.

System Options

System Options tool allows you to specify the File Locations Options which contain a list of folders referenced during a SolidWorks session. The default templates folder for a new installation on a local drive C:\ is located at: C:\Documents and Settings\All Users\Applications Data\ SolidWorks\ SolidWorks200x\templates. It is therefore important that you advice SolidWorks software where to find your customized templates as shown in Figure 1-19.

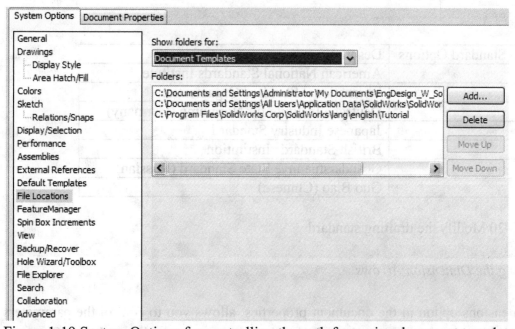

Figure 1-19 System Options for controlling the path for saving document templates

Document Properties

There are numerous settings that need to be made when you begin a modeling session. Document Properties tool offers users the resources to do this.

Modifying the Drafting Standard

For example, to choose a drafting standard, the Drafting Standard tool is accessed. The standards that are available in this drop-down list are ANSI, ISO, DIN, JIS, BSI, GOST, and GB as shown in Figure 1-20(a) and further expanded in Figure 1-20(b).

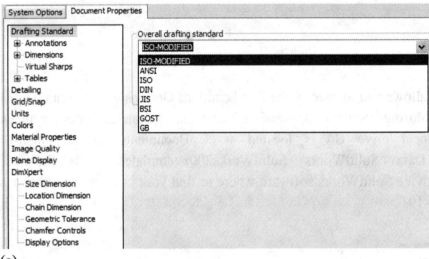

(a)

Drafting Standard Options	Description
ANSI	American National Standards Institute
ISO	International Standard Organization
DIN	Deutsche Institute fur Normumg (Germany)
JIS	Japanese Industry Standard
BSI	British Standards Institution
GOST	Gosndarstuennye State Standard (Russian)
GB	Guo Biao (Chinese)

(b)

Figure 1-20 Modify the drafting standard

Modifying the Dimension Arrows

The dimensions option in the document properties, allows you to control the parameters that define dimension arrows such as the height, width, and overall length (see Figure 1-21). It also allows you to specify whether dual dimensions are needed, and if so the precision can also be set. The text font can also be specified.

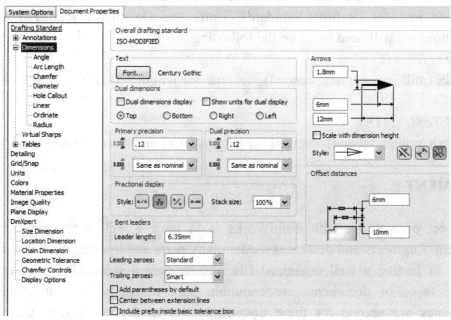

Figure 1-21 Modifying the dimension arrows

Modifying the Units Document Properties

The Units Document Properties assists the designer to define the Unit System, Length unit, Angular unit, Density unit, and Force unit of measurement for the Part document (see Figure 1-22). The Decimals option displays the number of decimal places for the Length and Angular units of measurement.

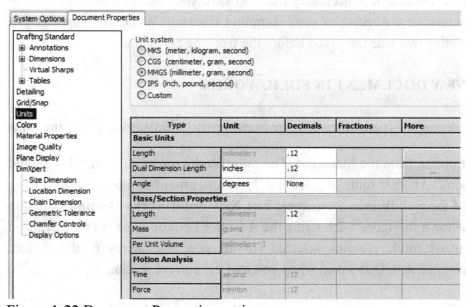

Figure 1-22 Document Properties settings

There are hundreds of document properties. However, the Document Properties that are commonly modified include: Drafting Standards, Units and Decimal Places. For a number of applications we will need to set up the following:

ANSI-MM-PART TEMPLATE

Choose the **MMGS** (millimeter, gram, second), decimal for length = 0.12 and None for Angle.

ANSI-INCH-PART TEMPLATE

Choose the **IPS** (inch, pound, second), decimal for length = 0.12 and None for Angle.

FILE MANAGEMENT

An important aspect of working with SolidWorks is to have a well organized file management system. Engineers and designers model many parts and it would be helpful to form the habit of having a well organized file management system. Generally in SolidWorks, three types of documents are common: part, assembly, and drawing. Customized templates are needed for these documents; let us decide to save these templates as MY-TEMPLATES. There are components that may be sources, so let us also have a folder for SOURCED-COMPONENTS. We will also decide to save our models in a particular folder under a known path, on our computer hard-drive. Other folders may be created for projects, exercises, etc. It is important to set up a file management system that would help us in a typical SolidWorks class.

Cautions Needed During SolidWorks Sessions

During SolidWorks sessions, it is necessary that you save your model from time to time because you may receive a surprise of your computer freezing. When this happens you might lose information that was not saved before the freezing takes place.

STARTING A NEW DOCUMENT IN SOLIDWORKS

To select a new document (part, assembly, or drawing) in SolidWorks, select the **New Document** option from the Menu bar. The SolidWorks screen of Figure 1-4 should be open at this point. Another route to select the **New Document** is through the **Getting Started** rollout of the SolidWorks Resources. The **New SolidWorks Document** dialog box displayed is shown in Figure 1-23. Click the Advanced button to select the advanced mode. The advanced mode remains selected for all new documents in the current SolidWorks session; the setting is saved when you exit the current session.

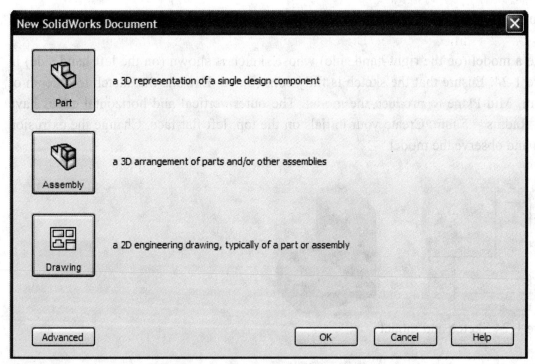

Figure 1-23 The **New SolidWorks Document** dialog box

Part

The **Part** button is chosen by default in the **New SolidWorks Document** dialog box. Choosing the **OK** button enables you to start a new part document to create solid models or sheet metal components.

Assembly

Choose the **Assembly** button and then the **OK** button from the **New SolidWorks Document** dialog box to start a new assembly document.

Drawing

Choose the **Drawing** button and then the **OK** button from the **New SolidWorks Document** dialog box to start a new Drawing.

MY FIRST PART

After understanding what SolidWorks is all about, let us now create our first part.

Example 1

Create a model (on the right-hand side) whose sketch is shown (on the left-hand side) in Figure 1-24. Ensure that the sketch is fully constrained. Extrude the sketch to a depth of 50 mm, Mid-Plane to produce the model. The outer vertical and horizontal edges have Fillet Radius = 5 mm. Create your initials on the top, left flat face. Change the extrusion depth and observe the model.

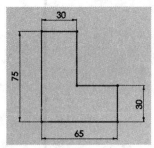 

Figure 1-24 Sketch and model

SolidWorks Solution

The following steps are recommended:

1. Create a **New** Document.
2. Ensure that you have set up the following:
   ANSI-MM-PART TEMPLATE: MMGS (millimeter, gram, second), decimal for length = 0.12 and None for Angle.
   ANSI-INCH-PART TEMPLATE: IPS (inch, pound, second), decimal for length = 0.12 and None for Angle.
3. Choose the **Front Plane**.
4. Starting from the origin, **sketch** an L-shape, 75 mm by 65 mm with 30 mm offset.
5. **Dimension** the sketch (see Figure 1-25).
6. **Extrude** it 50 mm (see Figure 1-25).

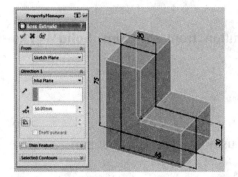

Figure 1-25 Boss Extrude PropertyManager

7. Click the **Fillet** option and select the seven out edges with **Fillet Radius = 10 mm** as shown in Figure 1-26. See the filleted model in Figure 1-27.

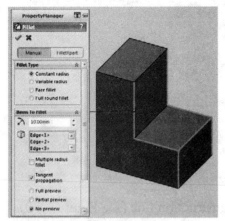

Figure 1-26 Fillet edges

Figure 1-27 Model has fillets

8. Select the topmost face, be in sketch mode and sketch two construction lines 25 mm apart (see Figure 1-28).
9. Click the **Sketch Text** tool (see Figure 1-29).

Figure 1-28 Sketch two construction lines

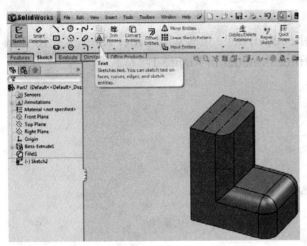

Figure 1-29 Text tool

10. In the **Curve** dialog box, select the right-side construction line (see Figure 1-30).

11. In the **Text** dialog box, write your initials (the acronym for computer-aided design, CAD is used) (see Figure 1-30).

12. Select the **Center** option for the text (see Figure 1-30).

13. Undo the **Use Document font** option (a Choose Font dialog box pops up) (see Figure 1-30).

14. Adjust **Font = Century Gothic, Font Style = Regular, Height Units = 10 mm, Height Points = 28** as desired (see Figure 1-30).

15. Click **OK** for the **Dialog Box** and **OK** for the **Sketch Text PropertyManager** to finish (see Figure 1-30).

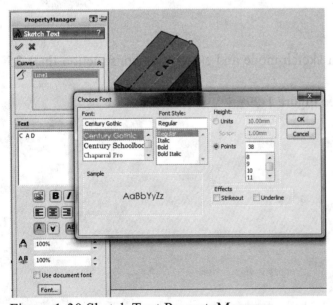

Figure 1-30 Sketch Text PropertyManager

16. Click Boss Extrude to extrude the Sketch Text with a Depth (Height) = 2 mm (see Figure 1-31 and Figure 1-32).

Figure 1-31 Extrude Sketch Text   Figure 1-32 Model with initials

USEFUL SOLIDWORKS RESOURCES

SolidWorks Tutorials tool (see Figure 1-33) which can be accessed through the **Help** tool in the SolidWorks Menu Bar is a very useful resource base. Explore the Tutorials.

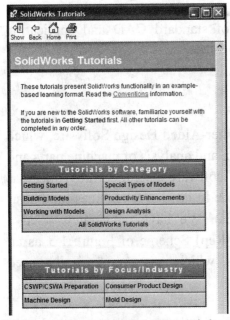

Figure 1-33 SolidWorks Tutorials

COMPATIBILITY OF SOLIDWORKS WITH OTHER SOFTWARE

SolidWorks interfaces well with a number of standard CAD and application software (see Figure 1-34). This means that while working with SolidWorks software, it is possible to import CAD files created using other software listed in Figure 1-34.

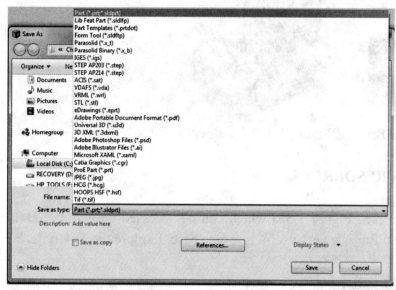

Figure 1-34 SolidWorks interface with a number of standard CAD and application software

Summary

This chapter gives an overview of SolidWorks Computer-Aided Design Software, which is one of the industry-standard software used for design and analysis of machine parts and assemblies. Industrial Designers will also find the software useful. SolidWorks has become very popular with manufacturing industries due to its user-friendliness and cost-effectiveness for small-to-medium-enterprises (SMEs). We have deliberately used a model created with the Boundary Representation (B-Rep) Scheme of Figure 1-3 as an example to show how easy it is to use SolidWorks, which is a parametrically-based design software.

Exercises

1. Create the sketch shown in Figure P1. Extrude the sketch to a depth of 1 inch to produce the model. Change the extrusion depth and observe the model. Part Name: Bracket. Material: Aluminum

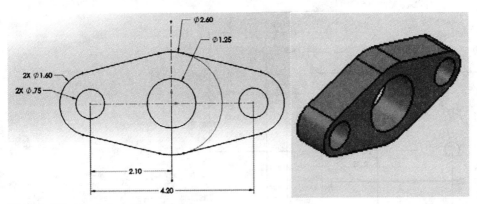

Figure P1 Sketch and model

2. Create the sketch shown in Figure P2. Part Name: Gasket. Material: 1 mm thick cork. Create the model.

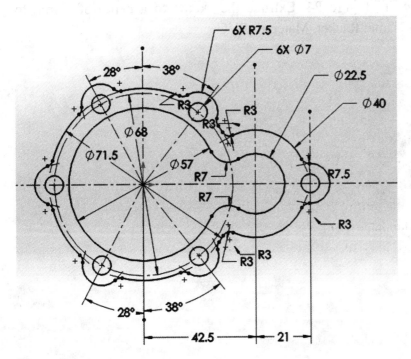

Figure P2

3. Create the sketch shown in Figure P3. Part Name: Gasket. Material: .0625 inch thick bronze. Create the model.

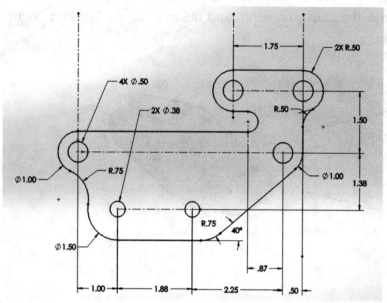

Figure P3

4. Create the sketch shown in Figure P4. Extrude the sketch to a depth of 5 mm to produce the model. Part Name: Racket. Material: PVC

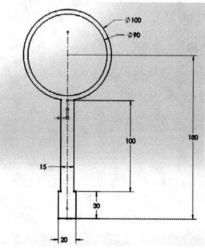

Figure P4

5. Create the sketch shown in Figure P5. Part Name: Die stamping. Material: 5 mm thick 1060 Aluminum. Create the model. Determine the mass properties.

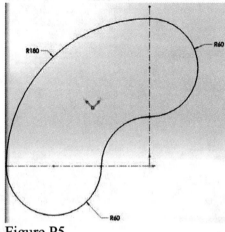

Figure P5

6. Create the sketch shown in Figure P6. Part Name: Die stamping. Material: 5mm thick Copper. Create the model. Determine the mass properties.

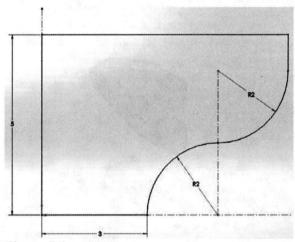

Figure P6

7. Create the sketch shown in Figure P7. Part Name: Pivot arm. Material: Aluminum. Create the model: base is 1 high; 4.25 OD is 1 high from base; 2.13 OD hole is .5 high from base; slot is through the base. Dimensions are in inch. Determine the mass properties.

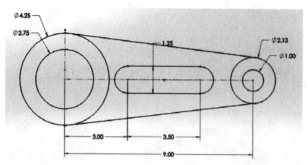

Figure P7

8. Create the sketch shown in Figure P8. Extrude the sketch to a depth of 15 mm to produce the model. Change the extrusion depth and observe the model.

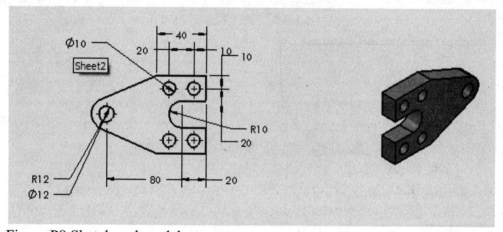

Figure P8 Sketch and model

9. Mirror the part about a plane that coincides with the two vertical rectangular faces.

Chapter 2
Geometric Construction Tools

Objectives:

In this chapter you will learn:

- About sketch entities in SolidWorks
- About sketch tools in SolidWorks
- The sketch tools used to modify sketch entities in order to produce parts

INTRODUCTION

SolidWorks uses *sketch entities* and *tools* to facilitate the creation of parts. While *sketch entities* have specific geometries (line, rectangle, parallelogram, slot, polygon, circle, arc, ellipse, parabola, spline, etc.), some of the *sketch tools* (fillet, chamfer, offset, convert entities, intersection curves, trim, extend, split, jog line, constructive geometry, mirror, stretch, move, rotate, scale, copy, pattern, etc.) are used to modify the shapes of sketch entities. Entities are grouped to define a boundary or profile, which are closed regions needed for creating extruded or revolved parts. SolidWorks sketch entities and tools can be accessed by clicking the Tools bar.

Sketch Entities include **line**, **rectangle** (2-opposite vertices, center, 2-opposite vertices, 3-point corner, 3-point center), **parallelogram**, **slot** (straight, center-point straight, 3-arc, center-point arc), **polygon**, **circle** (center-1-point, 3-points on perimeter), **arc** (center-2-point, tangent, 3-point arc), **ellipse** (full, partial), **parabola**, and **spline**.

Sketch Tools include **fillet**, **chamfer**, **offset**, **convert entities**, **intersection curves**, **trim**, **extend**, **split** entities, **jog line**, **construction geometry**, **make path**, **mirror** (straight, dynamic), **stretch** entities, **move** entities, **rotate** entities, **scale** entities, **copy** entities, and **pattern** (linear, circular).

SKETCH ENTITIES

Sketch entities are commonly used geometric shapes which are building blocks for modeling simple and complicated shapes. In general, these entities are grouped into line, rectangle, polygon, slot, arc, circle, ellipse, parabola, and spline. Figure 2-1 shows the **Sketch Entities** toolbar.

For most of the entities definitions in this section, it assumed that a new **Part** has already been started, and the appropriate **Plane** chosen from the **Feature Manager**. Therefore, a generic format for sketch entities presented in this chapter is as follows:

1. Start a new **Part** document, click **Sketch** group on the **Command Manager**, and select (appropriate) **Plane** from the **Feature Manager**.

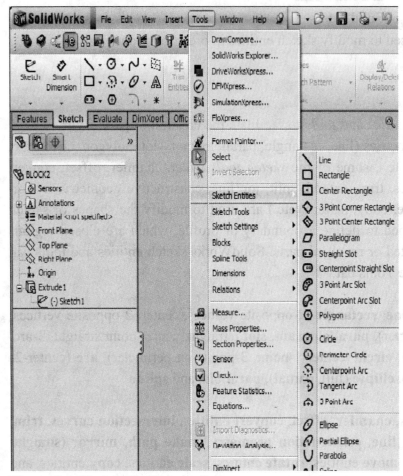

Figure 2-1 **Sketch Entities** toolbar

Line

Line is one of the most frequently used sketch entities in part modeling. There are basically two main types of line: solid and construction lines as shown in Figure 2-2.

1. Click the **Line** group on the **Command Manager**.
2. Select a starting point for the line and click the point.
3. Select other point and extend the line.
4. When the line is complete, right-click the mouse and click the **End chain** option.

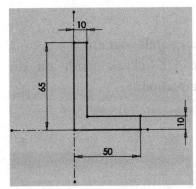

Figure 2-2 Solid and construction lines

Rectangle

There are a number of options for a rectangle entity: 2-opposite vertices, center, 2-opposite vertices, 3-point corner, 3-point center as shown in Figure 2-3. When a user is more interested in centering the rectangle about the origin of the graphics screen, then the **center rectangle** is the one to go for. Let us illustrate the center rectangle.

1. Click the **Rectangle** group on the **Command Manager**.
2. Select a center click the point.
3. Drag the cursor away from the center point to create a rectangle.
4. When the rectangle is complete, click the OK check mark on the PropertyManager to complete the rectangle construction.

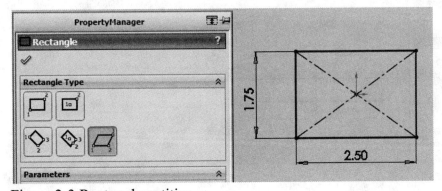

Figure 2-3 Rectangle entities

Parallelogram

Parallelogram is considered a special type of rectangle, hence it is grouped as a rectangle type as shown in Figure 2-4.

1. Click the **Rectangle** group on the **Command Manager**.

2. Select and click any two horizontal points.
3. Drag the cursor away from the second point to create a parallelogram.
4. When the parallelogram is complete, click the OK check mark on the PropertyManager to complete the parallelogram construction.

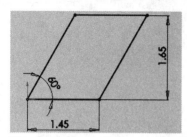

Figure 2-4 Parallelogram entities

Slot

There are a number of options for a slot entity: straight, center-point straight, 3-arc, center-point arc as shown in Figure 2-5.

1. Click the **Slot** group on the **Command Manager**.
2. Select and click any two horizontal points.
3. Drag cursor to the top or bottom of two points for the third point, to get the width of the slot.
4. When the slot is complete, click the OK check mark on the PropertyManager to complete sketching the slot.

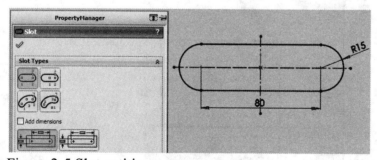

Figure 2-5 Slot entities

Polygon

Polygon has *n*-number of sides as shown in Figure 2-6. To sketch a polygon:

1. Click the **Polygon** group on the **Command Manager**.
2. Define the number of sides as six (hexagon); check Inscribed circle.

3. Click the OK check mark on the PropertyManager to complete sketching the polygon.

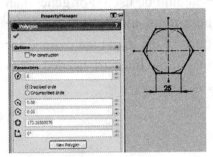

Figure 2-6 Polygon entities

Circle

There are generally two ways of defining a circle: center-1-point, 3-points on perimeter. See Figure 2-7.

1. Click the **Circle** group on the **Command Manager**.
2. Select and click a point.
3. Drag the cursor away from the center point to create a circle.
4. When the circle is complete, click the OK check mark on the PropertyManager.

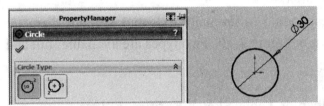

Figure 2-7 Circle entities

Arc

There are generally three ways of defining an arc: center-2-point, tangent, 3-point arc. See Figure 2-8.

Figure 2-8 Arc entities

When the center point and two other points are known, the **center-2-point** should be used. When two lines are already sketched and two end points of an arc are to coincide with the end points of the two lines, then **tangent** options should be used. For general an arc where the center point is not initially known, then the **3-point arc** option should be used. For example, in Figure 2-9, only two points (end points of the lines) are defined for the **tangent** arc. However, the center and the two end points of the lines are needed when the **center-2-point arc** option is used as in Figure 2-9.

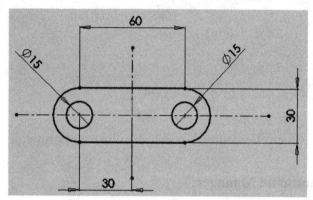

Figure 2-9 Arc entities for sketch definitions

Ellipse

An ellipse has a major diameter corresponding to its major axis and a minor diameter corresponding to its minor axis as shown in Figure 2-10. Two types are available: full and partial.

To create an ellipse:

1. Click **Ellipse** on the Sketch toolbar, or **Tools, Sketch Entities, Ellipse**.
2. Click in the graphics area to place the center of the ellipse.
3. Drag and click to set the major axis of the ellipse.
4. Drag and click again to set the minor axis of the ellipse.

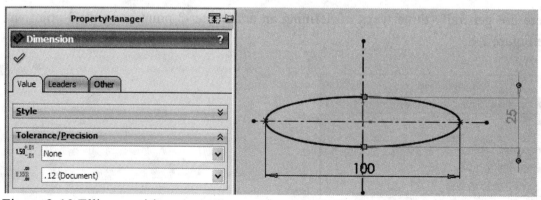

Figure 2-10 Ellipse entities

Ellipse can be used to model rugby ball by following these steps:
1. Trim half of the ellipse.
2. Sketch a line to close the shape.
3. Revolve the shape through the center line.

Parabola

A parabola is a loci of points in which the distance between a fixed point, the focus, and a fixed line, the directrix, are always equal. See Figure 2-11. It is a well-known geometry in elementary mathematics. To create a parabola:
1. Click Parabola (Sketch toolbar) or **Tools**, **Sketch Entities**, parabola.
2. Click to place the focus of the parabola and drag to enlarge the parabola. The parabola is outlined.
3. Click on the parabola and drag to define the extent of the curve.

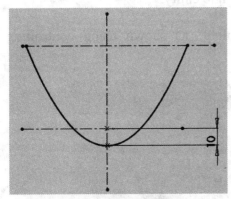

Figure 2-11 Parabola entity

Parabola can be used to model a satellite dish by following these steps (see Figure 2-12):
1. Trim half of the parabola.
2. Sketch horizontal line at the top and a vertical line through the focus.
3. Revolve the shape through the vertical center line.
4. Shell the object with thickness of 1 mm.

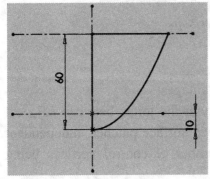

Figure 2-12 Half-parabola used for modeling satellite dish

Spline

Splines are geometries for modeling complex, general-form curves or surfaces as shown in Figure 2-13. Understanding the concept of splines is challenging and could be found in advanced CAD documentations. Free-form surfaces are extensively used in the automobile industry. The construction of aircraft, turbo-machinery, and automobiles, and recent applications in the advertising and animation industries, has become driving force behind the research into techniques for surface design. Splines have been heavily used in the automotive and aircraft industries and early work in the area began in those sectors for modeling of automotive bodies and fuselages.

Free-form surfaces are of different forms: quadratic or cubic spline (nonuniform rational B-spline) curve. To sketch a quadratic or cubic spline, specify:
1. First point
2. Next point (loops so that you can specify as many points as you want)
3. Complete the spline. The spline realized is a single entity.

The shapes modeled using splines can be "controlled" as shown using controlling polygons.

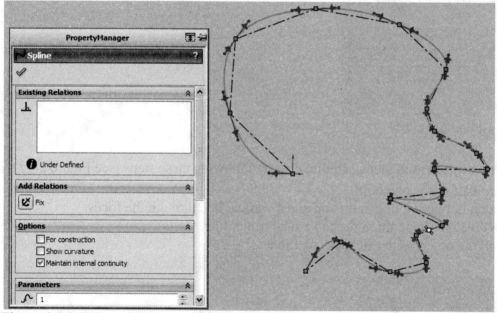

Figure 2-13 Spline entity

Parametric B-spline curves and surfaces have several advantages:
1) Ability to control the degree of continuity at the joints between adjacent curve segments, and at the borders between surface patches, independent of the order of the segments or the number of control vertices being approximated;

2) Ability to guarantee that smooth shapes would be generated from smooth data.

SKETCH TOOLS

Sketches are 2D in nature and Figure 2-14 shows the SolidWorks **Sketch Tools** toolbar mainly used for modifying them.

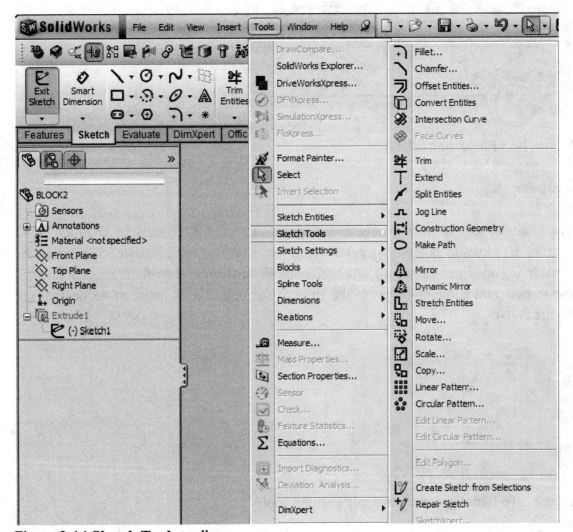

Figure 2-14 **Sketch Tools** toolbar

Fillet

The Fillet tool is used to create fillet between lines as desired in a model in order to remove sharp edges. The sketch shown in Figure 2-15 is filleted at a constant value of 5 mm radius between adjacent lines.

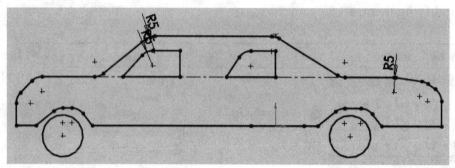

Figure 2-15 Illustrating fillet tool

Chamfer

The chamfer tool is used to create chamfer in a model. Generally, a chamfer of 45 degrees is common but other angles could be used. Let us illustrate chamfering by considering an object having all side horizontal or vertical. A chamfer is needed between the vertical and horizontal lines to the right of the object at an angle of 45 degree (see Figure 2-16).

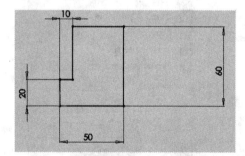

Figure 2-16 Initial geometry to apply chamfer tool

The resulting chamfered object is shown to have a vertical dimension of 30 mm and an angle of 45 degrees as shown in Figure 2-17.

1. Click the **Chamfer** group on the **Command Manager**.
2. Check the **Angle-Distance** option.
3. For the Distance, click the right vertical line; for the angle, specify 45 degrees.
4. When the chamfer is complete, click the OK check mark on the PropertyManager.

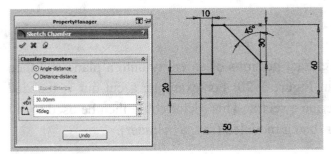

Figure 2-17 Chamfer tool

Offset

The **Offset** tool is used to draw entities parallel to existing entities of a sketch as shown in Figure 2-18. This tool is particularly useful and it can cut down time of modeling since all that is needed is the selection of the entities and the definition of the amount of offset.

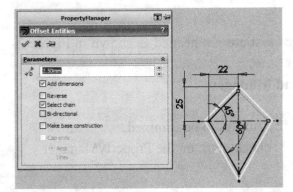

Figure 2-18 Offset tool

1. Click the **Offset** group on the **Command Manager**.
2. Select and click edges to be offset.
3. Specify the offset desired (2.5 mm in this case).
4. When the offset is complete, click the OK check mark on the PropertyManager.

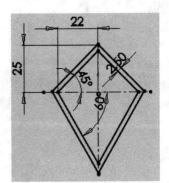

Figure 2-19 Offset geometry realized

Convert Entities

The **Convert Entities** tool is used to extract portions of an entity onto a plane and then used for further modeling as shown in Figure 2-20. For example, a cut-out is realized from a circle by using this tool to describe a sector. This sector could then be used to cut through the length or portion of the part being modeled (say, a cylinder).

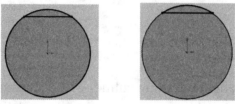

Figure 2-20 Illustrating Convert Entities tool

Trim

The **Trim** tool is used to clean up lines or arcs that are not needed as shown in Figure 2-22.

1. Click the **Trim** group on the **Command Manager**.
2. Select the **Power Trim** option.
3. Hold down and drag the cursor across the entities to be trimmed.
4. When the trim is complete, click the OK check mark on the PropertyManager.

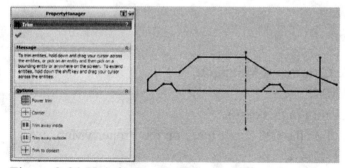

Figure 2-21 Use the Power Trim option

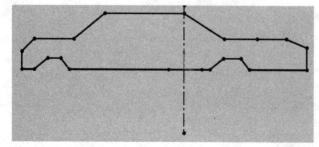

Figure 2-22 Trim entities tool

Extend

The **Extend** tool is used to extend an existing line to increase its length. See Figure 2-23. It is found in the Trim Entities group in the **Command Manager**.
1. Click the **Extend** group on the **Command Manager**.
2. Click the top and bottom lines to be extended.
3. When the extend task is complete, click the OK check mark on the PropertyManager.

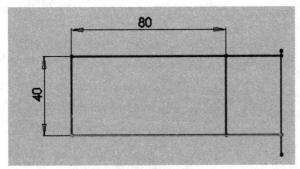

Figure 2-23 Extend entities tool

Split Entities

The Split Entities tool is found on the Sketching Tools. When it is chosen, click on the entity to trim approximately where you want the split. Figure 2-24 shows how this tool is used.

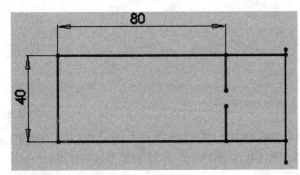

Figure 2-24 Split entities tool

Construction Geometry

It converts a solid line/circle/arc to construction line/ circle/arc.

Mirror

The **Mirror** tool is used to create a mirror image of an entity in a sketch. This tool is used when an axis, usually a line, exists about which an entity is to be mirrored. There are two forms of mirror tool: simple and dynamic. In the simple form, one-half of the entities are completed and mirrored about an axis as shown in Figure 2-25. In dynamic form, as an entity is sketch, it is dynamically mirrored about the chosen axis. The mirrored entities are show in Figure 2-26.

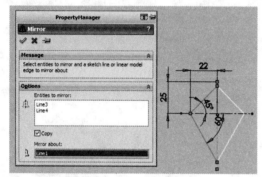

Figure 2-25 Mirror entities tool

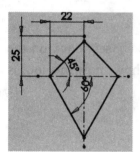

Figure 2-26 Mirrored entities

Stretch Entities

Stretch Entities tool stretches entities chosen; the value of stretch is based on the datum defined as shown in Figure 2-27. For example, the right-top, side and bottom lines are stretched about the left vertical line.
1. Click the **Stretch** group on the **Command Manager**.
2. Click the lines to be stretched.
3. Click the Base Define by clicking the left vertical line.
4. When the stretch task is complete, click the OK check mark on the PropertyManager.

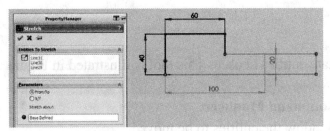

Figure 2-27 Stretch entities tool

The bottom line is stretched from 100 mm to 125 mm while the top-right line is stretched form 40 mm to 65 mm. See Figure 2-28 for stretched entities.

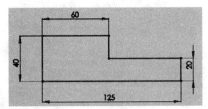

Figure 2-28 Illustrating stretched entities

Move Entities

The **Move Entities** tool is used to move entities chosen. An individual item or an entire object can be moved as shown in Figure 2-29.

1. Click the **Move** group on the **Command Manager**.
2. Click **Entities to Move** and Window the entities to be moved.
3. Uncheck the **Keep Relations**.
4. Click any point as starting point From Point Defined.
5. Drag object to another point and Click mouse at the End Point Defined.
6. When the move task is complete, click the OK check mark on the PropertyManager.

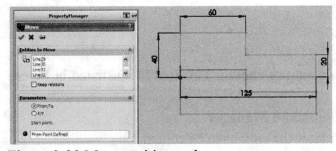

Figure 2-29 Move entities tool

Rotate Entities

The **Rotate Entities** tool is used to rotate entities chosen. This tool is illustrated in Figure 2-30.

1. Click the **Move** group on the **Command Manager**.
2. Click **Entities to Rotate** and Window the entities to be moved.
3. Uncheck the **Keep Relations**.
4. Click any point as Center of Rotation.
5. Define the Angle of rotation.
6. When the rotation task is complete, click the OK check mark on the PropertyManager.

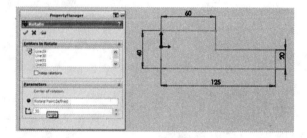

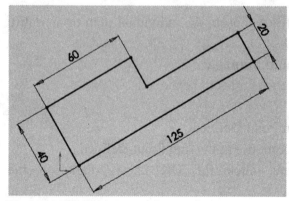

Figure 2-30 Rotate entities tool

Scale Entities

The **Scale Entities** tool is used to scale entities chosen. This tool is illustrated in Figure 2-31.

1. Click the **Scale** group on the **Command Manager**.
2. Click **Entities to Scale** and Window the entities to be copied.
3. Click any point as Scale Point Defined.
4. Define the scaling value.

5. When the scale task is complete, click the OK check mark on the PropertyManager.

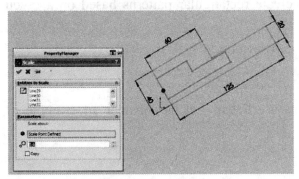

Figure 2-31 Scale entities tool

Copy Entities

The **Copy Entities** tool is used to copy entities chosen. An individual item or an entire object can be copied. This tool is illustrated in Figure 2-32.

1. Click the **Copy** group on the **Command Manager**.
2. Click **Entities to Copy** and Window the entities to be copied.
3. Uncheck the **Keep Relations**.
4. Click any point as starting point From Point Defined.
5. Drag object to another point and Click mouse at the End Point Defined.
6. When the copy task is complete, click the OK check mark on the PropertyManager.

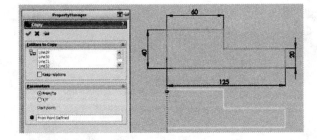

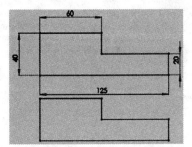

Figure 2-32 Copy entities tool

Pattern

The linear/circular pattern tool is used to create rectangular patterns based on a given model.

Linear Pattern

In linear pattern, directions for the patterns are linear. Let us consider an example as shown in Figure 2-33.

1. Sketch a geometry.
2. Sketch the seed pattern.
3. Click the **Linear Pattern** tool.
   The Linear Pattern Properties Manager appears.
4. Select the seed pattern.
5. For **Direction1>** select a horizontal edge for direction, 35 mm for Distance, and 4 for number of patterns. For **Direction2>** select a vertical edge for direction, 30 mm for Distance, and 3 for number of patterns.
6. Click OK to complete the patterns.

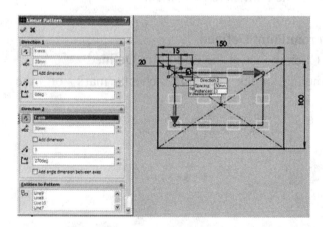

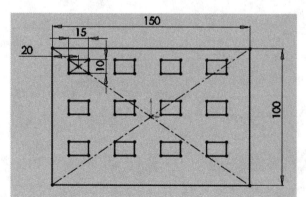

Figure 2-33 Linear patterns tool and patterns realized

Circular Pattern

In circular pattern, the patterns are created about an axis in a circular manner as shown in Figure 2-34.

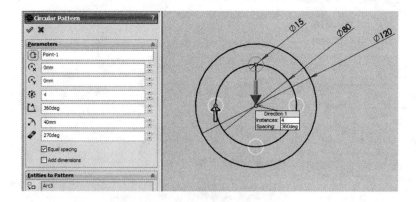

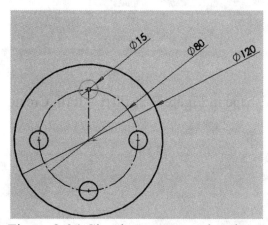

Figure 2-34 Circular pattern tool and patterns realized

Summary

This chapter discusses *sketch entities* and *tools* used in SolidWorks to facilitate the creation of parts. While *sketch entities* have specific geometries (line, rectangle, parallelogram, slot, polygon, circle, arc, ellipse, parabola, spline, etc.), some of the *sketch tools* (fillet, chamfer, offset, convert entities, intersection curves, trim, extend, split, jog line, constructive geometry, mirror, stretch, move, rotate, scale, copy, pattern, etc.) are used to modify the shapes of sketch entities. The *sketch entities* and *sketch tools* have been applied to a number of examples so that users can understand the principles involved.

Exercises

1. Use the given dimensions to redraw the given shape in Figure P-1. Create part models of the objects. Thickness = .5 inch

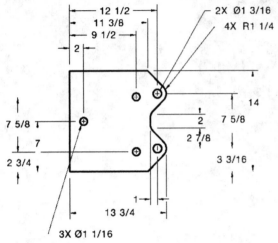

Figure P-1

2. Use the given dimensions to redraw the given shape in Figure P-2; fillet = R10. Create part models of the objects. Thickness = 25 mm

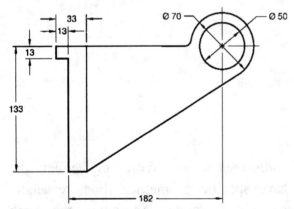

Figure P-2

3. Use the given dimensions to redraw the given shape in Figure P-3. Create part models of the objects. Thickness = 1.5 inch

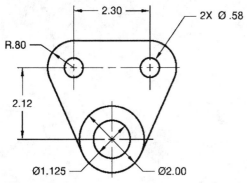

Figure P-3

4. Use the given dimensions to redraw the given shape in Figure P-4. Create part models of the objects. Thickness = 1 inch

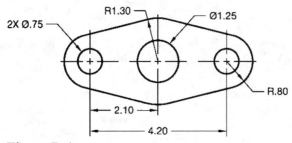

Figure P-4

5. Use the given dimensions to redraw the given shape in Figure P-5. Create part models of the objects. Thickness = 2 inch

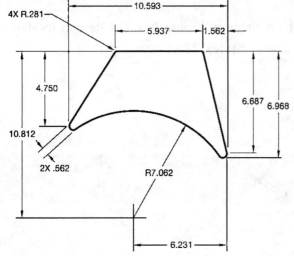

Figure P-5

6. Use the given dimensions to redraw the given shape in Figure P-6. Create part models of the objects. Thickness = 30 mm

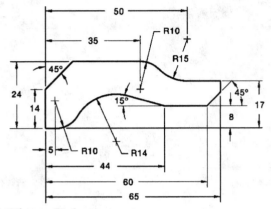

Figure P-6

7. Use the given dimensions to redraw the given shape in Figure P-7. Create part models of the objects. Thickness = .5 inch

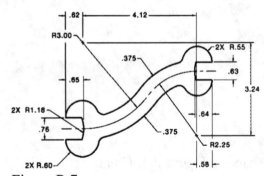

Figure P-7

8. Use the given dimensions to redraw the given shape in Figure P-8. Create part models of the objects (be sure to trim part of the .625-dia circle). Thickness = .5 inch

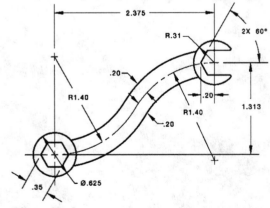

Figure P-8

9. Use the given dimensions to redraw the given shape in Figure P-9. Establish unknown dimensions to your own specifications. Create part models of the objects (be sure to trim part of the R1.600 arc). Thickness = 2 inch

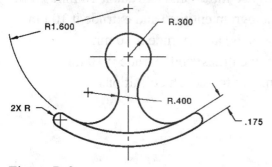

Figure P-9

10. Use the information in the ellipse section (refer to Figure 2-10) to create the rugby ball model shown in Figure P-10.

Figure P-10 Rugby ball

11. Use the information in the parabola section (refer to Figure 2-12) to create the satellite model shown in Figure P-11.

Figure P-11 Satellite dish

12. Create the sketch shown in Figure 2-2 (line entities) and extrude it 10 mm Mid-Plane.
13. Create the sketch shown in Figure 2-3 (rectangle entities) and extrude it 10 mm.
14. Create the sketch shown in Figure 2-4 (parallelogram entities) and extrude it 10 mm.
15. Create the sketch shown in Figure 2-5 (slot entities) and extrude it 10 mm.
16. Create the sketch shown in Figure 2-6 (polygon entities) and extrude it 10 mm.
17. Create the sketch shown in Figure 2-9 Arc entities for sketch definitions

Chapter 3
Features

Objectives:

In this chapter you will learn:

- About **Features** tools in SolidWorks
- How to create 3D objects using **Extrusion** Features tools
- How to create 3D objects using **Revolved** Features tools
- How to create 3D objects using **Lofted** Features tools
- How to create 3D objects using **Swept** Features tools
- How to use **Modification** Features tools
- How to **Edit Features** and hence able to trouble-shooting models
- How model **Sketch Driven Patterns**
- How model **Curve Driven Patterns**
- How model **Table Driven Patterns**
- How to use **Reference Planes**

INTRODUCTION

SolidWorks creates 3D objects based on **Features**. This chapter introduces **Features** tools (see Figure 3-1) and classifies them into five categories: **extrusion features** (extruded boss/base, draft, dome, rib, and extruded cut), **revolved features** (revolved boss/base, and revolved cut), **lofted features** (lofted boss/base, and lofted cut), **swept features** (swept boss/base, and swept cut), **modification features** (hole wizard, shell, fillet, chamfer, pattern, and mirror). In the first four categories, boss/base or cut models are realized. In the fifth category, tools for altering geometry of models are introduced. How to **edit features** work with **reference planes** to create more complex models is also introduced. Advanced **Patterns (Sketch Driven, Curve Driven, Table Driven)** tools are also introduced.

In illustrating all the features tools presented in this chapter, it is assumed that a new document has been opened for modeling and the **Document Properties** have been appropriately set to work with and appropriate design standard in mm/inch.

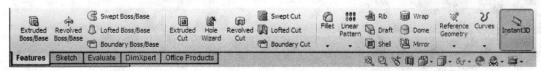

Figure 3-1 SolidWorks **Features** tools

EXTRUDED BOSS/BASE

The extruded boss/base tool is for adding height or thickness to an existing 2d sketch in order to realize a 3D model. It is an *addition* feature. To use an extruded boss/base tool:

1. Select the front plane and create Sketch1 as shown in Figure 3-2.
2. Click the **Features** tool.
3. Click the **Extruded Boss/Base** tool.
   The Extrude Properties Manager appears.
4. Define the extrusion height as 25mm. A real-time preview will appear (see Figure 3-3).
5. Click **OK** to complete the extrusion as shown in Figure 3-4.

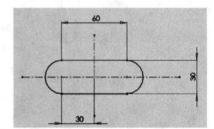

Figure 3-2 Sketch1

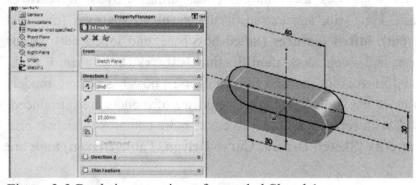

Figure 3-3 Real-time preview of extruded Sketch1

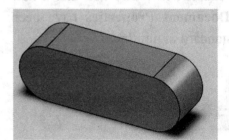

Figure 3-4 Part model obtained through extruded boss/base

DRAFT, DOME, RIB

Draft

The draft tool is used to create a slanted shape in a feature. Let us illustrate the tool with an example (See Figure 3-5).

1. Select the front plane and create Sketch1 (50 mm by 50 mm by 45 mm).
2. Click the **Features** tool.
3. Click the **Draft** tool.
   The Draft Properties Manager appears.
4. Click **Manual** for Type of Draft. **Neutral Plane** is chosen as default.
5. Define the **Draft Angle** as 30 degree.
6. Click upper face (Face<1>) as Neutral Plane. Arrow points upward. Correct it, if otherwise.
7. Click 2 adjacent faces (Face<2> and Face<3>) as **Faces to Draft**.
8. Click **OK** to complete the process of adding draft to a part model (see Figure 3-6).

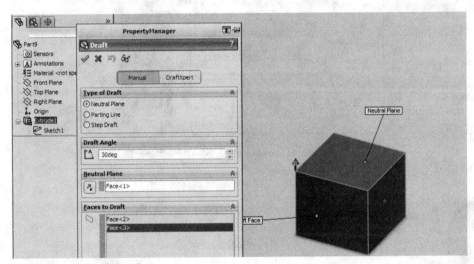

Figure 3-5 Draft tool

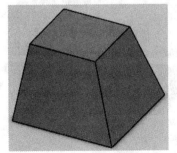

Figure 3-6 Adding draft features to a part model

Dome

The dome tool is used to add a dome shape to a feature. Let us illustrate the tool with an example (See Figure 3-7).

1. Select the front plane and create Sketch1.
2. Click the **Features** tool.
3. Click the top face of the cylinder.
4. Click the **Dome** tool.
   The Dome Properties Manager appears.
5. Define the dome height as 10 mm. A real-time preview will appear.
6. Click **OK** to complete the process of adding dome to a part model (see Figure 3-8).

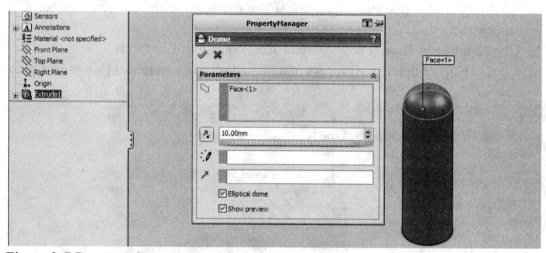

Figure 3-7 Dome tool

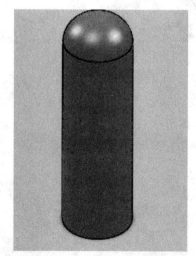

Figure 3-8 Adding dome feature to a part model

Rib

The rib tool is used to include a rib feature in part. Let there be an existing L-shaped model for which a rib is to be added.

1. Select the front plane (Sketch1) for the L-shape and define a reference plane, midway of the extruded length (See Figure 3-9).
2. Use the reference plane to sketch a slanting line.
3. Click the **Features** tool.
4. Click the **Rib** tool.
   The Rib Properties Manager appears (See Figure 3-10).
5. Check 'Both Sides' for the rib **Thickness**; Check 'Parallel to Sketch' for **Extrusion Direction**.
6. Set the rib thickness value as 10 mm. A real-time preview will appear.
7. Click **OK** to complete the rib and hide the reference plane (See Figure 3-11).

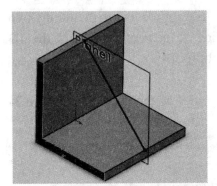

Figure 3-9 Sketching a slanting line on Plane1 of the L-shape to define a rib

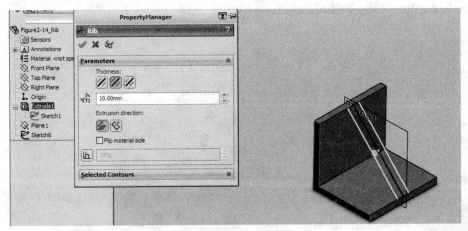

Figure 3-10 Rib Properties Manager

Figure 3-11 Adding rib feature to a part model

EXTRUDED CUT

The extruded cut tool is for removing portion of existing 2d sketch or part during 3D modeling. It is a *subtraction* feature. Let us illustrate the approach by including two holes, each 10 mm diameter located 30 mm from each side of the center of the of the 3D model created in Figures 3-2 to 3-4. To use an extruded cut tool:

1. Select the front plane and create Sketch2 (circle) to define the holes (see Figure 3-12).
2. Click the **Features** tool.
3. Click the **Extruded Cut** tool.
   The Extrude Properties Manager appears (see Figure 3-13).
4. Define the extrude cut distance as "All through". A real-time preview will appear.
5. Click **OK** to complete the extrude cut (see Figure 3-14).

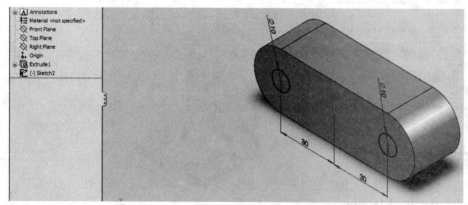

Figure 3-12 Creating circles, Sketch2 to define the holes

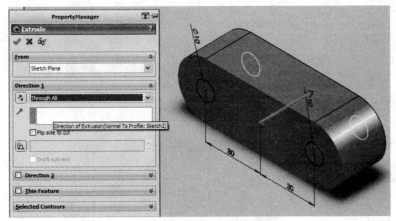

Figure 3-13 Preview for extruding Sketch2

Figure 3-14 Part model obtained through extrude cut

REVOLVED BOSS/BASE

The revolved boss/base tool rotates a contour about an axis. It is a useful tool when modeling parts that have circular contours. Let us illustrate the revolved boss/base concept as follows.

1. Select the front plane and create Sketch1 as shown in Figure 3-15.
2. Click the **Features** tool.
3. Click the **Revolved Boss/Base** tool.
   The Revolve Properties Manager appears (see Figure 3-16).
4. Define the revolved axis (Line1) as the vertical dimension line. A real-time preview will appear.
5. Click **OK** to complete the revolved part (see Figure 3-17).

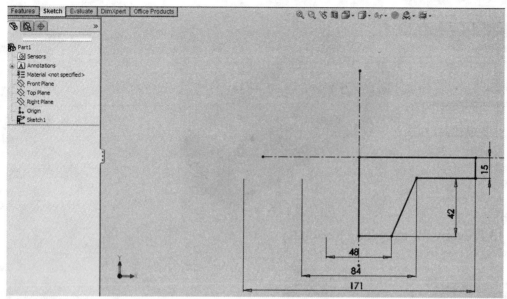

Figure 3-15 Sketch1

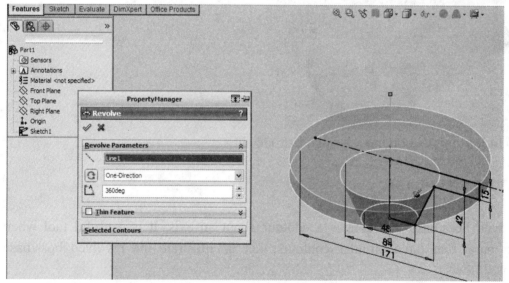

Figure 3-16 Preview

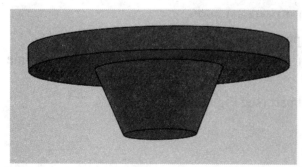

Figure 3-17 Revolved part, Extrude1

Creating Four Holes on the Revolved Part

The steps involved in creating four holes are as follows:
1. Sketch four holes, each 15 mm diameter as shown in Figure 3-18.
2. Extrude-cut each hole, Through All as shown in Figure 3-19. Final revolved part with holes is shown in Figure 3-20.

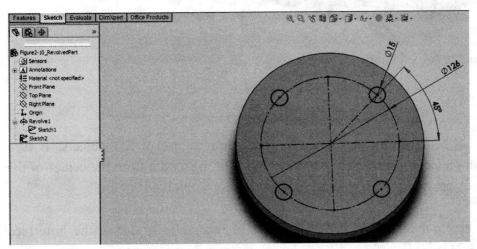

Figure 3-18 Sketches for four holes

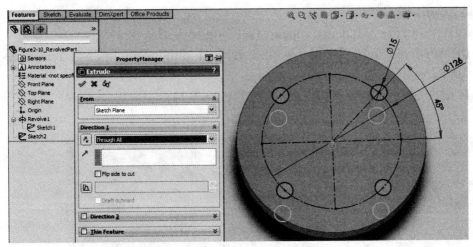

Figure 3-19 Extrude-Cut for holes

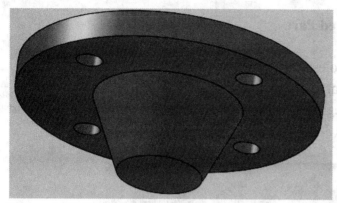

Figure 3-20 Final revolved feature

REVOLVED CUT

The revolved cut tool is for removing revolved sections out of 3D objects. It is a *subtraction* feature. Let us illustrate the approach by cutting a hole from the center of the 3D model already created in the previous section. To use a revolved cut tool:

1. Select the front plane and create Sketch3 (a rectangle) to define the hole (see Figure 3-21).
2. Click the **Features** tool.
3. Click the **Revolved Cut** tool.
   The Revolve Properties Manager appears (see Figure 3-22).
4. Define the revolved axis (Line1) as the vertical dimension line. A real-time preview will appear.
5. Click **OK** to complete the revolved cut (see Figure 3-23).

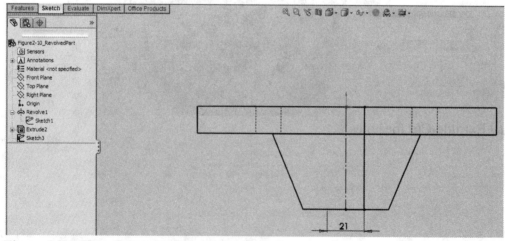

Figure 3-21 Sketch for revolve-cut

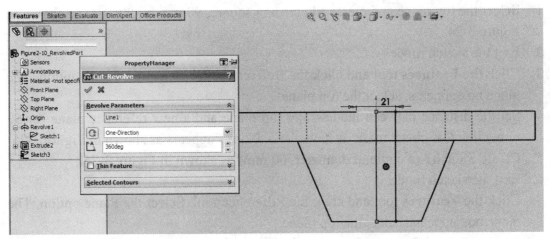

Figure 3-22 Revolve-cut

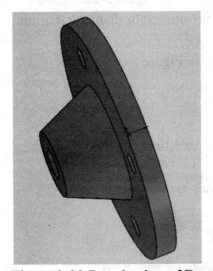

Figure 3-23 Revolved-cut 3D part

Although defining a circle and cutting through will still do the same work, the exercise has shown the steps required in a creating a revolved cut feature, which may be useful for more complicated modeling.

LOFTED BOSS/BASE

The lofted boss/base tool is used to create a shape between a number of planes, each of which contains a defined shape or geometry. The prerequisite for creating a 3D lofted model is to first sketch the shapes on the different planes. Let us illustrate lofted boss/base model using a square base, a circle, and an ellipse. There are no restrictions in the shapes that could be used. Let us illustrate the lofted boss/base concept as follows.

1. Select the top plane and create **Sketch1** (a square, 90 mm by 90 mm) as shown in Figure 3-24.
2. Exit the sketch mode.
3. Click the **Features** tool and click the Reference tool. Select the Plane option. The plane box appears; select the top plane.
4. Set the distance between the existing top plane and a new reference plane for 50 mm. click **OK** check mark. A new plane, Plane1 appears as shown in Figure 3-25.
5. Create **Sketch2** (a circle of diameter, 60 mm) as shown in Figure 3-25.
6. Exit the sketch mode.
7. Click the **Features** tool and click the Reference tool. Select the Plane option. The plane box appears; select the top plane.
8. Set the distance between Plane1 and a new reference plane for 50 mm. Click the OK check mark. A new plane, Plane2 appears as shown in Figure 3-26.
9. Create Sketch3 (an ellipse of major diameter, 80 mm and minor diameter, 65 mm) as shown in Figure 3-26.
10. Exit the sketch mode. All sketches appear as shown in Figure 3-27.
11. Click the **Lofted Boss/Base** tool.
    The Loft Properties Manager appears.
12. Right-click the Profiles box.
13. Click the square, then the circle, then the ellipse. A real-time preview will appear as shown in Figure 3-28.
14. Click OK to complete the lofted part. Hide the planes as shown in Figure 3-29.

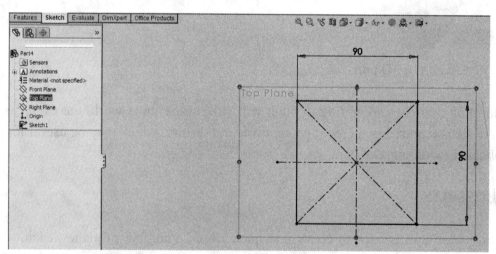

Figure 3-24 Bottom sketch for lofting (Sketch1)

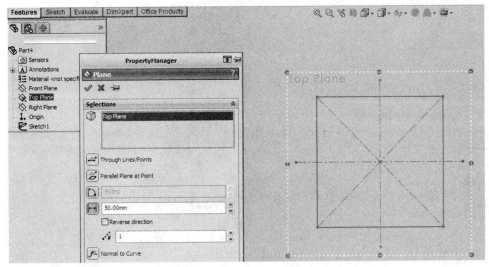

Figure 3-25 Middle sketch for lofting (Sketch2)

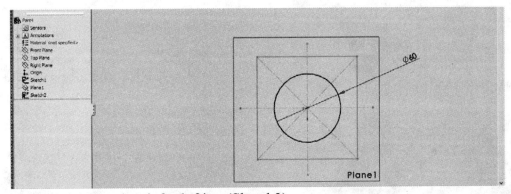

Figure 3-26 Top sketch for lofting (Sketch3)

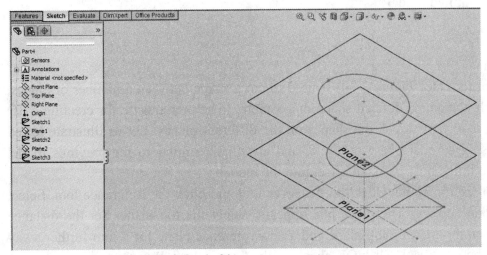

Figure 3-27 Three sketches for lofting

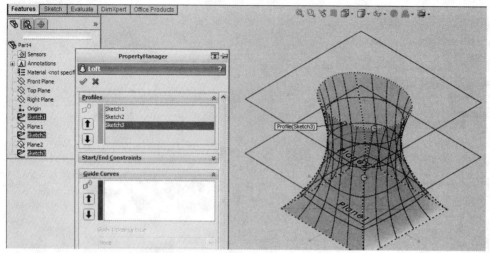

Figure 3-28 Loft based on Sketch1, Sketch2, and Sketch3

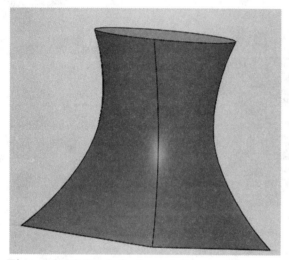

Figure 3-29 3D lofted model

LOFTED CUT

The lofted cut tool (see Figure 3-30) is used to cut a shape between a number of planes, each of which contains a defined shape or geometry. The prerequisite for creating a 3D lofted model is to first sketch the shapes on the different planes. Let us illustrate lofted cut model using a square base, a circle, and an ellipse similar to the previous model obtained from lofted boss/base but offset into the model.

1. Select the top plane. Click the **Features** tool and click the Reference tool. Select the Plane option. The plane box appears; select the top plane. Set the distance between the existing top plane and a new reference plane for 5 mm further away from the 3D model. Click OK check mark. A new plane, Plane3 appears.

2. Create Sketch4 (a square, 83 mm by 83 mm).

3. Exit the sketch mode.
4. Click the **Features** tool and click the Reference tool. Select the Plane option. The plane box appears; select the top plane.
5. Set the distance between the existing Plane1 and a new reference plane for 5 mm below. Click OK check mark. A new plane, Plane4 appears.
6. Create Sketch5 (a circle of diameter, 57 mm).
7. Exit the sketch mode.
8. Click the **Features** tool and click the Reference tool. Select the Plane option. The plane box appears; select the top plane.
9. Set the distance between Plane2 and a new reference plane for 5 mm above. Click the OK check mark. A new plane, Plane5 appears.
10. Create Sketch3 (an ellipse of major diameter, 67 mm and minor diameter, 60 mm).
11. Exit the sketch mode.
12. Click the **Lofted Cut** tool.
    The Loft Properties Manager appears.
13. Right-click the Profiles box.
14. Click the new square, then the new circle, then the new ellipse. A real-time preview will appear.
15. Click OK to complete the lofted cut part, which is now hollow. Hide the planes.

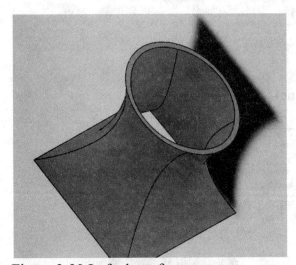

Figure 3-30 Lofted-cut features

SWEPT BOSS/BASE

The swept boss/base tool is used to sweep a profile through a path (arc, spline, etc.). As with lofting, there have to be existing shapes. The prerequisite for creating a 3D swept model is to first sketch the shapes on the different perpendicular planes. In the illustration presented here, a hexagon is the **profile** while a spline is the **path** as shown in Figure 3-31.

1. Select the top plane. Create Sketch1 (a hexagon with sides, 0.5 in).
2. Exit the sketch mode.
3. Select the front plane. Create Sketch2 (a spline with one end coinciding with the origin of the hexagon).
4. Exit the sketch mode.
5. Click the **Swept Cut** tool.
   The Swept Properties Manager appears (see Figure 3-32).
6. Right-click the **Profile** and **Path** box.
7. Click the hexagon as profile and the spline as path. A real-time preview will appear.
8. Click **OK** to complete the swept cut part, which is now hollow (see Figure 3-33). Hide the planes.

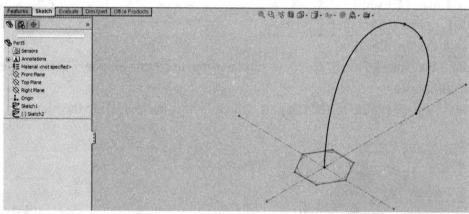

Figure 3-31 Profile (hexagon) and path (spline)

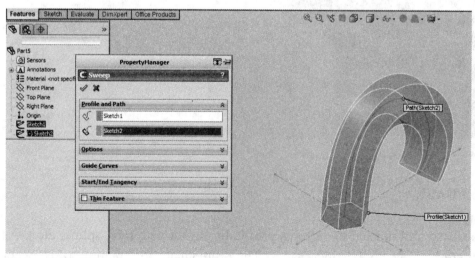

Figure 3-32 Preview

Figure 3-33 3D swept model

SWEPT CUT

The swept cut tool is used to cut a shape (profile) in one plane along a given path in another plane. The prerequisite for creating a 3D swept model is to first sketch the shapes on the different planes. Let us illustrate swept cut model using a hexagon as the profile while a spline is the path, similar to the previous model obtained from swept boss/base (see Figure 3-33). In this case the new hexagon is offset to be of smaller size than the one previously used.

1. Select the top plane. Click the **Features** tool and click the Reference tool. Select the Plane option. The plane box appears; select the top plane. Set the distance to be zero so that the new plane is collinear with existing top plane. Click **OK** check mark. A new plane, Plane3 appears.
2. Create Sketch2 (Sketch5) (a hexagon with sides offset inward by .05 in) [see Figure 3-34].
3. Exit the sketch mode.
4. Click the **Swept Cut** tool.
   The Swept Properties Manager appears (see Figure 3-35).
5. Right-click the Profile and Path box.
6. Click the hexagon as profile and the spline as path. A real-time preview will appear.
7. Click **OK** to complete the swept cut part, which is now hollow. Hide the planes (see Figure 3-36).

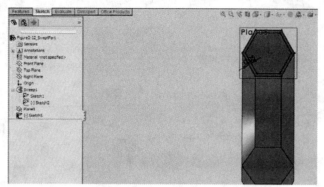

Figure 3-34 Sketch for cutting

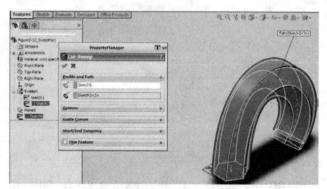

Figure 3-35 Preview

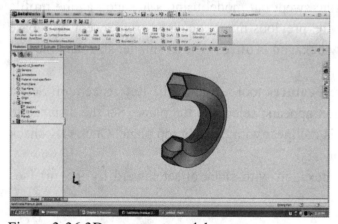

Figure 3-36 3D swept cut model

HOLE WIZARD

The hole wizard tool is used to add hole(s) to and existing 3D model as shown in Figure 3-37. Let us use the revolved boss/base model as an example; we want to add four 10 mm diameter holes using hole wizard tool.

1. Click the front face having four 15 mm diameter holes.
2. Click the **Features** tool and click the **Hole Wizard** tool.

The Hole Wizard Properties Manager appears (see Figure 3-38).

3. Click the **Type** button for the hole required. A clear hole was selected for our illustration.
4. Select the ANSI Metric for the Standard unit and 10 mm for the Size.
5. Click the **Position** button.
6. Click an approximate center point location for the hole.
7. Click **OK** check mark. A dialog box will appear (see Figure 3-39). Use the Smart Dimension tool to locate the center of the hole (see Figure 3-40).
8. Click **OK** in the dialog box.
9. The hole will be added to the model (see Figure 3-41).

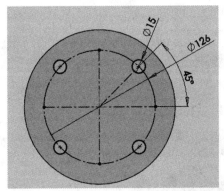

Figure 3-37 An existing model to which hole wizard is to be used to add extra holes

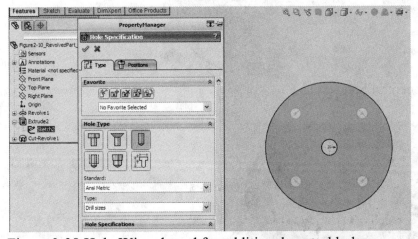

Figure 3-38 Hole Wizard used for additional central hole

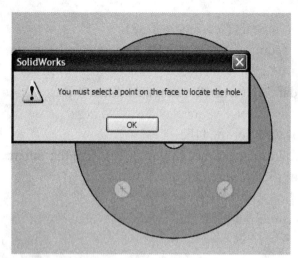

Figure 3-39 Hole Wizard Message

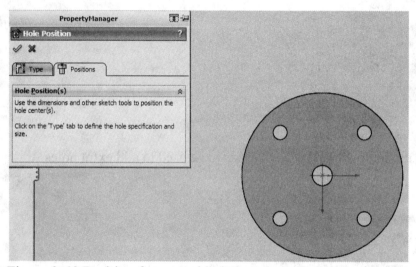

Figure 3-40 Position for central hole

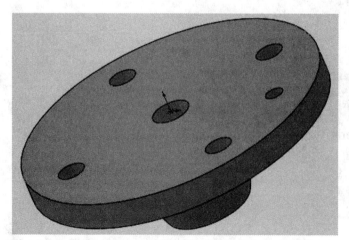

Figure 3-41 Hole created using Hole Wizard tool

SHELL

The shell tool is used to create a hollow shape in an existing 3D model, transforming it into a hollow object having uniform thickness. Let us use the lofted model for illustrating shell by applying the shell tool on the square base for a value of 5 mm thickness.

1. Select the square base (see Figure 3-42).
2. Click the **Shell** tool.
   The Shell Properties Manager appears (see Figure 3-43).
3. Apply 2.5 mm thickness.
4. Click **OK** to complete the shell part, which is now hollow as shown in Figure 3-44.

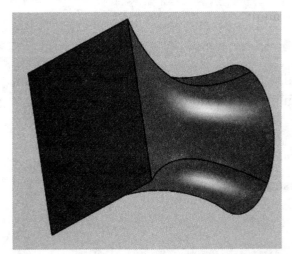

Figure 3-42 Bottom is chosen for shelling

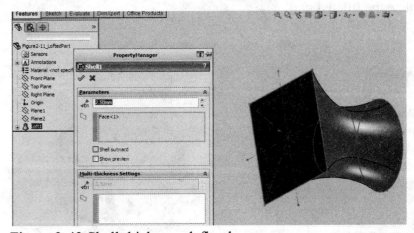

Figure 3-43 Shell thickness defined

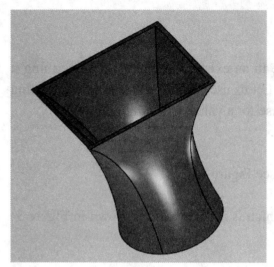

Figure 3-44 Shell tool for creating swept-cut features

FILLET TOOL

A fillet is a rounded corner. There are usually four ways of defining a fillet: constant radius or by variable radius or by face or by full round as shown in Figures 3-45—3-48.

Defining a Constant Radius Fillet

Defining a fillet using a constant radius is illustrated in Figure 3-45.

1. Click the **Fillet** tool.

   The Fillet Properties Manager appears.

2. Click the **Constant Radius** option.

3. Apply **5 mm** radius. A real-time preview will appear.

4. Click **OK** to complete the filleted part.

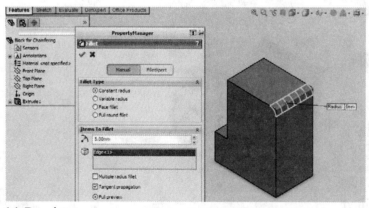 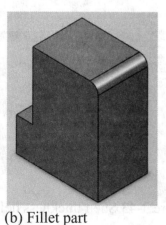

(a) Preview   (b) Fillet part

Figure 3-45 Fillet tool for creating constant radius fillets

Defining a Variable Radius Fillet

Defining a fillet using a variable radius is illustrated in Figure 3-46.
1. Click the **Fillet** tool.
   The Fillet Properties Manager appears.
2. Click the **Variable Radius** option.
3. Click the edge to apply the fillet.
   Two boxes appear on the screen, one at each end of the edge to accept the values.
4. Apply **2.5 mm** to the word **Unassigned** in the first box.
5. Apply **5 mm** to the word **Unassigned** in the second box. A real-time preview will appear.
6. Click **OK** to complete the filleted part.

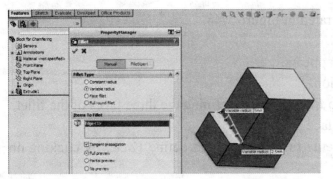

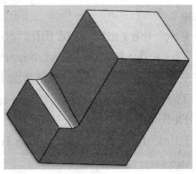

(a) Preview   (b) Fillet part

Figure 3-46 Fillet tool for creating variable radius fillets

Defining a Face Fillet

Defining a fillet using the face is illustrated in Figure 3-47.
1. Click the **Fillet** tool.
   The Fillet Properties Manager appears.
2. Click the **Face fillet** option.
   Two boxes appear in **Items to Fillet** box for defining the two faces of the fillet.
3. Apply **5 mm** radius.
4. Define *Face1* by clicking on a face as shown.
5. Click the second box in the **Items to Fillet** box and define *Face2* by clicking on the face as shown. A real-time preview will appear.
6. Click **OK** to complete the filleted part.

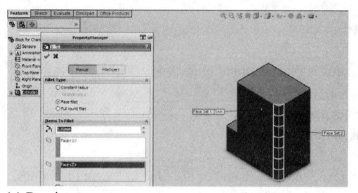

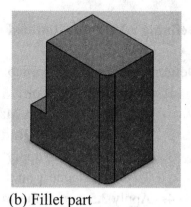

(a) Preview   (b) Fillet part

Figure 3-47 Fillet tool for creating variable radius fillets

Defining a Full Round Fillet

Defining a fillet using the face is illustrated in Figure 3-48.

1. Click the **Full round fillet** tool.
   The Fillet Properties Manager appears.
2. Click the **Full round fillet** option.
   Three boxes appear in **Items to Fillet** box for defining the three faces of the fillet.
3. Define Face1 by clicking on a face as shown.
4. Click the second box in the **Items to Fillet** box and define *Face2* by clicking on the face as shown.
5. Click the third box in the **Items to Fillet** box and define *Face3* by clicking on the face as shown. A real-time preview will appear.
6. Click **OK** to complete the filleted part.

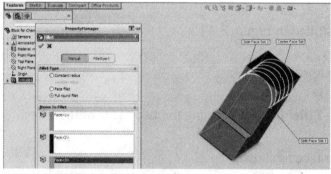

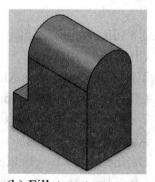

(a) Preview   (b) Fillet part

Figure 3-48 Fillet tool for creating full round fillets

CHAMFER TOOL

A chamfer is a slanted surface added to the corner of a part. Chamfers are usually manufactured at 45° but any other angle may be used. There are usually three ways of defining a chamfer: an angle and a distance (2.5×45°) or by two distances (2.5×2.5) or by a vertex as shown in Figures 3-49—3-51.

Defining a Chamfer Using an Angle and Distance

Defining a chamfer using an angle and distance is illustrated in Figure 3-49.
1. Click the **Chamfer** tool.
   The Chamfer Properties Manager appears.
2. Click the **Angle-distance** tool.
3. Apply 2.5 mm distance and accept the default angle 45°. A real-time preview will appear.
4. Click OK to complete the chamfered part.

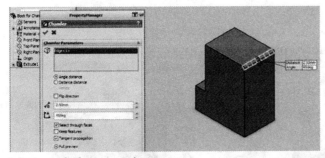 

(a) A real-time preview   (b) Chamfered part
Figure 3-49 Chamfer tool for creating chamfers defined using an angle and distance

Defining a Chamfer Using Two Distances

Defining a chamfer using two distances is illustrated in Figure 3-50.
5. Click the **Chamfer** tool.
   The Chamfer Properties Manager appears.
6. Click the **Distance-distance** tool.
7. Apply **2.5 mm** distances each. A real-time preview will appear.
8. Click **OK** to complete the chamfered part.

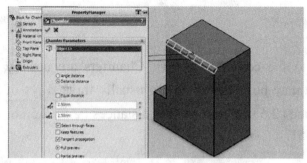 

(a) A real-time preview   (b) Chamfered part

Figure 3-50 Chamfer tool for creating chamfers defined using two distances

Defining a Chamfer Using a Vertex

Defining a chamfer using a vertex is illustrated in Figure 3-51.

1. Click the **Chamfer** tool.
   The Chamfer Properties Manager appears.
2. Click the **Vertex** tool. Three distance boxes will appear.
3. Define the three distances. Although **2.5 mm** is used, any other value could be used.
4. A real-time preview will appear.
5. Click **OK** to complete the chamfered part.

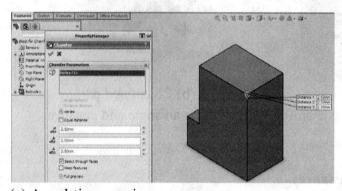 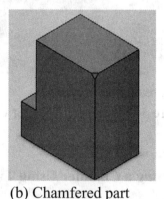

(a) A real-time preview   (b) Chamfered part

Figure 3-51 Chamfer tool for creating chamfers defined using two distances

LINEAR PATTERN

The linear pattern tool is used to create rectangular patterns based on a given model. Let us consider an example.

1. Sketch a rectangle, 100 mm by 50 mm and extrude it 5 mm.
2. Click the bottom and sketch one small rectangle, 5 mm by 5 mm; extrude it 50 mm.

3. Click the **Linear Pattern** tool.
   The Linear Pattern Properties Manager appears.
4. Select the 5 mm by 5 mm by 50 mm feature from the **Feature Manager** for the Feature to Pattern.
5. For **Direction1>** select a horizontal edge for direction, 70 mm for Distance, and 2 for number of patterns. For **Direction2>** select a vertical edge for direction, 36 mm for Distance, and 2 for number of patterns (see Figure 3-52).
6. Click **OK** to complete the patterns. Observe the object: a table as shown in Figure 3-53.

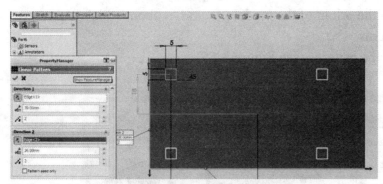

Figure 3-52 Defining distances and number of patterns in Direction 1 and Direction 2

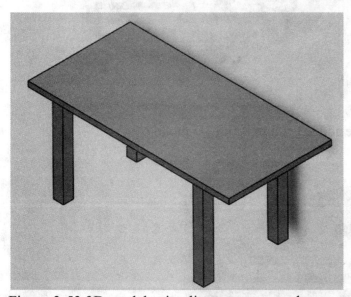

Figure 3-53 3D model using linear pattern tool

CIRCULAR PATTERN

The pattern tool is used to create circular pattern on a 3D model about an origin. The 10mm diameter hole created using the Hole Wizard is now to be duplicated into four patterns in a circular manner.

7. Click the **Circular Pattern** tool.
   The Circular Pattern Properties Manager appears (see Figure 3-54).
8. Select the 10mm diameter hole created using the Hole Wizard from the **Feature Manager** for the Feature to Pattern.
9. Click **View > Temporary Axis** to activate the temporary axes.
10. Select the axis through the origin of the model (Axis<1>) about which to pattern.
11. Define number of patterns.
12. Click **OK** to complete the patterns (see Figure 3-55).

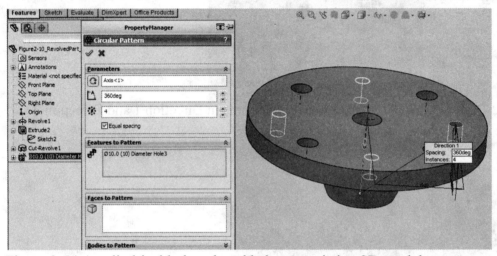

Figure 3-54 A cylindrical hole to be added to an existing 3D model

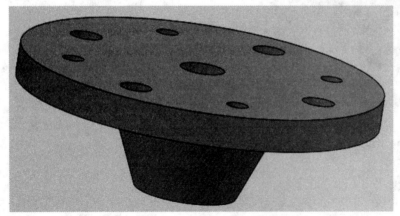

Figure 3-55 3D model using circular pattern tool

MIRROR

The mirror tool is used to create mirror images of features (see Figure 3-56). The axes for mirroring have to be defined. For example, if only one hole in the upper-right side of the object shown here was initially defined, the bottom-right hole can be obtained by mirroring about the horizontal center line. Using these two holes, the upper-left and the bottom-left holes can be obtained by mirroring about the vertical center line to obtain Figure 3-57.

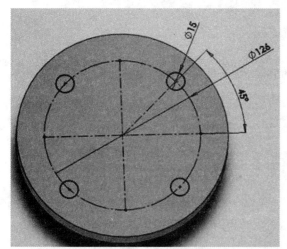

Figure 3-56 3D model illustrating mirror tool

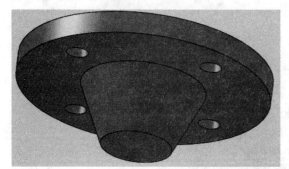

Figure 3-57 3D model with hole features obtained using mirror tool

EDITING FEATURES

SolidWorks **edit features** tools are extremely powerful also. The key to edit features tools is the extent to which you understand the **Feature Manager design tree**. The design tree gives us the history of how the components of a part were modeled as shown in Figure 3-58. Since features make up a part, and sketches make us a feature, we can easily edit a part by simply editing the features or the sketches. It is that easy, but you need to try it out for different parts and master the process for trouble-shooting your parts. Let us edit the sketch of lofted model and see how this will affect our target shape.

1. Right-click *Sketch2* in the **Feature Manager**.
2. Click **Edit Sketch**.
3. Change the dimension of the middle sketch (circle) from 60 mm to 100 mm (see Figure 3-59).
4. Click **Exit Sketch**. The model bulges outward as shown in Figure 3-60!

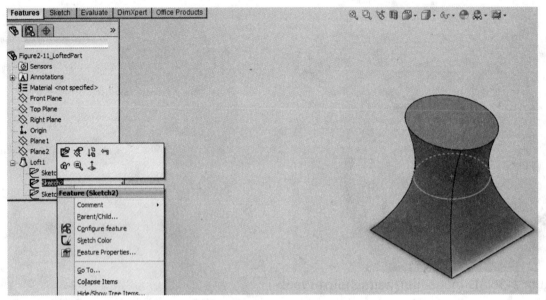

Figure 3-58 Design tree 3D lofted model

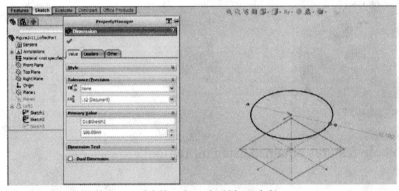

Figure 3-59 Editing middle sketch (Sketch2)

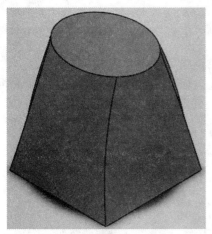

Figure 3-60 Edited model

SolidWorks **edit features** tools are powerful for editing model via the Design Tree. By merely changing the dimension of the middle sketch (circle) in the middle plane, a completely different shape is realized. The designer can change a number of dimensions to realize a suite of different designs. This is a useful tool for industrial designers.

TUTORIALS

Tutorial 1: Simple Part 3-1

Create the model shown in Figure 3-61. The sketch of the model is shown in Figure 3-62. Create the sketch and fully dimension it. Extrude the model to the depth of 1.25 in. Determine the center of mass for the model for 1060 Alloy material. Note the origin of the model.

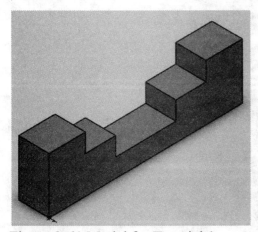

Figure 3-61 Model for Tutorial 1

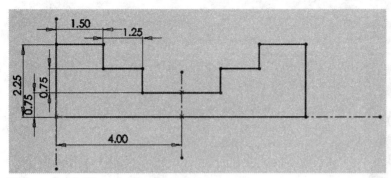

Figure 3-62 Sketch for Tutorial 1

SolidWorks Solution

1. Open a **New** SolidWorks part document.
2. **Set** the document properties for the model, with decimal places = 2.
3. Create **Sketch1** as shown in Figure 3-62.
4. Click the **Features** tool.
5. Click the **Extruded Boss/Base** tool.
   The Extrude Properties Manager appears.
6. Define the extrusion depth as 1.25 in. A real-time preview will appear.
7. Click **OK** to complete the extrusion, **Extrude1** as shown in Figure 3-61.
8. **Assign** 1060 Alloy material to the part modeled.
9. **Calculate** the mass properties of the part (see Figure 3-63).

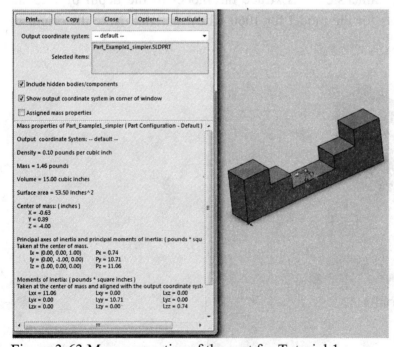

Figure 3-63 Mass properties of the part for Tutorial 1

Tutorial 2: Simple Part 3-2

Create the model shown in Figure 3-64. The sketch of the model is shown in Figure 3-65. Create the sketch and fully dimension it. Extrude the model to the depth of 1.25 in. Determine the center of mass for the model for 1060 Alloy material. Note the origin of the model.

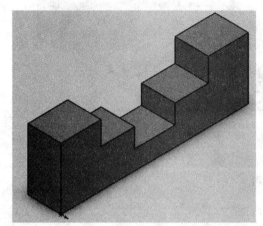

Figure 3-64 Model for Tutorial 2

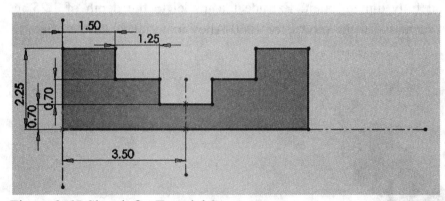

Figure 3-65 Sketch for Tutorial 2

SolidWorks Solution

1. Open a **New** SolidWorks part document.
2. **Set** the document properties for the model, with decimal places = 2.
3. Create **Sketch1** as shown in Figure 3-65.
4. Click the **Features** tool.
5. Click the **Extruded Boss/Base** tool.
   The Extrude Properties Manager appears.
6. Define the extrusion depth as 1.25 in. A real-time preview will appear.

7. Click **OK** to complete the extrusion, **Extrude1** as shown in Figure 3-64.
8. **Assign** 1060 Alloy material to the part modeled.
9. **Calculate** the mass properties of the part (see Figure 3-66).

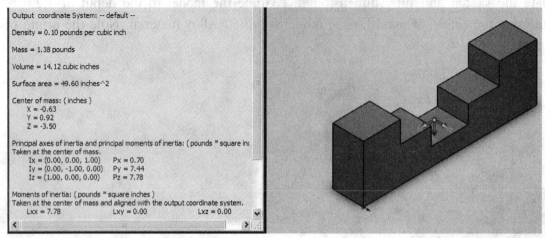

Figure 3-66 Mass properties of the part for Tutorial 2

Tutorial 3: Simple Part 3-3

Create the model shown in Figure 3-67. The sketch of the model is shown in Figure 3-68. Create the sketch and fully dimension it. Extrude the model to the depth of 1.25 in. Determine the center of mass for the model for 1060 Alloy material. Note the origin of the model.

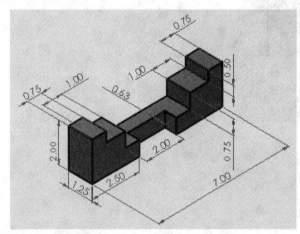

Figure 3-67 Model for Tutorial 3

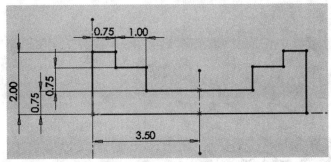

Figure 3-68 Sketch for Tutorial 3

SolidWorks Solution

1. Open a **New** SolidWorks part document.
2. **Set** the document properties for the model, with decimal places = 2.
3. Create **Sketch1** as shown in Figure 3-68.
4. Click the **Features** tool.
5. Click the **Extruded Boss/Base** tool.
    The Extrude Properties Manager appears.
6. Define the extrusion depth as 1.25 in. A real-time preview will appear.
7. Click **OK** to complete the first extrusion, **Extrude1** as shown in Figure 3-69.
8. Create **Sketch2** 2.00 in by 0.625 mm on top of inner face as shown in Figure 3-69.
9. **Extrude-cut** Sketch2 *All Through* as shown in Figure 3-70 to obtain the final model (see Figure 3-71).
10. **Assign** 1060 Alloy material to the part modeled.
11. **Calculate** the mass properties of the part (see Figure 3-71).

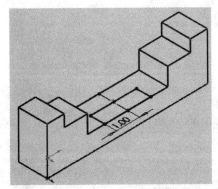

Figure 3-69 Intermediate solution

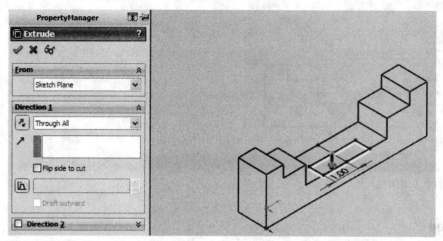

Figure 3-70 Extrude-cut of Sketch2 *All Through* to obtain the model shown in

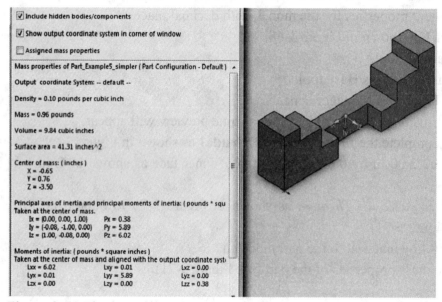

Figure 3-71 Final model and mass properties for Tutorial 3

Tutorial 4: Simple Part 3-4

Repeat Tutorial 3 with material being brass.

1. **Right-click** the material, 1060 Alloy on the FeatureManger.
2. Click **Edit Material**.
3. Select **Brass** and **Apply** its material properties.
4. **Calculate** the mass properties of the part (see Figure 3-72).

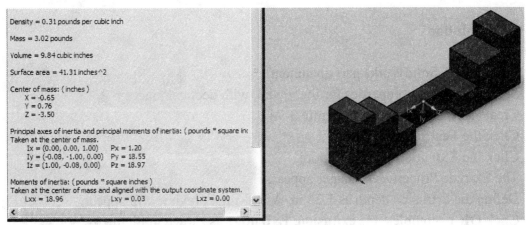

```
Density = 0.31 pounds per cubic inch

Mass = 3.02 pounds

Volume = 9.84 cubic inches

Surface area = 41.31 inches^2

Center of mass: ( inches )
    X = -0.65
    Y = 0.76
    Z = -3.50

Principal axes of inertia and principal moments of inertia: ( pounds * square inc
Taken at the center of mass.
    Ix = (0.00, 0.00, 1.00)    Px = 1.20
    Iy = (-0.08, -1.00, 0.00)   Py = 18.55
    Iz = (1.00, -0.08, 0.00)    Pz = 18.97

Moments of inertia: ( pounds * square inches )
Taken at the center of mass and aligned with the output coordinate system.
    Lxx = 18.96          Lxy = 0.03          Lxz = 0.00
```

Figure 3-72 Model and mass properties for Tutorial 4

Tutorial 5: Simple Part 3-5

Create the model shown in Figure 3-73. The sketch of the model is shown in Figure 3-74. Create the sketch and fully dimension it. Extrude the model to the depth of 1.25 in. Determine the center of mass for the model for 1060 Alloy material. Note the origin of the model.

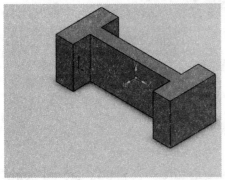

Figure 3-73 Model for Tutorial 5

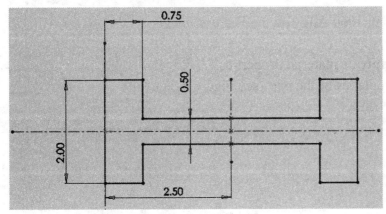

Figure 3-74 Sketch for Tutorial 5

SolidWorks Solution

1. Open a **New** SolidWorks part document.
2. **Set** the document properties for the model, with decimal places = 2.
3. Create **Sketch1** as shown in Figure 3-74.
4. Click the **Features** tool.
5. Click the **Extruded Boss/Base** tool.
   The Extrude Properties Manager appears.
6. Define the extrusion depth as 1.25 in. A real-time preview will appear.
7. Click **OK** to complete the extrusion, **Extrude1** as shown in Figure 3-73.
8. **Assign** 1060 Alloy material to the part modeled.
9. **Calculate** the mass properties of the part (see Figure 3-75).

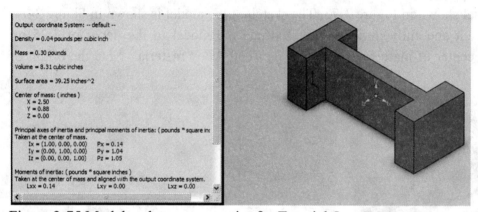

Figure 3-75 Model and mass properties for Tutorial 5

Tutorial 6: Simple Part 3-6

Repeat Tutorial 5 with height of sketch being 3.00 in (see Figure 3-76) and material being brass.

1. **Right-click** the material, 1060 Alloy on the FeatureManger.
2. Click **Edit Material**.
3. Select **Copper** and **Apply** its material properties.
4. **Calculate** the mass properties of the part (see Figure 3-77).

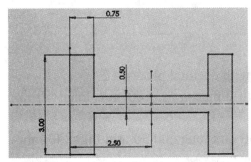

Figure 3-76 Sketch for Tutorial 6

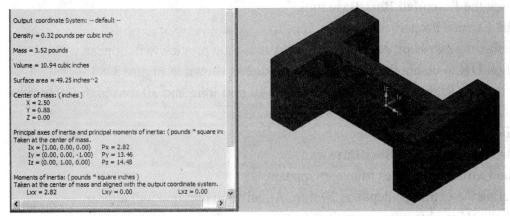

Figure 3-77 Model and mass properties for Tutorial 6

Tutorial 7: Simple Part 3-7

Create the model shown in Figure 3-78. Create the sketch and fully dimension it. Determine the center of mass for the model for Brass material. Note the origin of the model.

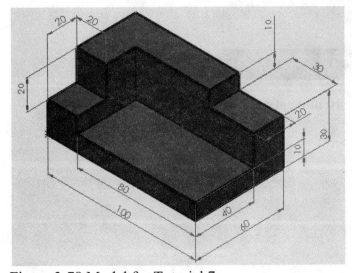

Figure 3-78 Model for Tutorial 7

SolidWorks Solution

1. Open a **New** SolidWorks part document.
2. **Set** the document properties for the model, with decimal places = 2.
3. Select the **Top Plane**; create **Sketch1** with dimensions, 100 mm long, 60 mm wide, and 10 mm high, to realize **Extrude1**.
4. Select the **Front Plane**; create **Sketch2**, 100 mm long and 30 mm high (40 mm – 10 mm) [30 mm by 10 mm cut out] (see Figure 3-79).
5. Click the **Features** tool.
6. Click the **Extruded Boss/Base** tool.
   The Extrude Properties Manager appears.
7. Define the extrusion depth as 20 mm. A real-time preview will appear.
8. Click **OK** to obtain the extrusion, **Extrude2** as shown in Figure 3-80.
9. Select the **Right Plane**; create **Sketch3**, 40 mm long and 30 mm high (20 mm by 20 mm cut out). (see Figure 3-81)
10. Click the **Features** tool.
11. Click the **Extruded Boss/Base** tool.
    The Extrude Properties Manager appears.
12. Define the extrusion depth as 20 mm. A real-time preview will appear.
13. Click **OK** to obtain the extrusion, **Extrude3** as shown in Figure 3-82.
14. **Assign** Brass material to the part modeled.
15. **Calculate** the mass properties of the part (see Figure 3-83).

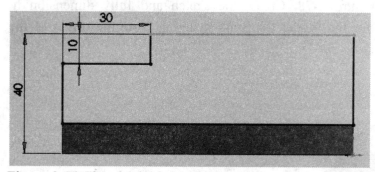

Figure 3-79 Sketch2 with 30 mm by 10 mm cut out

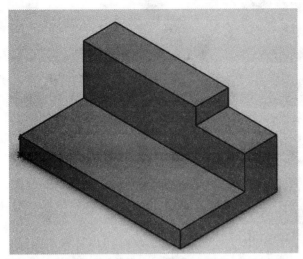

Figure 3-80 Sketch2 extruded 20 mm

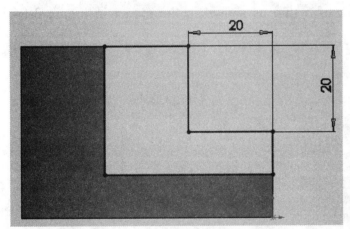

Figure 3-81 Sketch3 with 20 mm by 20 mm cut out

Figure 3-82 Part completed

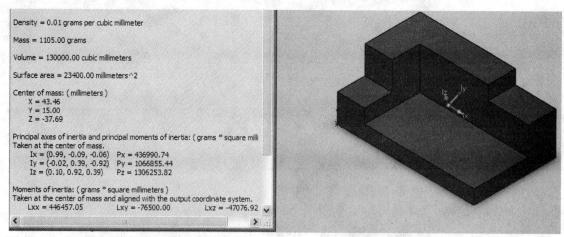

Density = 0.01 grams per cubic millimeter

Mass = 1105.00 grams

Volume = 130000.00 cubic millimeters

Surface area = 23400.00 millimeters^2

Center of mass: (millimeters)
   X = 43.46
   Y = 15.00
   Z = -37.69

Principal axes of inertia and principal moments of inertia: (grams * square milli
Taken at the center of mass.
   Ix = (0.99, -0.09, -0.06) Px = 436990.74
   Iy = (-0.02, 0.39, -0.92) Py = 1066855.44
   Iz = (0.10, 0.92, 0.39) Pz = 1306253.82

Moments of inertia: (grams * square millimeters)
Taken at the center of mass and aligned with the output coordinate system.
   Lxx = 446457.05   Lxy = -76500.00   Lxz = -47076.92

Figure 3-83 Model and mass properties for Tutorial 7

Tutorial 8: Simple Part 3-8

Repeat Tutorial 7 with fillet radius of 5 mm as shown in the model in Figure 3-84. Determine the mass properties.

Figure 3-84 Part in Tutorial 7 with fillet radius of 5 mm

SolidWorks Solution

1. Click **Fillet**.
2. Select **Constant radius** for **Fillet Type**.
3. Choose **Fillet radius, 5 mm**.
4. Select the **four edges**.
5. Click **OK** to obtain the part as shown in Figure 3-85.
6. **Calculate** the mass properties of the part (see Figure 3-86).

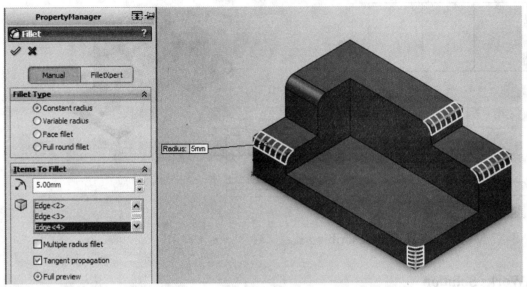

Figure 3-85 Preview of part having fillet radius of 5 mm for some edges

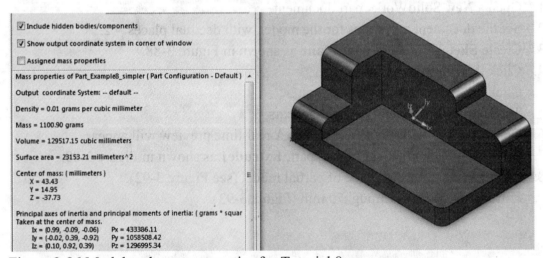

Figure 3-86 Model and mass properties for Tutorial 8

Tutorial 9: Simple Part 3-9

Create the model shown in Figure 3-87 for which the sketch is also described. Create the sketch and fully dimension it. Note the symmetry and origin of the model. Determine the center of mass for the model for 1060 Alloy material.

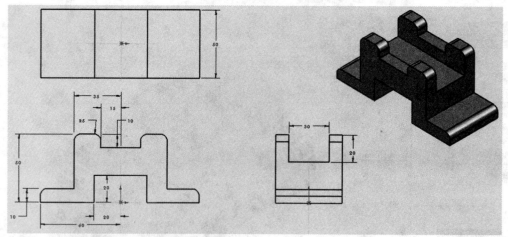

Figure 3-87 Model and sketch describing it

SolidWorks Solution

1. Open a **New** SolidWorks part document.
2. **Set** the document properties for the model, with decimal places = 2.
3. Create **Sketch1** on the **Front Plane** as shown in Figure 3-88.
4. Click the **Features** tool.
5. Click the **Extruded Boss/Base** tool.
   The Extrude Properties Manager appears.
6. Define the extrusion depth as 50 mm. A real-time preview will appear.
7. Click **OK** to complete the partial part, **Extrude1** as shown in Figure 3-89.
8. Create **Sketch2** on right side of partial model (see Figure 3-92).
9. Extrude-cut Sketch2 through 70 mm (Figure 3-93).

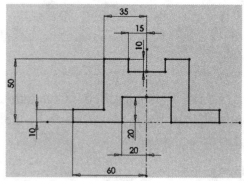

Figure 3-88 Sketch1

Figure 3-89 Sketch1 extruded 50 mm

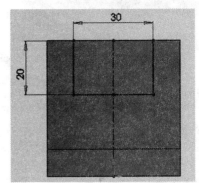

Figure 3-90 Sketch2 on right side of partial model

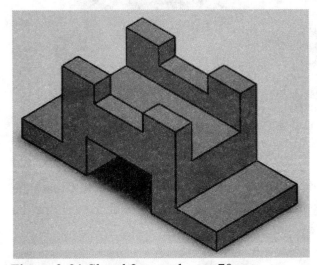

Figure 3-91 Sketch2 extrude-cut 70 mm

10. Click **Fillet**.
11. Select **Constant radius** for **Fillet Type**.
12. Choose **Fillet radius, 5 mm**.

13. Select the **four edges** on the top and **two edges** on the sides of the part (see Figure 3-92).

14. **Assign** 1060 Alloy material to the part modeled.

15. **Calculate** the mass properties of the part (see Figure 3-93).

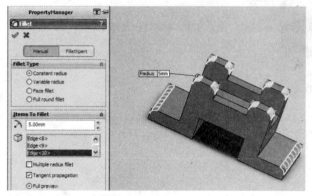 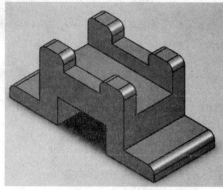

(a) Preview of filleting   (b) Part

Figure 3-92 Part with fillets

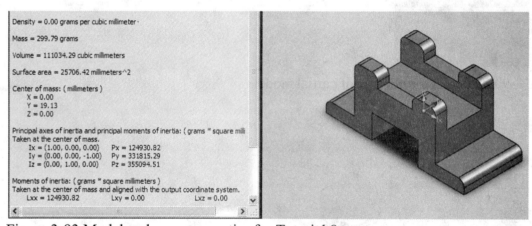

Figure 3-93 Model and mass properties for Tutorial 8

Tutorial 10: Simple Part 3-10

Create the model shown in Figure 3-94 for which the sketch is also described. Create the sketch and fully dimension it. Note the symmetry and origin of the model. Determine the center of mass for the model for 1060 Alloy material.

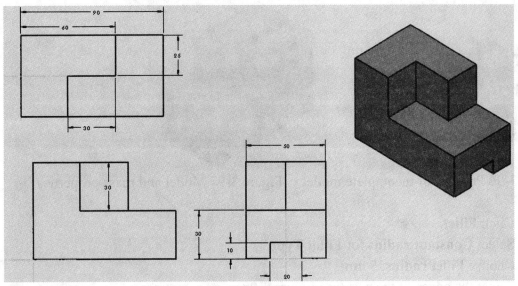

Figure 3-94 Model and sketch describing it

SolidWorks Solution

1. Open a **New** SolidWorks part document.
2. **Set** the document properties for the model, with decimal places = 2.
3. Create **Sketch1** as shown in Figure 3-95.
4. Click the **Features** tool.
5. Click the **Extruded Boss/Base** tool.
   The Extrude Properties Manager appears.
6. Define the extrusion depth as 90 mm. A real-time preview will appear.
7. Click **OK** to complete the partial part, **Extrude1** as shown in Figure 3-96.
8. Create **Sketch2** (L-shaped) on top of partial model (see Figure 3-96).
9. Extrude **Sketch2** through 30 mm to give completed model in Figure 3-97.

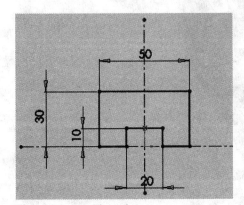

Figure 3-95 Sketch1

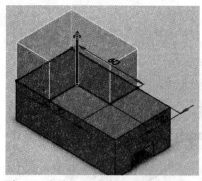
Figure 3-96 Preview of incomplete model

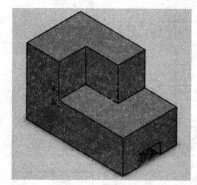
Figure 3-97 Model and mass properties

10. Click **Fillet**.
11. Select **Constant radius** for **Fillet Type**.
12. Choose **Fillet radius**, **5 mm**.
13. Select the **edges** of the part (see Figure 3-98).
14. **Assign** 1060 Alloy material to the part modeled.
15. **Calculate** the mass properties of the part (see Figure 3-99).

Figure 3-98 Model and mass properties for Tutorial 10

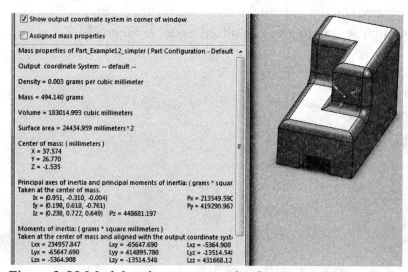

Figure 3-99 Model and mass properties for Tutorial 10

PATTERNS—ADVANCED METHODS

The patterns covered so far are quite basic: linear and circular patterns. In some cases, the sketch driven and curve driven pattern approaches are more appropriate. These will be discussed together with table driven patterns. The pros and cons of these approaches will be obvious as they are discussed.

Sketch Driven Pattern

1. Open a **New Part** document.
2. Select the **Top Plane** for sketching.
3. Sketch a circle, **Sketch1**, diameter 150 mm.
4. Extrude **Sketch1** using the **Mid Plane** option through **25 mm**.
5. Sketch a circle, **Sketch2**, diameter 10 mm with its center coinciding with that of **Sketch1**.
6. Extrude-cut **Sketch2** through **25 mm** (see Figure 3-100).

Figure 3-100 Feature to be patterned at the center of model

7. Click the top of the feature.
8. Sketch several points, **Sketch4** at locations of interest (see Figure 3-101).
9. **Exit** Sketch.

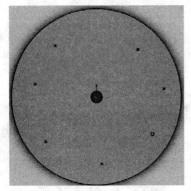

Figure 3-101 Points to drive pattern

10. Click **Feature > Linear Pattern > Sketch Driven Pattern** (see Figure 3-102).

The **Sketch Driven Pattern PropertyManager** automatically displayed; see Figure 3-103.

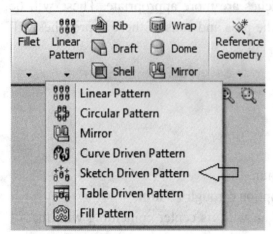

Figure 3-102 Sketch Driven Pattern option

11. In the Selections rollout, click Sketch4 (for the points created) [see Figure 3-103].

12. In the **Features to Pattern** rollout, click Extrude2 [see Figure 3-103].

13. Click **OK** (the completed patterns are shown in Figure 3-104).

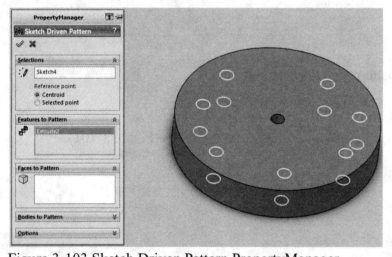

Figure 3-103 Sketch Driven Pattern PropertyManager

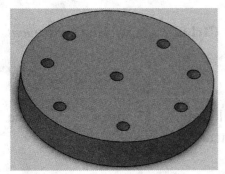

Figure 3-104 The resulting sketch driven pattern feature

Curve Driven Pattern

1. Open a **New Part** document.
2. Choose the **Top Plane** for sketching.
3. Sketch a slot profile, **Sketch1**, center-center distance 150 mm, width 100 mm (see Figure 3-105).
4. Extrude **Sketch1** using the **Mid Plane** option through **15 mm** (see Figure 3-106).

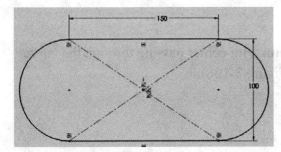

Figure 3-105 Base profile

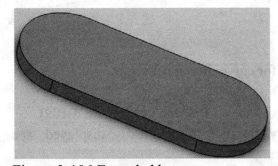

Figure 3-106 Extruded base

Case 1: Closed Curve

5. Click *the top face of the* **Extruded** base.

6. Click the **Sketch** command option.
7. Click *any edge*, followed by holding down the **Ctrl** key and *clicking subsequent edges.*
8. Click **Convert Entities** to extract the edges.
9. Click the **Offset Entities** command option.
10. Set the **Offset Distance** in the Parameters rollout to be **15 mm** and check the **Reverse** option (see Figure 3-107 for the extracted closed curve).
11. Exit Sketch.

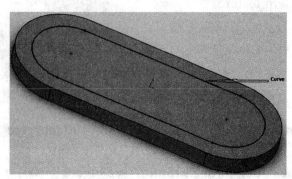

Figure 3-107 Closed curve to drive pattern

Create a seed feature

12. Select the top face of the base.
13. Sketch a circle, **Sketch3**, diameter **10 mm** with center passing through the curve.
14. Extrude **Sketch3** through 15 mm (see Figure 3-108).

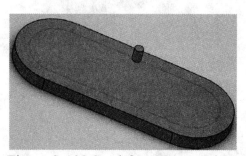

Figure 3-108 Seed-feature created on the curve for curve driven pattern

15. Click **Feature > Linear Pattern > Curve Driven Pattern** (see Figure 3-109). The **Curve Driven Pattern PropertyManager** automatically displayed; see Figure 3-109.
16. In the **Direction1** rollout, select **Sketch2** as the **Pattern Direction**.
17. For the **Number of Instances**, set it to **10**.
18. For the **Spacing**, set it to **50**.
19. In the **Features To Pattern** rollout, select **Extrude2**.
20. Click **OK** (see the model with pattern in Figure 3-110).

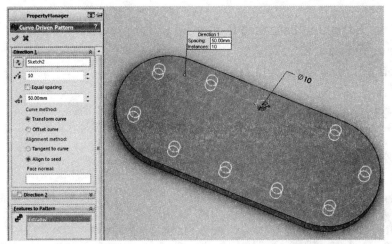

Figure 3-109 Curve driven pattern PropertyManager

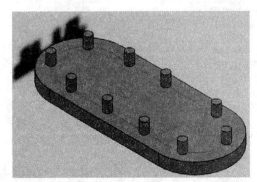

Figure 3-110 Resulting curve driven pattern feature

Mirror the resulting curve driven pattern feature
1. Click the **Mirror** command option.
2. For the **Mirror Face/Plane**, select the **Top Plane**.
3. For the **Features To Mirror**, select **CrvPattern1**.
4. Click **OK** (see the model with mirrored pattern in Figure 3-111).

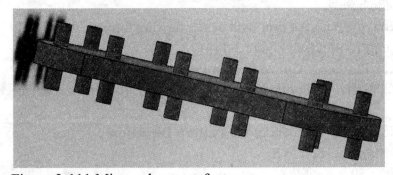

Figure 3-111 Mirrored pattern feature

Case 2: Open Curve

1. Click *the top face of the* **Extruded** base (see Figure 3-111 for previous model).
2. Click the **Sketch** command option.
3. Sketch a **Spline**, **Sketch2** (see Figure 3-112).
4. Exit **Sketch** mode.
   Repeat for **Line1** (see Figure 3-113).

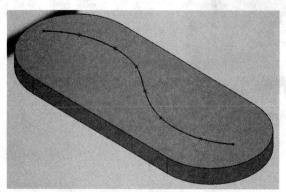

Figure 3-112 Sketch2 for Direction1 pattern driven curve

Figure 3-113 Line1 for Direction2 pattern driven curve

Create a seed feature

5. Select the top face of the base.
6. Sketch a circle, **Sketch3**, diameter **10 mm** with center passing through the curve.
7. Extrude **Sketch3** through 15 mm (see Figure 3-114).
8. Click **Feature > Linear Pattern > Curve Driven Pattern** (see Figure 3-109).
   The **Curve Driven Pattern PropertyManager** automatically displayed; see Figure 3-114.
9. In the **Direction1** rollout, select **Sketch2** as the **Pattern Direction**.
10. For the **Number of Instances**, set it to **5**.
11. For the **Spacing**, set it to **50**.
12. In the **Direction2** rollout, select **Line1@Sketch4** as the **Pattern Direction**.

13. For the **Number of Instances**, set it to **2**.

14. For the **Spacing**, set it to **15**.

15. In the **Features To Pattern** rollout, select **Extrude2**.

16. Click **OK** (see the model with pattern in Figure 3-115) .

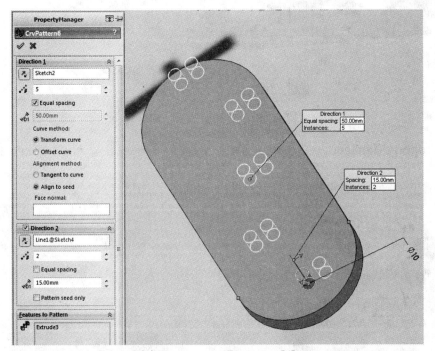

Figure 3-114 Curve driven pattern PropertyManager

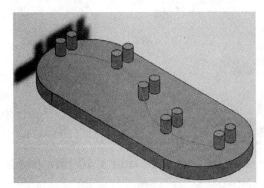

Figure 3-115 Resulting curve driven pattern feature

Mirror the resulting curve driven pattern feature

1. Click the **Mirror** command option.

2. For the **Mirror Face/Plane**, select the **Top Plane**.

3. For the **Features To Mirror**, select **CrvPattern6**.

4. Click **OK** (see the Mirror PropertyManager and mirrored pattern in Figure 3-116 and Figure 3-117 respectively).

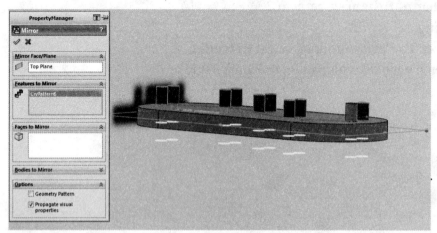

Figure 3-116 Mirror PropertyManager

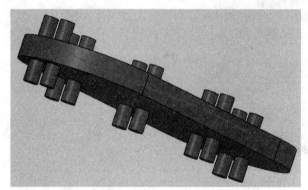

Figure 3-117 Mirrored pattern feature

Table Driven Pattern

1. Open a **New Part** document.
2. Select the **Top Plane** for sketching.
3. Sketch a rectangle, **Sketch1**, length of 150 mm, and width of 100 mm.
4. Extrude **Sketch1** using the **Mid Plane** option through **10 mm**.
5. Sketch a circle, **Sketch2**, **diameter 5 mm** with its center **10 mm x 10 mm** from one corner of **Sketch1**.
6. Extrude-cut **Sketch2** using the **Mid Plane** option through **10 mm** (see Figure 3-118).
7. Create a Coordinate System, **Coordinate System1**.
8. Click **Feature > Linear Pattern > Table Driven Pattern** (see Figure 3-109). The **Table Driven Pattern PropertyManager** automatically displayed; see Figure 3-118.

9. In the **Coordinate System** rollout, select **Coordinate System1** from the **FeatureManager**.

10. In the **Features To Copy** rollout, select **Extrude4**.

11. Enter the **X, Y Coordinates** in the **Table** for driving the Pattern.

12. Click **OK** (see the model with pattern in Figure 3-118).

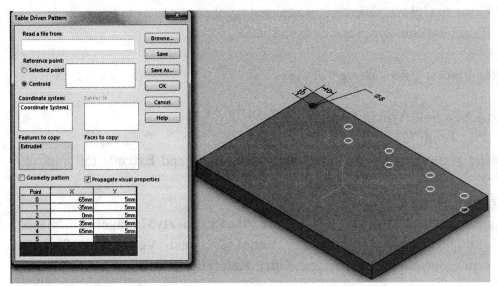

Figure 3-118 Table driven pattern PropertyManager

REFERENCE PLANES

The reference planes tool is a very powerful tool for modeling complex objects. Reference planes can be defined relative to the standard planes (top, right, and left) or relative to faces on a model from which other geometries are sketched to complete the part being modeled. These were used for lofting, as could be seen. They were also used in other models but hidden after completion of the modeling exercise. Reference planes are very useful and should be generously used.

The **Plane PropertyManager** which is new in **SolidWorks 2010** and newer versions provides the following selections: **First Reference**; **Second Reference**; **Third Reference**.

Select a face, plane or edge to create a reference plane. The following options are available:

Reference Entities: Displays the selected planes either from the FeatureManager or from the Graphics window.

Parallel: Creates a plane through a point parallel to a plane or a face.

Perpendicular: Creates a plane through a point perpendicular to a plane or a face.

Coincident: Creates a plane through a point coincident to a plane or a face.

Angle: Creates a plane through an edge, axis, or sketch line at an angle to a face or plane. Enter the angle value in the angle box.

Distance: Creates a plane parallel to a plane or a face, which is offset by a specified distance. Enter the *Offset distance* value in the *distance* box.

Reverse direction: Reverses the direction of the angle if needed.

Number of Plane to Create: Displays the selected number of planes to be created.

Mid Plane: Planes are equally spaced on both sides.

Tutorial 1 for Planes: Using Three Vertices

1. Open a **New SolidWorks Part** document.
2. Select the **Front Plane**.
3. Create a **rectangle** (100 mm long and 10 mm high) and **Extrude** (50 mm, mid-plane).
4. **Save** *extruded* part.
5. Click **Reference Geometry > Plane** [The **Plane PropertyManager** is displayed]
6. Click three Vertices (Vertex<1>, Vertex<2>, and Vertex<3>) for **First Reference**, **Second Reference**, and **Third Reference** respectively; (see Figure 3-119).
7. Click **OK** to complete the plane definition process.

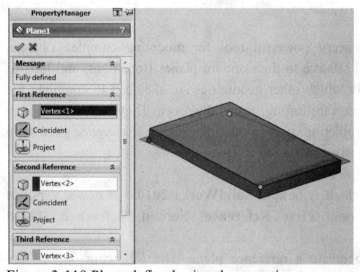

Figure 3-119 Plane defined using three vertices

Tutorial 2 for Planes: Angled Reference Plane

1. Open a **New SolidWorks Part** document
2. Open the *extruded part* previously created in Tutorial 1 for Planes.
3. Click **Reference Geometry > Plane** [The **Plane PropertyManager** is displayed]
4. Click **Right Plane** from the FeatureManager for **First Reference**
5. Click the **At Angle** button and enter **45**-deg for Angle
6. Click the **front vertical edge** of Extrude1 as **Second Reference** (see Figure 3-120).
7. Click **OK** to complete the plane definition process.

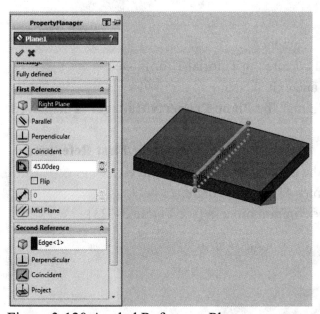

Figure 3-120 Angled Reference Plane

Tutorial 3 for Planes: Parallel Planes to Top Plane

1. Open a **New SolidWorks Part** document.
2. Click **Reference Geometry > Plane** [The **Plane PropertyManager** is displayed; see Figure 3-121].
3. Click **Top Plane** from the FeatureManager for **First Reference**.
4. Click the **Distance** button and enter **25** for Distance.
5. Click the **Number of Planes** button and enter **3** for Number of Planes.
6. Click **OK** to complete the plane definition process (see Figure 3-122).

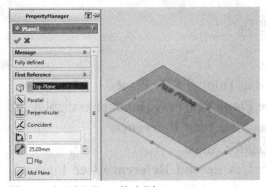

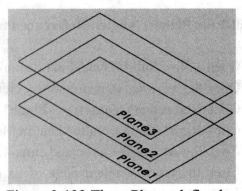

Figure 3-121 Parallel Planes   Figure 3-122 Three Planes defined

Tutorial 4 for Planes: Inclined Plane

1. Open a **New SolidWorks Part** document.
2. Open the *extruded part* previously created in Tutorial 1 for Planes.
3. Create a Sketch, which is a line, and exit sketch.
4. Click **Reference Geometry > Plane** [The **Plane PropertyManager** is displayed; see Figure 3-123].
5. Click the line (**Line4@Sketch2**) from the FeatureManager for **First Reference**.
6. Click the top face (Face<1>) of the parts as **Second Reference**.
7. Click the **At Angle** button and enter **45**-deg for Angle.
8. Click **OK** to complete the plane definition process (see Figure 3-123).

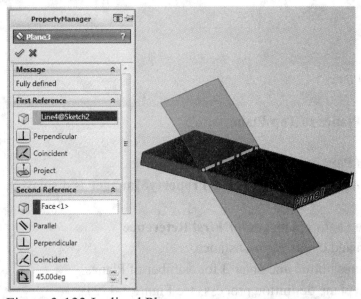

Figure 3-123 Inclined Plane

CREATING PATTERNS

Types of Pattern

There are basically three types of pattern: linear-, circular-, and feature-based patterns. Linear and circular patterns are most frequently used in part design. These are treated here.

Creating the Revolved Boss/Base

The revolved boss/base tool rotates a contour about an axis. It is a useful tool when modeling parts that have circular contours. Let us illustrate the revolved boss/base concept as follows.

1. Select the **Front Plane** and create **Sketch1** as shown in Figure 3-124a.
2. Click the **Features** tool.
3. Click the **Revolved Boss/Base** tool.
   The Revolve Properties Manager appears.
4. Define the revolved axis (Line1) as the vertical dimension line. A real-time preview will appear (see Figure 3-124b).
5. Click **OK** to complete the revolved part without fillet (see Figure 3-125).
6. Fillet with default radius of 2.5 mm (see Figure 3-126) to complete the revolved part.

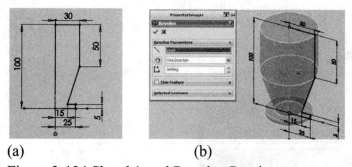

(a)   (b)

Figure 3-124 Sketch1 and Revolve Preview

Figure 3-125 Revolve1

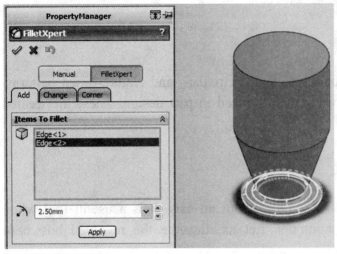
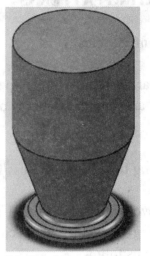

(a) Filleting   (b) Final revolved feature

Figure 3-126 Revolved boss/base tool for creating revolved features

Shelling

The next step is to shell the part from the top view.

7. Select the top face of Sketch1 as shown in Figure 3-127.
    Click the **Shell** tool. The Revolve Properties Manager appears.
    The Revolve Properties Manager appears.
8. Choose the shell thickness as 3 mm.
9. Click **OK** to complete the shelled part (see Figure 3-128).

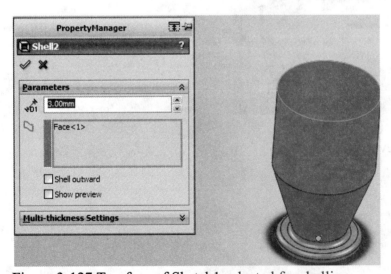

Figure 3-127 Top face of Sketch1 selected for shelling

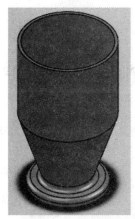

Figure 3-128 Creating revolved features with shelling operation included

Extruding a Thin Feature

10. Select the thin top plane of the shelled part.
11. Click the **Convert Entities** tool and Click the outer diameter of the top face.
    The circle having diameter equal to the outer diameter of the top face is extracted (see Figure 3-129).
12. Click the **Offset Entities** tool.
13. Choose the **Offset** value of 1 mm.
14. Click Reverse to offset the edge to the inside.
    A second offset circle is extracted.
15. Click **OK** to complete extraction.
16. Click **Extrude-cut**, choose Blind for a value of **5 mm**.
17. Click **OK** to complete (see Figure 3-130).

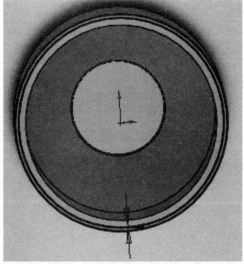

Figure 3-129 Extracting 2 circles

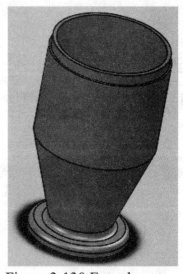

Figure 3-130 Extrude-cut

Creating a Slot

18. Create a **Reference Plane, Plane1** 30 mm from the Front Plane. See Figure 3-131.
19. Sketch a vertical center-line on Plane1. See Figure 3-132.
20. Create a slot Sketch on Plane1. See Figure 3-133.
21. Insert dimensions on the slot.   See Figure 3-134.
22. Extrude the slot Sketch. See Figure 3-135.

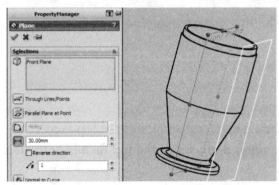

Figure 3-131 Creating a plane, Plane1   Figure 3-132 Vertical center-line on Plane1

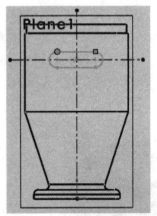

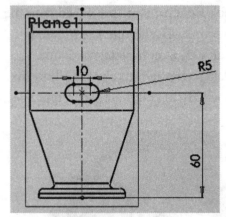

Figure 3-133 Create a slot Sketch on Plane1   Figure 3-134 Insert dimensions on the slot

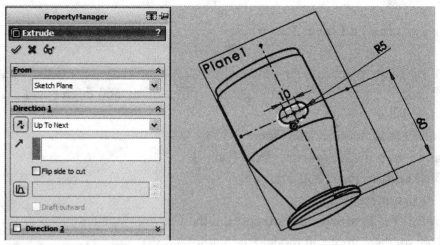

Figure 3-135 Creating a slot feature on the part

Creating the Linear Pattern

A linear pattern is now created using a temporary axis as the direction in which to create the linear pattern. In this case, we supply the spacing and set the number of instances that is desired.

1. Click **Linear Pattern** toolbar. See Figure 3-136.
2. Click **View > Temporary Axes**.
3. Choose **Direction 1** as **Temporary Axis**.
4. Set **Spacing** to 10 mm.
5. Set **Number of instances** to 4.
6. Click Extrude2 as the **Features to Pattern** from the FeatureManager.
7. Click OK.
8. Hide Plane1.

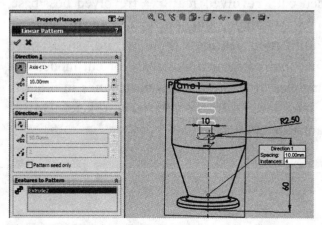

Figure 3-136 Linear-pattern created on the part

Creating a Circular Pattern of a Linear Pattern

A circular pattern of the linear pattern is now created using a temporary axis as the axis of revolution. In this case, we supply the total angle of revolution as 360 degree and set the number of instances that is desired.

1. Click **Circular Pattern** toolbar. See Figure 3-137.
2. Choose **Rotation Axis** as **Temporary Axis, Axis<1>**.
3. Accept default **Total Angle** as 360 degrees.
4. Set **Number of instances** to 3.
5. Click LPattern2 as the **Features to Pattern** from the FeatureManager.
6. Click **OK** to obtain the completed model (see Figure 3-138).

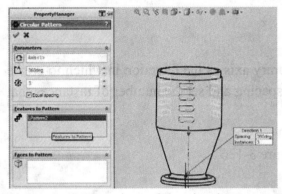

Figure 3-137 Preview of the circular pattern   Figure 3-138 Finished part

Summary

This chapter discusses in detail, the **Features** used in SolidWorks for creating 3D objects. These **Features** tools are classified into five categories: **extrusion features** (extruded boss/base, draft, dome, rib, and extruded cut), **revolved features** (revolved boss/base, and revolved cut), **lofted features** (lofted boss/base, and lofted cut), **swept features** (swept boss/base, and swept cut), **modification features** (hole wizard, shell, fillet, chamfer, pattern, and mirror). In the first four categories, boss/base or cut models are realized. Due to its importance, the principles of creating **reference planes** in order to create more complex models are also introduced. Advanced **Patterns** (Sketch Driven, Curve Driven, and Table Driven) tools are also introduced.

Exercises

1. Redraw the 3D solid model in Figure P1 based on the given dimensions.

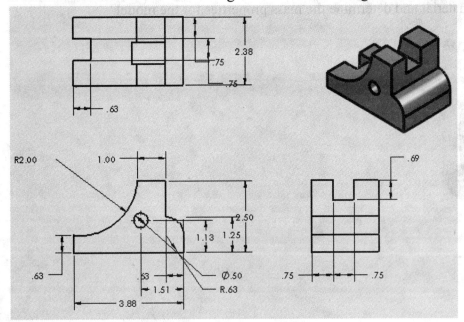

Figure P1

2. Redraw the 3D solid model in Figure P2 based on the given dimensions.

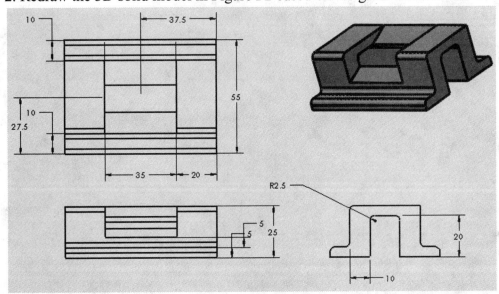

Figure P2

3. Repeat Tutorial 9 (Simple Part 3-9) and mirror the part produced about the Top Plane to obtain a new model. Determine the mass properties of the model created. Is the mass twice that obtained in Tutorial 9? Explain your answer.

4. For the model having patterns shown in Figure 3-138, suppress the slot patterns. Create a seed tapped hole (M5x0.8), 40 mm from the top lip using the Hole Wizard tool. Follow the same procedure used to create the patterns shown in Figure P3. Apply Brass as the material and determine the mass properties for the model.

Figure P3

Chapter 4
Part Modeling—CSWA Preparations

Objectives:

In this chapter you will learn:

- The level of expertise required for 2D CAD design in engineering
- How to utilize sketch tools, mirror, draft for part modeling
- How to model 3D parts using **Extrusion**, **Revolved**, features tools as well as using **Reference Planes**
- How to solve part modeling problems required for Certified SolidWorks Associate CSWA

INTRODUCTION

This goal of this chapter is to assist readers to achieve the level of expertise in 2D CAD design as it applies to engineering and to help them pass the Certified SolidWorks Associate (CSWA) which is synonymous with competence in SolidWorks at foundation and apprentice level of 2D CAD design and engineering practices and principles. A number of tutorials are presented in this chapter to achieve this goal.

Tutorial 4-1a Widget

Build the widget part shown in Figure 4-1. The lines and the arcs are tangential. Determine the center of mass for this part, if it is made from 1060 Aluminum.

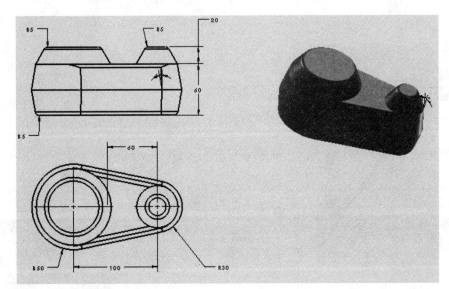

Figure 4-1 Widget

1. Open a **New** SolidWorks part document.
2. Sketch a horizontal center line through the origin.
3. Sketch a slanting line on one side of the center line.
4. Click **Mirror Tool**.
5. **Mirror** the slanting line about the horizontal center line.
6. Take the center of the 30 mm radius arc to be 60 mm to the right of the origin; and the center of the 50 mm radius arc to be 40 mm to the left of the origin.
7. Add a **Tangent Relation** between each of the lines and the two arcs. Trim any dangling edge. See Figure 4-2 for the sketch, **Sketch1**.

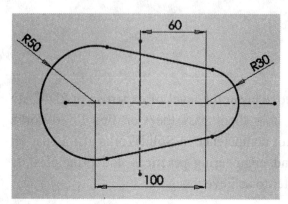

Figure 4-2 Sketch1

8. Click **Extruded Boss/Base**.
9. Set **Type** to **Mid Plane**, Depth to 60 mm, and Draft to 10 degree (ensure that Draft outward is cleared, if it is active) [see Figure 4-3].
10. Click **OK**.

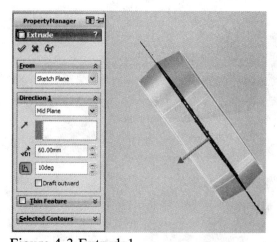

Figure 4-3 Extrude1

Add Bosses

11. Sketch two circles using two existing centers of the existing arcs (highlight the arcs to *awake* the centers).

12. Add **Coradial Relation** between the larger circle and the larger arc see (Figure 4-4).

13. Add **Coradial Relation** between the smaller circle and the smaller arc.

14. Click **Extruded Boss/Base**.

15. Set Type to **Blind**, Depth to 20 mm, and Draft to 30 **degree** (ensure that Draft outward is cleared, if it is active) [Figure 4-5].

16. Click **OK** (the modeled part is shown in Figure 4-6).

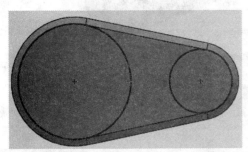

Figure 4-4 Sketches for second Extrude

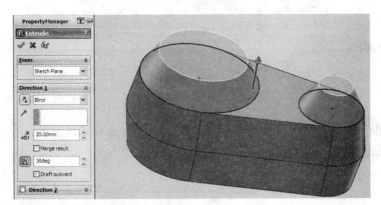

Figure 4-5 Preview

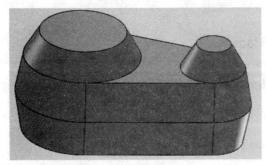

Figure 4-6 Completed part

Center of mass

Right-click **Material >Edit Material** in FeatureManager.

Choose **1060 Alloy** and **Apply**.

Click **Evaluate > Mass Properties** (see mass calculation output in Figure 4-7).

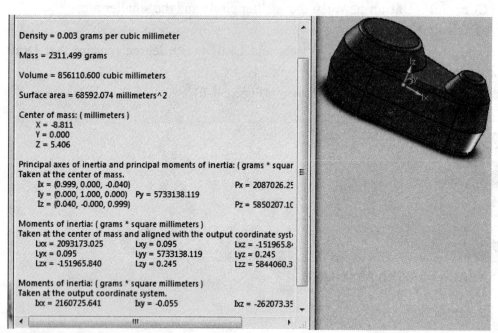

Figure 4-7 Part with mass properties

Tutorial 4-1b Widget

Repeat Tutorial 4-1a if the ends of the two slanting lines and the centers of the arcs are collinear (they have vertical relations).

Modeling

Similar to Tutorial 4-1a with the appropriate relations applied.

Center of mass

Right-click **Material >Edit Material** in FeatureManager.

Choose **1060 Alloy** and **Apply**.

Click **Evaluate > Mass Properties** (see mass calculation output in Figure 4-8).

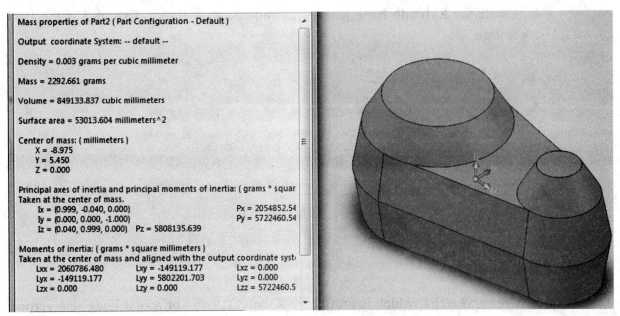

Figure 4-8 Part with mass properties

Tutorial 4-2

Build the part shown in Figure 4-9. Determine the center of mass for this part, if it is made from Cast Alloy Steel with density of 0.0073 g/mm^3.

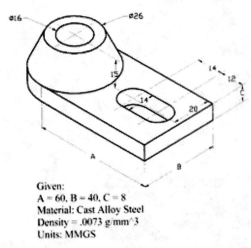

Given:
A = 60, B = 40, C = 8
Material: Cast Alloy Steel
Density = .0073 g/mm^3
Units: MMGS

Figure 4-9 Part for modeling

1. **Create** a New part in SolidWorks.
2. Set the document properties for the model.
3. Create **Sketch1**, which is profile for Extrude1; two horizontal line 40 mm apart, a vertical line joining them, an arc sketched using Tangent Arc tool and a slot inside. Select the Top Plane as the Sketch Plane. (see Figure 4-10)

4. Create the **Extrude Base** feature. Extrude depth = 8 mm. Extrude1 is the Base feature.

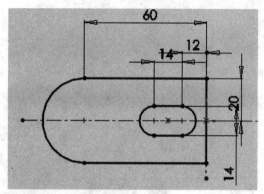

Figure 4-10 Sketch1

5. Create **Sketch2**, which is profile for Revolve1; two horizontal lines, one vertical line and one slanting line. Select the Front Plane as the Sketch Plane. (see Figure 4-11)

6. Create the **Revolved Base** feature. Select the centerline as the Axis of Revolution. (see Figure 4-12 for the preview and Figure 4-13 for the revolved part)

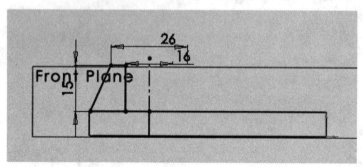

Figure 4-11 Sketch2

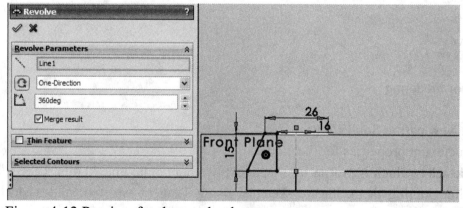

Figure 4-12 Preview for the revolved part

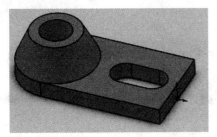

Figure 4-13 Revolved part

The mass properties are shown in Figure 4-14.

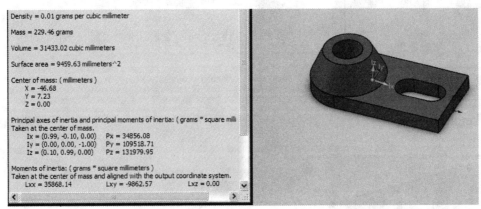

Figure 4-14 Mass properties for the part

Tutorial 4-3a

Build the part shown in Figure 4-15. Determine the center of mass for this part, if it is made from 6061 Alloy with density of 0.097 lb/in^3.

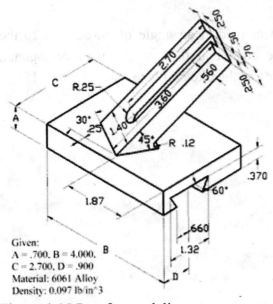

Figure 4-15 Part for modeling

1. **Create** a New part in SolidWorks.
2. Set the document properties for the model.
3. Create **Sketch1**, 4.00 in by 2.70 in. Select the Top Plane as the Sketch Plane. (see Figure 4-16)
4. Create the **Extrude Base** feature. Extrude depth = 0.7 in. Extrude1 is the Base feature. (see Figure 4-17)

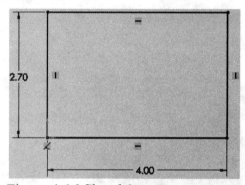

Figure 4-16 Sketch1

Figure 4-17 Extrude1

5. Create **Sketch2**, a line 1.40 in long, inclined at an angle of 30-degrees to the horizontal, located 1.87 in from one edge and 0.25 in from an orthogonal, adjacent edge. Select the top of Extrude1 as the Sketch Plane. (see Figure 4-18)

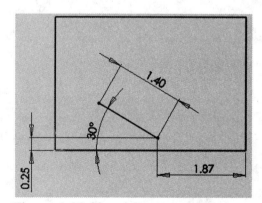

Figure 4-18 Sketch2

6. Create **Plane1**, passing through the inclined line and inclined to the top of Extrude1 at an angle of 45-degrees to the horizontal.

7. Create **Sketch3**, a rectangle with Sketch2 as width and having a length of 3.6 in on Plane1 (see Figure 4-19).

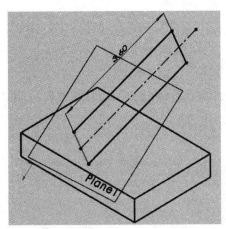

Figure 4-19 Sketch3

8. Create the **Extrude Boss** feature. Extrude depth = 0.56 in. Extrude2 is located on Plane1. (see Figure 4-20)

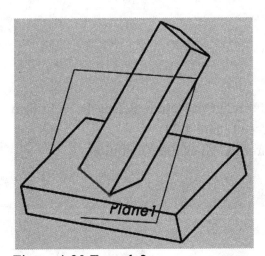

Figure 4-20 Extrude2

9. Create **Sketch4**, a profile for the first Extrude Cut feature. Select the top face of inclined Extrude2 as the Sketch Plane. (see Figure 4-21)

10. Create the **Extrude Cut** feature. Select Blind as End Condition, depth = 0.25 in.

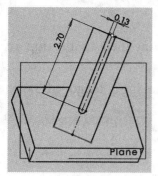

Figure 4-21 Sketch4

11. Create **Fillet** feature at the back edge of the inclined Extrude2, Radius = 0.12 in. (see Figure 4-22)

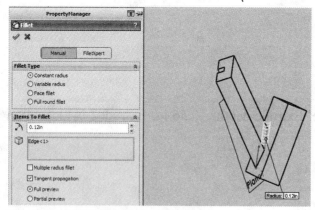

Figure 4-22 Fillet additions

12. Create **Sketch5**, a profile for the second Extrude Cut feature. Select the right face of inclined Extrude2 as the Sketch Plane. (see Figure 4-23)
13. Create the **Extrude Cut** feature. Select Through All as End Condition.

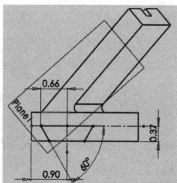

Figure 4-23 Sketch5

The completed part is shown in Figure 4-24 while the material properties are shown in Figure 4-25.

Figure 4-24 Completed part

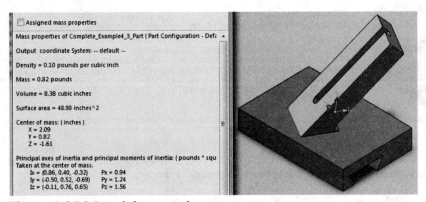

Figure 4-25 Material properties

Tutorial 4-3b

Modify the unit system of the part from IPS to MMGS. Modify the material from Cast Alloy Steel, 6061 Alloy to ABS. modify the plane1 angle from 45 degrees to 30 degrees. Determine the center of mass for this part.

The solution is shown in Figure 4-26 for the material properties.

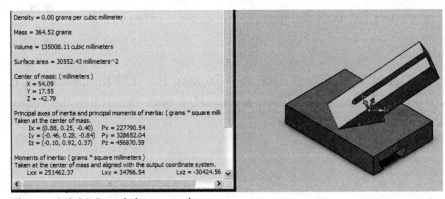

Figure 4-26 Material properties

Tutorial 4-4

Build the part for the previous Tutorial. Modify **Sketch2**, to be parallel to the edge with no inclination. Determine the center of mass for this part, if it is made from Cast Alloy Steel, 6061 Alloy with density of 0.097 g/mm^3.

The part is shown in Figure 4-27. The material properties are shown in Figure 4-28.

Figure 4-27 Modeled part

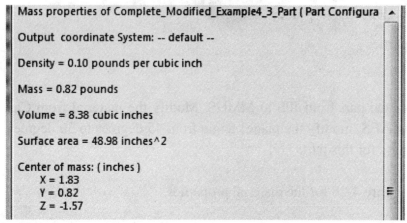

Figure 4-28 Material properties for modified part

Tutorial 4-5a

Build the part shown in Figure 4-29. Given data: A = 76 mm, B = 127 mm, Material is 2014 Alloy, Density = 0.0028 g/mm^3. All fillets are equal, 6 mm. Determine the center of mass for this part.

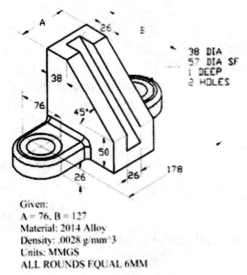

Given:
A = 76, B = 127
Material: 2014 Alloy
Density: .0028 g/mm^3
Units: MMGS
ALL ROUNDS EQUAL 6MM

Figure 4-29 Part for modeling

1. **Create** a New part in SolidWorks.
2. Set the document properties for the model.
3. Create **Sketch1**, a profile of two vertical lines, one horizontal line, and an inclined line. Select the Front Plane as the Sketch Plane. (see Figure 4-30)
4. Create the **Extrude Base** feature. Extrude depth = 76 mm. Extrude1 is the Base feature. (see Figure 4-31)

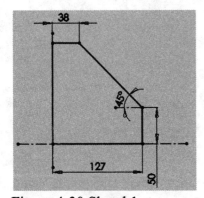

Figure 4-30 Sketch1

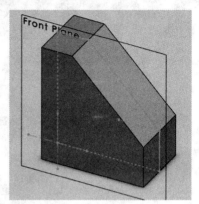

Figure 4-31 Extrude1

5. Create **Sketch2**, a square, 26 mm on each side. Select the flat top of Extrude1 as the Sketch Plane. (see Figure 4-32)

6. Create the first **Extrude Cut** feature. Select All Through as End Condition. Select and inclined edge as the Direction of Extrusion. (see Figure 4-32)

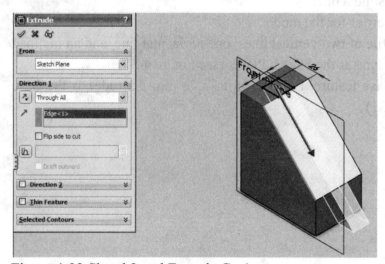

Figure 4-32 Sketch2 and Extrude Cut1

7. Create **Sketch3**, a profile of two vertical lines, an arc at their end points using Tangent Arc tool, and a circle. Select the bottom of Extrude1 as the Sketch Plane. (see Figure 4-33)

8. Create the **Extrude Boss** feature. Select Blind as End Condition. Extrude depth = 26 mm. Extrude2 is the Boss feature. (see Figure 4-34)

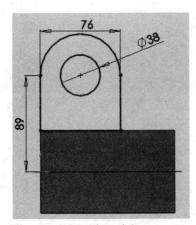

Figure 4-33 Sketch3

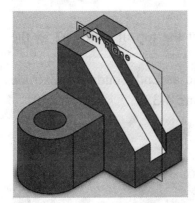

Figure 4-34 Boss feature, Extrude2

9. Create a **Mirror** of Extrude2 feature. Front Plane is used for Mirroring. (see Figure 4-35)

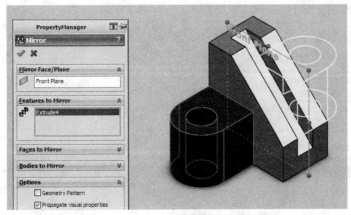

Figure 4-35 Mirror of Extrude2

10. Create **Fillets** on Extrude2 feature. Fillet radius is 6 mm. (see Figure 4-36)

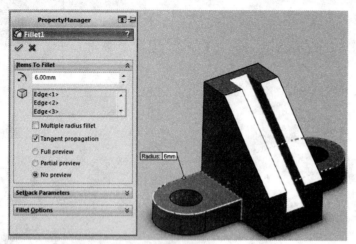

Figure 4-36 Fillets on Extrude2

11. Create **Sketch4**, a circle of 57 mm diameter. Select the top of Extrude2 as the Sketch Plane. (see Figure 4-37)

12. Create the second **Extrude Cut** feature. Select Blind as End Condition. Extrude depth = 1 mm. Extrude2 is the Boss feature. (see Figure 4-38)

Figure 4-37 Sketch4

Figure 4-38 Second Extrude Cut

13. Create a **Mirror** of Extrude Cut2 feature. Front Plane is used for Mirroring. (see Figure 4-39)

Material properties are shown in Figure 4-40

Figure 4-39 Completed part

Output coordinate System: -- default --

Density = 0.0028 grams per cubic millimeter

Mass = 3432.5988 grams

Volume = 1225928.1397 cubic millimeters

Surface area = 101032.4420 millimeters^2

Center of mass: (millimeters)
    X = 49.2493
    Y = 46.8736
    Z = -0.0009

Figure 4-40 Material properties

Tutorial 4-5b

Modify the fillet radius from 6 mm to 8 mm. Modify the material from 2014 Alloy to 6061 Alloy. Modify the plane1 angle from 45 degrees to 30 degrees. Determine the center of mass for this part.

The part is shown in Figure 4-41. The material properties are shown in Figure 4-42.

Figure 4-41 Modified part

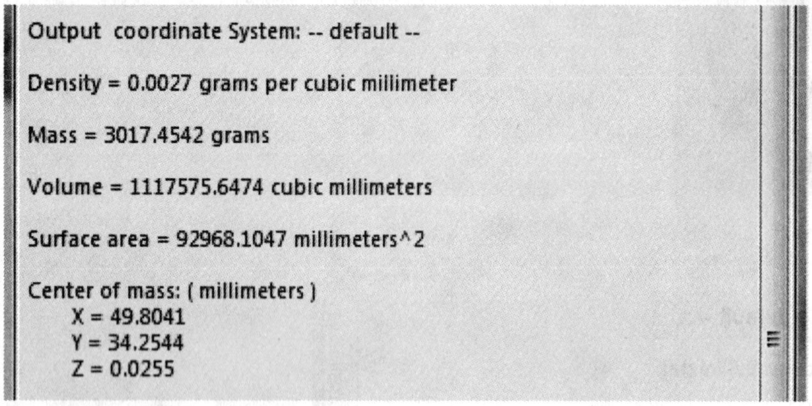

Output coordinate System: -- default --

Density = 0.0027 grams per cubic millimeter

Mass = 3017.4542 grams

Volume = 1117575.6474 cubic millimeters

Surface area = 92968.1047 millimeters^2

Center of mass: (millimeters)
    X = 49.8041
    Y = 34.2544
    Z = 0.0255

Figure 4-42 Material properties

Tutorial 4-6a

Build the part shown in Figure 4-43. Given data: A = 52 mm, B = 58 mm, Material is 6061 Alloy, Density = 0.0027 g/mm^3. All fillets are equal, 4 mm. Determine the center of mass for this part.

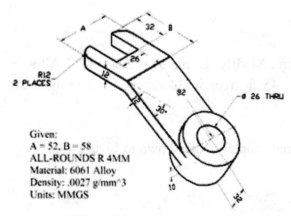

Given:
A = 52, B = 58
ALL-ROUNDS R 4MM
Material: 6061 Alloy
Density: .0027 g/mm^3
Units: MMGS

Figure 4-43 Part for modeling

1. **Create** a New part in SolidWorks.
2. Set the document properties for the model.
3. Create **Sketch1**, a profile of one horizontal line, and an inclined line at 30-degrees to the horizontal. Select the Front Plane as the Sketch Plane. (see Figure 4-44)
4. Create the **Extrude-Thin1** feature. Apply Symmetry. Select Mid Plane for End Condition in Direction1. Extrude depth = 52 mm. Thickness = 12 mm. Extrude1 is the Base feature. (see Figure 4-45)

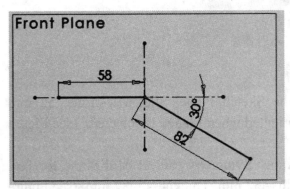

Figure 4-44 Sketch1

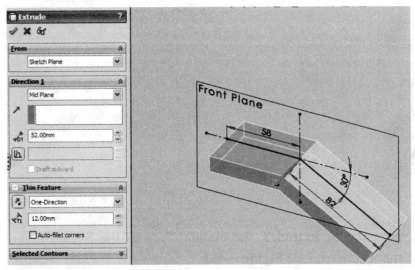

Figure 4-45 Extrude-Thin1

5. Create **Plane1**. Select the mid-point and the top face of the inclined edge of Extrude1. Plane1 is located at the middle of the top and bottom of faces of the inclined component of Edge1 (see Figure 4-46)

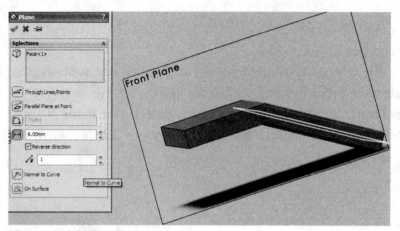

Figure 4-46 Plane1

6. Create **Sketch2**. Select Plane1 as the Sketch Plane. Sketch a circle, 52 mm diameter. Note the way Extrude1 is oriented when Plane1 is selected. (see Figure 4-47)

7. Create the **Extrude Boss** feature. Apply Symmetry. Select Mid Plane for End Condition in Direction1. Extrude depth = 52 mm. Thickness = 32 mm. (see Figure 4-48)

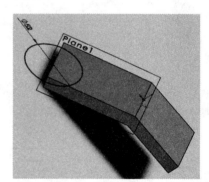

Figure 4-47 Sketch2

8. Create **Sketch3**. Select top of Extrude2, the circular face as the Sketch Plane. Sketch a circle, 26 mm diameter. (see Figure 4-48)

9. Create the first **Extrude Cut** feature. Select Through All End Condition in Direction1. (see Figure 4-49)

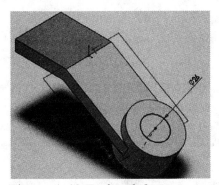

Figure 4-48 Exdtrude2

10. Create **Sketch4**. Select top of Extrude-Thin1 as the Sketch Plane. Sketch a rectangle, 26 mm by 32 mm. (see Figure 4-49)

11. Create the second **Extrude Cut** feature. Select Through All End Condition in Direction1. (see Figure 4-50)

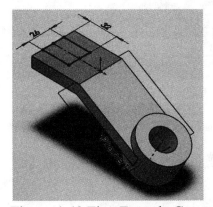

Figure 4-49 First Extrude Cut

12. Create **Fillet** features. (see Figure 4-50-Figure 4-52)

Figure 4-50 Extrude Cut2 and fillets

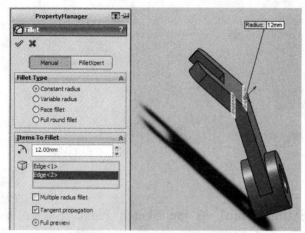

Figure 4-51 More 12mm radius fillets

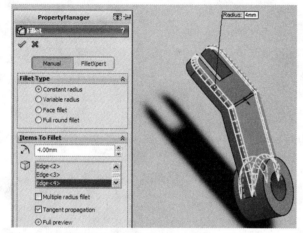

Figure 4-52 Fillets of 4 mm radius, Tangent propagation option chosen

Figure 4-53 Completed part

The material properties are shown in Figure 4-54.

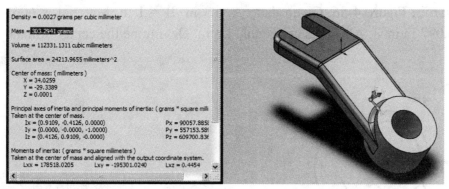

Figure 4-54 Material properties

Tutorial 4-6b

Modify the Fillet 1 radius from 12 mm to 10 mm; Fillet 2 and Fillet 3 radius from 4 mm to 2 mm. Modify the Sketch1 angle from 30 degree to 45 degree. Modify the Extrude-Thin 1 depth from 52mm to 38 mm. Modify the material from 6061 Alloy to ABS. Recalculate the location of the center of mass with reference to the origin.

	Modify From	Modify To
Fillet 1 radius	12 mm	10 mm
Fillet 2 and Fillet 3	4 mm	2 mm
Sketch1 angle	30 degree	45 degree
Extrude-Thin 1 depth	52 mm	38 mm
Material	6061 Alloy	ABS

The part and material properties are shown in Figure 4-55.

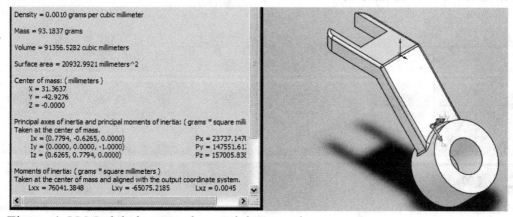

Figure 4-55 Modeled part and material properties

Tutorial 4-7a

Build the part shown in Figure 4-56. Given data: A = 3 in, B = 1 in, Material is 6061 Alloy, Density = 0.097 lb/in^3. All fillets are equal, 4 mm. Determine the center of mass for this part.

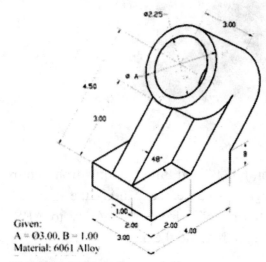

Figure 4-56 Part for modeling

1. **Create** a New part in SolidWorks.
2. Set the document properties for the model.
3. Create **Sketch1**, a rectangle of 3 in by 4 in. Select the Top Plane as the Sketch Plane. (see Figure 4-57)
4. Create the **Extrude Base** feature. Select Through All for End Condition in Direction1. Extrude depth = 1 in. Caution: Extrude direction is downward. Extrude1 is the Base feature.

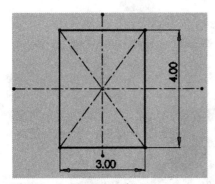

Figure 4-57 Extrude Base

5. Create **Plane1**. Select the mid-points of the top face of Extrude1 to add a construction line. Plane1 is defined using the construction line and the top face of Extrude1, with an Angle = 48-degrees. (see Figure 4-58)

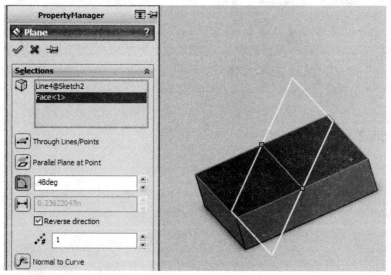

Figure 4-58 Plane1

6. Create **Sketch2**, made up of one horizontal line on Extrude1, two lines on Plane1 and an arc using Tangent Arc tool. Select Plane1 as the Sketch Plane. (see Figure 4-59)

7. Create the **Extrude Boss** feature. Select Up To Vertex for End Condition in Direction1. Select the top right vertex of Extrude1. Extrude2 is the Base Boss. (see Figure 4-60 for preview and Figure 4-61 for Extrude2)

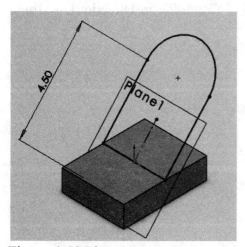

Figure 4-59 Plane1

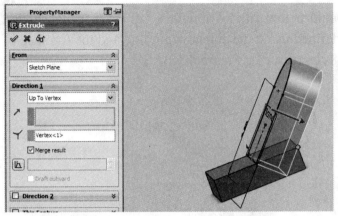

Figure 4-60 Preview of Extrude2

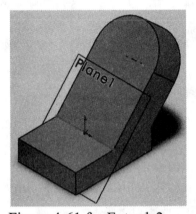

Figure 4-61 for Extrude2

8. Create **Sketch3**, a circle. Select the back angle of Extrude2 as the Sketch Plane. (see Figure 4-62)

9. Create the **Extrude Base** feature. Select Blind Condition in Direction1. Extrude depth = 3in. (see Figure 4-63)

Figure 4-62 Sketch3

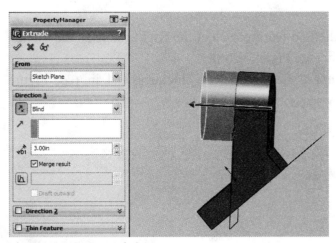

Figure 4-63 Extrude3

10. Create **Sketch4**, a circle of diameter 2.25 in. Select the face or back of Extrude2 (cylinder) as the Sketch Plane. (see Figure 4-64)

11. Create the **Extrude Cut** feature. Select Through All for End Condition in Direction1. (see Figure 4-65)

Figure 4-64 Sketch4

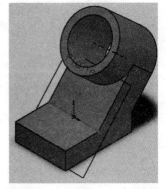

Figure 4-65 Extrude Cut

12. Create **Sketch5**, a profile for the Rib feature. Select the Right Plane as the Sketch Plane. Apply a Parallel relation. (see Figure 4-66)

13. Create the **Rib** feature. Use **Insert>Features>Rib** Thickness = 1 in. (see Figure 4-67 for the Rib feature preview)

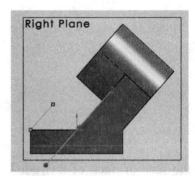

Figure 4-66 Sketch5

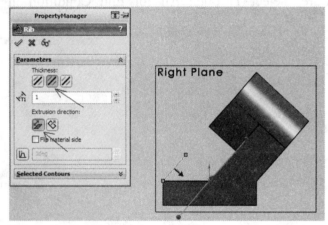

Figure 4-67 Rib feature preview

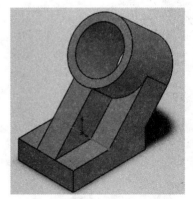

Figure 4-68 Completed part

14. Apply 6061 Alloy material.

15. Calculate the mass properties. Figure 4-69 shows the results.

Output coordinate System: -- default --

Density = 0.098 pounds per cubic inch

Mass = 2.989 pounds

Volume = 30.645 cubic inches

Surface area = 100.964 inches^2

Center of mass: (inches)
   X = 0.000
   Y = 0.729
   Z = -0.861

Figure 4-69 Mass properties

Tutorial 4-7b

Modify the Rib1 feature from 1.00 in to 1.25 in; depth of Extrude2 from 3.00 in to 3.25 in. Modify the Plane1 angle from 48 degree to 30 degree. Modify the material from 6061 Alloy to Copper. Recalculate the location of the center of mass with reference to the origin.

	Modify From	Modify To
Rib1 feature	1.00 in	1.25 in
Depth of Extrude2	3.00 in	3.25 in
Sketch1 angle	48 degree	30 degree
Material	6061 Alloy	Copper

The part and material properties are shown in Figure 4-70.

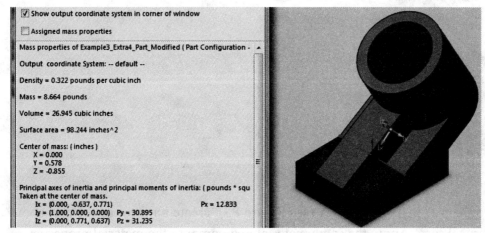

Figure 4-70 Modeled part and material properties

Summary

This chapter discusses part modeling at the level of CSWA and most of the examples are similar to the materials covered in the CSWA examinations. Students preparing for this exam will find this chapter helpful. Instructors should consider covering this chapter before moving to the next chapter which pitches at a higher level.

Exercises

1. Referring to the part in Tutorial 4-2 (see Figure P1), create a mirror of the part about the right vertical face. Apply the same material and compute the material properties of the part.

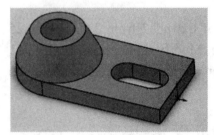

Figure P1

2. Referring to the part in Tutorial 4-3A (see Figure P2), change the angle of the vertical feature from 30-deg to 90-deg. Apply the same material and compute the material properties of the part.

Figure P2

3. Referring to the part in Tutorial 4-5A (see Figure P3), create a mirror of the part about the right vertical face. Apply the same material and compute the material properties of the part.

Figure P3

4. Referring to the part in Tutorial 4-7A (see Figure P4), change the angle of the vertical feature from 48-deg to 90-deg. Apply the same material and compute the material properties of the part.

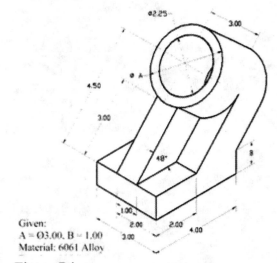

Given:
A = Ø3.00, B = 1.00
Material: 6061 Alloy

Figure P4

Chapter 5
Advanced Part Modeling—CSWA Preparations

Objectives:

In this chapter you will learn:

- About creating and manipulating a model coordinate system
- How to model advanced 3D parts using **Extrusion, Revolved, Lofted, Swept, Modification, Edit Features**, features tools as well as using **Reference Planes**
- How to apply **Advanced Modeling Tools**

INTRODUCTION

There is one difference between Advanced Part Modeling and Part Modeling: the complexity of the sketches involved and the number of dimensions and geometric relations and increased number of features. This means that the modeler has to be able to deal with significant amount of information in order to complete an advanced part modeling. Another difference between Advanced Part Modeling and Part Modeling is the complexity of features involved in the modeling. It is important to keep in mind the design intent. Take advantage of symmetric features and build in relations that would shorten design time. Maintenance of future design depends to a great extent on how well the current design has been carried out. In the first part of this chapter, we present some *Advanced Part Modeling tutorials* at the CSWA level.

Advanced Part Modeling is one of the five categories of the Certified SolidWorks Associate (CSWA) examination taken from the www.solidworks.com/cswa website. There is one question in this chapter taken from the CSWA category.

In providing SolidWorks solution to the problems or tutorials, we will first create a part based on a dimensioned drawing with the origin and coordinate axes annotated. We will then create the part, apply the correct material properties, and retrieve the mass and center of mass information. When building the model, we will ensure that it is oriented relative to the default coordinate system in the manner indicated in the problem. Knowledge of *Reference Plane* is essential in solving most CSWA problems. Characteristic of CSWA exam questions, care should be taken to locate the origin of the part, applying the material properties, and retrieving the mass properties. Creating Reference Axes to match those in the problem statement is essential when retrieving the center of mass of the model(s).

Advanced Part Modeling Tutorials

Tutorial 1: Block with hook

Create the model shown in Figure 5-1. Determine the overall mass and volume of the part, and the center of mass for the model for 1060 Alloy material. Note the origin of the model.

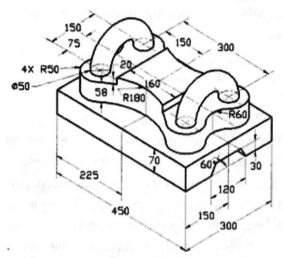

Figure 5-1 Model to be built

SolidWorks Solution

1. **Create** a New part in SolidWorks.
2. Set the document properties for the model.
3. Create **Sketch1**, which is 450 mm by 300 mm. Select the Top Plane as the Sketch Plane. Note that using the Center Rectangle tool is useful due to the origin of the part. (see Figure 5-2)
4. Create the **Extrude Base** feature. Extrude depth = 70 mm. Extrude1 is the Base feature. (see Figure 5-3)

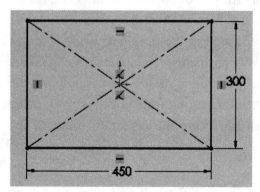

Figure 5-2 Sketch1

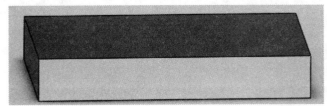

Figure 5-3 Extrude1

5. Create **Sketch2**. Select the right face of Extrude1 as the Sketch Plane. Sketch two parallel, horizontal lines and two inclined lines. (see Figure 5-4)
6. Create the first **Extrude Cut** feature. Extrude cut feature using Through All for End Condition. (see Figure 5-5)

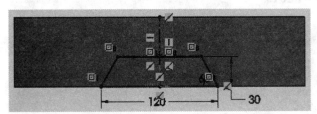

Figure 5-4 Sketch2

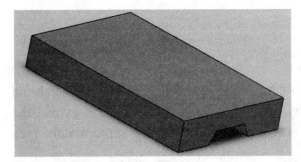

Figure 5-5 Extrude Cut1

7. Create **Sketch3**. Select the top face of Extrude1 as the Sketch Plane. Sketch the profile shown. (see Figure 5-6)
8. Create the second **Extrude Boss** feature. Extrude the feature using Blind End Condition, with depth of 58 mm. (see Figure 5-7)

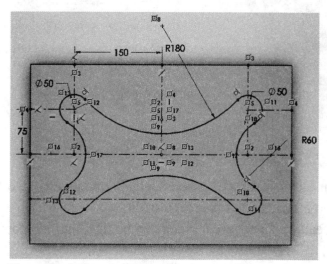

Figure 5-6 Sketch of profile on top of Extrude1

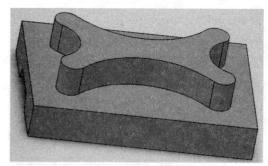

Figure 5-7 Extrude2 of sketched profile

9. Create **Sketch4**. Select the top face of Extrude2 as the Sketch Plane. Sketch the profile shown. This is easily done by using Convert Entities Tool to extract the two bounding curves, drawing two vertical lines, and trimming appropriately. (see Figure 5-8)

10. Create the third **Extrude Boss** feature. Extrude the feature using Blind End Condition, with depth of 20 mm. (see Figure 5-9)

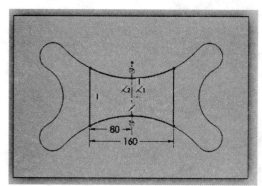

Figure 5-8 Sketch of profile on top of Extrude2

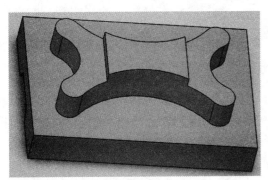

Figure 5-9 Extrude3 of sketched profile

11. Create **Sketch5**. Select the top face of Extrude2 as the Sketch Plane. Sketch a circle, diameter 50 mm. (see Figure 5-10)

12. **Exit Sketch5**.

13. Create **Plane1** cutting through the center of Sketch5. Select the Right Plane.

14. Create **Sketch6**. Select Plane1 as the Sketch Plane. Sketch an arc, radius 75 mm. (see Figure 5-11)

15. **Exit Sketch6**.

16. Create the first **Swept Boss** feature. **Sketch5** is the **Profile**, and **Sketch6** is the **Path**. (see Figure 5-12)

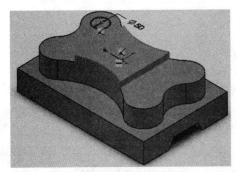

Figure 5-10 Sketch5: a circle on top of Extrude2

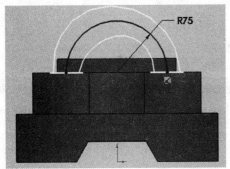

Figure 5-11 Sketch6: a circle on Plane1 on top of Extrude2

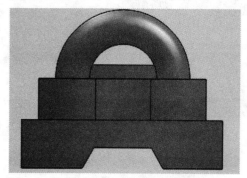

Figure 5-12 Swept feature

17. Create the **Mirror** of swept feature. Choose the Right Plane to **Mirror**. (see Figure 5-13 for the modeled part)

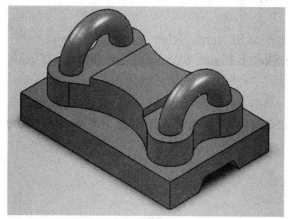

Figure 5-13 Model of part

The mass properties are given as follows:
Mass properties of hookedblock_gco (Part Configuration - Default)
Density = 0.003 grams per cubic millimeter
Mass = 37416.191 grams
Volume = 13857848.552 cubic millimeters
Surface area = 542149.374 millimeters^2
Center of mass: (millimeters) X = 0.000; Y = 70.936; Z = 0.000

Tutorial 2: Bracket 1
Create the model shown in Figure 5-14. Determine the overall mass and volume of the part, and the center of mass for the model for 6061 Alloy material. Note the origin of the model.

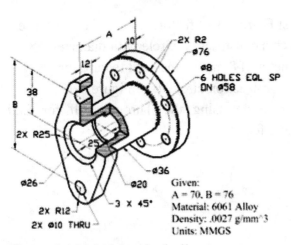

Figure 5-14 Model to be built

SolidWorks Solution

1. **Create** a New part in SolidWorks.
2. Set the document properties for the model.
3. Create **Sketch1**, which is made up of two circles, 76 mm and 20 mm diameter respectively. Select Front Plane as the Sketch Plane. (see Figure 5-15)
4. Create the **Extrude Base** feature. Extrude depth = 10 mm. Extrude1 is the Base feature. (see Figure 5-16)

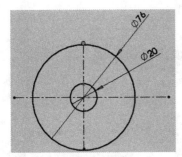

Figure 5-15 Sketch1

Figure 5-16 Extruded feature for Sketch1

5. Create **Sketch2**, the profile for the first Extrude Cut feature. Select the front face of Extrude1 as the Sketch Plane. Sketch a construction circle with diameter, 58 mm in diameter and a circle with diameter of 8 mm as the seed feature for Circular pattern with its center on the construction circle. (see Figure 5-17)

6. Create the **Extrude Cut** feature. Extrude using the Through All for End Condition. Extrude2 is the first bolt-hole feature.

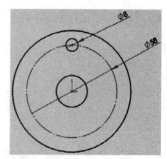

Figure 5-17 Sketch2

7. Create the **Circular Pattern** feature. Select the center axis for the Pattern axis. Enter 6 as Number of Instances, and Extrude2 as the Feature to Pattern. (see Figure 5-18)

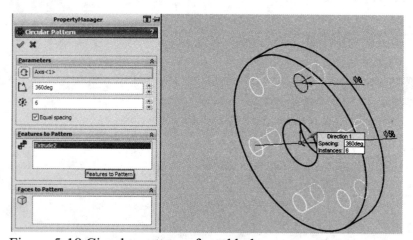

Figure 5-18 Circular pattern of seed hole

8. Create **Sketch3**, which is made up of two circles, 36 mm and 20 mm diameter respectively. Select the front face of Extrude1 as the Sketch Plane.

9. Create the **Extrude Boss** feature. Extrude depth = 48 mm. Extrude3 is the Boss feature, which is a hollow cylinder.

10. Create **Sketch4**. Select the front circular face of Extrude3 as the Sketch Plane. The profile of Sketch4 is shown in Figure 5-19.

11. Create the second **Extrude Boss** feature. Extrude depth = 12 mm. (see Figure 5-20 for the partly completed part)

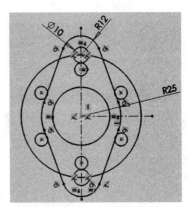

Figure 5-19 Profile of Sketch4

Figure 5-20 Partly finished part with the Extrude Boss

12. Create **Sketch5**. Select the front face of Extrude4 as the Sketch Plane. Sketch a circle with diameter of 26 mm. (see Figure 5-21)
13. Create the second **Extrude Cut** feature. Extrude depth = 25 mm.

Figure 5-21 Extrude Cut, the second in the part

14. Create the **Chamfer** feature. Select the top face of second ExtrudeCut as the Sketch Plane. Chamfer the inside edge. Distance = 3 mm and Angle = 45 degrees. (see Figure 5-22)

15. Create the **Fillet** feature. Select two circles of the second Extrude Boss. Distance = 3 mm and Angle = 45 degrees. (see Figure 5-23)

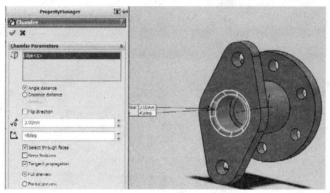

Figure 5-22 Preview of Chamfer PropertyManager

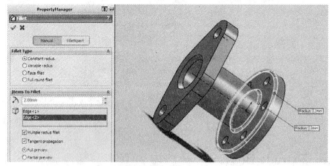

Figure 5-23 Fillets added

16. Assign the material.
17. Calculate the overall mass of the part.
18. Locate the Center of mass relative to the part Origin.

The final part and the material properties are shown in Figure 5-24.

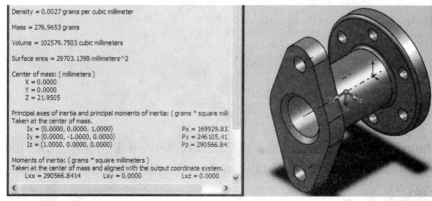

Figure 5-24 Mass properties

Tutorial 3: Bracket 2

Create the model shown in Figure 5-24. Determine the overall mass and volume of the part, and the center of mass for the model for 1060 Alloy material. Note the origin of the model.

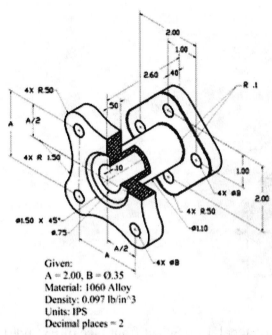

Given:
A = 2.00, B = 0.35
Material: 1060 Alloy
Density: 0.097 lb/in^3
Units: IPS
Decimal places = 2

Figure 5-25 Model to be built

SolidWorks Solution

1. **Create** a New part in SolidWorks.
2. Set the document properties for the model.
3. Create **Sketch1**, which is a profile of four circles and four lines connected by four arcs. Select Front Plane as the Sketch Plane. Center to center distance is 2 in. (see Figure 5-26)
4. Create the **Extrude Base** feature. Extrude depth = 0.4 in. Extrude1 is the Base feature. (see Figure 5-27)

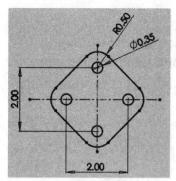

Figure 5-26 Sketch1

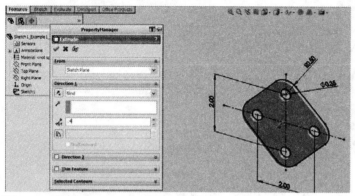

Figure 5-27 Preview of Extrude1

5. Create **Sketch2**, which is a circle of diameter, 1.1 in. Select front face of Extrude1 as the Sketch Plane. (see Figure 5-28)

6. Create the **Extrude Boss** feature. Extrude depth = 1.7 in [2.60 in – (0.50 in + 0.4 in)].

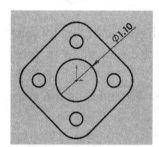

Figure 5-28 Sketch2

7. Create **Sketch3** feature. Select the front circular face of Extrude2 as the Sketch plane. Sketch a horizontal and a vertical construction lines. First create a circle, 0.35 in diameter. Mirror it about the vertical construction line (see Figure 5-29). Next, mirror both circles about the horizontal line to give four circles; then

include two arcs in the horizontal direction, two arcs in the vertical direction and four corner arcs (see Figure 5-30 and Figure 5-31 for different views).

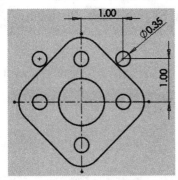

Figure 5-29 Mirror first circle, about the vertical construction line

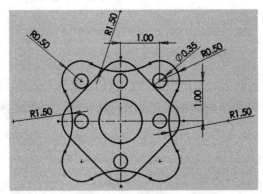

Figure 5-30 Sketch5 is complete

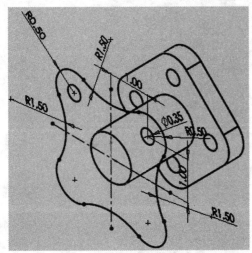

Figure 5-31 Part oriented in 3D to show Sketch2

8. Create the second **Extrude Boss** feature. Extrude depth = 0.50 in.

9. Create **Sketch4**. Select the front face of Extrude3 as the Sketch Plane. Sketch a circle with diameter of 0.75 in. (see Figure 5-32)

10. Create the first **Extrude Cut** feature. Select the Through All End Condition.

11. Create **Sketch5**. Select the front face of Extrude3 as the Sketch Plane. Sketch a circle with diameter of 1.5 in. (see Figure 5-32)

12. Create the second **Extrude Cut** feature. Extrude depth = 0.1 in.

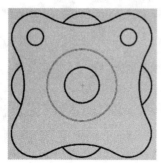

Figure 5-32 Sketch5

13. Create the **Chamfer** feature. Select the top face of second ExtrudeCut as the Sketch Plane. Chamfer the inside edge. Distance = 3 mm and Angle = 45 degrees. (see Figure 5-33)

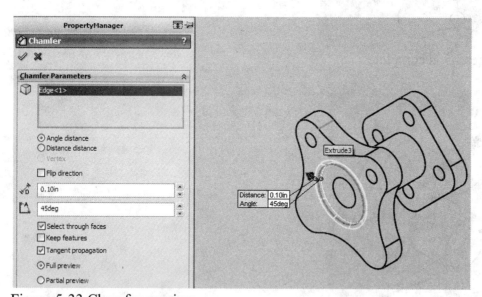

Figure 5-33 Chamfer preview

14. Create the **Fillet** feature. Select top circle of the second Extrude Boss. Distance = 0.1 in and Angle = 45 degrees. (see Figure 5-34)

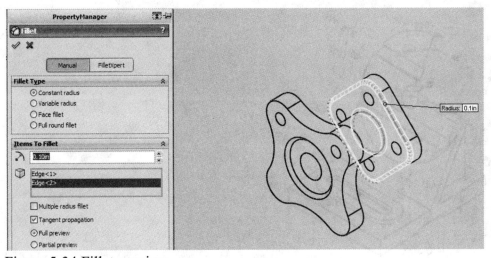

Figure 5-34 Fillet preview

1. Assign the material.
2. Calculate the overall mass of the part.
3. Locate the Center of mass relative to the part Origin.

The final part and the material properties are shown in Figure 5-35.

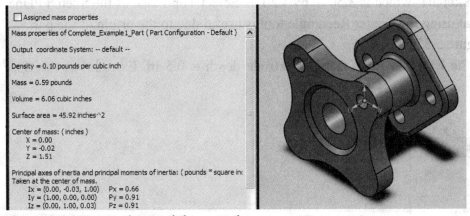

Figure 5-35 Part and material properties

Tutorial 4: Inclined Block

Create the model shown in Figure 5-36. Determine the overall mass and volume of the part, and the center of mass for the model for 1060 Alloy material. Note the origin of the model.

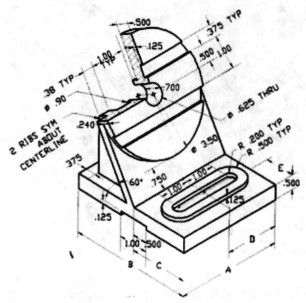

Figure 5-36 Model to be built

SolidWorks Solution

1. **Create** a New part in SolidWorks.
2. Set the document properties for the model.
3. Create **Sketch1**, which is 3.50 in by 4.20 in. Select Top Plane as the Sketch Plane. Note that using the Center Rectangle tool is useful due to the origin of the part. (see Figure 5-37)
4. Create the **Extrude Base** feature. Extrude depth = 0.5 in. Extrude1 is the Base feature.

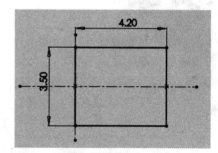

Figure 5-37 Sketch1

5. Create **Sketch2**. Select top face of Extrude1 as the Sketch Plane. Sketch a center line. (see Figure 5-38)
6. Create **Plane1**, which is inclined at 60 degrees. (see Figure 5-38)

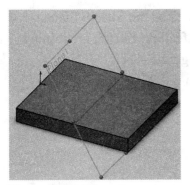

Figure 5-38 Plane1

7. Create **Sketch3**. Select Plane1 as the Sketch Plane. Sketch two equal vertical lines. Sketch arc joining the two vertical lines using Tangent Arc Tool. (see Figure 5-39)

8. Create the first **Extruded Boss** feature. Extrude depth = 0.26 in. [0.50 in – 0.24 in] (see Figure 5-40)

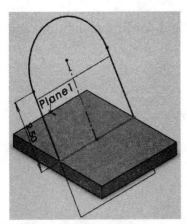

Figure 5-39 Sketch3

Figure 5-40 First Extruded Boss

9. Create **Sketch4**. Select the right angled face of Extrude2 as the Sketch Plane. Sketch a circle Coincident and Co-radial to Extrude2 feature. Sketch arc joining the two vertical lines using Tangent Arc Tool. (see Figure 5-41)

10. Create the first **Extruded Boss** feature. Extrude depth = 0.24 in.

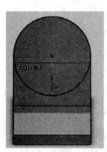

Figure 5-41 Sketch4

11. Create **Sketch5**, the profile for the Extrude Cut feature. Select the right angled face of Extrude3 as the Sketch Plane. Sketch four horizontal lines to cut the circle. Trim parts of the circle. (see Figure 5-42)

12. Create the **Extrude Cut** feature. Extrude using the Blind for End Condition, and depth of 0.125 in. (see Figure 5-43)

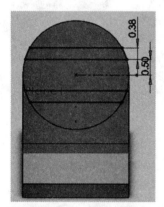

Figure 5-42 Sketch5

Figure 5-43 Second Extrude Cut

13. Create **Sketch6**. Select the left (back) angled face of Extrude2 as the Sketch Plane. Sketch a circle with diameter equal to 0.7 in. (see Figure 5-44)

14. Create the third **Extruded Boss** feature. Extrude depth = 0.20 in. [0.70 in – 0.50 in]

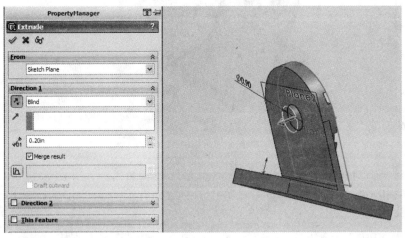

Figure 5-44 Back boss inserted

15. Create **Sketch7**. Select the right face (front) angled face of Extrude2 as the Sketch Plane. Sketch a circle of 0.625 in diameter (see Figure 5-45).

16. Create the fifth **Extrude Cut** feature. Extrude cut feature selecting Through All for End Condition. (see Figure 5-46 for preview, and Figure 5-47 for partially finished part)

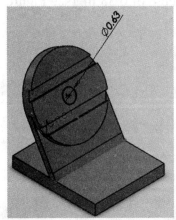

Figure 5-45 Inserting a circle on front face on incline feature

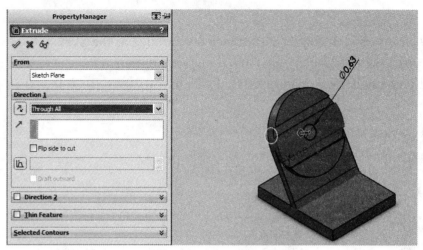

Figure 5-46 Hole preview

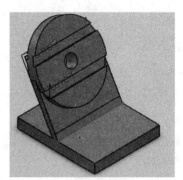

Figure 5-47 Partially finished part

17. Create **Rib** feature. Select the left angled face (back) angled face of Extrude2 as the Sketch Plane. Select Blind for End Condition and depth of 0.38 in. (see Figure 5-48)

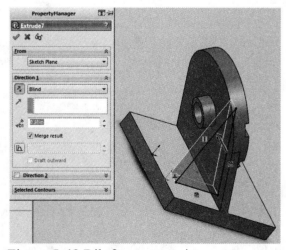

Figure 5-48 Rib feature preview

18. Create the **Mirror** feature. Select the Front Plane as the Mirror Plane for the Rib feature. (see Figure 5-49 for mirrored feature)

Figure 5-49 Mirrored rib

19. Create **Sketch8**. Select the bottom of Extrude1 as the Sketch Plane. Sketch two Slots as profiles. (see Figure 5-50)
20. Create the last Extrude Boss using Blind as End Condition through a depth of 0.625 in [0.50 in + 0.125 in] (see Figure 5-51 for completed part).

Figure 5-50 Slot profiles for extrude boss

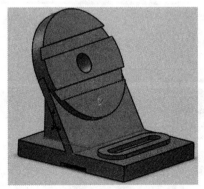

Figure 5-51 Completed part.

The mass properties are given as follows:

Mass properties of Complete_Example4_4_Part (Part Configuration - Default)

Output coordinate System: -- default --

Density = 0.098 pounds per cubic inch

Mass = 1.365 pounds

Volume = 13.990 cubic inches

Surface area = 79.772 inches^2

Center of mass: (inches): X = 1.595; Y = 0.692; Z = 0.000

Tutorial 5: Inclined Block

This example (Figure 5-52) was taken from the SolidWorks website, www.solidworks.com/cswa as an example of the Advanced Parts on the Certified SolidWorks Associate (CSWA) examination. The model has thirteen features and twelve sketches. Build this part. Calculate the overall mass and locate the center of mass of the given model.

Given: A = 63, B = 50, C = 100. Material: Copper. Units: MMGS. Density = 0.0089 g/mm^3. All holes are through all

It is worth noting where the origin is located in each example.

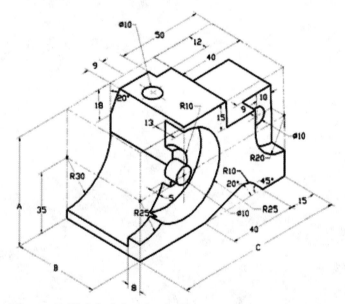

Figure 5-52 Model to be built

SolidWorks Solution

1. **Create** a New part in SolidWorks.

2. Set the document properties for the model.
3. Create **Sketch1**, which is 100 mm by 63 mm. Select Right Plane as the Sketch Plane. The part origin is at the left corner of the sketch. (see Figure 5-53)
4. Create the **Extrude Base** feature. Extrude depth = 50 mm. Extrude1 is the Base feature. (see Figure 5-54)

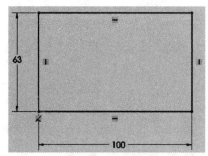

Figure 5-53 Sketch1

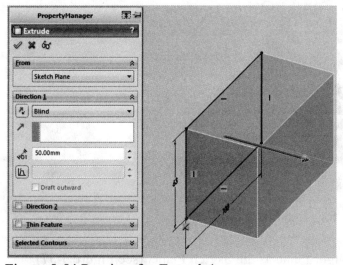

Figure 5-54 Preview for Extrude1

5. Create **Sketch2**. Select the right face of Extrude1 as the Sketch Plane. Sketch two parallel, vertical lines and use tangent arc tool to connect them, in addition to a third horizontal line. (see Figure 5-55)
6. Create the first **Extrude Cut** feature. Offset the extrude cut feature by 8 mm. Choose the outer face as Face<2> and an edge, Edge<1> for the direction. (see Figure 5-56)

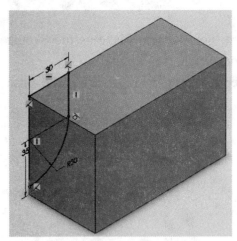

Figure 5-55 Sketch2

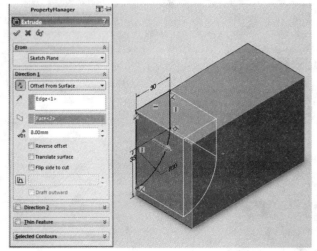

Figure 5-56 Preview of Extrude Cut for Sketch2

7. Create **Sketch3**. Select the Right Plane as the Sketch Plane. (see Figure 5-57)
8. Create the second **Extrude Cut** feature. Extrude using Through All **condition.** (see Figure 5-58)

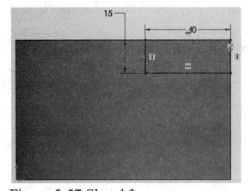

Figure 5-57 Sketch3

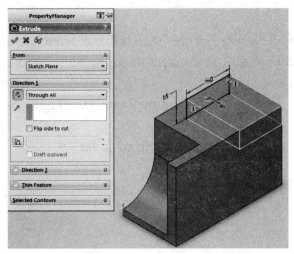

Figure 5-58 Preview of Extrude Cut for Sketch3

9. Create **Sketch4**. Select the top face of Extrude1 as the Sketch Plane. (see Figure 5-59)
10. Create the third **Extrude Cut** feature. Extrude using Through All condition. (see Figure 5-60)

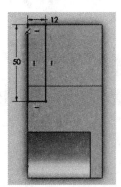

Figure 5-59 Sketch4

The partially completed model consists of these features defined so far.

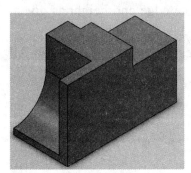

Figure 5-60 Extrude Cut for Sketch4

11. Create **Sketch5**. Select the right face of Extrude1 as the Sketch Plane. Sketch two parallel, vertical lines and use tangent arc tool to connect them, in addition to a third horizontal line. (see Figure 5-61)

12. Create the first **Extrude Cut** feature. Extrude cut feature by 9 mm. (see Figure 5-62)

The partially completed model consists of these features defined so far.

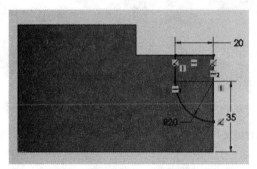

Figure 5-61 Sketch5

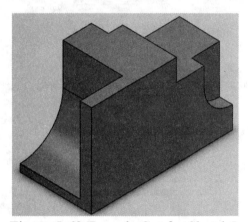

Figure 5-62 Extrude Cut for Sketch5

13. Create **Sketch6**. Select the right face of Extrude5 as the Sketch Plane. Sketch a circle of 10 mm diameter and insert it 10 mm from the edge and height as given. (see Figure 5-63)

14. Create the fifth **Extrude Cut** feature. Extrude cut feature selecting Through All for End Condition. (see Figure 5-64)

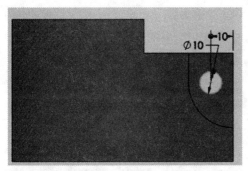

Figure 5-63 Extrude Cut for Sketch6

15. Create **Sketch7**. Select the right face of Extrude5 as the Sketch Plane. Select the top face of Extend1 as the Sketch Plane. Sketch a circle of 10 mm diameter as shown in Figure 5-64.

16. Create the sixth **Extrude Cut** feature. Extrude cut feature selecting Through All for End Condition. (see Figure 5-64)

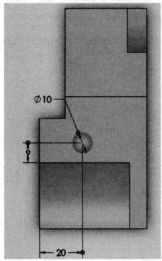

Figure 5-64 Extrude Cut for Sketch7

17. Create **Sketch8**. Select the right face of Extrude1 as the Sketch Plane. Sketch a triangle and insert a tangent arc (fillet the two intersecting lines) [see Figure 5-65].

18. Create the seventh **Extrude Cut** feature. Extrude cut feature selecting Through All for End Condition.

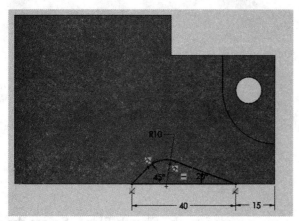

Figure 5-65 Sketch8

19. Create **Sketch9**. Select the right face of Extrude1 as the Sketch Plane. Select Hidden Lines Visible. Sketch two construction circles with center coinciding with the end of the arc. Sketch an arc using 3 Point Arc Sketch tool. Its center is at the same height with the construction circles. Complete the sketch by inserting two vertical lines and one horizontal line on the top. (see Figure 5-66)

20. Create the eight **Extrude Cut** feature. Extrude cut feature selecting Through All for End Condition.

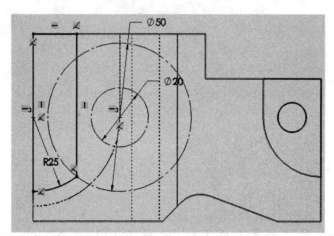

Figure 5-66 Sketch9

21. Create **Sketch10**. Select the right face of Extrude1 as the Sketch Plane. Sketch a circle with center coinciding with the end of the arc. Trim it appropriately. Insert a vertical line. (see Figure 5-67)

22. Create the ninth **Extrude Cut** feature. Extrude cut feature selecting Blind End Condition, with depth = 13 mm. (see Figure 5-68)

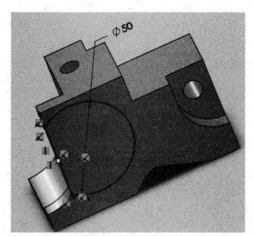
Figure 5-67 Sketch10

The partially completed model has all features so far defined is.

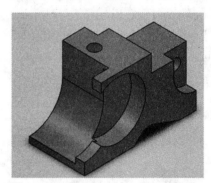
Figure 5-68 Extrude Cut of Sketch10

23. Create **Sketch11**. Select the top face of Extrude10 as the Sketch Plane. Sketch the rectangle to trim the part. (See Figure 5-69)
24. Create the eight **Extrude Cut** feature. Extrude cut feature selecting Blind End Condition, with depth of 13 mm. (See Figure 5-70)

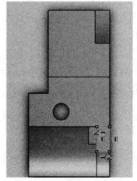
Figure 5-69 Sketch11

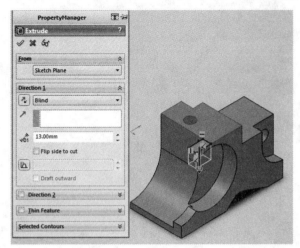

Figure 5-70 Preview of Extrude Cut of Sketch11

25. Create **Sketch12**. Select the right face of Extrude10 as the Sketch Plane. Sketch a circle. Trim it and extract left boundary features (line/arc). [See Figure 5-71]

26. Create the **Extrude Boss** feature, selecting Blind End Condition, with depth of 5 mm. (See Figure 5-72; and Figure 5-73 for 3D view)

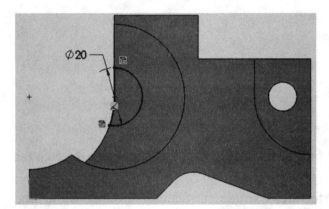

Figure 5-71 Sketch 12

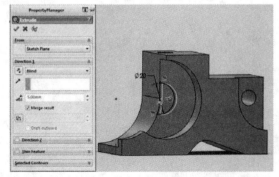

Figure 5-72 Preview of Extrude Boss of Sketch12

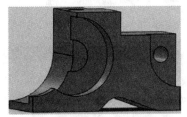

Figure 5-73 3D view of Extrude Boss of Sketch12

27. Create **Sketch13**. Select the right face of Extrude10 as the Sketch Plane. Sketch a circle. (See Figure 5-74)

28. Create an **Extrude Boss** feature, selecting Blind End Condition, with depth of up to the outer face. (Figure 5-75)

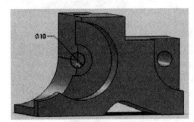

Figure 5-74 Sketch13

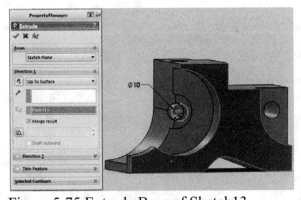

Figure 5-75 Extrude Boss of Sketch13

29. Create the **Chamfer**. Select the right face of Extrude10 as the Sketch Plane. Sketch a circle. Distance = 18 mm and Angle = 20 degrees. (See Figure 5-76)

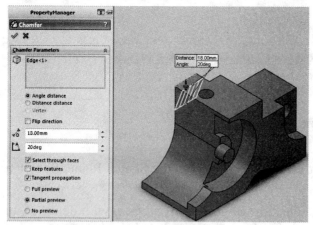

Figure 5-76 Chamfer inserted

The completed part is shown in Figure 5-77.

    30. Assign the material.

    31. Calculate the overall mass of the part.

    32. Locate the Center of mass relative to the part Origin.

Figure 5-77 Modeled part

The solutions are given as follows:

Mass properties of CSWApart (Part Configuration - Default)

Output coordinate System: -- default --

Density = 0.0089 grams per cubic millimeter

Mass = 1279.4834 grams

Volume = 143762.1768 cubic millimeters

Surface area = 26095.3206 millimeters^2

Center of mass: (millimeters): X = 26.8275, Y = 25.8163, Z = -56.3862

Tutorial 6: Inclined Block

Create the model shown in Figure 5-78. Determine the overall mass and volume of the part, and the center of mass for the model for ductile iron material. Note the origin of the model.

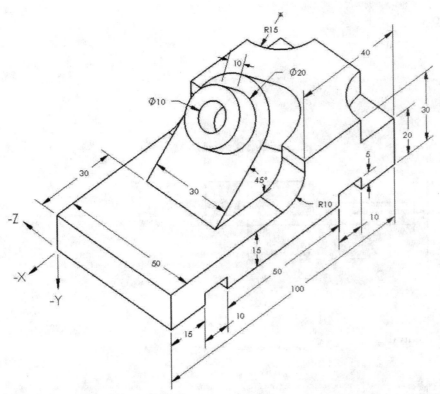

Figure 5-78 Part for modeling

SolidWorks Solution

1. **Create** a New part in SolidWorks.
2. Select the **Right Plane**
3. Create **Sketch1**. (see Figure 5-79)
4. Create **Fillet**, radius of **10 mm**. (see Figure 5-80)
5. Create the **Extrude Base** feature. Extrude depth = 50 mm. Extrude1 is the Base feature. (see Figure 5-81)

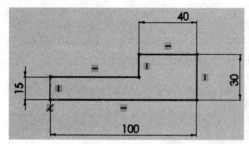

Figure 5-79 Sketch1 is created

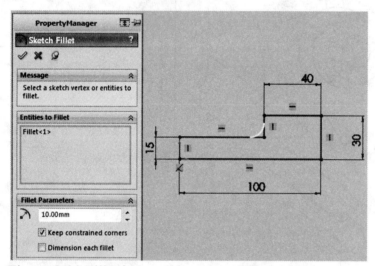

Figure 5-80 Fillet is created

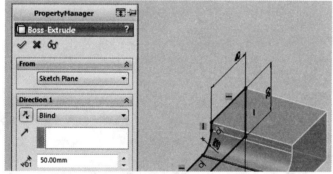

Figure 5-81 Extrude1 for Sketch1

6. Create a plane, **Plane1**, at a distance of **30 mm** from the front face. (see Figure 5-82)

7. Create an axis, **Axis1**, at the intersection of *Plane1* and *top of left-half* of *Extrud1*. (see Figure 5-83)

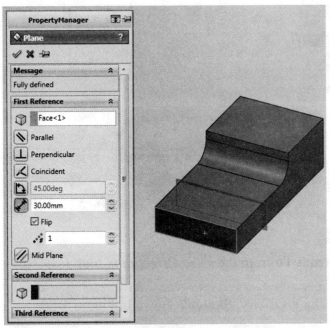

Figure 5-82 Plane1 is created

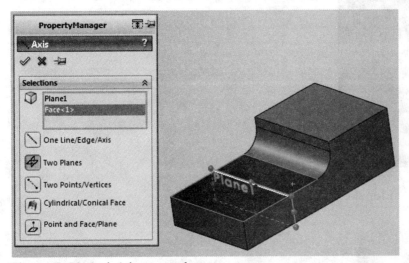

Figure 5-83 Axis1 is created

8. Create a plane, **Plane2**, through **Axis1** (**First Reference**) at an angle of **45-deg** to the *top of left-half* of *Extrud1* (Face<1>) [**Second Reference**] (see Figure 5-84).

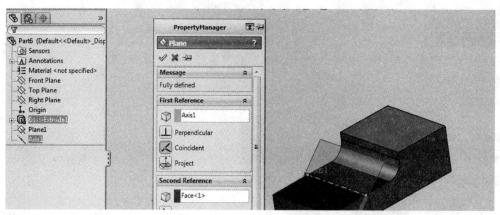

Figure 5-84 Plane2 is created

9. Select **Plane2**, and choose **Normal To** from the *View Orientation* tool. (see Figure 5-85)
10. Be in **Sketch** mode and sketch the geometry, **Sketch2** shown in Figure 5-86.

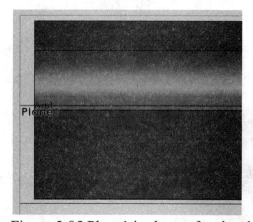

Figure 5-85 Plane1 is chosen for sketching

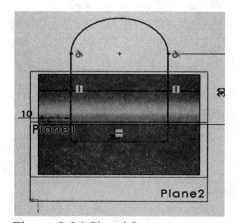

Figure 5-86 Sketch2

11. Select Isometric view for **Extrude1** and the new sketch, Sketch2. (see Figure 5-87)

12. Create the **Extrude Base** feature, **Extrude2**. Select **Up To Next** for **Direction1**. (see Figure 5-88)

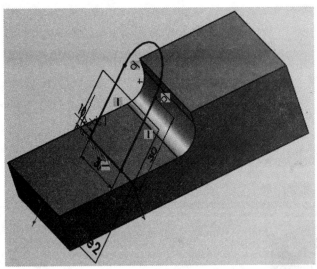

Figure 5-87 Isometric view of partial model

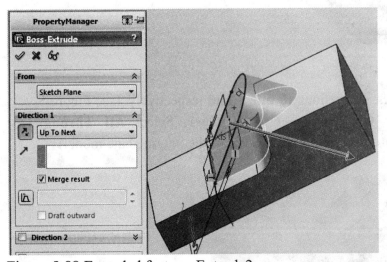

Figure 5-88 Extruded feature, Extrude2

13. Create two **Circles**, diameters **10 mm 20 mm** diameters respectively. (see Figure 5-89)

14. Create the **Extrude Boss** feature, **Extrude3**. Select **Blind** for **Direction1** and distance of **10 mm**; click the **reverse** button. (see Figure 5-90)

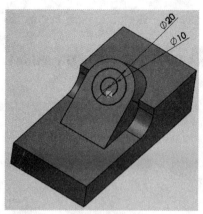

Figure 5-89 Sketch3 constitutes the two circles sketched

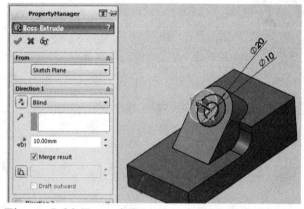

Figure 5-90 Extrude3

15. Create two **Rectangles**, dimensions **10 mm 5 mm** respectively. (see Figure 5-91)
16. Create the **Extrude Cut** feature, **Extrude-Cut1**. Select **All Through** for **Direction1**. (see Figure 5-92; and Figure 5-93 for the intermediate model)

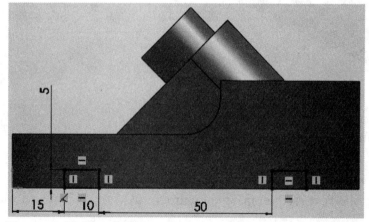

Figure 5-91 Sketch3 constitutes the two rectangles sketched

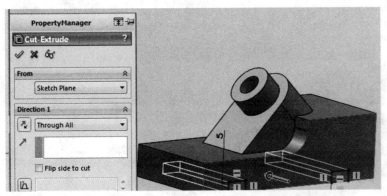

Figure 5-92 Extrude-Cut1

Figure 5-93 Intermediate model

17. Create a quarter-circle of radius 15 mm, **Sketch4**. (see Figure 5-94)

18. Create the **Extrude Cut** feature, **Extrude-Cut2**. Select **Blind** for **Direction1** and distance of **10 mm**. (see Figure 5-95)

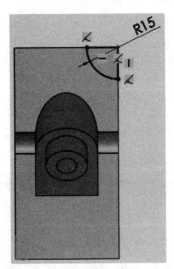

Figure 5-94 Sketch4

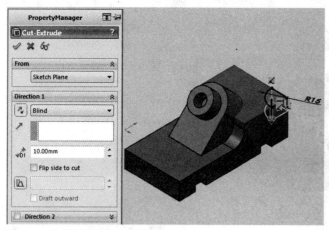

Figure 5-95 Extrude-Cut2

19. Create a plane, **Plane3**. (see Figure 5-96)
20. **Mirror Cut-Extrude3** about the plane, **Plane2**. (see Figure 5-96)

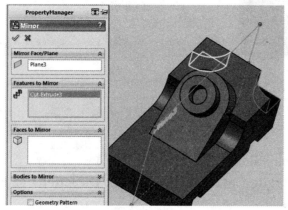

Figure 5-96 Mirror the feature, Cut-Extrude3 about a plane, Plane3

21. Apply **Material** as **Ductile Iron**. (see Figure 5-97)

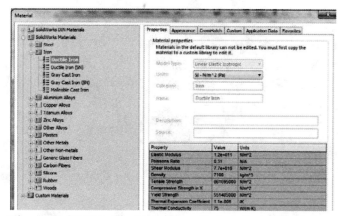

Figure 5-97 Ductile iron is applied as the material

The final model is shown in Figure 5-98, while the mass properties are shown in Figure 5-99.

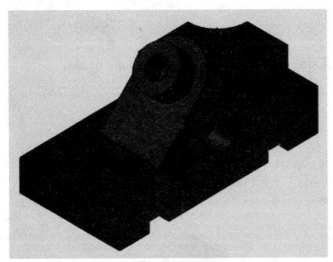

Figure 5-98 Model is complete

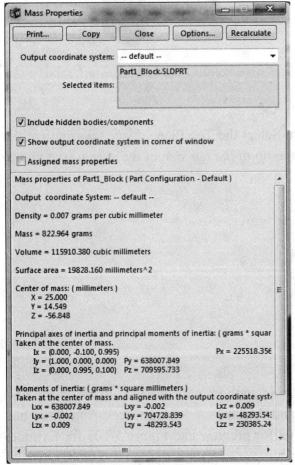

Figure 5-99 Mass properties of the completed model.

Tutorial 7: Bent Plate

Design this part in SolidWorks given the following information and Figure 5-99:

Units: MMGS

Material: 5MM, 6061 Alloy

Density: $0.0027 \ g/mm^3$

Part origin: middle of left side and right side of model. Note: All holes are 6MM.

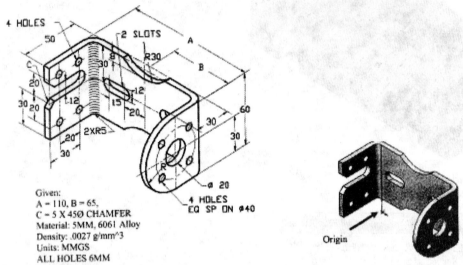

Figure 5-100 Part description

Solution

1. Create **Sketch1**, which is the base sketch. Select the Top Plane. Place the origin at the intersection of the *middle of back side* and the *tip of the left side* of the sketch (see Figure 5-101).

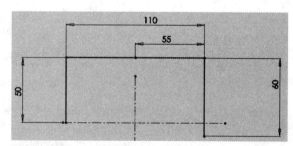

Figure 5-101 Sketch1

2. Create **Extrude-Thin1** feature. Symmetry is applied, with the Mid Plane as the End Condition in Direction 1. Depth = 60 mm and thickness = 5 mm. Check Auto-fillet box and define Radius = 5 mm. (see Figure 5-102 for preview and Figure 5-103 for Extrude-Thin1)

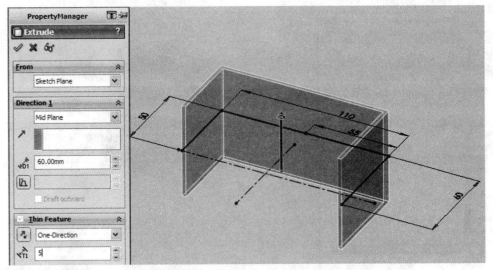

Figure 5-102

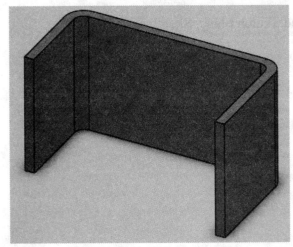

Figure 5-103 Extrude-Thin1

3. Create a **Fillet** feature. Fillet 1 is a full round fillet having diameter, 40 mm. Select the **Fillet Type** as Full Round Fillet, and choose 3 faces to define the fillet as shown in Figure 5-104.

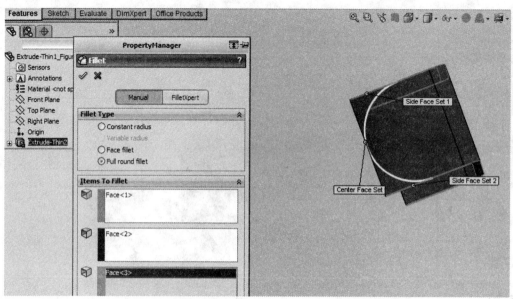

Figure 5-104 Fillet feature created

3. Create **Sketch2**. Select the right face as the Sketch plane. Sketch a circle with Diameter = 20mm. (see Figure 5-105)

4. Create first **Extrude Cut1** feature. Select Up To Next as the default End Condition.

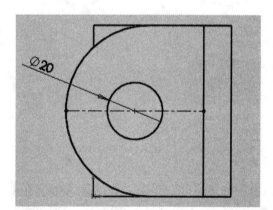

Figure 5-105 First Extrude Cut

5. Create **Sketch3**. Select the right face as the Sketch plane. Sketch a construction circle with Diameter = 40mm for the second set of circles. Create one seed of circle, radius = 6 mm. (see Figure 5-106)

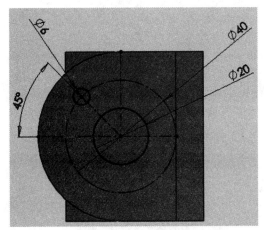

Figure 5-106 Sketch3, seed circle for circular pattern

6. Create second **Extrude Cut2** feature. Select Up To Next as the default End Condition.

7. Create **Circular Pattern** feature. Select Up To Next as the default End Condition. Activate the Temporary Axes. Use Axis at the center of the 20 mm diameter circle as axis of rotation (Axis<1>). Define the number of Instances = 4 and accept default angle = 360°. (see Figure 5-107 for preview, and Figure 5-108 for normal view)

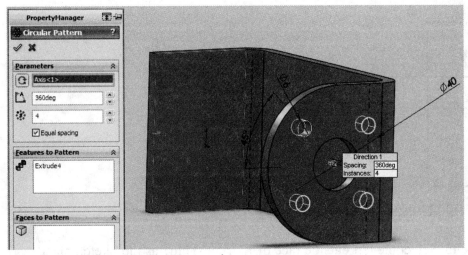

Figure 5-107 Circular pattern preview

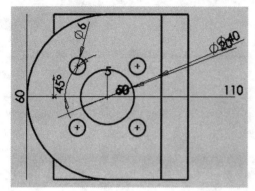

Figure 5-108 Normal view

8. Create **Sketch4**. Select the left outside face of Extrude-Thin1 as the Sketch plane. Sketch lines, 12 mm apart. The lower line should pass through the origin of the part. Both lines are horizontal and equal to 30 mm. Apply a Tangent Arc to the ends of these lines. Close the geometry by sketching a vertical line to the left. This results in a slot with a missing right hand arc. (see Figure 5-109)

9. Create third **Extrude Cut** feature. Select Up To Next as the default End Condition. (see Figure 5-109)

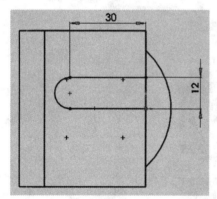

Figure 5-109 Third Extrude Cut

10. Create **Sketch5**. Select the left outside face of Extrude-Thin1 as the Sketch plane. Sketch two circles 20 mm apart, 20 mm vertical from the bottom of Sketch4 which passes through the origin; the center of the left circle is 30 mm from the right edge. (see Figure 5-110)

11. Create fourth **Extrude Cut** feature. Select Up To Next as the default End Condition.

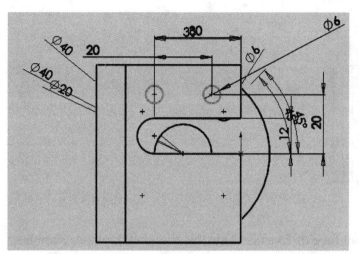

Figure 5-110 Fourth Extrude Cut

12. Create the first **Mirror** feature. Mirror the two top holes about the edge passing through the origin. (see Figure 5-111)

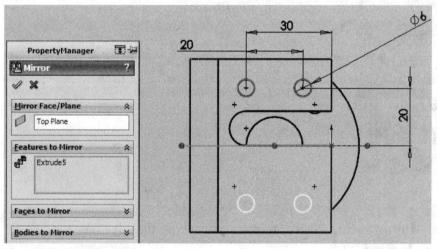

Figure 5-111 First Mirror

16. Create **Sketch6**. Select the front face of Extrude-Thin1 as the Sketch plane. Sketch a 3 Point Arc; the radius is 30 mm and its center is collinear with the origin. (see Figure 5-112)

17. Create fifth **Extrude Cut** feature. Select All Through as the default End Condition.

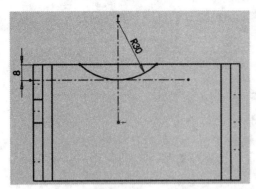

Figure 5-112 Sketch6

18. Create **Sketch7**. Select the front face of Extrude-Thin1 as the Sketch plane. Sketch a slot. The center is 30 mm from the top of the part. The center of the right arc is 20 mm from the origin. The slot is 15 mm long and 12 mm wide. (see Figure 5-113)

19. Create sixth **Extrude Cut** feature. Select All Through as the default End Condition.

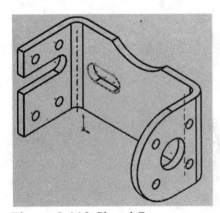

Figure 5-113 Sketch7

20. Create the second **Mirror** feature. Mirror the two slots about the edge passing through the origin. (see Figure 5-114)

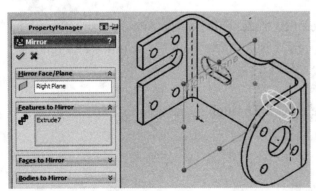

Figure 5-114 Second Mirror

21. Create the **Chamfer** feature. Apply the Angle-Distance option, with Angle = 45° and Distance = 5 mm. (see Figure 5-115)

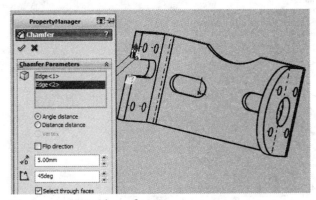

Figure 5-115 Chamfer

22. Assign **Material** to the part. Figure 5-116 shows the part and the material properties are listed.

Figure 5-116 Completed part

Mass = 135.48 grams; Volume = 50176.12 cubic millimeters
Surface area = 24647.71 millimeters^2
Center of mass: (millimeters): X = 1.78, Y = -0.86, Z = -35.65

Tutorial 8: Inclined Block

Design the part in SolidWorks given the following information and Figure 5-117:
Units: MMGS
$A = \phi 90$, top of right angled face and through other 2 features
Material: Gray Cast Iron
Density: $0.0072 \; g / mm^3$
Part origin: middle of left hand side
Note: All holes through unless otherwise noted.

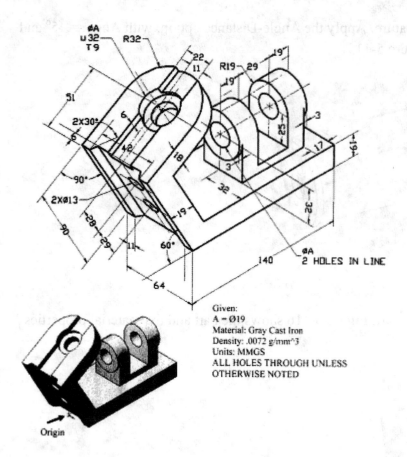

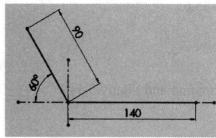

Figure 5-117 Part details

Solution

1. Create **Sketch1**, which is the base sketch. Select the right plane. Place the origin at the bottom of the left hand side of the sketch (see Figure 5-118).

Figure 5-118 Sketch1

2. Create **Extrude-Thin1** feature. Symmetry is applied, with the Mid Plane as the End Condition in Direction 1. Depth = 64 mm and thickness = 19 mm (see Figure 5-119 and Figure 5-120).

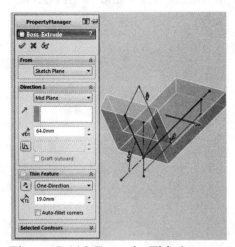

Figure 5-119 Extrude-Thin1

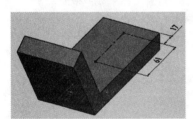

Figure 5-120 Extrude1

3. Create *center-line* for **Sketch2** on the *top face* of Extrude1 (see Figure 5-121).

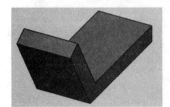

Figure 5-121 Center-line for Sketch2

4. Compete **Sketch2** (rectangle) on the *top face* of Extrude1 (see Figure 5-122).

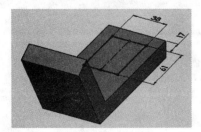

Figure 5-122 Sketch2

5. Create the **Extrude2** feature. The depth is 32 mm using the Blind as the default End Condition (see Figure 5-123 and Figure 5-124).

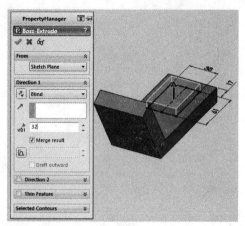

Figure 5-123 Boss-Extrude PropertyManager for Extrude2

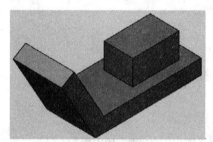

Figure 5-124 Extrude2

6. Create the **Plane1** 3 mm from right face of Extrude2 (see Figure 5-125).

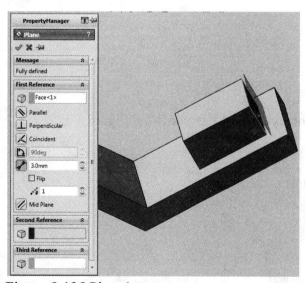

Figure 5-125 Plane1

7. Create Sketch3 (two circles) on **Plane1** (see Figure 5-126).
8. Create the **Extrude3** feature using Sketch3 on Plane1. The depth is 67 mm using the Blind as the default End Condition (see Figure 5-127).

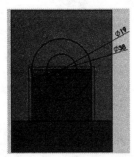

Figure 5-126 Sketch3 on Plane1

Figure 5-127 Boss-Extrude PropertyManager for Extrude3

9. Click **Plane1** and be in *sketch mode.*
10. Click the **Convert Entities** and select the arc and line as entities to convert, Sketch4. (see Figure 5-128).
11. Click **OK** to complete convert entities operation. (see and Figure 5-129)

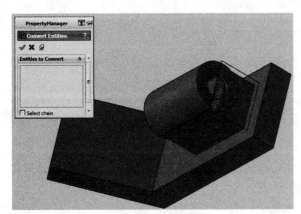

Figure 5-128 Convert Entities PropertyManager for arc and line (Sketch4) on Plane1

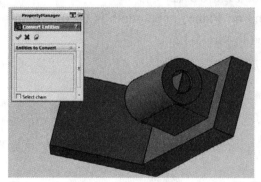

Figure 5-129 Convert Entities: arc and line (Sketch4)

12. Click the **Cut-Extrude** option to cut-extrude Sketch4 (see Figure 5-130 for Cut-Extrude1).

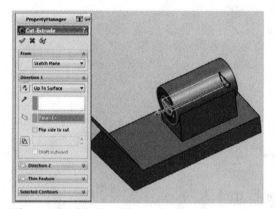

Figure 5-130 Cut-Extrude PropertyManager for convert entities features

13. Create the **Plane2** on the outer face of Extrude1 (see Figure 5-131).
14. Create **Sketch5** on **Plane2** (see Figure 5-132 and Figure 5-133).

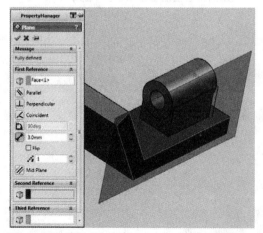

Figure 5-131 Plane2

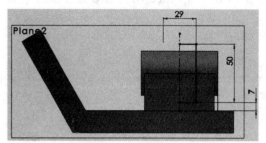

Figure 5-132 Incomplete Sketch5 on Plane2

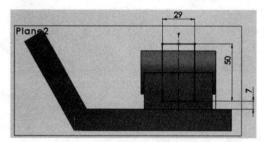

Figure 5-133 Completed Sketch5 on Plane2

15. Create the **Cut-Extrude2** feature using **Sketch5** on **Plane2**. Use **Up To Surface** (select the other face of Extrude2 away from Plane1) as the End Condition (see Figure 5-134).

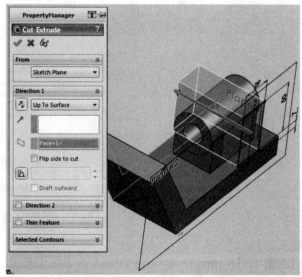

Figure 5-134 Cut-Extrude PropertyManager for Sketch5 on Plane2

16. Create **Sketch2**. Select the top of the face of **Extrude-Thin1** as the Sketch Plane. There are 3 lines and one arc (use Tangent Arc). The two opposite lines are

parallel and all lines and arc are collinear with the top face of **Extrude-Thin1** (see Figure 5-135, Figure 136 and Figure 137).

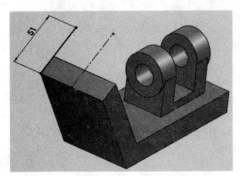

Figure 5-135 Incomplete Sketch6

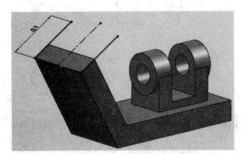

Figure 5-136 Lines added to incomplete Sketch6

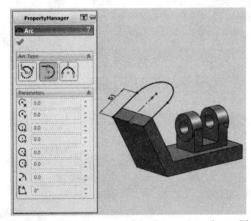

Figure 5-137 Arc added to complete Sketch6

17. Create the **Extrude4** feature. The depth is 18 mm using the **Blind as the default** End Condition (see Figure 5-138).

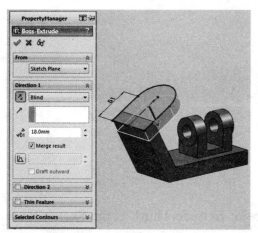

Figure 5-138 Boss-Extrude PropertyManager for Extrude4

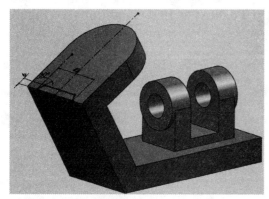

Figure 5-139 Sketch7

18. Create **Sketch7**. Select the top front angled face of Extrude-Thin1 as the Sketch Plane. Sketch the four-sided geometry using a center-line and take advantage of symmetry about the center-line (see Figure 5-140).

19. Create the third **Extrude Cut** feature. Select **Up To Next** as End Condition and the angle edge as vector for extrusion (see Figure 5-140 and Figure 5-141).

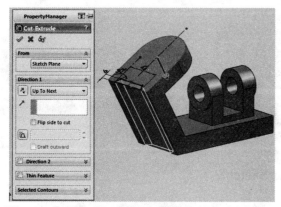

Figure 5-140 Cut-Extrude PropertyManager for Sketch7

Figure 5-141 Cut-Extrude3

20. Create **Sketch8**. Select the left angled face of Extrude-Thin1 as the Sketch Plane (third Extrude Cut). Sketch two circles 29 mm apart, each 13 mm in diameter (see Figure 5-142).

21. Create the **Extrude Cut** feature. Select **Up To Next** as End Condition (see Figure 5-143).

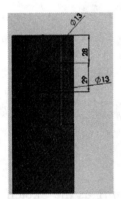

Figure 5-142 Sketch8—two circles

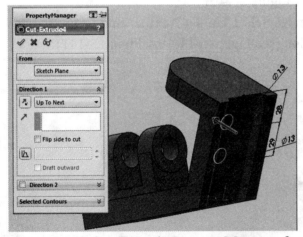

Figure 5-143 Cut-Extrude PropertyManager for Sketch8

22. Create Sketch9 (a circle) on the top face of **Extrude4** (see Figure 5-144).

23. Create the **Cut-Extrude** feature using Sketch9. The **Depth** is **9** mm using the **Blind** as the default End Condition (see Figure 5-145).

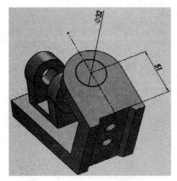

Figure 5-144 Sketch9

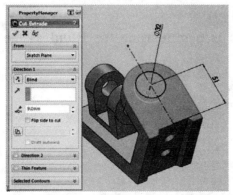

Figure 5-145 Cut-Extrude PropertyManager for Sketch9

24. Create Sketch10 (a circle) at the bottom face of the last **Cut-Extrude** (see Figure 5-146).
25. Create the **Cut-Extrude** feature using Sketch10. The **Up To Next** as the End Condition (see Figure 5-147).

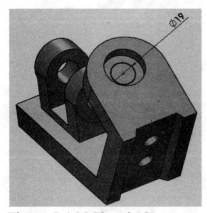

Figure 5-146 Sketch10

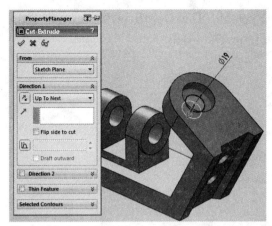

Figure 5-147 Cut-Extrude PropertyManager for Sketch10

26. Create **Sketch11**. Select the top of the face of **Extrude4** as the Sketch Plane for the rectangle (see Figure 5-148 and Figure 5-149).
27. Create the **Cut-extrude** feature. The **Depth** is **6 mm** using the **Blind** as the default End Condition (see Figure 5-150).

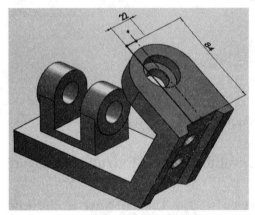

Figure 5-148 Incomplete Sketch11

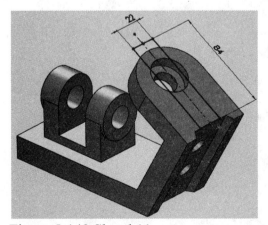

Figure 5-149 Sketch11

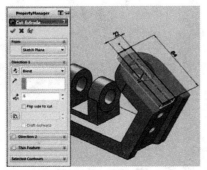

Figure 5-150 Cut-Extrude PropertyManager for Sketch11

The completed model and its mass properties are shown in Figure 5-151 and Figure 5-152 respectively.

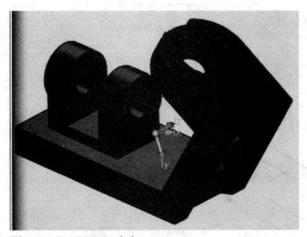

Figure 5-151 Model

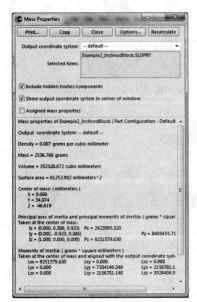

Figure 5-152 Mass properties for model

Tutorial 9: Model with Notched Offset Section View

Create the model shown in Figure 5-152.

Part Name: Mounting Plate
Material: AISI 1020
Fillets: R.03 unless otherwise specified.

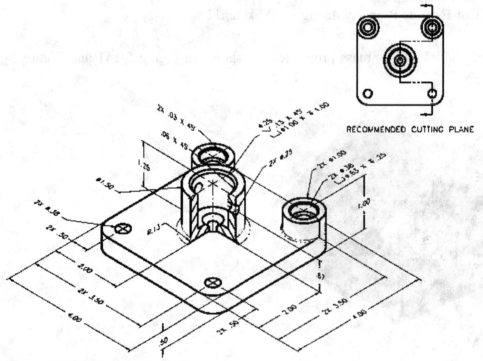

RECOMMENDED CUTTING PLANE

Figure 5-153 Model description

Solution

1. Create **Sketch1**, which is the base sketch. Select the Top Plane. Place the origin at the center of the sketch (see Figure 5-154).

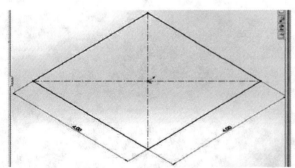

Figure 5-154 Sketch1 for the base of the model

2. Extrude base **.5**. (see Figure 5-155)
3. Create a **hole**, .38-dia as shown. (see Figure 5-155)
4. Use **Linear Pattern** tool to replicate the **hole .38-dia** as shown. (see Figure 5-156)

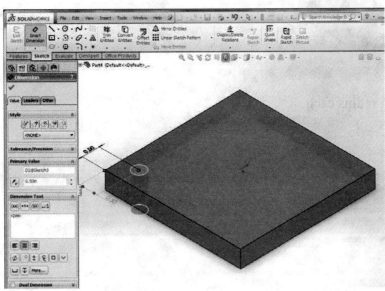

Figure 5-155 Extruded base

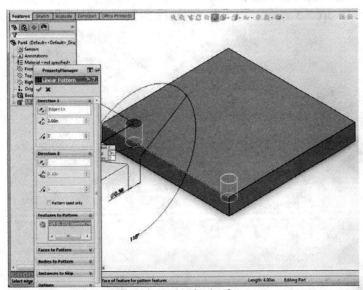

Figure 5-156 Duplicating the hole feature

2. Add fillet of .5 radius at each of the four corners. (see Figure 5-157)
3. Create boss 1.0 diameter height of .5 from top of base. (see Figure 5-158)

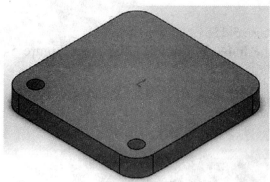

Figure 5-157 Four fillets of .5 radius each

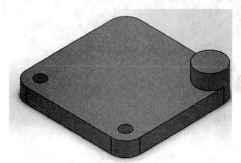

Figure 5-158 Boss added

4. Create a circle, .63 diameter on top of boss. (Figure 5-159)
5. Extrude Cut .25 downward to create a countersink. (Figure 5-160)

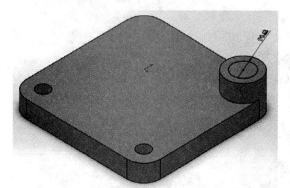

Figure 5-159 Sketch a circle

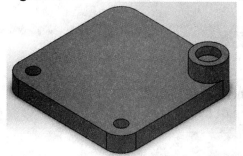

Figure 5-160 ExtrudeCut the circle

6. Create a circle, .38 diameter on top of countersink. (Figure 5-161)
7. Extrude Cut Through All. (Figure 5-162)

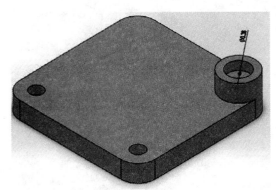

Figure 5-161 Countersink created

Figure 5-162 Hole right through created

8. Mirror the countersink and through hole about Right Plane. (Figure 5-163) [See Figure 5-164 for the mirrored features]

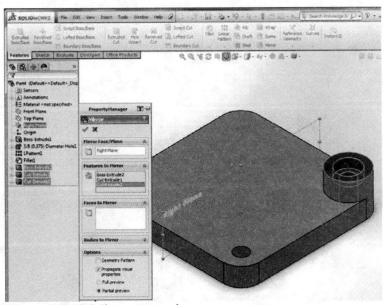

Figure 5-163 Mirror operation

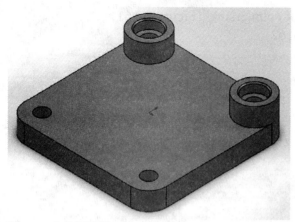

Figure 5-164 Mirrored features

9. Create central boss, 1.5 diameter, and 1.25 high from top of base. (Figure 5-165)
10. Sketch circle, 1 diameter on top of central boss. (Figure 5-166)

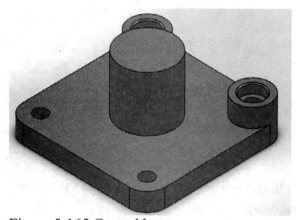

Figure 5-165 Central boss

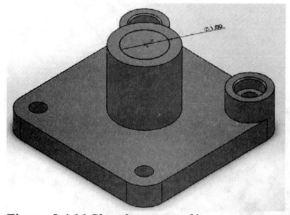

Figure 5-166 Sketch on top of boss

11. Extrude Cut, 1 downward to create a counter bore. (Figure 5-167)
12. Create a circle, .25 diameter. (Figure 5-168)
13. Extrude Cut right through. (Figure 5-169)

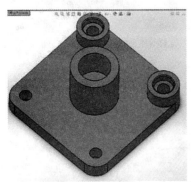

Figure 5-167 Central counterbore

Figure 5-168 Circle for through hole

14. Add Chamfers. (Figure 5-169; Figure 5-170)

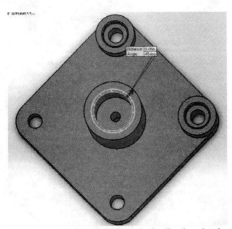

Figure 5-169 Through hole included and Chamfer added

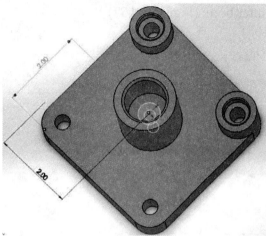

Figure 5-170 Add Chamfer

15. Add Material. (Figure 5-171)
16. Add Fillet to bottom of central boss. (Figure 5-172)

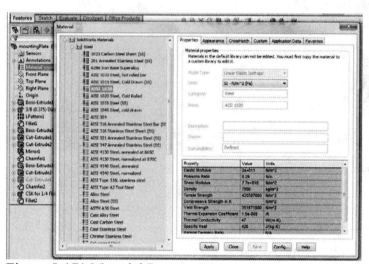

Figure 5-171 Material PropertyManager

Figure 5-172 Fillet added

17. Create Plane to coincide with extreme right vertical face. (see Figure 5-173)
18. Be in Sketch mode, and create a circle, .25 diameter on the Plane at Normal orientation. (see Figure 5-174)
19. Orient model in Isometric view. (see Figure 5-175)

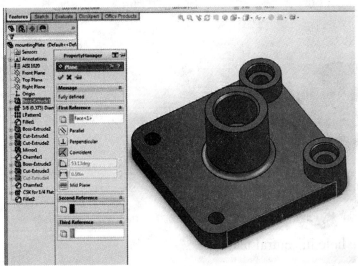

Figure 5-173 Plane1

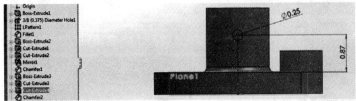

Figure 5-174 Circle on Plane1

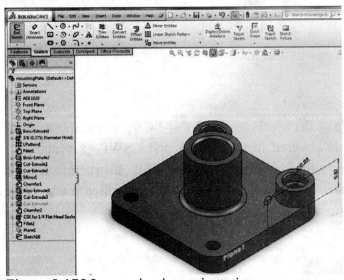

Figure 5-175 Isometric view orientation

20. Extrude Cut to opposite face (see Figure 5-176)
[Finished model is shown in Figure 5-177]

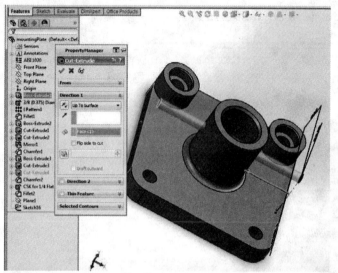

Figure 5-176 Extrude Cut to create hole in central feature

Figure 5-177 Finished model

Summary

This chapter discusses part modeling at the levels of CSWA and CSWP and most of the examples are similar to the materials covered in the CSWA and CSWP examinations. Students preparing for these exams will find this chapter helpful. Instructors should consider covering the previous chapter before moving to this chapter which pitches at a higher level.

Exercises

SolidWorks Corporation: CSWP Sample Exam
Certified SolidWorks Professional: Solid Modeling Specialist (CSWP/CORE)
SAMPLE EXAM – Part Modeling Portion
These questions are similar to the Parametric Part Modeling portion of the CSWP exam.

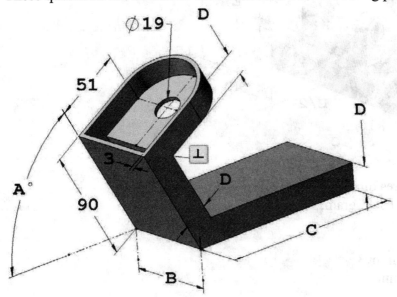

Design this part in SolidWorks.
Unit system: MMGS (millimeter, gram, second)
Decimal places: 2
Part origin: Arbitrary
Part material: Brass
Material Density: 0.0085 g/mm^3
Design note: the part is shelled throughout (single open face as shown)

Question 1:
A = 60 B = 64 C = 140 D = 19
What is the overall mass of the part (in grams)?

Question 2:
A = 50 B = 70 C = 160 D = 23
What is the overall mass of the part (in grams)?

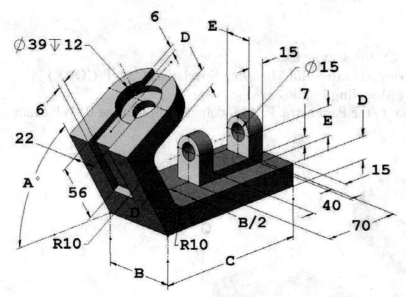

Update part with new features/dimensions.
Unit system: MMGS (millimeter, gram, second)
Decimal places: 2
Part material: Brass
Material Density: 0.0085 g/mm^3
Design note: no shell remaining

Question 3:
A = 60 B = 64 C = 140 D = 19 E = 25
What is the overall mass of the part (in grams)?
Question 4:
A = 70 B = 80 C = 130 D = 15 E = 40
What is the overall mass of the part (in grams)?

ANSWERS
1) 1006.91 grams
2) 1230.82 grams
3) 2859.51 grams
4) 3218.14 grams

ADVICE: You should be able to answer all four questions correctly within 20 to 30 minutes. Read through every question first. This will help you save time and make correct decisions when choosing which sketch plane to use and which sketch profile is best. Avoid sketch fillets in this particular design.

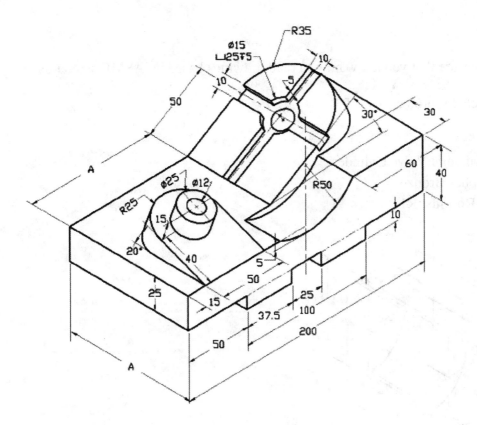

Build this part in SolidWorks.
Material: 6061 Alloy. Density = 0.0027g/mm^3
Unit system: MMGS (millimeter, gram, second)
Decimal places: 2.
Part origin: Arbitrary
A = 100.
All holes through all, unless otherwise specified

Question 4:
What is the overall mass of the part in grams?
Answers
a) 2040.57
b) 2004.57
c) 102.63
d) 1561.23

Projects

These projects ensure that you know how to read drawings based on ASME standards.

Create the models for projects P1—P3

P1:
Part Name: Hydraulic Valve Cylinder
Material: Phosphor Bronze
All Fillets and Rounds: R1

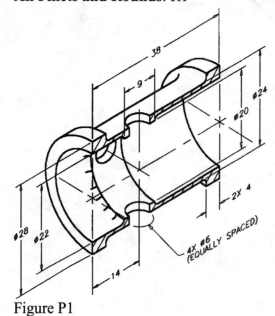

Figure P1

P2:

Part Name: Hub

Material: Cast Iron

Fillets: R.03 unless otherwise specified.

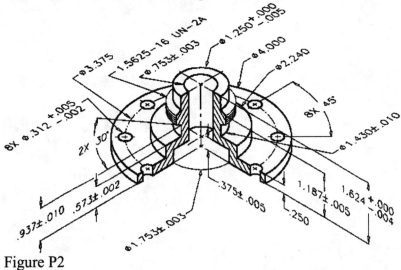

Figure P2

P3:

Part Name: Slide Bracket

Material: AISI 1020

Fillets: R.25 unless otherwise specified.

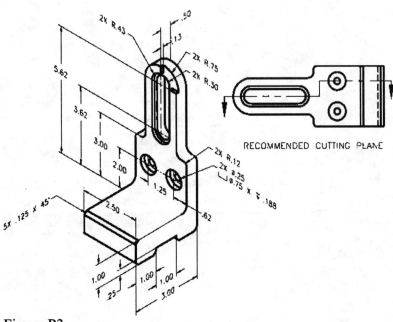

Figure P3

Resources:

http://www.eng.uwo.ca/designcenter/SWcertification/CSWA/CSWASampleExam2007.pdf

Chapter 6
Creating Revolved, Swept, and Lofted Parts

Objectives:
In this chapter you will learn:
- How to create 3D objects using **Revolved** Features tools
- How to use **Copy** Features tools
- How to create 3D objects using **Swept** Features tools
- How to use **Draft** Features tools
- How to create 3D objects using **Lofted** Features tools
- How to use **Circular Pattern** Features tools
- How to use **Reference Planes**
- How to use **Copy** Features tools

REVOLVED BOSS/BASE

The revolved boss/base tool rotates a contour about an axis. It is a useful tool when modeling parts that have circular contours. Let us illustrate the revolved boss/base concept as follows.

1. Select the front plane and create Sketch1 as shown in Figure 6-1.
2. Click the **Features** tool.
3. Click the **Revolved Boss/Base** tool.
   The Revolve Properties Manager appears (see Figure 6-2).
4. Define the revolved axis (Line1) as the vertical dimension line. A real-time preview will appear.
5. Click **OK** to complete the revolved part (see Figure 6-3).

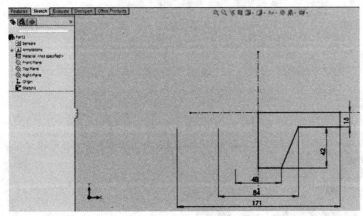

Figure 6-1 Sketch1

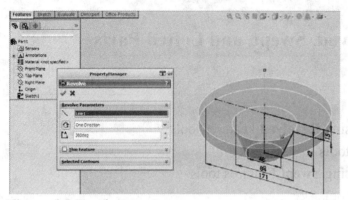

Figure 6-2 Preview

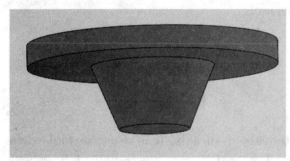

Figure 6-3 Extrude1

6. Click the top face of Extrude1
7. Sketch a **construction circle** of **126 mm** diameter, and four **circles**, each **15 mm** in diameter spaced out at 45 degrees (see Figure 6-4)
8. Select each circle, and click **Extrude-cut** to create a hole for each of the circle
9. See Figure 6-5 for the Extrude-Cut preview for the four holes and Figure 6-6 for the final part.

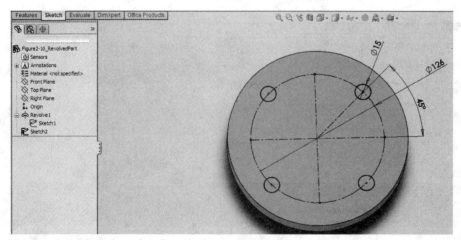

Figure 6-4 Sketches for four holes

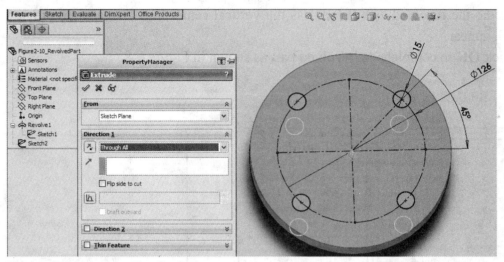

Figure 6-5 Extrude-Cut for holes

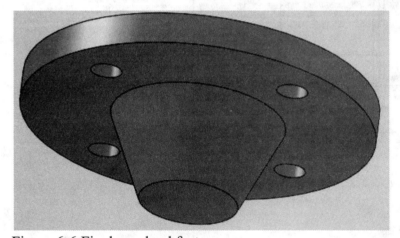

Figure 6-6 Final revolved feature

PRACTICAL EXAMPLES

Two practical examples are given based on the principles of revolved parts. One is the engine cylinder commonly used in automobile design and the other is pulley commonly used in power transmission.

ENGINE CYLINDER

1. Select the front plane and create Sketch1 as shown in Figure 6-7. Define the relations for the slots to ensure that the sketch is fully defined.
2. Click the **Features** tool.
3. Click the **Revolved Boss/Base** tool.
   The Revolve Properties Manager appears.

4. Define the revolved axis (**Line1**) as the vertical center line. A real-time preview will appear.
5. Click **OK** to complete the revolved part as shown in Figure 6-8.

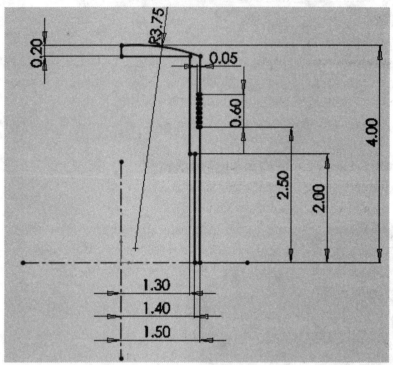

Figure 6-7 Sketch1

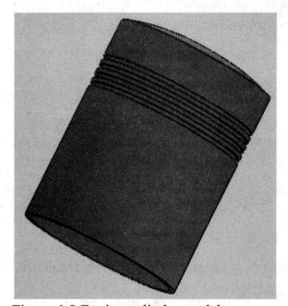

Figure 6-8 Engine cylinder model

PULLEY

1. Select the right plane and create Sketch1 as shown in Figure 6-9. The steps required for correctly defining the sketch are given in i)—vii).
2. Click the **Features** tool.
3. Click the **Revolved Boss/Base** tool.
   The Revolve Properties Manager appears.
4. Define the revolved axis (Line1) as the horizontal center line. A real-time preview will appear (see Figure 6-13 for steps [2—4]).
5. Click **OK** to complete the revolved part as seen in Figure 6-14.

The steps required for correctly defining the sketch are as follows:
   i)   Sketch a line to the left of the vertical construction line.
   ii)   Mirror this line about the vertical construction line.
   iii)   Dimension the line from end to end about the construction line, to be 10 mm.
   iv)   Sketch the first tooth-profile completely, and define relations for the three horizontal lines to be equal to 10 mm and the angles to be 60 degrees (see Figure 6-10 for steps [i—v]).
   v)   Copy part of the tooth-profile to increase the number of profiles equal to 2 and ensure that the end-condition relations are met (see Figure 6-11 for step v).
   vi)   Mirror the two tooth-profiles about the vertical construction line (see Figure 6-11 for step vi).
   vii)   Check that all points at the bottom are collinear, so are the points at the top of profiles. Also check that the sketch forms a closed loop.

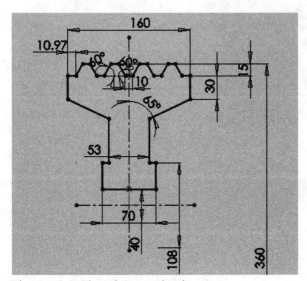

Figure 6-9 Sketch1 required

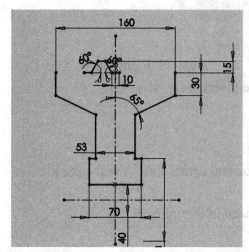

Figure 6-10 Steps (i) to (iv)

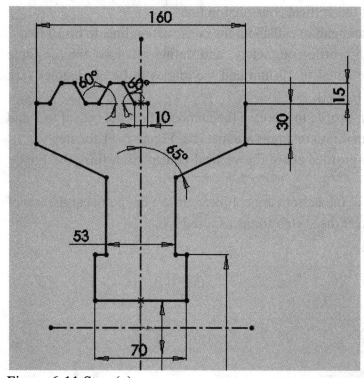

Figure 6-11 Step (v)

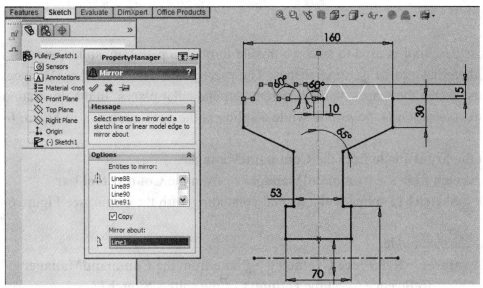

Figure 6-12 Step (vi)

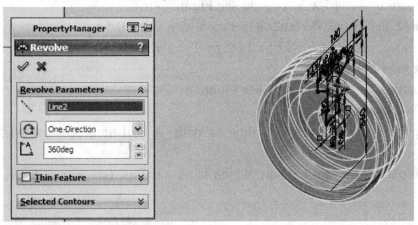

Figure 6-13 Steps 2 to 4

Figure 6-14 Pulley model

SWEPT BOSS/BASE

The swept boss/base tool is used to sweep a profile through a path (arc, spline, etc.). As with lofting, there have to be existing shapes. The prerequisite for creating a 3D swept model is to first sketch the shapes on the different perpendicular planes. In the illustration presented here, a hexagon is the *profile* while a spline is the *path* as shown in Figure 6-15.

1. Select the **Front Plane** from the **CommandManager**.
2. Click **Sketch** from the **CommandManager** or from the **Context tool bar**.
3. Create a **Sketch1** (a spline with one end coinciding with the origin; see Figure 6-15).
4. **Exit** the sketch mode.
5. Click **Features > Reference Geometry > Plane** from the **CommandManager**
6. For the **First Reference** select the **endpoint** of the spline, **Sketch1**.
7. For the **Second Reference** select the **spline, Sketch1** from the graphics window [SolidWorks enhanced features automatically creates the plane **Plane1**] (Note: this plane is normal to Sketch1 at any point; see Figure 6-16).
8. Right-click **Plane1** and create **Sketch2** (a hexagon with sides, 0.5 in).
9. **Exit** the sketch mode; see Figure 6-17 for both profile and path.
10. Click the **Swept boss/base** tool.
    The Swept Properties Manager appears (see Figure 6-17).
11. Right-click the Profile and *Path* box.
12. Click the hexagon as profile and the spline as path. A real-time preview will appear.
13. Click OK to complete the swept cut part, which is now hollow (see Figure 6-18). Hide the planes.

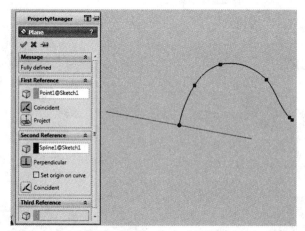

Figure 6-15 Path (Spline) and Plane1 created at the Spline left end-point

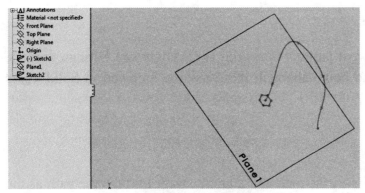

Figure 6-16 Profile (hexagon) and path (spline)

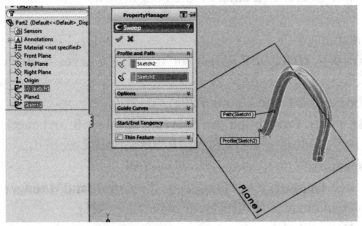

Figure 6-17 Preview

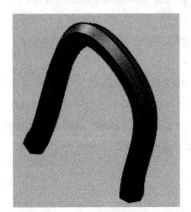

Figure 6-18 3D swept model

PRACTICAL EXAMPLES

Amongst the commonly used swept parts in industrial applications are O-rings, springs, and threaded parts (e.g. nuts and bolts, although these may be archived in SolidWorks library).

SPRING

Springs are modeled using a helix as the path and a circle swept through the path as the profile.

1. Select the **Top Plane**. Create **Sketch1** (a circle, radius 0.5 in) with center at the origin (see Figure 6-19).
2. Select the **Isometric** orientation.
3. Click on **Features > Curves > Helix and Spiral** (or **Insert > Curves > Helix and Spiral**).
   The **Helix/Spiral** dialog box appears (see Figure 6-20a).
4. Define Helix by **Height** (1.75 in); **Revolution** (6); **Starting Angle = 0**; and check Clockwise (see Figure 6-19 for values; and see Figure 6-20b for helix created).
5. Click OK to finish helix feature.
6. Click **Features > Reference Geometry > Plane** from the **CommandManager** [the Plane PropertyManager automatically displayed; see Figure 6-21].
7. Click the **endpoint** of the Helix, **Sketch1**.
8. Click the **Helix, Sketch1** from the FeatureManager [a plane normal to the Helix at its end-point is automatically created; see Figure 6-21].
9. Click **OK** to accept the plane **Plane1** created (Note: *Plane1 is normal to Sketch1* at any point).
10. Right-click **Plane1** and create **Sketch2** (a circle, diameter 0.125 in).
11. Use the **Relations** tool to make the center of the circle coincident with the origin of the helix, if necessary using pierce relation; click *center of circle* and *helix* as **Selected Entities** and choose **Pierce** as **Relation**) [see Figure 6-22].
12. **Exit** the sketch mode.
13. Click the **Swept boss/base** tool.
    The Swept Properties Manager appears.
14. Right-click the **Profile** and **Path** box.
15. Click the **circle** as **Profile** and the **helix** as **Path**. Note: It is preferred to do this through the **Feature Manager**. A real-time preview will appear (see Figure 6-23a).
16. Click **OK** to complete the swept cut part, which is now hollow as shown in Figure 6-23b. Hide the planes.

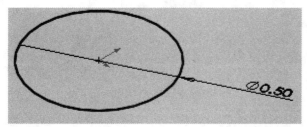

Figure 6-19 Sketch1

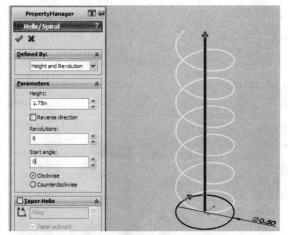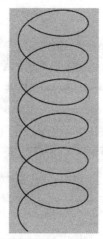

(a) Helix/spiral PropertyManager　　　　　　　　(b) Helix

Figure 6-20 Helix/spiral PropertyManager for creating a Helix feature

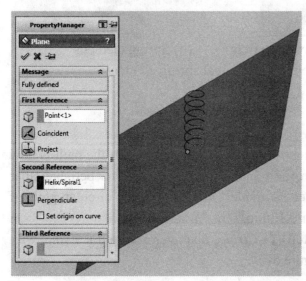

Figure 6-21 Defining normal plane at end point of helix

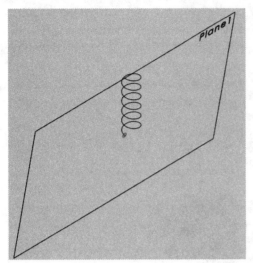

Figure 6-22 Sketch2, a circle on plane normal to helix

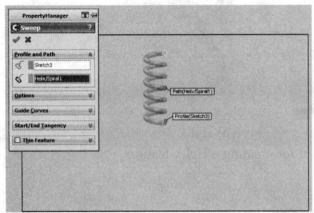 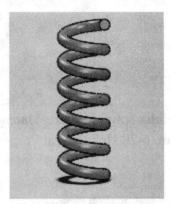

(a) Preview using path (helix/spiral) and profile (circle)   (b) Spring element

Figure 6-23 Swept boss/base tool for modeling mechanical spring element

O-RING

The procedure for modeling o-ring is similar to that of spring except that the path is now a circle (say on the top plane) while the profile remains a circle on another perpendicular plane (front plane). As an illustration, let us model an O-ring with circular path of diameter 5 in and cross-section of diameter 0.125 in.

1. Select the **Top Plane**. Create **Sketch1** (a *Circle*, diameter 5 in and a *Point*) with center at the origin as shown in Figure 6-24.
2. Select the **Isometric** orientation.
3. **Exit** the Sketch mode.
4. Click **Features > Reference Geometry > Plane** from the **CommandManager**.
5. For the **First Reference** select the **Curve** and the **Perpendicular** option.

6. For the **Second Reference** select the **Point** a.

7. Click **OK** to create the plane **Plane1** (Note: *Plane1 is normal to Sketch1* at any point).

8. Right-click **Plane1** and create **Sketch2** (a circle, diameter 0.125 in).

9. Add a **Pierce** relation by clicking the small circle center point, hold the Ctrl key down, Click on the large circle circumference and release the Ctrl key. Right click Make-Pierce from the dialog box. Click **OK** (see Figure 6-26).

10. **Exit** the Sketch mode.

11. Click the **Swept boss/base** tool.
    The Swept Properties Manager appears.

12. Right-click the *Profile* and *Path* box.

13. Click the small circle (**Sketch2**) as **profile** and the large circle (**Sketch1**) as **path** using the Feature Manager. A real-time preview will appear as shown in Figure 6-27.

14. Click **OK** to complete the swept cut part, which is now hollow as shown in Figure 6-28. Hide the planes.

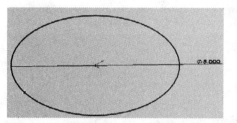

Figure 6-24 Path

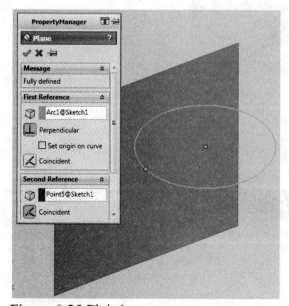

Figure 6-25 Plain1

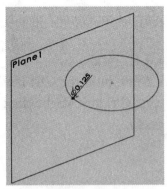

Figure 6-26 Plane definition with Profile (small circle) and path (large circle)

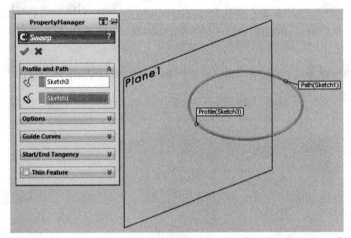

Figure 6-27 Sweep PropertyManager for O-ring preview

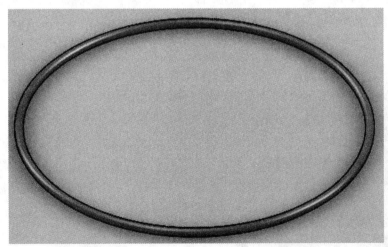

Figure 6-28 O-ring model

THREADED CAP

Threaded parts are modeled using a helix as the path and a shape of interest swept through the path, as the profile. As a small project, let us first model a cap having draft angle. Then, we will add a trapezoidal profile as an internal thread for a helical path. The procedure for achieving our objective could be simplified by considering two modules: (i) Cap without internal thread (steps [1]—[6]); (ii) Cap with internal thread (steps [7]—[11]). Let us consider these two modules.

Cap without internal thread
1. Select the **Front Plane**. Create **Sketch1** (a circle, radius 5 in) with center at the origin.
2. Click the **Extruded Boss/Base** feature tool.
   The Extrude PropertyManager is displayed with Blind as the default End Condition in Direction 1.
3. Enter **1.725 in** as **Depth** in Direction 1. Click the Draft On/Off button.
4. Enter **5 degree** as **Draft Angle**. Click the **Draft outward** box.
5. Click **OK** to accept the model (see Figure 6-29).
6. **Right-click** the front face of the Sketch plane.
7. Click **Sketch** from the toolbar. Then click the **Circle** Sketch tool for a circle centered at the origin (see Figure 6-30).
8. Using the **Smart Dimension** tool, dimension the circle to have a diameter of **3.875 in**.
9. Click **Extrude cut**.
10. Enter depth of **0.275 in** for Depth in Direction 1 (see preview in Figure 6-31).
11. Click **Draft On/Off** button and enter 5 degrees for **Angle**, accepting the default settings.
12. Click **OK** (see Figure 6-32).

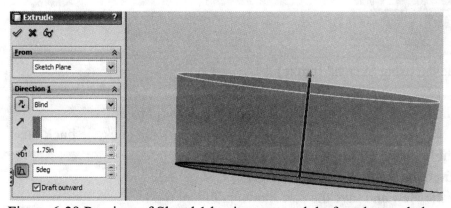

Figure 6-29 Preview of Sketch1 having outward draft and extruded

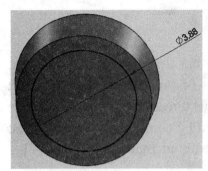

Figure 6-30 Creating Sketch2, a circle for and extrude-cut

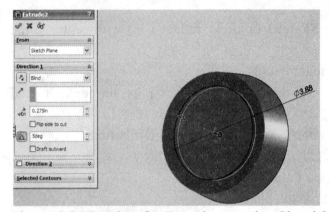

Figure 6-31 Preview for Extrude-cut using Sketch2 (circle)

Figure 6-32 Extrude-cut using Sketch2 (circle)

13. Click the **Shell** feature tool. The Shell1 PropertyManager pops up.

14. Click the front face of the **Front-Cut,** then rotate the part and click the **back face**.

15. Enter **0.15 in** for shell thickness (see Figure 6-33).

16. Click **OK** from the Shell1 PropertyManager.

17. Click isometric view and save the part shown in Figure 6-34.

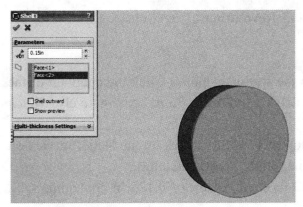

Figure 6-33 Preview for shelling operation

Figure 6-34 Completed part

Cap with internal thread

18. Select the **narrow back face**. Click the **Hidden Lines Removed** option.
19. Click **Feature > Reference Geometry > Plane**.
20. Enter **0.45 in** for Distance.
21. Click the **Reverse direction** box.
22. Click **OK** from the plane PropertyManager.
    Plane1 is displayed in the FeatureManager (see Figure 6-35).
23. **Right-click** Plane1 from the FeatureManager.
24. Click **Sketch** from the tool bar.
25. Click the **back inside circular edge of the Shell**.
26. Click **Convert Entities Sketch** tool. The **circular edge** is displayed on Plane1 (see Figure 6-36).
27. Click on **Features > Curves > Helix and Spiral** (or **Insert > Curves > Helix and Spiral**).
    The **Helix/Spiral** dialog box appears.

28. Define Pitch by **Pitch** (0.125 in) and **Revolution** (3) and check Clockwise (see Figure 6-37).

29. Click **OK** to complete the helix.

30. Create a plane, **Plane1 Normal To** the spring endpoint: Click the endpoint of the spring and click **Feature > Reference Geometry > Plane**. Alternatively: *Sketch on Right Plane.*

    The **Helix Property Manager** dialog box appears. Click on the Helix/Spiriall on the FeatureManager to which this endpoint, <Point1> belongs.

31. Click on Plane1 and create Sketch2 (a circle, diameter 0.125 in coinciding with the origin of the helix).

32. Exit the sketch mode.

33. Click the **Swept boss/base** tool.

    The Swept Properties Manager appears.

34. Right-click the Profile and Path box.

35. Click the circle as profile and the helix as path. Note: It is preferred to do this through the Feature Manager. A real-time preview will appear.

36. Click **OK** to complete the swept cut part, which is now hollow (see Figure 6-38). Hide the planes.

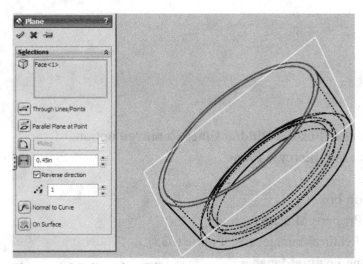

Figure 6-35 Creating Plane1

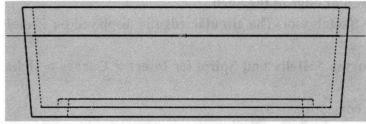

Figure 6-36 Extracting the circular edge using the Convert Entities Sketch tool

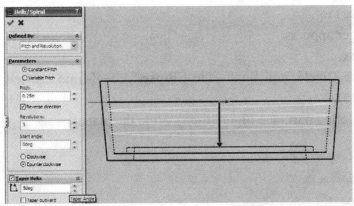

Figure 6-37 Preview of the helix for internal threading

Figure 6-38 Completed part with internal thread

LOFTED BOSS/BASE

The lofted boss/base tool is used to create a shape between a number of planes, each of which contains a defined shape or geometry. The prerequisite for creating a 3D lofted model is to first sketch the shapes on the different planes. Let us illustrate lofted boss/base model using a square base, a circle, and an ellipse. There are no restrictions in the shapes that could be used. Let us illustrate the lofted boss/base concept as follows.

1. Select the **Top Plane**, be in sketch mode and create **Sketch1** (a square, 90 mm by 90 mm) as shown in Figure 6-39.
2. **Exit** the sketch mode.
3. Click the **Features** tool and click the **Reference** tool. Select the Plane option. The plane box appears; select the top plane.
4. Set the distance between the existing **Top Plane** and a new reference plane for **50 mm**. Select **Number of Planes = 2**.Click **OK** check mark. Two new planes, **Plane1** and **Plane2** appear (see Figure 6-40).
5. Select the **Plane1**, be in sketch mode and create **Sketch2** (a **Circle** of diameter, **60 mm**) [see Figure 6-41a].
6. **Exit** the sketch mode.
7. Select the **Plane2**, be in sketch mode and create **Sketch3** (an ellipse of major diameter, 80 mm and minor diameter, 65 mm) [see Figure 6-41b].

8. **Exit** the sketch mode (see Figure 6-42 for the three profiles needed for lofting).

9. Click the **Lofted Boss/Base** tool.

   The Loft Properties Manager appears.

10. Right-click the **Profiles** box.

11. Click the **Square**, then the **Circle**, and finally the **Ellipse**. A real-time preview will appear (see Figure 6-43).

12. Click **OK** to complete the lofted part (see Figure 6-44). Hide the planes.

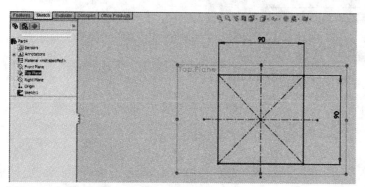

Figure 6-39 Bottom sketch for lofting (Sketch1)

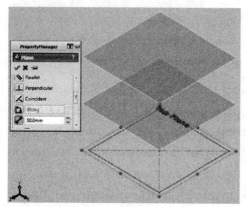

Figure 6-40 Plane1 and Plane2

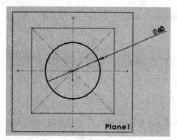

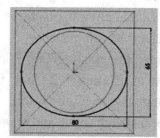

(a) Middle sketch for lofting (Sketch2)   (b) Top sketch for lofting (Sketch3)

Figure 6-41 Sketch2 and Sketch3 on Plane1 and Plane2 respectively

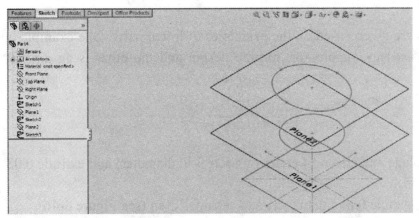

Figure 6-42 Three sketches for lofting

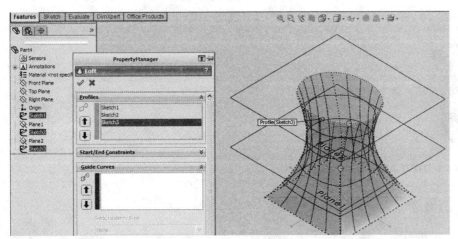

Figure 6-43 Loft based on Sketch1, Sketch2, and Sketch3

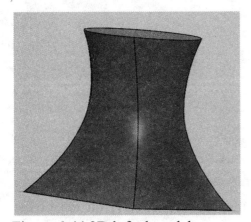

Figure 6-44 3D lofted model

PRACTICAL EXAMPLES

Two practical examples are given based on the principles of lofted parts. One example is an impeller commonly used in compressor, turbine design and the other is an aircraft wing.

Impeller

1. Select the front plane and create **Sketch1** (a circle 3 in diameter) and extrude 0.08 in (see Figure 6-45).
2. Create **Sketch2** (a circle 0.6 in diameter) and extrude 1.5 in (see Figure 6-46).

Figure 6-45 Extrude1 from Sketch1

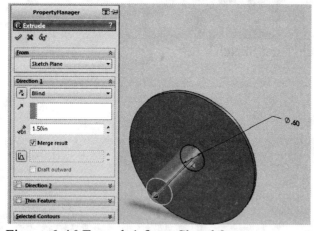

Figure 6-46 Extrude1 from Sketch2

3. Create **Sketch3** (2 arcs, 1.05 in and 1.03 in radii respectively) on top of the extruded face; the center of one of them is (0.75 in, 0.81 in) away from the center of Sketch1; the center of the other is offset 0.08 in from the first) [see Figure 6-47]. Use Convert Entities to extract the concentric circles (3 in and 0.6 in diameter respectively). Trim the circles from Sketch3 [see Figure 6-48].

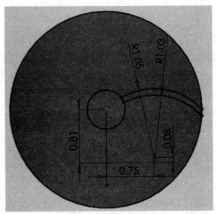

Figure 6-47Geometric definitions for fin profile on top of Extrude1

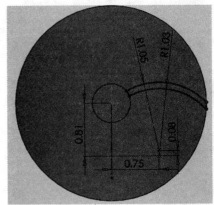

Figure 6-48 Trimmed geometries to fully define fin profile on top of Extrude1

4. Extrude **Sketch3** to **0.6 in** (see Figure 6-49)
5. Define 2 **Reference Planes**, Plane1 and Plane2 offset 0.68 in and 0.85 in respectively from the Front Plane (see Figure 6-49).
6. Insert **Sketch4** on Plane1, selecting all edges to extrude the fin and convert them to entities using **Convert-Entities** tool. Notice that Plane1 is active (see Figure 6-50).
7. Exit the sketch mode.
8. Insert **Sketch5** on Plane2. Create a circle, 1.77 in diameter. (see Figure 6-51)
9. Create **Sketch5** with two arcs with their ends touching the circles 1.77 in diameter and 0.62 in radius at an angle of 30 degrees; the centers are 0.08 offset from one another (see Figure 6-51). The geometry, Sketch5 is trimmed as shown in Figure 6-52. The fully defined Sketch5 is shown in Figure 6-53.

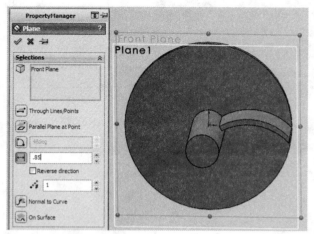

Figure 6-49 Extrude2 for fin profile and creating Plane1 on top of Extrude2

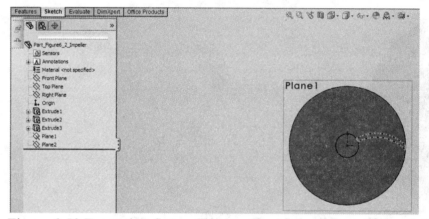

Figure 6-50 Extracting fin profile onto Plane1 from top of Extrude2

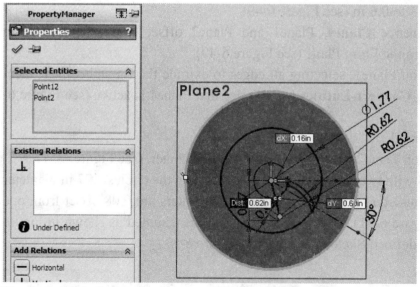

Figure 6-51 Defining geometries for fin profile on Plane2

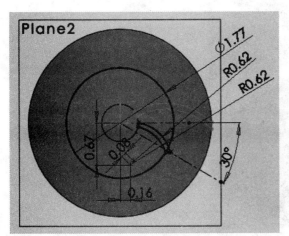

Figure 6-52 Geometries to be trimmed for fin profile on Plane2

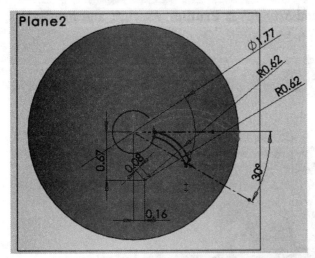

Figure 6-53 Fin profile on Plane2 fully defined

10. Return to isometric view.

11. Click the **Features** tool and click the Reference tool. Select the Plane through **Vertices** option. Create two planes, Plane3 (including left vertices of Sketch4 and Sketch5 and any other point) and Plane4 (including right vertices of Sketch4 and Sketch5 and any other point).

12. Sketch spline using 3D Sketch Tool on Plane3 to define Lofting Profile1 and another Lofting Profile2 on Plane4 as shown in Figure 6-54.

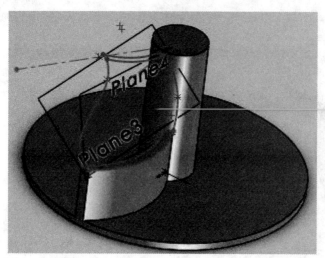

Figure 6-54 Creating Planes Plane3 and Plane4

13. Create **Loft base** using *Sketch4* and *Sketch5* as **Profiles**, *Profile1* and *Profile2* as **Guide Curves** as shown in Figure 6-55.

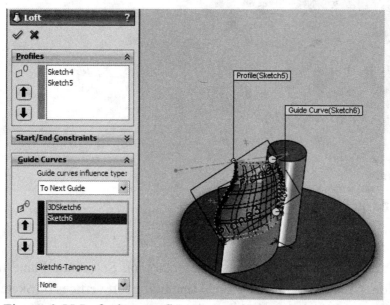

Figure 6-55 Lofted upper fin

14. Click **OK** and **Hide** Plane3 and Plane4.
15. Click **View > Temporary Axes**. (Axes are displayed; look out for the axis about the cylinder at its top. Note that it may be very small to detect.)
16. Click **Circular Pattern**, temporary axis, **Axis<2>** about which rotation takes place, **360 degrees** for angle, **12** for number of patterns and check **Equal Spacing** (see Figure 6-56). Click **OK**. The fully modeled part is shown in Figure 6-57.

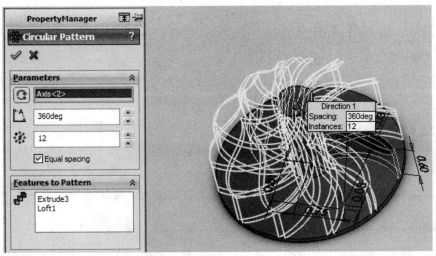

Figure 6-56 Circular pattern of fins

Figure 6-57 Completed impeller

Aircraft Wing

1. Select the **Right Plane** and create **Sketch1** as shown in Figure 6-58. A control polygon is used to help in the definition of the sketch.
2. Use Spline Tool to sketch a spline profile with length of 6 in.
3. Create **Plane1** 10 in from the Right Plane (see Figure 6-59).
4. On Plane1, select all edges of Sketch1 and convert them to entities using **Convert-Entities** tool. This ensures that we maintain similar profiles on Right Plane and Plane1.
5. Copy converted entities to start 4 in away from the origin. Note that the overall length is 6 in (see Figure 6-60).
6. Use Smart Dimension Tool to change 6 in to 3.5 in. Note: there are now to similar profiles on two planes (see Figure 6-61). Delete the larger profile to retain the smaller profile if entities converted are copied as in Figure 6-62.

7. **Exit** Sketch.
8. Create **Loft** using the two profiles (see Figure 6-63 for profiles; Figure 6-64 for preview; and Figure 6-65 for completed part).
9. Hide Plane1.

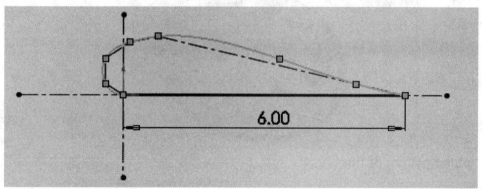

Figure 6-58 Sketch1

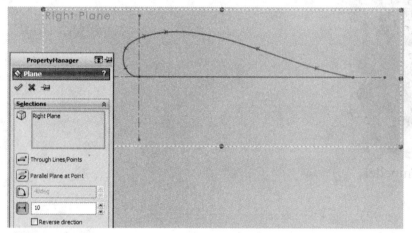

Figure 6-59 Plane1

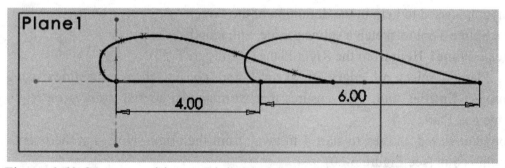

Figure 6-60 Convert entities on Right Plane to entities on Plane1 and copy entities to 4 in away

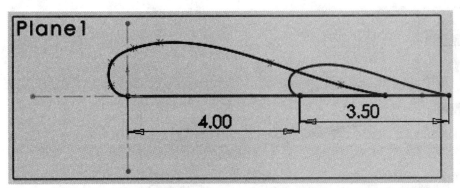

Figure 6-61 Change size of copied profile by resizing 6 in to 3.5 in

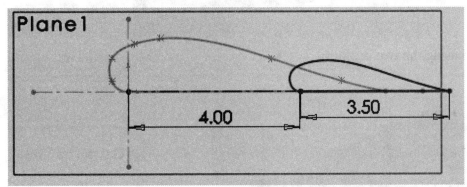

Figure 6-62 Delete larger profile and retain resized profile having length, 3.5 in and 4 in from origin

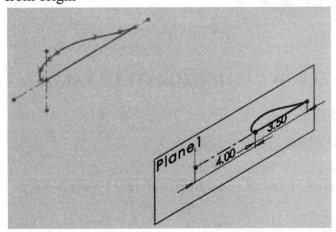

Figure 6-63 Two profiles on two planes (Right Plane and Plane1)

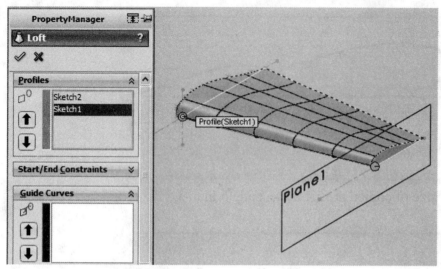

Figure 6-64 Loft using the two profiles

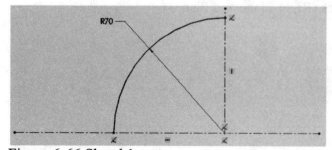

Figure 6-65 Lofted wing

PRACTICAL SWEPT FEATURE: ELBOW CASTING FOR STEAM VALVE

Sketch path for sweep

1. Open a new part document.
2. Select the front plane.
3. Sketch a quarter-circle, Sketch1, with radius equal to 70 mm (see Figure 6-66).
4. Exit sketch mode.

Figure 6-66 Sketch1

Create a plane normal to the endpoint of Sketch1

5. Click the left endpoint of Sketch1.
6. Select the reference geometry icon and click Features > Plane.
7. In the Section rollout, select Sketch1.
8. Select Normal To Curve.
9. Click OK to complete the definition of Plane1.

Sketch profile for sweep

10. Right-click Plane1 and click Normal To.
11. Sketch two concentric circles, Sketch2, with diameters of 82 mm and 66 mm, respectively (see Figure 6-67).
12. Exit sketch mode.

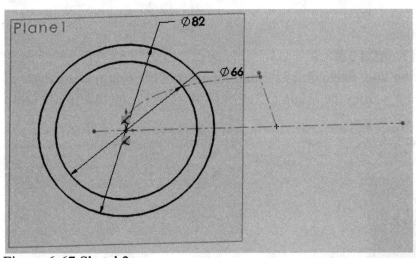

Figure 6-67 Sketch2

Sweep profile through the part

13. Click Features > Sweep Boss/Base (see the Sweep PropertyManager in Figure 6-68).
14. In the Sweep PropertyManager, define Sketch2 as the profile and Sketch1 as the path (see Figure 6-69).

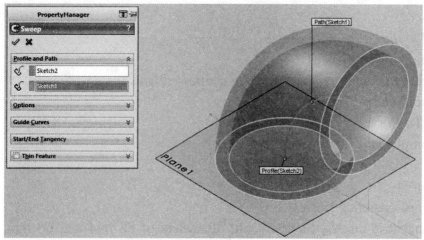

Figure 6-68 Sweep PropertyManager

Sketch a line at 45° to the horizontal (This line will be used to create a plane normal to its endpoint.)

15. Click the front plane.
16. Click Sketch and Normal To.
17. Sketch a dimension line, Sketch3, 152.7 mm long, from the origin at an angle of 45°, and dimension it from the origin (152.7 = (124 - 16)/Cosine(45°)), as shown in Figure 6-69.
18. Exit sketch mode.

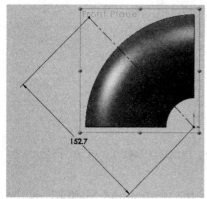

Figure 6-69 Line sketched for creating a plane

Create a plane normal to the endpoint of Sketch3: Plane2

19. Click the endpoint of Sketch3.
20. Select the reference geometry icon and click Features > Plane.
21. In the Section rollout, select Sketch3.
22. Select Normal To Curve.
23. Click OK to complete the definition of Plane2 (see Figure 6-70).

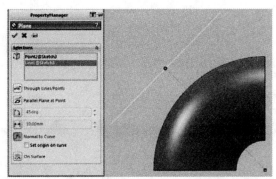

Figure 6-70 Plane created normal to line defined

Create Sketch4 on Plane2

24. Click Plane2 and rotate appropriately, but do not choose Normal To.

25. Create two circles; Sketch4, with diameters of 45 mm and 58 mm, respectively (see Figure 6-71).

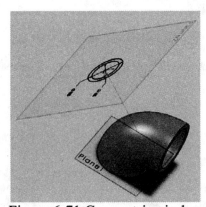

Figure 6-71 Concentric circles sketched on Plane2

Extrusion of concentric circles

26. Click Extrude.

27. In the Extrude PropertyManager, click Up Too Surface for Direction 1, and select the inner surface of the elbow (see Figure 6-72).

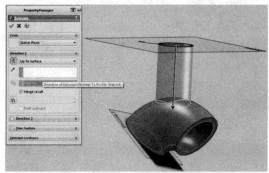

Figure 6-72 Extrude PropertyManager

Create right-hand flange for elbow

28. Click the right-hand face of the elbow and click Sketch, to start sketch mode.
29. Click Normal To; this makes the face selected normal to the viewer.
30. Sketch a circle with a diameter of 128 mm.
31. Use the Smart Dimension tool to dimension the center of the circle at 70 mm from the elbow (see Figure 6-73).

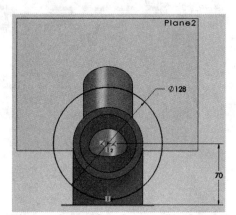

Figure 6-73 Circular profile for right-hand elbow flange

32. Click the Extrude tool from CommandManager.
33. Click Blind for Direction 1 and set the extrusion depth to 12 mm (see the extruded feature in Figure 6-74).

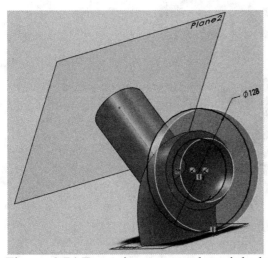

Figure 6-74 Extrusion to complete right-hand elbow flange

Create bottom flange for elbow

34. Click Plane1 at the bottom face of the elbow, and click Sketch to start sketch mode.

35. Click Normal To; this makes the face selected normal to the viewer.

36. Sketch a circle with a diameter of 125 mm (see Figure 6-75).

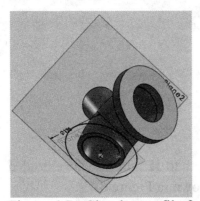

Figure 6-75 Circular profile for bottom elbow flange

37. Click the Extrude tool from CommandManager.

38. Click Blind for Direction 1 and set the extrusion depth to 12 mm (see the extruded feature in Figure 6-76).

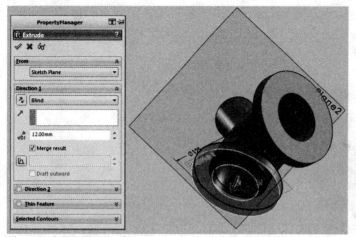

Figure 6-76 Extrusion to complete bottom elbow flange

Create top flange for elbow

39. Click Plane2 at the top face of the elbow and click Sketch to start sketch mode.
40. Click Normal To; this makes the face selected normal to the viewer.
41. Sketch a circle with a diameter of 88 mm (see Figure 6-77).

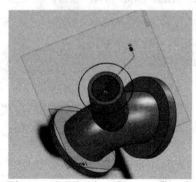

Figure 6-77 Circular profile for top elbow flange

42. Click the Extrude tool from CommandManager.
43. Click Blind for Direction 1 and set the extrusion depth to 12 mm (see the extruded feature in Figure 6-78). The final elbow model is shown in Figure 6-79.

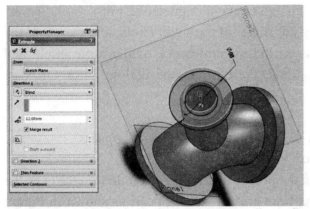

Figure 6-78 Extrusion to complete top elbow flange

Figure 6-79 Final elbow model

PRACTICAL SWEPT FEATURE: LATHE TAILSTOCK

Tailstock ring

1. Select the top plane. Create Sketch1 (a circle of diameter 176 mm) with center at the origin as shown in Figure 6-80.
2. Select the isometric orientation.
3. Exit sketch mode.
4. From CommandManager click Features > Reference Geometry > Plane.
5. Select the Normal to Curve option.
6. Click Sketch1.
7. Click OK to create Plane1, normal to Sketch1.

8. Right-click Plane1 and create Sketch2. (a circle of diameter 22 mm)
9. Add a piercing relation by clicking the center of the small circle, and then hold the Ctrl key down. Click somewhere on the circumference of the large circle and release the Ctrl key. Right-click Make Pierce from the dialog. Click OK (see Figure 6-81).
10. Exit sketch mode.
11. Click the Swept Boss/Base tool. The Sweep PropertyManager appears.
12. Right-click the Profile and Path box.
13. Click the small circle (Sketch2) as the profile and the large circle (Sketch1) as the path using FeatureManager. A real-time preview will appear, as shown in Figure 6-82.
14. Click OK to complete the swept cut part, which is hollow as shown in Figure 6-82. Hide the planes.

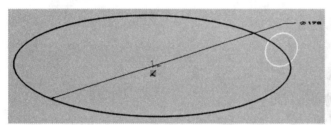

Figure 6-80 Profile (small circle) and path (large circle)

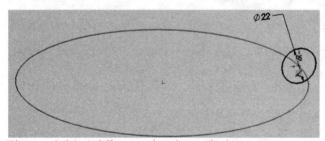

Figure 6-81 Adding a piercing relation

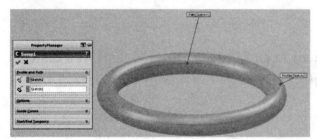

Figure 6-82 Sweep PropertyManager and preview of tailstock ring

Tailstock central boss

15. Select the right-hand plane.

16. Create Sketch3, 8 mm offset from the origin, as shown in Figure 6-83.
17. Revolve Sketch3 about the vertical dimension line (see Figure 6-84).

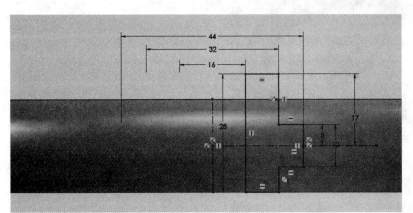

Figure 6-83 Sketch2 to create revolved central boss

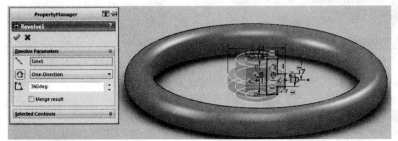

Figure 6-84 PropertyManager and preview of the revolved central boss

Create two planes

18. Select the right-hand plane.
19. Select the reference geometry icon and click Features > Plane.
20. In the Distance rollout, set a value of 18 mm (see Figure 6-85).
21. Click OK to complete the definition of the plane.

22. Select the right-hand plane.
23. Select the reference geometry icon and click Features > Plane.
24. In the Distance rollout, set a value of 82 mm (see Figure 6-86).
25. Click OK to complete the definition of the plane.

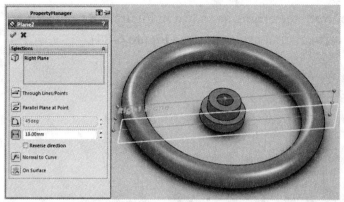

Figure 6-85 Plane2 definition

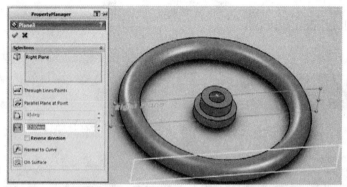

Figure 6-86 Plane3 definition

Lofting

26. Select Plane2, and create a rectangular profile, Sketch4 (see Figure 6-87).

27. Select Plane3, and create a rectangular profile, Sketch5 (see Figure 6-88).

28. Click the Lofted Boss/Base tool. The Loft PropertyManager appears.

29. Right-click the Profiles box.

30. Click Sketch4, then Sketch5. A real-time preview will appear (see Figure 6-89).

31. Click OK to complete the lofted feature (see Figure 6-89). Hide the planes.

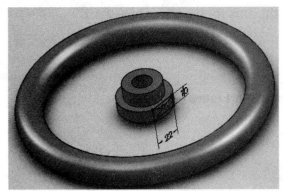

Figure 6-87 Sketch4 on Plane2

Figure 6-88 Sketch5 on Plane3

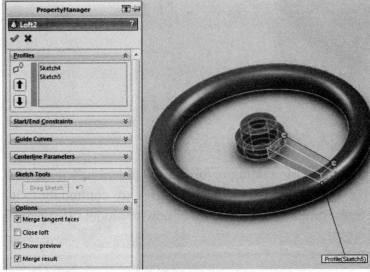

Figure 6-89 Preview of lofted rib

Create circular pattern of ribs

32. Click Circular Pattern, the Circular Pattern PropertyManager appears (see Figure 6-90).

33. Set the temporary axis, and select it as the axis for the circular pattern.
34. Set the number of instances to 4.
35. Select Loft2 as the Features to Pattern.
36. Add fillets.
37. Click OK to complete the design, as shown in Figure 6-91.

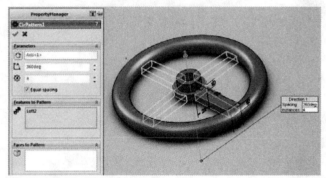

Figure 6-90 Circular Pattern PropertyManager

Figure 6-91 Final model of lathe tailstock

Summary

This chapter discusses the three methods of creating revolved, swept and lofted features, which are commonly encountered in machine parts. These features are commonly found in automotive assemblies, therefore a proper understanding of how to model these parts is essential.

Exercises

1. Repeat the design of the tail stock ring of Section 6.5. Create an ellipse with a major diameter of 22 mm and a minor diameter of 10 mm. Create another ellipse with a major diameter of 18 mm and a minor diameter of 10 mm. Loft between these features and use the Circular Pattern tool to replicate the lofted feature four times. Follow the steps shown in Figures 6-92 to 6-95.

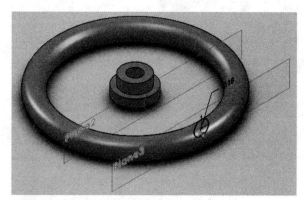

Figure 6-92 Ellipses

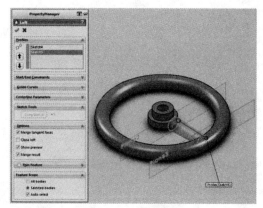

Figure 6-93 Preview of loft

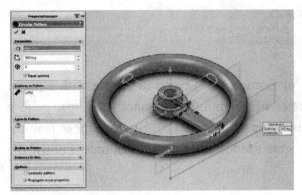

Figure 6-94 Preview of circular pattern

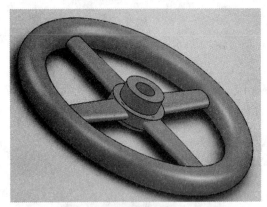

Figure 6-95 Final tailstock

2. Create a spring with the following parameters:
       Base circle for helix, radius 0.5 in
       Helix Height = 1.75 in
       Revolution = 8
       Starting Angle = 270-deg
       Helix Direction = Anticlockwise
       Diameter = 0.125 in

3. Create an O-ring with circular path of diameter 7.5 in and cross-section of diameter 0.125 in.

4. Create a lofted boss/base model using a square base, a circle, and an ellipse, with the following parameters:
       Distance between planes is 75 mm.
       The square is 100 mm by 100 mm dimension.
       The circle has a diameter of 70 mm)
       The ellipse has a major diameter, 90 mm and minor diameter, 75 mm

Chapter 7
Part Modeling with Equation Driven Curves

Objectives:
In this chapter you will learn:
- How to create **Equation Driven Curves** tool in SolidWorks
- How to create 3D objects using **Equation Driven Curves**
- How determine the surface areas and volumes of 3D objects created using **Equation Driven Curves**

INTRODUCTION

SolidWorks uses *sketch entities* such as line, rectangle, parallelogram, slot, polygon, circle, arc, ellipse, parabola, spline, etc. as the foundational building blocks for defining 3D objects. This chapter introduces a new concept of part modeling with the Equation Driven Curve tool in SolidWorks.

EQUATION DRIVEN CURVES

1. Open a **New SolidWorks** part document.
2. Choose a *Plane* (such as the **Front Plane**).
3. Click **Sketch** to be in sketch mode.
4. Click **Spline > Equation Driven Curves**. (See Figure 7-1)
   The **Equation Driven Curves** PropertyManager is displayed as in Figure 7-2.
5. In the **Enter and equation as a function of x**, enter the equation (see Figure 7-2).
6. In the **Enter start x value for the equation**, enter the start value (see Figure 7-2).
7. In the **Enter end x value for the equation**, enter the end value (see Figure 7-2).
8. Click **OK** to complete the procedure.

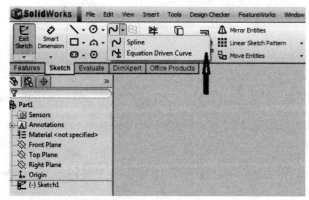

Figure 7-1 Equation Driven Curves tool

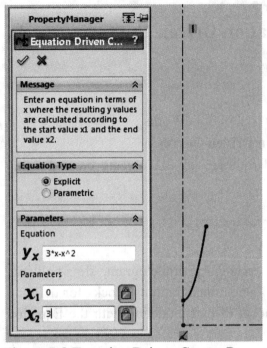

Figure 7-2 Equation Driven Curves PropertyManager

PROBLEM 1

The problem we solve is to define the shape made up of the first-quadrant area bounded by the curves $y = x^2 + 3$ $\quad y = 3x - x^2$ $\quad x = 0$ $\quad\quad x = 3$
This problem is from Chapter 31, Section 3, Example 9, of the referenced textbook.

We will first present the Integral Calculus solution and then follow the methodology described in this chapter to present the SolidWorks solution. The shape is then revolved about the y-axis to create a 3D part model.

Integral Calculus Solution for Area

Let: $f(x) = x^2 + 3$ $\quad g(x) = 3x - x^2$
Then, $f(x) - g(x) = (x^2 + 3) - (3x - x^2) = 2x^2 - 3x + 3$

The area between the curves is given as:

$$A = \int_0^3 [f(x) - g(x)]dx = \int_0^3 (2x^2 - 3x + 3)dx = \left[\frac{2x^3}{3} - \frac{3x^2}{2} + 3x\right]_0^3 = 18 - \frac{27}{2} + 9 = 13.5 \; sq.units$$

The next step is to use SolidWorks Equation Driven Curve tool to define the curves represented by the two equations used with the Integral Calculus method to ascertain the accuracy of SolidWorks.

SolidWorks Solution for Area

In this case, we use the Equation Driven Curve tool in SolidWorks to first define the two curves.
1. Open a **New SolidWorks** part document.
2. Choose the **Front Plane**.
3. Click **Sketch** to be in sketch mode. (Figure 7-3)
4. Click **Spline > Equation Driven Curves**. (See Figure 7-3)
   The **Equation Driven Curves** PropertyManager is displayed as in Figure 7-4.
5. In the **Enter and equation as a function of x,** enter the equation. (see Figure 7-4)
6. In the **Enter start x value for the equation**, enter the start value. (see Figure 7-4)
7. In the **Enter end x value for the equation**, enter the end value. (see Figure 7-4)
8. Click **OK** to complete the procedure.
9. Repeat step 1—8 for second curve. (see Figure 7-5)

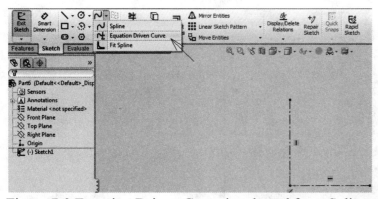

Figure 7-3 Equation Driven Curve is selected from Spline menu

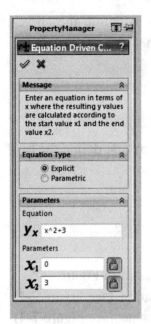

Figure 7-4 Equation 1

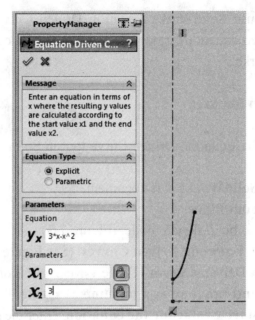

Figure 7-5 Equation 2

10. Sketch vertical lines at left and right ends of the two curves. (see Figure 7-6)

11. Click **Evaluate > Section Properties**. (see Figure 7-7 for the solution)

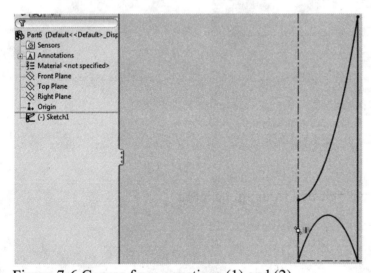

Figure 7-6 Curves from equations (1) and (2)

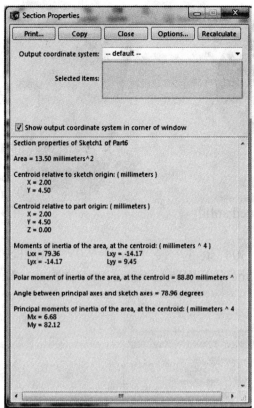

Figure 7-7 Section Properties

Comparing the values of the area enclosed by the two curves between the upper and lower limits shows that both Integral Calculus and SolidWorks have the same solution as shown in Table 7-1.

Table 7-1 Areas obtained

Integral Calculus	$A = 13.5 \ sq.units$
SolidWorks	$A = 13.5 \ sq.units$

Part Design Using the SolidWorks Equation Driven Curves

The part design is obtained by simply revolving the area already obtained about the y-axis. Figure 7-8 shows the sectioned and solid views of the revolved shape.

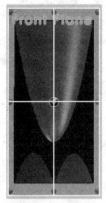 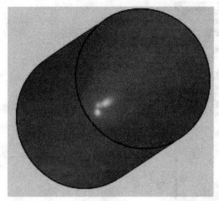 

Figure 7-8 Sectioned and solid views of the revolved solid

We apply material property and choose AISI 304 steel (see Figure 7-9), and then compute the mass properties. Figure 7-10 shows the SolidWorks mass properties for the solid generated in this study.

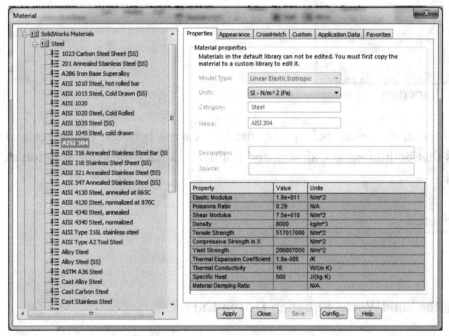

Figure 7-9 Material property: AISI 304 steel is selected

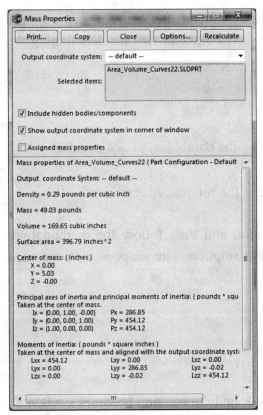

Figure 7-10 SolidWorks mass properties for the solid

Effect of Changing the Axis of Rotation

Here, we present the study of the effect of changing the position of the axis of rotation. By merely offsetting the axis of revolution from the y-axis, we obtain the solid generated in Figure 7-11.

Figure 7-11 Effect of changing the axis of rotation

Solving this problem using integral calculus could be quite challenging for such a simple solid. Therefore, SolidWorks offers the designer such a flexible tool for determining the solid properties during the design stage.

PROBLEM 2

The problem we solve is to find the area bounded by the parabolas $y^2 = 4x$ and $x^2 = 4y$

This problem is from Chapter 31: Exercise 3: #22 of the referenced textbook.

We will first present the Integral Calculus solution and then follow the methodology described in this chapter to present the SolidWorks solution. The shape is then extruded 25 mm to create a 3D part model.

Integral Calculus Solution for Area

To find the points of intersection $y^2 = 4x$ with $x^2 = 4y$,

$$\left(\frac{x^2}{4}\right)^2 = 4x \text{ or } x^4 - 64x = 0 \text{ leads to } x(x^3 - 64) = 0 : \text{ and the solution becomes x = 0, 4.}$$

Solving for y: $y = \frac{(0)^2}{4} = 0$; $y = \frac{(4)^2}{4} = 4$ leading to points of intersection $(0,0)$ and $(4,4)$

We integrate the functions taking limits as the values of x (0 and 4):

$$A = \int_0^4 \left[2x^{\frac{1}{2}} - \frac{x^2}{4} \right] dx = \left[\frac{4}{3} x^{\frac{3}{2}} - \frac{x^3}{12} \right]_0^4 = 5.333$$

SolidWorks Solution for Area

In this case, we use the Equation Driven Curve tool in SolidWorks to first define the two curves.
1.   Open a **New SolidWorks** part document.
2.   Choose the **Front Plane**.
3.   Click **Sketch** to be in sketch mode.
4.   Click **Spline > Equation Driven Curves**.
     The **Equation Driven Curves** PropertyManager is displayed as in Figure 7-12.

5. In the **Enter and equation as a function of x**, enter the equation. (see Figure 7-12)

6. In the **Enter start x value for the equation**, enter the start value. (see Figure 7-12)

7. In the **Enter end x value for the equation**, enter the end value. (see Figure 7-12)

8. Click **OK** to complete the procedure.

9. Repeat step 1—8 for second curve. (see Figure 7-13; and Figure 7-14 for curves)

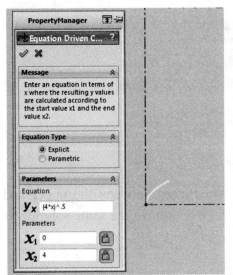

Figure 7-12 Equation 1

Figure 7-13 Equation 2

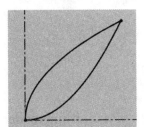

Figure 7-14 Curves are defined

10. Click **Evaluate > Section Properties**. (see Figure 7-15 for the solution)

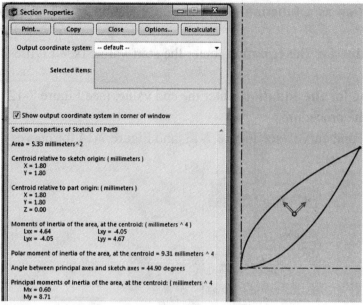

Figure 7-15 Section Properties

Comparing the values of the area enclosed by the two curves between the upper and lower limits shows that both Integral Calculus and SolidWorks have the same solution as shown in Table 7-2.

7-2 Areas obtained

Integral Calculus	$A = 5.33 \ sq.units$
SolidWorks	$A = 5.33 \ sq.units$

Part Design Using the SolidWorks Equation Driven Curves

The part design is obtained by extruding the area already obtained 25 mm, in Blind mode. Figure 7-16 shows the preview and solid views of the extruded shape.

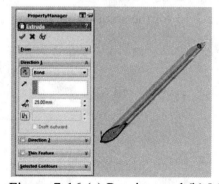

Figure 7-16 (a) Preview and (b) Model

We apply material property and choose AISI 304 steel and then compute the mass properties. Figure 7-17 shows the SolidWorks mass properties for the solid generated in this study.

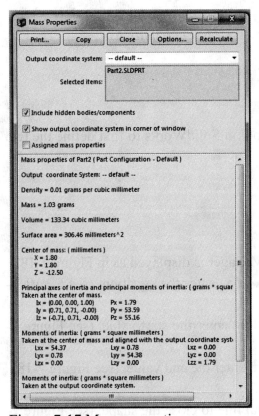

Figure 7-17 Mass properties

PROBLEM 3

The problem we solve is to find the volume generated when the area bounded by the curve $y = 8/x$, the x axis, and the lines x = 1 and x = 8 is rotated about the x axis.

This problem is from Chapter 31, Section 4, Example 16, of the referenced textbook.

We will first present the Integral Calculus solution and then follow the methodology described in this chapter to present the SolidWorks solution. The shape is then revolved about the x-axis to create a 3D part model.

Integral Calculus Solution for Volume

Since we are rotating the elemental area about the x-axis, the radius of the disc is equal to y, and the thickness *dh* of the disc is dx.

$$V = \pi \int_a^b y^2 \, dy = \pi \int_1^8 \left(\frac{8}{x}\right)^2 dx = 64\pi \int_1^8 x^{-2} \, dx = -64\pi \left[x^{-1}\right]_1^8 = 56\pi \quad cub.\,units$$

SolidWorks Solution for Area

In this case, we use the Equation Driven Curve tool in SolidWorks to first define the two curves.

1. Open a **New SolidWorks** part document.
2. Choose the **Front Plane**.
3. Click **Sketch** to be in sketch mode.
4. Click **Spline > Equation Driven Curves**.
   The **Equation Driven Curves** PropertyManager is displayed as in Figure 7-18.
5. In the **Enter and equation as a function of x**, enter the equation. (see Figure 7-18)
6. In the **Enter start x value for the equation**, enter the start value. (see Figure 7-18)
7. In the **Enter end x value for the equation**, enter the end value. (see Figure 7-18)
8. Click **OK** to complete the procedure.
9. Sketch two vertical lines and one horizontal line to close the shape. (see Figure 7-19)

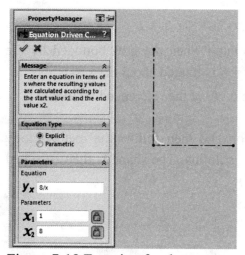

Figure 7-18 Equation for the curve

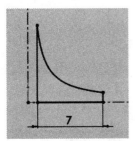

Figure 7-19 Curve is defined; vertical lines and horizontal line included

Part Design Using the SolidWorks Equation Driven Curves

The part design is obtained by simply revolving the area already obtained about the x-axis. Figure 7-20 shows the preview and solid views of the revolved shape.

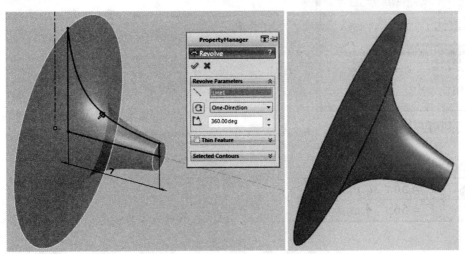

Figure 7-20 (a) Preview and (b) Model

We apply material property and then compute the mass properties. Figure 7-21 shows the SolidWorks mass properties for the solid generated in this study. Table 7-3 shows the results.

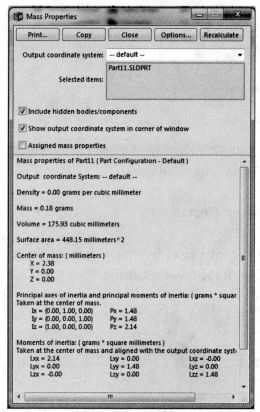

Figure 7-21 Mass properties

Table 7-3 Volumes obtained

Integral Calculus	$V = 56\pi \ sq.units$
SolidWorks	$V = 56\pi \ sq.units$

PROBLEM 4

The problem we solve is to find the area bounded by the curve $y = x^2 + 3$, the y axis, and the lines y = 7 and y = 12, which is rotated about the y axis.
This problem is from Chapter 31, Section 3, Example 14, of the referenced textbook.

We will first present the Integral Calculus solution and then follow the methodology described in this chapter to present the SolidWorks solution. The shape is then revolved about the y-axis to create a 3D part model.

Integral Calculus Solution for Area

$$dA = xdy = (y - 3)^{1/2} dy$$

$$A = \int_{7}^{12} \left[(y-3)^{1/2} \, dy \right] dx = \left[\frac{2(y-3)^{3/2}}{3} \right]_{7}^{12} = \frac{2}{3} \left[9^{3/2} - 4^{3/2} \right] = \frac{38}{3} \ sq.units$$

SolidWorks Solution for Area

In this case, we use the Equation Driven Curve tool in SolidWorks to first define the two curves.

1. Open a **New SolidWorks** part document.
2. Choose the **Front Plane**.
3. Click **Sketch** to be in sketch mode.
4. Click **Spline > Equation Driven Curves**.
   The **Equation Driven Curves** PropertyManager is displayed as in Figure 7-22.
5. In the **Enter and equation as a function of x**, enter the equation. (see Figure 7-22)
6. In the **Enter start x value for the equation**, enter the start value. (see Figure 7-22)
7. In the **Enter end x value for the equation**, enter the end value. (see Figure 7-2)
8. Click **OK** to complete the procedure.
9. Sketch two vertical line and one horizontal lines to close the shape. (see Figure 7-22)

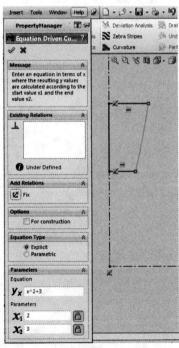

Figure 7-22 Curve is defined; vertical line and horizontal lines included

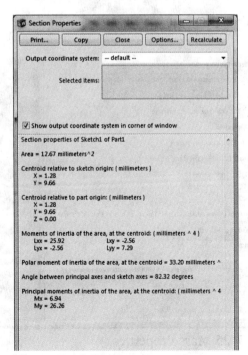

Figure 7-23 Section properties

We apply material property and then compute the mass properties. Figure 7-23 shows the SolidWorks section properties for the area generated in this study. Table 7-3 shows the comparative results.

Table 7-4 Areas obtained

Integral Calculus	$A = 38/3 \; sq.units$
SolidWorks	$A = 38/3 \; sq.units$

Revolve about y-axis

10. Click Revolve option and select the y-axis about which to revolve. (see Figure 7-24)
11. Click Evaluate for Mass Properties calculation. (see Figure 7-25)

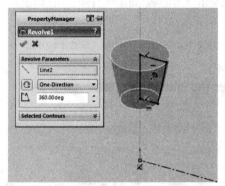

Figure 7-24 Revolve1

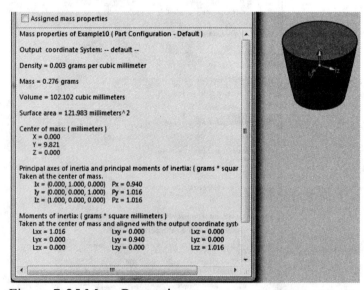

Figure 7-25 Mass Properties

PROBLEM 5

The problem we solve is to define the shape made up of the first-quadrant area bounded by the curves $y^2 = 12x$ $y^2 = 24x - 36$

This problem is from Chapter 31, Section 3, Example 9, of the referenced textbook.

We will first present the Integral Calculus solution and then follow the methodology described in this chapter to present the SolidWorks solution. The shape is then extruded to create a 3D part model.

Integral Calculus Solution for Area

The points of intersection are found by solving the simultaneous equations:

$12x = 24x - 36$

Yielding x = 3 and $y = \pm\sqrt{12x} = \pm 6$

Let: $x_1 = \dfrac{y^2}{12}$ $x_2 = \dfrac{y^2 + 36}{24}$

The area between the curves is given as:

$$A = \int_0^6 [x_1 - x_2]dx = \int_0^6 \left(\frac{y^2}{24} + \frac{36}{24} - \frac{y^2}{12} \right)dy = \int_0^6 \left(\frac{3}{2} - \frac{y^2}{24} \right)dy = \left[\frac{3y}{2} - \frac{y^3}{72} \right]_0^6 = \frac{3 \times 6}{2} - \frac{6^3}{72} = 6 \ sq.units$$

By symmetry the total area between the two curves is twice this value, or 12 square units.

The next step is to use SolidWorks Equation Driven Curve tool to define the curves represented by the two equations used with the Integral Calculus method to ascertain the accuracy of SolidWorks.

SolidWorks Solution for Area

In this case, we use the Equation Driven Curve tool in SolidWorks to first define the two curves.

1. Open a **New SolidWorks** part document.
2. Choose the **Front Plane**.
3. Click **Sketch** to be in sketch mode.

4. Click **Spline > Equation Driven Curves**.

The **Equation Driven Curves** PropertyManager is displayed as in Figure 7-26.

5. In the **Enter and equation as a function of x**, enter the equation. (see Figure 7-26)

6. In the **Enter start x value for the equation**, enter the start value. (see Figure 7-26)

7. In the **Enter end x value for the equation**, enter the end value. (see Figure 7-26)

8. Click **OK** to complete the procedure.

9. Repeat step 1—8 for second curve. (see Figure 7-27)

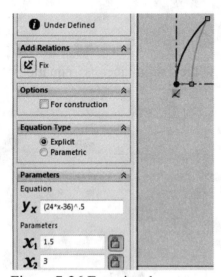

Figure 7-26 Equation 1

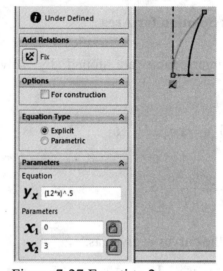

Figure 7-27 Equation 2

Mirror about x-axis

10. Click Mirror.

11. Select the two curves defined and click the horizontal construction line to mirror about it. (See Figure 7-28)

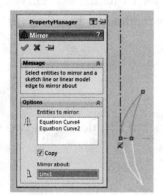

Figure 7-28 Curves are defined and mirrored about x-axis

12. Click **Evaluate > Section Properties**. (see Figure 7-29 for the solution)

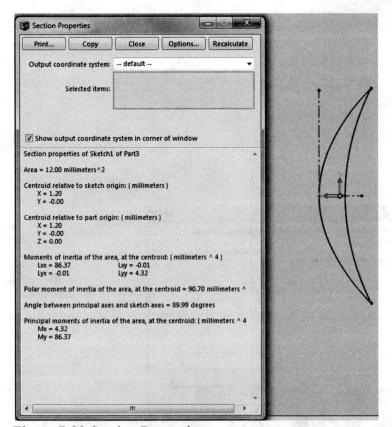

Figure 7-29 Section Properties

Comparing the values of the area enclosed by the two curves between the upper and lower limits shows that both Integral Calculus and SolidWorks have the same solution as shown in Table 7-5.

7-5 Areas obtained

Integral Calculus	$A = 12 \; sq.units$
SolidWorks	$A = 12 \; sq.units$

Part Design Using the SolidWorks Equation Driven Curves

The part design is obtained by extruding the area already obtained, in Blind mode. Figure 7-30 shows the solid of the extruded shape.

We apply material property (Figure 7-31) and then compute the mass properties. Figure 7-32 shows the SolidWorks mass properties for the solid generated in this study.

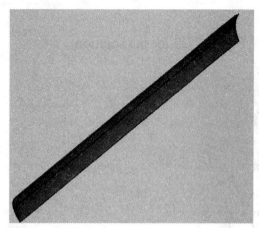

Figure 7-30 Part model

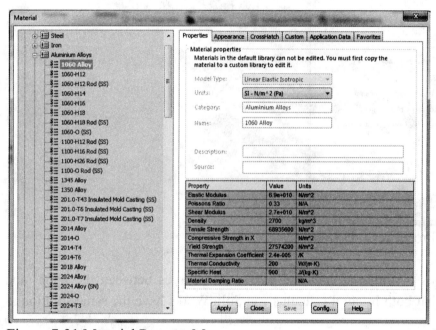

Figure 7-31 Material PropertyManager

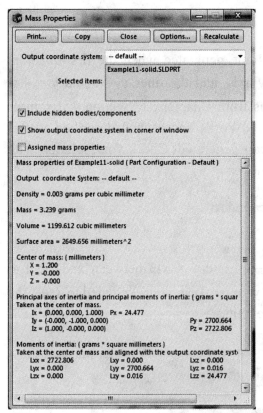

Figure 7-32 Mass properties

Summary

This chapter presents the steps involved in using SolidWorks software for design parts bounded by equation driven curves. The results for known functions show that the areas and volumes obtained using SolidWorks agree with those obtained using basic integral methods in mathematics. Integral calculus methods are limited in functionality because general-shaped objects may not have known mathematical definitions, and hence these methods may fail to compute the areas and volumes of such shapes. Numerical methods are used in such cases. This study shows that SolidWorks is a useful design tool that automatically computes the areas and volumes of parts being designed by a designer. We conclude that using SolidWorks to determine areas and volumes of objects is extremely useful in engineering because these parameters may be required for estimating costs involved in manufactured parts.

Reference

Calter, P. A., Calter M. A., 2008. Technical Mathematics with Calculus, Canadian Edition, John Wiley

Exercises

1. The problem we solve is to find the volume generated when the first-quadrant area bounded by the curves $y = x^2$ the y axis, and the lines y = 1 and y = 4 is rotated about the y axis. [This problem is from Chapter 31, Section 4, Example 16, of the referenced textbook]. Use SolidWorks approached described in this chapter to determine the volume of the part generated. Check your solution with the Integral Calculus solution given as follows:

$$V = \pi \int_a^b x^2 dy = \pi \int_1^4 y\, dy = \pi \left[\frac{y^2}{2} \right]_1^4 = 7.5\pi \ \ cub.units$$

2. Find the area bounded by the curves $y = \sqrt{x}$ and y = x-3 between x= 1 and 4. Revolve the shape obtained about the y axis. Test your knowledge (see the solutions in Figure P-2; area = 6.17 square units)

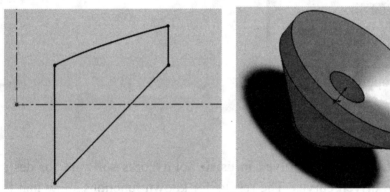

Figure P-2 (a) area between curves; (b) volume obtained by revolving area about y axis

3. Revolve the shape obtained in Question 2 about the left vertical edge in Figure P-2 (a).

4. Revolve the shape obtained in Question 2 about the right vertical edge in Figure P-2 (a).

5. Compare the surface areas and volumes if Question 2—4.

Chapter 8
Assembly Modeling—CSWA Preparations

Objectives:

In this chapter you will learn:

- The differences between **Top-down assembly modeling** and **Bottom-up assembly modeling** approaches
- How to apply **Bottom-up** approach to assembly modeling
- How to **Mate** components in an assembly
- How to assembly parts using the **Assembly Model Methodology**
- How to use **Assembly Analysis—Interference Analysis** to analyze how good an assembly is, and also to get a feel of the quality of the parts design
- How to use the **Exploded View Assembly Tool**
- How to **Animate the Exploded View**
- How to handle **Large Assemblies**

INTRODUCTION

Assembly modeling is the combining of part models into complex, interconnected solid models. There are two well-known approaches to assembly modeling: top-down and bottom-up.

Top-down assembly modeling

In Top-down assembly modeling approach, major design requirements are translated into assemblies, sub-assemblies and components.

Bottom-up assembly modeling

In Bottom-up assembly modeling approach, based on design requirements, components are developed independently and combined into sub-assemblies and assemblies. The three basic steps in Bottom-up assembly modeling approach are as follows:

- Create each component independent of any other component in the assembly;
- Insert the components in the assembly; and
- Mate the components in the assembly as they relate to the physical constraints of the design.

The bottom-up assembly modeling approach is used in this book. Since mating the components in an assembly is the new concept amongst the three steps involved, this is first presented and then the entire process of bottom-up assembly modeling approach is applied to typical assembly problems.

STARTING THE ASSEMBLY MODE OF SOLIDWORKS

There are two ways to start the assembly mode of SolidWorks: from new SolidWorks document or from an existing part which we wish to place first in the assembly document.

1. To start the assembly mode of SolidWorks, invoke the **New SolidWorks Document** dialogue box and choose the **Assembly** button and click **OK**, as shown in Figure 8-1.

Figure 8-1 The **New SolidWorks Document** dialogue box

The **Begin Assembly** PropertyManager pops up, as shown in Figure 8-2. Browse to open the first part to insert.

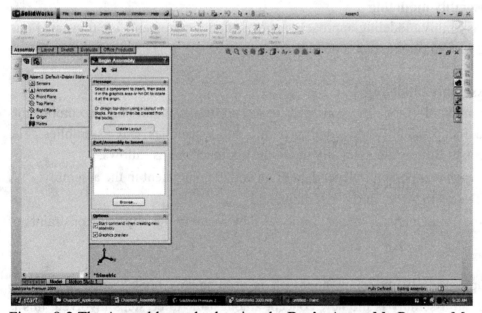

Figure 8-2 The Assembly mode showing the **Begin Assembly** PropertyManager

2. From an existing part document, click the **New** dialogue box as shown in Figure 8-3. Click **Make Assembly from Part/Assembly**. The **Begin Assembly** PropertyManager pops up, as shown in Figure 8-2. Browse to open the first part to insert.

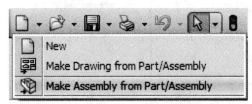

Figure 8-3 Accessing **Assembly** mode from the **New** dialogue box in an existing part document

INSERTING COMPONENTS IN THE ASSEMBLY DOCUMENT

There are several ways of inserting component in the assembly document of SolidWorks:

1. Click **Assembly > Insert Components** (See Figure 8-4)

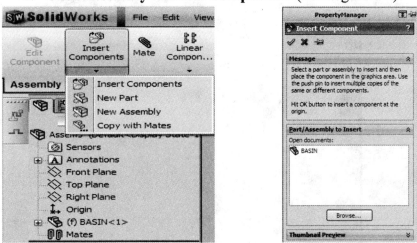

Figure 8-4 Inserting an existing component into an assembly document

2. Click **Insert > Component > Existing Part/Assembly** (See Figure 8-5)

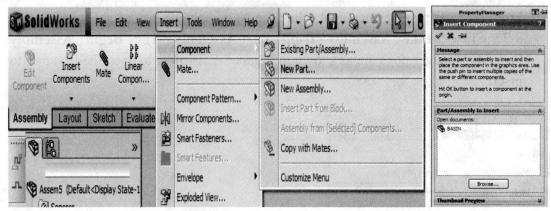

Figure 8-5 Inserting an existing component into an assembly

3. Inserting Components Using the Opened Document Window (See Figure 8-6)
4. In this case, there are currently opened part documents. Choose **Windows > Tile Horizontally or Vertically** from the Menu Bar menus. All opened SolidWorks document windows will be tilled accordingly, depending on the option that is chosen (See Figure 8-7).

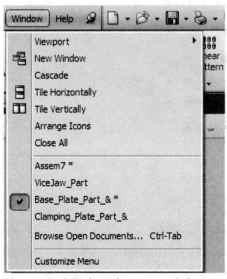

Figure 8-6 Using the opened document Window

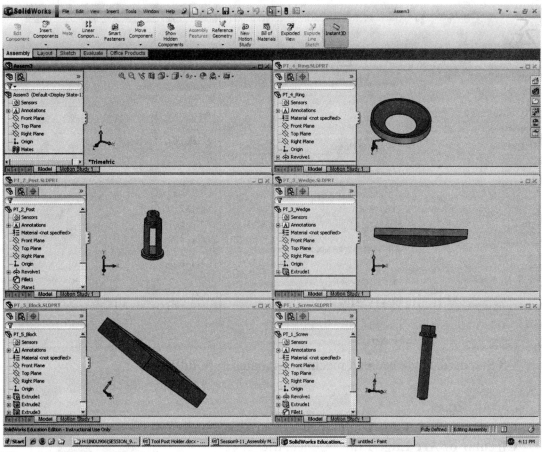

Figure 8-7 Tilled Window

MATES

Mates create geometric relationships between assembly components. There are three types of mates available in SolidWorks: standard, advanced and mechanical mates. See Figure 8-8. Standard mates create geometric relationships, such as coincident, parallel, perpendicular, tangent, concentric, lock, distance, and angle. Each mate is valid for specific combinations of geometry. A comprehensive list of possible mates for different part-types is given here.

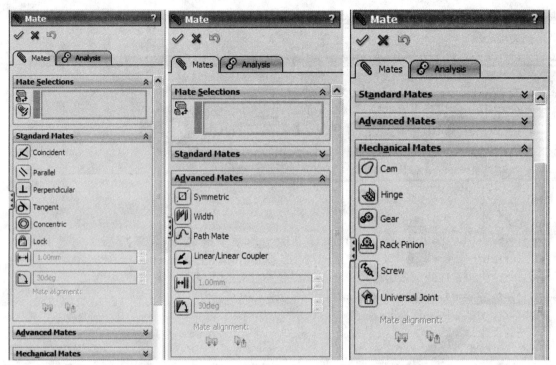

Figure 8-8 Standard, advanced and mechanical mates in SolidWorks

Circular or Arc Edge
- **Circular or Arc Edge/Cone** - Coincident, Concentric
- **Circular or Arc Edge/Line** - Concentric
- **Circular or Arc Edge/Cylinder** - Concentric, Coincident
- **Circular or Arc Edge/Plane** - Coincident
- **Circular or Arc Edge/Circular or Arc Edge** – Concentric

Cone
- **Cone/Circular or Arc Edge** - Coincident, Concentric
- **Cone/Cone** - Angle, Coincident, Concentric, Distance, Parallel, Perpendicular
- **Cone/Cylinder** - Angle, Concentric, Parallel, Perpendicular
- **Cone/Extrusion** - Tangent
- **Cone/Line** - Angle, Concentric, Parallel, Perpendicular
- **Cone/Plane** - Tangent
- **Cone/Point** - Coincident, Concentric
- **Cone/Sphere** – Tangent

Curve
- **Curve/Point** - Coincident, Distance

Cylinder
- **Cylinder/Cone** - Angle, Concentric, Parallel, Perpendicular

- **Cylinder/Cylinder** - Angle, Concentric, Distance, Parallel, Perpendicular, Tangent
- **Cylinder/Extrusion** - Angle, Parallel, Perpendicular, Tangent
- **Cylinder/Line** - Angle, Coincident, Concentric, Distance, Parallel, Perpendicular, Tangent
- **Cylinder/Plane** - Distance, Tangent
- **Cylinder/Point** - Coincident, Concentric, Distance
- **Cylinder/Sphere** - Concentric, Tangent
- **Cylinder/Circular Edge** - Concentric, Coincident
- **Cylinder/Surface** – Tangent

Extrusion
- **Extrusion/Cone** - Angle, Parallel, Perpendicular
- **Extrusion/Cylinder** - Angle, Parallel, Perpendicular, Tangent
- **Extrusion/Extrusion** - Angle, Parallel, Perpendicular
- **Extrusion/Line** - Angle, Parallel, Perpendicular
- **Extrusion/Plane** - Tangent
- **Extrusion/Point** – Coincident

Line
- **Line/Cone** - Angle, Concentric, Parallel, Perpendicular
- **Line/Cylinder** - Angle, Coincident, Concentric, Distance, Parallel, Perpendicular, Tangent
- **Line/Extrusion** - Angle, Parallel, Perpendicular
- **Line/Line** - Angle, Coincident, Distance, Parallel, Perpendicular
- **Line/Plane** - Coincident, Distance, Parallel, Perpendicular
- **Line/Point** - Coincident, Distance
- **Line/Sphere** - Concentric, Distance, Tangent
- **Line/Circular Edge** – Concentric

Plane
- **Plane/Cone** - Tangent
- **Plane/Cylinder** - Distance, Tangent
- **Plane/Extrusion** - Tangent
- **Plane/Line** - Coincident, Distance, Parallel, Perpendicular
- **Plane/Plane** - Angle, Coincident, Distance, Parallel, Perpendicular
- **Plane/Point** - Coincident, Distance
- **Plane/Sphere** - Distance, Tangent
- **Plane/Circular Edge** - Coincident
- **Plane/Surface** – Tangent

Point
- **Point/Cone** - Coincident, Concentric
- **Point/Curve** - Coincident, Distance
- **Point/Cylinder** - Coincident, Concentric, Distance

- **Point/Extrusion** - Coincident
- **Point/Line** - Coincident, Distance
- **Point/Plane** - Coincident, Distance
- **Point/Point** - Coincident, Distance
- **Point/Sphere** - Coincident, Concentric, Distance
- **Point/Surface** – Coincident

Sphere
- **Sphere/Cone** - Tangent
- **Sphere/Cylinder** - Concentric, Tangent
- **Sphere/Line** - Concentric, Distance, Tangent
- **Sphere/Plane** - Distance, Tangent
- **Sphere/Point** - Coincident, Concentric, Distance
- **Sphere/Sphere** - Concentric, Distance, Tangent

Surface
- **Surface/Cylinder** - Tangent
- **Surface/Plane** - Tangent
- **Surface/Point** - Coincident

ASSEMBLY MODELING METHODOLOGY

Two windows should be open: one for part and another for assembly

A. Open Part Window

Click **Open** > **Path** where part is located
Select **Part** for **Files of Type**: for example, Part*.sldprt
Click **View Menu** > check Thumbnails
Double-click **Part** of interest to be fixed. The **Part FeatureManager** is displayed.

B. Open Assembly Window

Click New ⬜▾
Double-click **Assembly** from the default **Templates** tab

Double-click **Part** in the **Open documents** 📂▾ box
Click **OK** from the **Begin Assembly** Property Manager
Click **Window** > **Part** > **File** > **Close**   [Close the Part and leave only Assembly open]

C. Set Assembly Units

Click **Options** > **Documents** > **Units** > **MMGS (IPS)** > **OK** > **Save** [to set the Assembly units]

D. Assemble Parts

For each Part to be inserted to the fixed Part (first in Graphics Window)
- Click **Assembly** > **Insert Components** > **Browse** for Existing Parts
- Double-click the **Part** from the **Path** as Part*.sldprt format
- Click a location to position the part
- Click the **Mate** Assembly Tool and check "Faces" to Mate ( )

Next Part

E. Exploded Assembly View Tool

For each Component to **Explode**
- Click the **Component**
- Drag the **Blue Manipulator Handle** in the appropriate **Direction**
- Click Done

Next Part

F. Animate the Exploded View

Right-click **ExplView1** from the **ConfigurationManager**

Click **Animate Explode**

Click **Stop**

Close the **Animator Controller**

Right-click **Collapse**

G. Exploded Assembly View Tool

Right-click the **Component** to view in the Graphics Window

Click **Open Part** from the shortcut toolbar

Click **Front Plane** (or any other Plane)

Click **Section View** for the **Heads-Up** View Toolbar

PROJECT

Let us start presenting an assembly methodology using the Tool post holder assembly as an example. The tool holder has five parts: PT1-Screw, PT2-Post, PT3-Wedge, PT4-Ring, and PT5-Block.

PLANNING THE ASSEMBLY

There is the need to plan how we are going to go about the assembly of parts in a bottom-up approach. We have to decide which part should be fixed while other parts are added in a sequential manner. In the tool post holder assembly, the following order applies:

Order of assembly	Part	Mate
1	PT2-Post	Fix this
2	PT5-Block	Mate the inner hollow part with the bottom of PT2
3	PT4-Ring	Mate the bottom part with the top of PT5
4	PT3-Wedge	Mate the curved part with the curved part of PT4
5	PT1-Screw	Concentric with the hole on the top of PT2, touching PT3

STARTING THE ASSEMBLY MODE OF SOLIDWORKS

There are two ways to start the assembly mode of SolidWorks: from new SolidWorks document or from an existing part which we wish to place first in the assembly document.

1. To start the assembly mode of SolidWorks, invoke the **New SolidWorks Document** dialogue box and choose the **Assembly** button and click **OK**, as shown in Figure 8-9.

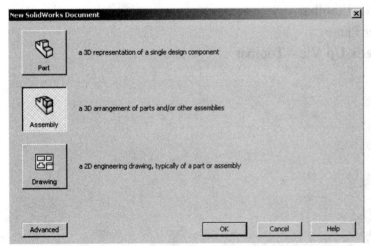

Figure 8-9 The **New SolidWorks Document** dialogue box

The **Begin Assembly** PropertyManager pops up, as shown in Figure 8-10. Browse to open the first part to insert.

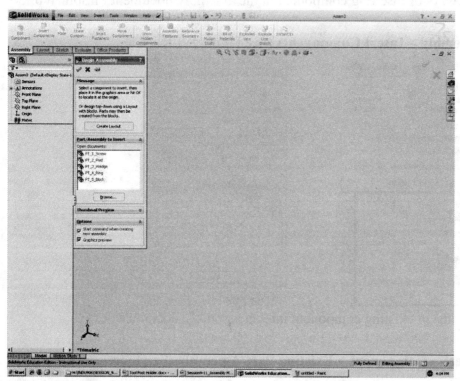

Figure 8-10 The Assembly mode showing the **Begin Assembly** PropertyManager

2. From an existing part document, click the **New** dialogue box as shown in Figure 8-11. Click **Make Assembly from Part/Assembly**.

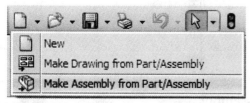

Figure 8-11 Accessing **Assembly** mode from the **New** dialogue box in an existing part document

INSERTING COMPONENTS IN THE ASSEMBLY DOCUMENT

There are several ways of inserting component in the assembly document of SolidWorks:

1. Click **Assembly > Insert Components** (See Figure 8-12)

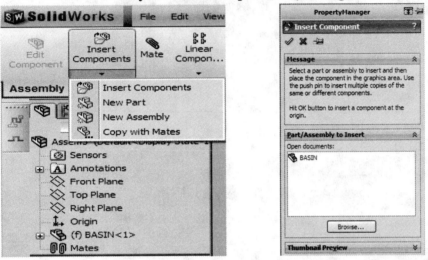

Figure 8-12 Inserting an existing component into an assembly document

2. Click **Insert > Component > Existing Part/Assembly** (See Figure 8-13)

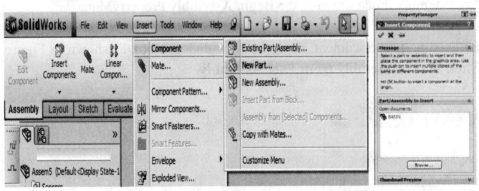

Figure 8-13 Inserting existing component into an assembly

3. Inserting Components Using the Opened Document Window (See Figure 8-14)
4. In this case, there are currently opened part documents. Choose **Windows > Tile Horizontally or Vertically** from the Menu Bar menus. All opened SolidWorks document windows will be tilled accordingly, depending on the option that is chosen (See Figure 8-15).

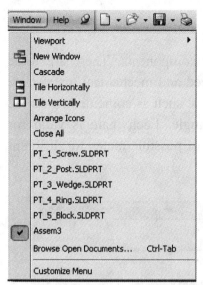

Figure 8-14 Using the opened document

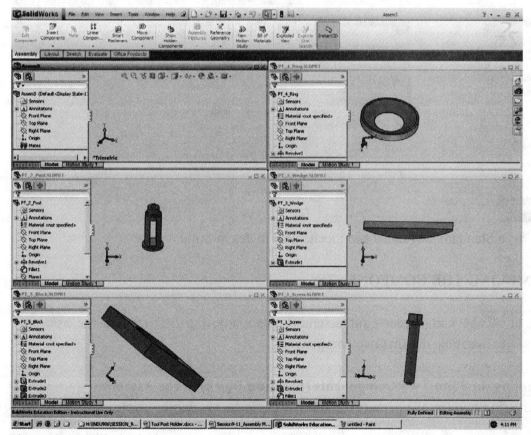

Figure 8-15 Tilled windows

MATES

Mates create geometric relationships between assembly components. There are three types of mates available in SolidWorks: standard, advanced and mechanical mates (See Figure 8-16). Standard mates create geometric relationships, such as coincident, parallel, perpendicular, tangent, concentric, lock, distance, and angle. Each mate is valid for specific combinations of geometry. A comprehensive list of possible mates for different part-types is given here.

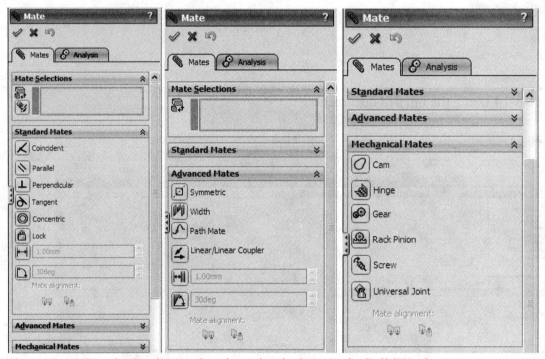

Figure 8-16 Standard, advanced and mechanical mates in SolidWorks

ASSEMBLING THE COMPONENTS

Now that all the parts needed for assembly are ready, the first step in the assembly process is to assemble the first two components.

Assembling the First Two Components (Post and Block) of the Assembly
Open the first two (or all) parts (Post and Block) to be assembled. Note: you are in part mode.

1. Start a **New** SolidWorks assembly document.
2. Click on the first part to be fixed, which is the PT2-Post (see Figure 8-17).
3. Click **Begin Assembly**.

4. Click **OK** to fix this first part, *PT2-Post* at the origin.

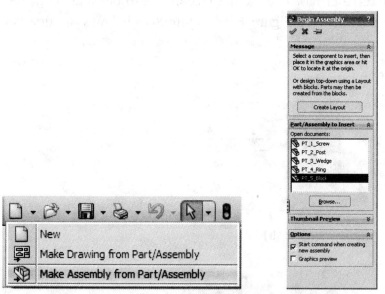

Figure 8-17 Begin assembly with the first part to be fixed

5. Click **Assembly > Insert Components** as already discussed (see Figure 8-18a). Select the *PT5-Block* from the Open documents selection box as shown in the preview (see Figure 8-18b).

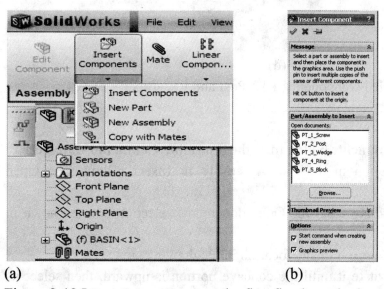

(a)   (b)

Figure 8-18 Insert a component to the first fixed part in the assembly

6. Place the inserted component in the required location on the first component. The **first** mate is that the cylindrical surface of PT2-Post is **concentric** with the inner surface of the hole of PT5-Block (see Figure 19a). The **second** mate is that the

inner surface of PT5-Block and the top of the base of PT2-Post are **coincident** (see Figure 19b). The **third** mate is that the flat face of PT5-Block and the flat cut face of PT2-Post are **parallel** (see Figure 19c). Figure 8-19d shows the first two assembled components.

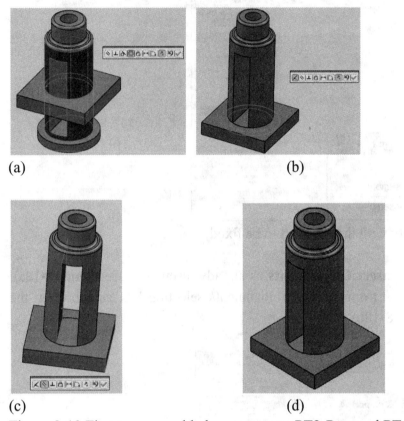

(a) (b)

(c) (d)

Figure 8-19 First two assembled components: PT2-Post and PT5-Block

Assembling the Ring
1. Click the **Insert Components** button from the **Assemble CommandManager**.
2. Click the **Browse** button in the **Part/Assembly to Insert** rollout. The Open dialogue box appears.
3. Double-click on *PT4-Ring* from the Open documents selection box as shown in the preview.
4. Place the inserted component in any location in the drawing area.
5. Select the Ring and rotate it until the concave portion is upward, then select its inner hollow surface and the outer surface of the cylindrical portion of the Post.
6. Apply the **Concentric** relation that is automatically chosen as default as shown in Figure 8-20. Click **OK** to accept it.

7. Apply the **Coincident** mate between the lower face of the Ring and the upper face of the Block as shown in Figure 8-21. The result of this sub-assembly process is shown in Figure 8-22.

Figure 8-20 Concentric mating between the Ring and the Post

Figure 8-21 Coincident mating between the Ring and the Block

Figure 8-22 Sub-assembly of first three components: PT2-Post, PT5-Block, and PT4-Ring

Assembling the Wedge

1. Click the **Insert Components** button from the **Assembly CommandManager**.

2. Click the **Browse** button in the **Part/Assembly to Insert** rollout. The Open dialogue box appears.

3. Double-click on *PT3-Wedge* from the Open documents selection box as shown in the preview.

4. Rotate only the Wedge inserted component towards the hole of the Post.

5. Apply the **Parallel** mate between one side flat face of the Wedge and the inner face of the hole of the Post.

6. Apply the **Parallel** mate between the other side flat face of the Wedge and the other inner face of the hole of the Post.

7. Apply the **Parallel** mate between the top flat face of the Wedge and the top flat face of the Ring.

8. Apply the **Parallel** mate between the front flat face of the Wedge and the side flat face of the Block.

9. Apply the **Distance** mate between the front flat face of the Wedge and the side flat face of the Block to be 0.625 inches [(4.00 - 2.75)/2].

10. Apply the **Distance** mate between one side flat face of the Wedge and the inner face of the hole of the Post to be 0.035 inches [(0.69 – 0.62)/2].

11. Apply the **Tangent** mate between the curved faces of the Wedge and the Ring. See Figure 8-23 for the resulting sub-assembly.

Figure 8-23 Sub-assembly: PT2-Post, PT5-Block, PT4-Ring, and PT3-Wedge

Assembling the Screw

1. Click the **Insert Components** button from the **Assemble CommandManager**.

2. Click the **Browse** button in the **Part/Assembly to Insert** rollout. The Open dialogue box appears.

3. Double-click on *PT1-Screw* from the Open documents selection box as shown in the preview.

4. Apply the **Concentric** relation that is automatically chosen as default as shown in Figure 8-24. Click **OK** to accept it. The final assembly is shown in Figure 8-25.

Figure 8-24 Preview of adding PT1-Screw to the assembly

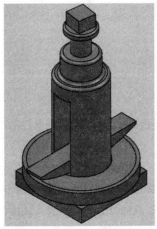

Figure 8-25 Final Assembly

ASSEMBLY ANALYSIS

It is necessary to determine how good the assembly task is by carrying out interference analysis. An assembly process may deceptively seem alright until an interference analysis is done only to find that there are some issues to be resolved. This step is important because it directs us to where problems are which need to be fixed before moving over to the expensive phase of machining the individual parts which make up the overall assembly. To analyze your assembly for interference detection, do the following:

Click **Evaluate > Interference Detection**
In the **Selected Component** click **Calculate** (See Figure 8-26 for the outcome)

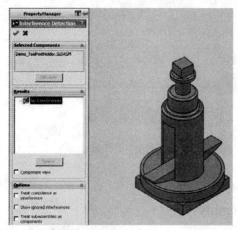

Figure 8-26 Interference detection

EXPLODED VIEW

1. Click the **Exploded View** Assembly Tool (see Figure 8-27)
2. For each part to explode
3. Click the part
4. Drag the **blue manipulator handle** in the appropriate direction (see Figure 8-28)
5. Click **Done**
6. Next
7. Click **OK** from the Explode Property Manager [Note: at this point, **ExplView1** is automatically found in the **ConfigurationManager** of the Assembly] (see Figure 8-29 for exploded view)

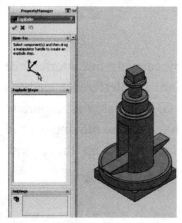

Figure 8-27 Exploded View Assembly tool

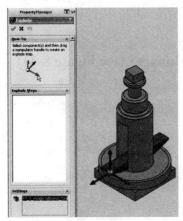

Figure 8-28 Exploding each part using the Triad

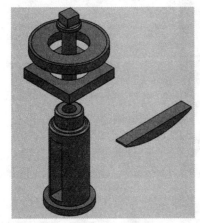

Figure 8-29 Exploded view

To Remove Exploded View

1. Right-click the **Graphics Window**
2. Click **Collapse** (see Figure 8-30)

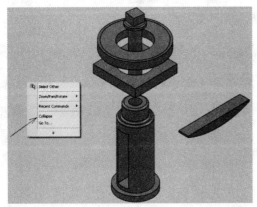

Figure 8-30 Collapsing parts in exploded view

ANIMATED EXPLODED VIEW

1. **Right-click** the **ExplView1** from the **ConfigurationManager** (see Figure 8-31)
2. Click **Animate Explode** (see Figure 8-31)
3. Click **Stop** (see Figure 8-32)
4. **Close** X the Animator Controller
5. **Right-click** the **Graphics Window**
6. Click **Collapse**
7. **Save** the document

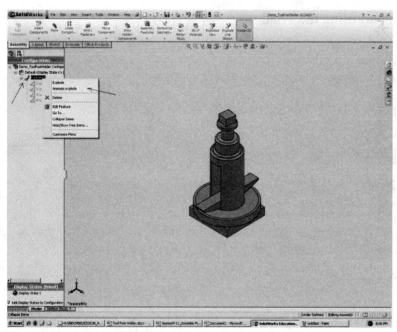

Figure 8-31 Animating the exploded view process

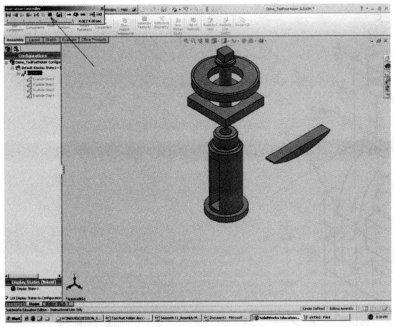

Figure 8-32 Stopping the animation session

TUTORIALS

Tutorial 8-1

Question 1: Model the parts and build the assembly shown in Figure 8-33. The assembly contains three parts: Base, Yoke, and Adjusting Pin. Apply the MMGS unit system. Material: 1060 Alloy for all parts. Density $= 0.0027\,g\,/\,mm^3$ [Note the origin. Fully constrain all sketches. Fully mate all parts]

Base: The distance between the front face of the Base and the front face of the Yoke = 60 mm.

Yoke: The Yoke fits inside the left and right square channels of the Base part; there is no clearance. The tope face of the Yoke contains a 12 mm diameter through-all hole.

Adjusting Pin: The bottom face of the Adjusting Pin head is located 40 mm from the top face of the Yoke part. The Adjusting Pin part contains a 5 mm diameter through-all hole.

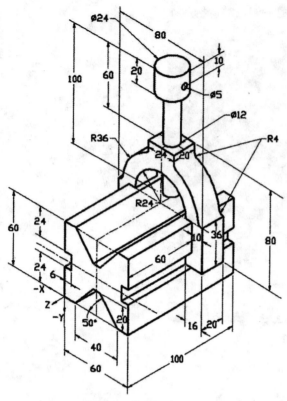

Figure 8-33

Question 2: Determine the following parameters for the assembly with respect to the illustrated coordinate system in Q1:

(i) Mass;
(ii) Volume;
(iii) Surface area;
(iv) Center of mass;

Solution to Tutorial 1

Solution to Tutorial 1, Question 1: Parts and assembly shown in Figure 8-33.

Base
1. **Create** a New part in SolidWorks.
2. **Set** the document properties for the model.
3. Create **Sketch1**, which is the Base sketch with overall dimensions of 60 mm by 60 mm.
4. Create the **Extruded Base** feature. Extrude1 is the Base feature obtained by extruding **Sketch1** through a Depth of 100 mm.

Yoke
1. **Create** a New part in SolidWorks.
2. **Set** the document properties for the model.
3. Create **Sketch1**, which is the sketch with overall dimensions of 80 mm by 80 mm.
4. Create the **Extruded Base** feature. Extrude1 is the Base feature obtained by extruding **Sketch1** through a Depth of 20 mm.

Pin
1. **Create** a New part in SolidWorks.
2. **Set** the document properties for the model.
3. Create **Sketch1**, which is the cylindrical sketch in the form of 24 mm diameter and 20 mm long; 12 mm diameter and 80 mm long respectively.
4. Create the **Revolved Base** feature. Revolved1 is the Base feature obtained by revolving **Sketch1** about the vertical axis.

   The base, yoke and pin are shown in Figures 8-34 (i), (ii) and (iii).

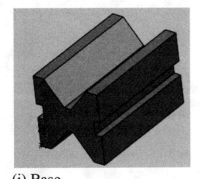

(i) Base   (ii) Yoke   (iii) Pin

Figure 8-34

Assembly Modeling
1. **Create** a New assembly in SolidWorks.
2. Click **Cancel** form the Begin Assembly PropertyManager.
3. **Set** the document properties for the model.
4. **Insert** the base as the first part in the assembly.
5. **Insert** the yoke as the second part in the assembly.
6. **Insert** Parallel and Concentric mates between the upper sides of the base and the notched part of the yoke in the bracket in the assembly.
7. **Insert** Distance mate of 60 mm between the front face of the Base and the front face of the Yoke.
8. **Insert** the pin as the third part in the assembly.
9. **Insert** Concentric mate between the pin and the yoke in the assembly.

10. **Insert** Distance mate of 40 mm between the bottom face of the Adjusting Pin head and the top face of the Yoke part.

The base, yoke and pin are shown in Figure 8-35.

Figure 8-35

Solution to Tutorial 1, Question 2: for the assembly in Q1:

    (i)   Mass = 843.22 grams

    (ii)   Volume; = 312304.68 cubic millimeters

    (iii)   Surface area = 54147.10 millimeters^2

    (iv)   Center of mass: X = 30.00; Y = 40.16; Z = -53.82

Tutorial 8-2

Question 1: The assembly shown in Figure 8-36 contains three machined brackets and two pins. Apply the MMGS (millimetre, gram, second) unit system. Decimal places: 2. Assembly origin is as shown.

Model the parts. [Note: Fully constrain all sketches]

Brackets: The identical brackets have 2 mm thickness, and equal size (holes through-all). Material: 6061 Alloy. Density = $0.0027\,g/mm^3$. The top edge of the notch is located 20 mm from the top edge of the machined bracket.

Pins: The identical pins are 5 mm in length and equal in diameter. Material: Titanium. Density = $0.0046\,g/mm^3$. Pins are mated concentric to bracket holes (no clearance). Pin end faces are coincident to bracket outer faces. There is a 1 mm gap between the brackets. Brackets are positioned with equal angle mates (45 degrees).

Question 2: Build the assembly of the parts described in Question 1 and shown in Figure 8-36.

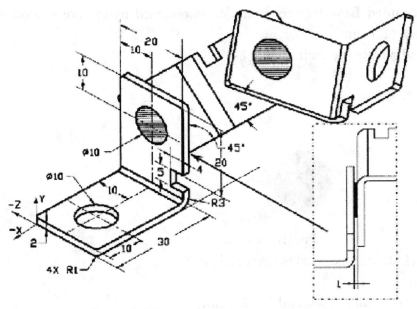

Figure 8-36

Solution to Tutorial 2, Question 1: Parts Modeling
Bracket

1. **Create** a New part in SolidWorks.
2. Select the **Right Plane** as the sketch plane.
3. Create **Sketch1**, which is the Base (bracket) sketch in the form of an L-shape (30 mm by 30 mm).
4. Create the **Extruded Base** feature. Extrude1, which is the Base feature, is obtained by extruding **Sketch1** through a Depth of 20 mm.
5. Create **Sketch2**, which is the second sketch in the form of a notch (4 mm by 5 mm).
6. Create the **Extrude Cut** feature. Extrude2, which is the Extrude cut feature, obtained by applying extrude cut to **Sketch2** through bracket's thickness of 2 mm.
7. Create **Sketch3**, which is the second sketch in the form of a circle (10 mm in diameter).
8. Create the **Extrude Cut** feature. Extrude3, which is the Extrude cut feature, obtained by applying extrude cut to **Sketch3** through bracket's thickness of 2 mm.
9. Create **Fillets**: 4 corners having fillet radius of 1 mm; 3 mm and 1 mm fillet radii for outer and inner bends of bracket.

Pin

1. **Create** a New part in SolidWorks.
2. Select the **Right Plane** as the sketch plane.
3. Create **Sketch1**, which is the pin sketch in the form of cylinder (10 mm in diameter).

4. Create the **Extruded Base** feature. Extrude1 is obtained by extruding **Sketch1** through a length of 5 mm.

   The bracket and pin are shown in Figure 8-37.

Bracket (right view)   Pin (front view)

Figure 8-37 Part model for the machined bracket and pin

Solution to Tutorial 2, Question 2: Assembly Modeling

1. **Create** a New assembly in SolidWorks.
2. Click **Cancel** form the Begin Assembly PropertyManager.
3. **Set** the document properties for the model.
4. **Insert** the bracket as the first part in the assembly.
5. **Insert** the pin as the second part in the assembly.
6. **Insert** a Concentric mate between the pin and the hole in the vertical part of the bracket in the assembly.
7. **Insert** a Distance mate of 1 mm gap between the brackets.
8. **Insert** an Angular mate 45 degrees between the edges of the first two brackets.
9. **Insert** the bracket as the third part in the assembly.
10. **Insert** the pin as the fourth part in the assembly.
11. **Insert** a Concentric mate between the pin and the hole in the inclined part of the bracket in the assembly.
12. **Insert** a Distance mate of 1 mm gap between the brackets.
13. **Insert** an Angular mate 45 degrees between the edges of the last two brackets.

    The assembly of the bracket and pin is shown in Figure 8-38.

    The FeatureManager information on mating of parts in assembly is shown in Figure 8-39.

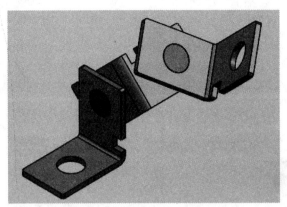

Figure 8-38 Assembly model for the machined brackets and pins

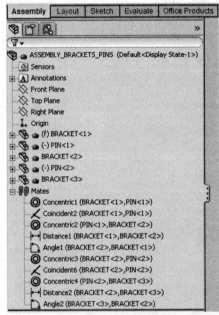

Figure 8-39 FeatureManager information on mating of parts in assembly

Tutorial 8-3

Repeat Tutorial 2 with straight edges for the simple brackets, a Distance mate of 1 mm gap between the brackets, and an Angular mate 45 degrees between the edges of the brackets.

Solution to Tutorial 3

The bracket and pin are shown in Figure 8-40.

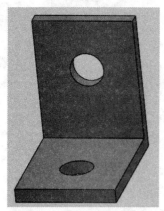

Simple Bracket   Pin for Bracket

Figure 8-40 Part model for the simple machined bracket and pin

Figure 8-41 Assembly for Simple Bracket and Pins

LARGE ASSEMBLIES

The controlling display performance in SolidWorks is split into two categories: central processing unit (CPU) processing and graphics processing unit (GPU) processing. This is in reality the difference between calculating the parametrics and geometry on one hand, and calculating the graphics and display on the other hand. Depending on the user's hardware, drivers, and system maintenance, either of the CPU processing or the GPU processing will be performed better.

There are four ways in which users attempt to minimize the load on CPU and the GPU in large assemblies. These are: suppressed, hidden, lightweight parts, and resolved.

Suppressed
When attempting to speed up the performance of an assembly, the biggest impact is made if the user can reduce the load on both the CPU and the GPU. This can be achieved by suppressing a part. When a part is suppressed, it is neither calculated for its parametrics and geometry nor displayed. Consequently, the load on each processor for that part is zero.

Hidden
When a part is hidden, the CPU still calculates its parametrics. However, since the part is hidden, it creates no load on the GPU. If the user has a good main processor but a weak video card, then benefits could be obtained by removing graphics load from the display by hiding them.

Lightweight parts
If a user is interested in showing a part but not calculating any of its parametric relations, then Lightweight parts should be used. Lightweight default settings can be found in **Options**, on both the assemblies and Performance pages. The user can make parts Lightweight through the right mouse button (RMB) menu.

Resolved
Resolved is the opposite of Lightweight. Resolved means that the part is fully loaded, its parametrics are loaded and calculated by the CPU, and its graphics display is calculated and shown by the GPU.

From this discussion, it is inferred that the optimal approach to manage large assemblies is *Lightweight parts*.

Automatic Setting to Lightweight

1. Click **Options > System Options > Assemblies** (see Figure 8-42) [Note: the number of assembly mode to improve performance is set by default to 500]

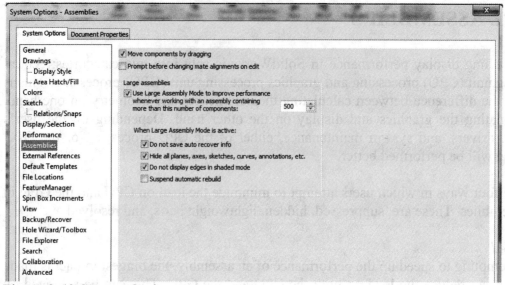

Figure 8-42 System Options

2. Click **Options > System Options > Performance** (see Figure 8-43)
3. Under **Assemblies** mode, check the box designated **Automatically load components lightweight** (see Figure 8-43)
4. Click **OK**

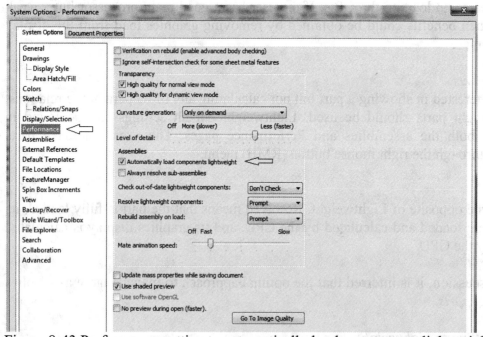

Figure 8-43 Performance setting to automatically load components lightweight

Manual Setting to Lightweight

Figure 8-44 shows the Resolved mode. To manually set to Lightweight:
  5. Right-click on the topmost resolved feature (see Figure 8-45)
  6. Click Set Resolved to Lightweight (see Figure 8-45)

The parts change to Lightweight mode with feathers attached (see Figure 8-46)

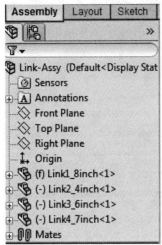

Figure 8-44 Resolved mode

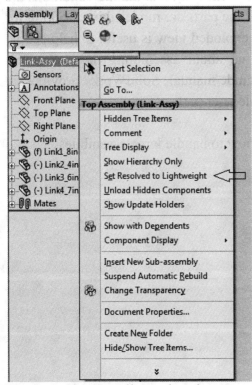

Figure 8-45 Manually setting the topmost resolved feature to Lightweight

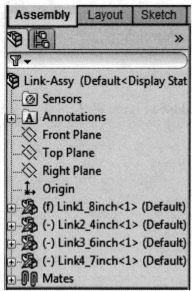

Figure 8-46 Lightweight mode

Summary

We have gone through the necessary steps for assembling parts in a bottom-up approach. We simply fix a major part and add other parts while ensuring that mating conditions are met. Thereafter, it is important to analyze how well the parts are modeled by checking for interference detection. To finish up, presenting an exploded view is useful to help people involved in the assembly to figure out how to go about assembling the parts. This information is normally included in the product guide/manual. SolidWorks provides an animation tool to help us visualize how we assembled our parts.

This chapter also covers another important aspect how to handle large assemblies.

Chapter 9

Part and Assembly Drawings—CSWA Preparations

Objectives:

In this chapter you will learn:
- The differences between **Part Drawing** and **Assembly Drawing**
- How to apply **Bottom-up** approach to assembly modeling
- How to create a new **Drawing Template**
- How to insert and position views on a **Drawing**
- How to use the **Exploded View Assembly Tool**
- How to **Animate the Exploded View**
- How to insert half-, offset-, and aligned-section views to drawings

INTRODUCTION

An engineering drawing is used to fully and clearly define requirements for engineered items. The main objective of an engineering drawing is to convey all the required information that will allow a manufacturer to produce that component. Engineering drawings are usually created in accordance with standard conventions for layout, nomenclature, interpretation, appearance, size.

Previous versions of SolidWorks have been limited to mainly handling mainly full-sectional views of drawings. The enhanced Section View tool now makes creating section views in drawings faster, with simple drag-and-drop placement. Section profiles can now be clicked, dragged, and jogged to modify section profiles on the fly.

This chapter, first deals with part and assembly drawing and then followed with describing the steps involved in inserting half-, offset-, and aligned-section views to drawings, which are enhancements in the most recent version of SolidWorks. Throughout this chapter, ASME standards for views, drawings, and dimensions are used. Although first-angle projection and third-angle projection are briefly discussed, third angle projection is used since this the standard mainly used in North America.

Orthographic Projection

An orthographic projection shows the object as it looks from the six sides (front, top, bottom, right, left, or back) and are position relative to each other according to the rules of either first-angle or third angle projection (see Figure 9-1).

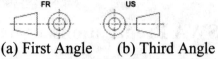

(a) First Angle   (b) Third Angle

Figure 9-1 Orthographic projections

First angle projection is the ISO standard and is primarily used in Europe. The 3D part is projected into 2D paper space as if one was looking at an X-ray of the object in which the top view is under the front view; the right view is at the left of the front view (see Figure 9-2).

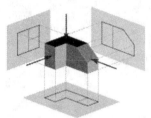

Figure 9-2 First Angle projection of a part

Third angle projection is primarily used in the United States and Canada, where it is the default projection system according to the BS 8888 (2006). The left view is placed on the left and the top view on the top.

Drawing Sizes

Sizes of drawing normally comply with either of two different standards of ISO (World Standard) or U.S. customary, according to Table 9-1.

Table 9-1 ISO (World Standard) or U.S. customary drawing sizes

ISO Drawing Sizes (mm)			U.S Customary Drawing Sizes	
A4	210x297		A	8.5"×11"
A3	297x420		B	11"×17"
A2	420x594		C	17"×22"
A1	594x841		D	22"×34"
A0	842x1189		E	34"×44"

CREATING A SOLIDWORKS DRAWING TEMPLATE

The Drawing Template is made up of three components: document properties, sheet properties, and title block.

Document Properties
1. Click **New**
2. Double-click **Drawing**
3. Click **Cancel X** from Model View Manager [If the *Start when creating new drawing* is checked, the Model View PropertyManager is selected by default (see Figure 9-3)]
4. Click **Options > Document Properties** from the Menu bar
5. Click **Drafting Standard > ANSI**
6. Click **Annotations > Font > Units** [enter 3 mm) > **OK** [Font-height] (see Figure 9-4)
7. Click **Dimensions** (enter 1 mm, 3 mm, 6 mm) > **OK** [Arrow-head for dimensioning] (see Figure 9-5)
8. Click **View Labels > Section** (enter 2 mm, 6 mm, 12 mm) > **OK**   [Arrow-head for sectioning] (see Figure 9-6)
9. Click **Units > MMGS** (select 0.12 basic unit length, None basic unit angle) (see Figure 9-7)
10. Click **Layer Properties** (select **Layers ON**) [If not active, right-click the CommandManager and activate it] (see Figure 9-8)
11. Click **Systems Options > File Location > Add** path and Click **OK > OK > OK** [Set System Options File Location) (see Figure 9-9)

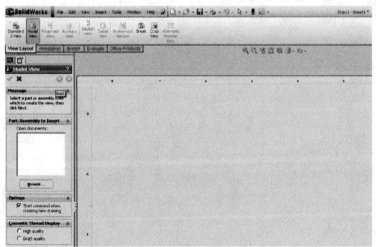

Figure 9-3 Clicking *Cancel X* from Model View Manager because a Template is being created

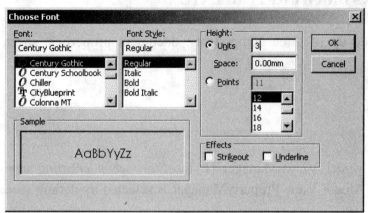

Figure 9-4 Clicking Annotations > Font > Units

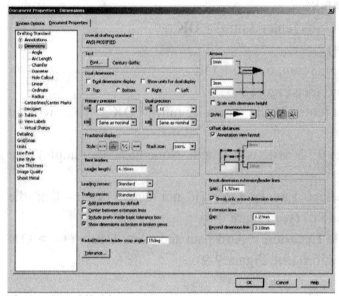

Figure 9-5 Clicking *Dimensions*

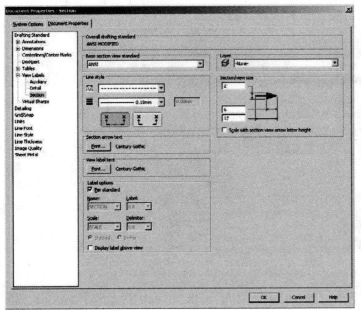

Figure 9-6 Click *View Labels > Section*

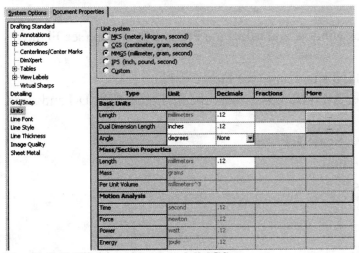

Figure 9-7 Clicking *Units > MMGS*

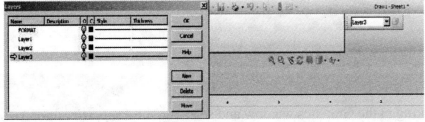

Figure 9-8 Clicking *Layer Properties*

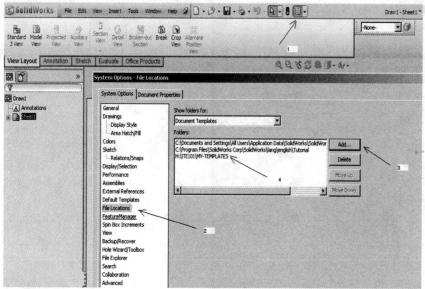

Figure 9-9 Clicking *Options > File Location > Add* path to set System Options File Location

Sheet Properties

12. Right-click in the Graphics window and select the Properties option (see Figure 9-10)

13. Click **Properties > Standard sheet** size (see Figure 9-11)

14. Select either A-Landscape, A-Portrait, B-Landscape, C-Landscape, D-Landscape, or E-Landscape

15. Check **Third Angle**; Select **Scale 1:1**

16. Uncheck **Display sheet format**

17. Click **OK**

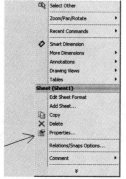

Figure 9-10 Right-clicking in the Graphics window and selecting the *Properties* option

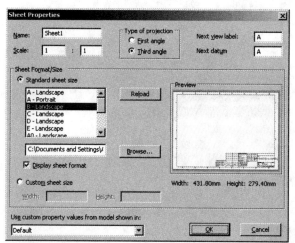

Figure 9-11 Clicking *Properties* and accessing *Standard sheet*

Title Block

18. Right-click in the Graphics window
19. Click **Edit Sheet Format** (see Figure 9-12)

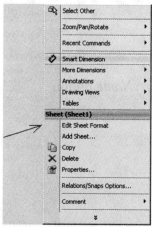

Figure 9-12 Right-clicking in the Graphics window and selecting the *Edit Sheet Format* option

20. Modify Tolerance Note, Angular Tolerance, etc.
21. Create a new Microsoft **Logo** and paste in Title Block.

Figure 9-13 Clicking *File > Properties*

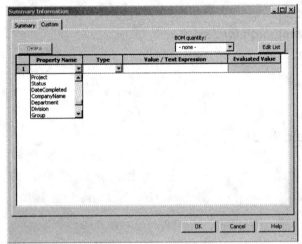

Figure 9-14 Clicking *Custom* from *Properties* and selecting *PropertyName* option

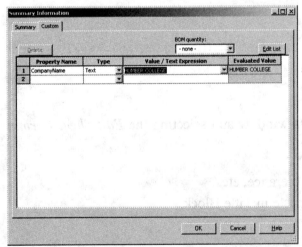

Figure 9-15 Modifying *ProperName* option

Saving the Template

22. Click File > **Save Sheet Format** > **CUSTOM-B.slddrt** in path [Save the Sheet Format]

23. Click **Save As > B-ANSI-MM.drwdot** in path [Save the Drawing Template] (see Figure 9-16)

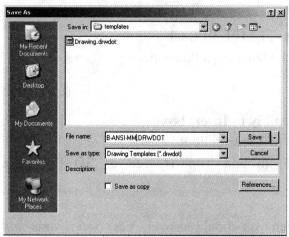

Figure 9-16 Save the Drawing Template

PART DRAWING OF TOOL POST

This section describes the steps required to generate a part drawing. Standard views are first obtained followed by the exploded view and bill of material (BOM). Let us examine some examples.

The assembly shown in Figure 9-17 contains five machined parts. The electronic files for the parts are available as a SolidWorks file in this book.

(i)   Build the assembly of the parts.
(ii)   Produce the Exploded View of assembly, the Bill of Materials (BOM
(iii) Produce the Drawing of each of the five parts to include necessary views.

Figure 9-17 Tool post holder

Screw: Standard Views

To display Drawing FeatureManager
1. Click **New** from the Menu bar
2. Double-click **B-ANSI-MM** from **MY-TEMPLATE** tab
3. Click **Cancel X** from the Model View Manager [if this appears]

To Insert Drawing View and Standard Views
4. Click **Model View** (see Figure 9-18)
5. Double-click Part from the **Part/Assembly to Insert** box
6. Click **Multiple Views** in the Number of Views rollout
7. Select **Standard views** needed: Front and Top as well as 3D from the **Orientation** rollout (see Figure 9-18)
8. Click **OK**

The following message may appear, to which you should answer, **Yes**: *SolidWorks has determined that the following view(s) may need Isometric (True) dimensions instead of standard Projected dimensions. Do you want to switch the view(s) to use Isometric (True) dimensions?*
(see Figure 9-19 for the query and Figure 9-20 for the views)

9. Click **Save As** from the Menu bar (give a name for the drawing) and **Save**.

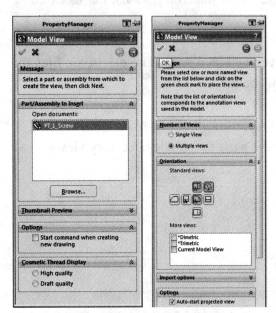

Figure 9-18 Multiple views selected

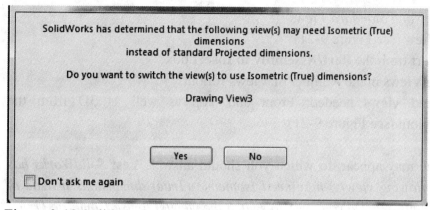

Figure 9-19 SolidWorks query

Import entire dimensions from source to destination

1. Click **Annotation > Model items**
2. Select **Entire model** for Source/Destination (see Figure 9-20)
3. Click **OK**

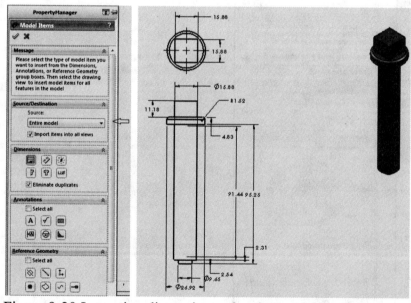

Figure 9-20 Importing dimensions of entire model

Post: Standard Views

To display Drawing FeatureManager
1. Click **New** from the Menu bar
2. Double-click **B-ANSI-MM** from **MY-TEMPLATE** tab
3. Click **Cancel X** from the Model View Manager [if this appears]

To Insert Drawing View and Standard Views

4. Click **Model View** (see Figure 9-21)
5. Double-click Part from the **Part/Assembly to Insert** box
6. Click **Multiple Views** in the Number of Views rollout
7. Select **Standard views** needed: Front and Top as well as 3D from the **Orientation** rollout (see Figure 9-21)
8. Click **OK**

The following message may appear, to which you should answer, **Yes**: *SolidWorks has determined that the following view(s) may need Isometric (True) dimensions instead of standard Projected dimensions. Do you want to switch the view(s) to use Isometric (True) dimensions?*

(see Figure 9-22 for the query and Figure 9-23 for the views)

9. Click **Save As** from the Menu bar (give a name for the drawing) and **Save**.

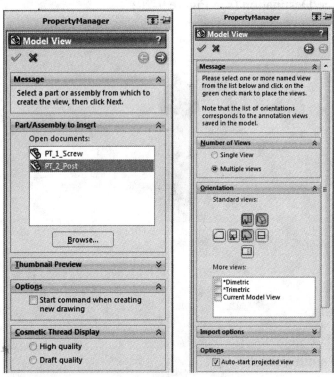

Figure 9-21 Multiple views selected

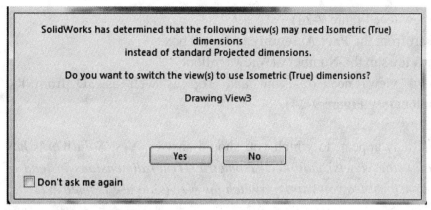

Figure 9-22 SolidWorks query

Import entire dimensions from source to destination

1. Click **Annotation > Model items**
2. Select **Entire model** for Source/Destination (see Figure 9-23)
3. Click **OK**

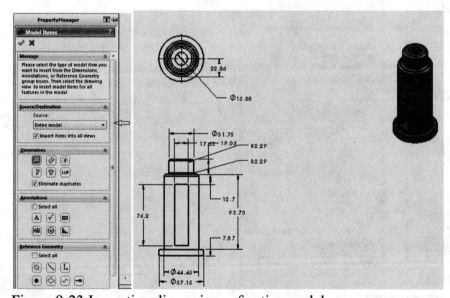

Figure 9-23 Importing dimensions of entire model

Wedge: Standard Views

To display Drawing FeatureManager
1. Click **New** from the Menu bar
2. Double-click **B-ANSI-MM** from **MY-TEMPLATE** tab
3. Click **Cancel X** from the Model View Manager [if this appears]

To Insert Drawing View and Standard Views

4. Click **Model View** (see Figure 9-24)
5. Double-click Part from the **Part/Assembly to Insert** box
6. Click **Multiple Views** in the Number of Views rollout
7. Select **Standard views** needed: Front and Top as well as 3D from the **Orientation** rollout (see Figure 9-24)
8. Click **OK**

The following message may appear, to which you should answer, **Yes**: *SolidWorks has determined that the following view(s) may need Isometric (True) dimensions instead of standard Projected dimensions. Do you want to switch the view(s) to use Isometric (True) dimensions?*

(see Figure 9-25 for the query and Figure 9-26 for the views)

9. Click **Save As** from the Menu bar (give a name for the drawing) and **Save**.

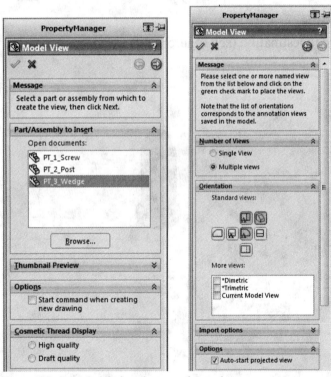

Figure 9-24 Multiple views selected

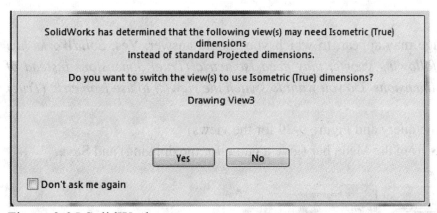

Figure 9-25 SolidWorks query

Import entire dimensions from source to destination

1. Click **Annotation > Model items**
2. Select **Entire model** for Source/Destination (see Figure 9-26)
3. Click **OK**

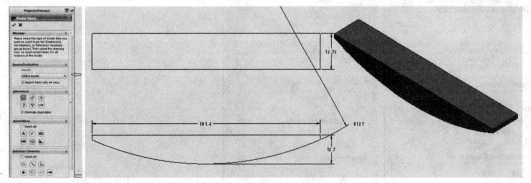

Figure 9-26 Importing dimensions of entire model

Ring: Standard Views

To display Drawing FeatureManager
1. Click **New** from the Menu bar
2. Double-click **B-ANSI-MM** from **MY-TEMPLATE** tab
3. Click **Cancel X** from the Model View Manager [if this appears]

To Insert Drawing View and Standard Views
4. Click **Model View** (see Figure 9-27)
5. Double-click Part from the **Part/Assembly to Insert** box
6. Click **Multiple Views** in the Number of Views rollout
7. Select **Standard views** needed: Front and Top as well as 3D from the **Orientation** rollout (see Figure 9-27)

8. Click **OK**

The following message may appear, to which you should answer, **Yes**: *SolidWorks has determined that the following view(s) may need Isometric (True) dimensions instead of standard Projected dimensions. Do you want to switch the view(s) to use Isometric (True) dimensions?*

(see Figure 9-28 for the query and Figure 9-29 for the views)

9. Click **Save As** from the Menu bar (give a name for the drawing) and **Save**.

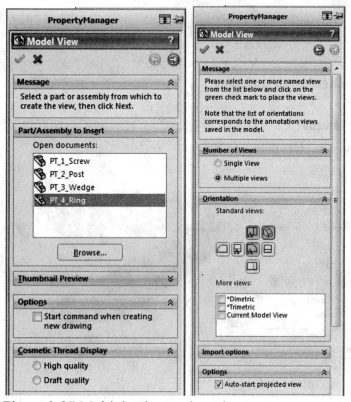

Figure 9-27 Multiple views selected

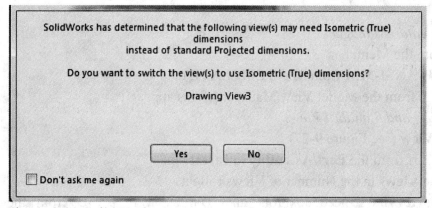

Figure 9-28 SolidWorks query

Import entire dimensions from source to destination

1. Click **Annotation > Model items**
2. Select **Entire model** for Source/Destination (see Figure 9-29)
3. Click **OK**

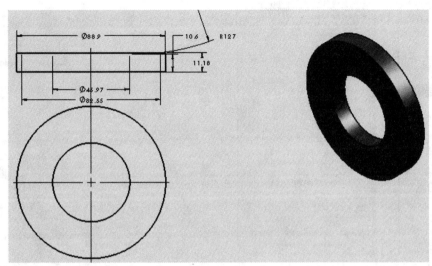

Figure 9-29 Importing dimensions of entire model

Block: Standard Views

To display Drawing FeatureManager
1. Click **New** from the Menu bar
2. Double-click **B-ANSI-MM** from **MY-TEMPLATE** tab
3. Click **Cancel X** from the Model View Manager [if this appears]

To Insert Drawing View and Standard Views
4. Click **Model View** (see Figure 9-30)
5. Double-click Part from the **Part/Assembly to Insert** box
6. Click **Multiple Views** in the Number of Views rollout
7. Select **Standard views** needed: Front and Top as well as 3D from the **Orientation** rollout (see Figure 9-30)
8. Click **OK**

The following message may appear, to which you should answer, **Yes**: *SolidWorks has determined that the following view(s) may need Isometric (True) dimensions instead of standard Projected dimensions. Do you want to switch the view(s) to use Isometric (True) dimensions?*
(see Figure 9-31 for the query and Figure 9-32 for the views)

9. Click **Save As** from the Menu bar (give a name for the drawing) and **Save**.

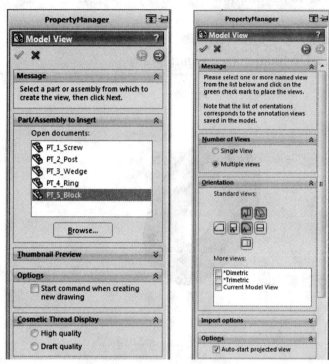

Figure 9-30 Multiple views selected

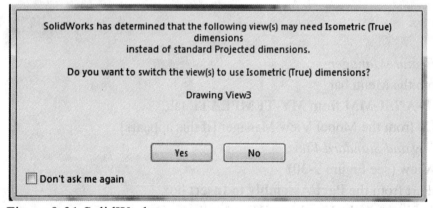

Figure 9-31 SolidWorks query

Import entire dimensions from source to destination

1. Click **Annotation > Model items**
2. Select **Entire model** for Source/Destination (see Figure 9-32)
3. Click **OK**

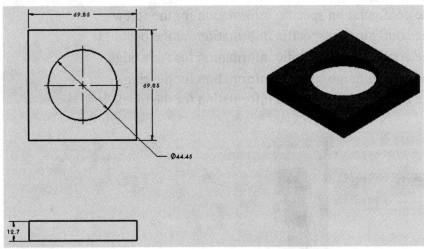

Figure 9-32 Importing dimensions of entire model

Assigning Properties through File > Properties

One way of assigning properties to a part is through **File > Properties** route (see Figure 9-33).

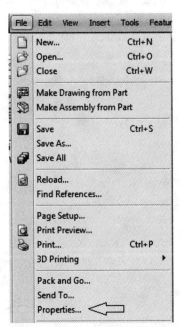

Figure 9-33 Assigning properties to a part: one route

1. Click **File > Properties > Custom** (see Figure 9-13)
2. Select **CompanyName, Revision, Number, DrawnBy, DrawnDate, Material, Mass, Description** and modifying them (see Figure 9-14 and Figure 9-15)
3. Link properties to Title Block

See Figure 9-34 for the configuration specific information for the screw
See Figure 9-35 for the configuration specific information for the post
See Figure 9-36 for the configuration specific information for the wedge
See Figure 9-37 for the configuration specific information for the ring
See Figure 9-38 for the configuration specific information for the block

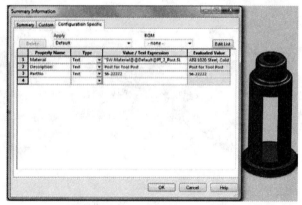

Figure 9-34 Screw configuration specific information

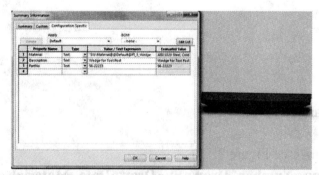

Figure 9-35 Post configuration specific information

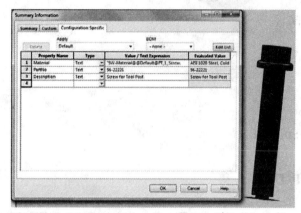

Figure 9-36 Wedge configuration specific information

Figure 9-37 Ring configuration specific information

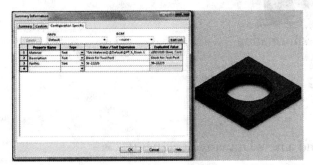

Figure 9-38 Block configuration specific information

Assigning Properties through the Configuration Manager

To assign properties through the configuration manager, the route to follow is shown in Figure 9-39. See Figure 9-40 for the configuration specific information for the screw.

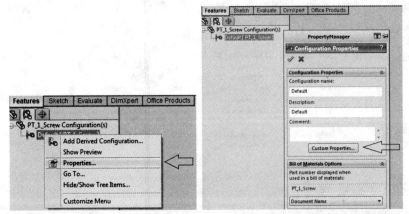

Figure 9-39 Accessing properties configuration for specific information

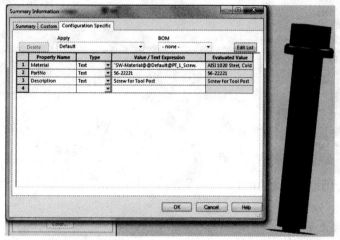

Figure 9-40 Screw configuration specific information

TOOL POST ASSEMBLY DRAWING

Exploded View

Two views must be open [the assembly and a new Drawing document].

Open the Assembly document already completed

1. Click **Windows > Close All**
2. Open the Assembly from appropriate folder (see Figure 9-41)

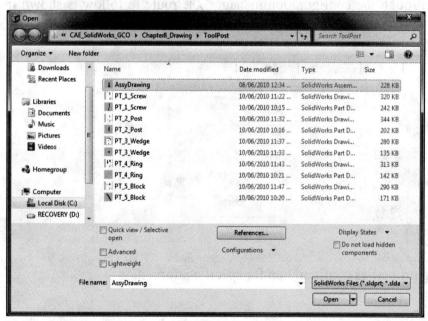

Figure 9-41 Opening the assembly

Create a new drawing

1. Click **Make Drawing from Part/Assembly from New** (see Figure 9-42)
2. Double-click **B-ANSI-MM** template from **MY-TEMPLATES** tab
3. Click **View Palette** tool from Task Pane (see Figure 9-43)
4. Click and drag Isometric view from **View Palette** to Sheet1 (see Figure 9-44)
5. Click **OK**

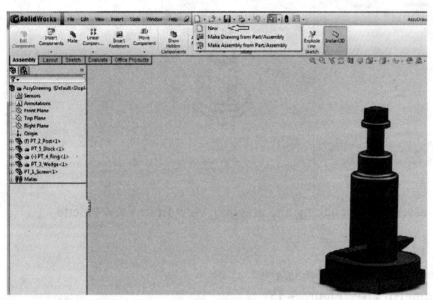

Figure 9-42 Making Drawing from an Assembly

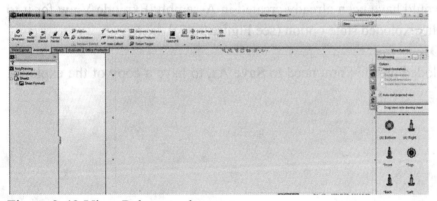

Figure 9-43 View Palette tool

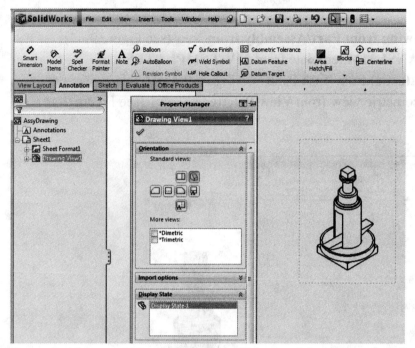

Figure 9-44 Imported assembly by clicking and dragging view from View Palette

Display the Exploded View
1. Click *inside the Isometric view boundary*
2. Right-click **Properties** (see Figure 9-45)
3. Click **Show in exploded state** (see Figure 9-46) [Note: The Exploded View, **ExplView1** would have been already created in Assembly-Explode View for it to be visible in the exploded state option (see Figure 9-47)]
4. Click **OK > OK**
5. **Save As** Exploded on file [You need to **Save As**, to have a copy of the exploded view]

Figure 9-45 Accessing Assembly Properties

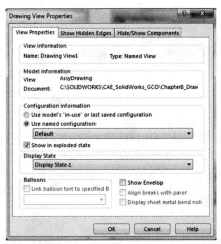

Figure 9-46 Checking Show in exploded state

Figure 9-47 Exploded view of tool post assembly

Balloons

1. Click **inside the isometric view boundary**
2. Click **Auto Balloon** from Annotation toolbar (see Figure 9-48)
3. Click **OK**
4. Select **Balloon Settings > Select Circular Split Line** (see Figure 9-49)
5. Click **OK** (see Figure 9-50 for the assembly balloon)
6. **Save**

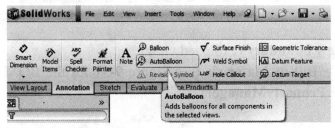

Figure 9-48 Auto Balloon tool

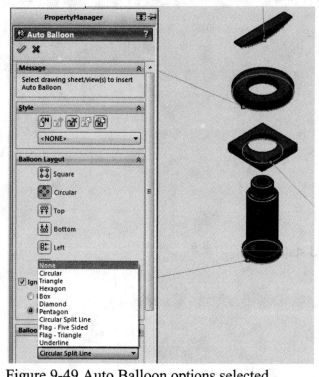

Figure 9-49 Auto Balloon options selected

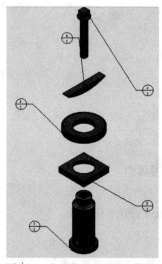

Figure 9-50 Auto Balloon of the assembly

Bill of Material (BOM)

1. Click **inside the Isometric view boundary** (exploded view)
2. Click **Annotation > Tables > Bill of Materials** (see Figure 9-51 for the **BOM** option and Figure 9-52 for the **PropertyManager**)

3. Click a position on any point within the graphics window and click the Return key; the Bill of Materials is shown in Figure 9-53.

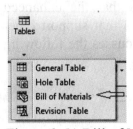

Figure 9-51 Bill of Materials option

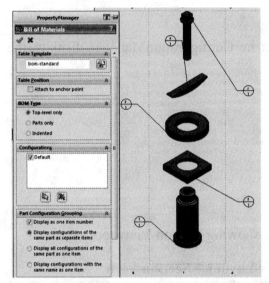

Figure 9-52 Bill of Materials PropertyManager

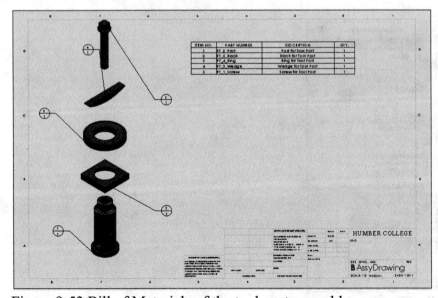

Figure 9-53 Bill of Materials of the tool post assembly

INSERTING SECTION VIEWS

SolidWorks 2013 now addresses customers' need to include sectional views other than only full section which it has supported previously. This means that the enhanced SolidWorks 2013 and later will compete with other CAD packages that support other options of section views other than the full section. This chapter discusses the following additional features of sectional views:

- Full Section View
- Half Section View
- Notched Offset Section View
- Aligned Section View

Inserting a Section View

Ensure that you click the View Layout so that he ConfigurationManager displays the section View tool as shown in Figure 9-54.

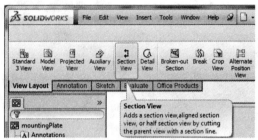

Figure 9-54 View Layout ConfigurationManager showing Section View tool

To insert a section view, in a drawing, click **View Layout > Section View**
[The Section View PropertyManager is automatically displayed with Half Section and Section options; see Figure 9-55]

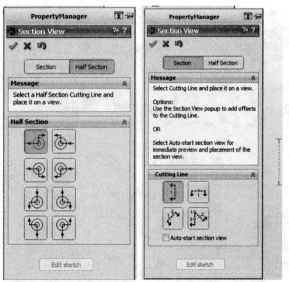

Figure 9-55 Section View PropertyManager

Let us now discuss the two options that users have to select: half section or section.

Half Section View

When the Half Section option is selected from the Section View PropertyManager (Figure 9-55), a number of configurations appears from which the user selects (see Figure 9-56).

Select the type of half section:

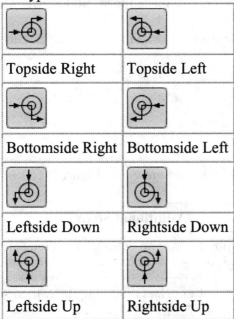

Topside Right	Topside Left
Bottomside Right	Bottomside Left
Leftside Down	Rightside Down
Leftside Up	Rightside Up

Figure 9-56 Half section options

Section View

When the Section option is selected from the Section View PropertyManager (Figure 9-55), a number of Cutting Line configurations appear from which the user selects (see Figure 9-57).

Select the cutting line:

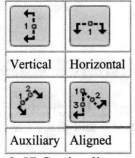

Vertical	Horizontal
Auxiliary	Aligned

Figure 9-57 Cutting line options

For example, to insert a vertical section view:
1. Click Section View   (Drawing toolbar).
2. In the Section View PropertyManager, click Section.
3. In Cutting Line, select Auto-start section view if not already selected.
4. Click Vertical and move the cutting line to the location as shown and click.

   If the Section View dialog box appears, click OK.

5. Drag the preview to the right and click ⬚ to place the section view.

After the user selects and places the cutting line in the drawing view, the Section View popup displays (see Figure 9-58).

Figure 9-58 Section View popup

Use the Section View popup to add offsets to the section view (see Figure 9-59).

Selection	Function	Additional Steps
	Add Arc Offset	Select first point of arc on cutting line, then select second point of arc.
	Add Single Offset	Select first point of offset on cutting line, then select second point of offset.
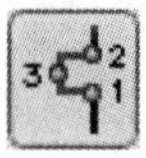	Add Notch Offset	Select first point of notch on cutting line, select second point on cutting line for width of notch, then select third point for depth of notch.
	Step Back	
	OK (Add the view)	
	Cancel (Cancel the view)	

Figure 9-59 Using the Section View popup to add offsets to the section view

If you select Auto-start section view in the Section View PropertyManager, the Section View popup does not appear, allowing you to immediately preview and place the section view in the drawing.

- You can add multiple offsets to a section view. Notch offset may be applied to any cutting line segment. Single offset and Arc offset may only be applied to one of the two outer cutting line segments.
- The cutting line inferences to the drawing's geometry.

Now that we have discussed how to go about sectioning, some examples will now follow in order to clarify the concepts. Sectioning is now made very easy in the enhanced SolidWorks CAD software, which now competes with other CAD software such as Inventor, etc., for this particular functionality.

Example A: Half Section

Create a half section for the model shown in Figure 9-60.

Part Name: Rod Support
Material: 6061-T6 aluminum
Fillets: R.03 unless otherwise specified.

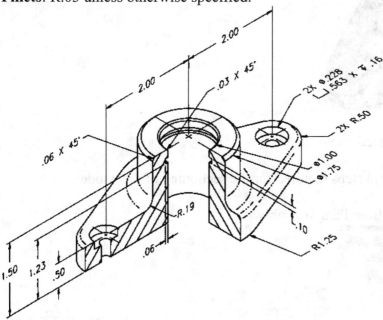

Figure 9-60 Model description for half sectioning

SolidWorks Solution

Figure 9-61 shows the partial model dimensions for the necessary sketches, while Figure 9-62 shows the solid model. These steps are not part of sectioning but are the pre-requisites to produce model required, based on initial dimensions given in Figure 9-60. In other words, these pre-requisite steps are useful to users to consolidate their 3D modeling experience. You may skip these steps depending on your level of model capability.

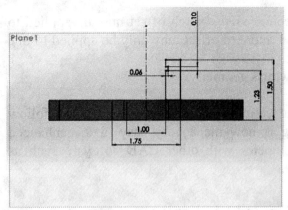

Figure 9-61 Partial model dimensions for the necessary sketches

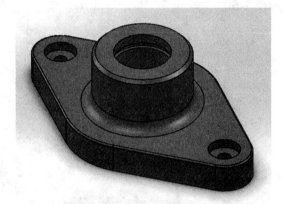

Figure 9-62 Solid model for sectioning

Now, let us proceed to the main steps required for the sectioning of this model.

1. Click Make Drawing from Part/Assembly

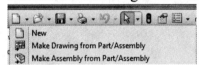

2. **Pin** the View Palette
3. **Drag** and **Drop** Views

To create a half section view:
1. Highlight the bounding box enclosing the view of interest.
2. Click **View Layout > Section View**.
3. In the Section View PropertyManager, click **Half Section**. (see Figure 9-63)
4. In **Half Section**, click **Topside Right**.
5. Move the pointer to the location as shown and click to place it (see Figure 9-64).
6. Drag the preview to the right and click to place the section view (see Figure 9-65).

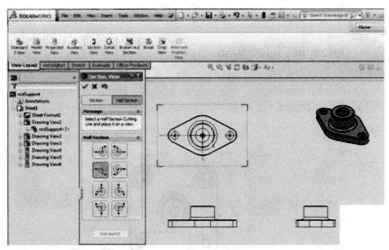

Figure 9-63 Section View option chosen

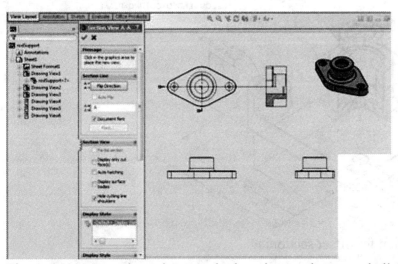

Figure 9-64 Move the pointer to the location as shown and click to place it

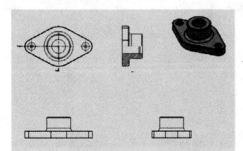

Figure 9-65 Drag the preview to the right and click to place the section view

Example B: Notched Offset Section View

Create a half section for the model shown in Figure 9-66.

Part Name: Mounting Plate
Material: AISI 1020
Fillets: R.03 unless otherwise specified.

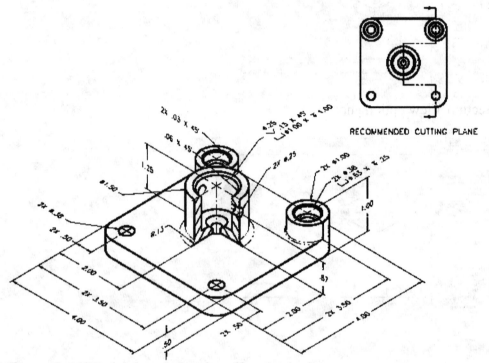

RECOMMENDED CUTTING PLANE

Figure 9-66 Model description for offset sectioning

SolidWorks Solution

Figure 9-67 shows the 3D model.

Figure 9-67 3D Model created from definition for offset sectioning

1. Click Make Drawing from Part/Assembly

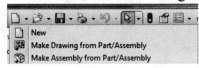

2. **Pin** the View Palette
3. **Drag** and **Drop** Views

To insert a section view with a notched offset:
1. Click **View Layout > Section View**.
2. In the Section View PropertyManager, click **Section**. (see Figure 9-68)
3. In **Cutting Line**, clear **Auto-start section view**. This eliminates the automatic insertion of the section view and lets you add additional offsets to the view.

4. Click Vertical ⬚ and move the cutting line to the location as shown and click to place the line.

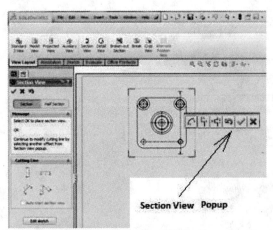

Figure 9-68 The Section View popup appears.

5. Click ⬚ to add a notched offset. (see Figure 9-69)
6. Move the pointer to the location as shown and click to select the first and second points of the notch. These points must be on the cutting line.

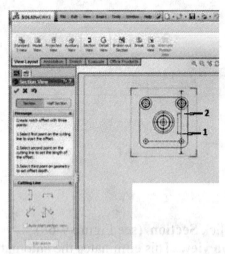

Figure 9-69 Notched offset is added

7. Move the pointer to the location as shown and click to select the depth of the notch. The Section View popup appears. At this point, you could add additional offsets to the view. (see Figure 9-70)

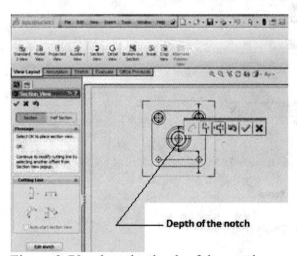

Figure 9-70 select the depth of the notch

8. Click ☑ to close the Section View popup.
9. Drag the preview to the location as shown and click to place the section view. [Figure 9-71 shows the notched offset]

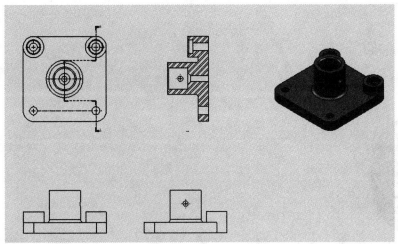

Figure 9-71 Notched offset

Example C: Aligned Section View

Create an aligned section for the model shown in Figure 9-72.

Part Name: Hub
Material: SAE 3145
Fillets: R.03 unless otherwise specified.

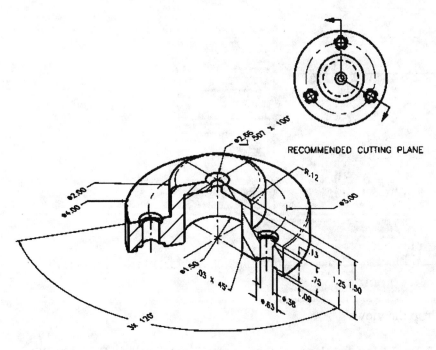

RECOMMENDED CUTTING PLANE

Figure 9-72 Model description for offset sectioning

SolidWorks Solution

Figure 9-73 shows the 3D model.

Figure 9-73 3D Model created from definition for aligned sectioning

1. Click **Make Drawing from Part**
2. Pin the **View Palette**
3. Drag and drop the views (see Figure 9-74)

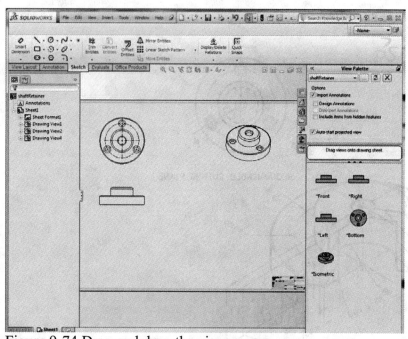

Figure 9-74 Drag and drop the views

4. Click **Drawing View1** bounding box containing the Top View (see Figure 9-75)
5. Click **View Layout > Section View**
6. Select **Section**
7. Click **Cutting Line > Aligned** (see Figure 9-76a)

8. Select center of central circle as 1; center of vertical circle as 2; and center of bottom right circle as 3 (see Figure 9-76b)
9. Click **OK**
10. Drag Aligned View to the right to complete (see Figure 9-77)

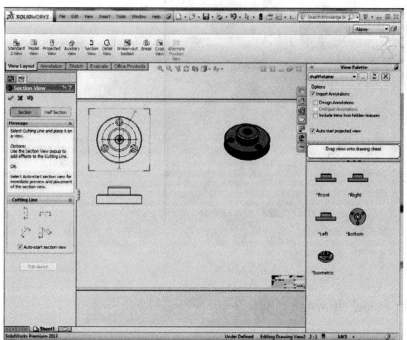

Figure 9-75 Click *Drawing View1* bounding box containing the Top View

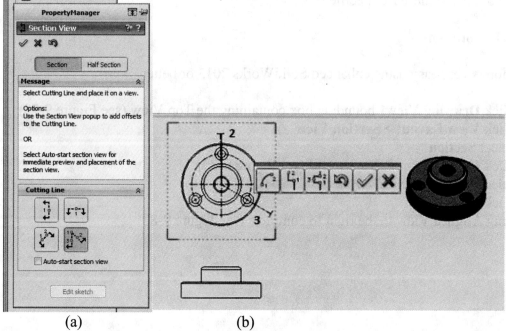

(a)   (b)

Figure 9-76 Click 'Cutting Line' and select 'Aligned'

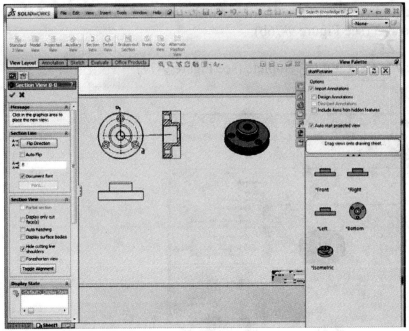

Figure 9-77 Aligned view

Example D: Full Section

Create a half section for the model shown in Figure 9-60.

Part Name: Rod Support
Material: 6061-T6 aluminum
Fillets: R.03 unless otherwise specified.

SolidWorks Solution

The solution is very easy using enhanced SolidWorks 2013 or better.

1. Click **Drawing View1** bounding box containing the Top View (see Figure 9-78)
2. Click **View Layout > Section View**
3. Select **Section**
4. Click **Cutting Line > Horizontal** (see Figure 9-79)
5. Select *center of central circle*
6. Click **OK**
7. Drag Aligned View to the right to complete (see Figure 9-80)

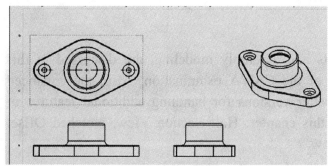

Figure 9-78 Top View highlighted

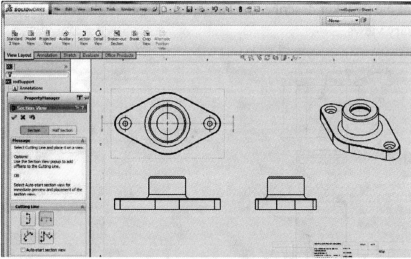

Figure 9-79 Click 'Cutting Line' and select 'Horizontal'

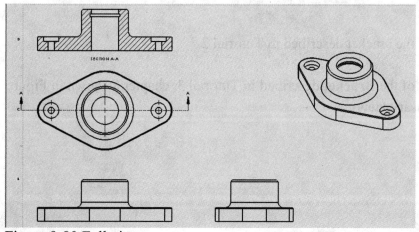

Figure 9-80 Full view

Summary

The basic principles involved in parts and assembly modeling, are discussed in this chapter. This is an important aspect of the CSWA examination. Also, the enhanced capability of SolidWorks 2013 and better versions for handling additional features of sectional views are now included in this chapter: Half Section View; Notched Offset Section View; and Aligned Section View.

Exercises

1: Produce the Drawing of the **Bracket** described in Tutorial 2, chapter 7 shown in Figure 9-54 to include necessary views.

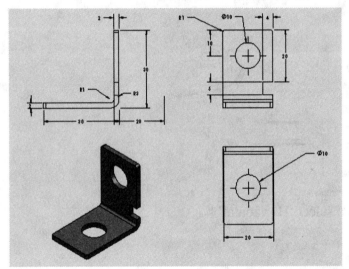

Figure 9-54 Drawing of the bracket described in Tutorial 2

2: Produce the Drawing of the **Bracket** described in Tutorial 3, chapter 8 shown in Figure 9-55 to include necessary views.

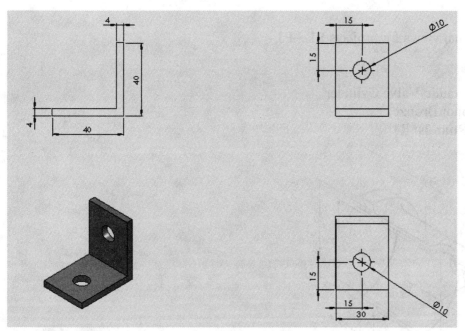

Figure 9-55 Drawing of the simple bracket described in Tutorial 3

3: The assembly shown in Figure 9-56 contains five machined parts (see Example 3). The electronic files for the parts are available as a SolidWorks file in this book. Produce the following views for each of the five parts:

(i)   Auxiliary view (if necessary)
(ii)   Sectional view
(iii)   Detail view
(iv)   Crop view, and
(v)   Detailed drawing.

Figure 9-56 Tool post holder

Projects

Create the sectional views for projects P1—P3

P1:

Part Name: Hydraulic Valve Cylinder
Material: Phosphor Bronze
All Fillets and Rounds: R1

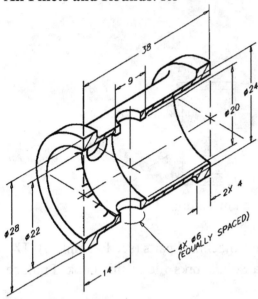

Figure P1

P2:

Part Name: Hub
Material: Cast Iron
Fillets: R.03 unless otherwise specified.

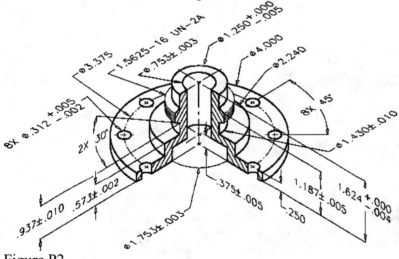

Figure P2

P3:
Part Name: Slide Bracket
Material: AISI 1020
Fillets: R.25 unless otherwise specified.

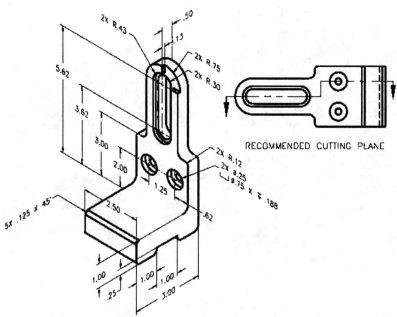

RECOMMENDED CUTTING PLANE

Figure P3

Chapter 10
Reverse Engineering Using Auto Trace and FeatureWorks

Objectives:

In this chapter you will learn:

- The concept of reverse engineering in a competitive market place
- The functionalities of SolidWorks reverse engineering tools
- How to import graphic images such as company logos and scanned geometric designs into SolidWorks
- How to convert graphic images such as company logos and scanned geometric designs into digital data and trace them for reverse engineering
- The FeatureWorks Add-In and Options
- How to import Geometry from outside the SolidWorks environment
- How to import Diagnostic tools to eliminate gaps between adjacent faces
- How to carry out Automatic Recognition of Features
- How to carry out Interactive Recognition of Features

REVERSE ENGINEERING

Engineering is the profession involved in designing, manufacturing, constructing, and maintaining of products, systems, and structures. At a higher level, there are two types of engineering: forward engineering and reverse engineering.

Forward engineering is the traditional process of moving from high-level abstractions and logical designs to the physical implementation of a system. In some situations, there may be a physical part without any technical details, such as drawings, bills-of-material, or without engineering data, such as thermal and electrical properties.

The process of duplicating an existing component, subassembly, or product, without the aid of drawings, documentation, or computer model is known as reverse engineering.

Reverse engineering can be viewed as the process of analyzing a system to:
1. Identify the system's components and their interrelationships
2. Create representations of the system in another form or a higher level of abstraction
3. Create the physical representation of that system

Reverse engineering is very common in such diverse fields as software engineering, entertainment, automotive, consumer products, microchips, chemicals, electronics, and mechanical designs. For example, when a new machine comes to market, competing manufacturers may buy one machine and disassemble it to learn how it was built and how it works. A chemical company may use reverse engineering to defeat a patent on a competitor's manufacturing process. In civil engineering, bridge and building designs are copied from past successes so there will be less chance of catastrophic failure. In software engineering, good source code is often a variation of other good source code.

In some situations, designers give a shape to their ideas by using clay, plaster, wood, or foam rubber, but a CAD model is needed to enable the manufacturing of the part. As products become more organic in shape, designing in CAD may be challenging or impossible. There is no guarantee that the CAD model will be acceptably close to the sculpted model. Reverse engineering provides a solution to this problem because the physical model is the source of information for the CAD model. This is also referred to as the part-to-CAD process.

Another reason for reverse engineering is to compress product development times. In the intensely competitive global market, manufacturers are constantly seeking new ways to shorten lead-times to market a new product. Rapid product development (RPD) refers to recently developed technologies and techniques that assist manufacturers and designers in meeting the demands of reduced product development time. For example, injection-moulding companies must drastically reduce the tool and die development times. By using reverse engineering, a three-dimensional product or model can be quickly captured in digital form, re-modelled, and exported for rapid prototyping/tooling or rapid manufacturing.

Following are reasons for reverse engineering a part or product:
1. The original manufacturer of a product no longer produces a product
2. There is inadequate documentation of the original design
3. The original manufacturer no longer exists, but a customer needs the product
4. The original design documentation has been lost or never existed
5. Some bad features of a product need to be designed out. For example, excessive wear might indicate where a product should be improved
6. To strengthen the good features of a product based on long-term usage of the product
7. To analyze the good and bad features of competitors' product
8. To explore new avenues to improve product performance and features
9. To gain competitive benchmarking methods to understand competitor's products and develop better products
10. The original CAD model is not sufficient to support modifications or current manufacturing methods
11. The original supplier is unable or unwilling to provide additional parts
12. The original equipment manufacturers are either unwilling or unable to supply replacement parts, or demand inflated costs for sole-source parts
13. To update obsolete materials or antiquated manufacturing processes with more current, less-expensive technologies

Reverse engineering enables the duplication of an existing part by capturing the component's physical dimensions, features, and material properties. Before attempting reverse engineering, a well-planned life-cycle analysis and cost/benefit analysis should be conducted to justify the reverse engineering projects. Reverse engineering is typically cost effective only if the items to be reverse engineered reflect a high investment or will be reproduced in large quantities. Reverse engineering of a part may be attempted even if it is not cost effective, if the part is absolutely required and is mission-critical to a system.

Reverse engineering of mechanical parts involves acquiring three-dimensional position data in the point cloud using laser scanners or computed tomography (CT). Representing geometry of the part in terms of surface points is the first step in creating parametric surface patches. A good polymesh is created from the point cloud using reverse engineering software. The cleaned-up polymesh, NURBS (Non-uniform rational B-spline) curves, or NURBS surfaces are exported to CAD packages for further refinement, analysis, and generation of cutter tool paths for CAM. Finally, the CAM produces the physical part.

It can be said that reverse engineering begins with the product and works through the design process in the opposite direction to arrive at a product definition statement (PDS). In doing so, it uncovers as much information as possible about the design ideas that were used to produce a particular product.

SOLIDWORKS REVERSE ENGINEERING TOOLS

SolidWorks offers some reverse engineering capabilities:
• Reverse Engineering – Scan concept sketches or data into SolidWorks using **ScanTo3D** and complete the product design in SolidWorks.
• Reverse Engineering – Insert a picture into SolidWorks **Sketch Picture** and trace it using **Auto Trace** tool for reverse engineering. Insert pictures (**.bmp**, **.gif**, **.jpg**, **.jpeg**, **.tif**, **.wmf**).
• Feature Recognition – Import non-SolidWorks CAD data, preserve design intent, and make changes. Increase the value of translated files, while reducing the time spent rebuilding existing 3D models.

We will describe the Auto Trace tool first and later describe the feature recognition tool.

CREATE AUTO TRACE TOOL

SolidWorks Auto Trace tool helps to convert raster data into vector data. Company logos and scanned geometric designs can be converted into SolidWorks digital data using Auto Trace Add-In tool, which allows users to insert a picture into SolidWorks **Sketch Picture** and trace it for reverse engineering. SolidWorks **Sketch Picture** PropertyManager enables you to trace outlines or select areas by colour to create vector data. This tool creates a sketch that you can save and edit as needed. Auto Trace tool inserts (**.bmp**, **.gif**, **.jpg**, **.jpeg**, **.tif**, **.wmf**) format pictures.

This tool can help convert raster data to vector data. In **Tools > Sketch Tools > Sketch Picture**, open a document and click the **Next** icon to select conversion options. Options include:

-Trace Settings
-Display Options
-Adjustments

Once you convert the document to vector data, you have a sketch that you can modify, save, and used as a basis for creating a 3D model. The steps involved can be summarized as follows:

    (a) Open raster data
    (b) Trace shape outline
    (c) Convert raster data to vector data
    (d) Modify sketch
    (e) Create 3D model

1.   Open **New Part SolidWorks** document as shown in Figure 10-1.

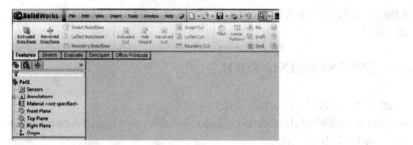

Figure 10-1 A New SolidWorks document

2.   Click **Add-In** (see Figure 10-2)

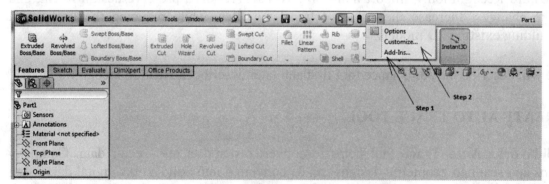

Figure 10-2 Click Add-In from the Feature CommandManager

The **Add-In PropertyManager** is displayed (see Figure 10-3)

3.   Select **Autotrace** option to add-in (see Figure 10-3)

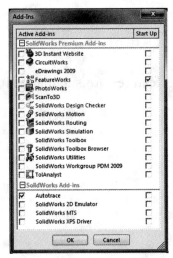

Figure 10-3 Add-In PropertyManager

4. Click **Customize > Commands > Sketch** (see Figure 10-2 and Figure 10-4)

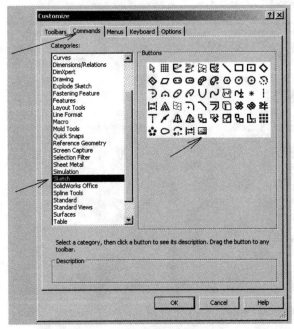

Figure 10-4 Click Customize from the Feature CommandManager to access Sketch

5. Drag **Sketch Picture** to the CommandManager (see Figure 10-5)

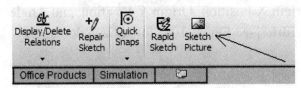

Figure 10-5 Customizing Sketch Picture

Methodology for Importing and Extracting Image Features

A four-phase methodology for importing and extracting image features are summarized as follows:

Phase 1: Import Image (by clicking '*Sketch Picture*')
Phase 2: Image Extraction
Phase 3: Image Repair
Phase 4: Extrude Features

Phase 1: Import Image

6. Click **Front Plane** > **Sketch** [see Figure 10-6; be in *Sketch mode* to activate **Sketch Picture**]

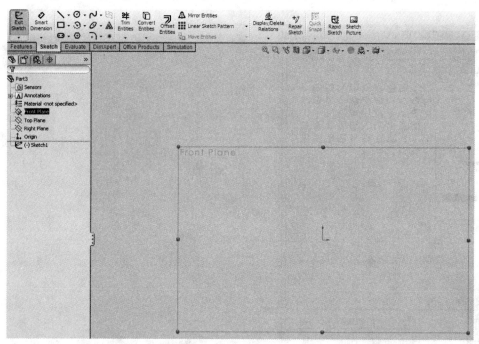

Figure 10-6 Front Plane is chosen

7. Click **Sketch Picture** > **SolidWorks Logo.bpm** > **Open** from the appropriate directory
8. Enter **0** for the first three entries (Origin X Position, Origin Y Position, and Angle respectively) and **100 mm** for the **Width** [see Figure 10-7 for resized document]

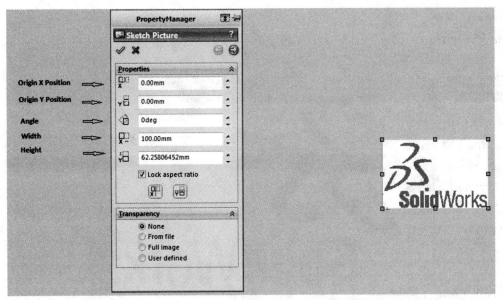

Figure 10-7 Importing a picture to SolidWorks within Sketch Picture environment

9. Click **Next** (arrow head) to select conversion options [see Figure 10-8]
   [Sketch Picture Property Manager appears showing conversion options as in Figure 10-9]

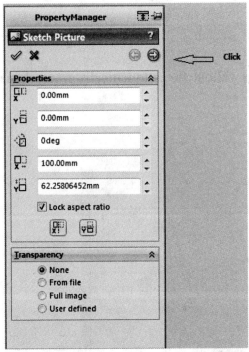

Figure 10-8 Options for Trace Settings, Display Options and Adjustments

Figure 10-9 Sketch Picture PropertyManager

Phase 2: Image Extraction

10. Press the "**f**" key to enlarge the image on the screen

11. Click **Use to select rectangular area** in **Trace Settings** [see Step 1 in Figure 10-10]

12. Use the **Rectangular Selection Tool** to sketch a bounding box around the features (see Figure 10-10)

13. Click **Begin Trace** in the **Trace Settings** callout [to automatically trace shape outlines] (see Figure 10-10)

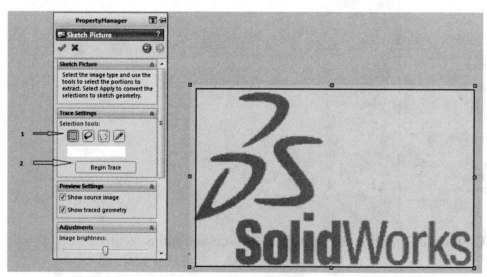

Figure 10-10 Using Selection Tool to extract image automatically

14. Click **Apply** at the bottom of the **Trace Settings** callout (see Figure 10-11)
15. Click **OK** on the top right side of the Sketch Picture PropertyManager (see Figure 10-11)

[The extracted images are shown in Figure 10-12]

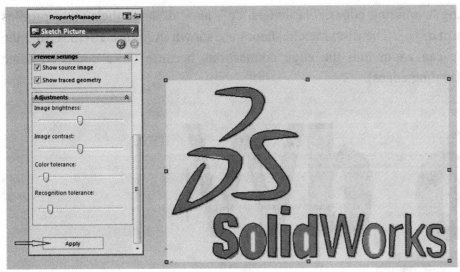

Figure 10-11 Automatic tracing of shape outlines

Figure 10-12 Extracted images

Phase 3: Image Repair

Fault Diagnosis

Automatic tracing of shape outlines may result in some missing features as well as "open contours" as shown in Figure 10-12. The extracted images have to be repaired. We could use line or Spline tools to connect open contours and complete the profiles. For example, the words "S", "o", "d", "W", and "D" in italic are not correctly extracted. "S", "W", and "D" have dangling or missing edges. The letters, "o", and "d" have their inner profiles missing in the form of "o". The ill-extracted shapes are shown in Figure 10-13. Using the zooming tool we can zoom into the edge connections because there could be some missing edges (dangling edges).

Figure 10-13 Ill-extracted shapes

Fault Repair

Since these shapes are SolidWorks feature, we could then use Line or Spline tools to correct the missing or ill-extracted edges.

Right-click **Sketch1** from the **FeatureManager** (see Figure 10-14)
Click **Edit Sketch** to edit the ill-extracted features.

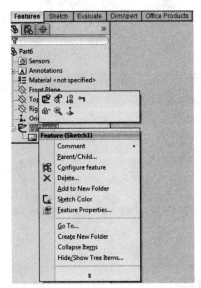

Figure 10-14 Sketch1

The corrected shapes are shown in Figure 10-15.

Figure 10-15 Corrected shapes

This completes the process of converting the raster data into vector data which can now be used as basis for a SolidWorks 3D model.

Phase 4: Extrude Features

To create the SolidWorks 3D model, we follow the normal steps:

16. Click **Extruded Boss/Base** in the **FeatureManager** (The **Extrude PropertyManager** is displayed as shown in Figure 10-16)

17. Accept the Blind option and give a Distance for extrusion as 10 mm (Figure 10-17 shows the Extruded features)

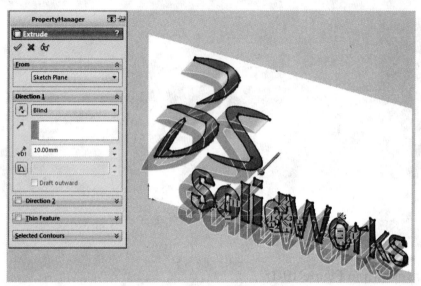

Figure 10-16 Extrude PropertyManager

Figure 10-17 Extruded features

Expanding the Solid Bodies folder in the FeatureManager shows that there are fourteen solid bodies (see Figure 10-18). It is worthwhile further investigating the FeatureManager. There is one sketch, Sketch1 which composes the fourteen profiles extracted. We notice that the Sketch Picture1 tool icon is attached to Sketch1, showing how the sketch was created.

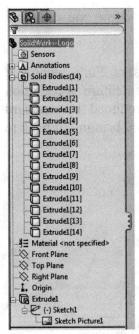

Figure 10-18 Fourteen solid bodies in the Solid Bodies folder

FEATUREWORKS TOOL

FeatureWorks Product Overview

FeatureWorks® software is feature recognition software that is fully integrated with SolidWorks 3D CAD software. FeatureWorks software is the first parametric feature recognition solution for CAD users. By applying intelligence to translated 3D CAD files, FeatureWorks brings static 3D data to life, making it ready for use with SolidWorks 3D CAD software. Automatic feature recognition applies intelligence to static geometric data from standard 3D translators. Once feature recognition is complete, the part is fully editable with SolidWorks software. There is additional time saving through automatic recognition of linear, rectangular, and circular hole patterns (see Figure 10-37 and Figure 10-38).

Ease sharing of 3D models between organizations that use different CAD systems. Leverage the value of legacy data. Make a complete transition to a SolidWorks solution more quickly. FeatureWorks software reduces time spent rebuilding models, resulting in better product designs, faster development cycles, and lower costs.

Why spend hours rebuilding designs? Standard translators allow you to share geometric data with other people and organizations that use different CAD systems, but making changes to that data and performing "what if" analyses are not so easy. To do so, you typically need to rebuild designs manually, introducing new intelligence or recreating intelligence that was lost during the translation process. Life would be simpler if you could add intelligence to static 3D models more quickly and easily. Now you can, with FeatureWorks software.

FeatureWorks software is the first software of its kind for CAD users. Fully integrated with SolidWorks software, FeatureWorks is the first parametric feature recognition software for CAD users. By recognizing features from files produced by standard translators, FeatureWorks applies intelligence to static geometric data, bringing it back to life and making it ready to use in SolidWorks.

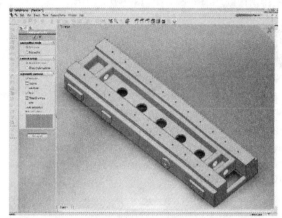

Figure 10-19 Automatic feature recognition

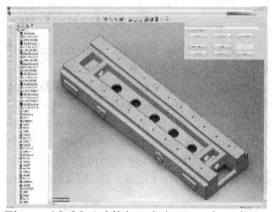

Figure 10-20 Additional time saving through automatic recognition of linear, rectangular, and circular hole patterns

FeatureWorks Software Capabilities:
a) Modify the size and location of features easily.
b) Once recognition of features – including holes, cuts, chamfers, fillets, extrusions, sheet-metal features, ribs, and sketch patterns – is complete, you can easily fine-tune the design using SolidWorks software.
c) Features recognized by FeatureWorks are fully editable, associative, and parametric, and you can create new features at any time.
d) FeatureWorks enhances the value of legacy data and enables easier, more productive sharing of 3D models between different CAD systems.

e) Preserve design intent, maintain quality. FeatureWorks gives you the flexibility to make changes to static geometric data, and helps preserve or introduce new design intent. For example, a hole originally created as "blind" or "through all" will regain the essential specifications that it may have lost through the translation process, keeping the design intent intact for all downstream modifications and maintaining quality.

f) Choose automatic or interactive methods. FeatureWorks provides both automatic and interactive feature recognition capabilities. Automatic feature recognition requires no user intervention. The interactive method provides a dialog that lets you control or specify the design intent easily by selecting and clicking on a face or the edges of a cut or boss. The model checker indicates any changes to underlying imported geometry before and after feature recognition. You can perform automatic recognition before or after interactive recognition. All feature recognition steps can be automated using the SolidWorks API (Application Programming Interface).

g) FeatureWorks requires easy setup, easy use, fully integrated with SolidWorks software. You can access all the controls for FeatureWorks from the SolidWorks menu bar. The FeatureManager® design tree in SolidWorks software automatically keeps track of features recognized by FeatureWorks, so the entire design process stays consistent and intuitive. FeatureWorks provides the same Windows® look-and-feel that has made SolidWorks the easiest-to-learn-and-use 3D CAD software available.

h) Save time through parametric feature recognition. FeatureWorks captures all imported data and recognizes features from files produced by standard translators such as STEP, IGES, SAT (ACIS®), VDA-FS, and Parasolid® files. Best suited for geometrically regular parts, FeatureWorks recognizes, and bring static translated file data to life through the feature recognition of parts that contain holes, cuts, bosses, fillets, chamfers, sketch patterns, curve-driven patterns, sheet-metal features, and shells (see Figure 10-39):
• Extrusion features such as bosses and cuts of the following sketch entities: lines, circles, and circular arcs
• Revolved features, which are conical or cylindrical
• Sweep features
• Hole patterns including linear, rectangular, and circular patterns
• Any standard hole-types, such as simple, tapered, and counter-bored
• Sheet-metal features including edge flange, sketch and bend, hem, and base features
• Random sketch patterns of features on a plane
• Shell features such as uniform wall and shell inward only
• Ribs and draft features
• Combination of features and imported geometry
• Constant- and variable-radius fillets
• Applied features such as chamfers and fillets
• Multibody part construction

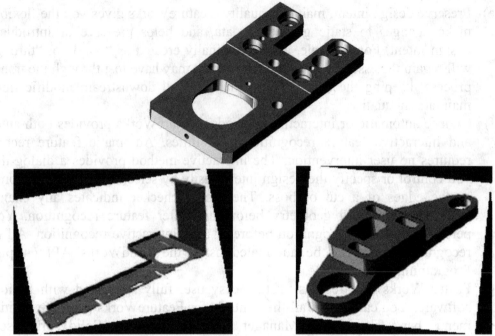

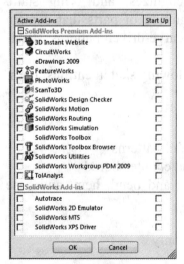

Figure 10-21 Feature recognition of parts from static translated file data

FeatureWorks Add-In

To enable the FeatureWorks application and set the SolidWorks option:
1. Click **Tools, Add-Ins** (see Figure 10-22).
2. In the dialog box, select **FeatureWorks**, then click **OK**.

Active Add-ins	Start Up
SolidWorks Premium Add-Ins	
3D Instant Website	
CircuitWorks	
eDrawings 2009	
☑ FeatureWorks	
PhotoWorks	
ScanTo3D	
SolidWorks Design Checker	
SolidWorks Motion	
SolidWorks Routing	
SolidWorks Simulation	
SolidWorks Toolbox	
SolidWorks Toolbox Browser	
SolidWorks Utilities	
SolidWorks Workgroup PDM 2009	
TolAnalyst	
SolidWorks Add-ins	
Autotrace	
SolidWorks 2D Emulator	
SolidWorks MTS	
SolidWorks XPS Driver	
OK Cancel	

Figure 10-22 SolidWorks Add-Ins

FeatureWorks Options

1. Click **FeatureWorks > Options** (see Figure 10-23 for the FeatureWorks toolbar).
2. In the dialog box:
   - For **General** (see Figure 10-24: top-left):
     - o **Select Create new file.**
     - o Select **Prompt for feature recognition as part opens**.
   - For **Dimensions/Relations** (see Figure 10-24: top-right), under **Relations**, select **Add constraints to sketch** to fully define the sketch.
   - For **Advanced Controls** (see Figure 10-24: bottom-right):
     - o Under **Diagnose**, select **Allow failed feature creation** to allow creation of features that have rebuild errors.
     - o Under **Performance**, clear both check boxes.
3. Click **OK**.

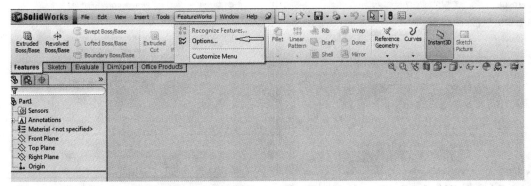

Figure 10-23 SolidWorks FeatureWorks toolbar

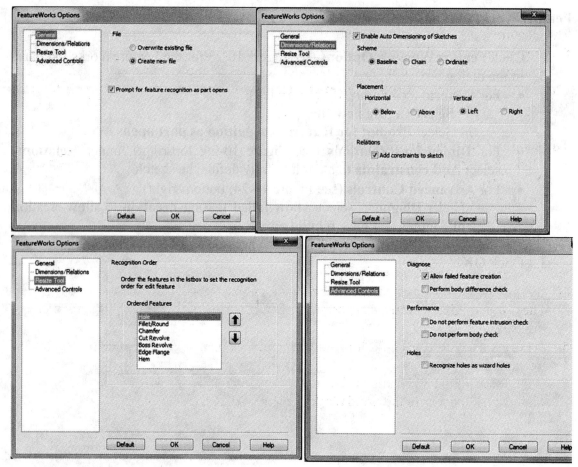

Figure 10-24 SolidWorks FeatureWorks Options

FeatureWorks PropertyManager

The **FeatureWorks** PropertyManager can be used to set most of the FeatureWorks recognition options. Features can be automatically or interactively recognized. You can use *step-by-step recognition* with automatic and interactive feature recognition or a combination of these methods. Standard features, or sheet metal features can also be recognized. FeatureWorks cannot recognize entities in the **Surface Bodies** folder.

In the subsequent sections, we will discuss:
- Automatic Feature Recognition
- Interactive Feature Recognition

Problem Description

Use the *SolidWorks Automatic Feature Recognition* and *Interactive Feature Recognition* tools to extract and recognize the *IGES* file, named *holder.igs*.

Automatic Feature Recognition Methodology

The FeatureWorks software attempts to automatically recognize and highlight as many features as possible. The advantage to this method is the speed at which features are recognized because you do not select faces or features. If the FeatureWorks software can automatically recognize most or all of the features in your model, then use **Automatic Feature Recognition**.

To recognize features automatically:

1. Click **Recognize Features** (FeatureWorks toolbar) or click **FeatureWorks > Recognize Features**.
   The **FeatureWorks** PropertyManager appears.
2. Under **Recognition Mode**, click **Automatic**.
3. Under **Feature Type**, click one of these options:
   - *Standard features*
   - *Sheet metal features*
4. Click **Next** (arrow head) to automatically recognize the selected features.
   The **Intermediate State** PropertyManager appears with the list of **Recognized Features**.
5. If necessary, you can Find Patterns, Combine Features, or Re-Recognize Features as alternate features.
6. Click to recognize the features. To exit without recognizing the features, click.
   The features appear in the SolidWorks FeatureManager design tree.

Import Geometry

1. **Open** a file with **File Name: HOLDER.IGS** while selecting **Files of type: IGES (*.igs.*.iges)** [see Figure 10-25]
2. Click **OK** [see Figure 10-26 for the **New SolidWorks** Part document PropertyManager]
3. Click **OK** [see Figure 10-27 for the imported geometry]

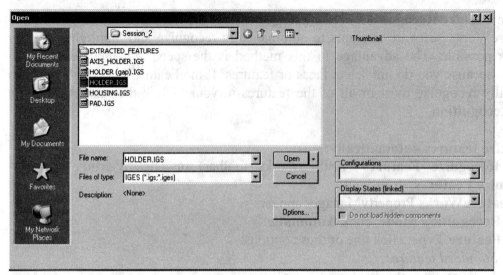

Figure 10-25 Opening a foreign file to SolidWorks (IGES file)

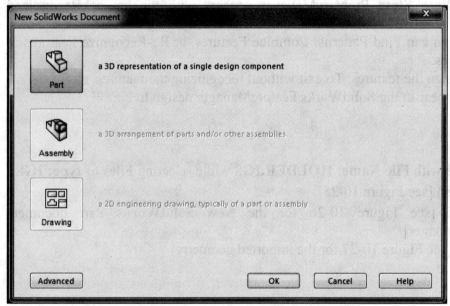

Figure 10-26 New SolidWorks Part document PropertyManager

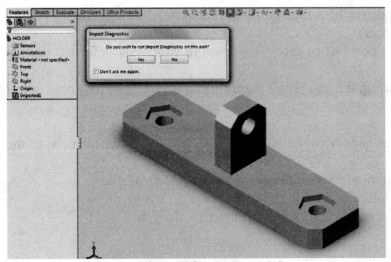

Figure 10-27 Import Diagnostics PropertyManager

Import Diagnostics

Import diagnostics repairs faulty surfaces, knits repaired surfaces into closed bodies, and makes closed bodies into solids.

When a part is imported, the Import Diagnostics PropertyManager appears as shown in Figure 10-27 together with a query which reads: "Do you wish to run Import Diagnostics on this part?" Answer "Yes" if you wish this to run it, or "No" if otherwise.

The Import Diagnostics PropertyManager opens.
If you click **Yes** this repair capability is needed because imported surface data often has problems that prevent surfaces from being converted into valid solids. These problems include:
- Bad surface geometry.
- Bad surface topology (trim curves).
- Adjacent surfaces whose edges are close to each other but do not meet, thus creating gaps between the surfaces.

Import Diagnostics finds problems by:
- Running the check used in **Tools**, **Check**, plus
- Running additional checks, such as overlapping surfaces, plus
- Checking for accurate, unsimplified surfaces, which are B-splines that are planar, cylindrical, and so on and therefore, can be replaced with equivalent analytic surfaces, improving performance and making the model easier to reference.

Import Diagnostics repairs errors in geometry (the underlying surface) and topology (the boundaries) of faces by doing one or more of the following:

- Recreating the trim boundaries of a face based on the surrounding geometry (which often fixes overlapping faces).
- Trimming away defective portions of faces (for cases in which the defective portion is not used in the model).
- Removing the face and using the gap repair algorithm to fill the resulting hole (a last resort).

Import Diagnostics eliminates gaps between adjacent faces by doing one or more of the following:
- Replacing two close but non-intersecting edges with one "tolerant" edge.
- Creating a fill surface or lofted surface to fill the gap.
- Extending two adjacent faces into each other to eliminate the gap.

Additional functionality:
- Converts unsimplified surfaces into analytic surfaces.
- Knits repaired faces into the rest of the surface body, if possible.
- Converts the body into a solid if the surface body is closed (without gaps). This is done automatically when you click **OK** in the dialog box.

General approach to using the Import PropertyManager

  a) Click **Attempt to Heal All**.
  b) Repair faces. Right-click a face in the list and select a command.
  c) Repair gaps. Right-click a gap in the list and select a command or the **Gap Closer** tool.

1. Click **Yes** (if desired) for the imported part, which results in the **Import Diagnostic PropertyManager** appearing as shown in Figure 10-28.
2. Click **OK** to continue (see Figure 10-29 in which the Feature Recognition Query appears)
   A query which reads: "Do you want to proceed with feature recognition?" Answer "Yes" if you wish this to proceed, or "No" if otherwise.

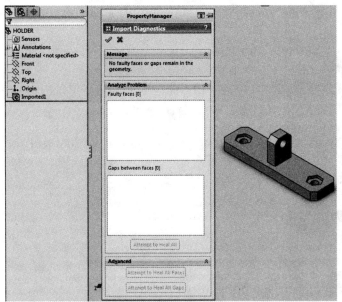

Figure 10-28 Import Diagnostic PropertyManager

Figure 10-29 FeatureWorks PropertyManager

Automatic Feature Recognition

1. Click **Yes** for the query in Figure 10-29 to proceed with feature recognition (see Figure 10-30 in which the Feature Recognition PropertyManager appears)
2. Select **Automatic** for the **Selection Mode** (see Figure 10-30)
3. Click **OK** (see Figure 10-31 for the recognized feature and the FeatureManager)

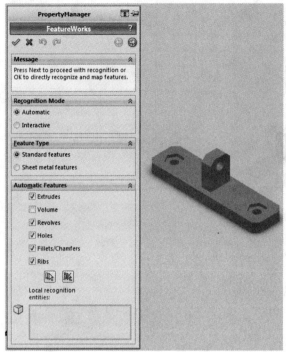

Figure 10-30 FeatureWorks PropertyManager

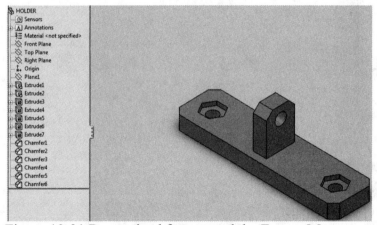

Figure 10-31 Recognized feature and the FeatureManager

Interactive Feature Recognition Methodology
You select the feature type and the entities that make up the feature that you want to recognize.

The advantage to this method is the control that you have over the features that are recognized. For example, you can decide if you want to recognize a cylindrical cut as an extrusion, a revolve, or a hole. Additionally, you can determine the location and complexity of the sketches of your features by the faces and edges that you select.

To recognize features interactively:
1. Click **Recognize Features** (FeatureWorks toolbar) or click **FeatureWorks**, **Recognize Features**.

The **FeatureWorks** PropertyManager appears.
2. Under **Recognition Mode**, click **Interactive**.
3. Under **Feature Type**, click one of these options:
   - Standard features
   - Sheet metal features
4. Under **Interactive Features**, choose the **Feature type**.
5. Under **Selected entities**, select geometry from the graphics area to recognize as the selected **Feature type**. You do not have to select every face of a feature to recognize it.
6. Select from the following options, which appear depending on the selected feature type:
   - **Chain chamfer faces**. (Chamfer features only). Select this check box to have FeatureWorks find additional faces for a chamfer feature adjacent to the face you select.
   - **Chain fillet faces**. (Fillet features only). Select this check box to have FeatureWorks find additional fillet faces tangent to the fillet face you select. You can select a chain of fillets with different radii on each edge. Variable radius fillets can be included in a chain of fillets. The selected chain is recognized as a single feature. If the fillet faces do not chain automatically, you may be able to manually select them to create a chain as a single feature.
   - **Chain revolved faces**. (Revolve and Hole features only). Select this check box if you want the FeatureWorks software to determine the faces for a revolved feature from a minimum set of faces you select. For an illustration of the effect of this check box.
   - **End Face 1** and **End Face 2**. (*Loft* and *sweep* features only). Select a start and end face for these features.
   - **Neutral face**. (Draft features only) Select a face for the neutral plane of the **Draft** feature.
   - **Normal to sketch**. (Rib features only). You can interactively recognize ribs that are extruded normal to sketch.
   - **Recognize similar**. (Extrudes, Revolves, Ribs, and Hole features only). Select this check box to recognize features with similar characteristics. For example, you have several boss extrudes with rectangular cross sections. Select the face of one boss, and these features are recognized at the same time, but as separate features.
   - **Up to face**. (Extrudes only) Select a face for termination of the feature. The FeatureWorks software extends the feature from the sketch plane to the selected face.
   - **Fixed face** (Miter flanges only). The fixed face must meet and be on the same side (inner or outer) as the selected miter flange faces.
7. If you want to delete one or more faces, click *Delete Faces*. You can use this prior to feature recognition to get rid of complicated or unwanted geometry. If you delete faces that are necessary for previously recognized features, FeatureWorks will not be able to recreate those features.
8. Click **Recognize** to interactively recognize the selected features.
   If successful, the features are removed from the imported body in the graphics area.

9. If you want to undo the recognition of a feature, click **Anticlockwise Arrow** in the FeatureWorks PropertyManager. Click **Clockwise Arrow** to recreate the undone feature.

10. Continue to recognize features of different feature types.

11. Click **Next** (forward arrow head) or **Recognize**.
    The *Intermediate Stage* PropertyManager appears with the list of **Recognized Features**.

12. Click **Next** (backward arrow head) to complete feature recognition and create the new features.

The following steps are common to both Automatic and Interactive Feature Recognition methods: FeatureWorks Add-In, Options, Import non-SolidWorks Geometry, Import Diagnostics. Therefore, these steps are not repeated here. We will concentrate on the Interactive Feature Recognition method

1. Select **Interactive** for the **Recognition Mode** from the **FeatureWorks PropertyManager** shown in Figure 10-32 similar to Figure 10-30 (Note: **Boss Extrude** is default **Feature type**)

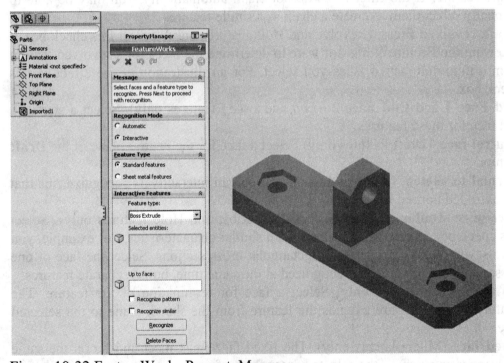

Figure 10-32 FeatureWorks PropertyManager

Recognize Chamfer features on the Base

2. Select **Chamfer** from the drop down button of the **Feature type** (see Figure 10-33)

3. Click the **face** of one chamfer feature (see Figure 10-33)
4. Click the **Recognize** button (see Figure 10-33)

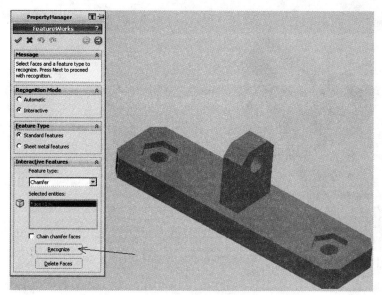

Figure 10-33 Recognition first chamfer feature

5. Click the **face** of the second chamfer feature (see Figure 10-34)
6. Click the **Recognize** button (see Figure 10-34)

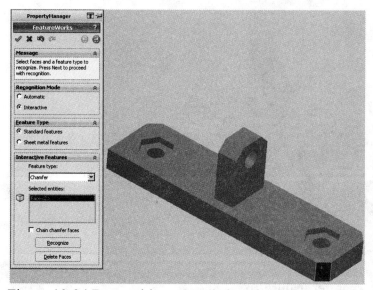

Figure 10-34 Recognition second chamfer feature

7. Click the **face** of the third chamfer feature (see Figure 10-35)
8. Click the **Recognize** button (see Figure 10-35)

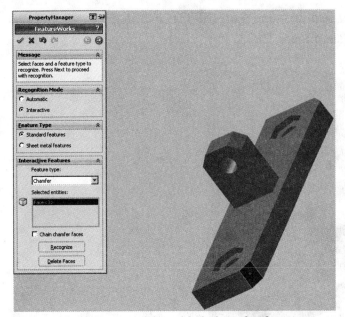

Figure 10-35 Recognition third chamfer feature

9. Click the **face** of the fourth chamfer feature (see Figure 10-36)
10. Click the **Recognize** button (see Figure 10-36)

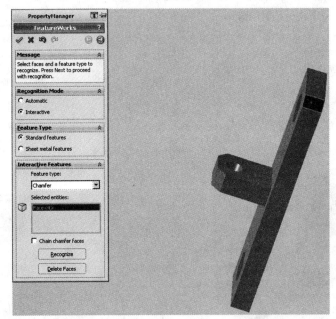

Figure 10-36 Recognition fourth chamfer feature

Recognize Cut Extrude features on the Base and Boss

11. Select **Cut Extrude** from the drop down button of the **Feature type** (see Figure 10-37)
12. Click the **face** of one cut extrude feature (see Figure 10-37)

13. Click the **Recognize** button (see Figure 10-37)

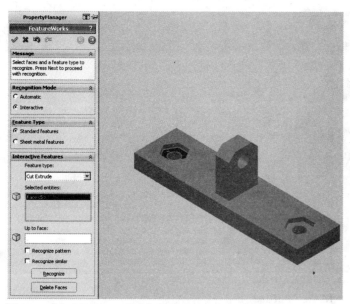

Figure 10-37 Recognition first cut extrude feature

14. Click the **face** of the second cut extrude feature (see Figure 10-38)
15. Click the **Recognize** button (see Figure 10-38)

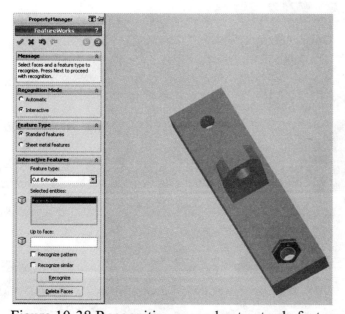

Figure 10-38 Recognition second cut extrude feature

16. Click the **face** of third cut extrude feature (see Figure 10-39)
17. Click the **Recognize** button (see Figure 10-39)

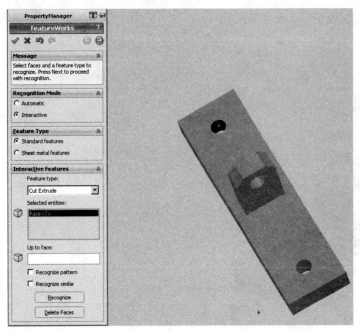

Figure 10-39 Recognition third cut extrude feature

18. Click the **face** of one cut extrude feature (see Figure 10-40)
19. Click the **Recognize** button (see Figure 10-40)

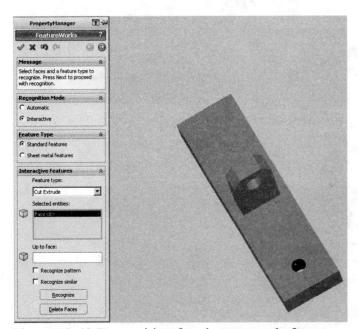

Figure 10-40 Recognition fourth cut extrude feature

20. Click the **face** of fifth cut extrude feature (see Figure 10-41)
21. Click the **Recognize** button (see Figure 10-41)

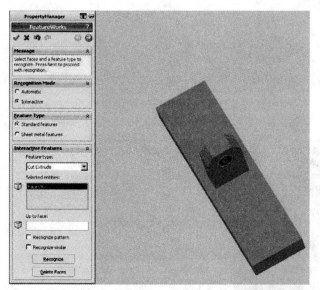

Figure 10-41 Recognition fifth cut extrude feature

Recognize Chamfer features on the Boss
22. Select **Chamfer** from the drop down button of the **Feature type** (see Figure 10-42)
23. Click the **face** of one chamfer feature (see Figure 10-42)
24. Click the **Recognize** button (see Figure 10-42)

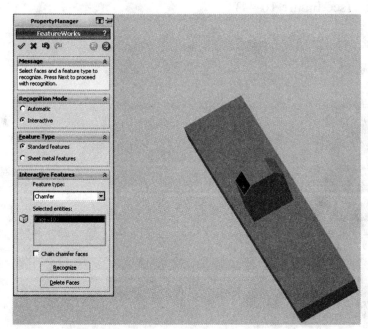

Figure 10-42 Recognition first boss chamfer feature
25. Click the **face** of the second boss chamfer feature (see Figure 10-43)
26. Click the **Recognize** button (see Figure 10-43)

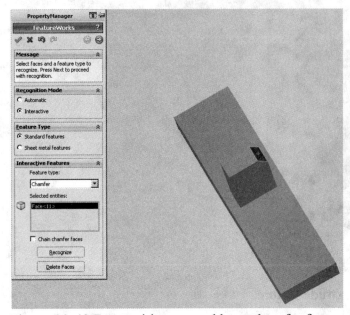

Figure 10-43 Recognition second boss chamfer feature

Recognize Boss Extrude

27. Select **Boss Extrude** from the drop down button of the **Feature type** (see Figure 10-44)
28. Click the **face** of top boss extrude feature (see Figure 10-44)
29. Click the **Recognize** button (see Figure 10-44)

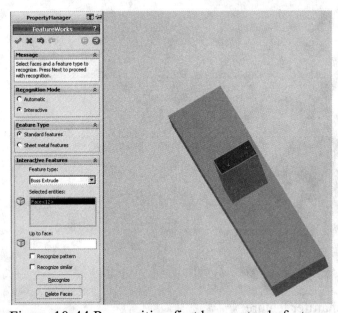

Figure 10-44 Recognition first boss extrude feature

30. Click the **face** of base boss extrude feature (see Figure 10-45)
31. Click the **Recognize** button (see Figure 10-45)

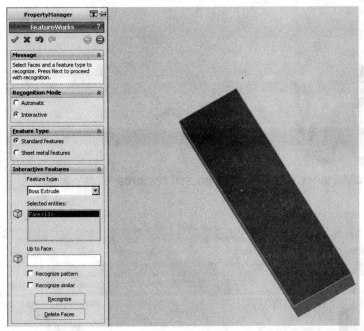

Figure 10-45 Recognition second boss extrude feature

Figure 10-46 shows the recognized features listed in the FeatureWorks PropertyManager. Figure 10-47 shows the recognized features while Figure 10-48 shows the SolidWorks FeatureManager having the part renamed.

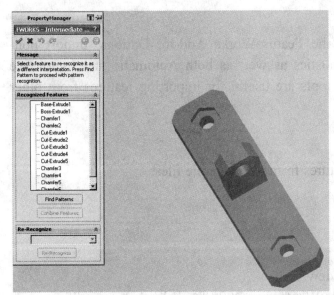

Figure 10-46 Recognized features listed in FeatureWorks PropertyManager

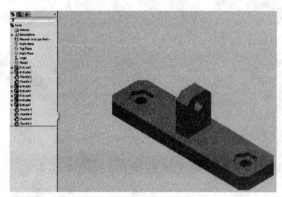

Figure 10-47 SolidWorks FeatureManager showing recognized features

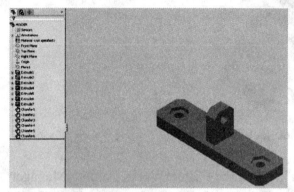

Figure 10-48 SolidWorks FeatureManager showing part renamed

Summary

In this chapter, we have presented the FeatureWorks Add-In, Options, Import non-SolidWorks Geometry, Import Diagnostics as well as both Automatic and Interactive Feature Recognition methods. These tools are useful for importing features from other CAD environments to SolidWorks.

Exercises

Reconstruct the features following features from the available files:

(i) housing

(ii) sheetmetal

References

http://www.npd-solutions.com/reoverview.html

http://files.solidworks.com/Supportfiles/Whats_new/2008/English/whatsnew.pdf

http://help.solidworks.com/2010/English/SolidWorks/sldworks/SW_Sketch/Sketch_Picture.htm?

http://images.google.ca/images?

*www.**solidworks**academic.de/**solidworks**/.../swx_2007_**Featureworks**.pdf*

Chapter 11
Top-Down Design

Objectives:

In this chapter you will learn:

- The concept of *Top-Down Design* approach
- How to use the *Top-Down Design* approach to develop products from within the assembly

The *Top-Down Design approach* is a conceptual approach used to develop products from within the assembly. The concept is applied to the design of a cabinet containing electronic parts as well as to the design of a seal from a lid. Generally, there are two ways in which the Top-Down Design approach could be implemented: designing from layout, or designing from part outline. These two approaches will be illustrated through examples that now follow.

DESIGNING FROM LAYOUT

Layout of the CABINET

Layout of the CABINET involves sketching its 2D profile and dimensioning it. This involves the following steps:

1. Click **New** from the Menu bar.
2. Click the **MY-TEMPLATES** tab.
3. Double-click **ASM-MM-ANSI**.
4. Click **Cancel X** from the Begin Assembly PropertyManager.
5. Save the model **CABINET**
6. Right-click **Front Plane** form the FeatureManager
7. Click **Sketch** from the Context toolbar. The Sketch tool bar is displayed.
8. Sketch a rectangle using the **Corner Rectangle** option starting from the origin and stretching the top-right corner away from the origin (see Figure 11-1).
9. Click **Smart Dimensions** from the Sketch toolbar.
10. Click one of the horizontal edges and enter the value of **300** as the width (see Figure 11-2).
11. Click one of the vertical edges and enter the value of **400** as the length (see Figure 11-2).

Figure 11-1 Profiles of CABINET   Figure 11-2 Dimensions of CABINET

Create Shared Values

Shared Values are linked in a design using Shared Values. The use of Shared Values here is to build design constraints between the layout of the CABINET and the subassemblies of power supply, microcontroller, and cooling unit. Later, we will see how to use Shared Values for configuration management.

12. Right-click the vertical dimension of the CABINET
13. Click **Link Value** to open the **Shared Values** dialog box (see Figure 11-3)
14. In the **Name** option, type Cabinet_Height and click OK
15. Click **OK** on the Dimension dialog box to complete the process.

Repeat the process for the width of the CABINET
Notice the red shapes that appear beside each of the dimensions (see Figure 11-4)

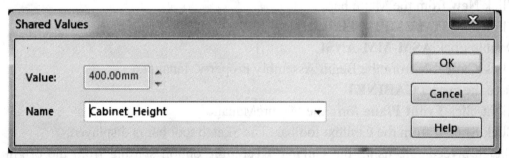

Figure 11-3 Shared Values dialog box

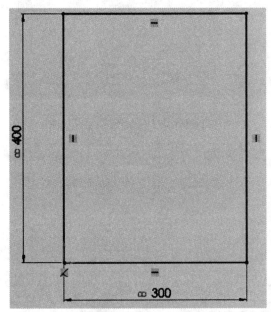

Figure 11-4 Shared Values have red signs attached to them

Sketch the 2D Profile of the Power Supply

16. Click **Sketch** from the Context toolbar. The Sketch tool bar is displayed.
17. Sketch a rectangle using the **Corner Rectangle** option starting from a point towards the top-left, inside the CABINET and stretching the top-right corner away from the starting point (see Figure 11-5).

Dimension the 2D Profile of the Power Supply

18. Click **Smart Dimensions** from the Sketch toolbar.
19. Click one of the horizontal edges and enter the value of **75** as the width (see Figure 11-5).
20. Click one of the vertical edges and enter the value of **150** as the length (see Figure 11-5).

Gaps for the Power Supply Profile

21. Click the **Smart Dimensions** from the Sketch toolbar.
22. Click the top horizontal edges of the power supply profile and the CABINET, and enter the value of **20** as the gap (see Figure 11-5).
23. Click the left (right) vertical edges of the power supply profile and the CABINET, and enter the value of **20** as the gap (see Figure 11-5).

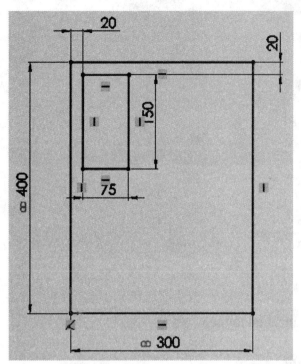

Figure 11-5 Power supply profile, dimensions, and gaps

Sketch the 2D Profile of the Cooling Unit

24. Click **Sketch** from the Context toolbar. The Sketch tool bar is displayed.
25. Sketch a rectangle using the **Corner Rectangle** option starting from a point towards the bottom-left, inside the CABINET and stretching the top-right corner away from the starting point (see Figure 11-6).

Dimension the 2D Profile of the Cooling Unit

26. Click **Smart Dimensions** from the Sketch toolbar.
27. Click one of the horizontal edges and enter the value of **75** as the width (see Figure 11-6).
28. Click one of the vertical edges and enter the value of **100** as the length (see Figure 11-6).

Gaps for the Cooling Unit

29. Click the **Smart Dimensions** from the Sketch toolbar.
30. Click the top horizontal edges of the power supply profile and the CABINET, and enter the value of **20** as the gap (see Figure 11-6).

31. Click the left (right) vertical edges of the power supply profile and the CABINET, and enter the value of **20** as the gap (see Figure 11-6).

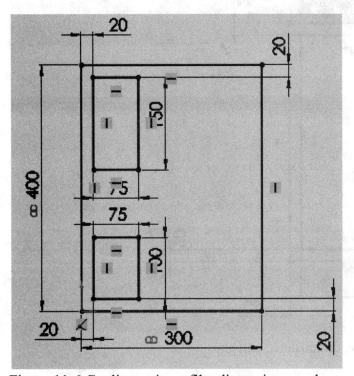

Figure 11-6 Cooling unit profile, dimensions, and gaps

Sketch the 2D Profile of the Microcontroller

32. Click **Sketch** from the Context toolbar. The Sketch tool bar is displayed.
33. Sketch a rectangle using the **Corner Rectangle** option starting from a point towards the bottom-right, inside the CABINET and stretching the top-right corner away from the starting point (see Figure 11-7).

Gaps for the Microcontroller

34. Click the **Smart Dimensions** from the Sketch toolbar.
35. Click the top horizontal edges of the microcontroller profile and the CABINET, and enter the value of **20** as the gap (see Figure 11-7).
36. Click the left (right) vertical edges of the power supply profile and the CABINET, and enter the value of **20** as the gap (see Figure 11-7).
37. Click the right vertical edge of the power supply profile and the left vertical edge of the microcontroller, and enter the value of **30** as the gap (see Figure 11-7).

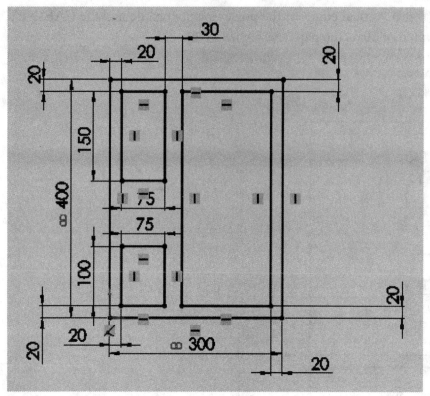

Figure 11-7 Microcontroller profile, dimensions, and gaps

38. Click **Exit Sketch**
39. Rename **Sketch1** to **Design_Layout** (see Figure 11-8: FeatureManager)
40. Click **Save** to save the design layout (see Figure 11-9 for the design layout)

(a) Before renaming

(b) After renaming

Figure 11-8 Renaming Sketch1 to Design_Layout

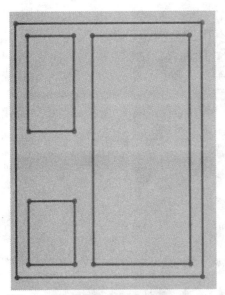

Figure 11-9 Design layout

41. Right-click the **Annotations** folder in the FeatureManager (see Figure 11-10)
42. Click **Show Feature Dimensions** (see Figure 11-10)
43. Right-click any of the gaps of value **20 mm**
44. Click **Link Values**
45. Enter **Gap** as Name in the Shared Values dialog box
46. Click **OK**

Repeat the process for all other 20 mm gap dimensions (or Hold the **Ctrl** key down for the multiple selection process)

Notice the red shapes that appear beside each of the dimensions (see Figure 11-11)

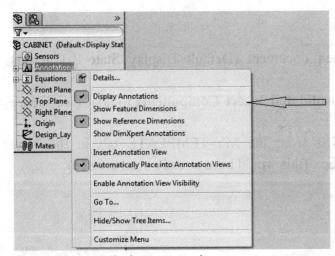

Figure 11-10 Echoing annotations

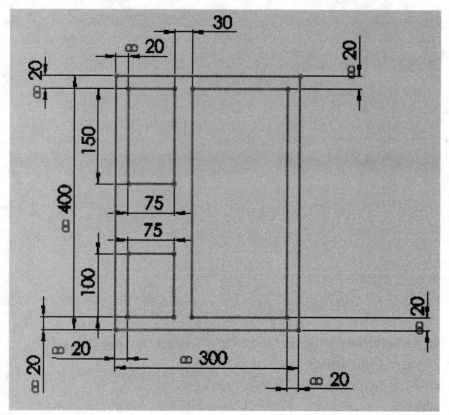

Figure 11-11 Gaps are linked

If any of the gap value is changed, all gaps change accordingly. There is the need to **Rebuild** the graphics window in order to effect the changes made in the new value of gap.

Microcontroller-Insert Component

The CABINET assembly is the open document (Default<Display State-1>) at this juncture.

47. Click **New Part** from the **Consolidated Insert Components** toolbar (see Figure 11-12)
48. Double-click **PART-MM-ANSI** from the MY-TEMPLATE tab in the New SolidWorks Document dialog box (this would have already been created).

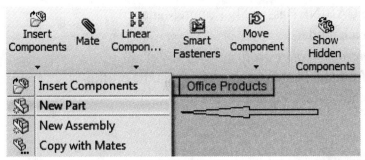

Figure 11-12 Inserting **New Part** from the **Consolidated Insert Components** toolbar

The new part is displayed in the FeatureManager design tree with the new name in the format [Part#^*AssemblyName*]<#>. Let us explain the syntax because it is important to understand this. (1) The square bracket shows that the part is a virtual component.
(2) # is the number of virtual components.
(3) *AssemblyName* is the assembly name.

In the current illustration, the first virtual part is **[Part**1^CABINET]<1>.

The gateway between the assembly and the Component added In-Context is Edit Component feature. In other words, the **Edit Component** is the switch between the assembly and the component edited In-Context (see Figure 11-13).

It is extremely important to note this gateway. For example when **[Part**1^CABINET]<1> is clicked and **Edit Component** is clicked, **[Part**1^CABINET]<1> becomes light blue. This means that we are in the *Component added In-Context* level.

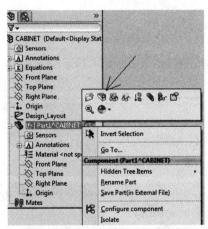

Figure 11-13 Switching to the *Component added In-Context* level

Create the Sketch for the [Part1^CABINET]

49. Click **Front Plane** in the CABINET assembly FeatureManager.
50. Click **Sketch** to be in sketch mode
51. Select the *edges of the microcontroller profile*
52. Click **Convert Entities** from the Sketch toolbar to extract the profile
53. Click **OK** to extract the entities (see Figure 11-14)

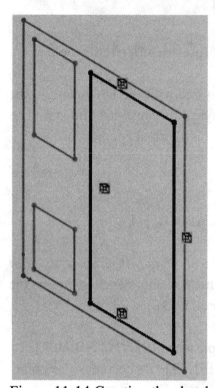

Figure 11-14 Creating the sketch for the microcontroller

Insert an Extrude Base for the [Part1^CABINET]

54. Click **Extrude Boss/Base** from the FeatureManager toolbar. The Extrude PropertyManager is displayed (see Figure 11-15)
55. Enter **15 mm** Depth in Direction1
56. Click **OK** to extrude
57. Rename **Extrude1** to **Base Extrude**.

Notice now that [Part1^CABINET]<1>->, Base Extrude->, and Sketch1-> all have the "->" symbol indicating External References to the CABINET assembly.

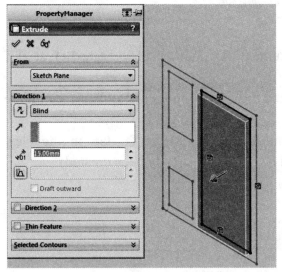

Figure 11-15 Extrude PropertyManager

To save the assembly:
  58. Click **Edit Component** [This returns you to the CABINET assembly]
  59. Click **Save**

To save the [Part1^CABINET]<1>-> to MICROCONTROLLER:
  60. Right-click **[Part1^CABINET]<1>->** (see Figure 11-16 for the part)
  61. Click **Save As**
  62. Click **OK** for "*Resolve Ambiguity*" dialog box
  63. Click **OK** for the "*Virtual Component*" referring to dialog box
  64. Enter in the **File Name** box
  65. **Close** the part.
  66. Return to the CABINET assembly.

Figure 11-16 Save the MICROCONTROLLER using **Save As** option

Cooling Unit-Insert Component

The CABINET assembly is the open document (Default<Display State-1>) at this juncture.

67. Click **New Part** from the **Consolidated Insert Components** toolbar (see Figure 11-17)
68. Double-click **PART-MM-ANSI** from the MY-TEMPLATE tab in the New SolidWorks Document dialog box (this would have already been created).

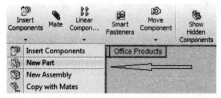

Figure 11-17 Inserting **New Part** from the **Consolidated Insert Components** toolbar

Create the Sketch for the [Part1^CABINET]

69. Click **Front Plane** in the CABINET assembly FeatureManager.
70. Click **Sketch** to be in sketch mode
71. Select the *edges of the cooling unit*
72. Click **Convert Entities** from the Sketch toolbar to extract the profile
73. Click **OK** to extract the entities (see Figure 11-18)

Insert an Extrude Base for the [Part1^CABINET]

74. Click **Extrude Boss/Base** from the FeatureManager toolbar. The Extrude PropertyManager is displayed (see Figure 11-18)
75. Enter **10 mm** Depth in Direction1
76. Click **OK** to extrude
77. Rename **Extrude1** to **Base Extrude**.

Notice now that [Part1^CABINET]<1>->, Base Extrude->, and Sketch1-> all have the "->" symbol indicating External References to the CABINET assembly.

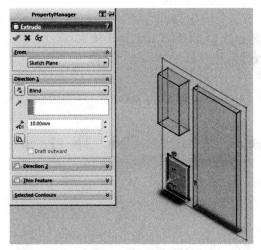

Figure 11-18 Extrude PropertyManager for cooling unit

To save the assembly:

78. Click **Edit Component** [This returns you to the CABINET assembly]

79. Click **Save**

Power Supply-Insert Component

The CABINET assembly is the open document (Default<Display State-1>) at this juncture.

80. Click **New Part** from the **Consolidated Insert Components** toolbar (see Figure 11-19)

81. Double-click **PART-MM-ANSI** from the MY-TEMPLATE tab in the New SolidWorks Document dialog box (this would have already been created).

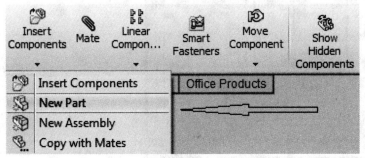

Figure 11-19 Inserting **New Part** from the **Consolidated Insert Components** toolbar

Create the Sketch for the [Part1^CABINET]

82. Click **Front Plane** in the CABINET assembly FeatureManager.

83. Click **Sketch** to be in sketch mode

84. Select the *edges of the power supply*
85. Click **Convert Entities** from the Sketch toolbar to extract the profile
86. Click **OK** to extract the entities (see Figure 11-20)

Insert an Extrude Base for the [Part1^CABINET]

87. Click **Extrude Boss/Base** from the FeatureManager toolbar. The Extrude PropertyManager is displayed (see Figure 11-20)
88. Enter **35 mm** Depth in Direction1
89. Click **OK** to extrude
90. Rename **Extrude1** to **Base Extrude**.

Notice now that [Part1^CABINET]<1>->, Base Extrude->, and Sketch1-> all have the "->" symbol indicating External References to the CABINET assembly.

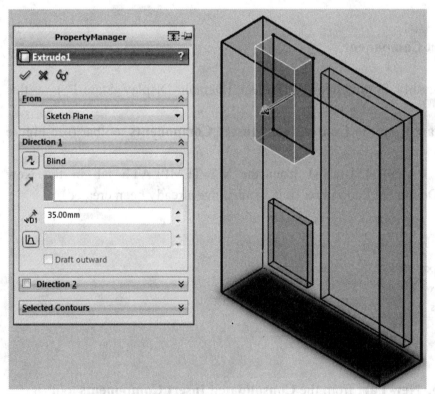

Figure 11-20 Extrude PropertyManager for power supply

To save the assembly:
91. Click **Edit Component** [This returns you to the CABINET assembly]
92. Click **Save**

Housing-Insert Component

The CABINET assembly is the open document (Default<Display State-1>) at this juncture.

93. Click **New Part** from the **Consolidated Insert Components** toolbar (see Figure 11-21)

94. Double-click **PART-MM-ANSI** from the MY-TEMPLATE tab in the New SolidWorks Document dialog box (this would have already been created).

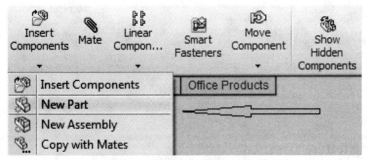

Figure 11-21 Inserting **New Part** from the **Consolidated Insert Components** toolbar

Create the Sketch for the [Part1^CABINET]

95. Click **Front Plane** in the CABINET assembly FeatureManager.
96. Click **Sketch** to be in sketch mode
97. Select the *edges of the housing*
98. Click **Convert Entities** from the Sketch toolbar to extract the profile
99. Click **OK** to extract the entities (see Figure 11-22)

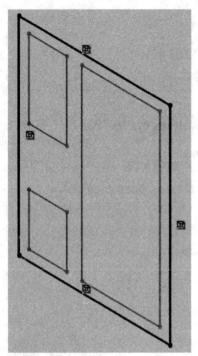

Figure 11-22 Edges of the housing feature extracted

Insert an Extrude Base for the [Part1^CABINET]

100. Click **Extrude Boss/Base** from the FeatureManager toolbar. The Extrude PropertyManager is displayed (see Figure 11-23)
101. Enter **120 mm** Depth in Direction1
102. Click **OK** to extrude
103. Rename **Extrude1** to **Base Extrude**.

Notice now that [Part1^CABINET]<1>->, Base Extrude->, and Sketch1-> all have the "->" symbol indicating External References to the CABINET assembly.

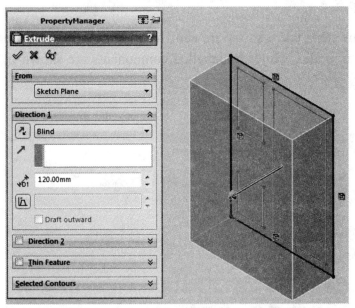

Figure 11-23 Extrude PropertyManager for housing

Shelling Operation for the Housing Feature

104.　　Click **Feature > Shell in the Feature CommandManager**

105.　　Click *top face of the housing feature* (**Face<1>@HOUSING-1**) [see Figure 11- 24]

106.　　Supply the **Thickness** of **1.00 mm**

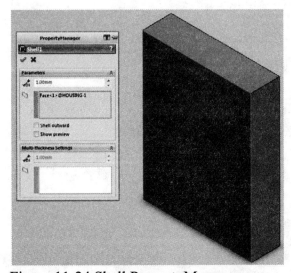

Figure 11-24 Shell PropertyManager

To save the assembly:

1. Click **Edit Component** [This returns you to the CABINET assembly]
2. Click **Save**

The FeatureManager details for the steps taken so far are shown in Figure 11-25. Figure 11-26 Completed top-down design model, while the labelled components are shown in Figure 11-27.

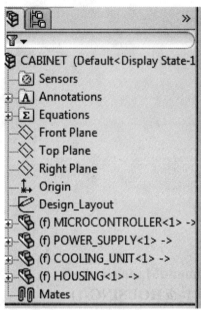

Figure 11-25 FeatureManager details for the steps taken so far

Figure 11-26 Completed top-down design model

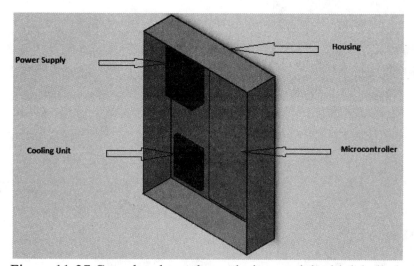

Figure 11-27 Completed top-down design model with labelled components

DESIGNING FROM PART OUTLINE

Part Model

In the designing from part outline approach, a part exists from which the outline is extracted to create another part in an assembly. Let us commence with a lid (see Figure 11-28) and then create a seal.

Figure 11-28 Lid model

Modelling In-Context

1. Click **New Assembly** document (see Figure 11-29)
2. Click *Lid* as the **Open documents** in the **Part/Assembly to Insert** rollout (see Figure 11-29)
3. Click **OK** to insert the *Lid*

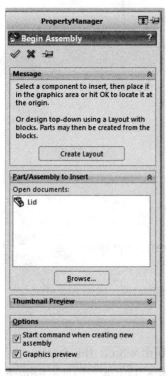

Figure 11-29 New Assembly document with the lid opened

The **Assem1**assembly is the open document (Default<Display State-1>) at this juncture.

4. Click **New Part** from the **Consolidated Insert Components** toolbar (see Figure 11-30)

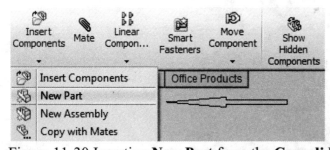

Figure 11-30 Inserting **New Part** from the **Consolidated Insert Components** toolbar

The new part is displayed in the FeatureManager design tree with the new name in the format [Part#^*AssemblyName*]<#>. Let us explain the syntax because it is important to understand this. (1) The square bracket shows that the part is a virtual component.

(2) # is the number of virtual components.

(3) *AssemblyName* is the assembly name.

In the current illustration, the first virtual part is **[Part**1^Assem1**]**<1>-->.

The gateway between the assembly and the Component added In-Context is Edit Component feature. In other words, the **Edit Component** is the switch between the assembly and the component edited In-Context (see Figure 11-31).

It is extremely important to note this gateway. For example when **[Part**1^Assem1]<1>--> is clicked and **Edit Component** is clicked, **[Part**1^Assem1]<1>--> becomes light blue. This means that we are in the *Component added In-Context* level.

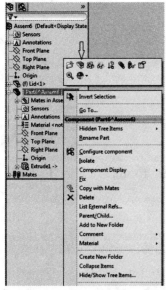

Figure 11-31 Switching to the *Component added In-Context* level

Create the Sketch for the [Part1^Assem1]

5. Click **Top Plane** in the Assem1 assembly FeatureManager.
6. Click **Sketch** to be in sketch mode
7. Select the *edges of the Lid profile*
8. Click **Convert Entities** from the Sketch toolbar to extract the profile
9. Click **OK** to extract the entities (see Figure 11-32)

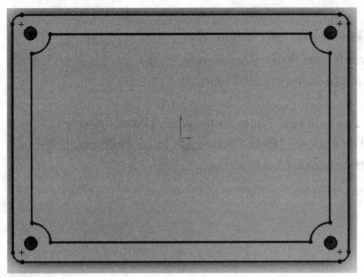

Figure 11-32 In-context sketch for designing the seal

Insert an Extrude Base for the [Part1^Assem1]

10. Click **Extrude Boss/Base** from the FeatureManager toolbar. The Extrude PropertyManager is displayed (see Figure 11-33)
11. Enter **0.1-in** Depth in Direction1
12. Click **OK** to extrude
13. Rename **Extrude1** to **Base Extrude**.

Notice now that [Part1^Assem1]<1>-->, Base Extrude->, and Sketch1-> all have the "-->" symbol indicating External References to the Lid assembly.

Figure 11-33 Extrude PropertyManager

Notice that there are now two parts, one of them is Lid<1>, the other is [Part1^Assem1]<1>-->.

Colour Coding in Design Levels

It is important to understand this nomenclature.

   a) When [Part1^Assem1]<1>--> and the sub-nodes are in **blue** colour, we are in Part level.
   b) When [Part1^Assem1]<1>--> and the sub-nodes are in **dark** colour, we are in Assembly level (see Figure 11-34).

Right-click **[Part1^Assem1]<1>-->** and select **Edit** to switch from **assembly** to **part** level.
Click **Edit Component** in the **CommandManager** to switch from **part** to **assembly** level.

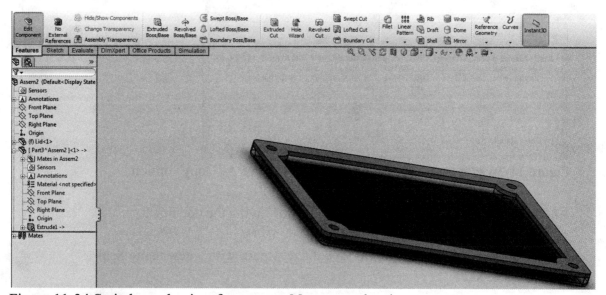

Figure 11-34 Switch mechanism from **assembly** to **part** level

Saving the New Part

Using the Top-Down Design approach, we have designed a seal from the profile of the lid. The new part now has to be saved.

   14. Right-click **[Part1^Assem1]<1>-->** and select **Edit** to switch from **assembly** to **part** level.
   15. Click **File > Save As**

The Resolve Ambiguity window shown in Figure 11-35 automatically appears highlighting the part and awaiting the user to confirm by clicking the OK button.

16. Click **OK**

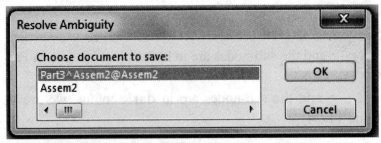

Figure 11-35 Resolve Ambiguity window

Another window appears (see Figure 11-36) displaying the message suggesting the usage of "*Save As Copy*" option.

17. Click **OK**

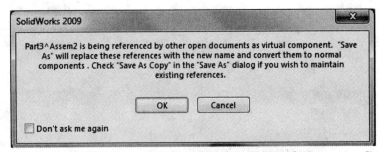

Figure 11-36 Message suggesting the usage of "Save As Copy" option

Another window appears (see Figure 11-37) for saving the document.

18. Browse for the directory to save the new part, with a new name **Seal**
19. Click **Save**

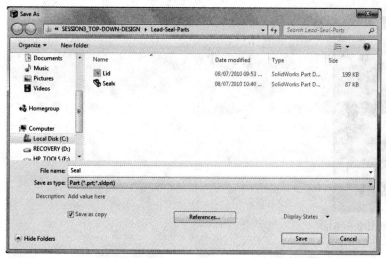

Figure 11-37 Window for saving new part created and the "Save As Copy" option

The **AssemblyManager** during and after saving the new part are shown in Figure 11-38.

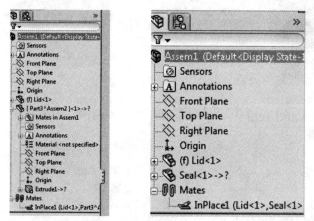

Figure 11-38 AssemblyManager during and after saving the new part created

Further modification of the seal is shown in Figure 11-39 and the assembly of the lid and seal is shown in Figure 11-40. The materials are assigned (see Figure 11-40) and the mass properties are computed (see Figure 11-41).

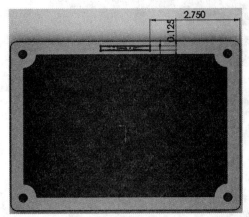

Figure 11-39 Modifications of the seal

Figure 11-40 Material assignment to the lid and seal

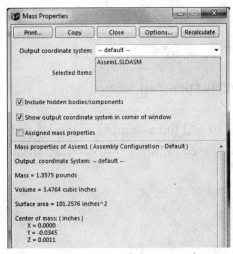

Figure 11-41 Material properties computed

Mold Design Using Top-Down Approach

In this chapter, a new method is introduced for designing molds based on the top-down paradigm. This is the author's contribution to mold design using SolidWorks for parts with a specific set of features.

Create Lower Lid from Lid already available [Figure 11-42— Figure 11-44]
1. Open **Lid <file name>** as active part
2. Start **New SolidWorks Assembly** document
3. Open **Lid** in *Assembly* environment
4. Click **OK**
5. Save **Assembly** with a name
6. **Right-click (+)Lid<1> (Default…)**
7. Select **Edit Part** [The tree for *Lid* turns blue; because we are in part mode]
8. Check **Save As**
9. Check **OK** for **Resolve Ambiguity** message
10. Check **OK** for **Reference as Virtual Part**
11. Save as **lidLower<1> (Default…)**

Creating Mold for lidLower [Figure 11-45—Figure 11-52]
12. Define a Plane using three points on the part (0.118 from the *flat face* and 0.132 from the *indented face*)
13. Be in **Sketch** mode
14. Sketch a *Rectangle* using **Center Rectangle** tool to enclose **lidLower**
15. **Dimension** the box as **7.5** by **6.5** (inches)
16. **Extrude** the box inward toward the user through **0.15**
17. Uncheck '**Merge result**' to create two **Solid Bodies** (*Fillet 1 and Boss-Extrude1*)
18. Click **Insert>Features>Combine** [The Combine1 PropertyManager appears]
19. Select **Subtract**
20. Expand the **SolidBodies** and select **Boss-Extrude1** as **Main Body** from the **SolidBodies(2)**
21. Select **Fillet1** as **Bodies to Combine** from the **SolidBodies(2)**
22. Suppress **lidLower**
23. Check **Edit Component** to be in Assembly mode

Create Upper Lid from Lid already available [Figure 11-53]
24. Click **Insert Component**
25. Open **Lid** in *Assembly* environment
26. Click **OK**
27. Save **Assembly** with a name

28. **Right-click (+)Lid<2> (Default...)**
29. Select **Edit Part**
30. Check **Save As**
31. Check **OK** for **Resolve Ambiguity** message
32. Check **OK** for **Reference as Virtual Part**
33. Save as **lidUpper<1> (Default...)**

Create Mold for lidUpper [Figure 11-54— Figure 11-57]

34. Define a Plane using three points on the part (0.118 from the *flat face* and 0.132 from the *indented face*)
35. Be in **Sketch** mode
36. Sketch a *Rectangle* using **Center Rectangle** tool to enclose **lidUpper**
37. **Dimension** the box as **7.5** by **6.5** (inches)
38. **Extrude** the box outward away from the user through **0.20**
39. Uncheck '**Merge result**' to create two **Solid Bodies** (*Fillet 1 and Boss-Extrude1*)
40. Click **Insert>Features>Combine** [The Combine1 PropertyManager appears]
41. Select **Subtract**
42. Expand the **SolidBodies** and select **Boss-Extrude1** as **Main Body** from the **SolidBodies(2)**
43. Select **Fillet1** as **Bodies to Combine** from the **SolidBodies(2)**
44. Check **Edit Component** to be in Assembly mode

Figure 11-58 shows the complete upper and lower molds.

Figure 11-42 Begin Assembly   Figure 11-43 Open lid as part

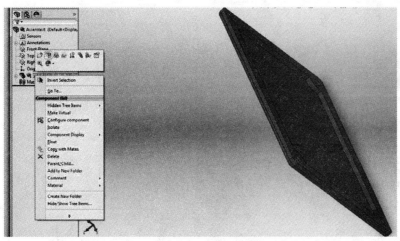

Figure 11-44 Edit Part mode

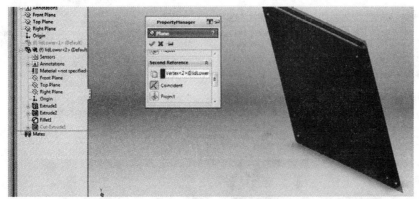

Figure 11-45 Create a Plane using 3 vertices, 0.118 from one face and 0.132 from the other

Figure 11-46 Create parting plane 7.5 x 6.5

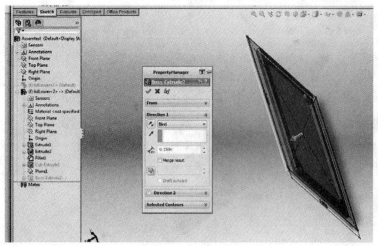

Figure 11-47 Extrude toward the user's view

Figure 11-48 Access Boolean operations tool using Insert>Features>Combine

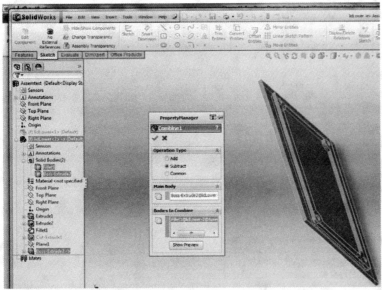

Figure 11-49 Subtract Fillet1 from Boss-Extrude1, using SolidBodies in Boolean operation

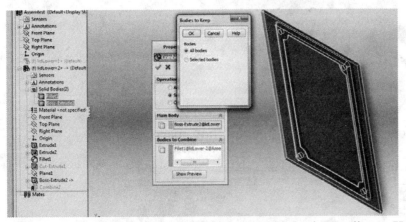

Figure 11-50 Accept All Bodies if prompted on the Bodies to Keep

Figure 11-51 Lower mold (lidLower)

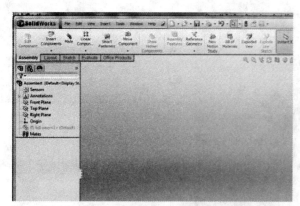

Figure 11-52 Lower mold suppressed

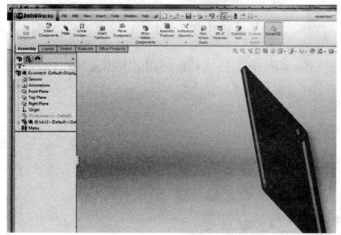

Figure 11-53 Original lid opened and named Upper lid (lidUpper)

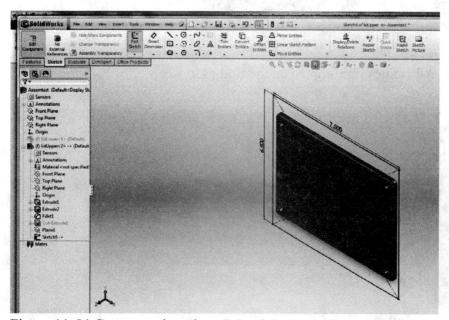

Figure 11-54 Create parting plane 7.5 x 6.5

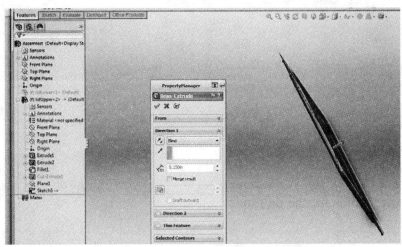

Figure 11-55 Extrude away from the user's view

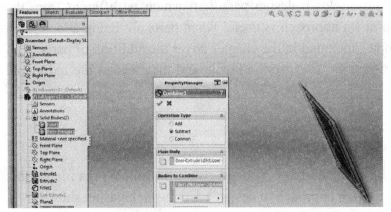

Figure 11-56 Subtract Fillet1 from Boss-Extrude1, using SolidBodies in Boolean operation

Figure 11-57 Upper mold (lidUpper)

Figure 11-58 Upper and lower molds for the lid model

Summary

This chapter has discussed the top-down design paradigm which is different from the bottom-up approach. The top-down approach is useful when parts are being added to an existing assembly. The examples included in the chapter cover the addition of parts to an existing assembly, and also where we start from a layout and then design the individual components in turn.

Exercises

1. Figure P1 shows the model of a ribbed-base. You are given the SolidWorks file for this model. Use the *Top-Down Design* approach to design a 1 mm-thick gasket shown.

Figure P1

2. Figure P2 shows the model of a connecting rod bushing. You are given the model SolidWorks file. Use the *Top-Down Design* approach to design 1 mm-thick gaskets shown.

Figure P2

Chapter 12
Surface Modeling

Objectives:

In this chapter you will learn:

- How to create **freeform** surfaces
- How to use **control polygons** for freeform surface design
- How to use **control** freeform surfaces using **control polygons**
- How to create **extrude surfaces**
- How to create **boundary surfaces**
- How to create **lofted surfaces**
- How to create **revolved surfaces**

GENERALIZED METHODOLOGY FOR FREEFORM SURFACE DESIGN

In this section, the author presents a generalized methodology for **Freeform Surface Design**. In SolidWorks, there are at least two ways of freeform design: (i) extracting an existing surface from a 3D part and creating a Freeform Surface; (ii) creating a freeform surface from scratch. The second method is not popularly used because users of this method should be fairly conversant with the knowledge of how standard Surface Modeling Methods work. The well known methods are based on Coons, Bezier, and NURBS (Non-Uniform Rational B-Spline); the treatment of these is outside the scope of this course. SolidWorks freeform surface is based on NURBS.

In this section, the concept of **Control Polygon** is presented from which **Freeform Surface Design** is carried out. **Control Polygon** is the key for a flexible and robust **Freeform Surface Design** methodology.

CONTROL POLYGON

1. Click **Insert > 3D Sketch**
2. Click **Front Plane**
3. Sketch **3DSketch1** that defines a set of 4 (or more) **control points** of interest as shown in Figure 12-1
4. Create 4 (or more) other Planes resulting in Plane1, Plane2, Plane3, and Plane4 (see Figure 12-2)
5. **Exit 3D Sketch**
6. Select **Plane1, Right-click** and **Click 3D Sketch On Plane**
7. Choose **Normal To,** to make the plane normal

8. Sketch lines collinear to the ones on Front Plane (choosing Normal To is helpful)
9. Select **Plane2**, **Right-click** and **Click 3D Sketch On Plane** [Repeat procedure]
10. Select **Plane3**, **Right-click** and **Click 3D Sketch On Plane** [Repeat procedure]
11. Select **Plane4**, **Right-click** and **Click 3D Sketch On Plane** [Repeat procedure]

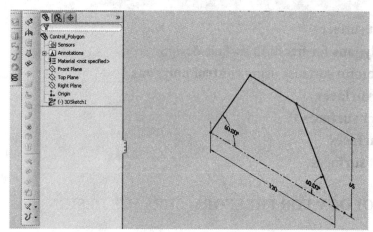

Figure 12-1 Control points on first plane (Front Plane)

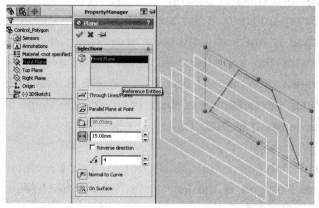

(a) Plane1

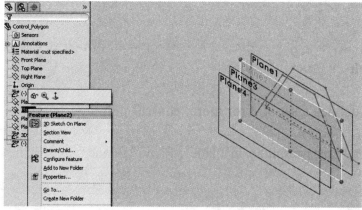

(b) Front Plane, Plane1,..., Plane4

Figure 12-2 Planes defining control polygon

At this point, our control vertices are ready as shown in Figure 12-3. There are 20 vertices, four on each plane; there are five planes. Notice that there are 5 **3DSketches**. This means that we can control each control independently. This is important in **Surface Design**. For example, **3DSketch1** can be changed independent of **3DSketch2**; **3DSketch2** can be changed independent of **3DSketch2**; **3DSketch3** can be changed independent of **3DSketch4**, etc.

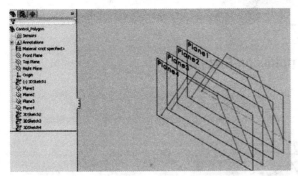

Figure 12-3 Simple **Control Polygon**

LOFTING B-SPLINES USING A CONTROL POLYGON

From the control vertices, we can also create B-Splines that pass through these vertices as shown in Figure 12-4.
1. Click **3DSketch1**
2. Click **Spline,** Click the vertices on **3DSketch1**, Click **OK,** and **Exit 3DSketch**
3. Click **3DSketch2**
4. Click **Spline,** Click the vertices on **3DSketch2**, Click **OK,** and **Exit 3DSketch**
5. Click **3DSketch3**
6. Click **Spline,** Click the vertices on **3DSketch3**, Click **OK,** and **Exit 3DSketch**
7. Click **3DSketch4**
8. Click **Spline,** Click the vertices on **3DSketch4**, Click **OK,** and **Exit 3DSketch**

The reason we exit **3DSketch** each time is because we are switching a **different Plane.** This is a catch! The lofted B-splines using control polygon are shown in Figure 12-5.

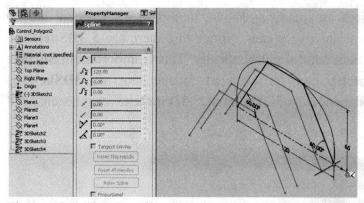

Figure 12-4 First B-spline based on control points on first plane

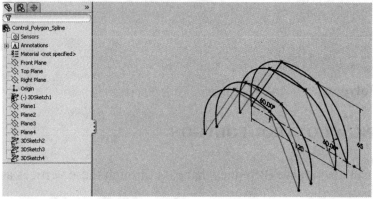

(a) Dimensions shown

(b) Exit Sketch

Figure 12-5 B-Spline using **Control Polygon**

FREEFORM SURFACE DESIGN

Now, let us design surfaces based on the **Control Polygon** that we have created. What it now seems, is that we have created **Lofting** of **B-Splines** based on the **Control Polygon** realized. We will use the **Boundary Surface** option with the **Control Polygon**. If we design from scratch, this is the only option that is active.

1. Click **Insert > Surface > Boundary Surface**
2. Click **3DSketch_Spline1** in the **Direction1** rollout (see Figure 12-6)
3. Click **3DSketch_Spline2**
4. Click **3DSketch_Spline3**
5. Click **3DSketch_Spline4**
6. Click **3DSketch_Spline5** (see Figure 12-6 for the preview of the surface)
7. Click **OK** (Figure 12-6 for surface realized)

We have now created our first freeform surface from scratch as shown in Figure 12-7! Notice that a new folder, Surface Bodies(1) is now in existence, and the **FeatureManager** now has a surface definition, Boundary-Surface1 which as well contains all the **3DSketch_Spline1,..., 3DSketch_Spline5**.

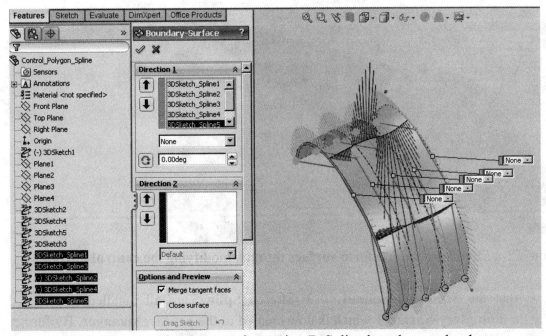

Figure 12-6 Pre-view of freeform surface using B-Spline based control polygon

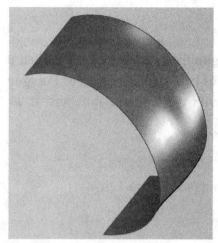

Figure 12-7 Freeform surface using B-Spline based control polygon

EFFECT OF MODIFYING CONTROL POLYGON ON FREEFORM SURFACE

If we can modify the **control polygon** and see the effect of the modification on the freeform surface, that will offer us a flexible way of shape design. See in Figure 12-6, the effect of modifying the **control polygon** Figure 12-8! This modification is done through **3DSketch1, not through 3DSketch_Spline1**.

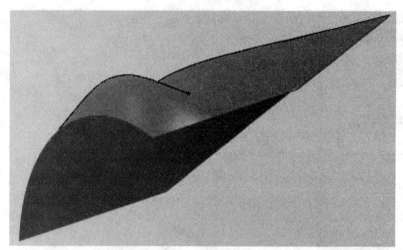

Figure 12-8 Modifying the **freeform surface** through modifying the **control polygon**

Notice that the **3DSketch_Spline1**,..., **3DSketch_Spline5**.are all bundled and placed under the **Boundary-Surface1** which is now created in the **FeatureManager**. By further modifying the control vertices as shown in Figure 12-9, we can then have a modified shape (see Figure 12-10).

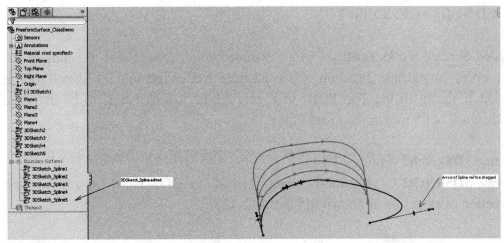

Figure 12-9 Modified control vertices

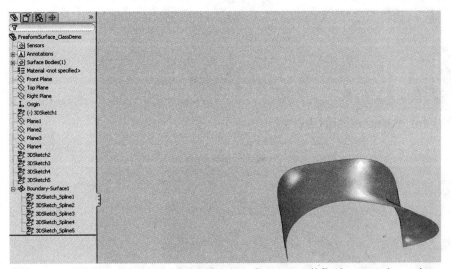

Figure 12-10 Modified shape resulting from modified control vertices

Notice that when the surface model is complete, **Surface Bodies(1)** now shows up in the **FeatureManager** at the top, while **Boundary-Surface(1)** shows up at the bottom. This now shows that we have Surface Bodies. The number in parenthesis shows the number of Surface Bodies.

In this chapter, we have presented a generalized methodology for freeform surface design. We have also shown that by modifying the Splines obtained using the control vertices by dragging the handle vertices on the Spline vertices, it is possible to obtain significantly different freeform surface. This generalized approach to freeform design is heavily used in practical applications in the automotive, ship, and aircraft industries for designing car bodies, ship hulls, aero plane fuselages, etc.

EXTRUDED SURFACE: TYPE I

The Extruded Surface works exactly like an extruded solid, except that the ends of the surface are open. An extrude direction is needed here. Let us use the 3D Sketch tool to define a sketch shown in the Top Plane in Figure 12-11, which needs to be extruded through a distance of 65 mm in the Front Plane.

1. Create **3DSketch1** (Figure 12-11)
2. Create **3DSketch2**   (a straight line vertical to 3DSketch1 specifying the direction of extrusion as shown in Figure 12-12)

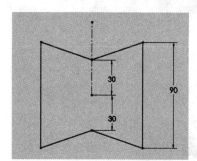

Figure 12-11 Sketch1 for extruding surface

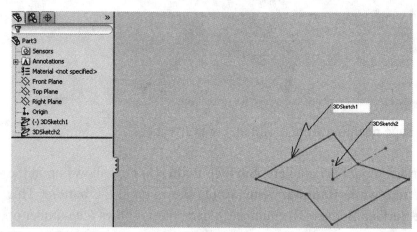

Figure 12-12 Vertical line: direction for extrusion

8. Choose **3DSketch1** in the **FeatureManager**
9. Click **Insert > Surface > Extrude**
10. From the **Selected Contours** rollout, highlight the geometry of **3DSketch1** in the Graphics Window (see Figure 12-13)
11. From the **Direction 1** rollout, click **3DSketch2** [A **Preview** pops up]   (see Figure 12-13)
12. Give the value of the extrusion in **Direction1** in the **Distance** spinner as 65 mm

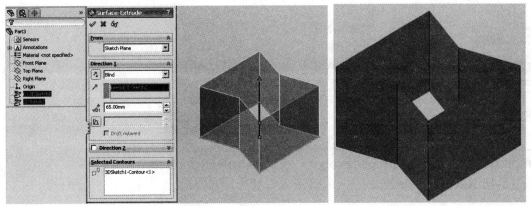

(a) The preview of the extruded surface   (b) The extruded surface

Figure 12-13 Extruded surface

REVOLVED SURFACE: TYPE I

The **Revolved Surface** works exactly like a revolved solid, except that the ends of the surface are open. A revolve direction is also needed as in solid. Let us use the 2D Sketch tool to define a sketch shown in Figure 12-14 in the Front Plane, which needs to be revolved about a vertical construction line or axis. Fillet radius is 1mm as shown.

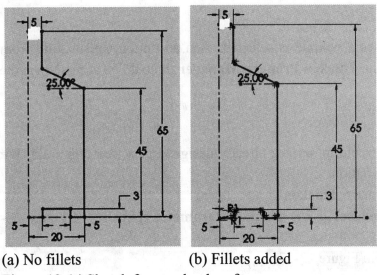

(a) No fillets   (b) Fillets added

Figure 12-14 Sketch for revolved surface

1. Click **Insert > Surface > Revolve**
2. Select the contour of **Sketch1 (Sketch1-Contour<1>)** from the Graphics Window
3. Select the direction, **Line1** about which to revolve the contour (see Figure 12-15)

4. Click **OK**

(a) PropertyManager for surface-revolve   (b) Revolved surface
Figure 12-15 Revolved surface

KNITTING MULTIPLE SURFACES

When we design different surfaces, they become knitting multiple **Surfaces Bodies**, just like we have **Solid Bodies** which are Multiple Bodies. To *sew together* Surfaces Bodies, **Knit Surface** is used just like a tailor sews pieces of clothes together.

If the knit operation results in a watertight volume, the Fill Surface option turns the volume into a solid.

THICKEN FEATURE

If a surface body that encloses a volume is selected, then an option Create solid from enclosed volume pops us on the **Thicken PropertyManager**. It could be accessed via the route of:
Insert > Boss/Base > Thicken

Let us convert the modified freeform surface already designed to a freeform solid. We will use the **Thicken Feature** option.
1. Click **Insert > Boss/Base > Thicken**
2. Choose **Boundary-Surface1** in the **Thicken Parameter** spinner (see Figure 12-16)
The converted solid is shown in Figure 12-17.

Figure 12-16 Process of converting the surface model into a solid model using **Thicken Feature**

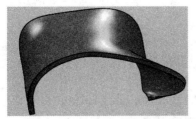

Figure 12-17 Solid model realised using **Thicken Feature**

Once we have converted the surface model into a solid model using **Thicken Feature**, notice that two things happen:
  (1) The **Surface Bodies (1)** previously at the top of the **FeatureManager** as well as the **Boundary-Surface (1)** at the bottom now disappear.
  (2) The thicken1 feature is added to the bottom of the **FeatureManager**.
  (3) These observations are important: we now only have solids, no more reference to surface bodies.

FILL SURFACE

The **Fill Surface** has an option to merge the fill with a solid or to knit it into a surface body.

Create a Hole
  1. Create **Plane5**, 60 mm from the Top Plane
  2. Create **3DSketch6**, a circular profile 15 mm diameter
  3. Extrude **3DSketch6 Up To** the top face of the solid, **Thicken1** in the Direction of **3DSketch7** resulting in a hole (see Figure 12-18)

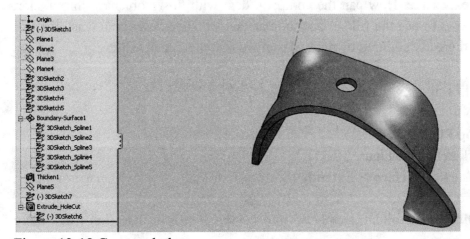

Figure 12-18 Create a hole

Create a Hole

Let us fill this hole using **Fill Surface** option.

Click **Insert > Surface > Fill Surface** (see Figure 12-19 for preview)

Click the *cut-out* in the Graphics Window for the **Patch Boundary** rollout; this is the **Extrude_HoleCut**. **Edge<1>Contact-50** appears in the Patch Boundary rollout and the cut is filled at the top (see Figure 12-20). It is amazing. Notice that the solid is not filled; the top surface of the solid is filled. This is the similar principle used in "Shut-off Surfaces" used in Mold design.

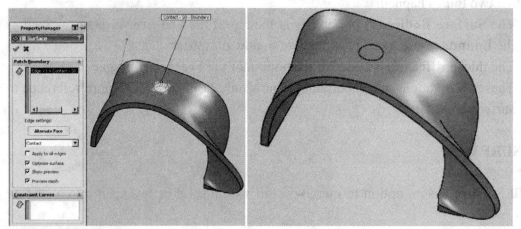

Figure 12-19 Preview for Fill Surface   Figure 12-20 Repaired surface

Fill Surface tool is of primary importance in the manufacturing industry. A company receives an order from another contracting company requesting a job description for filling a hole on the rim of an automobile wheel which is for mass production. A wrong hole was initially drilled. This hole is to be filled and drilled elsewhere on the rim. Redesigning is expensive. How can the company deal with this problem within a short time? The answer is to use the fill surface toolbar that we have described. It is effective and efficient, and greatly admired by many designers for what it can achieve.

Extruded Surface

1. Click **Top Plane**
2. Create **Sketch1** (see Figure 12-21)
3. Click **Insert > Surface > Extrude** (Surface-Extrude1 PropertyManager appears; see Figure 12-22)
4. In the **Direction1** rollout, supply **35** mm for the **Depth** of extrusion (see Figure 12-22)
5. Click **OK** (Surface model appears; see Figure 12-23)

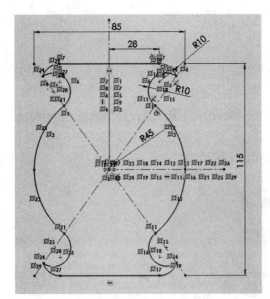

Figure 12-21 Sketch1

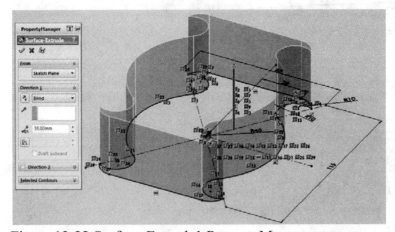

Figure 12-22 Surface-Extrude1 PropertyManager

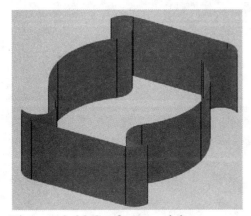

Figure 12-23 Surface model

Revolved Surface

1. Click **Front Plane**
2. Create **Sketch1** (see Figure 12-24)
3. Click **Insert > Surface > Revolve** (Surface-Revolve1 PropertyManager appears; see Figure 12-25)
4. Click **OK** (Surface model appears; see Figure 12-26)

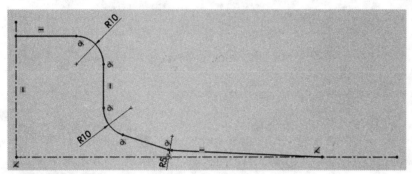

Figure 12-24 Sketch1

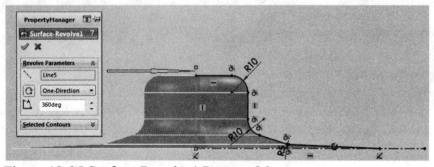

Figure 12-25 Surface-Revolve1 PropertyManager

Figure 12-26 Surface model

Swept Surface

Rectangular Section

1. Click **Front Plane**
2. Create a 3D-sketch **3DSketch1** (see Figure 12-27)
3. Exit Sketch
4. Click end of **3DSketch1** (**Point9@3DSketch1**)
5. Click **Features > Plane**
6. In the Selections rollout click **Normal to Curve** (the **Plane PropertyManager** appears as in Figure 12-28)
7. Click the arc close to the end point already selected [**Arc3@3DSketch1** is added automatically; see Figure 12-28]
8. Exit Sketch
9. Click **Insert > Surface > Sweep** (Figure 12-29)
10. The Surface-Sweep PropertyManager appears; see Figure 12-30
11. Click **OK** (Surface model appears; see Figure 12-31)

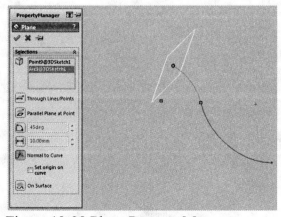

Figure 12-27 Sketch1

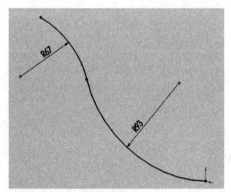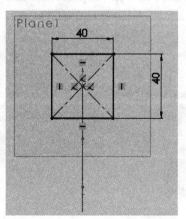

Figure 12-28 Plane PropertyManager

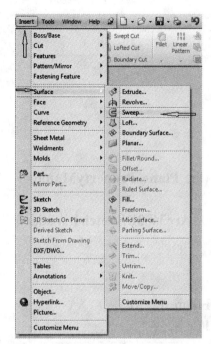

Figure 12-29 Surface sweep option

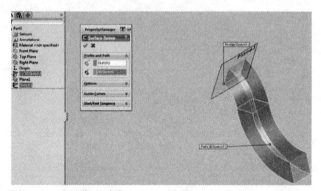

Figure 12-30 Surface sweep PropertyManager

Figure 12-31 Surface model

Circular Section

1. Click **Front Plane**
2. Create a 3D-sketch **3DSketch1** (see Figure 12-32)
3. Exit Sketch
4. Click end of **3DSketch1** (**Point9@3DSketch1**)
5. Click **Features > Plane**
6. In the Selections rollout click **Normal to Curve** (the **Plane PropertyManager** appears as in Figure 12-33)
7. Click the arc close to the end point already selected [**Arc3@3DSketch1** is added automatically; see Figure 12-33]
8. Exit Sketch
9. Click **Insert > Surface > Sweep** (Figure 12-34)
10. The Surface-Sweep PropertyManager appears; see Figure 12-35
11. Click **OK** (Surface model appears; see Figure 12-36)

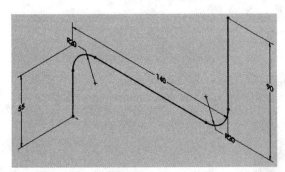

Figure 12-32 Sketch1

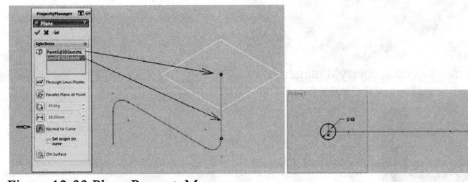

Figure 12-33 Plane PropertyManager

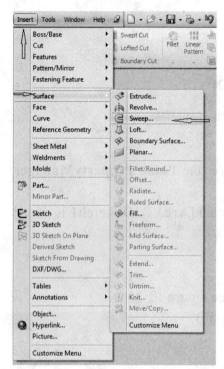

Figure 12-34 Surface sweep option

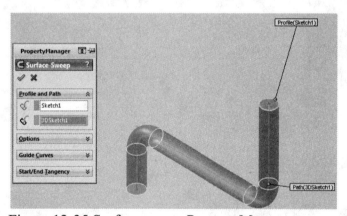

Figure 12-35 Surface sweep PropertyManager

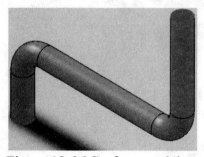

Figure 12-36 Surface model

Loft Surface

1. Create a 3D-sketch **3DSketch1** (100 mm by 100 mm) in **YZ** Plane (see Figure 12-37)
2. **Exit** sketch, **3DSketch1**
3. Create **Plane1** to correspond to **3DSketch1** using a point and a line
4. Create **Plane2** at a distance **175 mm**
5. On **Plane2** create a 3D-sketch **3DSketch2** (50 mm by 50 mm) in **YZ** Plane (see Figure 12-38)
6. **Exit** sketch, **3DSketch2**

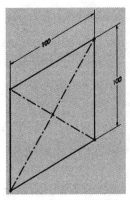

Figure 12-37 3DSketch1 on YZ Plane

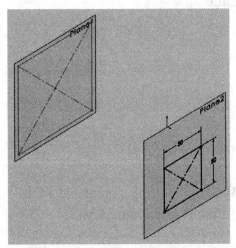

Figure 12-38 3DSketch2 on YZ Plane

7. Click **Insert > Surface > Loft**
   The Surface-Loft PropertyManager appears; see Figure 12-39
8. Click **OK** (Surface model appears; see Figure 12-40)

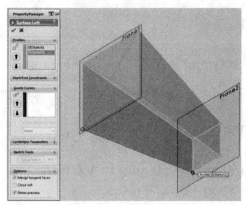

Figure 12-39 Surface-Loft PropertyManager

Figure 12-40 Surface model

Free-Form Surface Design: Boundary Surface

Control Polygons

1. Start a **New SolidWorks Part** document
2. Select the **Front Plane**
3. Click Sketch **3DSketch** on Plane
4. Create a 3D-sketch **3DSketch1** on **XY** Plane (see Figure 12-41)
5. **Exit** sketch, **3DSketch1**
6. Create **Plane1** on the same plane containing **3DSketch1** using a point and a line
7. Create three more planes **Plane2**, **Plane3**, and **Plane4** (see Figure 12-42)

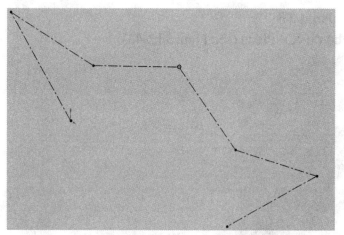

Figure 12-41 Control polygon with control vertices

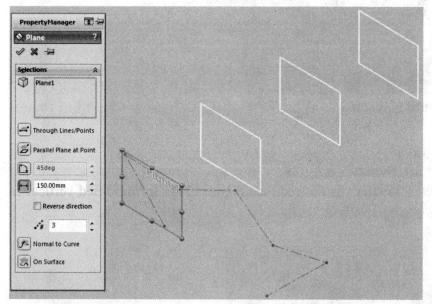

Figure 12-42 Three extra planes created Plane2, Plane3, and Plane4

8. Click **Plane2 > 3D-Sketch** on Plane
9. Click **View Orientation > Normal To**
10. Create a 3D-sketch **3DSketch2** on **XY** Plane (see Figure 12-43)
11. **Exit** sketch, **3DSketch2**

12. Click **Plane3 > 3D-Sketch** on Plane
13. Click **View Orientation > Normal To**
14. Create a 3D-sketch **3DSketch3** on **XY** Plane (see Figure 12-43)
15. **Exit** sketch, **3DSketch3**

16. Click **Plane4 > 3D-Sketch** on Plane

17. Click **View Orientation > Normal To**
18. Create a 3D-sketch **3DSketch4** on **XY** Plane (see Figure 12-43)
19. **Exit** sketch, **3DSketch4**

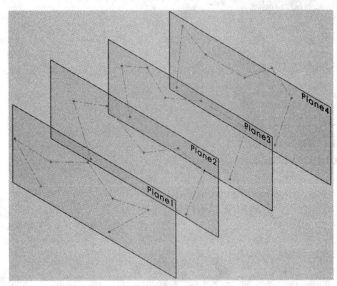

Figure 12-43 Four control polygons

Modifying Control Polygons

20. Click **Plane1 > 3D-Sketch**
21. Modify 3D-sketch **Vertices** as desired (see Figure 12-44 for modified vertices in Plane1 and Plane4, especially)

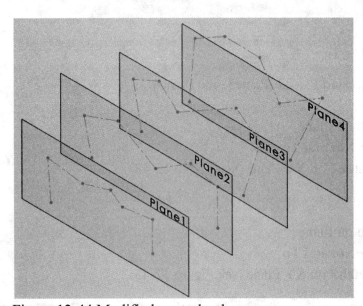

Figure 12-44 Modified control polygons

U-direction Control Curves

22. Click **Insert > Curve > Curve Through Reference Points** (see Figure 12-45)
    The **Curve Through PropertyManager** automatically appears (see Figure 12-46)

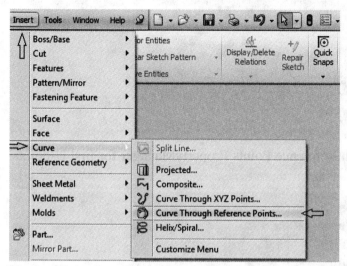

Figure 12-45 Access Spline Curve Through Reference Points tool

23. Click vertices of the first set of Control Vertices (see Figure 12-46)
24. Click **OK**

Repeat for Second Set of Control Vertices

25. Click vertices of the second set of Control Vertices (see Figure 12-47)
26. Click **OK**

Repeat for Third Set of Control Vertices

27. Click vertices of the third set of Control Vertices (see Figure 12-48)
28. Click **OK**

Repeat for Fourth Set of Control Vertices

29. Click vertices of the fourth set of Control Vertices (see Figure 12-49)
30. Click **OK**

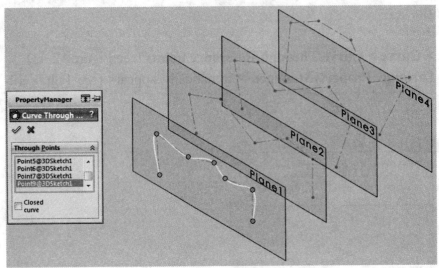

Figure 12-46 Spline Curve Through Reference Points PropertyManager for first U-points

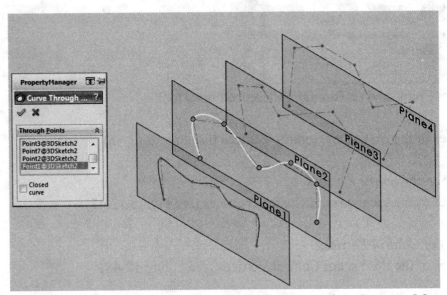

Figure 12-47 Spline Curve Through Reference Points PropertyManager for second U-points

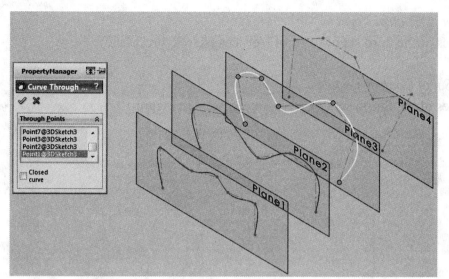

Figure 12-48 Spline Curve Through Reference Points PropertyManager for third U-points

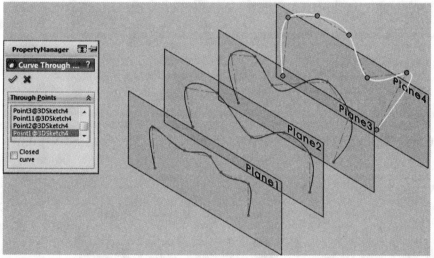

Figure 12-49 Spline Curve Through Reference Points PropertyManager for fourth U-points

U-direction Control Curves

31. Click **Insert > Curve > Curve Through Reference Points**
    The **Curve Through PropertyManager** automatically appears (see Figure 12-50)
32. Click vertices of the first set of Control Vertices (see Figure 12-50)
33. Click **OK**

Repeat for Second Set of Control Vertices
34. Click vertices of the second set of Control Vertices (see Figure 12-51)
35. Click **OK**

Repeat for Third Set of Control Vertices

36. Click vertices of the third set of Control Vertices (see Figure 12-52)

37. Click **OK**

Repeat for Fourth Set of Control Vertices

38. Click vertices of the fourth set of Control Vertices (see Figure 12-53)

39. Click **OK**

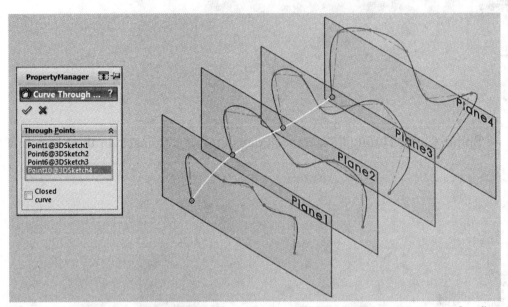

Figure 12-50 Spline Curve Through Reference Points PropertyManager for first V-points

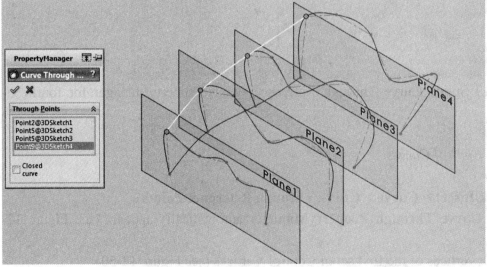

Figure 12-51 Spline Curve Through Reference Points PropertyManager for second V-points

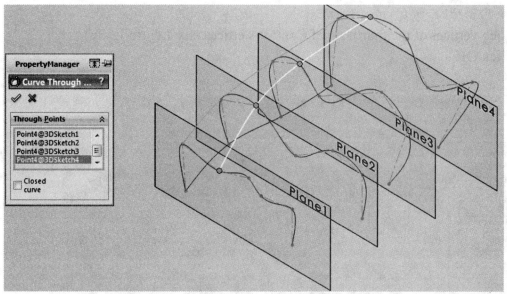

Figure 12-52 Spline Curve Through Reference Points PropertyManager for third V-points

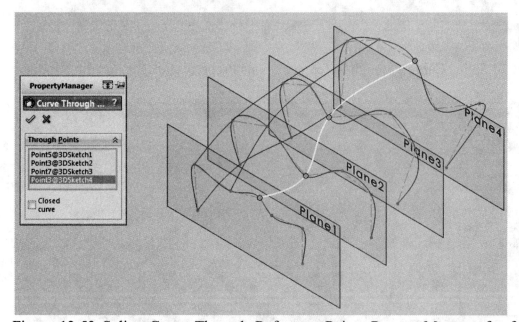

Figure 12-53 Spline Curve Through Reference Points PropertyManager for fourth V-points

Repeat for Second Set of Control Vertices

40. Click vertices of the second set of Control Vertices (see Figure 12-54)

41. Click **OK**

Repeat for Third Set of Control Vertices

42. Click vertices of the third set of Control Vertices (see Figure 12-55)

43. Click **OK**

Repeat for Fourth Set of Control Vertices

44. Click vertices of the fourth set of Control Vertices (see Figure 12-56)
45. Click **OK**

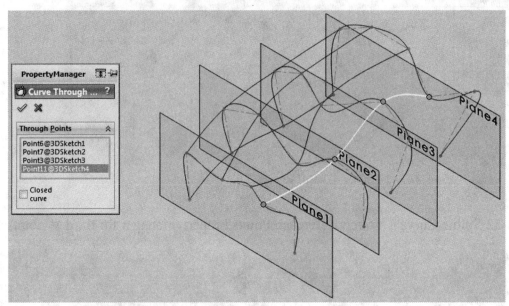

Figure 12-54 Spline Curve Through Reference Points PropertyManager for fifth V-points

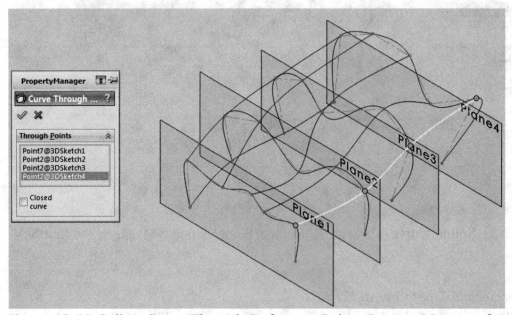

Figure 12-55 Spline Curve Through Reference Points PropertyManager for sixth V-points

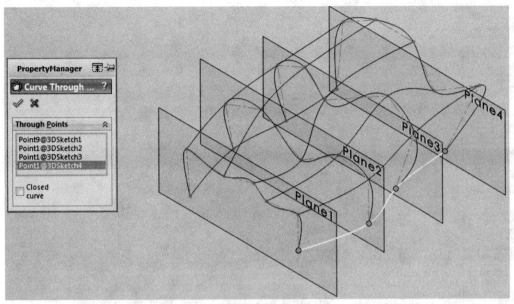

Figure 12-56 Spline Curve Through Reference Points PropertyManager for seventh V-points

Creating Boundary Surface using Control Curves

46. Click **Insert > Surface > Boundary Surface** (see Figure 12-57)
    The **Boundary Surface PropertyManager** automatically appears (see Figure 12-58)
47. Select **Curve1,..,Curve4** for *Dir1 Curves Influence* (see Figure 12-58)
48. Select **Curve5,..,Curve11** for *Dir2 Curves Influence* (see Figure 12-58)

Figure 12-57 Insert Boundary Surface

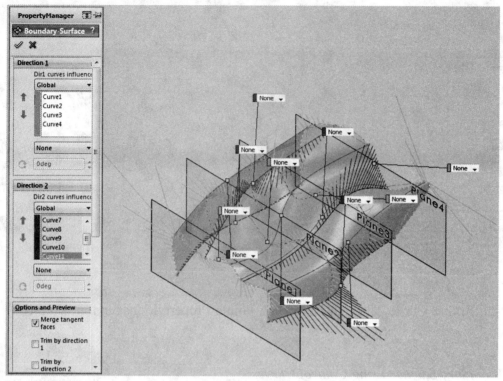

Figure 12-58 Boundary Surface PropertyManager

The surface model created is shown Figure 12-59. By modifying the control vertices, a modified surface model created is shown Figure 12-60. The FeatureManager for the surface design is shown in Figure 12-61.

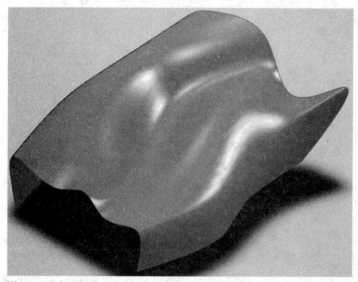

Figure 12-59 Surface model created

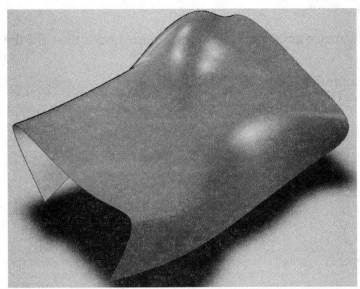

Figure 12-60 Modified surface model created by modifying some control vertices

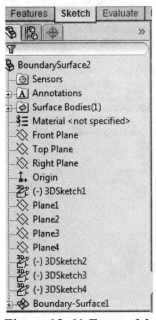

Figure 12-61 FeatureManager for the surface design

Summary

In summary, we have been presented with three ways of realizing solids from surfaces. Try these options. After all, a solid are made up of pieces of surfaces on its boundary, therefore, in general it is natural to piece together surfaces into a solid. On the other hand, the outer parts of a solid can be extracted for a number of bounding surfaces. We have also presented a very useful tool for filling surfaces. This is a very useful tool in the manufacturing industry.

Exercises

1. Create (drill) a hole, 10 mm diameter anywhere on top of Figure 12-59; then fill the hole.
2. Repeat the above process for Figure 12-60.
3. How is the process of filling a hole useful in manufacturing?

Chapter 13
Toolboxes and Design Libraries

Objectives:

In this chapter you will learn:

- The usefulness of **SolidWorks Toolbox** and **Design Library**
- Modeling and analyzing **Structural Steel** using **SolidWorks Toolbox**
- How to add **Grooves** for O-rings and Retaining Rings to components
- How to use the **SolidWorks Design Library** to add standard mechanical parts (nuts, bolts, screws, etc.) to an assembly
- How to use the **SolidWorks Toolbox** to design gears (spurs, helical, and bevels)
- How to use the **SolidWorks Toolbox** to design gearing systems (gears, shafts, bearing selection, etc.)

Introduction

The goals of this chapter are to encourage engineers and designers to take advantage of the design tools available in SolidWorks, and to extend their understanding of this robust and flexible CAD package beyond mere shape design (modeling).

SolidWorks Toolbox Add-Ins

1. Open a **New Part** document
2. Click the **Options** pull-down menu
3. Select SolidWorks Toolbox "**Add-Ins**" options (see Figure 13- 1)
   The **Add-Ins PropertyManager** appears as shown in Figure 13- 2
4. Check (select) **SolidWorks Toolbox** and **SolidWorks Toolbox Browser** (see Figure 13- 2)

Figure 13- 1 Select *Add-Ins* options

Figure 13- 2 SolidWorks Toolbox "Add-Ins"

How to Use the SolidWorks Design Library & Toolbox

SolidWorks software is useful for creating different types of standard mechanical parts. There are two ways of using the **Toolbox**. One way is to access the **Toolbox** once it is added-in through the **SolidWorks CommandManager** (see Figure 13- 3) or through the **Design Library** (to be discussed later). More features are available to the user when the Toolbox is accessed the **Design Library**.

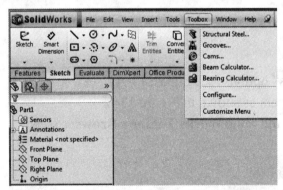

Figure 13- 3 SolidWorks Toolbox accessed through the CommandManager

Features Available in the Toolbox via the CommandManager
- Structural Steel
- Grooves
- Cams
- Beam Calculator
- Bearing Calculator

Features Available in the Toolbox via the Design Library
- Bearings
- Bolts and Screws
- Jig Bushings
- Keys
- Nuts
- O-rings
- Pins
- Power Transmission (Chain Sprockets, Gears, Timing Belt Pulleys)
- Retaining Rings
- Structural Members
- Washers

In the subsequent sections, we will discuss some of the SolidWorks Toolbox accessed through the CommandManager and present an overview of the SolidWorks Toolbox accessed through the Design Library.

Structural Steel

1. Open a **New Part** document
2. Click **Toolbox > Structural Steel** (see Figure 13- 3)
3. Select **ANSI Inch** (see Figure 13- 4)
4. Select **RECT Tube > TS4x2x0.25** (see Figure 13- 4)
5. Click **Create > Done** (the cross-section, **Sketch1** is created as shown in Figure 13- 5)

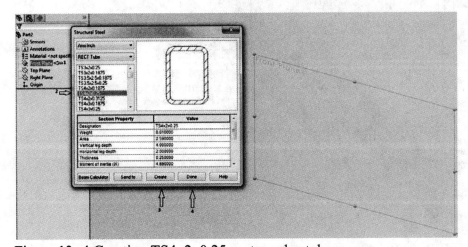

Figure 13- 4 Creating TS4x2x0.25-rectangular-tube

Figure 13- 5 Cross-section of TS4x2x0.25 rectangular-tube

6. Click **Sketch1** from the FeatureManager
7. Click **Edit Sketch** to be in *sketch mode* (see Figure 13- 6)
8. Click **Features > Extruded Boss/Base** (see the **Extrude PropertyManager** in Figure 13- 7)
9. In the **Direction1** rollout, accept **Blind** and specify **500** for the extrusion **Distance**

The rectangular tube created *Extrude1*, is shown in Figure 13- 8

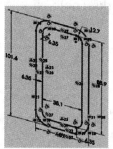

Figure 13- 6 Sketch1 in sketch mode

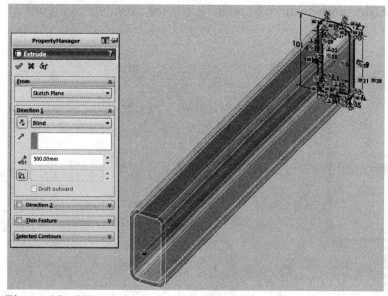

Figure 13- 7 Extrude PropertyManager

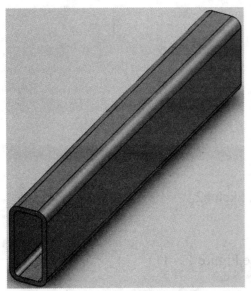

Figure 13- 8 TS4x2x0.25 rectangular-tube created, Extrude1

10. Click the front face of the rectangular-tube (see Figure 13- 9)
11. Click **Toolbox > Structural Steel** (see Figure 13- 9)
12. Select **C Channel > C3x4.1** (see Figure 13- 9)
13. Click **Create > Done** (the cross-section, **Sketch2** is created as shown in Figure 13- 10)

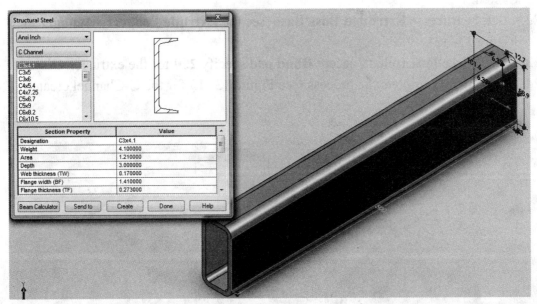

Figure 13- 9 Creating C3x4.1 C-Channel

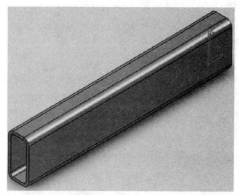

Figure 13- 10 Cross-section of C3x4.1 C-Channel, Sketch2

14. Click **Sketch2** from the FeatureManager
15. Click **Edit Sketch** to be in *sketch mode* (see Figure 13- 11)
16. Click **Add Relations**
17. Select the top of the **C-Channel** and top edge of the hole of the **rectangular tube** (see Figure 13- 11)
18. Click **OK** to add the relations
19. Click **Add Relations**
20. Select the left edge of the **C-Channel** and left edge of the hole of the **rectangular tube** (see Figure 13- 11)
21. Click **OK** to add the relations (see Figure 13- 12 for the proper positioning of Sketch2)
22. Click **Features > Extruded Boss/Base** (see the **Extrude PropertyManager** in Figure 13- 13)
23. In the **Direction1** rollout, accept **Blind** and specify **250** for the extrusion **Distance**
24. Click **OK** to complete the process (see Figure 13- 13 for the C-Channel created *Extrude2*)

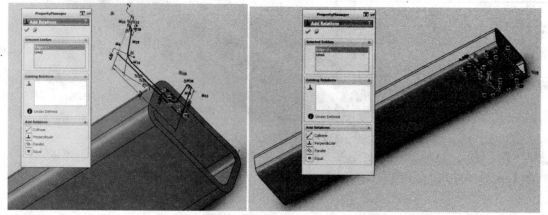

Figure 13- 11 Cross-section of C3x4.1 C-Channel, Sketch2 in sketch mode

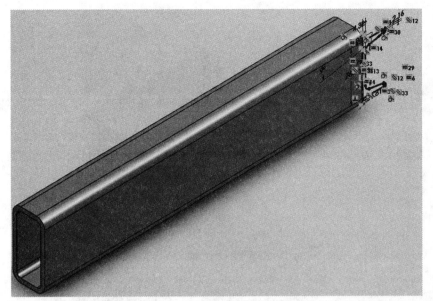

Figure 13- 12 Sketch2 placed in correct position using appropriate relations

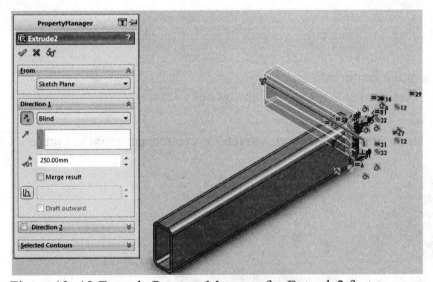

Figure 13- 13 Extrude PropertyManager for Extrude2 feature

25. Create **Plane1, 250 mm** from one end of the rectangular tube (see Figure 13- 14)
26. Click **Features > Mirror** (the Mirror PropertyManager is displayed as in Figure 13- 14)
27. Select **Plane1** as the **Mirror Face/Plane**
28. Select **Extrude2** as the **Bodies to Mirror**
29. Click **OK** to complete mirroring

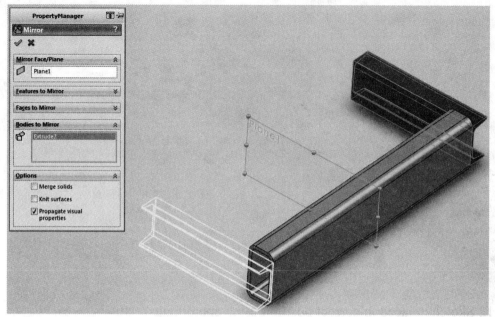

Figure 13- 14 Mirror PropertyManager

30. Create **Plane2** using any three outer vertices of the mirrored C-channel (see Figure 13- 15)
31. Click **Plane2** from the FeatureManager
32. Click **Toolbox > Structural Steel** (see Figure 13- 16)
33. Select **C Channel > C3x4.1** (see Figure 13- 16)
34. Click **Create > Done** (the cross-section, **Sketch3** is created as shown in Figure 13- 17)

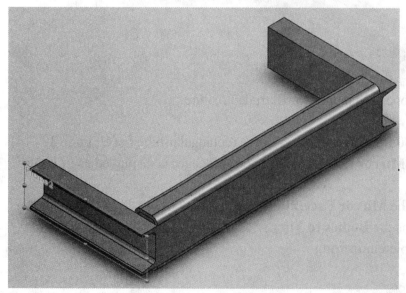

Figure 13- 15 Plane2 defined using any three outer vertices of the mirrored C-channel

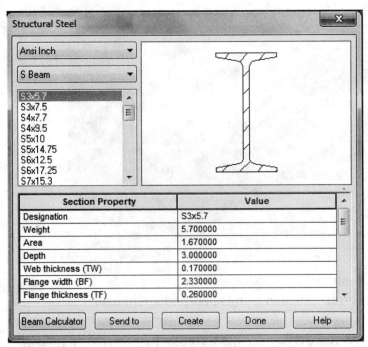

Figure 13- 16 Creating S3x5.7 S-beam

Figure 13- 17 Cross-section of S3x5.7 S-beam

35. Click **Sketch3** from the FeatureManager
36. Click **Edit Sketch** to be in *sketch mode* (see Figure 13- 18)
37. Click **Add Relations**
38. Select the bottom outer vertex of the **S3x5.7 S-beam** and bottom left (outer) vertex of the mirrored **C-channel** (see Figure 13- 18)
39. Click **OK** to add the relations

Figure 13- 18 Sketch3 placed in correct position using appropriate relations

40. Click **Features > Extruded Boss/Base** (see the **Extrude PropertyManager** in Figure 13- 19)
41. In the **Direction1** rollout, select **Up To Surface** and select *outer face* of **C-Channel**
42. Click **OK** to complete the process (see Figure 13- 20 for the S-beam created *Extrude3*)

Figure 13- 20 shows the FeatureManager showing the four solid bodies created

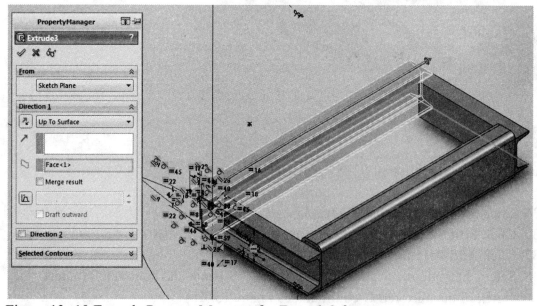

Figure 13- 19 Extrude PropertyManager for Extrude3 feature

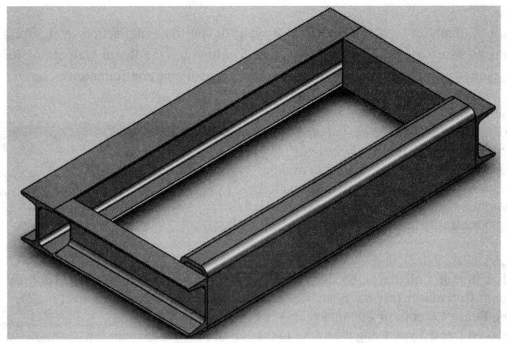

Figure 13- 20 Completed structural steel model

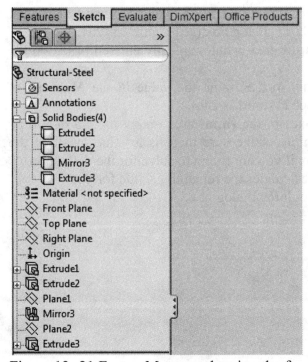

Figure 13- 21 FeatureManager showing the four solid bodies created

Beam Calculator

The **Beam Calculator** dialog box allows you to perform deflection and stress calculations on structural steel cross sections. The **Toolbox** has the **Beam Calculator** for calculating the structural section properties for different available configurations.

The available load options include:
- (1) Fixed at one end, loaded at the other end;
- (2) Fixed at one end, uniformly loaded;
- (3) Supported at both ends, loaded in middle;
- (4) Supported at both ends, uniformly loaded;
- (5) Supported at both ends, unsymmetrical load;
- (6) Supported at both ends, two symmetrical loads.

To perform a beam calculation:
1. Click **Beam Calculator** on the SolidWorks Toolbox toolbar, or click **Toolbox**, **Beam Calculator** (see the Beam Calculator PropertyManager in Figure 13- 22). The **Beam Calculator** dialog box appears.
2. Select a **Load Type** using the slider to the left of the preview window
3. Under **Type of Calculation**, select **Deflection** or **Stress**. The **Input** area updates to show the boxes appropriate for your selection.
3. Click **Beams**, select a beam in the **Structural Steel** dialog box, and then click **Done** to return to the **Beam Calculator** dialog box (see Figure 13- 23). Some of the information in the **Input** area is automatically entered based on the beam that you select.
4. Select an **Axis** (X or Y local axis) to determine the value in the **Moment of inertia** or **Section modulus** box (see Figure 13- 24a).
5. Type a value in the rest of the boxes in the **Input** area *except for the one to be solved*, and click **Solve**. For example, make sure there is a value in all of the boxes except for the **Deflection** box if you are trying to solve for the deflection. The **Beam Calculator** dialog box calculates the remaining value for you.
6. Click **Done** to close the **Beam Calculator** dialog box. Solutions are displayed in Figure 13- 24b.

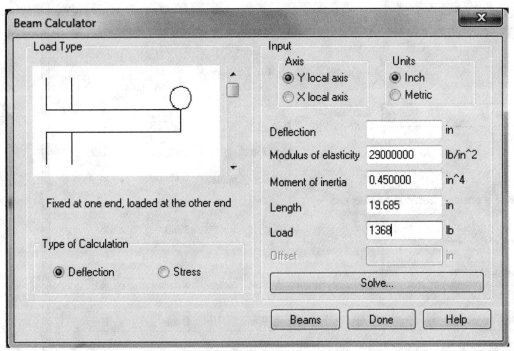

Figure 13- 22 Beam Calculator PropertyManager

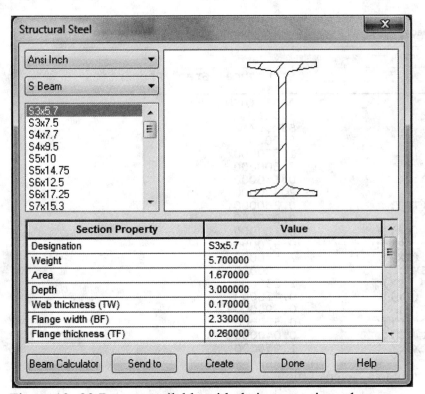

Figure 13- 23 Beams available with their properties values

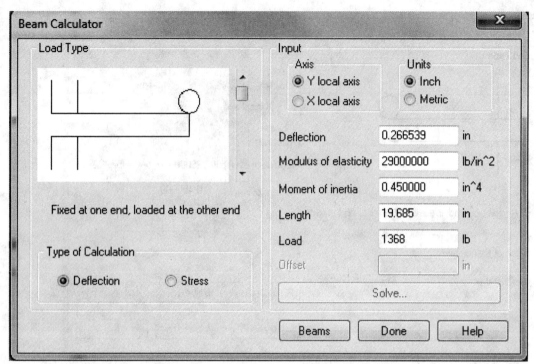

(a) Deflection output

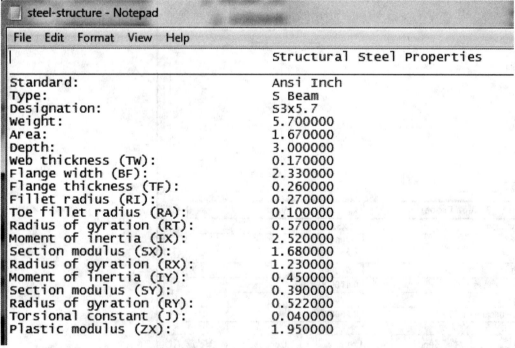

(b) Section properties output to a Notepad file

Figure 13- 24 Solutions generated

Grooves

Industry standard O-ring grooves can be created on your cylindrical model. The gateway to access the **Grooves** option in the **Toolbox** is shown in Figure 13- 25.

To create an O-ring groove:
1. Select a cylindrical face on a part where the groove is to be placed.
   By pre-selecting a cylindrical face, the SolidWorks software determines the diameter for the groove and suggests appropriate groove sizes.
2. Click **Grooves** on the SolidWorks Toolbox toolbar, or click **Toolbox, Grooves** (see Figure 13- 25)
   The **Grooves** dialog box appears (see Figure 13- 26). ANSI Inch Male Static Groove
3. On the **O-Ring Grooves** tab, do the following:
   a. Select a **Standard** (ANSI Inch), a **Groove Type** (Male Static Groove), and an available **Groove Size** (AS 568-338) from the lists on the top left of the tab.
      The fields in the **Property** and **Value** columns are updated.
   b. Notice the **Selected Diameter** (**3.5**) is set for you because you selected a cylindrical face in Step 1.
   c. Notice the **Mate Diameter** (**3.5**). This is a reference value for the diameter of the non-grooved mating part that completes the seal.
4. Notice the values for the **Groove Diameter** (3.18), **Width** (0.281), and **Radius** (0.275).
5. Click **Create** to add the groove.
   The groove is cut into the model. A feature appears in the FeatureManager design tree with a name (*Groove for AS 568-338, O-Ring1*) that matches the **Description**.
6. Click **Done (OK)** to close the dialog box (see Figure 13- 27 for the model with groove).

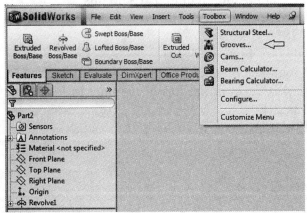

Figure 13- 25 Gateway to access the Grooves option in the toolbox

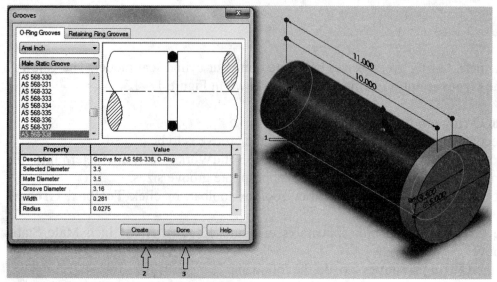

Figure 13- 26 Grooves PropertyManager

Figure 13- 27 Groove created in a model

The next step is to locate the groove at the exact position required. To do this,

1. Right-click **Sketch2** in the **FeatureManager** under Groove for **AS 568-338, O-Ring1** Feature tree (see Figure 13- 28)
2. Click **Edit Sketch** to be sketch mode (see Figure 13- 28)
3. Position the part using **Normal To** tool (see Figure 13- 28)
4. Dimension the *edge of the Groove profile from the top of the part* to locate the desired position (7.5) [see Figure 13- 29]
   The final part is shown in Figure 13- 30.

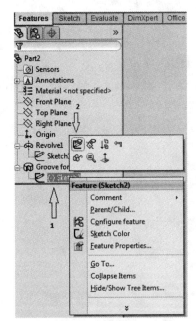

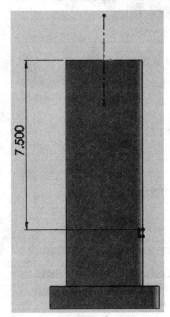

Figure 13-28 Editing Groove location   Figure 13-29 Re-dimensioning Groove position

Figure 13- 30 Final part with groove position adjusted

O-Ring Grooves: Retaining Ring Grooves

Industry standard retaining ring grooves can be created on your cylindrical model using exactly the same gateway as in o-ring grooves. The **Grooves** dialog box shown in Figure 13- 31 is for both types of grooves (o-ring and retaining ring).

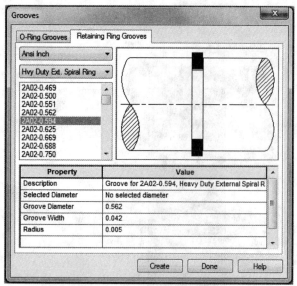

Figure 13- 31 Grooves PropertyManager

Creating Standard Parts Using SolidWorks Design Library & Toolbox

SolidWorks software is useful for creating different types of standard mechanical parts. As many as eighteen Standards are available in the SolidWorks Toolbox from which the designer can choose (see Figure 13-32). To access these standards, click **Design Library>Toolbox**.

The Toolbox offers quite a number of design tools for bearings, bolts and screws, jig bushings, keys, nuts, O-rings, power transmission elements (chain sprockets, gears, timing belt pulleys), retaining rings, structural members, and washers, as shown in Figure 13-33. These design tools assist the design engineer to perform his/her work more effectively and efficiently.

The first step in using the Toolbox in the Design Library is to decide on the Standard to use: ANSI (Inch/Metric), BSI, CISC, DIN, GB, IS, ISO, JIS, KS, MIL, PEM (Inch/Metric), SKF, Torrington (Inch/Metric), Truarc, or Unistrut. The first ten are national/internal standards while the remaining five are registered companies of international reputations that produce specific products.

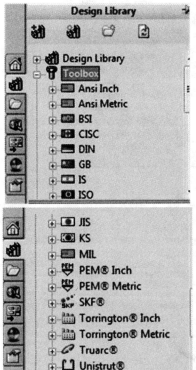

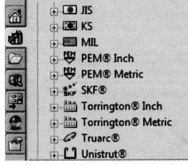

Figure 13- 32 SolidWorks Toolbox Standards

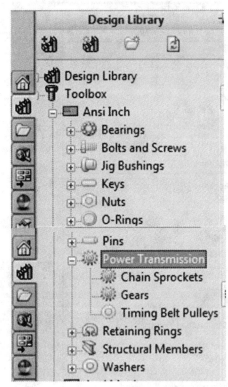

Figure 13- 33 Toolbox design tools

Adding Set Screws to the Collar of a Shaft

As an illustration, we consider adding set screws to the collar of a shaft. Figure 13- 34 shows the Set Screw selection from the Design Library Toolbox and how it is dragged into the sub-assembly of a shaft and collar.

To access set screws, do the following
1. Open the collar and shaft sub-assembly
2. Click **Design Library > Toolbox > ANSI Inch > Bolts and Screws > Set Screws (Slotted)**
3. Select the **Slotted Set Screw Cup Point** option and click and drag the set screw into the drawing window (see Figure 13- 34)
4. Define the size of the set screw as #10-24 and the length as 0.315
5. Click OK to complete insertion and specification
6. Use Mate tool and insert the set screws into the collar and shaft
7. Save the assembly shown in Figure 13- 35

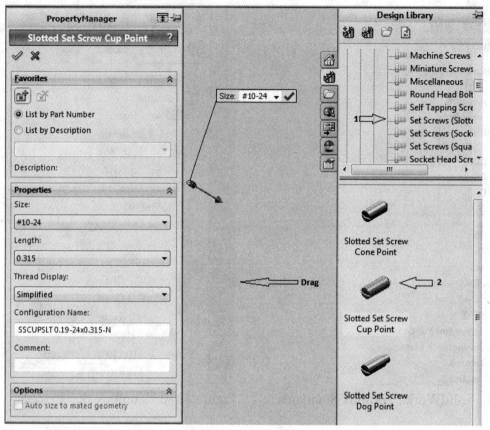

Figure 13- 34 Set screw selection from the Design Library Toolbox

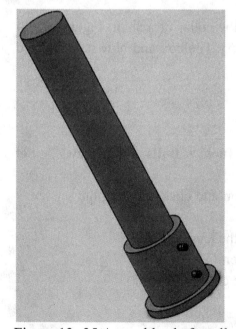

Figure 13- 35 Assembly shaft, collar, and set screws

Gear Design Using SolidWorks

Gears are used to transmit rotary motion, torque, and power from one shaft to another. Gears are the most rugged and durable means of power transmission compared to various other means, such as belts and chains. They have transmission efficiency as high as 98%, but are more expensive than belts and chains.

Types of Gears

The four main types most commonly used in practical application are: *spur*, *helical*, *bevel* and *worm* gears.

Spur gears are the simplest.

Helical gears, like spur gears, are cut from a cylindrical blank and have involute teeth. The difference is that their teeth are at some helix angle to the shaft axis. These gears are used to transmit power between parallel or nonparallel shafts.

Bevel gears are cut on conical blanks to be used to transmit motion between intersecting shafts. The simplest bevel gear type is the straight-tooth bevel gear or straight bevel gear.

Worm gear-set consists of a worm (similar to a screw) and the worm gear (a special helical gear). The shafts on which the worm and gear are mounted are usually oriented 90-degrees to each other. Worm gearing can be employed to transmit motion between nonparallel nonintersecting shafts.

Generally, spur and helical gears have teeth parallel and inclined to the axis of rotation, respectively.

Design Methodology for Gears

Two modes of failure affect gear teeth: *fatigue fracture due to fluctuating bending stress* at the root of the tooth and fatigue (*wear*) of the tooth surface. Both modes of failure must be checked when designing the gears. The shapes and sizes of the teeth are standardized by the American Gear Manufacturers Association (AGMA). The methods of AGMA are widely used in design and analysis of gear sets. The AGMA approach requires extensive use of charts and graphs together with equations that facilitate the application of computer-aided design.

In a gearing system, three tasks have to be performed:
   1) Check the gear pairs for the two main modes of failure: AGMA approach is used;

2) Size the shaft carrying the gears based on gear loading: AGMA approach is used;

3) Select bearings carrying the shaft based on gear loading: SKF, ANSI, ISO, etc.

SolidWorks Solution Procedure

In this chapter, we consider the most critical steps. The author has worked out the details of the '*black box*.' Utilization of the AGMA approach for checking the gear pairs for the two main modes of failure is treated as a '*black box*.' Utilization of the AGMA approach for sizing the shaft carrying the gears based on gear loading is treated as a '*black box*.' The reason for labelling these design decisions as black-boxes is due to the fact that the details are not included in this chapter as they are outside the scope of this chapter. The procedure is given to show how **SolidWorks** or any other CAD design software can be used for gearing system design rather than the mere shape design which are mainly covered by users.

The general solution procedure involves the following major components (note where **SolidWorks** could be applied):

1) Sizing of the gearbox based on the design specifications (supports, housing, etc.) [Use **SolidWorks**]

2) Check the gear pairs for the two main modes of failure [**AGMA** approach is used; treat this as a '*black box*' since this is not covered in this chapter; Use **SolidWorks Simulation** as an alternative]

3) Size the shaft carrying the gears based on gear loading [**AGMA** approach is used; treat this as a '*black box*' since this is not covered in this chapter; Use **SolidWorks Simulation** as an alternative]

4) Select bearings carrying the shaft based on gear loading [Use **SolidWorks Toolbox** to select bearings after initial loading analysis has been completed]

5) Models gears [Use **SolidWorks**]

6) Assemble Parts (include keyways, keys, etc.) [Use **SolidWorks**]

7) Animate gear assemble [Use **SolidWorks**]

8) Create Drawings and BOM [Use **SolidWorks**]

We will now commence SolidWorks gear design procedure by first considering spur gears, then helical gears, and finally bevel gears. Note that worm gears are not supported in the SolidWorks Design Library/Toolbox. Another observation is that that ANSI Inch supports more elements for power transmission than ANSI mm. Therefore, designers should consider using ANSI Inch where more mechanical elements such as chain sprockets and timing belt pulleys are required. It is feasible to convert from ANSI Inch to ANSI mm, if the latter is required.

Spur Gear Design

Let us consider spur gears which are the simplest of the different classes of gear. In this example, we will use SolidWorks to design the spur gears from the design specifications given. Other details for sizing the gear box, checking that AGMA specifications are met, are not shown.

Problem Description

A simple gearing system consists of a plate ($5 \times 4 \times 0.5$), two shafts each ($\phi\, 0.5 \times 1.7$), and a pair of spur gears defined as follows:

Gear 1:	Gear 2:
Diametral pitch = 24	Diametral pitch = 24
Number of teeth = 30	Number of teeth = 60
Pressure angle = 20-deg.	Pressure angle = 20-deg.
Face width = 0.5	Face width = 0.5
Hub Style = One side	Hub Style = One side
Hub diameter = 1.00	Hub diameter = 1.00
Overall length = 0.70	Overall length = 0.70
Nominal shaft diameter = ½	Nominal shaft diameter = ½
Key = None	Key = None

Use SolidWorks for designing the gearing system.

SolidWorks Solution Procedure

The pitch diameter of the pinion is: $D_1 = \dfrac{N_{t1}}{P_d} = \dfrac{30}{24} = 1.25''$

The pitch diameter of the gear is: $D_2 = \dfrac{N_{t2}}{P_d} = \dfrac{60}{24} = 2.5''$

The center-to-center distance is: $c = \dfrac{(D_1 + D_2)}{2} = \dfrac{(1.25 + 2.5)}{2} = 1.875''$

Note that for spur gears, the center-to-center distance calculated agrees with the value that should be used. In helical gears, this may not be the case.

Support

Model the support (see Figure 13-36)

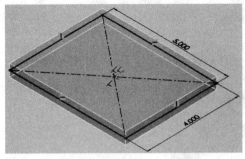

(i)

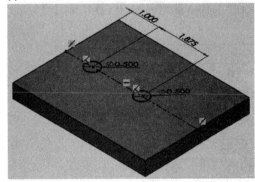

(ii)

Figure 13-36 Support part

Shaft

Model the shaft (see Figure 13-36)

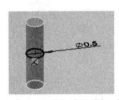 

Figure 13-37 Shaft

Pinion

1. Open a **New SolidWorks Part** document
2. Click **Design Library > Toolbox > ANSI Inch > Power Transmission > Gears**
3. Right-click **Spur Gear** (see Figure 13-38)
4. Select **Create Part** [Note: this is the preferred route used in this book; do not *drag and drop*' parts from the Design Library] (see Figure 13-38)

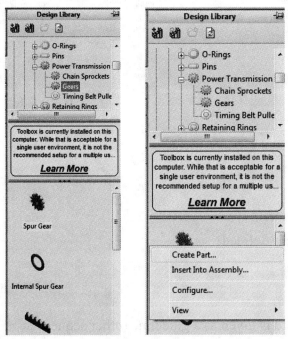

Figure 13-38 Creating Helical gears

The **Spur Gear PropertyManager** appears immediately (see Figure 13-39). Based on the design specification, fill in the properties as shown in Figure 13-39.

5. Click **OK** when complete

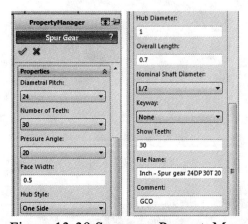

Figure 13-39 Spur gear PropertyManager (pinion defined)

Gear

Repeat as in pinion (see Figure 13-40 for the PropertyManager)

Figure 13-40 Spur gear PropertyManager (gear defined)

Assembly Modeling

To assemble the parts, the following procedure is given as a guideline (other sequences could be used to arrive at an assembly solution):

1. Open a **New SolidWorks Assembly** document
2. **Insert** the base as the first part (see Figure 13-41)
3. **Insert** the shaft twice since two are needed (see Figure 13-41)

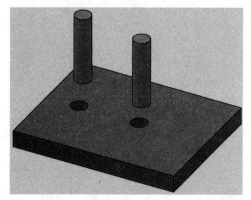

Figure 13-41 Insert support and shafts

Concentric Mating for Shafts

4. Click *each shaft* and *each hole*, and apply **Concentric Mate** condition (see Figure 13-42 and Figure 13-43)

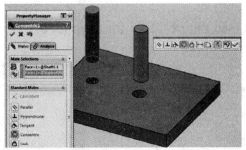

Figure 13-42 Concentric mating for one shaft

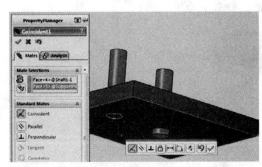

Figure 13-43 Concentric mating for second shaft

Coincident Mating for Shafts

5. Click *end face of each shaft* and *bottom of support plate*, and apply **Coincident Mate** condition (see Figure 13-44 and Figure 13-45)

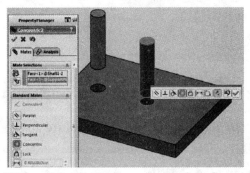

Figure 13-44 Coincident mating for one shaft

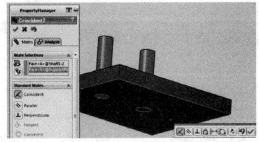

Figure 13-45 Coincident mating for second shaft

Insert Pinion

6. **Insert** the gear (or pinion) as the fourth part (see Figure 13-46 for the pinion)

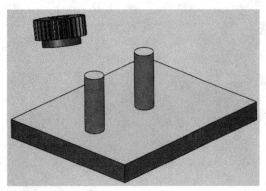

Figure 13-46 Insert the pinion

Concentric Mate for Pinion and Shaft

7. Click *inside of bore surface of pinion* and *shaft* and apply **Concentric Mate** (see Figure 13-47)

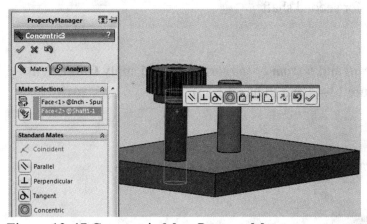

Figure 13-47 Concentric Mate PropertyManager

Insert Gear

8. **Insert** the gear (or pinion) as the fifth part (see Figure 13-48 for the gear)

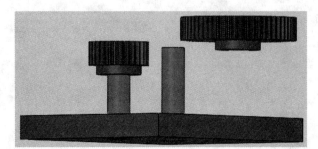

Figure 13-48 Insert the gear

Concentric Mate for Gear and Shaft

9. Click *inside of bore surface of gear* and *shaft* and apply **Concentric Mate** (see Figure 13-49)

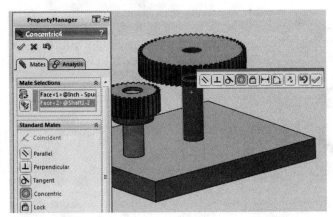

Figure 13-49 Concentric Mate PropertyManager

Distance Mate for Pinion/Gear and Top of Support Plate

10. Click *end face of hub for pinion/gear* and *top face of support plate* and apply **Distance Mate** with value equal to **0.5** (see Figure 13-50 and Figure 13-51)

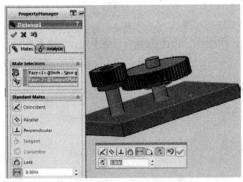

Figure 13-50 Distance Mate PropertyManager

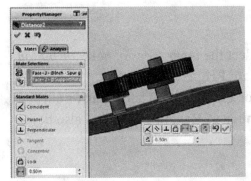

Figure 13-51 Distance Mate PropertyManager

Align the Teeth on Pinion and Gear

    11. Use **Zoom to Area** tool to zoom teeth of pinion and gear in the area of mesh

    12. Align the teeth of Pinion and Gear to ensure that they mesh (see Figure 13-52)

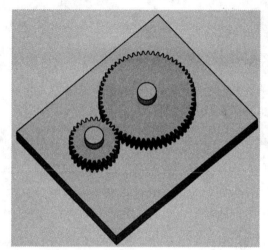

Figure 13-52 Align teeth of Pinion and Gear

Temporarily Suppress Coincident Mates for Shafts

    13. Right-click the **Coincident Mates** for Shafts

    14. Select **Suppress** tool to suppress them

    15. Pull the shafts down to expose the bore of the pinion and gear (see Figure 13-53)

Figure 13-53 Suppress Coincident Mates for shafts and pull shafts

Mechanical Mates

    16. Click **Mates** and for the **Mate Selection**, select the *inner faces of bore for pinion and gears* (see Figure 13-54 for the **GearMate PropertyManager**)

    17. Define the **Ratio** using **Number of Teeth** for **Pinion (= 30)** and **Gear (= 60)** respectively; their **Pitch Diameters** or **Number of Revolutions** could also be used (see Figure 13-54)

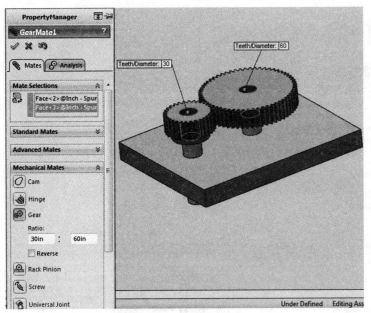

Figure 13-54 GearMate PropertyManager

Un-Suppress Coincident Mates for Shafts

18. Right-click the **Coincident Mates** for Shafts
19. Select **Suppress** tool to un-suppress them (see Figure 13-55 for model)

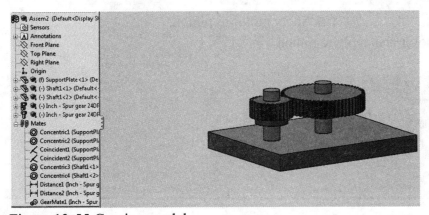

Figure 13-55 Gearing model

Animation

1. Click **Motion Study1** at the bottom left of the Window
2. For the **Type of Study** select **Animation** (see Figure 13-56)
3. Click the **Motor** tool to define the motor; select the Rotary Motor, with Pinion chosen as driver (see Figure 13-57)
4. Click **Calculate** to calculate the Motion Study (see Figure 13-58)

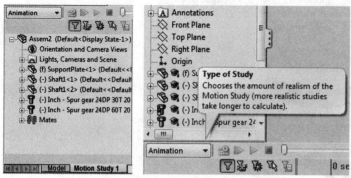

Figure 13-56 Select Type of Study

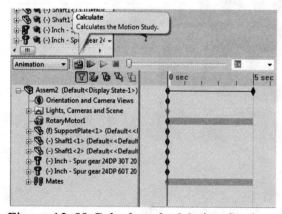

(i) Motor tool   (ii) Apply motor to pinion

Figure 13-57 Define motor and apply to pinion

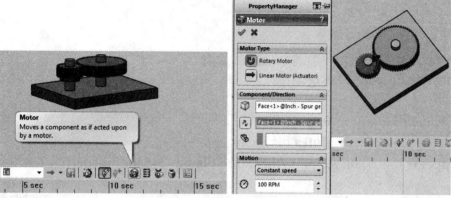

Figure 13-58 Calculate the Motion Study

Helical Gear Design

A motor running at $n = 2400$ rpm and delivering 122 kW (164-hp) power drives a machine by means of a helical gear-set as shown in Figure 13-58. The gears have the following geometric quantities: $P_n = 5\,in^{-1}.$, $\phi = 20^o$, c (center-center distance) = 9-inch, $N_1 = 30$, $N_2 = 42$, and b (face-width) = 2-in. The gears are made from SAE 1045 steel, water-quenched and tempered (WQ&T), and hardened to 200 BHN. Use SolidWorks for designing the gearing system.

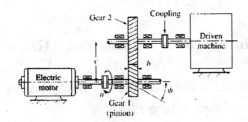

Figure 13-58 Helical gear-set

Initial Sizing

$P_n = P_d / Cos\,\psi$ [Note: there is difference between Normal Pitch and Diametral Pitch]

$$P_d = \frac{(N_{t1} + N_{t2})}{2c} = \frac{(30 + 72)}{2(9)} = 4$$

The Diametral Pitch becomes 4. We need to compute the pitch diameters based on the value of Diametral pitch of 4.

The pitch diameter of the pinion is: $D_1 = \dfrac{N_{t1}}{P_d} = \dfrac{30}{4} = 7.5''$

The pitch diameter of the gear is: $D_2 = \dfrac{N_{t2}}{P_d} = \dfrac{42}{4} = 10.5''$

The center-to-center distance is: $c = \dfrac{(D_1 + D_2)}{2} = \dfrac{(7.5 + 10.5)}{2} = 9.0''$

Note that this value matches the given value in the problem definition. We need to determine the Helix Angle, given as: $Cos\,\psi_1 = \dfrac{P_d}{P_n} = \dfrac{4}{5} = 0.8$

The arc-cosine of 0.8 is equal to 36.9-deg or 37-deg. But note that due to Virtual Values, our measured diameters from SolidWorks may be different. We will use Imperial.

Support (Housing) Sizing

Length of support, $L = b + 2b_w + 2\varepsilon_l$

Width of support, $W = d_1 + d_2 + \varepsilon_w$

Thickness of support, $T = \varepsilon_T$

Pinion

1. Open a **New SolidWorks Part** document
2. Click **Design Library > Toolbox > ANSI Inch > Power Transmission > Gears**
3. Right-click **Helical Gear** (see Figure 13-59)
4. Select **Create Part** [Note: this is the preferred route used in this book; do not *'drag and drop'* parts from the Design Library] (see Figure 13-59)

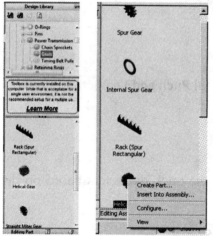

Figure 13-59 Creating Helical gears

The **Helical Gear PropertyManager** appears immediately (see Figure 13-60). Based on the design specification, fill in the properties as shown in Figure 13-60.

5. Click **OK** when complete (see Figure 13-61 for the pinion)

Figure 13-60 Helical gear PropertyManager

Figure 13-61 Pinion created

Gear

Repeat as in pinion (see Figure 13-62 for the PropertyManager and Figure 13-63 for the gear)

Figure 13-62 Helical gear PropertyManager

Figure 13-63 Gear created

Support

Model the support (see Figure 13-64)

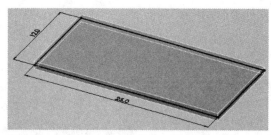

(i)

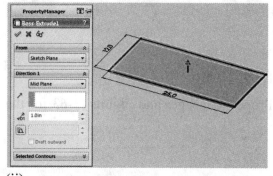

(ii)

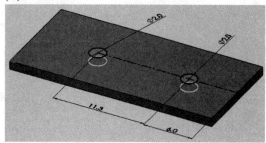

(iii)

Figure 13-64 Support part

Assembly Modeling

To assemble the parts, the following procedure is given as a guideline (other sequences could be used to arrive at an assembly solution):
1. Open a **New SolidWorks Assembly** document
2. **Insert** the support as the first part (see Figure 13-65)
3. **Insert** the shaft twice since two are needed

Concentric Mating for Shafts
4. Click *each shaft* and *each hole*, and apply **Concentric Mate** condition (see Figure 13-66 for shafts mated to support)

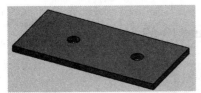

Figure 13-65 Support is the first part inserted

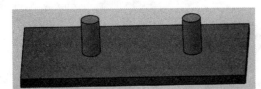

Figure 13-66 Two shafts inserted to the support

Insert Pinion
1. **Insert** the gear (or pinion) as the fourth part (see Figure 13-67 for the pinion)

Figure 13-67 Pinion is inserted

Concentric Mate for Pinion and Shaft
1. Click *inside of bore surface of pinion* and *shaft* and apply **Concentric Mate** (see Figure 13-68)

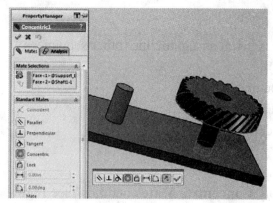

Figure 13-68 Hole in pinion and shaft are made concentric

Insert Pinion

1. **Insert** the gear (or pinion) as the fifth part (see Figure 13-69 for the pinion)

Figure 13-69 Gear is inserted

Concentric Mate for Gear and Shaft

1. Click *inside of bore surface of gear* and *shaft* and apply **Concentric Mate** (see Figure 13-70)

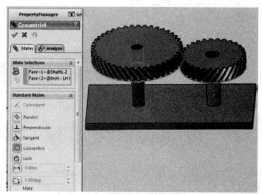

Figure 13-70 Hole in gear and shaft are made concentric

Coincident Mating for Shafts

1. Click *end face of each shaft* and *bottom of support plate*, and apply **Coincident Mate** condition (see Figure 13-71)

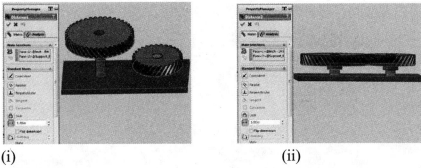

(i)   (ii)

Figure 13-71 Fix distance between the top face of support and bottom face of pinion/gear

Mechanical mate is important for pinion and gear to rotate when one of them is rotated. Generally, choosing the holes in the pinion and gear will achieve this. We could also use features from the pinion and gear respectively; this still works. For our mechanical mate, we use holes in the pinion and gear as shown in Figure 13-72.

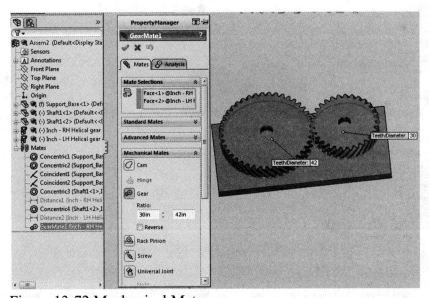

Figure 13-72 Mechanical Mate

Figure 13-73 Assembly of pinion, gear, shafts and support

Figure 13-74 shows the **AssemblyManager** with details

Figure 13-74 AssemblyManager showing details

Animation

See steps in Figure 13-75 to Figure 13-76. Pinion is chosen as driver.

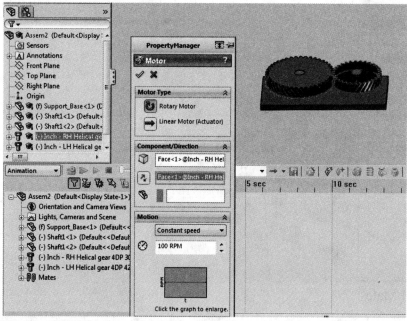

Figure 13-75 Pinion is chosen as driver

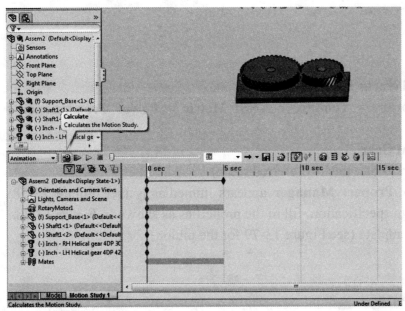

Figure 13-76 Calculate Motion

Bevel Gear Design

Let us consider bevel gears as another class of applications. In this example, we will use SolidWorks to design the gears from the design specifications given. Other details for sizing the gear box, checking that AGMA specifications are met are not shown. These extra details are given as assignments.

Problem Description

A set of bevel gears having pressure angle $\phi = 20^o$ is used to transmit 20-hp from a pinion operating at 500 rpm to a gear mounted on a shaft rotating at 200 rpm that inserts at an angle of 90-degrees as shown in Figure 13-77. Use SolidWorks for designing the gearing system.

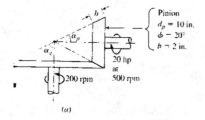

Figure 13-77 Helical gear-set

SolidWorks Solution

Pinion

1. Open a **New SolidWorks Part** document
2. Click **Design Library > Toolbox > ANSI Metric > Power Transmission > Gears**
3. Right-click **Helical Gear**
4. Select **Create Part** [Note: this is preferred route]
   The **Helical Gear PropertyManager** appears immediately (see Figure 13-78). Based on the design specification, fill in the properties as shown in Figure 13-78.
5. Click **OK** when complete (see Figure 13-79 for the pinion)

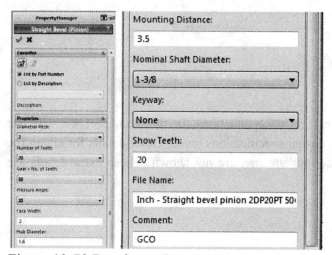

Figure 13-78 Bevel gear PropertyManager for the pinion

Figure 13-79 Pinion created by SolidWorks Toolbox

Gear

Repeat as in pinion (see Figure 13-80 for the PropertyManager and Figure 13-81 for the gear)

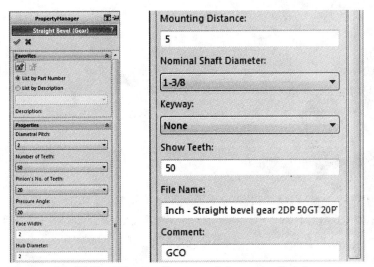

Figure 13-80 Bevel gear PropertyManager for the gear

Figure 13-81 Gear created by SolidWorks Toolbox

Save the pinion and gear as part document in a directory that you created. Do not save in SolidWorks directory.

Assembly

To assemble the parts, the following procedure is given as a guideline (other sequences could be used to arrive at assembly solution):

1. Open a **New SolidWorks Assembly** document
2. Insert a shaft for the pinion (or gear) as the first part (see Figure 13-82)
3. Insert the pinion (or gear) as the second part (see Figure 13-82)
4. Insert a shaft for the gear (or pinion) as the third part (see Figure 13-82)
5. Insert the gear (or pinion) as the fourth part (see Figure 13-82)

Figure 13-82 Pinion, gear, shaft (twice)

Mating

6. **Mate** the shaft and pinion hole as being **Concentric** (see Figure 13-83)
7. **Mate** the shaft and the gear hole as being **Concentric** (see Figure 13-84)
8. **Mate** the two shafts at 90-degrees to each other (alternatively use the back faces of the gears for mating; check how they are oriented) (see Figure 13-85)
9. **Mechanical mate** is added (use the holes in pinion and gear, or other features from pinion and gear) (see Figure 13-86)
10. **Mate** end of shaft and face of pinion face/gear face (see Figure 13-87 and Figure 13-88)
11. **Mate** teeth-teeth clearance using **distance** (see Figure 13-89)

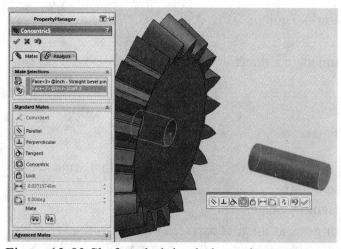

Figure 13-83 Shaft and pinion hole mating

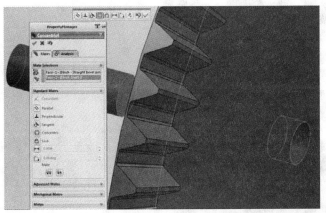

Figure 13-84 Shaft and gear hole mating

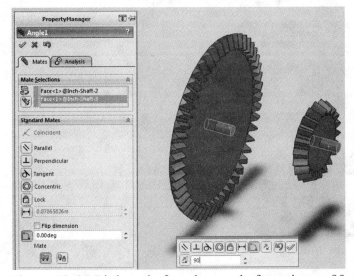

Figure 13-85 Pinion-shaft and gear-shaft mating at 90-degrees (alternatively, faces could be used)

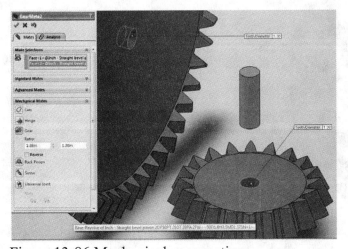

Figure 13-86 Mechanical gear mating

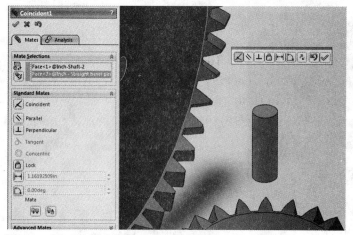

Figure 13-87 Shaft-end and gear face mating

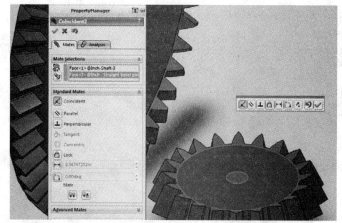

Figure 13-88 Shaft-end and pinion face mating

Figure 13-89 Teeth alignment for distance mating

Summary

Spur, helical and bevel gears have been considered. There is an observation. For gear manufacturing, the gears created using **SolidWorks Toolbox** need to be revisited for practical functionality. The chapter concentrates on giving the engineers and designer an in-depth understanding of *SolidWorks Toolbox/Design Library* which is extremely useful in practice for designers.

Exercises

Project 1 [measurements in inches]

1. Create four shafts, 0.375-in diameter and 3.00-in long.
2. Model the rectangular support plate shown in Figure P1. Consider modeling the shaft supports.
3. Access the SolidWorks Design Library and create three Gear 1s and Gear 2s.

 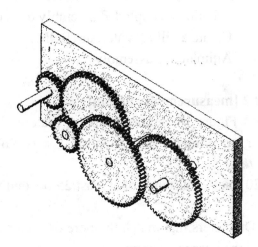

Figure P1 Spur gear train

The gears are defined as follows:
Gear 1:
Diametral pitch = 12
Number of teeth = 18
Pressure angle = 14.5
Face width = 0.25
Hub Style = One side
Hub diameter = 0.50

Overall length = 0.50

Nominal shaft diameter = 3/8

Key = None

Gear 2:

Diametral pitch = 12

Number of teeth = 48

Pressure angle = 14.5

Face width = 0.25

Hub Style = One side

Hub diameter = 0.50

Overall length = 0.50

Nominal shaft diameter = 3/8

Key = None

4.   Add #6-32 threaded holes to each gear hub 0.19 from the top hub surface.

5.   Assemble the gears onto the shafts so that Gear 1 and Gear 2 are 0.50 offset from the support plate and Gear 3 and Gear 4 are 1.25 offset from the support plate.

6.   Insert a #6-32 Slotted Set Screw with an Oval Point into each hole.

7.   Creating an exploded assembly drawing

8.   Create a bill of materials (BOM)

9.   Animate the assembly

Project 2 [measurements in mm]

Based on Figure P1 define a support plate and shafts that support the following gears. Consider modeling the shaft supports. Use two of each gear.

Parameters:

Plate: 20 thick, a distance of at least 25 beyond the other edge of the gears to the edge of the plate.

Shafts: Diameters that match the bore diameter of the gear; minimum offset between the plate and the gear is 20 or greater.

Gear 1:

Module = 2.0

Number of teeth = 25

Pressure angle = 14.5

Face width = 12

Hub Style = One side

Hub diameter = 25

Overall length = 30

Nominal shaft diameter = 20

Key = None

Gear 2:

Diametral pitch = 2.0

Number of teeth = 60

Pressure angle = 14.5

Face width = 12

Hub Style = One side

Hub diameter = 30

Overall length = 30

Nominal shaft diameter = 20

Key = None

1. Add M4 threaded holes to each gear hub 12 from the top hub surface.
2. Assemble the gears onto the shafts so that Gear 1 and Gear 2 are 10 offset from the support plate and Gear 3 and Gear 4 are parallel to the ends of the support plate.
3. Insert an M4 Slotted Set Screw with an Oval Point into each hole.
4. Creating an exploded assembly drawing
5. Create a bill of materials (BOM)
6. Animate the assembly

Project 3 [measurements in mm]

Carry out a preliminary design (sizing) for the gearbox of Figure P2. The design outcomes are similar to Project 1 (#1-#9). Size the gearbox of Figure P2. Consider modeling the shaft supports.

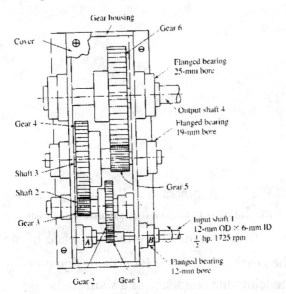

Figure P2 Spur gear train

A 0.5-hp, 1725 rpm electric motor drives the input shaft 1 at 95% efficiency. All gears have $\psi = 20°$ pressure angle. Shafts 1 or 2, 3, and 4 are supported by 12, 19, and 25-mm bore flanged bearings, respectively. The pinions are made of carburized 55 R_c steel. Gears are Q&T, 180 BHN steel.

Data:

	Module m (mm)	Number of teeth N	Pitch diameter d (mm)	Face width b (mm)
Gear 1 (pinion)	1.3	15	20	14
Gear 2	1.3	60	80	14
Gear 3 (pinion)	1.6	18	28.8	20
Gear 4	1.6	72	115.2	20
Gear 5 (pinion)	2.5	15	37.5	32
Gear 6	2.5	60	150	32

Project 4 [measurements in inches]
A motor running at $n = 2400$ rpm drives a machine by means of a helical gear-set as shown in Figure P3. The gears have the following geometric quantities: $P_n = 5in.^{-1}$, $\psi = 20°$, $c = 9$-in, $N_1 = 30$, $N_2 = 42$, $b = 2$-in. The gears are made of SAE 1045 steel, water-quenched and tempered (WQ&T), and hardened to 200 BHN. Size the gearbox of Figure P3. The design outcomes are similar to Project 1 (#1-#9). Consider modeling the *couplings* and *shaft supports*.

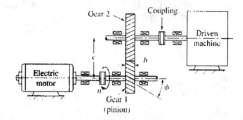

Figure P3 Helical gear-set

Project 5 [measurements in inches]
A turbine rotates at $n = 8000$ rpm drives a 250-kW (335-hp) generator at 1000rpm by means of a helical gear-set as shown in Figure P4. The gears have the following geometric quantities: gear-set angle $\psi = 30°$, $\phi_n = 20°$, $P_n = 10in.^{-1}$ and $b = 8$-in. The pinion is made of steel with 150 BHN and gear is cast iron. Size the gearbox of Figure P4. The design outcomes are similar to Project 1 (#1-#9). Consider modeling the *couplings* and *shaft supports*.

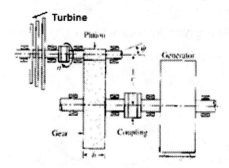

Figure P4 Helical gear-set

Project 6 [measurements in inches]

A set of straight bevel gears having pressure angle $\psi = 20^o$ is to be used to transmit 20-hp from a pinion operating at 500 rpm to a gear mounted on a shaft that intersects at an angle of 90-degrees as shown in Figure P5. Size the gearbox of Figure P5. The design outcomes are similar to Project 1 (#1-#9). Consider modeling *shaft supports*.

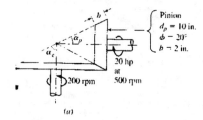

Figure P5 Bevel gears

BASIC GEAR KINEMATICS

The Nomenclature used in the basic kinematics of gears is given as follows:

P: Diametral pitch

m: Module

p_c: Circular pitch

D: Circular pitch diameter

N_t: Number of teeth

ϕ: Pressure angle

ψ: Helix angle (for helical gears only)

c: Center-center distance

Spur Gears

(1) $P_d = \dfrac{N_t}{D}$: Imperial unit

(2) $m = \dfrac{D}{N_t}$: SI unit

(3) $p_c = \dfrac{\pi D}{N_t}$

(4) $P_d \times p_c = \pi$

Helical Gears

(1) $P_n = P_d / Cos\psi$

(2) $P_a = P_n / Sin\psi = P_n \times Cot\psi$

(3) $P_d = \dfrac{N_t}{D}$

(4) $c = \dfrac{D_1 + D_2}{2} \Rightarrow P_d = \dfrac{\left(N_{t1} + N_{t2}\right)}{2c}$

Bevel Gears

(1) $D_p = \dfrac{N_{tp}}{P}$; $D_g = \dfrac{N_{tg}}{P}$

(2) $\tan\alpha_p = \dfrac{N_{tp}}{N_{tg}}$; $\tan\alpha_g = \dfrac{N_{tg}}{N_{tp}}$

(3) $r_s = \dfrac{N_{tg}}{N_{tp}} = \dfrac{N_{tp}}{N_{tg}} = \tan\alpha_p = Cot\alpha_g$

Chapter 14
Animation with Basic Motion

Objectives:

In this chapter you will learn:

- The different types of **Motion Studies**
- How to model Linkages
- How to animate the Linkages using **Basic Motion**

Different Types of Motion Studies

The **MotionManager Interface** is accessed in the lower left of the graphics window (see Figure 14-1). **SolidWorks** uses different types of motion studies. We will briefly examine these.

Animation - Animation uses the key frame method, in which the software interpolates between positions established by mates, free-hand drag, or positioning via Triad or XYZ values.

Basic Motion - Basic Motion uses motors, springs, 3D contacts, and gravity (*Physical Simulation*); it does not use frames. It includes *Physical Dynamics*, which is the calculation of motion due to collision.

Motion Analysis - Motion Analysis is the highest level of motion study, and is an *Add-In* to **SolidWorks**.

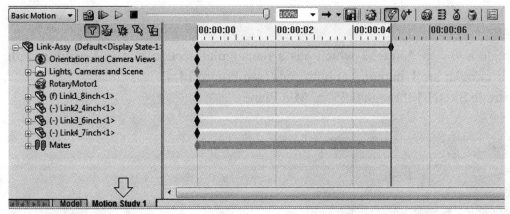

Figure 14-1 MotionManager Interface

We will model simple linkages, assembly them into a mechanism, and then carry out motion studies using Basic Motion.

Modeling of Linkages

Model Link1

1. Open a **New Part** document
2. Create a sketch, **Sketch1** which has a rectangular section that is 8-in long with half-circular arc 1-in radius at both ends (see Figure 14-2)
3. Extrude **Sketch1** through 0.25-in, Mid Plane (see Figure 14-3)

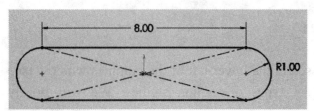

Figure 14-2 Sketch1

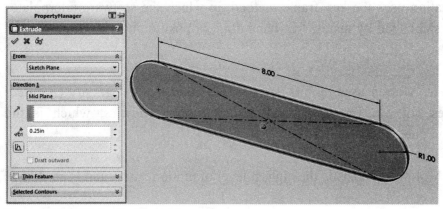

Figure 14-3 Extrude Sketch1

Model Link2

1. Create a sketch, **Sketch2** which has a rectangular section that is 4-in long with half-circular arc 1-in radius at both ends (see Figure 14-4)
2. Extrude **Sketch1** through 0.25-in, Mid Plane

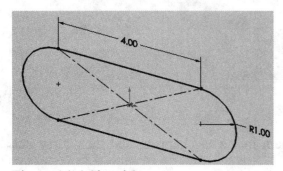

Figure 14-4 Sketch2

Model Link3

1. Create a sketch, **Sketch3** which has a rectangular section that is 6-in long with half-circular arc 1-in radius at both ends (see Figure 14-5)
2. Extrude **Sketch1** through 0.25-in, Mid Plane

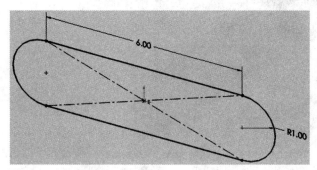

Figure 14-5 Sketch3

Model Link4

1. Create a sketch, **Sketch4** which has a rectangular section that is 7-in long with half-circular arc 1-in radius at both ends (see Figure 14-6)
2. Extrude **Sketch1** through 0.25-in, Mid Plane

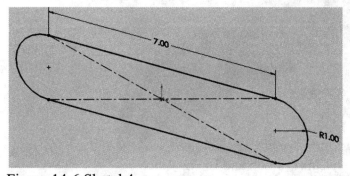

Figure 14-6 Sketch4

Assembly Modeling of Linkages

1. Open a **New Assembly** document
2. Fix the first part, **Link1_8inch**
3. Insert **Link2_4inch**
4. Create **Concentric Mate** between **Link1_8inch** and **Link2_4inch** (see Figure 14-7)
5. Create **Coincident Mate** between **Link1_8inch** and **Link2_4inch** (see Figure 14-8)

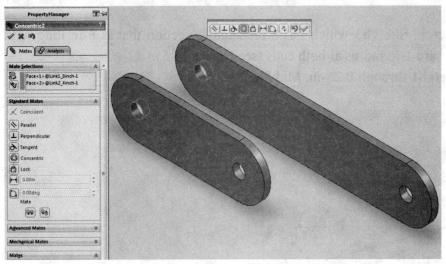

Figure 14-7 Concentric Mate between Link1_8inch and Link2_4inch

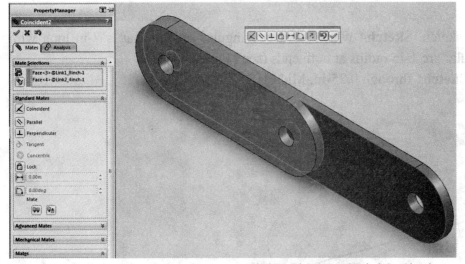

Figure 14-8 Coincident Mate between Link1_8inch and Link2_4inch

6. Insert **Link3_6inch**
7. Create **Concentric Mate** between **Link1_8inch** and **Link3_6inch**   (see Figure 14-9)
8. Create **Coincident Mate** between **Link1_8inch** and **Link3_6inch**   (see Figure 14-10)

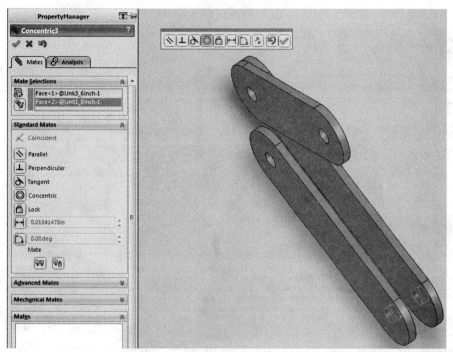

Figure 14-9 Concentric Mate between Link1_8inch and Link2_4inch

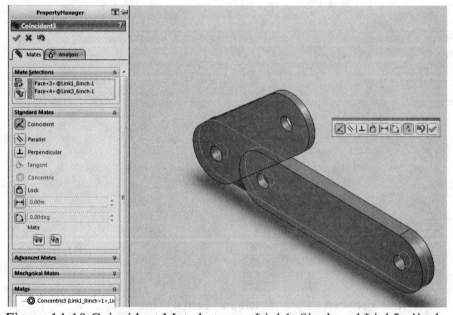

Figure 14-10 Coincident Mate between Link1_8inch and Link2_4inch

9. Insert **Link4_7inch**

10. Create **Concentric Mate** between **Link2_4inch** and **Link4_7inch** (see Figure 14-11)

11. Create **Coincident Mate** between **Link2_4inch** and **Link4_7inch** (see Figure 14-12)

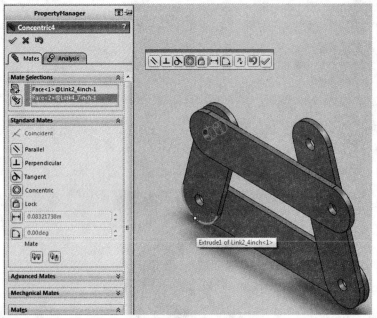

Figure 14-11 Concentric Mate between Link2_4inch and Link4_7inch

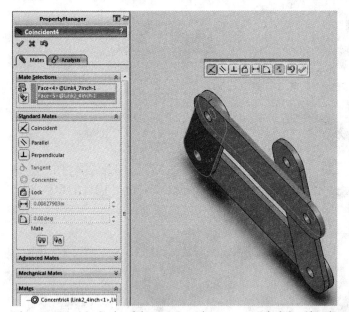

Figure 14-12 Coincident Mate between Link2_4inch and Link4_7inch

12. Create **Concentric Mate** between **Link2_4inch** and **Link3_6inch**   (see Figure 14-13)

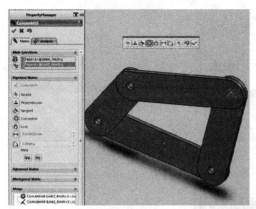

Figure 14-13 Create **Concentric Mate** between **Link2_4inch** and **Link3_6inch**

Figure 14-14 shows the mechanism realized.

Figure 14-14 Mechanism realized

MotionManager Interface

The **MotionManager Interface** is accessed in the lower left of the graphics window (see Figure 14-15). There are four *Physical Simulation* elements used: (1) **Gravity**; (2) **3D contacts**; (3) **Springs**; and (4) **Motors** (see Figure 14-15 and Figure 14-16 for their PropertyManagers).

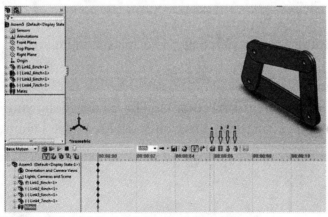

Figure 14-15 MotionManager Interface

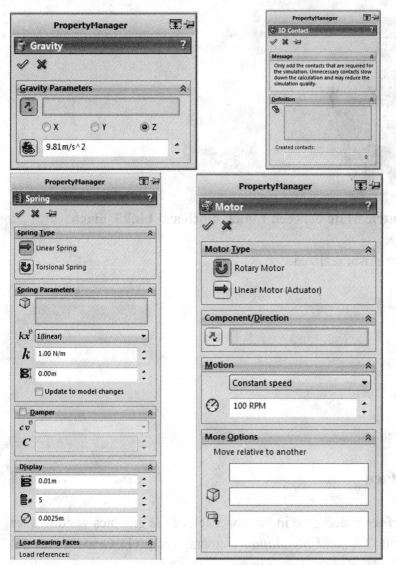

Figure 14-16 PropertyManagers for Gravity, 3D contacts, Springs, and Motors

Using Motors

1. Click the Motor option (The **Motor PropertyManager** is displayed in Figure 14-17)
2. Select **Rotary Motion** (see Figure 14-17)
3. Click the **face of Link2** for the **Component/Direction** field [a red arrow showing the direction of rotation is displayed; change the direction if required] (see Figure 14-17)
4. Click **OK** (see Figure 14-17)

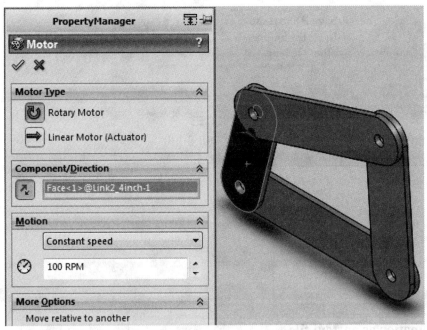

Figure 14-17 Motor PropertyManager

5. Click the **Calculate** option to *calculate* the motion study (see Figure 14-18).

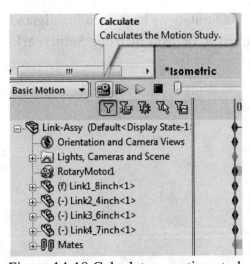

Figure 14-18 Calculate a motion study

The motion studies can be saved as a Microsoft *.avi file by clicking the **Save** option in the **MotionManager Interface** (see Figure 14-19).

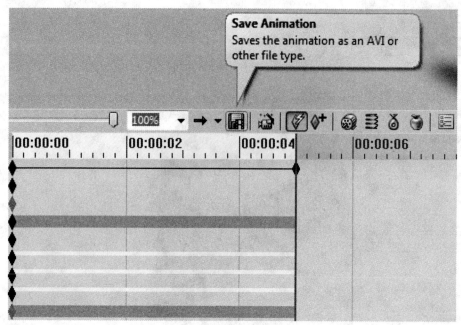

Figure 14-19 Save Animation as an *avi file

Summary

Animation with Basis Motion has been discussed. Its limitations have been highlighted. For more meaningful simulations, a premium price has to be paid by using **SolidWorks Motion Analysis**.

Chapter 15
Animation with SolidWorks Motion

Objectives:

In this chapter you will learn:

- An overview of SolidWorks Motion
- About SolidWorks Motion Add-Ins
- An overview of slider-crank assembly created in SolidWorks
- Kinematic analysis of slider-crank mechanism using SolidWorks Motion
- Interference analysis of slider-crank mechanism using SolidWorks Motion
- Dynamic analysis of slider-crank mechanism using SolidWorks Motion

Types of Motion Studies

Motion studies are graphical simulations of motion for assembly models. Visual properties such as lighting and camera perspective can be incorporated into motion studies. Motion studies do not change an assembly model or its properties. They simulate and animate the motion the user prescribes for a model. SolidWorks *mates* can be used to restrict the motion of components in an assembly when motion is modeled.

From a motion study, MotionManager, a timeline-based interface can be used that includes the following motion study tools:

(1) Animation (available in core SolidWorks). Animation can be used to animate the motion of assemblies:

Add *motors* to drive the motion of one or more parts of an assembly.

Prescribe the positions of assembly components at various times using set *key points*. Animation uses interpolation to define the motion of assembly components between key points.

(2) Basic Motion (available in core SolidWorks). Basic Motion can be used for approximating the effects of *motors*, *springs*, *contact*, and *gravity* on assemblies. Basic Motion takes mass into account in calculating motion. Basic Motion computation is relatively fast, so you can use this for creating presentation-worthy animations using physics-based simulations.

(3) Motion Analysis (available with the SolidWorks Motion™ add-in to SolidWorks Premium). Motion Analysis can be used for accurately simulating and analyzing the effects of motion elements (including *forces*, *springs*, *dampers*, and *friction*) on an assembly. Motion Analysis uses computationally strong kinematic solvers, and accounts for material properties as well as mass and inertia in the computations. Motion Analysis can also be used to plot simulation results for further analysis.

Generally, animation outputs can be posted as AVI (Audio Video Interleave) files; AVI is a multimedia container format introduced by Microsoft.

Deciding Which Type of Study to Use

Use Animation to create presentation-worthy animations for motion that does not require accounting for mass or gravity.

Use Basic Motion to create presentation-worthy approximate simulations of motion that account for mass, collisions, or gravity.

Use Motion Analysis to run computationally strong simulations that take the physics of the assembly motion into account. This tool is the most computationally intensive of the three options. The better the user understands the physics of the motion required, the better the results obtained. Motion Analysis can be used to run impact analysis studies to understand component response to different types of forces.

Differentiating between Animation, Basic Motion & Motion Analysis

There are some differences between the animation and motion capabilities of the various SolidWorks modules, namely: Animation, Basic Motion and Motion Analysis. These differences need to be understood by end-users so that they can determine for themselves which is the right one to use. A nice feature is that the interface pretty much stays the same, and changing from one type of output to the other might only take changing the solver type (*Animation*, *Basic Motion* or *Motion Analysis*). In this subsection, we discuss classification of motion studies based on Solvers used.

Animation (or Assembly Motion) uses the **3DDCM** (3D Dimensional Constraint Manager) from D-Cubed.

The 3DDCM is commonly used to position the parts in an assembly or mechanism. Fast, fully three-dimensional, non-sequential solving, comprehensive geometry, dimension and constraint support enables designers to build, modify and animate the most demanding of assemblies and mechanisms efficiently.

Animation is used to create simple animations that use interpolation to specify point-to-point motion of parts in assemblies.

Basic Motion (or Physical Simulation) uses **Ageia PhysX.**

Ageia PhysX is a physics solver primarily used in games. It simulates how objects move and react; how they behave. It simulates life-like motion and interaction. With its Ageia PhysX, SolidWorks Physical Simulation focuses on making the simulation look real.

Basic Motion is used for approximating the effects of motors, springs, collisions, and gravity on assemblies. Basic Motion takes mass into account in calculating motion. Basic Motion computation is relatively fast, so you can use this for creating presentation-worthy animations using physics-based simulations.

Motion Analysis (or SolidWorks Motion) uses the ADAMS solver.

The ADAMS solver can analyze the complex behavior of mechanical assemblies. With this solver, Motion focuses on *accurately* analyzing the forces, torques, contact forces, power consumption and so on in your mechanism. You can plot any of the resultant kinematic quantities over time (or versus other parameters) in the analysis.

SolidWorks Motion comes in the top level of our design software, SolidWorks Premium, and is also included in both SolidWorks Simulation Professional & Simulation Premium. You must first turn on the Add-In before using Motion Analysis.

Motion Analysis is used to accurately simulate and analyze the motion of an assembly while incorporating the effects of Motion Study elements (including forces, springs, dampers, and friction). A Motion Analysis study combines motion study elements with mates in motion calculations. Consequently motion constraints, material properties, mass, and component contact are included in the SolidWorks Motion kinematic solver calculations. A Motion Analysis study also calculates loads that can be used to define load cases for structural analyses.

Now that the differences between the animation and motion capabilities in the various SolidWorks modules, we will proceed to discuss the SolidWorks Motion overview, SolidWorks Motion Add-In, four-bar linkage mechanism, slider-crank mechanism, and then proceed to motion analysis of a slider-crank mechanism using SolidWorks Motion.

SolidWorks Motion Overview

SolidWorks Motion is the standard virtual prototyping Add-In package in SolidWorks Premium, SolidWorks Simulation Professional, and SolidWorks Simulation Premium, for engineers and designers interested in understanding the performance of their assemblies. The most popular virtual prototyping tool for SolidWorks, SolidWorks Motion simulator lets you make sure your designs will work before you build them.

SolidWorks Motion enables engineers to size motors/actuators, determine power consumption, layout linkages, develop cams, understand gear drives, size springs/dampers, and determine how contacting parts behave.

The result is of motion simulation and analysis is a quantitative reduction in physical prototyping costs and reduced product development time. SolidWorks Motion also provides qualitative benefits such as the ability to consider more designs, risk reduction, and the availability of valuable information early in the design process.

SolidWorks Motion *Add-In*

1. Open **SolidWorks**
2. Open the **model file**
3. Click the **Add-Ins** tool (see Figure 15-1a)
4. Check **SolidWorks Motion** (see Figure 15-1b)
5. Click **OK** (Motion Manager is added; see Figure 15-2)

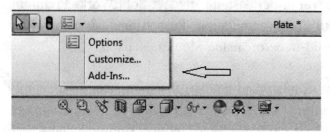

(a) Add-Ins tool is clicked

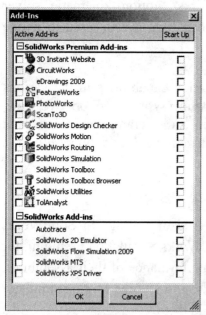

(b) SolidWorks Motion tool is clicked
Figure 15-1 SolidWorks Motion Add-In

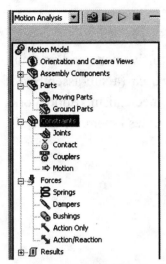

Figure 15-2 SolidWorks Motion Manager

Four-bar Linkage Mechanism and Slider-Crank Mechanism

One of the simplest examples of a constrained linkage is the *four-link mechanism*. A variety of useful mechanisms can be formed from a four-link mechanism through slight variations, such as changing the character of the pairs, proportions of links, *etc.* Furthermore, many complex link mechanisms are combinations of two or more such mechanisms. The majority of four-link mechanisms fall into one of the following two classes:

1. The four-bar linkage mechanism, and
2. The slider-crank mechanism.

The four-bar mechanism has some special configurations created by making one or more links infinite in length. The slider-crank (or crank and slider) mechanism shown in Figure 15-3 is a four-bar linkage with the slider replacing an infinitely long output link. This configuration translates a rotational motion into a translational one. Most mechanisms are driven by motors, and slider-cranks are often used to transform rotary motion into linear motion.

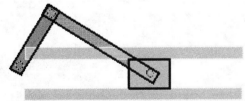

Figure 15-3 Slider-crank mechanism

Problem Description

A slider-crank mechanism designed using SolidWorks consists of five parts and one sub-assembly. They are *bearing*, *crank*, *rod*, *pin*, *piston*, and *rodandpin* (a sub-assembly of rod and pin). Figure 15-4 shows the exploded view of the mechanism. SolidWorks Motion is used for motion analysis of the mechanism, which includes kinematic analysis, interference analysis and dynamic analysis.

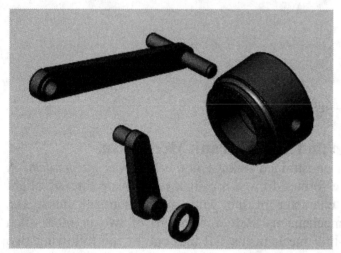

Figure 15-4 Model to be studied using SolidWorks Motion

SolidWorks Parts and Assembly

The first step in the process of Motion Analysis is to have the parts and assembly available. For our study, Figure 15-5 shows the AssemblyManager of the slider-crank mechanism.

Figure 15-5 AssemblyManager of parts and assembly of model for the motion analysis

Using SolidWorks Motion

The Motion Model contains five branches (nodes) as shown in Figure 15-6. These are:

1. **Assembly Components**: contains all parts and subassembly defining the assembly
2. **Parts**: contains Moving Parts and Ground Parts
3. **Constraints**: contains joints, contact, couplers, motion
4. **Forces**: contains springs, dampers, bushings, action Only, Action/Reaction
5. **Results**

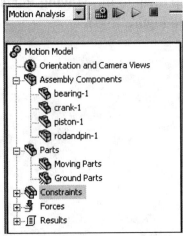

Figure 15-6 Five branches (nodes) of the Motion Model

Methodology for Motion Analysis Using SolidWorks Motion

The basic steps for a motion analysis using SolidWorks Motion are as follows:

1. Defining Bodies
2. Driving Joints
3. Turning off Gravity
4. Running Simulation

Defining Bodies

Before defining the bodies, we need to classify the parts as Moving or Grounded. This means that we need decide which part(s) should be placed in the Ground Parts node and which part(s) should be placed in the Moving Parts node of the Parts branch of the Motion Model Manager. In the current example, the bearing will be grounded, while other parts will move.

To define the bodies, we require **Assembly Components** and **Parts**. The steps involved in defining the bodies are as follows:

1. Expanding the **Assembly Components** (there would appear the four components: *bearing-1*, *crank-1*, *piston-1*, and *rodandpin-1*)

2. Expanding the **Parts** (there would appear the two types: *Moving Parts* and *Ground Parts*)

3. Click *bearing-1* and drag it from **Assembly Components** and drop it to the **Ground Parts** in the **Parts** branch of the Motion Model Manager (see Figure 15-7).

4. Select *crank-1*, *piston-1*, and *rodandpin-1* at the same time using the Shift key, and drag them from **Assembly Components** and drop them to the **Moving Parts** in the **Parts** branch of the Motion Model Manager (see Figure 15-7).

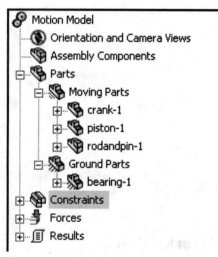

Figure 15-7 Bodies defined

Driving Joints

The **constraints** branch has **Joints**, **Contact**, **Couplers**, and **Motion** as sub-modules (see Figure 15-8). For defining the driving joints, we will examine **Joints** could be one of the following types: *concentric*, *revolute*, or *translational* (see Figure 15-9).

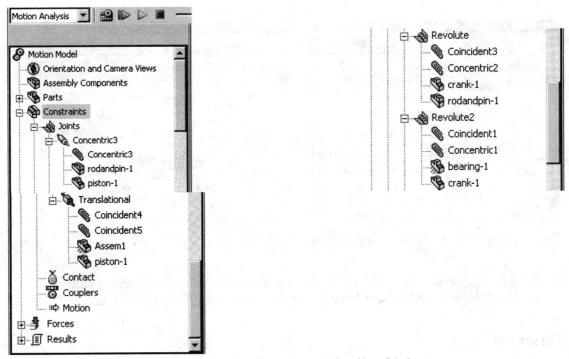

Figure 15-8 Components of Constraints branch and details of Joints

1. Right-click the **Revolute** node and choose Properties (see Figure 15-9)
   The **Edit Mate-Defined Joint** dialog box is automatically displayed (see Figure 15-10)
2. Choose **Velocity** for **Motion Type**, **Constant** for **Function**, and enter **360** degrees/sec for **Angular Velocity** in the **Motion** tab of the **Edit Mate-Defined Joint** dialog box (see Figure 15-10)

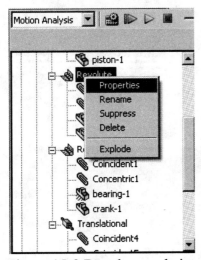

Figure 15-9 Revolute node is used to define the type of motion

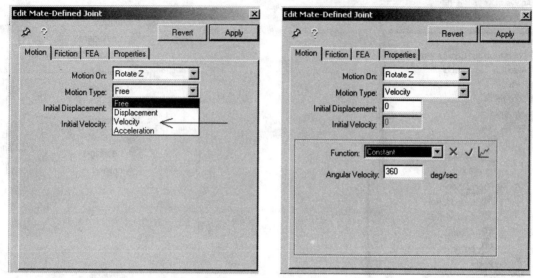

Figure 15-10 Edit Mate-Defined Joint dialog box and definitions for Motion

Turning off Gravity

There are cases in which gravity effect is not needed. In order to **turn off Gravity**, do the following:

1. Right-click the **Motion ModelManager** at the bottom-left side of the window (see Figure 15-11)
2. Click **System Defaults** (The SolidWorks Motion Manager is automatically displayed as shown in Figure 15-12

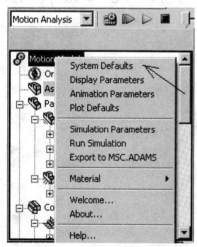

Figure 15-11 Systems Defaults to be accessed

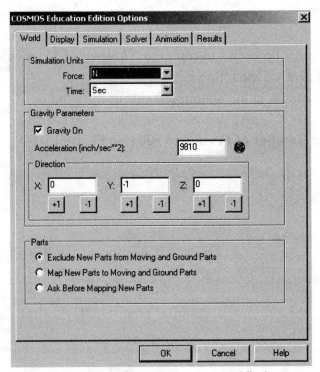

Figure 15-12 Gravity Parameter modified

3. In the **Simulation Units**, select **Force Unit** as **lbf** (see Figure 15-13)
4. Uncheck the **Gravity On** in the **Gravity Parameter**s options (see Figure 15-13)
5. Click **OK**

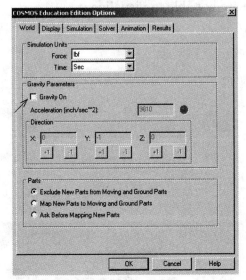

Figure 15-13 Gravity Off

Running Motion Analysis

Before running the Motion Analysis, it may be useful to reset the **Number of Frames**. Let is set the value to 500. To reset the value, do the following:

1. Right-click the **Motion ModelManager** at the bottom-left side of the window
2. Click **System Defaults**
3. Click **Simulation** and change the **Number of Frames** to 500 (see Figure 15-14)

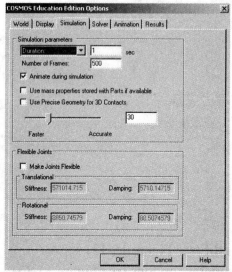

Figure 15-14 Resetting the Number of Frames

This step is useful if we want to visualize what is actually happening. If the **Number of Frames** is small, the motion may be too fast that we are not able to visualize it.

To run Motion Analysis:

4. Click the **Calculate** icon (see Figure 15-15)

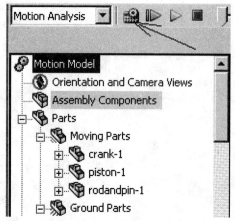

Figure 15-15 Running the Motion Analysis

The results are obtained by right-clicking a part or joint of interest and plotting the output(s) as shown in Figure 15-16.

5. Right-click **piston-1 > Plot > CM Position > X Component** (see Figure 15-16)
6. Right-click **piston-1 > Plot > CM Velocity > X Component** (see Figure 15-16)
7. Right-click **piston-1 > Plot > CM Acceleration > X Component** (see Figure 15-16)

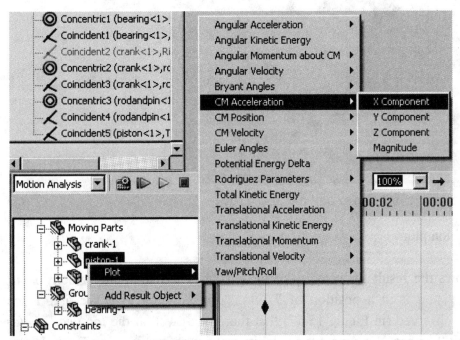

Figure 15-16 Process of generating Results

Kinematic Analysis

The study setup so far is for the kinematic analysis of the slider-crank mechanism. In this case, no effect of loading is considered; we are only interested in the motion of the machine members without considering the inertial effects.

Figures 15-17, 15-18, and 15-19 show the results for position, velocity, and acceleration respectively, for the piston. Similar results can be obtained for any part of the mechanism that we are interested in.

Figure 15-17 shows the result for position of the piston.

In Figure 15-17, it could be observed that the piston moves from minimum of 5 in to maximum of 11 in, resulting in a stroke of 6 in (11 − 5). Initially, the piston is at a position of 7.3 in, progressively increasing within 0.3 sec to 11 in. Then it progressively decreases until 5 in for the next 0.5 sec (0.8 − 0.3). It then moves back to the starting point within the next 3 sec. It could be therefore inferred that the *bottom dead-center* is at a position, 5 in, while the *top dead-center* is at a position, 11 in. There is a dwell at the *top dead-center* (at 0.3 s) for about 0.05 sec. Similarly, there is a dwell at the *bottom dead-center* (at 0.8 s) for about 0.025 sec.

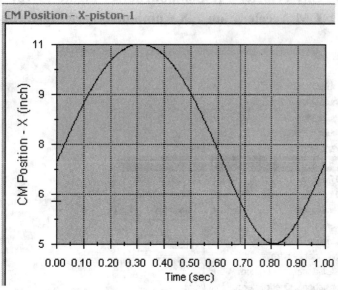

Figure 15-17 Position plot

Figure 15-18 shows the result for velocity of the piston. The maximum velocity is 19 in/sec when the piston is at a position of 7.3 in, corresponding to 0 sec and 1 sec respectively. We observed (in Figure 15-17) that there is a dwell at the *top dead-center* (at 0.3 s) for about 0.05 sec. We expect the velocity to be zero in this case. Similarly, we observed (in Figure 15-17) there is a dwell at the *bottom dead-center* (at 0.8 s) for about 0.025 sec. We also expect the velocity to be zero in this case. Figure 15-18 confirms that the velocity at 0.3 s and 0.8 s is zero.

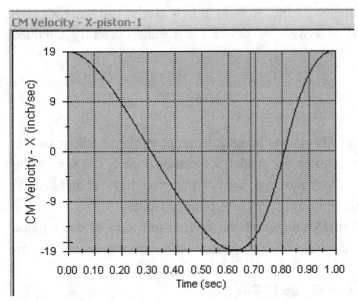

Figure 15-18 Velocity plot

Figure 15-19 shows the result for acceleration of the piston. There is a basin between 0 s and 0.6 s, with constant and minimum acceleration (deceleration) of $-86\,in/s^2$ between 0.25 s and 0.35 s, corresponding to the *top dead-center*. There is a similar scenario between 0.8 s and 0.85 s with a smaller basin for maximum acceleration of $189\,in/s^2$, corresponding to the *bottom dead-center*.

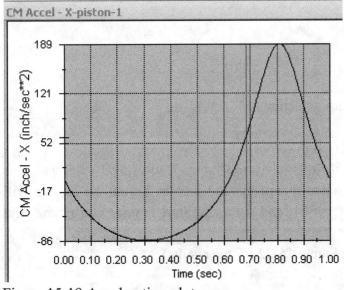

Figure 15-19 Acceleration plot

Our kinematic analysis is now complete. Note: to have a new study, use the **Calculate** icon. SolidWorks will ask you if you want to delete the results currently obtained. Answer "Yes" and continue.

Interference Check

Our second study is Interference Check. Although, it is possible to carry out an interference check in the SolidWorks assembly model, we can do exactly the same using SolidWorks Motion when the parts are moving. Ensure that you have completed the kinematic study before going to this new study. For Interference Check:

1. Right-click the **Motion ModelManager** at the bottom-left side of the window (Notice in Figure 15-20 that the options are now different because there are Results available)
2. Click **Interference Check** (see Figure 15-20)

Figure 15-20 Interference Check study selection

In the **Select Parts to test** text field (red in colour):

3. Click *each part/sub-assembly* (piston-1, rodandpin-1, bearing-1, etc) [see the **Find Interferences Over Time PropertyManager** in Figure 15-21; we will accept the default values of 1, 501, and 2 for the Start Frame, End Frame, and Increment, respectively]
4. Click **Find Now** button (see Figure 15-22 for the results)

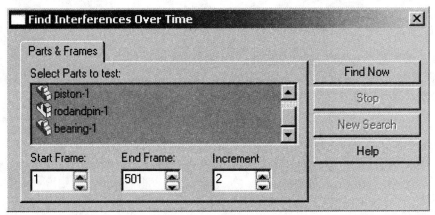

Figure 15-21 Find Interferences Over Time PropertyManager

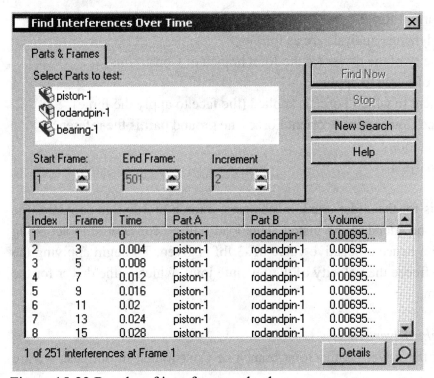

Figure 15-22 Results of interference check

Dynamic Analysis

Our third study is Dynamic Analysis. Ensure that you delete the current Results before continuing. To delete the current results:

1. Right-click the **Motion ModelManager** at the bottom-left side of the window
2. Click **Delete Results** (see Figure 15-23)

Figure 15-23 Delete current Results

The steps involved in dynamic analysis are as follows:

a) Freeze the velocity of the driver (at the Joint branch of Constraints)
b) Select the type of Force to apply
c) Select Component to which Force is applied (the face to apply the force)
d) Select Reference Component to orient Force (the ground part is the reference)
e) Select Force Function
f) Run Motion Analysis

In the dynamic analysis for the slider-crank mechanism, a force of 3 lb that simulates the engine firing load will be added to the piston. This load will be considered to act along the negative X-direction hence a negative value of -3 lbf is given. To begin applying the force, we need to first freeze the velocity of the revolute joint, which is the driver for the slider-crank mechanism.

Freeze the velocity of the driver

Freeze the velocity of the driver (at the Joint branch of Constraints; in our case we are looking at Revolve)

3. Click **Revolve > Properties > Motion Type** and select to **Free** to freeze the velocity (see Figure 15-24)

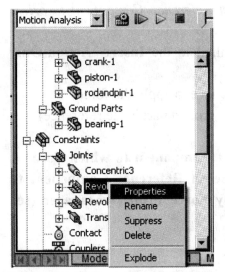 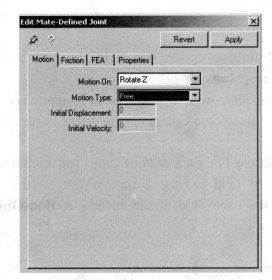

Figure 15-24 Freezing the velocity

Select the type of Force to apply

There are a number of types of **Forces** (*Springs*, *Dampers*, *Bushings*, *Action-Only Force*, and *Action-Only Moment*). There is therefore the need to select the type of Force to apply. We are interested in *Action-Only Force*.

    4. Click **Forces > Add Action-Only Force** to Add Forces (see Figure 15-25)
        The **Insert- Action-Only Force PropertyManager** (see Figure 15-26)

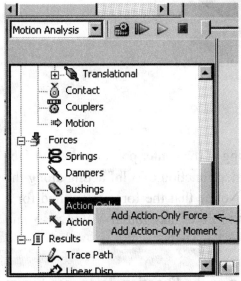

Figure 15-25 Add Force

Select Component to which Force is applied & Select Reference Component to orient Force

From the **Definition** option, two fields have to be filled in the **Insert- Action-Only Force PropertyManager**:

a) Select Component to which Force is applied (the face to apply the force)

b) Select Reference Component to orient Force (the ground part is the reference)

5. Select the *End face of the Piston* for the **Select Component to which Force is applied** field and the *Ground Parts* for the **Select Reference Component to orient Force** field of the **Insert- Action-Only Force PropertyManager** (see Figure 15-26)

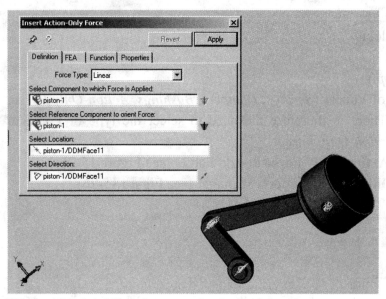

Figure 15-26 Adding force on the face of the piston

Select Force Function

The force will be defined as a point force (load) acting at the center point on the end face of the piston. Therefore, the force is simulated as a step function of 3 lbf acting along the negative X-direction and applied for 0.1 seconds. Notice that the force is applied for a short period. The Type of Function will be Step; the Force has Initial Value = -3 and Final Value = 0; the Start Step Time = 0 and End Step Time = 0.1.

6. Select the **Function Option** and choose **Step** as the **Function Type** (see Figure 15-27).

7. For the **Force (pound-force) Value**, supply **-3** as **Initial Value** of force (lbf) and **0.1** as **End Step Time** [Note: accept **0** as **Final Value** of force (lbf) and **0** as **Start Step Time**] (see Figure 15-27)

8. Click *Apply* (see results in Figure 15-28)

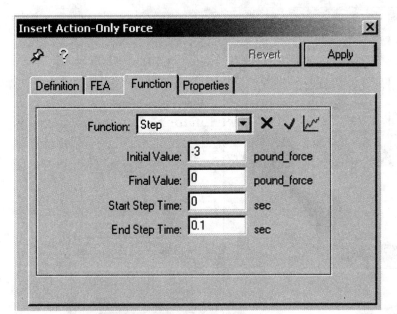

Figure 15-27 Defining the force function

Run Motion Analysis

We are now ready to run the Motion Analysis. To run Motion Analysis:

1. Click the **Calculate** icon

The results shown in Figure 15-28 are automatically generated for position, velocity, and acceleration of the piston for the dynamic loading. It could be observed that the piston moves in the negative X-direction for 0.15 s and then change direction moving in the positive direction until 0.45 s when reverses direction until 0.8 in, and moves in the positive X-direction again until 1 s.

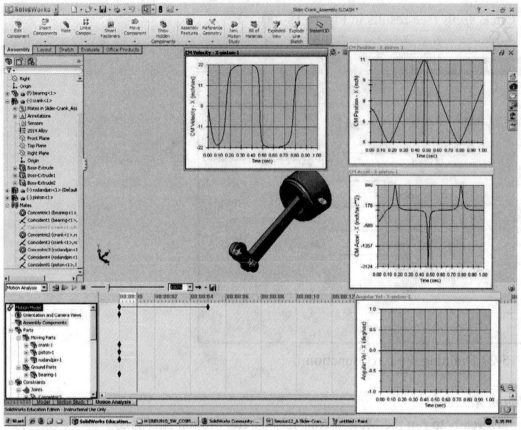

Figure 15-28 Screen shot of position, velocity, and acceleration for dynamic loading

Validating the Results

Validating the results obtained using SolidWorks Motion cannot be overemphasized. This is true for using any software. Therefore, we need to check that we are correct by comparing our results with results from know methods. The results obtained for these motion analyses are consistent with analytical methods found in dynamics textbooks.

Summary

We have presented SolidWorks Motion for solving simple and complex parts or assemblies. The differences between SolidWorks Motion and Animation or Basic Motion have been discussed in detail.

Exercises

1. What is the difference between SolidWorks Motion and Animation or Basic Motion?
2. Are we able to obtain the position, velocity, or acceleration for the slider-crank mechanism using Animation or Basic Motion?
3. Are we able to carry out dynamic analysis for the slider-crank mechanism using Animation or Basic Motion?

References

(1) Chang, K-H, Motion Simulation and Mechanism Design with COSMOSMotion 2007, SDC Publications, 2008.

(2)
   http://www.me.unlv.edu/~mbt/320/SolidWorks/CrankSlider SW Animation.htm

(3)
   http://cimar.mae.ufl.edu/~carl/eml2023_spring09/pages/docs/cosmos_motion/CM_Student_Workbook-ENG-2008.pdf

(4) http://www.cs.cmu.edu/~rapidproto/mechanisms/chpt5.html#fourlink

(5)
   https://forum.solidworks.com/community/solidworks_simulation/motion_studies/blog/2010/02/08/solvers-used-for-animation-basic-motion-motion-analysis

Chapter 16

Rendering

Objectives:

In this chapter you will learn:

- How to use **Zebra Stripes options** to render a part or assembly
- How to use **Curvature options** to render a part or assembly
- How to use **PhotoWorks** toolbar to render photo-realistic images

Introduction

The **Zebra Stripes** tool allows the user to see small changes in a surface that may be hard to see with a standard display. Zebra Stripes simulate the reflection of long strips of light on a very shiny surface. With Zebra Stripes, the user can easily see wrinkles or defects in a surface, and can verify that two adjacent faces are in contact, are tangent, or have continuous curvature.

The **Curvature** tool allows the user to display a part or assembly with the surfaces rendered in different colours according to the local radius of curvature. Curvature is defined as the reciprocal of the radius (1/radius), in current model units. By default, the greatest curvature value displayed is 1.0000, and the smallest value is 0.0010. As the radius of curvature decreases, the curvature value increases, and the corresponding colour changes from black (0.0010), through blue, green, and red (1.0000). As the radius of curvature increases, the curvature value decreases. A planar surface has a curvature value of zero because the radii of flat faces are infinite.

The **PhotoWorks Studio** allows the user to render a model in an existing scene with lights. The user selects one of the studios and the scene and lights are automatically added. The lights and the scene automatically scale to the size of the model. The floor of the scene positions itself on the bottom of the model relative to the current view orientation.

Surface Model

1. Click **New Part** document
2. Create **Sketch1** (see Figure 16-1)

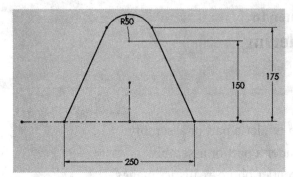

Figure 16-1 Sketch1

3. Click **Insert > Surface > Extrude** (see Figure 16-2 for the Surface-Extrude PropertyManager)
4. In the **Direction1** rollout, set the **Extrude Thickness** as **100 mm** (see Figure 16-2)

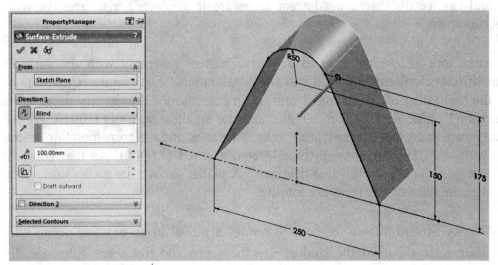

Figure 16-2 Surface-Extrude PropertyManager

Zebra Stripes

Inserting the Zebra Stripes Tool

5. Right-click the top-right empty space in the **CommandManager**
6. Select the **Customize** option (see Figure 16-3)

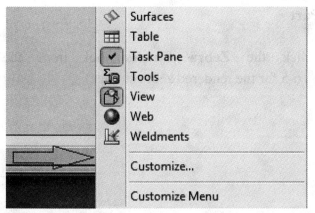

Figure 16-3 Select Customize option

7. In the **Customize PropertyManager**, click **Commands > View** (see Figure 16-4)
8. Drag the **Zebra** button to the CommandManager (see Figure 16-4)

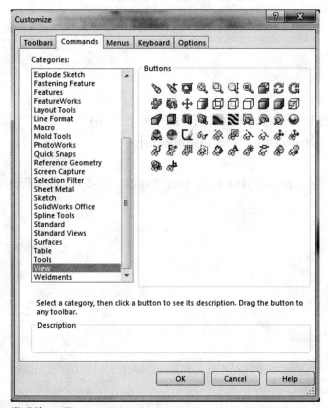

(i) View Buttons

(ii) Zebra Stripes tool

Figure 16-4 Zebra Stripes tool

Including Zebra Stripes Effects on a Part

9. With the **surface** active, click the **Zebra Stripes** tool from the **CommandManager** (see Figure 16-5 for the rendered zebra surface)

Figure 16-5 Rendered zebra surface

Removing Zebra Stripes Effects

10. Right-click the surface having Zebra Stripes effects (see Figure 16-6)
11. Click **Zebra Stripes** (see Figure 16-6) [the effect disappears]
    OR
12. Click **Zebra Stripes** from the **CommandManager** (see Figure 16-6) [the effect disappears]

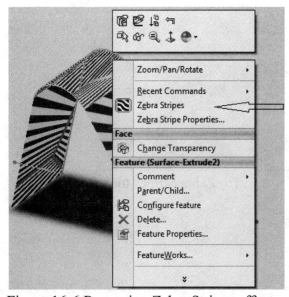

Figure 16-6 Removing Zebra Stripes effects

Curvature

Inserting the Curvature Tool

The procedure is similar to the Zebra Stripes, except that the **Curvature** tool is selected and dragged to the CommandManager.

Including Curvature Effects on a Part

1. With the **surface** active, click the **Curvature** tool from the **CommandManager** (see Figure 16-7 for the rendered surface with the curvature depicted)
   Notice: Curvature = 1/Radius of curvature

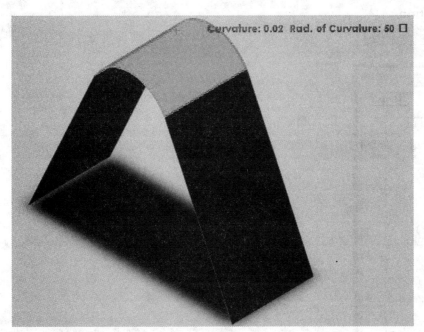

Figure 16-7 Rendered surface with the curvature (1/Radius of curvature) depicted

Removing Curvature Effects

2. Click **Curvature** from the **CommandManager** (the effect disappears)

PhotoWorks Toolbar

Inserting the PhotoWorks Tool

1. Click a **New** Part
2. Click **Add-Ins** (see Figure 16-8)
3. Select or check **PhotoWorks** from the **Add-Ins PropertyManager** (see Figure 16-9)

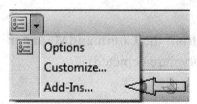

Figure 16-8 Add-Ins options

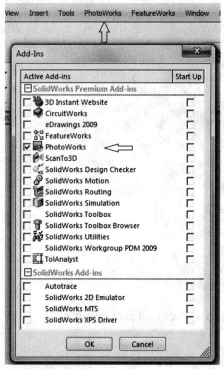

Figure 16-9 PhotoWorks selection from the Add-Ins PropertyManager

4. Click the **PhotoWorks Studio** tool from the PhotoWorks Studio toolbar (see Figure 16-10)

   The PhotoWorks Studio PropertyManager is displayed; see Figure 16-11)

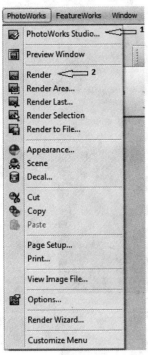

Figure 16-10 PhotoWorks Studio toolbar

5. In the **Scenery** rollout, select **Office Space** using the drop-down menu (Figure 16-11)
6. Click **Render** from the PhotoWorks Studio toolbar (see Figure 16-10)
7. Click **OK**. View the rendered model in the Graphics window (see Figure 16-12).

Figure 16-11 Office Space option selection

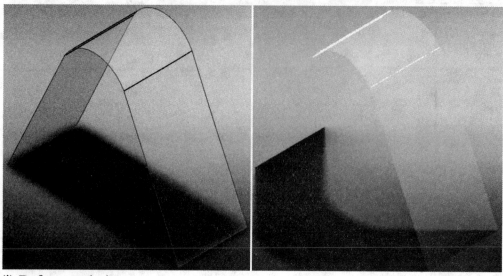

(i) Before rendering   (ii) After rendering

Figure 16-12 Rendered model

Summary

This chapter presents the Zebra Stripes and Curvature tools as well as the PhotoWorks Studio for rendering surface models. The Curvature tool can suggest which area of a surface is under more stress that the others because it is related to the inverse of the radius of curvature. These tools are mainly for aesthetic design and are useful at the design stage for exploring the best surfaces required for a product.

Exercises

1. Use the Zebra Stripes tool and PhotoWorks Studio to render the surface shown in Figure 12-7 in chapter 12.

2. Use the Zebra Stripes tool and PhotoWorks Studio to render the surface shown in Figure 12-16 in chapter 12.

3. Use the Zebra Stripes tool and PhotoWorks Studio to render the surface shown in Figure 12-59 in chapter 12.

Chapter 17
Mold Design

Objectives:

In this chapter you will learn:

- The terminology and concepts of **Draft**, **Parting Line**, **Draft Analysis**, **Shut-Off Surfaces**, **Parting Surface**, and **Tooling Split** used in mold design
- How to create **Parting Line**
- How to create **Parting Surface**
- How to carry out **Tooling Split** and create cavity and core blocks for injection molds

MOLD DESIGN BACKGROUND

Mold design is a special area of manufacturing processes which considers the process for creating the lower half and upper-half of the mold required for producing forged, cast, and plastic parts. Due to its specialty, there is very limited information available for proven methodology using an automated software approach. Mold design is one of the important applications of SolidWorks. Earlier versions of SolidWorks followed long-winded approaches, but most recent versions of SolidWorks are quite effective in handling a reasonably good number of mold designs. The SolidWorks Mold Tools are available to help users create cavity and core blocks for injection molds. They do not provide libraries for building the entire mold or mold components. Most recent versions of SolidWorks offer significant enhancements in mold design and these enhancements are covered in this book.

It is a known fact that Parting Surface in SolidWorks works best on planar parting lines that are convex throughout the part and that mold designers have to create their Parting Surfaces for 70% or more of the involvement in mold design. To put in different words, SolidWorks Mold Tools are not reliable for concave parting lines/surfaces or non-planar lines/surfaces, which are commonly encountered in complex parts. It is important to note some of the limitations of SolidWorks in mold design. SolidWorks Mold Tools are semi-automated tools. It should helpful to know that creating moderately complex mold requires some level of manual intervention to get the SolidWorks Mold Tools to deliver reasonably usable results. Several experienced mold designers tend to use different techniques, ranging from cutting away bits of solids, to utilizing surface modeling, to using about 80% Mold Tools techniques and the rest manual surfacing.

The remaining part of this chapter presents the application of SolidWorks to mold design. The pre-requisite is that the part for which the mold design is to be carried out, should have been already modeled. Let us now follow step-by-step, the method used in SolidWorks Mold Tools for designing mold and we will use the basin, pulley, bowl, plastic cover, and sump parts that we have already modeled.

MOLD DESIGN TOOLS OVERVIEW

Mold analysis tools are used by designers of molded plastic parts and by designers of the mold tools used to manufacture those parts. You create a mold using a sequence of integrated tools that control the mold creation process. You can use these mold tools to analyze and correct deficiencies with either SolidWorks or imported models of parts to be molded. Mold tools span from initial analysis to creating the tooling split. The result of the tooling split is a multi-body part containing separate bodies for the molded part, the core, and the cavity, plus other optional bodies such as side cores. The multi-body part file maintains your design intent in one convenient location. Changes to the molded part are automatically reflected in the tooling bodies.

The following overview from SolidWorks lists typical mold design tasks and the SolidWorks functions that provide solutions to help users complete those tasks.

Tasks	Solutions
When you are not using models built with SolidWorks, import parts into SolidWorks.	Use *Import/Export* tools to import models into SolidWorks from another application. The model geometry in imported parts can include imperfections such as gaps between surfaces. The SolidWorks application includes an *import diagnostic* tool to address these issues.
Determine if a model (imported or built in SolidWorks) includes faces without draft.	Use the *Draft Analysis* tool to examine the faces to ensure sufficient draft. Additional functionality includes: **Face classification**. Display color-coded count of faces with positive draft, and straddle faces. **Gradual transition**. Display the draft angle as it changes within each faced.
Check for undercut areas.	Use the *Undercut Detection* tool to locate trapped areas in a model that prevent ejection from the mold. These areas require a mechanism called a "side core" to produce the undercut relief. Side cores eject from the mold as it is opened.
Scale the model.	Resize the model's geometry with the *Scale* tool to account for the shrink factor when plastic cools. For odd shaped parts and glass filled plastic, you can specify nonlinear values.

Select the parting lines from which you create the parting surface.	Generated parting lines with the *Parting Lines* tool that selects a preferred parting line around the model.
Create shut-off surfaces to prevent leakage between core and cavity.	Detect possible sets of holes and automatically shut them off with the *Shut-off Surfaces* tool. The tool creates surfaces to fill the open holes using no fill, tangent fill, contact fill, or a combination of the three. The no fill option is used to exclude one or more though holes so you can manually create their shut-off surfaces. You can then create the core and cavity.
Create the parting surface, from which you can create the tooling split.\n\nWith certain models, use the ruled surface tool to create interlock surfaces along the edges of the parting surface.	Use the *Parting Surface* tool to extrude surfaces form the parting lines generated earlier. These surfaces are used to separate the mold cavity geometry from the mold core geometry.
Add interlock surfaces to the model.	Apply these solutions for interlock surfaces:\nSimpler models. Use the automated option that is part of the *Tooling Split* tool.\nMore complex models. Use the *Ruled Surface* tool to create the interlock surfaces.
Perform tooling split to separate core and cavity.	Crate the core and cavity automatically with the *Tooling Split* tool. The Tooling Split tool uses the parting line, shut off surfaces, and parting surfaces information to create the core and cavity, and allows you to specify the block sizes.
Create side cores, lifters, and trimmed ejector pins.	Use *Core* to extract geometry from the tooling solid to create a core feature. You can also create lifters and trimmed ejector pins.
Display the core and cavity transparently, enabling you to view the model inside.	Assign different colors to each entity with the *Edit Color* tool. The **Edit Color** tool also manipulates optical properties such as transparency.
Display the core and cavity separated.	Separate the core and cavity at a specified distance with the *Move/Copy* Bodies tool.

MOLD DESIGN METHODOLOGY

1. Click **Insert > Part > Name*.sldprt**
2. Click **Draft > DraftXpert > Add** {check **Auto paint**}
3. Click **Scale** > [1.2]   {check **Uniform Scaling**}
4. Click **Parting Line > Pull Direction** (Mold Parameter) [Using Temporary Axis; note direction]
    -**Draft Analysis** [Check "**Use for Core/Cavity Split**" > **OK**]
    -Pick all lines/curves defining the **Parting Line > OK** [An Arrow moves along the Parting Line contour. It should be manually guided]
5. Click **Shut-Off Surfaces > OK** [Clear "Knit option" if advised. If REDUNDANT Shut-OFF Surfaces exist, DELETE them]
6. Click **Parting Surface > Top View > Value** <1-50> {Check **Perpendicular to Pull**}
    -Check "Knit all surfaces" IF there is a warning
7. Click **TOP PLANE (or other plane)** and sketch base (normally rectangular) of **TOOLING SPLIT**
    –Exit Sketch
8. Check **TOOLING SPLIT > PLANE** in Step 6 and define **Heights** UP/DOWN from this PLANE which passes the origin
    -Define height of tooling split upward (mm) from datum
    -Define height of tooling split downward (mm) from datum
9. Right-click **Surface Bodies** and HIDE them
10. Expand **Solid Bodies** in the **FeatureManager**
11. Click **Tooling Split [1] > Insert > FeatureManager > Move-Copy**
    -move **Triad** vertical axis in the direction to pull out
12. Repeat Step 10 for the other **Tooling Split [2]**

Enhancements in SolidWorks for Mold Design

One area where most recent versions of SolidWorks significantly differ from their predecessors is in Mold Design. We summarize the new steps for mold design here, for a part, *basin*:

Access Model: **BASIN**

1. Open a **New** SolidWorks part document [Note: Mold Tool should be activated]
2. **Set** the document properties for the model, with decimal places = 2.
3. Click **Insert > Part > BASIN*.sldprt > OK**

Mold Design Procedure

Step 1: Click Draft from the Mold Tools CommandManager (see Figure 17-1)
Step 2: Enter a draft angle and check the Auto part dialogue box (see Figure 17-2)

Figure 17-1 Draft tool

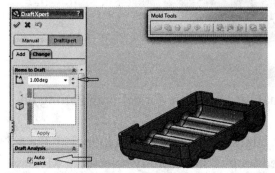

Figure 17-2 Draft angle and Auto part check

Step 3: Click the Scale tool and enter the Scale parameter box (see Figure 17-3)

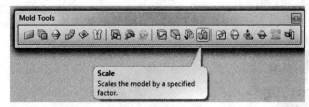

Figure 17-3 Scale factor

Step 4: Click the Parting line tool (see Figure 17-4)

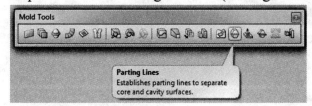

Figure 17-4 Parting lines

Step 5: When the Parting line PropertyManager appears, click a vertical line for pull direction; reverse direction if needed (see Figure 17-5)

Step 6: Click the Draft Analysis tool (see Figure 17-5)

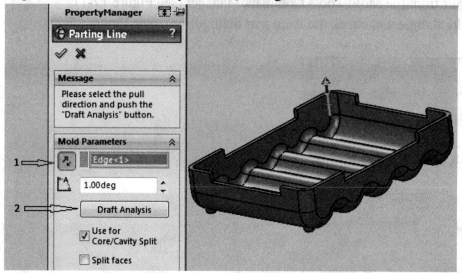

Figure 17-5 Choose Pull direction and Draft Analysis to prepare for defining Parting line

Step 7: When the colored model appears, select edges that form a closed loop with the aid of the 'GPS'(see Figure 17-6). When the closed loop is successfully selected a Message is displayed (see Figure 17-7).

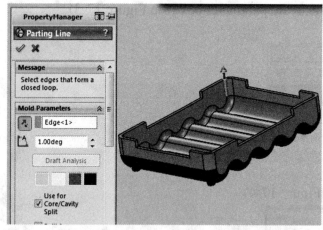

Figure 17-6 Select edges that form a closed loop

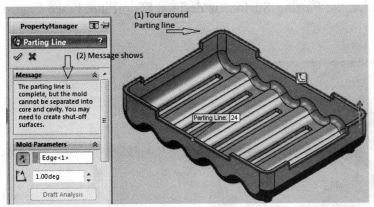

Figure 17-7 Message is displayed to show that parting line is complete

Step 8: Click the Shut-off Surface tool (see Figure 17-8)

Figure 17-8 Shut-off Surface

Step 9: Click the Parting Surface tool (see Figure 17-9)

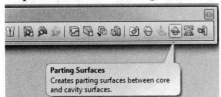

Figure 17-9 Parting Surface

Step 10: Adjust the Parting Surface Parameter [15mm or any other larger value] (see Figure 17-10)

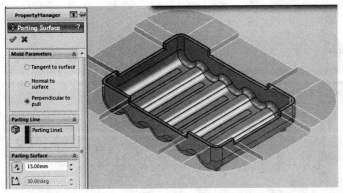

Figure 17-10 Adjust the Parting Surface Parameter to a suitable value [e.g. 15 mm]

Step 11: Click the Plane on which the Parting Surface is defined [Top Plane] (see Figure 17-11)

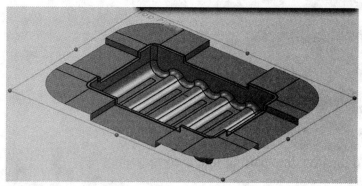

Figure 17-11 Plane defining Parting Surface is selected

Step 12: Be in Sketch Mode and sketch a rectangle to define Tooling Split box (see Figure 17-12)

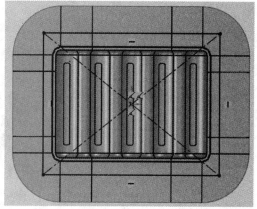

Figure 17-12 Sketch a rectangle to define Tooling Split box

Step 13: Exit Sketch Mode [This step is imperative] (see Figure 17-13)

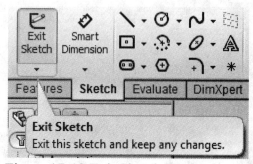

Figure 17-13 Exit Sketch Mode

Step 14: Click the Tooling Split icon (see Figure 17-14)

Figure 17-14 Click the Tooling Split icon

Step 15: Click any edge of the Tooling Split box (see Figure 17-15)

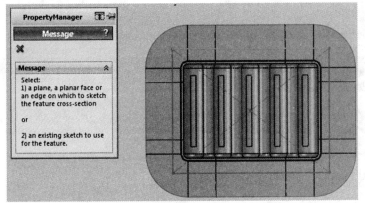

Figure 17-15 Click any edge of the Tooling Split box

Step 16: When the Tooling Split PropertyManager appears, adjust the Block Size (see Figure 17-16).

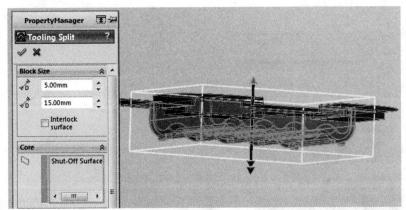

Figure 17-16 Adjust the Block Size from the Tooling Split PropertyManager

Step 17: From the **FeatureManager**, **hide** the **Surface Bodies**.
Step 18: From the **FeatureManager**, **hide** the **Parting Line**.
Step 19: From the **FeatureManager**, expand the **Solid Bodies**.

Step 20: Click **Tooling Split[1] > Insert > Features > Move/Copy**

Step 21: Click **Translate/Rotate** to activate the **Triad** [This step is mandatory for the Triad to appear]

Step 22: When the Triad appears, pull the Arrow to move part of the Box (see Figure 17-17).

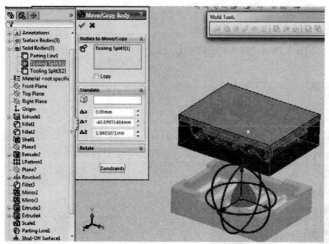

Figure 17-17 Pull Arrow of Triad to move part of the Box

Step 22: Click **Tooling Split[2] > Insert > Features > Move/Copy**

Step 23: Click **Translate/Rotate** to activate the **Triad** [This step is mandatory for the Triad to appear]

Step 24: When the Triad appears, pull the Arrow to move part of the Box (see Figure 17-18).

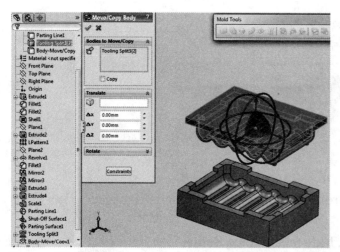

Figure 17-18 Pull Arrow of Triad to move part of the Box

The mold design process is complete (see Figure 17-19). Electronic files of the molds have to be sent to the manufacturing division for manufacture while the mold model is retained in the design division for archiving and future revisions.

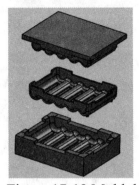

Figure 17-19 Mold design is complete

Summary

The chapter presents some of the significant enhancements that have been made in most recent versions of SolidWorks for Mold Design. Such enhancements have made SolidWorks to be very user-friendly, efficient, and effective in mold design. A step-by-step example of the processes involved in mold design is included in this chapter and following these steps, user should be able to design molds for similar parts encountered in practice.

Exercises

Design the molds for producing the parts shown in Figure P-1 to P-4; files are available in the resources archive for this book.

1. Pulley

Figure P-1 Part for which the mold is being designed: pulley

2. Bowl

Figure P-2 Part for which the mold is being designed: bowl

3. Plastic cover

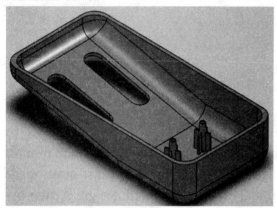

Figure P-3 Part for which the mold is being designed: plastic cover

4. Sump

Figure P-4 Part for which the mold is being designed: sump

Chapter 18
Sheet Metal Parts—I

Objectives:

In this chapter you will learn:

- The differences between **Insert Bends** and **Base Flange** approaches in **Sheet Metal Parts**
- How to create sheet metal parts using the **Insert Bends** approach
- About **Sheet Metal Part** tools
- How to insert a **Rip** feature
- How to insert a **Sheet Metal Bend** feature
- How to insert a **Flange** feature
- How to insert a **Hem** feature
- How to insert a **Miter Flange** feature
- How to insert a **Vent** features and make some manufacturing decisions.
- How to create sheet metal parts using the **Base Flange** approach

There are a number of manufacturing functions for which SolidWorks has tools for industrial applications. Some of these manufacturing functions include mold design, sheet metal work, weldments, hinges, etc. Sheet metal work is one of the several aspects of manufacturing process which requires specific attention.

Sheet Metal Manufacturing Processes

The success of forming is in relation to two things, the flow and stretch of material. As a die forms a shape from a flat sheet of metal, there is a need for the material to move into the shape of the die. The flow of material is controlled through pressure applied to the blank and lubrication applied to the die or the blank. If the form moves too easily, wrinkles will occur in the part. To correct this, more pressure or less lubrication is applied to the blank to limit the flow of material and cause the material to stretch or thin. If too much pressure is applied, the part will become too thin and break. Drawing metal is the science of finding the correct balance between wrinkles and breaking to achieve a successful part.

There are several methods involved in sheet metal work, amongst which are the following: bending, roll forming, deep drawing, bar drawing, tube drawing, wire drawing, and plastic drawing.

Bending is a common _metalworking_ technique to process _sheet metal_ as shown in Figure 18-1. It is usually done by hand on a _box_ and _pan brake_, or industrially on a _brake press_ or _machine brake_. Typical products that are made like this are boxes such as _electrical enclosures_, and rectangular _ductwork_. Usually bending has to overcome both tensile stresses as well as compressive stresses. When bending is done, the residual stresses make it spring back towards its original position, so we have to over-bend the sheet metal keeping in mind the residual stresses. When sheet metal is bent, it stretches in length. The bend deduction is the amount the sheet metal will stretch when bent as measured from the outside. A bend has a radius. The term bend radius refers to the inside radius. The bend radius depends upon the dies used, the metal properties, and the metal thickness.

In sheet metal parts, knowledge of the following is important:
- Bending phenomenon (effect of bend radius, material thickness, and bend angle)
- Stress Relief methods (rectangular, tear, and obround configurations)

Many software packages refer to the K-factor for bending sheet metal. K-factor is a ratio that represents the location of the neutral sheet with respect to the inside thickness of the sheet metal part. The bend allowance is the length of the arc of the neutral axis between the tangent points of a bend in any material.

$$B_d = 2*(R+T)-B_a$$
$$B_a = \pi*(R+K*T)*\alpha/180$$
$$K = (180*B_a)(\pi*\alpha*T)-R/T$$

where:
- B_a = bend allowance
- R = inside bend radius
- K = K-Factor, which is t / T
- T = material thickness
- t = distance from inside face to neutral sheet
- A = bend angle in degrees (the angle through which the material is bent)

Figure 18-1 Sheet metal bending setup

Roll forming is a continuous bending operation in which a long strip of _metal_ (typically coiled _steel_) is passed through consecutive sets of rolls, or _stands_, each performing only an incremental part of the bend, until the desired cross-section profile is obtained (see Figure 18-2). Roll forming is ideal for producing parts with long lengths or in large quantities.

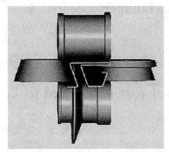

Figure 18-2 Sheet metal roll forming bending setup

Deep drawing

Drawing can also be used to pull metal over a _die_ (male mold) to create a specific shape. For example, _stainless steel kitchen sinks_ are formed by drawing the stainless steel _sheet metal_ stock over a form (the die) in the shape of the sink. _Beverage cans_ are formed by drawing _aluminum_ stock over can-shaped dies. By comparison, _hydroforming_ forces metal into a female mold using pressure.

There are many other manufacturing processes applied to sheet metal part design.

There are basically two approaches to sheet metal part design. One is referred to as the **Insert Bends Method**; this is the traditional method. The other is the **Base Flange Method**, which is the more recent one. These approaches are now presented.

SHEET METAL PART DESIGN METHODOLOGY USING INSERT BENDS

EXAMPLE 1 SHEET METAL PARTS

CREATE A SHELL

1. Create a **shell** [Note: a shell is not a sheet metal; it is a thin-walled part having constant thickness]
2. Click the **MY-TEMPLATE** tab.
3. Double-click **ANSI-MM-PART**.
4. Click **Top Plane** (or other appropriate plane)
5. Sketch and dimension the part profile (a rectangle, 350 mm by 450 mm).
6. Click **Extruded Boss/Base**.
7. Enter value (**100 mm**) for Depth in Direction1.
   [In this case a box (350 mm by 450 mm by 100 mm)] (see Figure 18-3).
8. Click **OK**
9. Click the **front face** of the **Extrude1** feature

10. Click **Shell** for the features toolbar. The **Shell1 PropertyManager** appears.
11. Click the **Shell outward** box.
12. Enter **1mm** (or other value) for Thickness.
13. Click **OK** from the **Shell1 PropertyManager**.

Shell1 is displayed in the FeatureManager and a shelled part is obtained as in Figure 18-3.

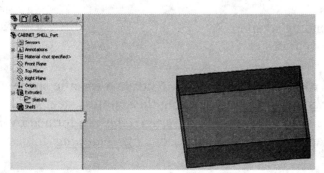

Figure 18-3 Shell1 PropertyManager

As already mentioned, creating a shell is not sheet metal work. A thin-walled part (shell) needs to be available as the starting point for sheet metal part design using the **Insert Bends** method.

INSERT A RIP FEATURE

A **Rip** Feature is normally inserted in a part to create a cut of no thickness along the edges of the Extruded Base feature.

1. Click **Rip** from the Sheet Metal toolbar. The **Rip PropertyManager** appears (see Figure 18-4).
2. Click the **inside vertical edges**. The selected edges are displayed in the **Edges to Rip/Rip Parameters** box. Accept the default **Rip Gap** (0.10 mm).
3. Click **OK** from the **Rip PropertyManager**. Rip1 appears in the **FeatureManager**.

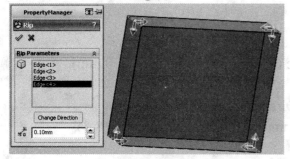

Figure 18-4 Inserting a rip feature

The gateway that is used into the Sheet Metal toolbox is the **Feature > Insert > Sheet Metal** (see Figure 18-5). This route enables the sheet metal tool box when a part (shell) is the starting point.

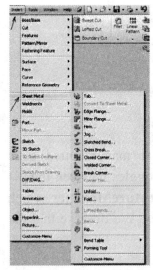

Figure 18-5 The Insert Sheet Metal Tool bar gate way

INSERT THE SHEET METAL BENDS

1. Click the inside **bottom face** to remain fixed.
2. Click **Insert Bend**s from the Sheet Metal toolbar. The **Bends PropertyManager** appears (see Figure 18-6). Face<1> is displayed.
3. Enter Bend Radius (**2.00 mm**)
4. Enter K-factor (**0.45 mm**)
5. Select **Rectangle** for **Auto Relief Type** and value of **0.5 mm**
6. Click OK from the **Bends PropertyManager**.
7. Click **OK** to the message "Auto relief cuts were made for one or more bends"
8. Click **Isometric view** from the Heads-up View toolbar.
9. Click **Save**.

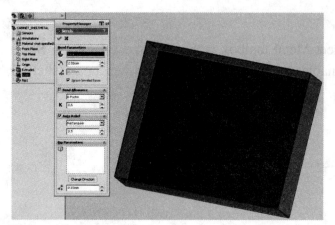

Figure 18-6 Inserting the sheet metal bends

The part that has been created is in its 3D formed state. The 2D flat (manufactured) state is obtained using the **Flatten** sheet metal tool. The **Flatten tool** toggles between the 3D formed state and the 2D flat (manufactured) state. Notice the **FeatureManager** which now shows the Rip1, Flatten-Bends1 and Process-Bends1 features. We observe that the Sheet Metal features start after the Rip1 feature.

10. Click **Flatten** from the **Sheet Metal toolbar** to display the **Flat State** (see Figure 18-7).

11. Click **Flatten** from the **Sheet Metal toolbar** to display the **fully Formed State** (see Fig. 18-8).

(a) FeatureManager shows the Flatten-Bends1 and Process-Bends1 Sheet Metal features

(b) Flat State obtained by clicking Flatten option

Figure 18-7 The flattened state

Figure 18-8 The fully Formed State obtained by clicking Flatten option again (it toggles)

INSERT THE EDGE FLANGE FEATURES

Inserting Edge Flange Feature on the left side of cabinet

12. Click the **front vertical left edge (Edge<1>)** of the cabinet.

13. Click **Edge-Flange** from the **Sheet Metal toolbar** (see Figure 18-9).

14. Select **Blind** from the **Flange Length** and Enter **25 mm** for length. An arrow appears; reverse the direction if needed.

15. Click **OK**.

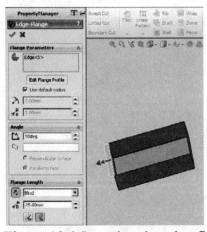

Figure 18-9 Inserting the edge flange features

Inserting Edge Flange Feature on the right side of cabinet

16. Click the **front vertical right edge (Edge<1>)** of the cabinet.

17. Click **Edge-Flange** from the **Sheet Metal toolbar** (see Figure 18-10).

18. Select **Blind** from the **Flange Length** and Enter **25 mm** for length. An arrow appears; reverse the direction if needed.

19. Click **OK**.

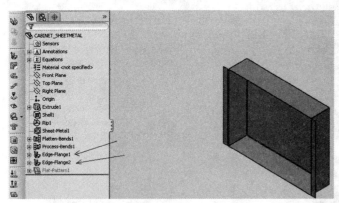

Figure 18-10 Edge Flange features on two sides of the cabinet

INSERT THE HEM FEATURES

Inserting Hem Feature on the left side of cabinet

20. Click the **left Edge Flange (Edge-Flange1)** of the cabinet.
21. Click **Hem** from the **Sheet Metal toolbar** (see Figure 18-11).
22. Select **Material Inside**
23. Click the **Reverse Direction** button (Zoom to see the effects of choice)
24. Accept **default (Open)** or select as required from the **Type and Size**
25. Enter **8 mm** for Length
26. Enter **0.1 mm** for Gap Distance
[Observe the preview]
27. Click **OK**.

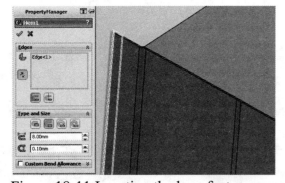

Figure 18-11 Inserting the hem features

Inserting Hem Feature on the right side of cabinet

28. Click the **right Edge Flange (Edge-Flange1)** of the cabinet.
29. Click **Hem** from the **Sheet Metal toolbar**.
30. Select **Material Inside**

31. Click the **Reverse Direction** button (Zoom to see the effects of choice as shown in Figure 18-12)
32. Accept **default (Open)** or select as required from the **Type and Size**
33. Enter **8 mm** for Length
34. Enter **0.1 mm** for Gap Distance
35. [Observe the preview]
36. Click **OK**. The completed sheet metal cabinet with edge flange and hem features is shown in Figure 18-13
37. Rename **Hem1** as **Hem1_Left**
38. Rename **Hem2** as **Hem2_Right**
39. Click **Save**

Zooming gives a clear view of the hem as shown in Figure 18-12 and the final cabinet is shown in Figure 18-13.

Figure 18-12 A clear view of hem

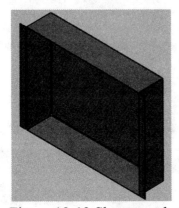

Figure 18-13 Sheet metal cabinet with edge flange and hem features

INSERT VENTILATION FEATURES

There are several ways of including ventilation features: d-cutout and louvers from SolidWorks library; holes, and patterns cutouts made in-house. All these options require manufacturing and cost considerations.

Louvers

40. Click **Design Library > Forming Tools > Louvers**

41. To apply the **louver** to the sheet metal part, drag the louver to the front face of the sheet metal part. Do *not* drop the forming tool yet until you are done (see Figure 18-14a).

42. To rotate the positioning sketch 90°, click **Tools > Sketch Tool > Modify**

43. Use relation to make the centre of the louver to be collinear with the midpoint of the height of the cabinet

44. Dimension this centre to be **90 mm** from the bottom edge of the cabinet (see Figure 18-14b).

45. Click **Finish** to complete inserting the louver.

46. Create **4 patterns** of the louver **25 mm** apart (see Figure 18-14c).

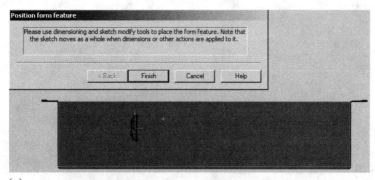

(a)

(b) Inserting a louver

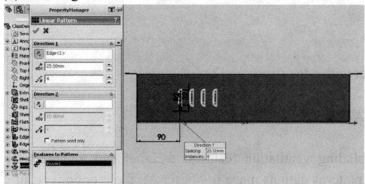

(c) Linear pattern for several louvers

Figure 18-14 Louvers created

D-cutout

47. Click **Design Library > Features > Sheetmetal**
48. To apply the **d-cutout** to the sheet metal part, drag the d-cutout to the front face of the sheet metal part. Do *not* drop the forming tool yet until you are done.
49. To rotate the positioning sketch 90°, click **Tools > Sketch Tool > Modify**
50. Use relation to make the top edge of the d-cutout to be horizontal
51. Dimension the centre of the d-cutout to be **50 mm** from the right-edge of the cabinet and **60 mm** from the bottom of the cabinet.
52. Click **Finish** to complete inserting the d-cutout as shown in Figure 18-15.

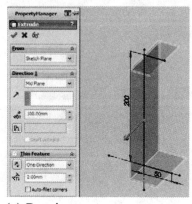

Figure 18-15 D-cutout and louver features in the cabinet

EXAMPLE 2 SHEET METAL PARTS

Let us follow exactly the procedure for the Insert Bend to illustrate another example for a channel sheet metal part design.

Extruding Thin Feature

1. Create a **U-sketch** (200x50) and **extrude** it **100 mm** to define a channel as shown in Figure 18-16.

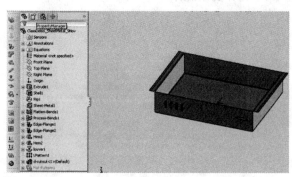

(a) Preview   (b) Part

Figure 18-16 U-channel part

Inserting Sheet Metal Bends

2. Click the inside **bottom face** to remain fixed.
3. Click **Insert Bend**s from the Sheet Metal toolbar. The **Bends PropertyManager** appears (see Figure 18-17). Face<1> is displayed.
4. Enter Bend Radius (**2.00 mm**)
5. Enter K-factor (**0.45 mm**)
6. Select **Rectangle** for **Auto Relief Type** and value of **0.5 mm**
7. Click OK from the **Bends PropertyManager**.
8. Click **OK** to the message "Auto relief cuts were made for one or more bends"
9. Click **Isometric view** from the Heads-up View toolbar.
10. Click **Save**.

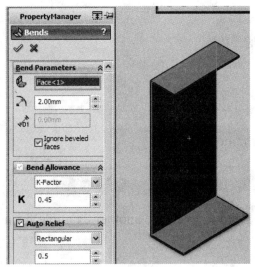

Figure 18-17 Clicking the inside bottom face to remain fixed

Click the **Flatten** tool to obtain the flatten state as shown in Figure 18-18

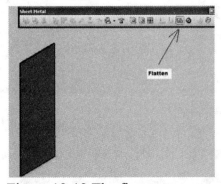

Figure 18-18 The flatten state

Inserting the holes using Hole Wizard

The Hole Wizard tool is used to create four holes as shown in Figure 18-19

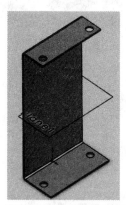

Figure 18-19 Create four holes using the Hole Wizard tool

Applying the Sheet Metal Forming Tool
11. Click **Design Library > Forming Tools > Louvers**
12. To apply the **louver** to the sheet metal part, drag the louver to the front face of the sheet metal part. Do *not* drop the forming tool yet until you are done (see Figure 18-20a).
13. To rotate the positioning sketch 90°, click **Tools > Sketch Tool > Modify** (see Figure 18-20b, c).
14. Use relation to make the centre of the louver to be collinear with the centre of the cabinet (see Figure 18-20d).
15. Dimension this centre to be **40 mm** from the edge of the cabinet (see Figure 18-20d).
16. Click **Finish** to complete inserting the louver.
17. Create **4 patterns** of the louver **40 mm** apart (see Figure 18-20e, f).
    The channel part is shown in Figure 18-20g.

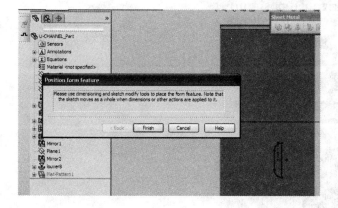

(a) A louver dragged from the design library

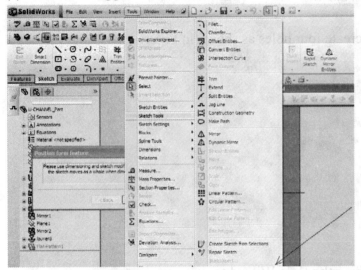

(b) Tool for modifying the orientation of the louver

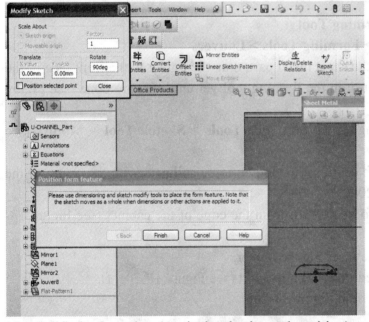

(c) Modified orientation (vertical to horizontal position)

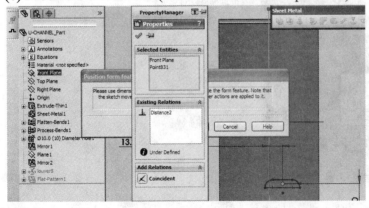

(d) Positioning louver through dimensioning

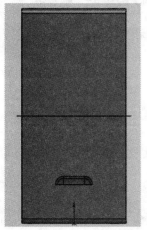

(e) Seed louver for linear pattern

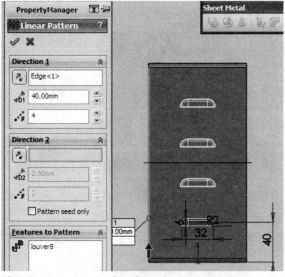

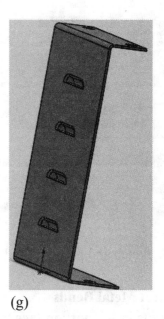

(f) Linear pattern for four instances   (g)

Figure 18-20 Inserting louvers

EXAMPLE 3 SHEET METAL PARTS

This time, let us follow exactly the procedure for the Insert Bend to illustrate yet another example for a channel sheet metal part design.

Extruding Thin Feature

1. Create on the **Right Plane** a slanting **U-sketch** (75x60 bent at an angle of 120 degrees) and **extrude** it **100 mm** to define a channel as shown in Figure 18-21.

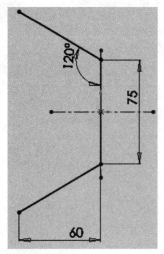

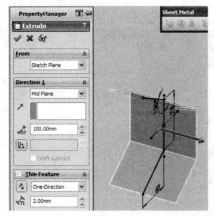

(a) Sketch

(b) Preview   (c) Part

Figure 18-21 Sketch and part required for sheet metal work

Inserting Sheet Metal Bends

2. Click the inside **bottom face** to remain fixed.
3. Click **Insert Bend**s from the Sheet Metal toolbar. The **Bends PropertyManager** appears (see Figure 18-22). Face<1> is displayed.
4. Enter Bend Radius (**2.00 mm**)
5. Enter K-factor (**0.45 mm**)
6. Select **Rectangle** for **Auto Relief Type** and value of **0.5 mm**
7. Click OK from the **Bends PropertyManager**.
8. Click **OK** to the message "Auto relief cuts were made for one or more bends"
9. Click **Isometric view** from the Heads-up View toolbar.
10. Click **Save**.

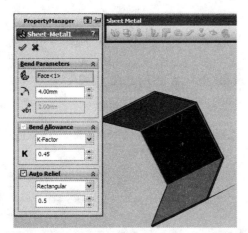

Figure 18-22 Specifying the face to remain fixed during bending

11. Click the **Flatten** tool to obtain the flatten state as shown in Figure 18-23.
12. Click the **Flatten** tool again to obtain the 3D-formed state.

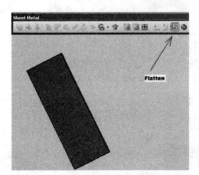

Figure 18-23 The flattened condition

Inserting a Reference Plane

13. Click the **Reference Plane** tool and select **an edge** as well as **a vertex** as shown in Figure 18-24.

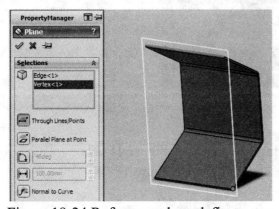

Figure 18-24 Reference plane define

Create Tabs

14. Select the **Reference Plane** and sketch as well as dimension the first **Tab** as shown in Figure 18-25.

15. **Extrude the Tab toward the rear of the part** as shown in Figure 18-26.

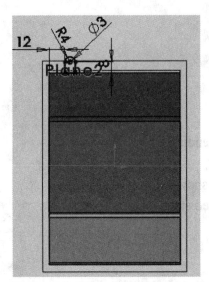

Figure 18-25 Creating sketch for a tab

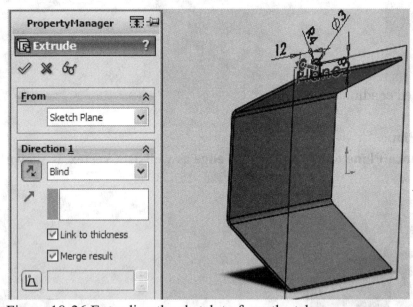

Figure 18-26 Extruding the sketch to form the tab

16. **Mirror** the first Tab about the **Right Plane** as shown in Figure 18-27.

17. **Mirror** the two Tabs about the **Top Plane** as shown in Figure 18-28.

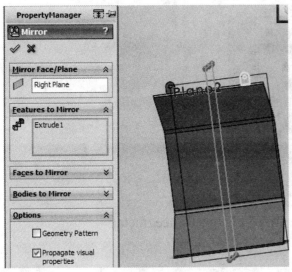

Figure 18-27 Duplication of the tab through mirroring

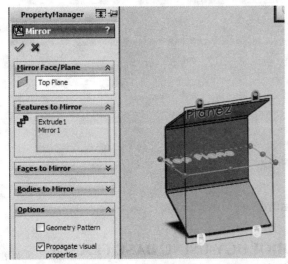

Figure 18-28 Further duplication of the tab through mirroring

The formed sheet metal is now shown in Figure 18-29.

18. Click the **Flatten** tool to obtain the **flatten state** as shown in Figure 18-30.

19. Drag the **Rollback Bar** to just below the **Flatten Bend** in the **FeatureManager**.

20. Sketch a circle, 30 mm in diameter on the **flatten state** as shown in Figure 18-30.

21. Drag the **Rollback Bar** to the end of the **FeatureManager** to show the cut feature as shown in Figure 18-31.

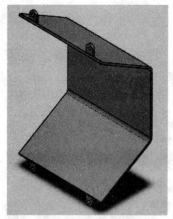

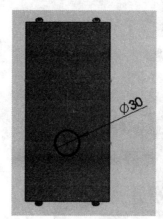

Figure 18-29 Formed sheet metal   Figure 18-30 Flattened sheet metal

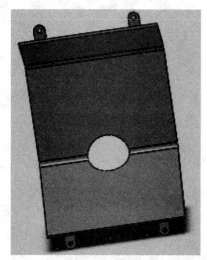

Figure 18-31 Formed sheet metal with cut feature

SHEET METAL PART DESIGN METHODOLOGY USING BASE FLANGE

In this approach, the starting point is a base flange, which when applied to the cabinet under consideration is the bottom face (a rectangle, 350 mm by 450 mm).

1. Click the **MY-TEMPLATE** tab.
2. Double-click **ANSI-MM-PART**.
3. Click **Front Plane** (or other appropriate plane).
4. Sketch and dimension the base flange, **Sketch1** (a rectangle, 350 mm by 450 mm).
5. Click **Base Flange** from the Sheet Metal toolbar. The **Base Flange PropertyManager** appears (see Figure 18-32).

   Accept default value of sheet metal thickness (Notice: there is an option to choose Gauge Table)

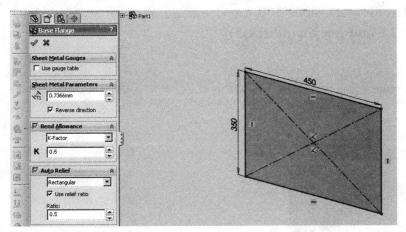

Figure 18-32 Sketch1

Notice that **Base-Flange1** appears after **Sheet-Metal1** in the **FeatureManager** (see Figure 18-33)

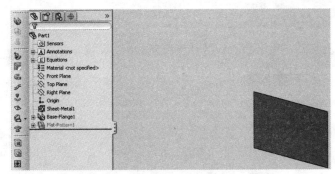

Figure 18-33 Base Flange appears after sheet metal in the FeatureManager

The steps involved in creating Miter Flange are as follows:

   a) Click any edge of the Base Flange

   b) Select the Line tool from the Sketch toolbar and sketch the profile for the miter flange

   c) Without exiting sketch mode, click Miter tool and select each edge of the Base Flange to create the Miter feature (the first one is automatically created on the first edge initially selected) [Note: If you exit the sketch, then it has to be selected for the Miter function]

Create an Edge Flange

6. **Click one of the edges of the Base Flange and then select the Line tool from the Sketch toolbar** (see Figure 18-34). [Notice that a perpendicular plane for sketching the line is automatically selected; this is very useful in this approach.]

7. Create an L-sketch with dimensions **100 mm** long and **35 mm** wide, **Sketch2**, with fillet radius of **2.5 mm** (see Figure 18-35)

8. **Exit** sketch.

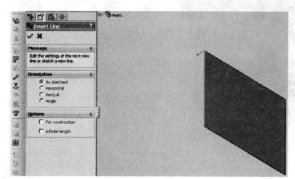

Figure 18-34 Effect of selecting line tool

Figure 18-35 Creating profile sketch

Create Miter Flange Features

9. Select **Sketch2**

10. Click the **Miter Flange** button on the **Sheet Metal toolbar**, while the sketch is still active.

11. Select the **four edges of the Base Flange**, which are not automatically dimensioned to have height of **100 mm** as the height of the Sketch as shown in Figure 18-36.

12. Click OK from the **Miter Flange Property** toolbar

13. Hide **Plane1**

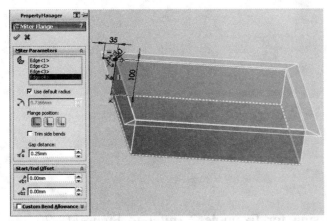

Figure 18-36 Miter flange feature

Alternatively, still be in sketch mode after the L-shape is sketch and access Miter Flange. Our design based on **Base Flange** approach is complete at this stage as shown in Figure 18-37, which seems to have more capabilities than the alternative *insert bends* design approach. Other venting features already discussed can now be included.

Figure 18-37 Completed part using Base Flange approach

Summary

The chapter has discussed the differences between **Insert Bends** and **Base Flange** approaches in sheet metal part design and considered some examples. The **Insert Bends** approach does not match the natural way sheet metal design is carried out on the shop floor; whereas the **Base Flange** approach does. The next chapter uses the **Base Flange** approach to solve a number of problems of practical relevance.

Exercises

1. Repeat the sheet metal part design for Example 1 (refer to Figure 18-15 and Figure P1) using the *Base Flange* approach

Figure P1

2. Repeat the sheet metal part design for Example 2 (refer to Figure 18-20 and Figure P2) using the *Base Flange* approach

Figure P2

3. Repeat the sheet metal part design for Example 3 (refer to Figure 18-31 and Figure P3) using the *Base Flange* approach

Figure P3

Chapter 19
Sheet Metal Parts—II

Objectives:

In this chapter you will learn:

- How to create sheet metal parts using the **Base Flange** approach

Comparing Sheet Metal Design Methods

There are three ways to create a sheet metal part:

- **Convert a solid part to a sheet metal part.**
  You can convert a solid or surface body, or an imported part.
- **Create the part as a sheet metal part using sheet metal-specific features.**
  When you create a part initially out of sheet metal you use two features: Base-Flange and Miter Flange. This eliminates extra steps because you create a part as sheet metal from the initial design stage.
- **Build a part, shell it, and then convert it to sheet metal.**
  If you build a solid, then convert it to sheet metal, you need more features: Base Extrude, Shell, Rip, and Insert Bends. However, there are instances when it is preferable to build a part and then convert it to sheet metal.

Advantages of the Base Flange Approach

The Base Flange approach has some advantages which are summarized:

1. A part is created as sheet metal from the initial design stage
2. The method is quite intuitive and consistent with the manner in which sheet metal work is done in practice
3. Designing sheet metal using this approach is very flexible and efficient
4. When some sheet metal tools are used, all the tools necessary for defining sketches are available, and could be used

The remaining parts of this chapter concentrate on the *Base Flange* approach for sheet metal part design which is preferred to the *Insert Bend* approach. Several tutorials are discussed to show how Base Flange approach can be applied to a number of sheet metal part-design.

This chapter discusses several Tutorials for sheet metal design based on Base Flange approach. It is expected that students will become competent in sheet metal part design after covering all the Tutorials. Detailed step-by-step procedures have been discussed in such a way that students can reproduce the solutions of the problems being solved. The standard of the sheet metal part design problems discussed in this chapter, is at par with the CSWA and CSWP examinations.

TUTORIALS ON BASE FLANGE APPROACH FOR SHEET METAL DESIGN

The following Tutorials are discussed in detail in the subsequent subsections of this chapter:

Tutorial 1: General Sheet Metal Part
Tutorial 2: P1
Tutorial 3: P2
Tutorial 4: Hanger Support
Tutorial 5: Jogged Sheet Metal Part
Tutorial 6: Lofted Sheet Metal
Tutorial 7: P9
Tutorial 8: General Sheet Metal
Tutorial 9: CSWP-SMTL

The Sheet Metal User Interface

The Sheet Metal User Interface is shown in Figure 19-1, with the definitions of each tool described. The most used tools used in the Base Flange approach are Edge Flange, Sketched Bend, and Flatten.

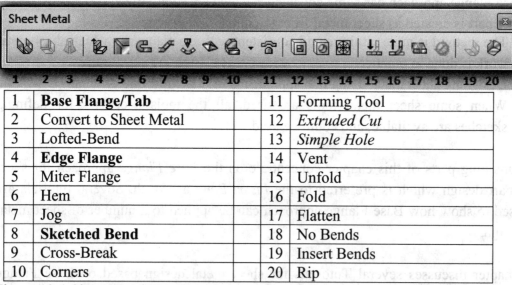

1	**Base Flange/Tab**	11	Forming Tool
2	Convert to Sheet Metal	12	*Extruded Cut*
3	Lofted-Bend	13	*Simple Hole*
4	**Edge Flange**	14	Vent
5	Miter Flange	15	Unfold
6	Hem	16	Fold
7	Jog	17	Flatten
8	**Sketched Bend**	18	No Bends
9	Cross-Break	19	Insert Bends
10	Corners	20	Rip

Figure 19-1 Sheet Metal User Interface

Tutorial 1: General Sheet Metal Part

In this tutorial, we will create the sheet metal part shown at the top-right, with its views and dimensions shown in Figure 19-2. The flat pattern of the sheet metal part is shown in Figure 19-3.

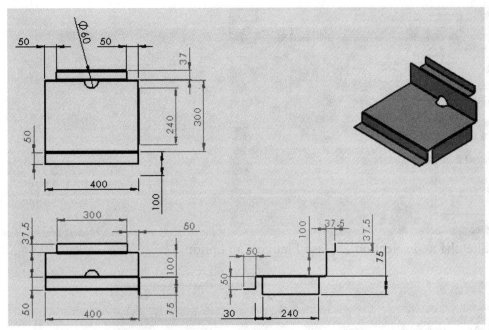

Figure 19-2 Part and drawing views and dimensions for Tutorial 1

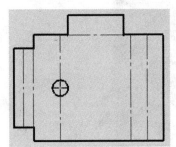

Figure 19-3 Flat pattern of the sheet metal part for Tutorial 1

SolidWorks Solution to Tutorial 1

Create the Base Flange

1. Start a **New SolidWorks Part** document
2. Select the **Top Plane**
3. Be in sketch mode and create Sketch1, 500 mm by 400 mm (see Figure 19-4)
4. Click the **Base Flange/Tab** option from the **Sheet Metal CommandManager** (see Figure 19-4)

[Note: The **Sheet Metal CommandPropertyManager** is automatically displayed; see Figure 19-5]

5. Set the values of the following parameters: **Thickness = 1.5; K-Factor = 0.5; Ratio = 0.5**

6. Click **OK**

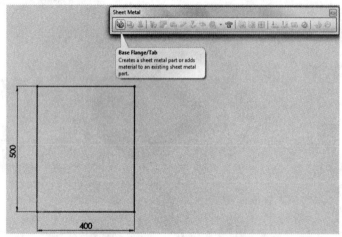

Figure 19-4 Sketch1 and selection of Base Flange/Tab option

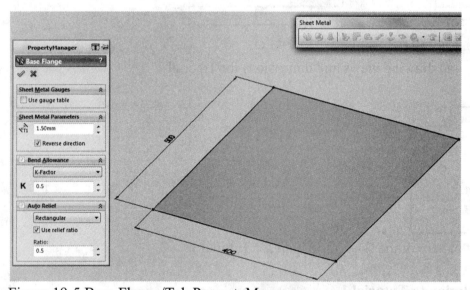

Figure 19-5 Base Flange/Tab PropertyManager

Create the First Sketched Bend

7. Click top of the **Base Flange**

8. Be in sketch mode and create **Sketch2** on the Base Flange for the first bending operation, a line **100 mm** *from one edge* (see Figure 19-6)

9. Click the **Sketch Bend** tool (see Figure 19-7)

10. Accept the default **Bend radius** of **2 mm** and **Angle = 90**-deg

11. Click the **Fixed Face** (**Face<1>**) *to one side of the line* (Sketch2) for the **Bend Parameters** rollout (the **Sketched Bend PropertyManager** is automatically displayed; see Figure 19-8)

12. Click **OK** to complete the sketched bend operation (see Figure 19-9 for bend created)

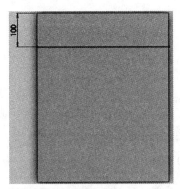

Figure 19-6 Sketch2

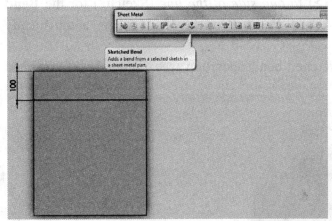

Figure 19-7 Sketched Bend tool is used for bend operation

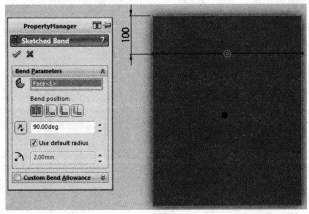

Figure 19-8 Sketched Bend PropertyManager

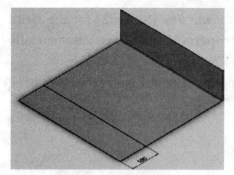

Figure 19-9 Bend created

Create the Second Sketched Bend

13. Click top of the **Base Flange**
14. Be in sketch mode and create **Sketch3** on the Base Flange for the first bending operation, a line **100 mm** *from one edge* (see Figure 19-9)
15. Click the **Sketch Bend** tool (see Figure 19-7)
16. Accept the default **Bend radius** of **2 mm** and **Angle = 90**-deg
17. Click the **Fixed Face (Face<1>)** *to one side of the line* (Sketch2) for the **Bend Parameters** rollout (the **Sketched Bend PropertyManager** is automatically displayed; see Figure 19-10)
18. Click **OK** to complete the sketched bend operation (see Figure 19-11 for bend created)

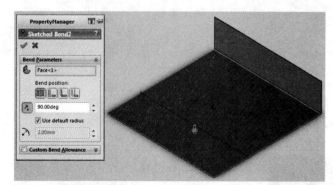

Figure 19-10 Sketched Bend PropertyManager

Figure 19-11 Bend created

Create the First Edge Flange

19. Select the *top-edge* of the first **Sketched Bend** (see Figure 19-12)

20. Set **Length** of **Edge Flange = 75** and **Angle = 90**-deg (see Figure 19-12)

21. Click **Edit Flange Profile** button from the **Edge Flange PropertyManager** (see Figure 19-12)

22. Click **OK** if the following message appears: *"The automatic relations inferred by this operation would over define the sketch. They will not be added."*

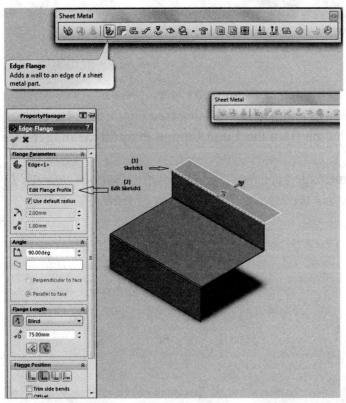

Figure 19-12 PropertyManager for creating Edge Flange

23. Adjust the **Width** of the **Edge Flange** created by dragging the end points of the edge to new positions (**50 mm** from each end) and using sketch tool to add dimensions (see Figure 19-13)

[**Note:** *When the Profile Sketch window appears, do not click **Finish** until the length of the Edge Flanged is fully adjusted*]

24. Click **Finish**

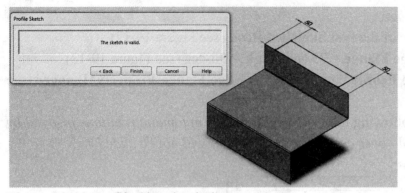

Figure 19-13 Profile Sketch window

Create the Second Edge Flange

25. Select the *top-edge* of the first **Sketched Bend** (see Figure 19-14)
26. Set **Length** of **Edge Flange = 75** and **Angle = 90**-deg (see Figure 19-14)
27. Click **Edit Flange Profile** button from the **Edge Flange PropertyManager** (see Figure 19-14)
28. Click **OK** if the following message appears: *"The automatic relations inferred by this operation would over define the sketch. They will not be added."*

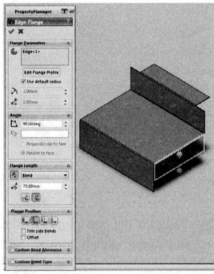

Figure 19-14 PropertyManager for creating Edge Flange

29. Adjust the **Width** of the **Edge Flange** created by dragging the end points of the edge to new positions (**30 mm** from each end) and using sketch tool to add dimensions (see Figure 19-15)
    [**Note:** *When the Profile Sketch window appears, do not click **Finish** until the length of the Edge Flanged is fully adjusted*]
30. Click **Finish** (see Figure 19-16 for the two edge flanges)

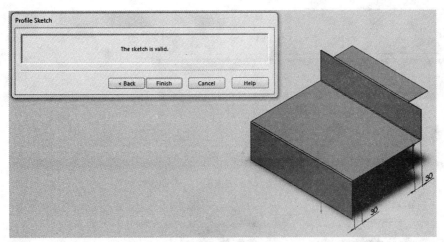

Figure 19-15 Profile Sketch window

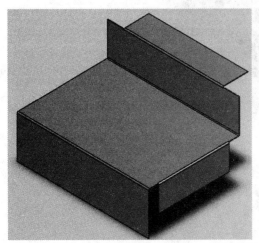

Figure 19-16 Model has the two edge flanges created

Unfold the First Sketched Bend

31. Click **Unfold** button (the **Unfold PropertyManager** is automatically displayed (see Figure 19-17)

32. Select **Face<1>** as the **Fixed Face** and **SketchBend1** as the **Bends to unfold** (see Figure 19-17)

33. Click **OK** to unfold the bend (see Figure 19-18)

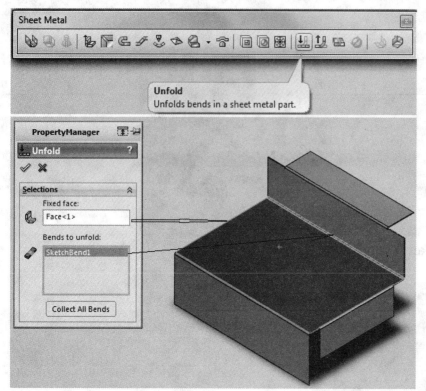

Figure 19-17 Unfold PropertyManager

Figure 19-18 Unfolded bend

Create a Circular Hole Mid-point Along of the First Sketched Bend

    34. Be in sketch mode, and create **Sketch6**, a Circle having diameter of **60** mm (see Figure 19-19)

    35. **Extrude-cut** up to Next (see Figure 19-20)

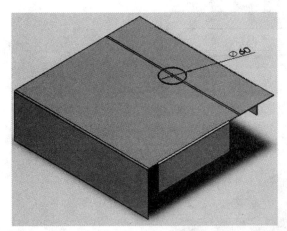

Figure 19-19 Sketch6, a circle

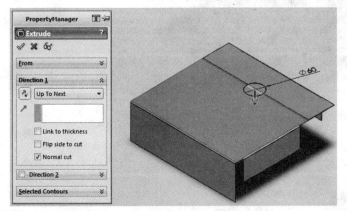

Figure 19-20 Extrude-cut to create a hole

Fold the First Sketched Bend

36. Click **Fold** button (the **Fold PropertyManager** is automatically displayed (see Figure 19-21)
37. Select **Face<1>** as the **Fixed Face** and **SketchBend1** as the **Bends to Fold** (see Figure 19-21)
38. Click **OK** to fold the bend (see Figure 19-22)

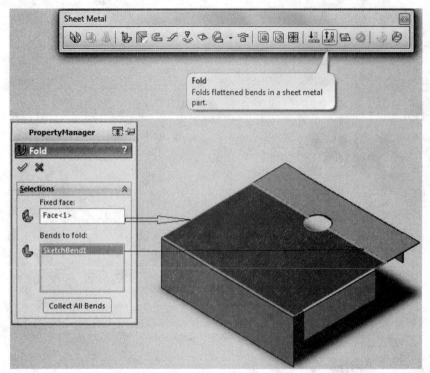

Figure 19-21 Fold PropertyManager

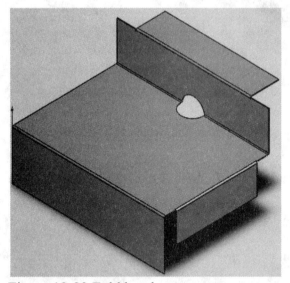

Figure 19-22 Fold bend

Create the Third Sketched Bend

39. Click bottom **Edge Flange**
40. Be in sketch mode and create **Sketch7** on the bottom Edge Flange for the third bending operation, a line **mid-point** *from one edge* (see Figure 19-23)
41. Click the **Sketch Bend** tool
42. Accept the default **Bend radius** of **2 mm** and **Angle = 90**-deg

43. Click the **Fixed Face** (**Face<1>**) *to one side of the line* (Sketch2) for the **Bend Parameters** rollout (the **Sketched Bend PropertyManager** is automatically displayed; see Figure 19-23)

44. Click **OK** to complete the sketched bend operation (see Figure 19-24 for bend created)

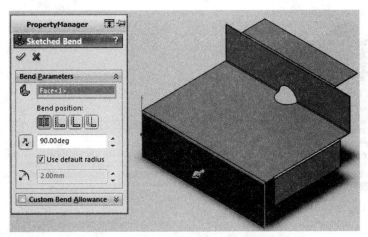

Figure 19-23 Sketched Bend PropertyManager

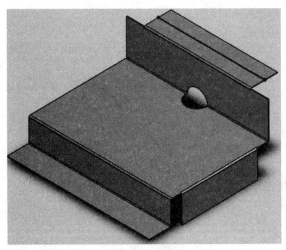

Figure 19-24 Bend created

Create the Fourth Sketched Bend

45. Click top **Edge Flange**

46. Be in sketch mode and create **Sketch8** on the bottom Edge Flange for the third bending operation, a line **mid-point** *from one edge* (see Figure 19-25)

47. Click the **Sketch Bend** tool

48. Accept the default **Bend radius** of **2 mm** and **Angle = 90**-deg

49. Click the **Fixed Face (Face<1>)** *to one side of the line* (Sketch2) for the **Bend Parameters** rollout (the **Sketched Bend PropertyManager** is automatically displayed; see Figure 19-25)

50. Click **OK** to complete the sketched bend operation (see Figure 19-26 for bend created)

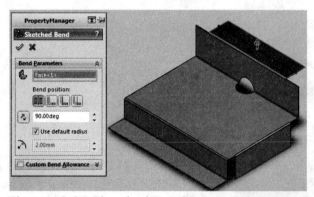

Figure 19-25 Sketched Bend PropertyManager

Figure 19-26 Bend created

Create the Flatten State

51. Click the **Flatten** tool (the flatten state appears as shown in Figure 19-27)

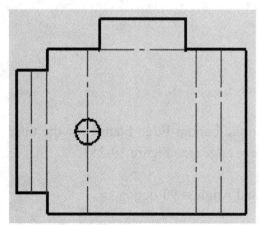

Figure 19-27 Flatten state

Tutorial 2: P1

In this tutorial, we will create the sheet metal part shown at the top-right, with its views and dimensions shown in Figure 19-28. The flat pattern of the sheet metal part is shown in Figure 19-29.

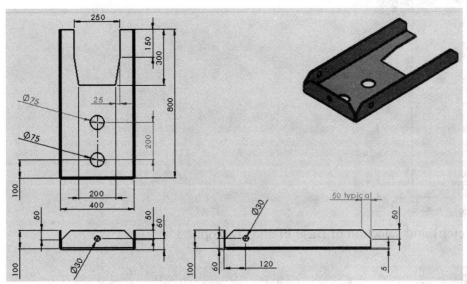

Figure 19-28 Sheet metal part with drawings and dimensions for Tutorial 2

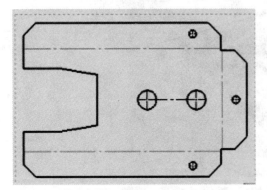

Figure 19-29 Flat pattern of the sheet metal part for Tutorial 2

SolidWorks Solution to Tutorial 2

Create the Base Flange
1. Start a **New SolidWorks Part** document
2. Select the **Top Plane**
3. Be in sketch mode and create Sketch1, 800 mm by 400 mm (see Figure 19-30)
4. Click the **Base Flange/Tab** option from the **Sheet Metal CommandManager** (see Figure 19-31)

5. Set the values of the following parameters: **Thickness = 5; K-Factor = 1; Ratio = 0.5**

6. Click **OK**

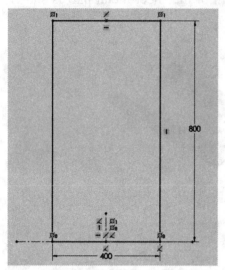

Figure 19-30 Sketch1 and selection of Base Flange/Tab option

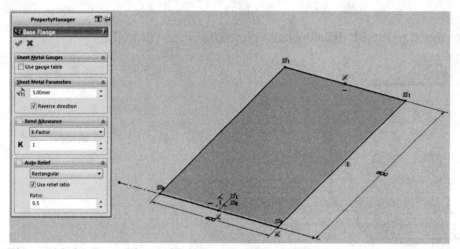

Figure 19-31 Base Flange/Tab PropertyManager

Create the First Edge Flange

7. Select the *left-edge* of the first **Base Flange** (see Figure 19-32 for the **Edge Flange PropertyManager**)

8. Set **Length** of **Edge Flange = 100** and **Angle = 90**-deg (see Figure 19-32)

9. Click **OK**

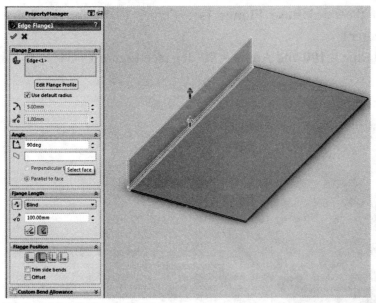

Figure 19-32 PropertyManager for creating first Edge Flange

Create the Second Edge Flange

10. Select the *left-edge* of the second **Base Flange** (see Figure 19-33 for the **Edge Flange PropertyManager**)
11. Set **Length** of **Edge Flange = 100** and **Angle = 90**-deg (see Figure 19-33)
12. Click **OK**

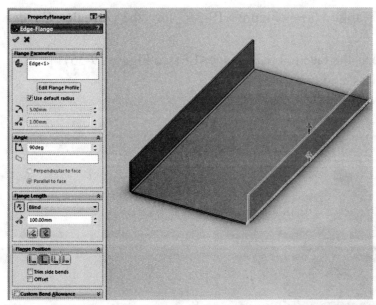

Figure 19-33 PropertyManager for creating second Edge Flange

Create the Third Edge Flange

13. Select the *left-edge* of the third **Base Flange** (see Figure 19-34 for the **Edge Flange PropertyManager**)
14. Set **Length** of **Edge Flange = 100** and **Angle = 90**-deg (see Figure 19-34)
15. Click **OK**

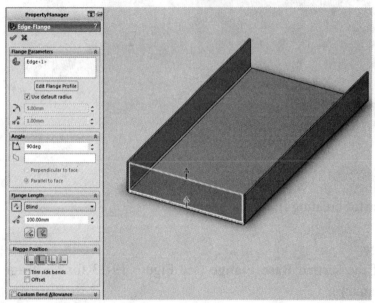

Figure 19-34 PropertyManager for creating third Edge Flange

Create the First Break Corner

16. Select an **Edge Flange** (see Figure 19-35 for the **Break Corner PropertyManager**)
17. Select the **Edge Flange** as the face to break, **Face<1>** (see Figure 19-35)
18. Set break **Distance = 50** (see Figure 19-35)
19. Click **OK**

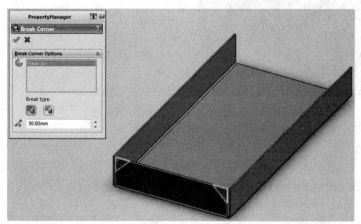

Figure 19-35 PropertyManager for creating first Break Corner

Create the Second Break Corner

20. Select an **Edge Flange** (see Figure 19-36 for the **Break Corner PropertyManager**)
21. Select the **Edge Flange** as the face to break, **Face<1>** (see Figure 19-36)
22. Set break **Distance = 50** (see Figure 19-36)
23. Click **OK**

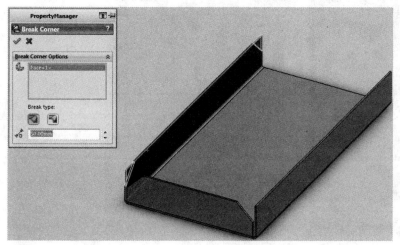

Figure 19-36 Second Break Corner PropertyManager

Create the Third Break Corner

24. Select an **Edge Flange** (see Figure 19-37 for the **Break Corner PropertyManager**)
25. Select the **Edge Flange** as the face to break, **Face<1>** (see Figure 19-37)
26. Set break **Distance = 50** (see Figure 19-37)
27. Click **OK**

Figure 19-37 Third Break Corner PropertyManager

Create Extrude-Cut features

28. Create a sketch on top of **Base Flange** and Extrude-Cut (see Figure 19-38)
29. Create sketches (circles) on top of **Base Flange** and Extrude-Cut (see Figure 19-39)

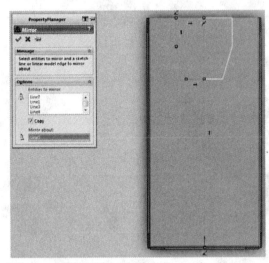
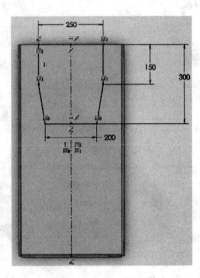

Figure 19-38 Sketch for Extrude-Cut

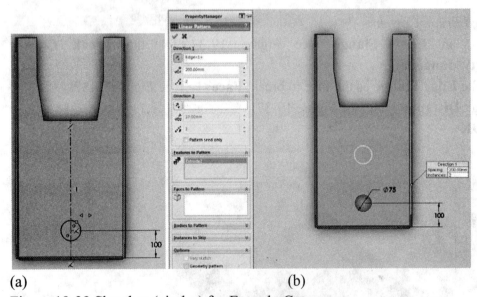

(a)   (b)

Figure 19-39 Sketches (circles) for Extrude-Cut

30. Create a sketch on end view of **Edge Flange** and Extrude-Cut (see Figure 19-40)
31. Create a sketch on end view of **Edge Flange** and Extrude-Cut (see Figure 19-41)
    The completed of the sheet metal part is shown in Figure 19-42.

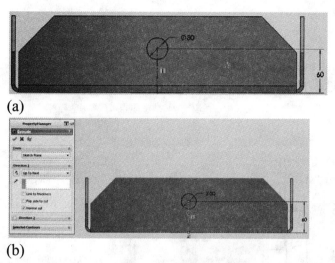

(a)

(b)

Figure 19-40 Sketch (circle) for Extrude-Cut

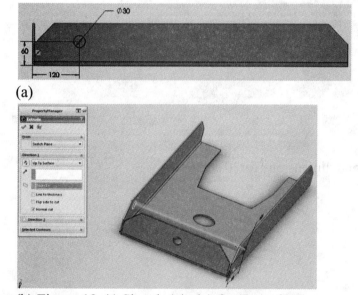

(a)

(b) Figure 19-41 Sketch (circle) for Extrude-Cut

Figure 19-42 Sheet metal part

Tutorial 3: P2

In this tutorial, we will create the sheet metal part shown at the top-right, with its views and dimensions shown in Figure 19-43a. The flat pattern of the sheet metal part is shown in Figure 19-43b.

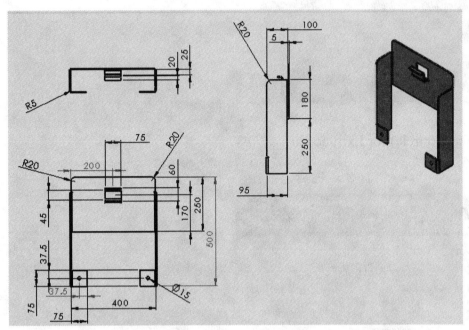

(a) Sheet metal part with drawings and dimensions for Tutorial 3

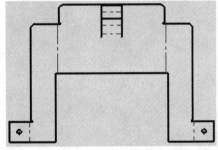

(b) Flat pattern of the sheet metal part for Tutorial 3

Figure 19-43

Create the Base Flange

1. Start a **New SolidWorks Part** document
2. Select the **Front Plane**
3. Be in sketch mode and create Sketch1, 400 mm by 250 mm (see Figure 19-44)
4. Click the **Base Flange/Tab** option from the **Sheet Metal CommandManager** [Note: The **Sheet Metal CommandPropertyManager** is automatically displayed; see Figure 19-45]

5. Set the values of the following parameters: **Thickness = 5; K-Factor = 1; Ratio = 0.5**
6. Click **OK**

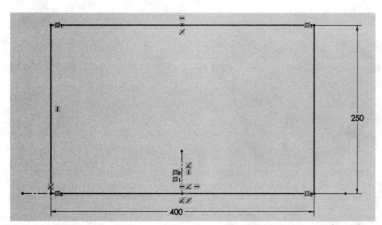

Figure 19-44 Sketch1 and selection of Base Flange/Tab option

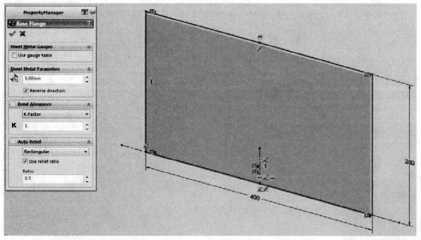

Figure 19-45 Base Flange/Tab PropertyManager

Create the First Edge Flange

7. Select the *right-edge* of the first **Sketched Bend** (see Figure 19-46)
8. Set **Length** of **Edge Flange = 100** and **Angle = 90**-deg (see Figure 19-46)
9. Click **Edit Flange Profile** button from the **Edge Flange PropertyManager** (see Figure 19-46)
10. Click **OK** if the following message appears: "*The automatic relations inferred by this operation would over define the sketch. They will not be added.*"
11. Adjust the **Width** of the **Edge Flange** created by dragging one end point of the edge to a new position (**180 mm**) and using sketch tool to add dimensions [**Note:**

When the Profile Sketch window appears, do not click **Finish** *until the length of the Edge Flanged is fully adjusted*]

12. Click **Finish** (see Figure 19-47 for the Edge Flange)

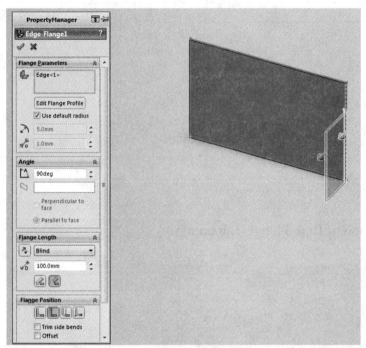

Figure 19-46 PropertyManager for creating Edge Flange

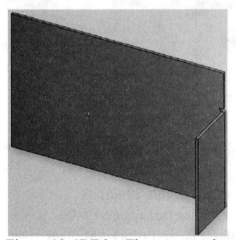

Figure 19-47 Edge Flange created

Create the First Tab

13. Select the **Edge Flange** just and sketch a rectangle, **250 mm** by **95 mm** (see Figure 19-48)

14. Click the **Base Tab** tool to create a tab (see Figure 19-49)

[Note: The **Tab** feature is automatically created as shown in Figure 19-50]

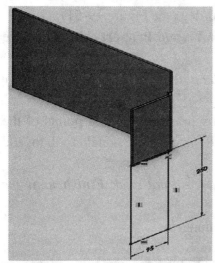

Figure 19-48 Sketch2 create

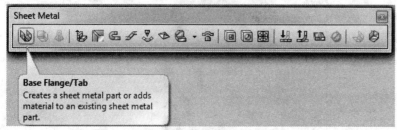

Figure 19-49 Base Tab tool used to create a tab

Figure 19-50 Tab tool used to create a tab

Create the Second Edge Flange

15. Select the *bottom-edge* of the right **Flange Edge** (see Figure 19-51)
16. Set **Length** of **Edge Flange** = **75** and **Angle** = **90**-deg (see Figure 19-51)
17. Click **Edit Flange Profile** button from the **Edge Flange PropertyManager** (see Figure 19-51)
18. Click **OK** if the following message appears: *"The automatic relations inferred by this operation would over define the sketch. They will not be added."*
19. Adjust the **Width** of the **Edge Flange** created by dragging the end points of the edge to new positions (**75 mm** from each end) and using sketch tool to add dimensions

    [**Note:** *When the Profile Sketch window appears, do not click* **Finish** *until the length of the Edge Flanged is fully adjusted*]
20. Click **Finish** (see Figure 19-52 for the two edge flanges)

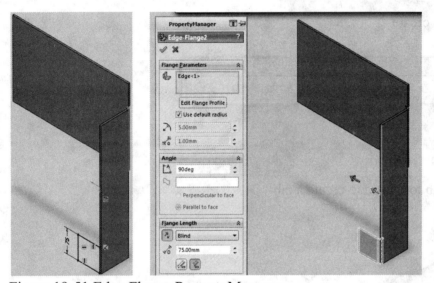

Figure 19-51 Edge Flange PropertyManager

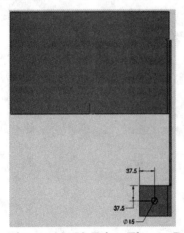

Figure 19-52 Edge Flange PropertyManager

Create a Circular Hole

21. Click the *face* of the second Edge Flange
22. Be in sketch mode, and create a Sketch, **Circle** (see Figure 19-52)
23. Click **Extrude-Cut** and choose **Next** to create the hole (see Figure 19-53)

Fillet Edges

24. Click **Fillet** and select corners on the right of the model
25. Ser **Radius of fillet = 20 mm**
26. Click **OK**

Mirror of second edge flange

27. Click the **Mirror** tool
28. For the **Mirror Face/Plane**, select the **Right Plane**
29. For **Features to Mirror**, select *all the features for the right leg* (see Figure 19-53)
30. Click **OK**

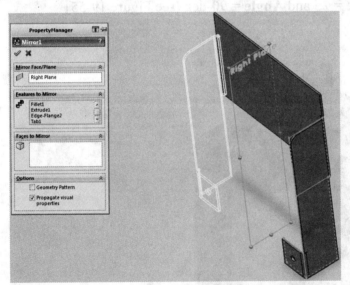

Figure 19-53 Hole created on second edge flange

Create the Second Extrude-Cut

31. Click the *face* of the **Base Flange**
32. Be in sketch mode, and create a Sketch, **Rectangle** (see Figure 19-54)
33. Click **Extrude-Cut** and choose **Next** to create the slot (see Figure 19-55)

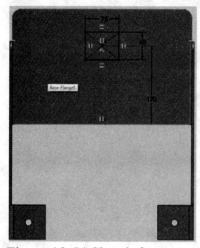

Figure 19-54 Sketch for second Extrude-Cut

Create First Edge Flange for Rectangular Slot

    34. Select the *bottom-edge* of the Rectangular Slot created (see Figure 19-55)

    35. Set **Length** of **Edge Flange = 25** and **Angle = 90**-deg (see Figure 19-55)

    36. Click **OK**

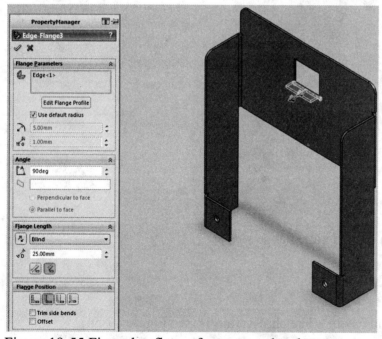

Figure 19-55 First edge flange for rectangular slot

Create Second Edge Flange for Rectangular Slot

    37. Select the *edge* of the Edge Flange created at the Slot (see Figure 19-56)

    38. Set **Length** of **Edge Flange = 45** and **Angle = 90**-deg (see Figure 19-56)

    39. Click **OK**

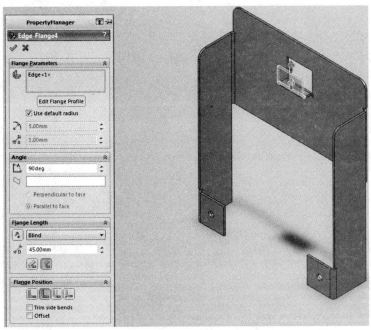

Figure 19-56 Second edge flange for rectangular slot

Create Third Edge Flange for Rectangular Slot

40. Select the *edge* of the second Edge Flange created at the Slot (see Figure 19-57)
41. Set **Length** of **Edge Flange = 20** and **Angle = 90**-deg (see Figure 19-57)
42. Click **OK** (see Figure 19-58 for the completed sheet metal model)

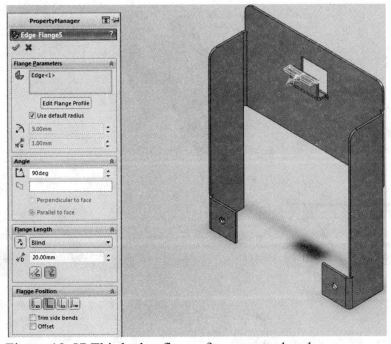

Figure 19-57 Third edge flange for rectangular slot

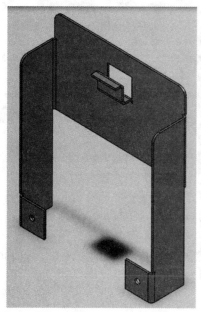

Figure 19-58 Sheet metal part

Tutorial 4: Hanger Support

In this tutorial, we will create the sheet metal part shown at the top-right, with its views and dimensions shown in Figure 19-59. The flat pattern of the sheet metal part is shown in Figure 19-60.

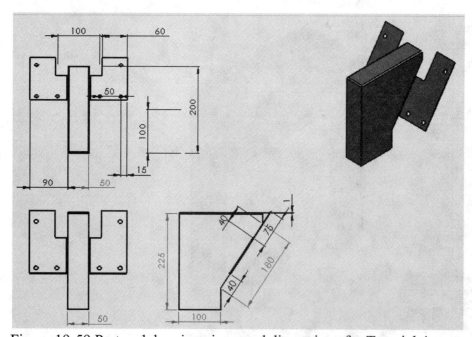

Figure 19-59 Part and drawing views and dimensions for Tutorial 4

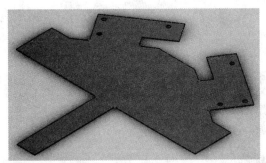

Figure 19-60 Flat pattern of the sheet metal part for Tutorial 4

SolidWorks Solution to Tutorial 4

Create the Base Flange

1. Start a **New SolidWorks Part** document
2. Select the **Top Plane**
3. Be in sketch mode and create Sketch1 (see Figure 19-61)
4. Click the **Base Flange/Tab** option from the **Sheet Metal CommandManager** (see Figure 19-61)

   [Note: The **Sheet Metal CommandPropertyManager** is automatically displayed; see Figure 19-62]
5. Set the values of the following parameters: **Thickness = 1; K-Factor = 1; Ratio = 0.5**
6. Click **OK**

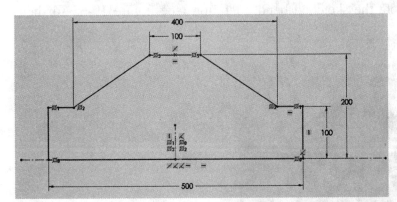

Figure 19-61 Sketch1 and selection of Base Flange/Tab option

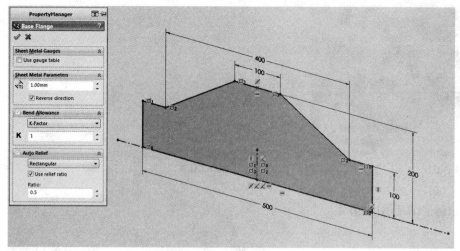

Figure 19-62 Base Flange/Tab PropertyManager

Create the First Sketched Bend

7. Click top of the **Base Flange**
8. Be in sketch mode and create **Sketch2** on the Base Flange for the first bending operation, a line **25 mm** *from the centre of the sketch* (see Figure 19-63)
9. Click the **Sketch Bend** tool
10. Accept the default **Bend radius** of **2 mm** and **Angle = 90**-deg
11. Click the **Fixed Face (Face<1>)** *to one side of the line* (Sketch2) for the **Bend Parameters** rollout (the **Sketched Bend PropertyManager** is automatically displayed; see Figure 19-64)
12. Click **OK** to complete the sketched bend operation (see Figure 19-65 for bend created)

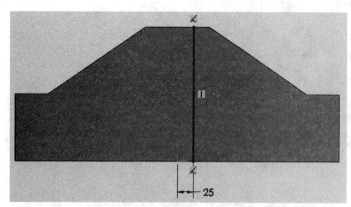

Figure 19-63 Sketch used for bend operation

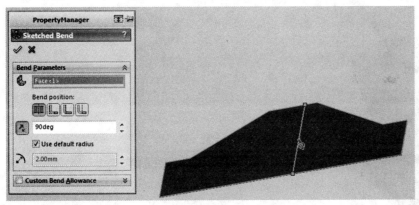

Figure 19-64 Sketched Bend PropertyManager

Figure 19-65 Bend created

Create the First Sketched Bend

13. Click top of the **Base Flange**

14. Be in sketch mode and create **Sketch3** on the Base Flange for the first bending operation, a line **25 mm** *from the centre of the sketch* (see Figure 19-66)

15. Click the **Sketch Bend** tool

16. Accept the default **Bend radius** of **2 mm** and **Angle = 90**-deg

17. Click the **Fixed Face (Face<1>)** *to one side of the line* (Sketch2) for the **Bend Parameters** rollout (the **Sketched Bend PropertyManager** is automatically displayed; see Figure 19-67)

18. Click **OK** to complete the sketched bend operation (see Figure 19-68 for bend created)

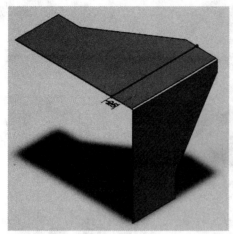

Figure 19-66 Sketch used for bend operation

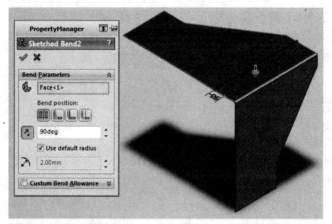

Figure 19-67 Sketched Bend PropertyManager

Figure 19-68 Bend created

Create the First Edge Flange

19. Select the *right-edge* of the first **Sketched Bend** (see Figure 19-69)
20. Set **Length** of **Edge Flange = 90** and **Angle = 90**-deg (see Figure 19-69)
21. Click **Edit Flange Profile** button from the **Edge Flange PropertyManager** (see Figure 19-69)

22. Click **OK** if the following message appears: "*The automatic relations inferred by this operation would over define the sketch. They will not be added.*"

23. Adjust the **Width** of the **Edge Flange** created by dragging one end point of the edge to a new position (**40 mm**) and using sketch tool to add dimensions (see Figure 19-70) [**Note:** *When the Profile Sketch window appears, do not click* **Finish** *until the length of the Edge Flanged is fully adjusted*]

24. Click **Finish** (see Figure 19-71 for the Edge Flange)

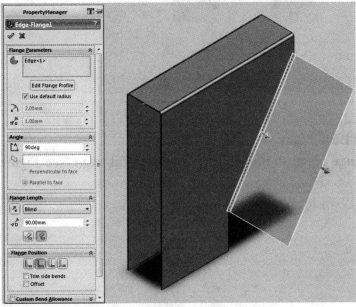

Figure 19-69 Edge Flange PropertyManager

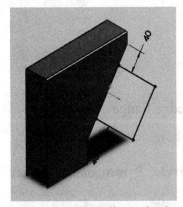

Figure 19-70 Adjusted edge

Figure 19-71 First Edge Flange created

First Base Tab created

25. Click the *right edge flange* created and sketch a rectangle, 60 mm by 75 mm (see Figure 19-72a)

26. Click the **Base Tab** tool (see Figure 19-72b for the **Base Tab** created)

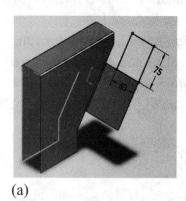
(a)

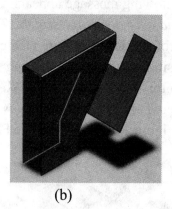
(b)

Figure 19-72 First Base Tab created

Create the Third Edge Flange

27. Click the **Base Flange** tool
28. Select the *top-edge* of the **Base Flange** (see Figure 19-73)
29. Set **Length** of **Edge Flange** equal to the length of the vertical *edge* (see Figure 19-73)
30. Click **Finish** (see Figure 19-74 for the Edge Flange)

Figure 19-73 Upper horizontal edge chosen for creating third edge flange

Create a Sketch, Circle

31. Click the *right edge flange* created and sketch a **Circle, 9 mm** diameter (see Figure 19-74)
32. Click the Linear **Pattern** tool and replicate the circular sketch **2** on **x-direction** and **2** on **y-direction** (see Figure 19-75)

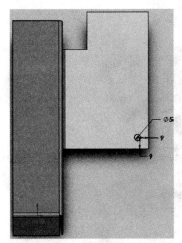

Figure 19-74 Circular sketch on the right edge flange

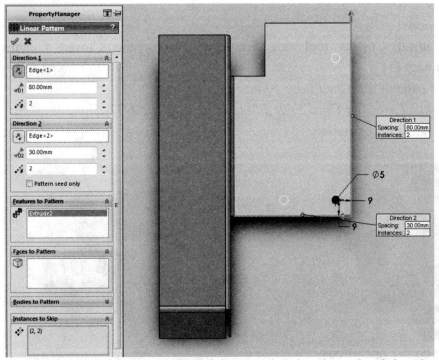

Figure 19-75 Linear patterning of the circular sketch on the right edge flange

Mirror Features

33. Click the *right edge flange* created and sketch a **Mirror Features** tool (see Figure 19-76 for the **Mirror Features PropertyManager**)

34. Select all the features for mirror operation (see Figure 19-76)

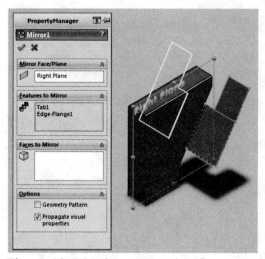

Figure 19-76 Mirror operation for some features created

Closed corner operations

35. Click the **Closed Corner** tool (see Figure 19-77 for the **Closed Corner PropertyManager**)
36. Select the *left edge* of the *Third Edge Flange* (see Figure 19-77)
37. Select the *right edge* of the *Third Edge Flange* (see Figure 19-77)
38. Click **OK** to finish the operation

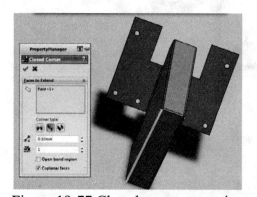

Figure 19-77 Closed corner operations

Welded corner operations

39. Click the **Welded Corner** tool (see Figure 19-78 for the **Welded Corner PropertyManager**)
40. Select the *left edge* of the *Third Edge Flange* (see Figure 19-78)
41. Select the *right edge* of the *Third Edge Flange* (see Figure 19-78)
42. Click **OK** to finish the operation

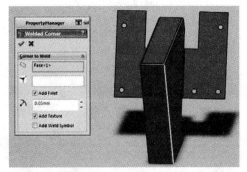 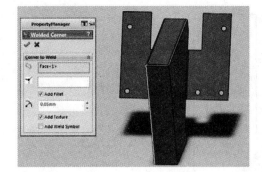

Figure 19-78 Welded corner operations

Flattened State

Click the **Flatten** tool (see Figure 19-79 for the **Flattened** state of the sheet metal)

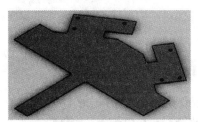

Figure 19-79 Flattened state of the sheet metal

Tutorial 5: Jogged Sheet Metal Part

In this tutorial, we will create the sheet metal part shown at the top-right, with its views and dimensions shown in Figure 19-80. The flat pattern of the sheet metal part is shown in Figure 19-81.

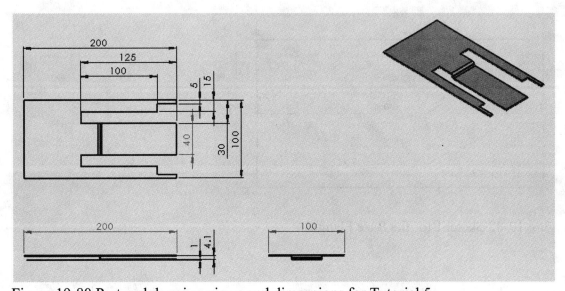

Figure 19-80 Part and drawing views and dimensions for Tutorial 5

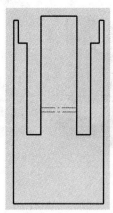

Figure 19-81 Flat pattern of the sheet metal part for Tutorial 5

SolidWorks Solution to Tutorial 4

Create the Base Flange
1. Start a **New SolidWorks Part** document
2. Select the **Top Plane**
3. Be in sketch mode and create Sketch1, 100mm by 200 mm (see Figure 19-82)
4. Click the **Base Flange/Tab** option from the **Sheet Metal CommandManager** (see Figure 19-83)

   [Note: The **Sheet Metal CommandPropertyManager** is automatically displayed; see Figure 19-83]
5. Set the values of the following parameters: **Thickness = 3.0; K-Factor = 1; Ratio = 0.5**
6. Click **OK**

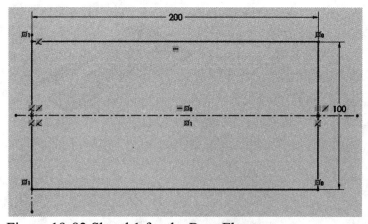

Figure 19-82 Sketch1 for the Base Flange

(a) Sheet Metal CommandManager

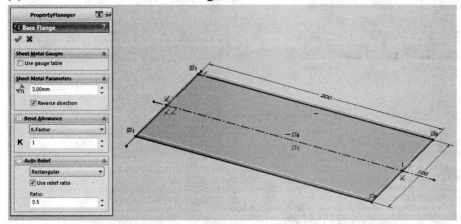

(b) Base Flange PropertyManager

Figure 19-83 Base Flange

Create Sketch for the Extrude-Cut

7. Click the *top face* of the **Base Flange** (see Figure 19-84)
8. Be in sketch mode and create **Sketch2** (see Figure 19-85)
9. Click **Extrude-Cut**
10. For the **Distance** for **Extrude-Cut**, choose **Up To Next** (see Figure 19-86)

Figure 19-84 Top face of the Base Flange is selected for sketch

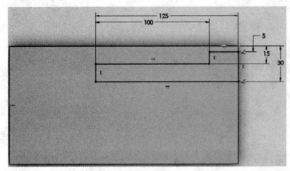

Figure 19-85 Sketch2

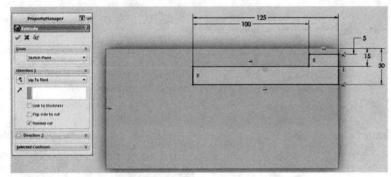

Figure 19-86 Extrude-Cut of Sketch2

Mirror the Extrude-Cut Feature

    11. Click **Mirror** tool to mirror tool

    12. Select the **Extrude1** as **Feature to Mirror** (see Figure 19-87)

    13. Select the **Front Plane** as the **Mirror Face** (see Figure 19-87)

    14. Click **OK**

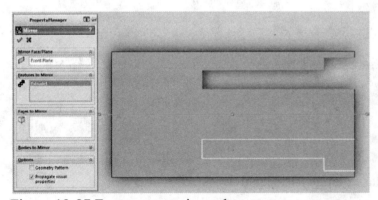

Figure 19-87 Features are mirrored

Sketch a line for jogging

    15. Select the *top face of the mid-feature* (see Figure 19-88)

    16. Be in sketch mode and create **Sketch3** a line for jogging (see Figure 19-88)

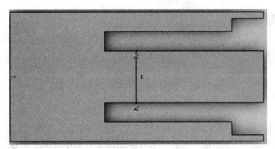

Figure 19-88 Sketch3

Exit line Sketch
17. Click **Exit** to exit Sketch3 [Note: this is extremely important]

Create a Jog feature
18. Select **Sketch3** created
19. Click **Jog** (Jog PropertyManager appears as shown in Figure 19-89)
20. In the **Jog Offset** rollout, select the **Inside Offset** for the **Dimension Position**
21. *Case 1: Jog Offset of 4.05 mm at an angle of 90 degrees*
22. Set the **Jog Offset (Blind Distance)** to **4.05 mm**
23. Reverse the **Blind Direction** (if jog is in an opposition direction to the one desired)
24. Accept the **Jog Angle** to be **90 degrees**
25. In the **Selections** rollout, click any point on the surface to the right (or left) of the **Jog Line (Sketch)** to indicate the **Fixed Face (Face<1>)** [a **Black Sphere** appears on the fixed face and jog is created to the right (or left) of the **Jog Line**; see Figure 19-89] [The jog feature created in Figure 19-90]

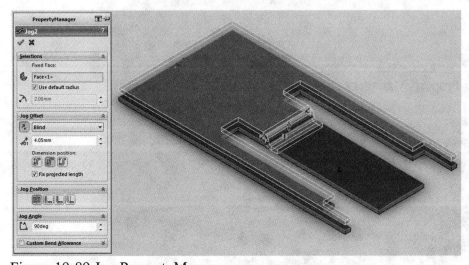

Figure 19-89 Jog PropertyManager

Figure 19-90 Sheet metal with jog feature is created

Let us consider another jog feature by changing some of the settings on the Jog PropertyManager.

Case 2: Jog Offset of 35 mm at an angle of 135 degrees
Right-click **Jog1** in the **FeatureManager**
Select **Edit Feature** from the In-Context Menu that is displayed
Set the Jog Offset to **35 mm** at an angle of **135** degrees (see Figure 19-91)
Click OK (see Figure 19-92)

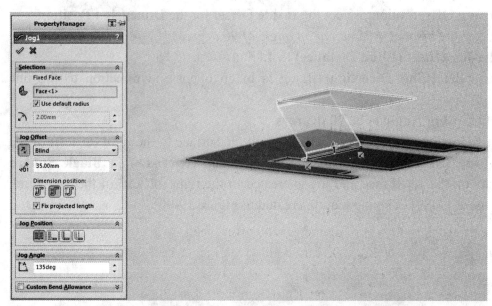

Figure 19-91 Jog PropertyManager

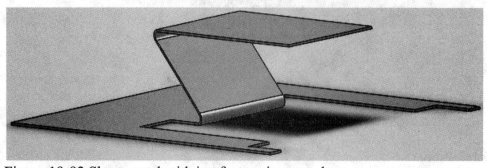

Figure 19-92 Sheet metal with jog feature is created

Tutorial 6: Lofted Sheet Metal

In this tutorial, we will create the sheet metal part shown at the top-right, with its views and dimensions shown in Figure 19-93.

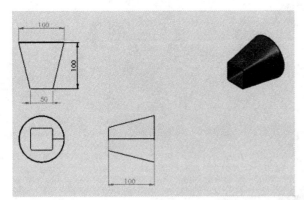

Figure 19-93 Part and drawing views and dimensions for Tutorial 6

Create Lofted Boss/Base

1. Select the **Front Plane** and create **Sketch1** (a square, 50 mm by 50 mm) as shown in Figure 19-94a.
2. Create a **Split** on Sketch1 (0.02 mm width) [see Figure 19-94b]
3. **Exit** the sketch mode.
4. Click the **Features** tool and click the **Reference** tool. Select the **Plane** option. The plane box appears; select the Front Plane.
5. Set the distance between the existing **Front Plane** and a new reference plane for **100 mm**. click **OK** check mark. A new plane, **Plane1** appears (see Figure 19-95).
6. Click **Plane1** and be in sketch mode
7. Create **Sketch2** (a **Circle** of diameter, **100 mm**) [see Figure 19-96a].
8. Create a **Split** on Sketch2 (0.02 mm width) [see Figure 19-96b]
9. **Exit** the sketch mode (see Figure 19-97 for the two sketches).
   [Note: It is essential to *break* Sketch1 and Sketch2 **Split Entities** tool]

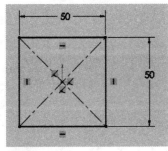
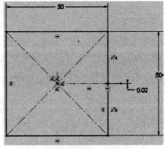

(a) Sketch1   (b) Split Sketch1 (0.02 mm width)
Figure 19-94 Sketch1 for lofting

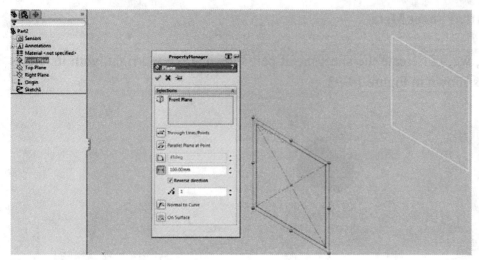

Figure 19-95 Plane1 is created

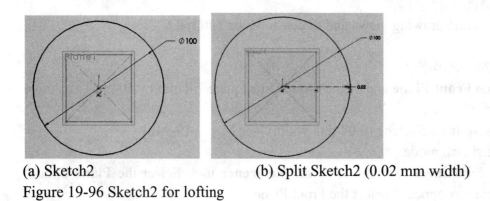

(a) Sketch2   (b) Split Sketch2 (0.02 mm width)

Figure 19-96 Sketch2 for lofting

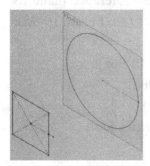

Figure 19-97 Sketches for lofting

Fillet the square shape to remove sharp corners (SolidWorks requires smooth corners)
1. Click Fillet tool and select the four edges of the square shape (see Figure 19-98)
2. Select a **Fillet Radius** of 5 mm
3. Click **OK** to complete filleting

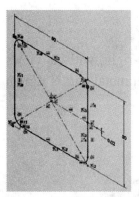

Figure 19-98 Edges of the square feature are filleted

Create Lofted Bend

1. Click the **Lofted Bend** tool (see Figure 19-99).
   The Lofted Bend Properties Manager appears.
2. Right-click the **Profiles** box.
3. Click the **Square**, and the **Circle**. A real-time preview will appear (see Figure 19-100).
4. Click **OK** to complete the lofted part (see Figure 19-101). Hide the planes.

Figure 19-99 Lofted Bend tool

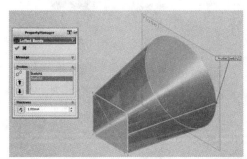

Figure 19-100 Lofted Bend PropertyManager

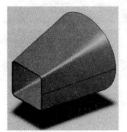

Figure 19-101 Lofted sheet metal

Tutorial 7: P9

In this tutorial, we will create the sheet metal part shown at the top-right, with its views and dimensions shown in Figure 19-102. The flat pattern of the sheet metal part is shown in Figure 19-103.

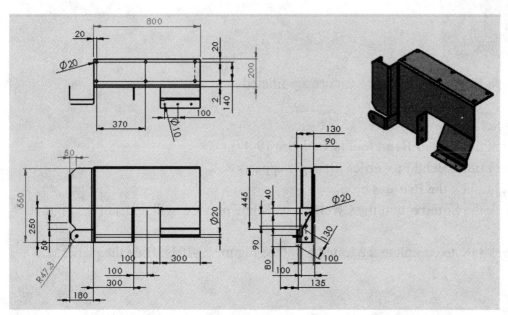

Figure 19-102 Part and drawing views and dimensions for Tutorial 7

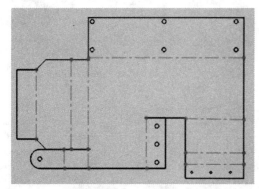

Figure 19-103 Flat pattern of the sheet metal part for Tutorial 7

SolidWorks Solution to Tutorial 7

Create the Base Flange

1. Start a **New SolidWorks Part** document
2. Select the **Top Plane**
3. Be in sketch mode and create Sketch1 (see Figure 19-104)

4. Click the **Base Flange/Tab** option from the **Sheet Metal CommandManager** [Note: The **Base Flange PropertyManager** is automatically displayed; see Figure 19-105]

5. Set the values of the following parameters: **Thickness = 2; K-Factor = 1; Ratio = 0.5**

6. Click **OK** (see Figure 19-106 for the base flange)

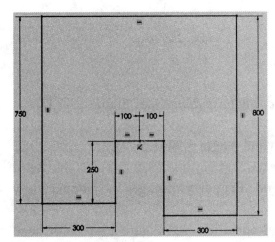

Figure 19-104 Sketch1

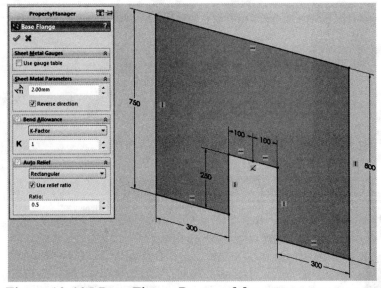

Figure 19-105 Base Flange PropertyManager

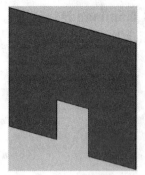

Figure 19-106 Base Flange

Creating the First Sketched Bend

7.   Create a line **200 mm** *from the top edge of the base flange* (see Figure 19-107)

8.   Click the **Sketch Bend** tool

9.   Accept the default **Bend radius** of **2 mm** and **Angle = 90**-deg

10. Click the **Fixed Face (Face<1>)** *to one side of the line* (Sketch2) for the **Bend Parameters** rollout (the **Sketched Bend PropertyManager** is automatically displayed; see Figure 19-1085)

11. Click **OK** to complete the sketched bend operation (see Figure 19-109 for bend created)

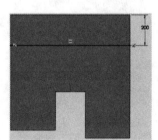

Figure 19-107 Sketch for the first Sketched Bend

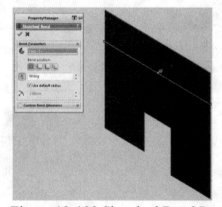

Figure 19-108 Sketched Bend PropertyManager

Figure 19-109 First sketched bend created

Creating the Second Sketched Bend

12. Create a line, collinear with the top of the cut on the first sketch bend feature (see Figure 19-110)

13. Click the **Sketch Bend** tool

14. Accept the default **Bend radius** of **2 mm** and **Angle = 90**-deg

15. Click the **Fixed Face (Face<1>)** *to one side of the line* for the **Bend Parameters** rollout (the **Sketched Bend PropertyManager** is automatically displayed; see Figure 19-110)

16. Click **OK** to complete the sketched bend operation (see Figure 19-111 for bend created)

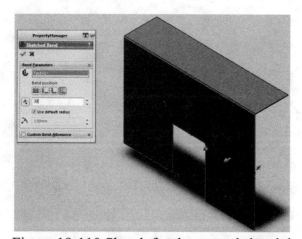

Figure 19-110 Sketch for the second sketch bend

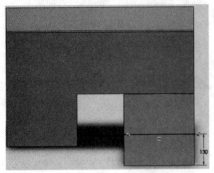

Figure 19-111 Second sketched bend created

Creating the Third Sketched Bend

17. Create a line, mid-way of the first sketch bend feature (see Figure 19-112)
18. Click the **Sketch Bend** tool
19. Accept the default **Bend radius** of **2 mm** and **Angle = 90**-deg
20. Click the **Fixed Face (Face<1>)** *to one side of the line* for the **Bend Parameters** rollout (the **Sketched Bend PropertyManager** is automatically displayed; see Figure 19-112)
21. Click **OK** to complete the sketched bend operation (see Figure 19-113 for bend created)

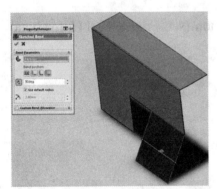

Figure 19-112 Sketch for the third sketch bend

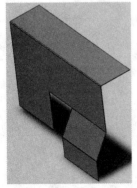

Figure 19-113 Third sketched bend created

Creating the Fourth Sketched Bend

22. Create a line, **80 mm** from bottom of the first sketch bend feature (see Figure 19-114)

23. Click the **Sketch Bend** tool

24. Accept the default **Bend radius** of **2 mm** and **Angle = 90**-deg

25. Click the **Fixed Face (Face<1>)** *to one side of the line* for the **Bend Parameters** rollout (the **Sketched Bend PropertyManager** is automatically displayed; see Figure 19-115)

26. Click **OK** to complete the sketched bend operation (see Figure 19-116 for bend created)

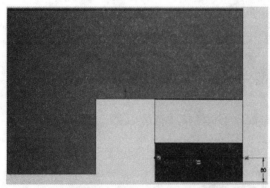

Figure 19-114 Sketch for the fourth sketch bend

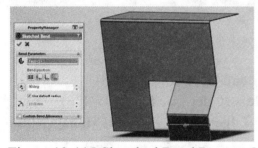

Figure 19-115 Sketched Bend PropertyManager

Figure 19-116 Fourth sketched bend created

Creating the First Edge Flange

27. Select the *left-edge* of the first cut feature of the first **Sketched Bend** (see Figure 19-117)
28. Set **Length** of **Edge Flange = 100** and **Angle = 90**-deg (see Figure 19-117)
29. Click **OK** to finish the operation

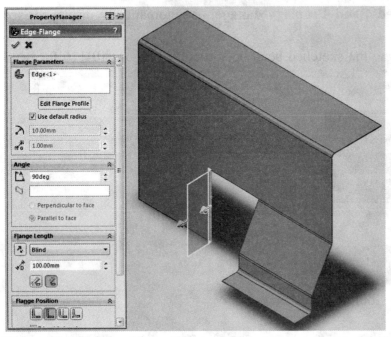

Figure 19-117 Edge Flange PropertyManager

Creating the Second Edge Flange

30. Select the *right-edge* of the first **Sketched Bend** (see Figure 19-118)
31. Set **Length** of **Edge Flange = 90** and **Angle = 90**-deg (see Figure 19-118)
32. Click **Edit Flange Profile** button from the **Edge Flange PropertyManager** (see Figure 19-118)
33. Click **OK** if the following message appears: "*The automatic relations inferred by this operation would over define the sketch. They will not be added.*"
34. Adjust the **Width** of the **Edge Flange** created by dragging one end point of the edge to a new position (**445 mm**) and using sketch tool to add dimensions (see Figure 19-119) [**Note:** *When the Profile Sketch window appears, do not click* **Finish** *until the length of the Edge Flanged is fully adjusted*]
35. Click **Finish** (see Figure 19-120 for the Edge Flange)

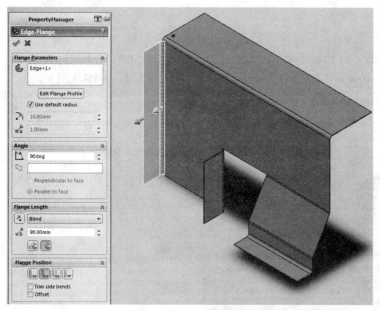

Figure 19-118 Edge Flange PropertyManager

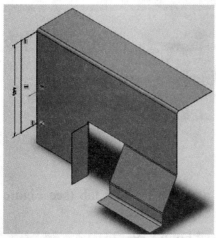

Figure 19-119 Width adjustment for the edge flange

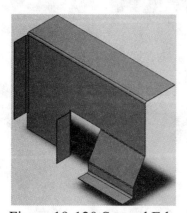

Figure 19-120 Second Edge Flange

Creating the Third Edge Flange

36. Select the *left-bottom edge* of the second edge flange (see Figure 19-121)
37. Set **Length** of **Edge Flange = 130** and **Angle = 90**-deg (see Figure 19-121)
38. Click **OK** to finish the operation

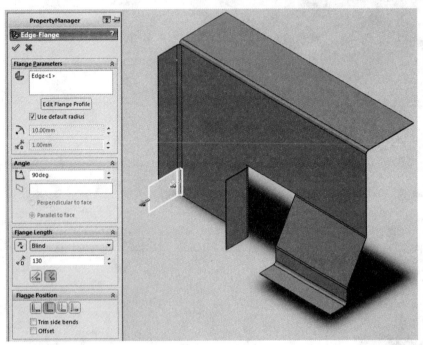

Figure 19-121 Third edge flange

Creating the First Tab

Be in sketch mode on the third edge flange and create a sketch for first tab (see Figure 19-122)

Click the Base Flange/Tab tool to produce the first tab (see Figure 19-123)

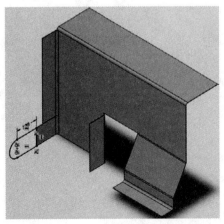

Figure 19-122 Sketch for first Tab

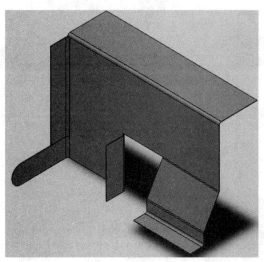

Figure 19-123 First Tab

Creating the Fourth Edge Flange

39. Select the *left-outer bottom edge* of the third edge flange (see Figure 19-124)
40. Set **Length** of **Edge Flange = 180** and **Angle = 90**-deg (see Figure 19-124)
41. Click **OK** to finish the operation

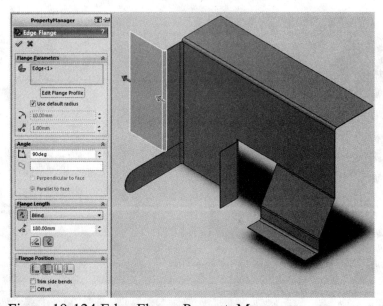

Figure 19-124 Edge Flange PropertyManager

Creating the First Break Corner

42. Click the **Break Corner** tool
43. Select the *outer face* (**Face<1>**) of the fourth edge flange (see Figure 19-125)
44. Set **Distance = 50** (see Figure 19-125)

45. Click **OK** to finish the operation

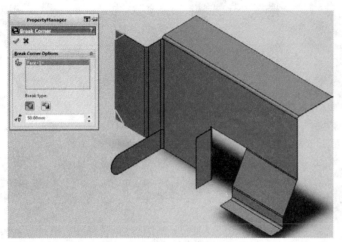

Figure 19-125 Break Corner PropertyManager

Creating the Fifth Edge Flange

46. Select the *left-outer bottom edge* of the third edge flange (see Figure 19-126)
47. Set **Length** of **Edge Flange = 100** and **Angle = 90**-deg (see Figure 19-126)
48. Click **OK** to finish the operation

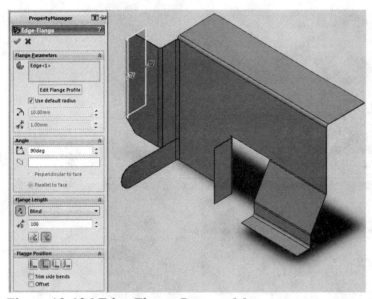

Figure 19-126 Edge Flange PropertyManager

Creating the Holes of Features

49. Click *top* of the **Base Flange** and be in sketch mode, create a circle **20 mm** diameter, located 20 mm by 20 mm from the outer left vertex (see Figure 19-127)
50. Click **Extrude-Cut** to create a hole from the circle; choose **Up To Next**

51. Create Linear Pattern using the seed hole and select **3** and **2** for **Number** of features for **Direction 1** and **Direction 2** respectively (see Figure 19-127)

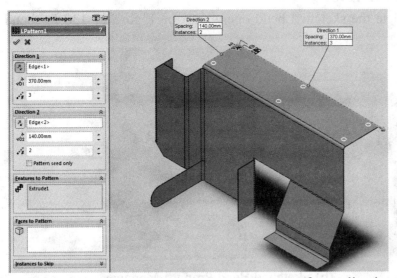

Figure 19-127 Linear Pattern PropertyManager for replicating holes

Figure 19-128 shows a number of holes created in other features of the sheet metal part.

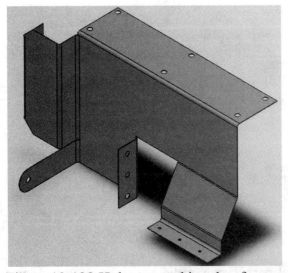

Figure 19-128 Holes created in other features

Creating the Second Sketch Bend

52. Create a line **135 mm** *from the hole of the tab* (see Figure 19-1296a)
53. Click the **Sketch Bend** tool
54. Accept the default **Bend radius** of **2 mm** and **Angle = 90**-deg

55. Click the **Fixed Face (Face<1>)** *to one side of the line* (Sketch2) for the **Bend Parameters** rollout (the **Sketched Bend PropertyManager** is automatically displayed; see Figure 19-129b)

56. Click **OK** to complete the sketched bend operation (see Figure 19-130 for bend created)

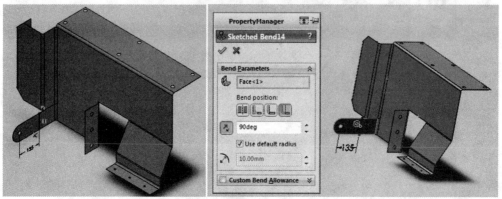

(a) Sketch for second bend   (b) Sketched Bend PropertyManager

Figure 19-129 Sketch and Sketched Bend PropertyManager for second bend

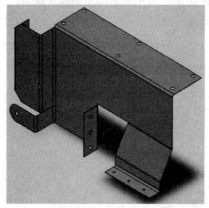

19-130 Sheet metal part completed

Tutorial 8: General Sheet Metal

In this tutorial, we will create the sheet metal part shown at the top-right, with its views and dimensions shown in Figure 19-131. The flat pattern of the sheet metal part is shown in Figure 19-132.

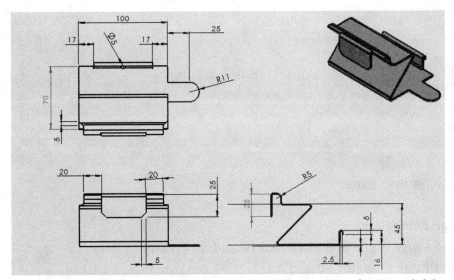

Figure 19-131 Part and drawing views and dimensions for Tutorial 8

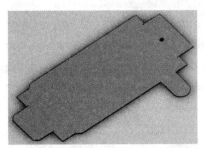

Figure 19-132 Flat pattern of the sheet metal part for Tutorial 8

SolidWorks Solution to Tutorial 8

Create the Base Flange
1. Start a **New SolidWorks Part** document
2. Select the **Top Plane**
3. Be in sketch mode and create Sketch1 (see Figure 19-133)
4. Click the **Base Flange/Tab** option from the **Sheet Metal CommandManager**
5. Set the values of the following parameters: **Thickness = 1; K-Factor = 0.5; Ratio = 0.5**
6. Click **OK**

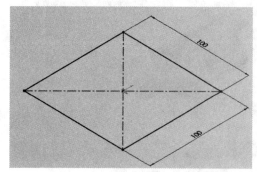

Figure 19-133 Sketch for base flange

Create the First Edge Flange

7. Select the *right-edge* of the first **Sketched Bend** (see Figure 19-134)
8. Set **Length** of **Edge Flange** = **90** and **Angle** = **90**-deg (see Figure 19-134)
9. Click **Edit Flange Profile** button from the **Edge Flange PropertyManager** (see Figure 19-134)
10. Click **OK** if the following message appears: "*The automatic relations inferred by this operation would over define the sketch. They will not be added.*"
11. Adjust the **Width** of the **Edge Flange** created by dragging one end point of the edge to a new position (**16 mm**) and using sketch tool to add dimensions (see Figure 19-134) [**Note:** *When the Profile Sketch window appears, do not click* **Finish** *until the length of the Edge Flanged is fully adjusted*]
12. Click **Finish**

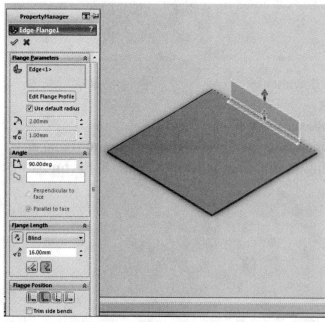

Figure 19-134 Edge Flange PropertyManager

Unfold the First Edge Flange

13. Click the **Unfold** tool
14. Click the **Fixed Face (Face<1>)** and **Bends to Unfold (EdgeBend1)** (see Figure 19-135)
15. Click **OK** to unfold the edge

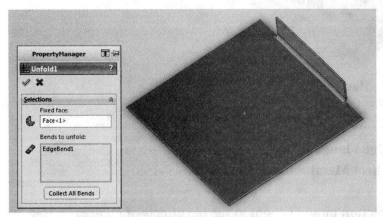

Figure 19-135 Unfold PropertyManager

Create a Hole along First Edge Flange

16. Click top of the Base Flange and be in sketch mode
17. Sketch a circle **5 mm** in diameter mid-way of unfolded bent feature (see Figure 19-136)
18. **Extrude-Cut** the **Circle Up To Next** (see Figure 19-136)

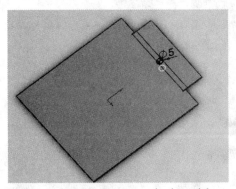

Figure 19-136 Create a hole mid-way of unfolded bent feature

Fold the First Edge Flange

1. Click the **Fold** tool
2. Click the **Fixed Face (Face<1>)** and **Bends to fold (EdgeBend1)** (see Figure 19-137)
3. Click **OK** to fold the edge

Figure 19-137 Unfold PropertyManager

Inserting Hem Feature on the right edge flange

1. Click the *top of the* **Edge Flange (Edge-Flange1)**.
2. Click **Hem** from the **Sheet Metal toolbar** (see Figure 19-138).
3. Select **Material Inside**
4. Click the **Reverse Direction** button (Zoom to see the effects of choice)
5. Accept **default (Open)** or select as required from the **Type and Size**
6. Enter **5 mm** for Length
7. Enter **2.5 mm** for Gap Distance
   [Observe the preview]
8. Click **OK**.

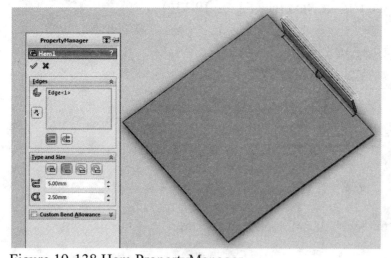

Figure 19-138 Hem PropertyManager

Create a Jog

9. Click the top face of the Base Flange, be in sketch mode and sketch a **Line 30 mm** from the edge for the Jog Feature (see Figure 19-139)
10. Click the Jog tool (see Figure 19-140)

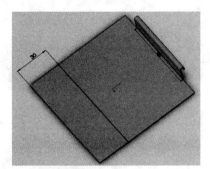

Figure 19-139

11. Click the **Fixed Face** on the *right side of the sketch* on the **Base Flange**
12. Set **Jog Offset** equal to **45**
13. Set **Jog Angle** equal to **135**
14. Set **OK** to finish

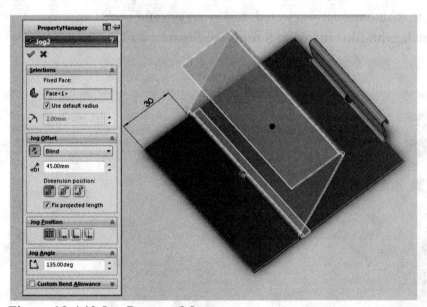

Figure 19-140 Jog PropertyManager

Create Break Corner

15. Select the *outer face* (**Face<1>**) of the fourth edge flange (see Figure 19-141)
16. Set **Distance = 5** (see Figure 19-141)
17. Click **OK** to finish the operation

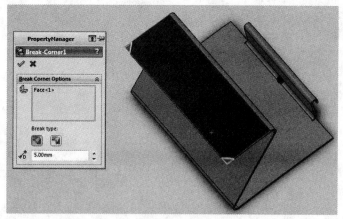

Figure 19-141 Break Corner PropertyManager

Create Sketch for Miter Flange

18. **Click one of the edges of the Base Flange and then select the Line tool from the Sketch toolbar** (see Figure 19-142). [Notice that a perpendicular plane for sketching the line is automatically selected; this is very useful in this approach.]

19. Create an L-sketch, with fillet radius of **5 mm** (see Figure 19-142)

20. **Exi**t sketch.

Figure 19-142 Sketch for miter flange

Create Miter Flange Features

21. Select **Sketch2**

22. Click the **Miter Flange** button on the **Sheet Metal toolbar**, while the sketch is still active.

23. Select the **Jog edge**, at the top as shown in Figure 19-143.

24. Click OK from the **Miter Flange Property** toolbar

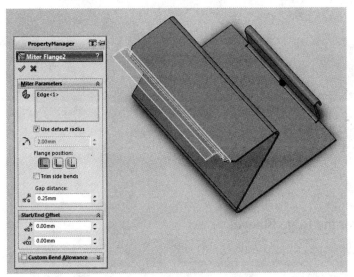

Figure 19-143 Miter Flange PropertyManager

Create the Second Edge Flange

25. Select the *right-edge* of the first **Sketched Bend** (see Figure 19-144)

26. Set **Length** of **Edge Flange** = **25** and **Angle** = **90**-deg (see Figure 19-144)

27. Click **Edit Flange Profile** button from the **Edge Flange PropertyManager** (see Figure 19-144)

28. Click **OK** if the following message appears: "*The automatic relations inferred by this operation would over define the sketch. They will not be added.*"

29. Adjust the **Width** of the **Edge Flange** created by dragging one end point of the edge to a new position (**16 mm**) and using sketch tool to add dimensions (see Figure 19-145) [**Note:** *When the Profile Sketch window appears, do not click* **Finish** *until the length of the Edge Flanged is fully adjusted*]

30. Click **Finish**

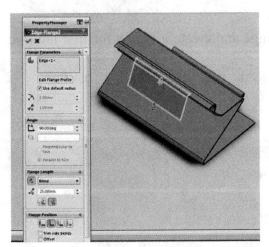

Figure 19-144 Edge Flange PropertyManager

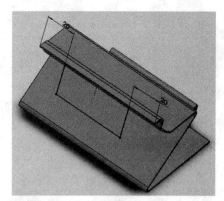

Figure 19-145 Width adjustment for the Edge Flange

Second Break Corners

31. Click the **Break Corner** tool
32. Select the *outer face* (**Face<1>**) of the fourth edge flange (see Figure 19-1463)
33. Set **Distance = 5** (see Figure 19-146)
34. Click **OK** to finish the operation

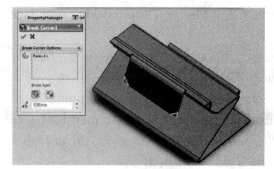

Figure 19-146 Break Corner PropertyManager

First Tab

35. Be in sketch mode on the third edge flange and create a sketch for first tab (see Figure 19-14)
36. Click the **Base Flange/Tab** tool to produce the first tab (see Figure 19-148)

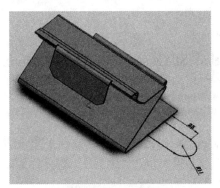

Figure 19-147 Sketch for creating tab feature

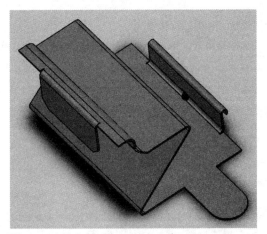

Figure 19-148 Sheet metal part

The Flatten state is shown in Figure 19-149. This is important for fabricating the sheet metal part on the shop floor.

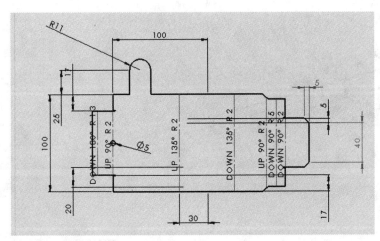

Figure 19-149 Flatten state

Tutorial 9: Hanger

A hanger support shown in Figure 19-150 is to be modeled. Show step-by-step procedure for the design.

Figure 19-150 Sheet metal model

SolidWorks Sheet Metal Procedure

1. Start a **New Part** document
2. Select the **Top** view
3. Sketch the base profile, **Sketch1** (see Figure 19-151)

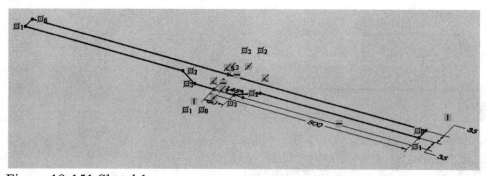

Figure 19-151 Sketch1

Base Flange
4. With base profile (**Sketch1**) active, click **Base Flange/Tab** (see Figure 19-152)
5. Set the **Thickness** as **5 mm** (see Figure 19-152)
6. Accept the **K-Factor** and **Ratio** default values (see Figure 19-152)

7. Click **OK** to complete Base Flange

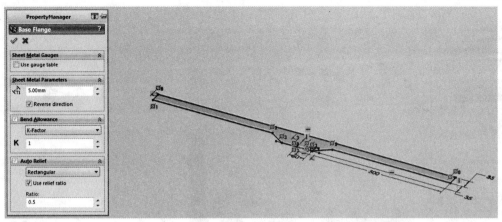

Figure 19-152 Base Flange PropertyManager

First Sketched Bending Operation

8. Sketch a **line, Sketch2** on the Base Flange for the first bending operation (see Figure 19-153 for Sketched Bend PropertyManager)
9. Click the **Sketched Bend** tool from the **SheetMetal CommandManager**
10. Click the **Fixed Face (Face<1>)** *to the left of the line* (Sketch2) in the **Bend Parameters** rollout (see Figure 19-153)
11. Click **OK** to complete the sketched bend operation (see Figure 19-153 for Sketched Bend)

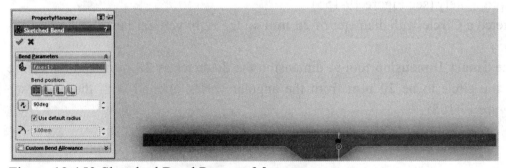

Figure 19-153 Sketched Bend PropertyManager

Second Sketched Bending Operation

12. Sketch another **line, Sketch2** on the Base Flange for the second bending operation (see Figure 19-154 Sketched Bend PropertyManager)
13. Click the **Sketched Bend** tool from the **SheetMetal CommandManager**
14. Click the **Fixed Face (Face<1>)** *to the right of the line* (Sketch2) in the **Bend Parameters** rollout (see Figure 19-154)

15. Click **OK** to complete the sketched bend operation (see Figure 19-154 for Sketched Bend)

Figure 19-154 Sketched Bend PropertyManager

Create A Circle on the Right Vertical Face

16. Click the right vertical face of the model and use **Normal To** tool to position it appropriately (see Figure 19-155)

17. Sketch a **Circle** with diameter of **25 mm** on the right vertical face (see Figure 19-155)

18. Use **Smart Dimension** tool to dimension the diameter as **25 mm**, and the centre of the circle to be **20 mm** from the angular vertex aligned with the edge (see Figure 19-155)

Figure 19-155 Circle sketched on right vertical face of model

Create an Extrude Feature

19. Click **Feature > Extrude** (see Figure 19-156 for the Extrude PropertyManager)
20. In the **Direction1** rollout, select **Up To Vertex** (see Figure 19-156 for Vertex at the top)
21. Click **OK** to complete this extrusion

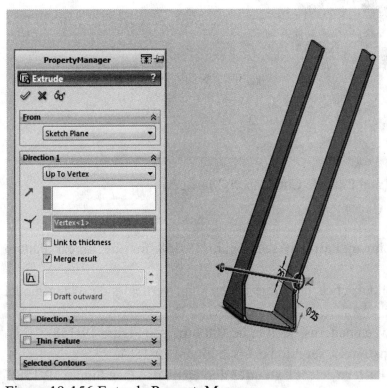

Figure 19-156 Extrude PropertyManager

Create another Circle on the Right Vertical Face

22. Sketch another concentric **Circle** with diameter of **15 mm** (see Figure 19-157)

23. Use **Smart Dimension** tool to dimension the diameter as **15 mm** (see Figure 19-157)

Create an Extrude Cut Feature

24. Click **Feature** > **Extrude Cut** (see Figure 19-157 for the Extrude PropertyManager)

25. In the **Direction1** rollout, select **Up To Vertex** (see Figure 19-157 for Vertex at the top)

26. Click **OK** to complete this extrusion

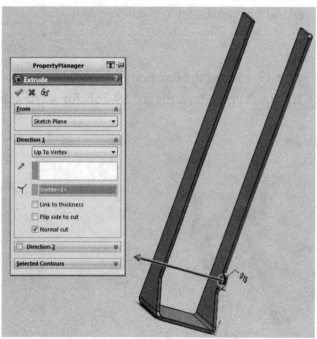

Figure 19-157 Circle created and Extrude Cut PropertyManager

Linear Pattern

27. Click **Features** > **Linear Pattern** (see Figure 19-158 for the Linear Pattern PropertyManager)

28. In the **Direction1** rollout, click the Edge of the right vertical side of the model (see Figure 19-158)

29. For the **Distance** between patterns, set it to be **180 mm** (see Figure 19-158)

30. For the **Number of Instances**, set it to be **3** (see Figure 19-158)

31. For the **Features To Pattern** select **Extrude3** and **Extrude4** (see Figure 19-158)

32. Click **OK** to complete the patterns (see Figure 19-158)

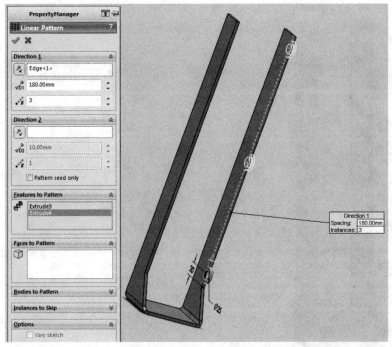

Figure 19-158 Linear Pattern PropertyManager

Mirror

33. Click **Features > Mirror** (see Figure 19-156 for the Mirror PropertyManager)
34. For the **Mirror/Face Plane**, select the **Right Plane** (see Figure 19-159)
35. For the **Features Mirror** select **LPattern2** (see Figure 19-159)
36. Click **OK** to complete the mirror operation (see Figure 19-159)

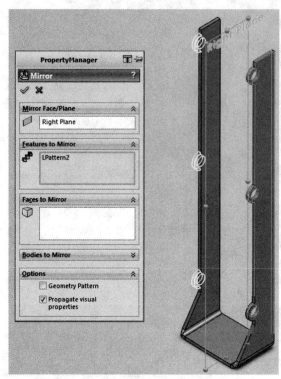

Figure 19-159 Mirror operation

Edge Flange

37. Create a **Rectangular profile** of **length 390 mm** *from the Top right corner* (see Figure 19-160)

38. Click the **Edge-Flange** tool (see Figure 19-161)

39. For the **Flange Parameter**, click the *Edge of the Rectangle common with the model* (see Figure 19-161)

40. For the **Flange Length**, set it to a value of **75.00 mm** (see Figure 19-161)

41. Click **OK** (see Figure 19-161)

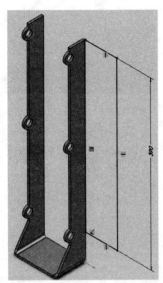

Figure 19-160 Rectangular profile for Edge Flange feature

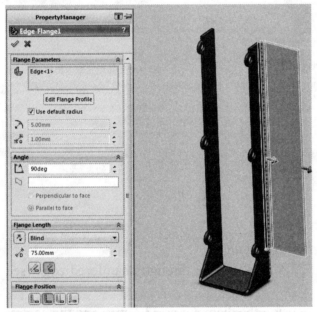

Figure 19-161 Edge Flange PropertyManager

Chamfer

42. Click **Features > Chamfer** (see Figure 19-162 for the Chamfer PropertyManager)
43. Select the **Distance** option (see Figure 19-162)
44. Select an **Edge** and for **Distance** set the value to **70.00 mm** (see Figure 19-162)
45. Click **OK** to complete the chamfer operation (see Figure 19-162)

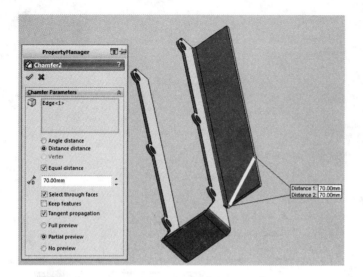

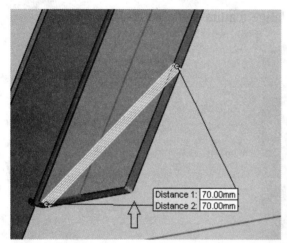

Figure 19-162 Chamfer PropertyManager

Create a Circle on the Front Face of Right Edge Flange

46. Sketch a **Circle** with diameter of **33.4 mm** passing through chamfered edge (see Figure 19-163)

47. Use **Smart Dimension** tool to dimension the diameter as **33.4 mm** and the centre, a distance of **148.85** mm from the bottom of model (see Figure 19-163)

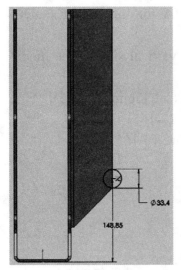

Figure 19-163 Circle on Right Edge Flange

Create an Extrude Cut Feature

48. Click **Feature > Extrude Cut** (see Figure 19-164 for the Extrude Cut PropertyManager)
49. In the **Direction1** rollout, select **Up To Next** (see Figure 19-164)
50. Click **OK** to complete this extrusion

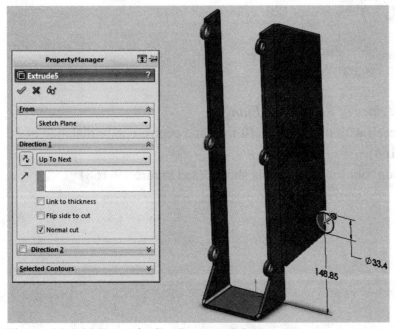

Figure 19-164 Extrude Cut PropertyManager

Linear Pattern

51. Click **Features > Linear Pattern** (see Figure 19-165 for the Linear Pattern PropertyManager)

52. In the **Direction1** rollout, click the Edge of the right vertical side of the model (see Figure 19-165)

53. For the **Distance** between patterns, set it to be **130 mm** (see Figure 19-165)

54. For the **Number of Instances**, set it to be **3** (see Figure 19-165)

55. For the **Features To Pattern** select **Extrude5** (see Figure 19-165)

56. Click **OK** to complete the patterns (see Figure 19-165)

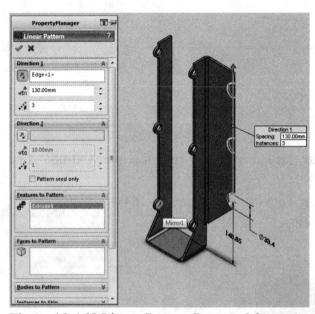

Figure 19-165 Linear Pattern PropertyManager

Create a Circle on the Front Face of Right Edge Flange

57. Sketch two **Circles** each with diameter of **10 mm** and centre-centre distance of **35 mm** (see Figure 19-166)

58. Use **Smart Dimension** tool for dimensions shown (see Figure 19-166)

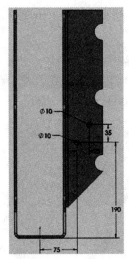

Figure 19-166 Two circles for Extrude Cut

Create Extrude Cut Feature

59. Click **Feature > Extrude Cut** (see Figure 19-167 for the Extrude Cut PropertyManager)
60. In the **Direction1** rollout, select **Up To Next** (see Figure 19-167)
61. Click **OK** to complete this extrusion

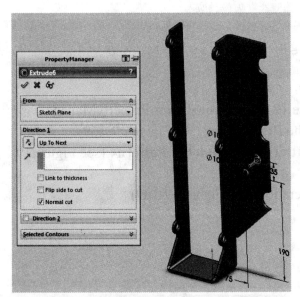

Figure 19-167 Extrude Cut PropertyManager

Linear Pattern on Right Edge Flange

1. Click **Features > Linear Pattern** (see Figure 19-168 for the Linear Pattern PropertyManager)

2. In the **Direction1** rollout, click the Edge of the right vertical side of the model (see Figure 19-168)
3. For the **Distance** between patterns, set it to be **210 mm** (see Figure 19-168)
4. For the **Number of Instances**, set it to be **2** (see Figure 19-168)
5. For the **Features To Pattern** select **Extrude6** (see Figure 19-168)
6. Click **OK** to complete the patterns (see Figure 19-168)

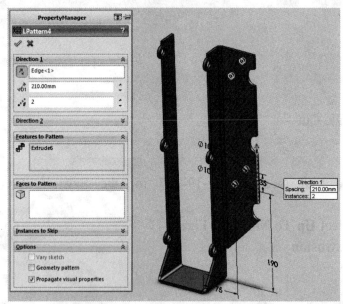

Figure 19-168 Linear Pattern PropertyManager

Mirror

1. Click **Features > Mirror** (see Figure 19-169 for the Mirror PropertyManager)
2. For the **Mirror/Face Plane**, select the **Right Plane** (see Figure 19-169)
3. For the **Features Mirror** select **LPattern3**, **Extrude6**, **LPattern4** (see Figure 19-169)
4. Click **OK** to complete the mirror operation (see Figure 19-169)

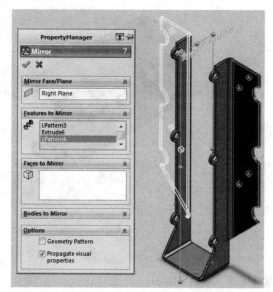

Figure 19-169 for the Mirror PropertyManager

The flattened state for the sheet metal is shown in Figure 19-170.

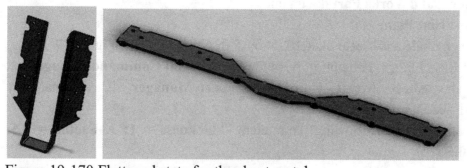

Figure 19-170 Flattened state for the sheet metal

Tutorial 10: CSWP-SMTL

Design the part shown in Figure 19-171 using SolidWorks Sheet Metal features. The part material is Aluminium, 1060 Alloy. Sheet metal thickness is 1.20 mm and inner bend radius is 1.00 mm. The part origin is arbitrary. Unit system: MMGS (millimetre, gram, second). Decimal places: 2. The following dimensions are used for the design: A = 175, B = 100, C = 50, D = 15.

i. What is the overall *mass* of the part (in grams)?

ii. What are the overall measured *length* (X) and *width* (Y) for the flattened state?

iii. Produce the *Flattened State Drawing* for this part.

[Note: These questions are similar to the primary part portion of the Certified SolidWorks Professional-SMTL examination]

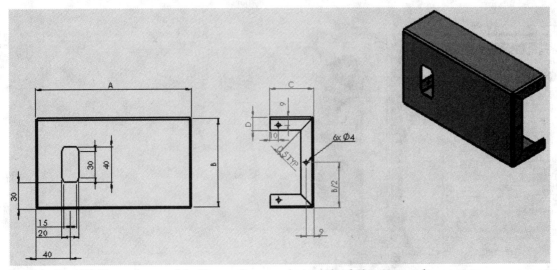

Figure 19-171 Drawings with dimensions and model of sheet metal

SolidWorks Solution

Create Base Flange

1. Start a **New SolidWorks Part** document
2. Select the **Front Plane**
3. Be in sketch mode and create Sketch1, *A* by *B* in dimension (see Figure 19-172)
4. Click the **Base Flange/Tab** option from the **Sheet Metal CommandManager** [Note: The **Sheet Metal CommandPropertyManager** is automatically displayed; see Figure 19-172]
5. Set the values of the following parameters: **Thickness = 1; K-Factor = 0.5; Ratio = 0.5**
6. Click **OK**

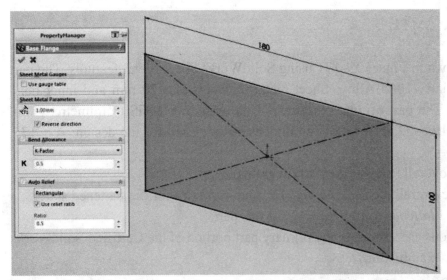

Figure 19-172 Sketch1 and selection of Base Flange/Tab option

Creating the First Edge Flange

7. Select the *top edge* of the base flange (see Figure 19-173)
8. Set **Length** of **Edge Flange** = **50** and **Angle** = **90**-deg in the **Edge Flange PropertyManager** (see Figure 19-173)
9. Click **OK** to finish the operation

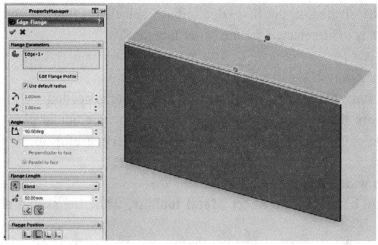

Figure 19-173 Edge Flange PropertyManager

Creating the Second Edge Flange

10. Select the *bottom edge* of the base flange (see Figure 19-174)
11. Set **Length** of **Edge Flange** = **50** and **Angle** = **90**-deg in the **Edge Flange PropertyManager** (see Figure 19-174)
12. Click **OK** to finish the operation

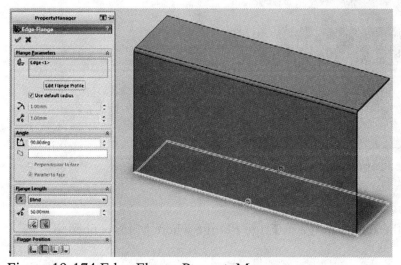

Figure 19-174 Edge Flange PropertyManager

The steps involved in creating Miter Flange are as follows:
a) Click any edge of the Base Flange or the Edge Flange where Miter is needed.
b) Select the Line tool from the Sketch toolbar and sketch the profile for the Miter flange
c) Without exiting sketch mode, click Miter tool and select each edge of the Base Flange or the Edge Flange where Miter is needed to create the Miter feature (the first one is automatically created on the first edge initially selected) [Note: If you exit the sketch, then it has to be selected for the Miter function]

Create the First Miter Flange Feature

13. Click **any Edge** of the **Base Flange** or **Edge Flange** where Miter is needed
14. Select the **Line tool from the Sketch toolbar**. [Notice that a perpendicular plane for sketching the line is automatically selected; this is very useful in this approach.]
15. Create a sketch **15 mm** wide, **Sketch2** (see Figure 19-175)
16. Click the **Miter Flange** button on the **Sheet Metal toolbar**, while the sketch is still active.
17. Select the **three Edges** of the **Base Flange/Edge Flange** (see Figure 19-175).
18. Click **OK** from the **Miter Flange Property** toolbar

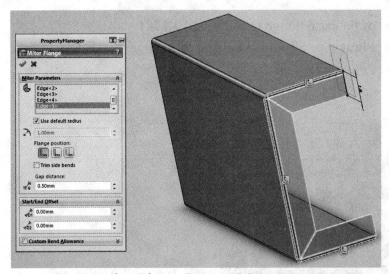

Figure 19-175 Miter Flange PropertyManager

Create the First Miter Flange Feature

19. Click **any Edge** of the **Base Flange** or **Edge Flange** where Miter is needed

20. Select the **Line tool from the Sketch toolbar**. [Notice that a perpendicular plane for sketching the line is automatically selected; this is very useful in this approach.]

21. Create a sketch **15 mm** wide, **Sketch3** (see Figure 19-176)

22. Click the **Miter Flange** button on the **Sheet Metal toolbar**, while the sketch is still active.

23. Select the **three Edges** of the **Base Flange/Edge Flange** (see Figure 19-176).

24. Click **OK** from the **Miter Flange Property** toolbar

25. Hide **Plane1**

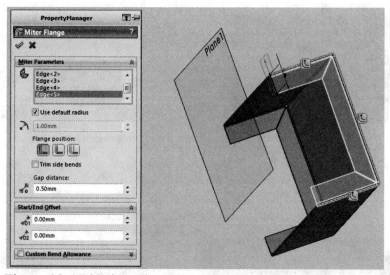

Figure 19-176 Miter Flange PropertyManager

Create Sketch for Extrude Cut

26. While in sketch mode, select the inner face of the **Base Flange**, and create a partial sketch (see Figure 19-177)

27. Select the partial sketch and **Mirror** about the horizontal **Construction Line** (see Figure 19-178)

28. Select the partial sketch and **Mirror** about the horizontal **Construction Line** (see Figure 19-179)

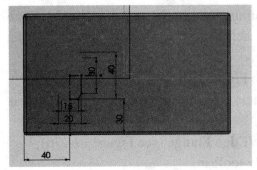

Figure 19-177 Sketch for Extrude-Cut

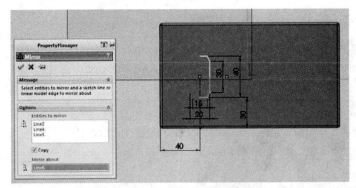

Figure 19-178 Mirror PropertyManager

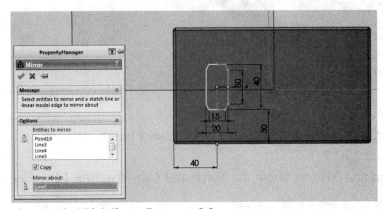

Figure 19-179 Mirror PropertyManager

Create Extrude Cut

29. Click the **Extrude-Cut** option
30. Select the **Up To Next** for **Direction1** (see Figure 19-180)
31. Click **OK** to complete the extrusion process

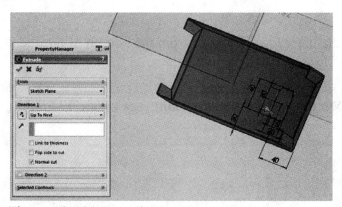

Figure 19-180 Extrude-Cut PropertyManager

Create Circular Extrude Cuts

32. Create a **circle**, **4-mm** diameter located **9 mm** by **10 mm** from the open end of the sheet metal (see Figure 19-181)

33. Click **Extrude-Cut** option

34. Select the **Extrude-Cut** and **Mirror** about the **Top Plane** (see Figure 19-182)

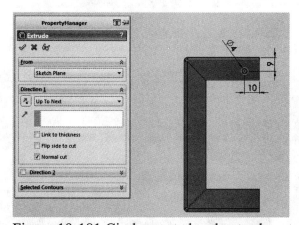

Figure 19-181 Circle created and extrude cut

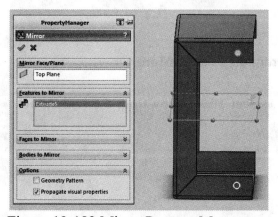

Figure 19-182 Mirror PropertyManager

35. Create another **circle**, **4-mm** diameter located **9 mm** from the bottom of the sheet metal (see Figure 19-183)
36. Click **Extrude-Cut** option
37. Select the **Extrude-Cut** and **Mirror** about the **Right Plane** (see Figure 19-184)

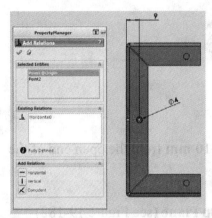

Figure 19-183 Another circle created for extrusion

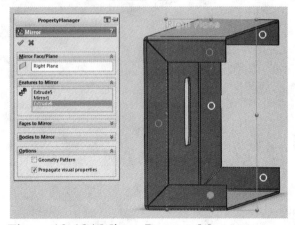

Figure 19-184 Mirror PropertyManager

Apply Material

38. Right-click **Material <not specified>** from the **FeatureManager**
39. Select **Edit Material**
40. From the **Material PropertyManager**, select **1060 Alloy** from the **SolidWorks** *Materials Database* (see Figure 19-185)
41. Click **Apply** to apply the Material
42. Click **Close** to complete the process

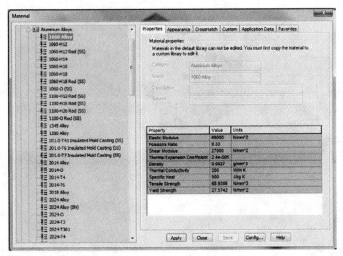

Figure 19-185

Compute Mass Properties

43. Click **Evaluate > Mass Properties** (see Figure 19-186 for the values)

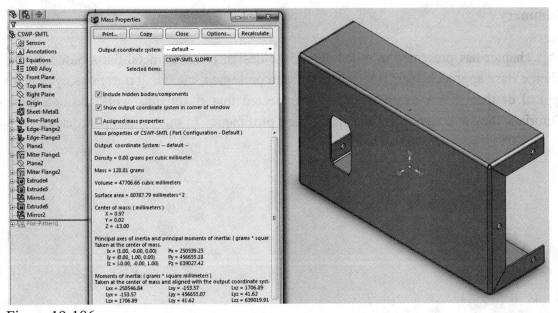

Figure 19-186

Create Flattened State Drawing

Figure 19-187 shows the **Flattened** state of the sheet metal part.

The overall measured *length* (X) and *width* (Y) for the flattened state are:

X = 206.23 mm; Y = 201.03 mm

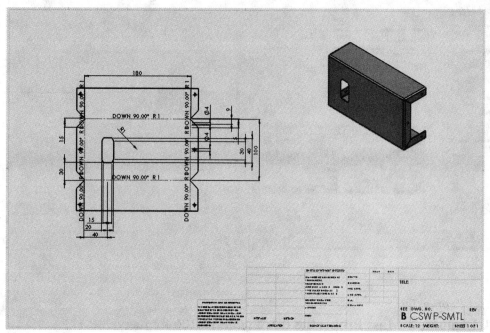

Figure 19-187 Flattened state

Summary

This chapter has presented in much detail, the design of sheet metal parts based on the Flange Base approach. Ten Tutorials have been presented, including questions, which are typical of the CSWA examination. It is expected that if students work through these Tutorials, they will significantly enhance their proficiency in sheet metal part design.

Exercises

1. Apply 1060 Alloy material from the SolidWorks to the sheet metal in Tutorial 1 (see Figure P1) and determine the mass.

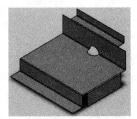

Figure P1

2. Apply 1060 Alloy material from the SolidWorks to the sheet metal in Tutorial 1 (see Figure P2) and determine the mass.

Figure P2

3. For the sheet metal in Tutorial 2 (see Figure P3) apply 1060 Alloy material and determine the mass. Can you create a mirror about a plane A-B?

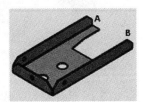

Figure P3

4. For the sheet metal in Tutorial 8 (see Figure P4) apply 1060 Alloy material as material, and determine the mass. Create part drawing.

Figure P4

5. Repeat the CSWP-SMTL sheet metal part in Tutorial 9 (see Figure P5) with the following dimensions used for the design: A = 180, B = 100, C = 50, D = 15.

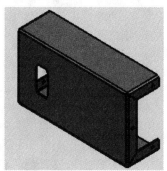

Figure P5

Chapter 20
Weldments

Objectives:
In this chapter you will learn:
- About **Weldment** tools
- How to define the basic weldment framework using **3DSketch**
- How to insert a **Structural Member**
- How to insert a **Fillet Bead** feature
- How to insert a **Trim/Extend** feature
- How to insert an **End Cap** feature
- How to insert a **Gusset** feature
- How to apply **Weldment** to part design

INTRODUCTION

Weldments play a significant role in joining structural members, and hence are of vital importance in the civil engineering discipline. Also, weldments constitute one of the several aspects of the manufacturing process which requires specific attention. We will now consider weldments. Weldments functionality enables you to design a weldment structure as a single multibody part. The basic approach is to use 2D and 3D sketches to define the basic framework. Then create structural members containing groups of sketch segments. Features that can added include gussets, end caps, etc., using tools on the **Weldments toolbar**. This chapter also considers creating weldments from a part design.

CREATING PARTS WITH A 3-D SKETCH

Since the paths of weldments are mainly in 3D, a good grasp of the 3DSketch tool is a prerequisite for creating weldments. From the main menu, select the **3DSketch tool** (see Figure 20-1) by clicking on the **Sketch tab** of the **CommandManager**. Select the **Line Tool**. Note that beside the cursor, the plane that the line will be displayed.

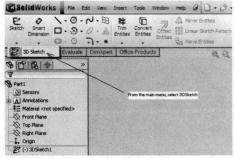

Figure 20-1 3DSketch tool

Tutorial 1

Model a bent tube with 0.5 inch outer diameter and 0.375 inner diameter to join the ends of two tubes as shown in Figure 20-2. Follow the route shown by the center lines in Figure 20-2 and add 1 inch radius fillets to the corners.

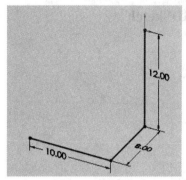

Figure 20-2 Specified route

Solution

1. Select the **3DSketch tool** by clicking on the **Sketch tab** of the **CommandManager**.
2. Select the **Line Tool**. Note that beside the cursor, the plane that the line will be displayed.
3. Press the tab key until when the plane selected is **YZ**
4. Sketch a line **12 in** long from the origin along **Y**
5. Sketch a line **8 in** long along **Z**
6. Press the tab key until when the plane selected is **ZX**
7. Sketch a line **10 in** long along **X**
8. **3DSketch1** is complete (see Figure 20-3).
9. Exit **3DSketch**

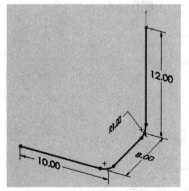

Figure 20-3 3DSketch of route

10. Click the **top vertex** of the vertical line which is 12 in long
11. Click **Features > Reference Geometry**
12. Select **top vertex** and vertical line connected to it, for **Selections**
13. Select **Normal to Curve** to complete defining **Plane1**
14. Select **Plane1**
15. Right-click and select Sketch tool to sketch the two circles with 0.5 inch outer diameter and 0.375 inner diameter, as Sketch1; dimension them (see Figure 20-4).
16. Exit **Sketch**

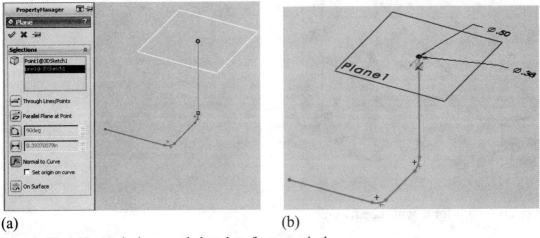

(a)   (b)

Figure 20-4 Normal plane and sketches for two circles

17. Click **Features > Sweep**
18. Select **Sketch1** as the Profile and **3DSketch1** as the Path (see Figure 20-5)
19. Click **OK**

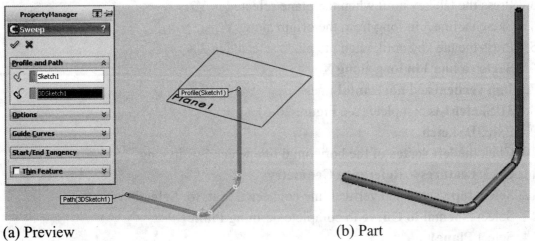

(a) Preview   (b) Part

Figure 20-5 Part for Exercise 1

Tutorial 2

Model a bent tube with 0.5 inch outer diameter and 0.375 inner diameter to join the ends of two tubes as shown in Figure 20-6. Follow the route shown by the center lines in Figure 20-6 and add 1 inch radius fillets to the corners.

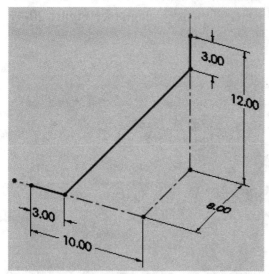

Figure 20-6 Path for a bent tube model

Solution

1. Select the **3DSketch tool** by clicking on the **Sketch tab** of the **CommandManager**.
2. Select the **Line Tool**. Note that beside the cursor, the plane that the line will be displayed.
3. Press the tab key until when the plane selected is **YZ**
4. Sketch a line **3 in** long from the origin along **Y**
5. Press the tab key until when the plane selected is **ZX**
6. Sketch a line **3 in** long along **X**
7. Join **vertical** and **horizontal** lines
8. **3DSketch1** is complete (see Figure 20-6).
9. Exit **3DSketch**
10. Click the **left vertex** of the horizontal line which is 3 in long
11. Click **Features > Reference Geometry**
12. Select **top vertex** and vertical line connected to it, for **Selections**
13. Select **Normal to Curve** to complete defining **Plane1**
14. Select **Plane1**
15. Right-click and select Sketch tool to sketch the two circles with 0.5 inch outer diameter and 0.375 inner diameter, as Sketch1; dimension them (see Figure 20-7).

16. Exit **Sketch**

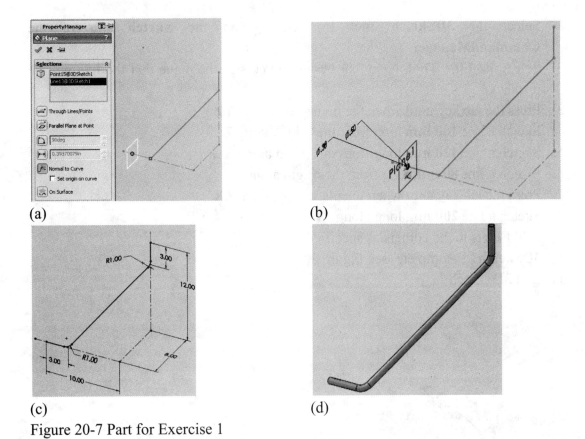

(a)

(b)

(c)

(d)

Figure 20-7 Part for Exercise 1

Tutorial 3

Model handlebars tube with 25.4 mm outer diameter and 23.4 mm inner diameter to join the ends of two tubes as shown in Figure 20-8. Follow the route shown by the center lines in Figure 20-8 and add fillets to the corners as specified.

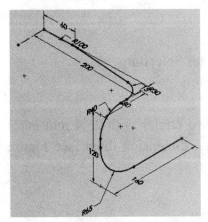

Figure 20-8 Specified route

Solution

1. Select the **3DSketch tool** by clicking on the **Sketch tab** of the **CommandManager**.
2. Select the **Line Tool**. Note that beside the cursor, the plane that the line will be displayed.
3. Press the tab key until when the plane selected is **YZ**
4. Sketch a line **160 mm** long from the origin along **Z**
5. Sketch a line **120 mm** long from the origin along **Y**
6. Sketch a line **80 mm** long from the origin along **-Z**
7. Press the tab key until when the plane selected is **ZX**
8. Sketch a line **200 mm** long along **-X**
9. Add **Fillets** to the corners as specified
10. **3DSketch1** is complete (see Figure 20-9).
11. Exit **3DSketch**

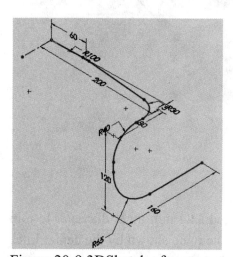

Figure 20-9 3DSketch of route

12. Click the end of the **160 mm** long line
13. Click **Features > Reference Geometry**
14. Select **top vertex** and vertical line connected to it, for **Selections**
15. Select **Normal to Curve** to complete defining **Plane1**
16. Select **Plane1**
17. Right-click and select Sketch tool to sketch the two circles with 25.4 mm outer diameter and 23.4 mm inner diameter, as Sketch1; dimension them (see Figure 20-10)
18. Exit **Sketch**

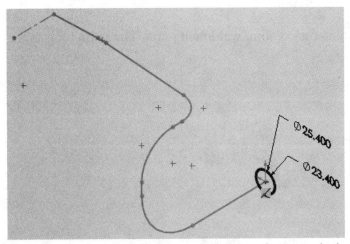

Figure 20-10 Normal plane and sketches for two circles

Figure 20-11 shows the preview while Figure 20-12 shows the final model.

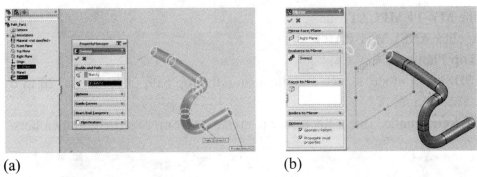

(a)   (b)

Figure 20-11 Preview of model

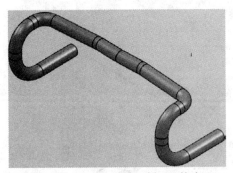

Figure 20-12 Model of handlebars

Now that we have a good grasp of 3DSketch tool which is a prerequisite for creating weldments, it becomes logical to now present weldment tool bar.

WELDMENTS TOOLBAR

The **Weldments** toolbar provides tools for creating weldment parts. The main tools are:

Weldment

Structural Member

Gusset

End Cap

Fillet Bead

Trim/Extend

STRUCTURAL MEMBER

The first step is to define the paths for which different profiles will be created. The paths are created using 3DSketch.

1. Click the **MY-TEMPLATE** tab.
2. Double-click **ANSI-MM-PART**.
3. Click **Top Plane**.
4. Using **3DSketch** mode, sketch and dimension the top path (a rectangle, 20 in by 12 in). This is in the X-Y plane (see Figure 20-13).
5. Exit **3DSketch** mode. This is necessary to create a **Group** of structural members.

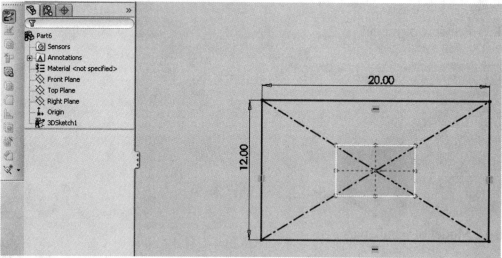

Figure 20-13 Top path (a rectangle, 20 in by 12 in) in the X-Y plane

6. Click **Top Plane**.
7. Click **3DSketch** in **CommandFeature**

8. Pick one of the vertices of the Top rectangular feature and Sketch a line (switch to YZ plane by pressing Tab key)

9. Sketch the other legs and use relations to make all four legs **parallel** and **equal**

10. Dimension one of them to be **10 in**

11. Add a relation that one of the legs and the top members are **perpendicular** (90°) (see Figures 20-14 and 20-15). The complete sketch is shown in Figure 20-15.

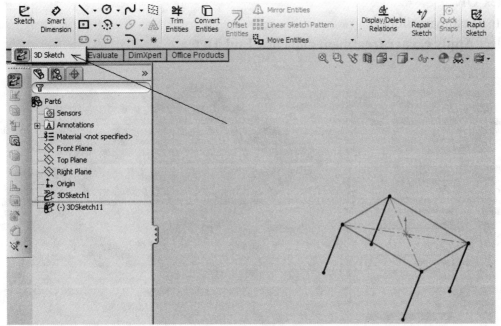

Figure 20-14 3DSketch in CommandFeature necessary for creating weldments

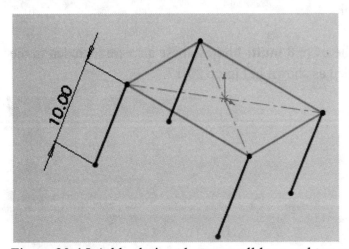

Figure 20-15 Add relations between all legs and top path

12. Exit **3DSketch**

13. Click **Structural Member** toolbar.

14. In the Selection rollout, specify the profile of the structural member by selecting (see Figure 20-16):
15. **Standard**. Select **ansi inch**.
16. **Type**. Select a **Profile Type, square tube**.
17. **Size**. Select a **Profile**, such as **2 x 2 x 0.25**.
18. Select all **4 members** of the Top elements as **Group1**
19. Click **New Group** button and select all **4 legs** as **Group2**
20. Click **OK**
21. In the Settings rollout,
22. Select **Apply corner treatment** and click **End Meter**

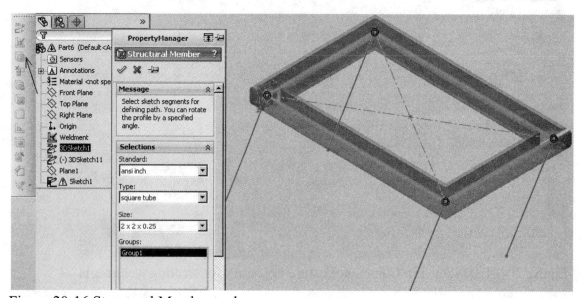

Figure 20-16 Structural Member tool

Expanding the **Cut list** shows that there are **8 multi-bodies**; these also are included in the **Structural Member1** if it is expanded as shown in Figure 20-17.

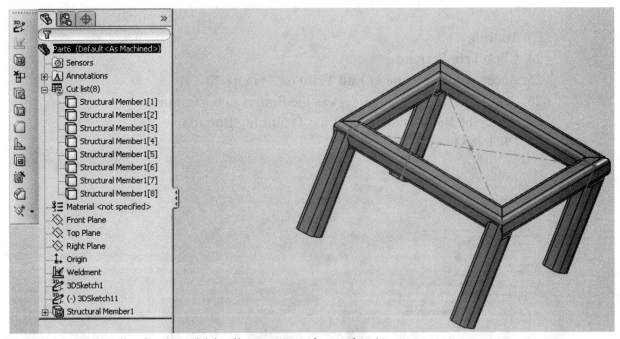

Figure 20-17 Cut list for 8 multi-bodies structural members

TRIMMING THE STRUCTURAL MEMBERS

There are cases in which structural members have to be trimmed. For example, if instead of defining Group1 and Group2 at the same time of defining structural members, they are defined as two different structural members then the need for trimming may arise. This scenario is shown in Figure 20-18. Notice, there are **Structural Member1** and **Structural Member2**. However, trimming is now needed because some solid bodies are *entering* into other solid bodies, which is not allowed in practice.

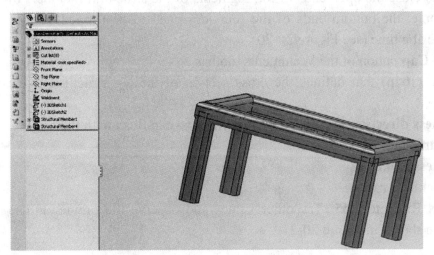

Figure 20-18 Structural Member requiring trimming operation

23. To trim,
24. Click **Trim/Extend**
25. Accept **Corner Type** as **End Trim** (see Figure 20-19)
26. Select **one of the vertical legs** as the **Bodies to be Trimmed**
27. Select the **Bodies** radio button for **Trimming Boundary**
28. Click the **bounding surfaces**

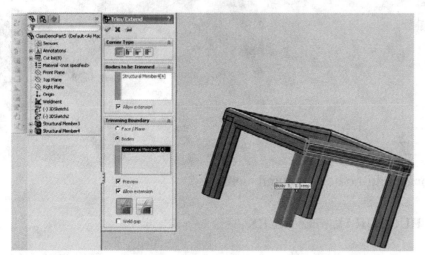

Figure 20-19 Trim/Extend option

Repeat the process for all other legs.

ADDING END CAPS TO STRUCTURAL MEMBERS

Let us add end caps to close the open ends of the segments of the structural members of interest. In this example, the bottom ends of the four legs need to be capped so they should be selected one at a time (see Figure 20-20).

29. Click the **End Cap** option of the Weldments toolbar
30. Click the **face (strip)** that defines the cross section of the leg structure as the **Parameter**
31. Select **Thickness direction** to **Inward** to make the end cap flush with the original extent of the structure.
32. Set the **thickness** to **0.25 in**
33. Select **Use thickness ratio**
34. Set **Thickness Ratio** to **0.65** (Try other values and observe the preview). The capped legs are shown in Figure 20-21.

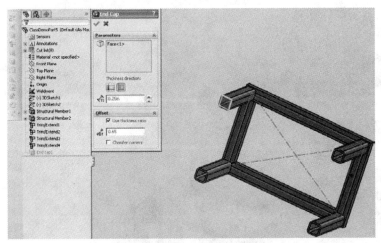

Figure 20-20 End cap option

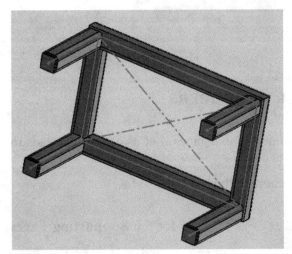

Figure 20-21 Structural Members with end caps

ADDING GUSSETS TO STRUCTURAL MEMBERS

Gussets features which may be triangular or polygonal profiles can be added to two adjoining planar faces. Let us add gussets to the corners of the four legs.

35. Click **Gusset** option of the Weldments toolbar
36. Click the two faces (Face<1> and Face<2>) as shown for the **Supporting Faces** (see Figure 20-22)
37. Under **Profile,** Click **Triangular Profile**
38. Set **Profile Distance1** and **Profile Distance2** to 1 in each
39. Select Thickness to **inner Side**
40. Set Gusset **thickness** to **0.25 in**
41. Select **Profile Locates at Mid Point** for Location

Repeat steps 35—41 for each leg

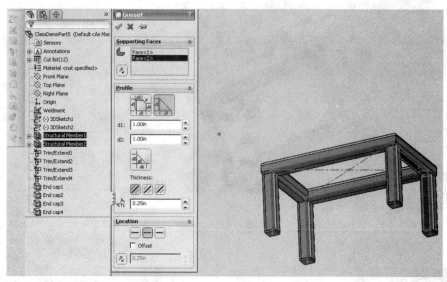

Figure 20-22 Gusset option

ADDING FILLET BEADS TO STRUCTURAL MEMBERS

Fillet beads features can be added to two adjoining planar faces. Let us add fillet beads to the corners of the four legs.

42. Click **Fillet Bead** option of the Weldments toolbar
43. Click **Gusset** face
44. Click the two faces (Face<1> and Face<2>) as shown for the **Supporting Faces** (see Figure 20-23)

Repeat for each leg

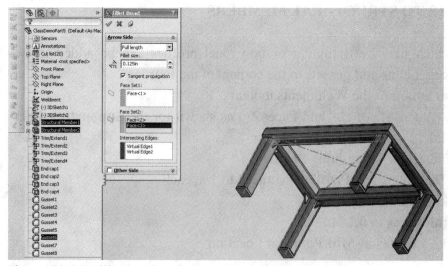

Figure 20-23 Fillet bead option

WELDMENT OF PARTS

In this subsection, it is demonstrated that weldment can be applied to part design. We will first create a part which is made up of an inverted channel shape as the base and two vertical brackets. Figure 20-24 shows *Sketch1* for the base, while Figure 20-25 shows the extruded base of *Sketch1*.

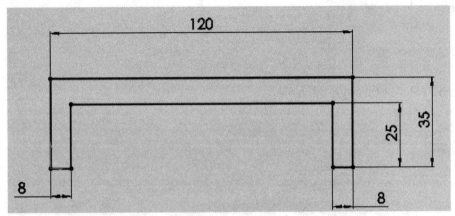

Figure 20-24 Sketch1 for the base

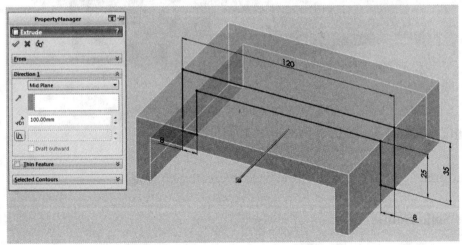

Figure 20-25 Extruded base of Sketch1

A rectangular sketch, Sketch2, 70 mm by 10 mm which is offset 15 mm from the horizontal top edges is used to create a slot as shown in Figure 20-26 and Figure 20-27.

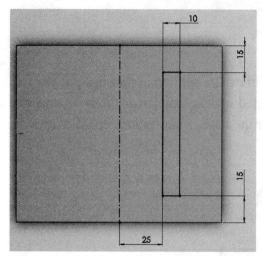

Figure 20-26 Sketch2 for slot through the base

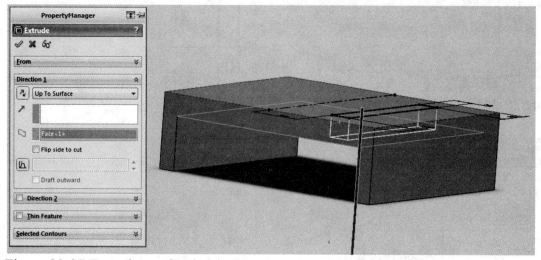

Figure 20-27 Extrude-cut for the slot

Extrude-cut is mirrored about the centre of the base to create two slots.

Assembly versus Solid Bodies

When an Assembly of parts is created, the weldment tool does not work. However, when Solid Bodies are created, Weldment tool functions appropriately. The point made here is important: use solid bodies for weldment of parts. The principle is now illustrated.

The edges of the Extrude-cut features are extracted using **Convert Entities** tool and used to create side features by extrusion. The **Merge Results** options are unchecked during extrude operation in order to create solid bodies.

1. Click the bottom face of the horizontal upper portion of the base created.
2. Be in sketch mode and select the *four edges of the right slot (Extrude-cut feature)* already created.
3. Click the **Convert Entities** tool to create a rectangular profile
4. Click the **Extrude Boss/Base** tool; ensure that the **Merge Results** options are unchecked

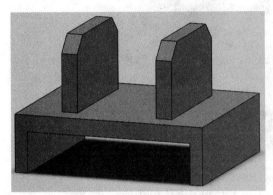

Figure 20-28 Base and side features as three solid bodies

Fillet beads are now created for the two vertical features.

5. Click Weldment tool to enable the weldment environment
6. Click **Fillet Bead** tool and select one **face** of the left **side feature** as well as the top of the **base**

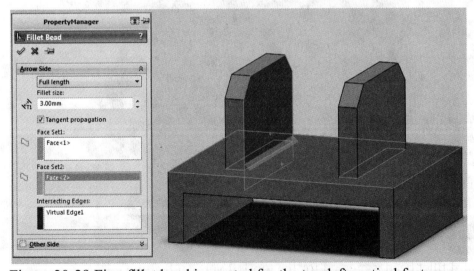

Figure 20-29 First fillet bead is created for the top-left vertical feature

7. Click **Fillet Bead** tool and select one **face** of the left **side feature** as well as the top of the **base**

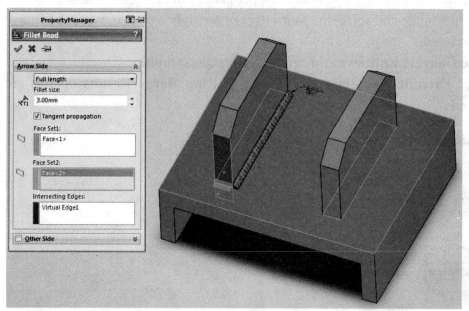

Figure 20-30 Second fillet bead is created for the top-left vertical feature

8. Click **Fillet Bead** tool and select one **face** of the left **side feature** as well as the top of the **base**

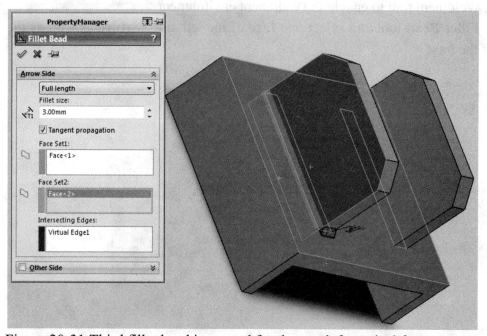

Figure 20-31 Third fillet bead is created for the top-left vertical feature

9. Click **Fillet Bead** tool and select one **face** of the left **side feature** as well as the top of the **base**

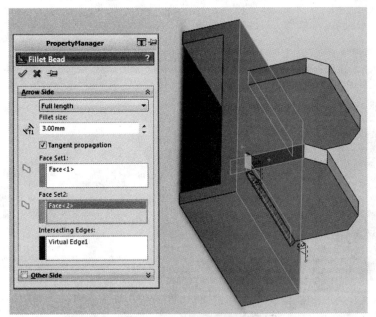

Figure 20-32 Fourth fillet bead is created for the top-left vertical feature

10. Click **Fillet Bead** tool and select one **face** of the right **side feature** as well as the top of the **base**

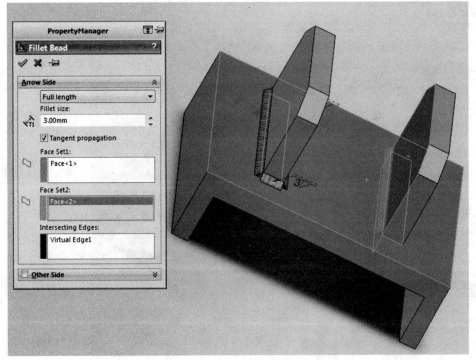

Figure 20-33 First fillet bead is created for the top-right vertical feature

11. Click **Fillet Bead** tool and select one **face** of the right **side feature** as well as the top of the **base**

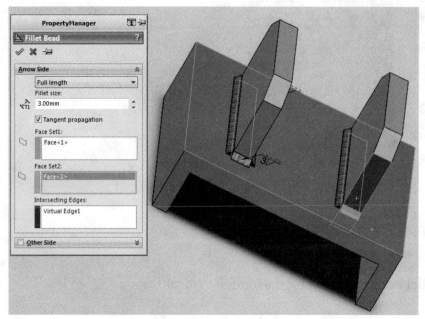

Figure 20-34 Second fillet bead is created for the top-right vertical feature

12. Click **Fillet Bead** tool and select one **face** of the right **side feature** as well as the top of the **base**

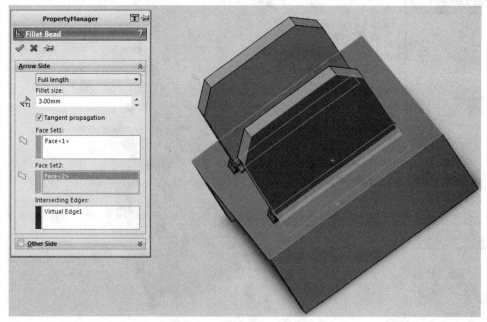

Figure 20-35 Third fillet bead is created for the top-right vertical feature

13. Click **Fillet Bead** tool and select one **face** of the right **side feature** as well as the top of the **base**

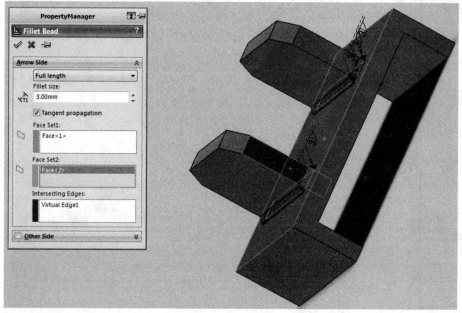

Figure 20-36 Fourth fillet bead is created for the top-right vertical feature

The completed weldment model is shown in Figure 20-37. It is important to note that there are 11 members in the weldment Cut list (see Figure 20-38); *three* from the part model and *four* each from the fillet beads around the *two* vertical features [3 + 4 + 4 =11].

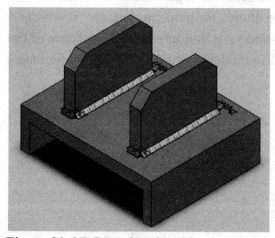

Figure 20-37 Completed weldment of base and two side features

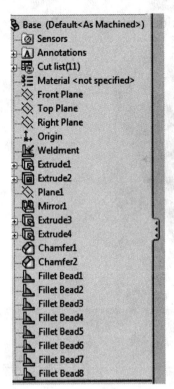

Figure 20-38

Summary

In this chapter, we have described methods for creating weldments from defined paths using the 3D Sketch tool, and also creating weldments from part designs. These are two approaches. The first approach is considered the choice for modeling trusses. The second approach is the choice when we are modeling solid parts and intend welding some of the parts together. Weldments are extremely useful in modeling trusses and beams for stress analysis using the finite element method, FEM.

Exercises

1. Create the truss structure shown in Figure P-1. The material is steel pipe, NPS1$\frac{1}{2}$″, Schedule 40.

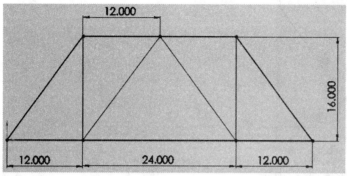

Figure P-1

2. Create the truss structure shown in Figure P-2. The material is steel pipe, NPS1$\frac{1}{2}$″, Schedule 40.

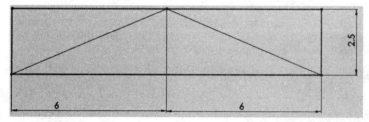

Figure P-2

3. Create the truss structure shown in Figure P-3. The material is steel pipe, NPS1$\frac{1}{2}$″, Schedule 40.

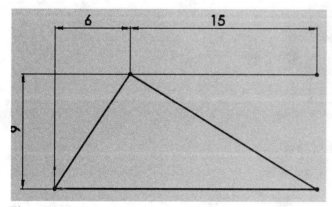

Figure P-3

4. Create the truss structure shown in Figure P-4. The material is steel pipe, NPS$1\frac{1}{2}''$, Schedule 40.

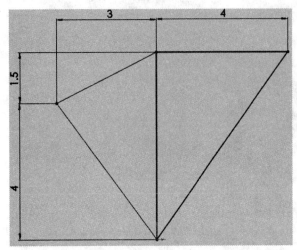

Figure P-4

5. Create the truss structure shown in Figure P-5. The material is steel pipe, NPS$1\frac{1}{2}''$, Schedule 40.

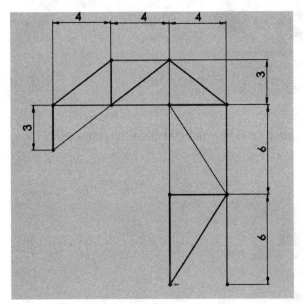

Figure P-5

6. Create the truss structure shown in Figure P-6. The material is steel pipe, NPS1$\frac{1}{2}''$, Schedule 40.

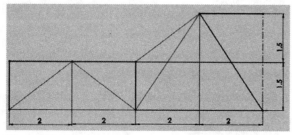

Figure P-6

7. Create the truss structure shown in Figure P-7. The material is steel pipe, NPS1$\frac{1}{2}''$, Schedule 40.

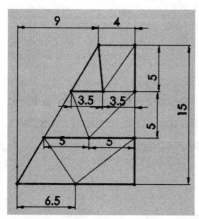

Figure P-7

8. Create the truss structure shown in Figure P-8. The material is steel pipe, NPS1$\frac{1}{2}''$, Schedule 40.

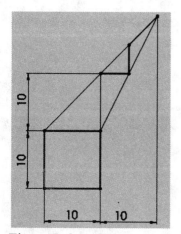

Figure P-8

9. Create the truss structure shown in Figure P-9. The material is steel pipe, NPS$1\frac{1}{2}''$, Schedule 40.

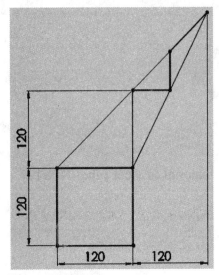

Figure P-9

10. Create a plate, 120 mm by 100 mm by 10 mm thick, placed on top the two vertical brackets shown in Figure 9-10. Create fillet beads to hold the plate to the top faces of the vertical brackets. Refer to the section on weldment of parts.

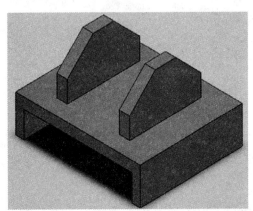

Figure P-10 Assembly of base and side features

Chapter 21
Routings in Piping and Tubing

Objectives:

In this chapter you will learn:

- About **customizing routing templates**
- How to **add parts to routing library**
- How to **start a route**
- How to **create the route** for pipes and tubes

INTRODUCTION

SolidWorks Routing enables designers to create a special type of sub-assembly that builds a path of pipes, tubes, or electrical cables between components. SolidWorks Routing also includes harness flattening and detailing capabilities, so that designers can develop 2D harness manufacturing drawings from 3D electrical route assemblies.

A route sub-assembly is always a component of a top-level assembly. When you insert certain components into an assembly, a route sub-assembly is created automatically. Unlike other types of sub-assemblies, you do not create a route assembly in its own window and then insert it as a component in the higher-level assembly.

You model the route by creating a 3D sketch of the centerline of the route path. The SolidWorks software generates the pipe, tube, or cable along the centerline.

The SolidWorks software makes extensive use of design tables to create and modify the configurations of route components. The configurations are distinguished by different dimensions and properties. If you are unfamiliar with these concepts, see Design Tables.

ACTIVATING THE SOLIDWORKS ROUTING ADD-INS

The starting point for utilizing the routing tool is to activate the SolidWorks Routing adds-in. To activate SolidWorks Routing:

1. Click **Tools > Adds-Ins**
2. Select **SolidWorks Routing** to activate it for the current session in the **Active Adds-Ins**
3. Click **OK** to add SolidWorks Routing (see Figure 21-1)

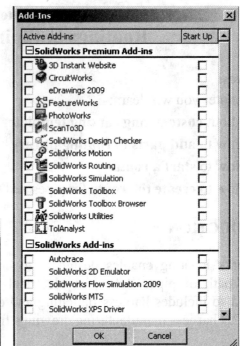

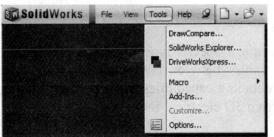

Figure 21-1 SolidWorks Routing add-ins

BACKGROUND

It should be noted that a route is always a component of a top-level assembly. This means that when we insert components into an assembly, a route sub-assembly is created automatically. There is a way of switching from the sub-assembly to the top-level assembly. We will consider this later.

CUSTOMIZING ROUTING TEMPLATES

Now create a custom routing template and set its units to inches. If your organization's policy allows, you could save the custom template in the default template location, but for our current purpose, you save it in a new folder that you create.

1. In Windows Explorer, create a folder on your local drive called **H:\MyRouting**.
2. In SolidWorks, click **Open**.
3. In the **Open** dialog box:
   a. For **Look in**, browse to your default template location (typically **C:\Documents and Settings\All Users\Application Data\SolidWorks\SolidWorks**<*version*>**\templates**).
      If your default template location is different, browse to that location.
   b. In **File of type**, select **Template (*.prtdot;*.asmdot;*.drwdot)**.
   c. Select **routeAssembly.asmdot**.
   d. Click **Open**.

   Now save a copy of the template and change some settings in it.
1. Click **File, Save As**.

2. In the **Save As** dialog box:
   a. For **Save in**, browse to **H:\MyRouting**.
   b. For **File name**, type **MyRouteAssembly**.
   c. For **Save as type**, select **Assembly Templates (*.asmdot)**.
   d. Click **Save**.
3. Click **Options**.
4. In the dialog box:
   a. On the **Document Properties** tab, select **Units**.
   b. Under **Unit system**, select **IPS (inch, pound, second)**.
   c. Click **OK**.
5. Click **Save** (Standard toolbar).

ADDING PARTS TO THE ROUTING LIBRARY

The Routing Library contains parts (such as flanges, fittings, and pipes) for you to use in routes you create. By default, the Routing Library is located in a folder named **routing** in the Design Library. You can add components to existing folders in the Routing Library, or create new folders. You must have write access to your Design Library to create folders and add parts

Create a new folder in the Routing Library and add an *assembly fitting without acp* assembly.
1. In the Task Pane:
   a. Click the **Design Library** tab.
   b. Browse to **Design Library\routing\assembly fittings**.
2. At the top of the Task Pane, click **Create New Folder**.
3. Type **MyLibrary** for the folder name and press **Enter**.

Let us consider some illustrations on routing.

ILLUSTRATION 1

Now add **assembly fitting without acp.sldasm** to the **MyLibrary** folder (see Figure 21-2).
1. At the top of the Task Pane, click **Add to Library**.
2. In the PropertyManager:
   a. For **Items to Add**, select **assembly fitting without acp.sldasm** at the top of the flyout FeatureManager design tree.
   b. Under **Save To**, make sure the **MyLibrary** folder is selected under **Design Library folder**.
   c. Click.
      The part is added to the Routing Library, and is available for selection when you create a route.
3. Close the part.

STARTING A ROUTE

Add some pipe and tube routes to an assembly.

1. Browse to **C:\Documents and Settings\All Users\Application Data\SolidWorks\SolidWorks<*version*>\designlibrary\routing\assembly fittings\MyLibrary**
2. Save the assembly as **MyAssyFitting.sldasm**.
   The assembly normally will already contain some fittings that need to be connected by pipe or tube routes.

Start the first route by dragging a flange into the assembly. Figure 21-2 shows a preview of the Design Library **Assembly Fitting**. You can use tools on the **View toolbar** to zoom, rotate, and pan the model view to facilitate working with the model.

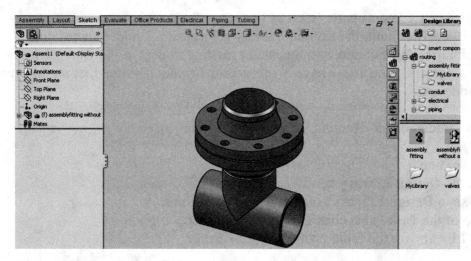

Figure 21-2 Assembly fitting without acp.sldasm

Click **Start by Drag/Drop** (Piping toolbar [see Figure 21-3]).
   The Design Library opens to the **piping** section of the Routing Library.
2. In the lower panel, double-click the **flanges** folder.
3. **Drag slip on weld flange.sldprt** from the library to the flange face on the regulator.
4. **Drop** the flange when it snaps into place (see Figure 21-4).
5. In the dialog box:
   a. Select **Slip On Flange 150-NPS2**.
   b. Click **OK**.
The **Route Properties** PropertyManager appears.

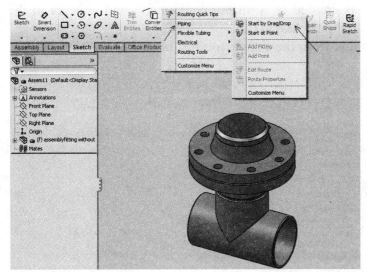

Figure 21-3 Drag/Drop option

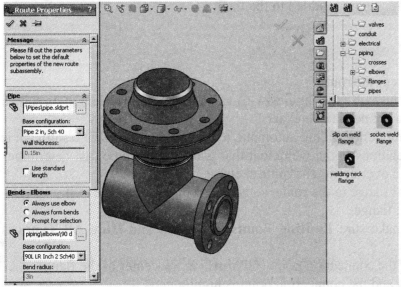

Figure 21-4 Flange for dragging/dropping on the right of Window

In the **Route Properties** PropertyManager, you specify the properties of the route you are about to create. Some of the items you can specify include:

- Which pipe or tube parts to use
- Whether to use elbows or bends

  For this session, use the default settings.

1. Click.
2. If a message asks if you want to turn off the option **Update component names when documents are replaced**, click **Yes**.

   The following happens:

- A 3D sketch opens in a new route sub-assembly.

- The new route sub-assembly is created as a virtual component, and appears in the FeatureManager design tree as **[Pipe1-Assem1]**.
- A stub of pipe appears, extending from the flange you just placed as shown in Figure 21-5.

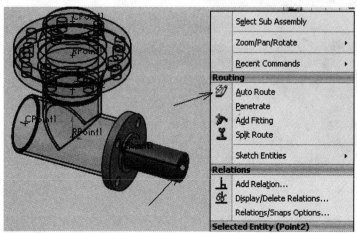

Figure 21-5 Starting a route: a pipe is added to the flange

CREATING A ROUTE

Start creating the segments of the route.

1. Drag the endpoint of the stub (see Figure 21-6) to increase the pipe length as shown in Figure 21-6. You do not need to be exact.
2. If a message appears about not adding automatic relations, click **OK**. (The software is trying to add sketch relations to the weldment that is behind the pipe, but determines that the relations would over define the route sketch.)
   Now add the horizontal flange to the route, so you can connect the pipe to it.
3. Zoom to the horizontal flange.
   On the **View** menu, make sure **Routing Points** is *selected* and **Hide All Types** is *cleared*.
4. Move the pointer over the connection point (**CPoint1**) in the center of the flange.
   The pointer changes to and the connection point is highlighted.
5. Right-click **CPoint1** and select **Add to Route**.

A stub of pipe extends from the flange.

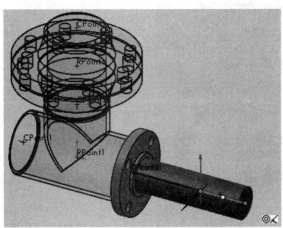

Figure 21-6 Pipe lengthens

ILLUSTRATION 2

Let us switch to **assembly fitting.sldasm**. The sub-assembly has a Tee and flanges (see Figure 21-7). In this case, we can commence our routing beginning with three pipes. We will do the following:

1. Click CPoint1 and extend the pipe to the right (see Figure 21-8)
2. Click CPoint2 and extend the pipe to the left (see Figure 21-8)
3. Click CPoint1 on the right, and insert a line using 3DSketch along Y on XY plane (see Figure 21-9)
4. Click CPoint2 on the left, and insert a line using 3DSketch along Z on YZ plane (see Figure 21-9)

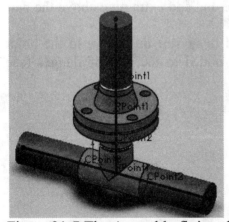

Figure 21-7 The Assembly fitting.sldasm

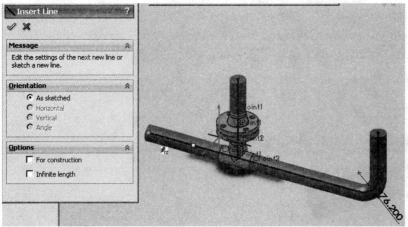

Figure 21-8 Extending right-hand pipe vertically using 3DSketch tool

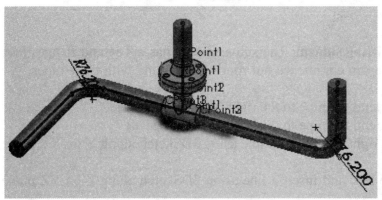

Figure 21-9 Extending left-hand pipe horizontally using 3DSketch tool

We will now add a pair of flanges on the vertical pipe and add extra pipe above the pair of flanges.

5. Click end (**CPoint1**) of the vertical pipe, and **drag slip on flange** to the point (**CPoint1**). Note that a pipe is automatically added to the pair of flanges (see Figure 21-10).

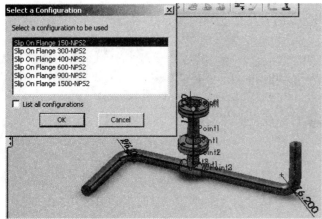

Figure 21-10 Dragging slip from Library unto flange at the top of the third vertical pipe

6. Click end (**CPoint1**) of the vertical pipe, and extend it (see Figure 21-11).
7. Click **CPoint1**, and insert a line using 3DSketch along Z on YZ plane (see Figure 21-11)

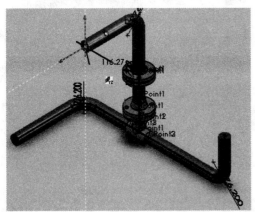

Figure 21-11 Extending third pipe vertically and along Z-direction on the YZ-plane

8. Click end (**CPoint1**) of the vertical pipe, and **drag slip on flange** to the point (**CPoint1**) as shown Figure 21-12.

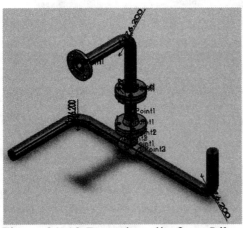

Figure 21-12 Dragging slip from Library unto flange third vertical pipe

It should be noted that so far, we are creating a sub-assembly in a top-level assembly. The sub-assembly is in blue color. To move to the top-level assembly, click **Edit Assembly**. This concept is shown in Figure 21-13. The routing solution is shown in Figure 21-14. The FeatureManager contains details of the routing operations.

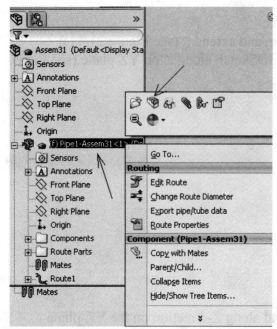

Figure 21-13 Switching to the top-level assembly

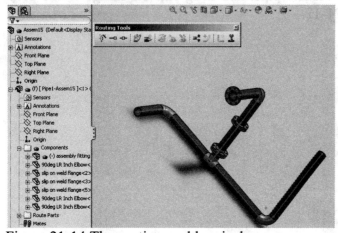

Figure 21-14 The routing problem is done.

ROUTE DRAWING

When the routing exercise is complete, a new drawing document is opened for presenting the drawing of the route. The same procedure for drawing parts applies here, with the bill of materials added. This is left as an exercise.

Chapter 22
Power Transmission Elements

Objectives:

In this chapter you will learn:

- The available Design Tools for power transmission systems
- How to size Supporting Plates and Shafts for power transmission systems
- To model an assembly of **Pinion and Gear (Spur-type)** transmission system
- To model an assembly of **Rack and Pinion** transmission system
- To model an assembly of **Belt and Pulley** transmission system
- To model an assembly of **Chain and Sprocket** transmission system
- To model an assembly of **Bevel Gear** transmission system

Power is generated from an engine, motor, or windmill. The power is then transmitted to a mechanism to perform some function. Transmission is generally through the use of elements such as gears, pulleys, and chains. For example, power is generated in the engine of an automobile, and then transmitted to the wheels via the gear box. These power transmission elements are considered in this chapter. We discuss how SolidWorks software is used to model these transmission elements.

Gears and Power Transmission

A **gear** is a rotating machine part having cut *teeth*, or *cogs*, which *mesh* with another toothed part in order to transmit torque. Two or more gears working in tandem are called a *transmission* and can produce a mechanical advantage through a gear ratio and thus may be considered a simple machine. Geared devices can change the speed, magnitude, and direction of a power source. The most common situation is for a gear to mesh with another gear; however, a gear can also mesh a non-rotating toothed part, called a rack, thereby producing translation instead of rotation.

When two gears of unequal number of teeth are combined a mechanical advantage is produced, with both the rotational speeds and the torques of the two gears differing in a simple relationship.

In transmissions which offer multiple gear ratios, such as bicycles and cars, the term **gear**, as in *first gear*, refers to a gear ratio rather than an actual physical gear. The term is used to describe similar devices even when gear ratio is continuous rather than discrete, or when the device does not actually contain any gears, as in a continuously variable transmission.

The gears in a transmission are analogous to the wheels in a pulley. An advantage of gears is that the teeth of a gear prevent slipping.

The remaining sections of this chapter discuss the methodology for the assembly modeling of pinion and gear, rack and pinion, belt and pulley, and chain and sprocket transmission systems.

Spur Gears

Spur gears or *straight-cut gears* are the simplest type of gear. They consist of a cylinder or disk, and with the teeth projecting radially, and although they are not straight-sided in form, the edge of each tooth thus is straight and aligned parallel to the axis of rotation. These gears can be meshed together correctly only if they are fitted to parallel axles.

Creating Gears Using SolidWorks

SolidWorks software is useful for creating different types of gears such as spur, bevel, and helical gears. As many as eighteen standards are available in the SolidWorks Toolbox from which the designer can choose (see Figure 22-1). To access these standards, Click **Design Library > Toolbox**

Note: You must have the Toolbox license in order to access Toolbox Add-Ins. First, click the **Options** tab to make changes in the settings for SolidWorks:

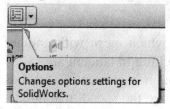

Select the **Add-Ins** option and tick off the following options:
SolidWorks Toolbox
SolidWorks Toolbox Browser

The Toolbox offers quite a number of design tools for bearings, bolts and screws, jig bushings, keys, nuts, O-rings, power transmission elements (chain sprockets, gears, timing belt pulleys), retaining rings, structural members, and washers, as shown in Figure 22-2. These design tools assist the design engineer perform his/her work more effectively and efficiently. In this chapter, we discuss the use SolidWorks for modelling power transmission elements.

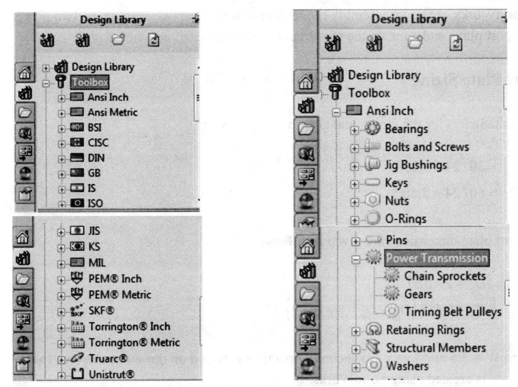

Figure 22-1 SolidWorks Toolbox Standards Figure 22-2 Toolbox design tools

Problem Description

A gear system consists of the pinion (Gear 1) and gear (Gear 2) and the specifications relating to their geometry are given as follows:

Gear 1: Pinion
Diametral pitch = 24
Number of teeth = 30
Face thickness = 0.5
Bore = 0.5 diameter
Hub = 1.0 diameter
Pressure angle = 20 deg.

Gear 2: Gear
Diametral pitch = 24
Number of teeth = 60
Face thickness = 0.5
Bore = 0.5 diameter
Hub = 1.0 diameter
Pressure angle = 20 deg.

Using SolidWorks, create an assembly model consisting of the two spur gears, two pins and a support plate, and animate the movement of the gears.

Support Plate Sizing

The pitch diameters for the pinion and gear are respectively:

$$D_p = 30/24 = 1.25''$$
$$D_g = 60/24 = 2.50''$$

The support plate dimensions are given as follows:

$$W = (D_g + 2 \times 0.5)$$
$$L = [(D_p + 0.5) + (D_g + D_p)/2 + W/2]$$

Leading to W = 3.5 and L = 5.375 inches respectively. Based on these dimensions, the support plate is created using SolidWorks.

Gear Assembly Modeling Using SolidWorks

The gear assembly modelling consists of three main steps: modelling of the support plate, modelling of the pin, and assembly of the support plate, pin, and gears.

Support Plate Model
1. Create a **New Part** document
2. Select the **Top Plane**
3. Sketch a rectangular profile **Sketch1** of **5.4** inch by **3.5** inch (see Figure 22-3)
4. Extrude **Sketch1** through **0.5** inch to get **Extrude1**
5. Create a circle, **Sketch2** on top of **Extrude1** at a point (**1.75, 1.00**) [see Figure 22-4]
6. Extrude-cut this circle through the thickness, to get **Extrude2**

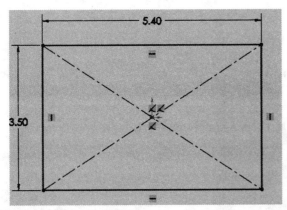

Figure 22-3 Sketch1

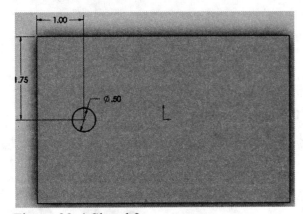

Figure 22-4 Sketch2

Create a Linear Pattern of Extrude2

7. Click Features > Linear Pattern (The Linear Pattern PropertyManager is displayed as shown in Figure 22-5)
8. Click a horizontal edge (**Edge <1>**) as Direction1
9. Set the **Number of Instance**s equal to **2**
10. Select **Extrude2** as the **Features to Pattern**
11. Click **OK**
12. **Save** the document

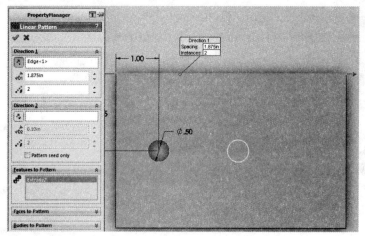

Figure 22-5 Linear Pattern PropertyManager

Pin Model

1. Create a **New Part** document
2. Select the **Top Plane**
3. Sketch a circular profile **Sketch1** of **0.5** inch diameter
4. Extrude **Sketch1** through **1.5** inch to get **Extrude1**
5. Click **OK**
6. **Save** the document

Assembly of the Support Plate, Pin, and Gears

Assembly of the support plate and two pins

1. Create a **New Assembly** document
2. Create an assembly of the support plate and two pins (see Figure 22-6)

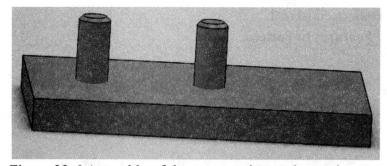

Figure 22-6 Assembly of the support plate and two pins

Adding Gears to the assembly of the support plate and two pins

3. Click **Design Library Toolbox > ANSI Inch > Power Transmission > Gears** (see Figure 22-7)

4. Right-click the **Spur Gear** tool and select **Create Part** (the Spur Gear PropertyManager is automatically displayed for the pinion and gear as shown in Figure 22-8)

5. Enter the data for pinion and gear as shown in Figure 22-8.

6. Click **OK**

7. Click any point on the graphics drawing area (a duplicate of the gear appears; see Figure 22-9)

8. Click **Cancel** in the Insert Components PropertyManager

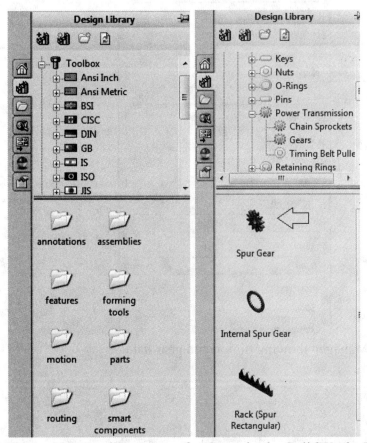

Figure 22-7 Toolbox access for Gears in the SolidWorks Design Library

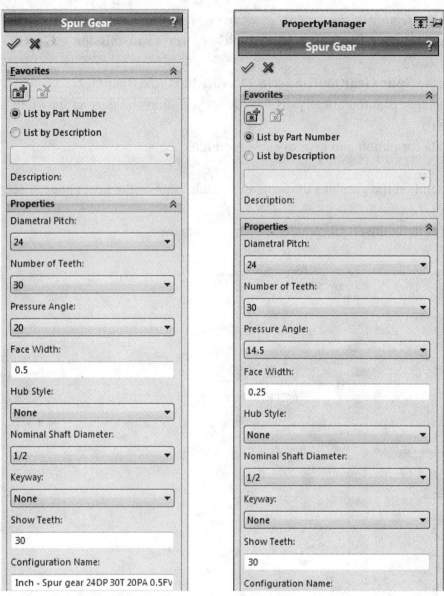

Figure 22-8 Spur Gear PropertyManager showing pinion and gear data

Figure 22-9 Duplicate spur gears created

Ordinary Mating

9. **Rotate** the individual pinion and gear

10. Click **Mate**

11. Select the hole in the pinion and the outer surface of the pin and apply **Concentric** mate

12. Select the top of the pinion and the top surface of the support and apply **Distance** mate of 1.0 (see Figure 22-10)

    Repeat for the gear (see Figure 22-11)

    Repeat See Figure 22-12 for the meshed pinion and gear

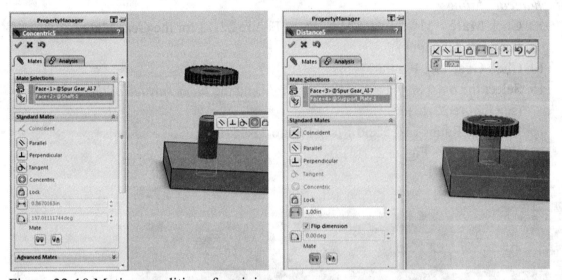

Figure 22-10 Mating conditions for pinion

Figure 22-11 Mating conditions for gear

Figure 22-12 Meshed pinion and gear

Mechanical Mating

13. Click **Mate > Mechanical Mates** (see Figure 22-13 for the **GearMate PropertyManager**)

14. Click **Gear** (see Figure 22-13)

15. Select the *inner surface of the pinion hole* and the *inner surface of the gear hole* (see Figure 22-13)

16. Enter the Ratios as 0.5 and 1 (see Figure 22-13)

17. Click **OK** (see Figure 22-13)

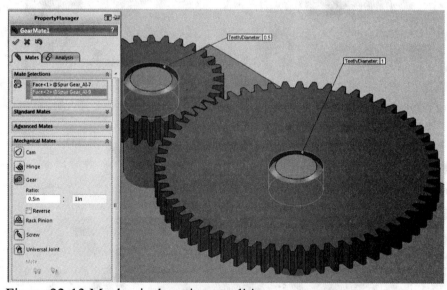

Figure 22-13 Mechanical mating conditions

Animation

Click **Motion Study1** icon at the bottom right corner of the graphics window.

Click the **Motor** icon (see Figure 22-14)

Click the top of the pinion as the **Component** (see Figure 22-14)

Set the **Motion Speed** as required (**3000 rpm**) [see Figure 22-14)

Figure 22-14 Motion of pinion and gear

Rack and Pinion Gears

A rack is a toothed bar or rod that can be thought of as a sector gear with an infinitely large radius of curvature. Torque can be converted to linear force by meshing a rack with a pinion: the pinion turns; the rack moves in a straight line. Such a mechanism is used in automobiles to convert the rotation of the steering wheel into the left-to-right motion of the tie rod(s). Racks also feature in the theory of gear geometry, where, for instance, the tooth shape of an interchangeable set of gears may be specified for the rack (infinite radius), and the tooth shapes for gears of particular actual radii then derived from that. The rack and pinion gear type is employed in a rack railway.

Problem Description

A rack-and-pinion system consists of the rack and pinion and the specifications (Imperial Units are used) relating to their geometry are given as follows:

Rack
Diametral pitch = 24
Face Width = 0.25
Pitch Height = 1.5
Length = 5
Pressure angle = 14.5 deg.

Pinion
Diametral pitch = 24
Number of teeth = 20
Face Width = 0.25
Hub Style: One Side
Hub Diameter = 1.0
Overall Length = 1.0
Nominal Shaft Diameter = 1/2
Pressure angle = 14.5 deg.

Shaft
Shaft Diameter = 1/2
Shaft Length = 2.25

Using SolidWorks, create an assembly model consisting of the rack, pinion and shaft, and animate the movement of the gears.

Gear Assembly Modeling Using SolidWorks

The gear assembly modelling consists of four main steps: insert the shaft, insert the pinion from Design Library and assemble it to the shaft to form a sub-assembly, insert the rack from Design Library, and assembly of the sub-assembly and rack.

Insert Shaft in Assembly
1. Create a **New Assembly** document
2. Click **Assembly > Insert Components**
3. **Insert** Shaft (see Figure 22-15)

Figure 22-15 Shaft inserted first in the assembly

Sub-Assembly of Shaft and Inserted Pinion from Design Library

4. Click **Design Library Toolbox > ANSI Inch > Power Transmission > Gears** (see Figure 22-16)
5. Right-click the **Spur Gear** tool and select **Create Part** (the Spur Gear PropertyManager is automatically displayed for the pinion and gear as shown in Figure 22-17)
6. Enter the data for spur gear (pinion) as shown in Figure 22-17.
7. Click **OK**

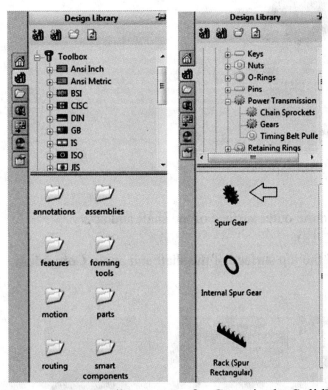

Figure 22-16 Toolbox access for Gears in the SolidWorks Design Library

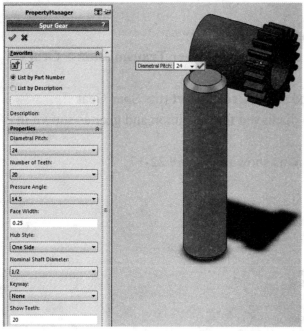

Figure 22-17 Spur Gear PropertyManager

8. **Rotate** the pinion appropriately
9. Click **Mate**
10. Select the hole in the pinion and the outer surface of the shaft and apply **Concentric** mate(see Figure 22-18)
11. Select the top of the pinion and the top surface of the shaft and apply **Coincident** mate (see Figure 22-19)

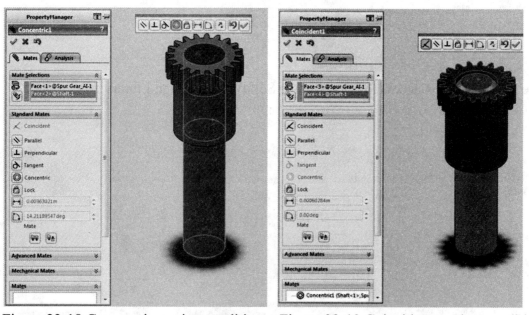

Figure 22-18 Concentric mating condition   Figure 22-19 Coincident mating condition

Insert Rack in Assembly

12. Click **Design Library Toolbox > ANSI Inch > Power Transmission > Gears** (see Figure 22-16)
13. Right-click the **Rack (Spur Rectangular)** tool and select **Create Part** (the Rack PropertyManager is automatically displayed for the pinion and gear as shown in Figure 22-20)
14. Enter the data for pinion and gear as shown in Figure 22-20.
15. Click **OK**

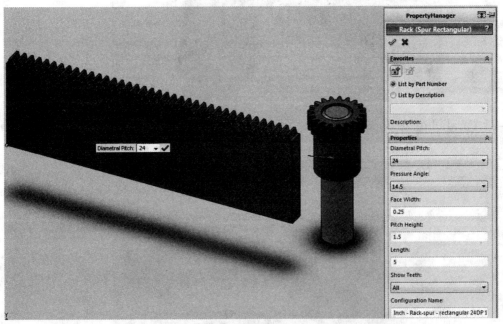

Figure 22-20 Rack PropertyManager

Ordinary Mating

16. Click **Mate**
17. Select top of the pinion and the outer flat surface of the rack and apply **Parallel** mate (see Figure 22-21)
18. Select top of the pinion and the outer flat surface of the rack and apply **Coincident** mate (see Figure 22-22)
19. Select the bottom tooth of the rack and the top tooth of the pinion and apply **Tangent** mate (see Figure 22-23)

Figure 22-21 Parallel mate condition

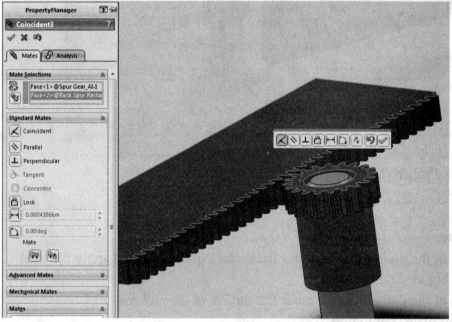

Figure 22-22 Coincident mate condition

Figure 22-23 Tangent mate condition

Mechanical Mating

20. Click **Mate > Mechanical Mates** (see Figure 22-24 for the **Rack Pinion PropertyManager**)
21. Click **Rack Pinion** (see Figure 22-24)
22. Select the *top edge of the rack* and the *side face of the pinion* (see Figure 22-24)
23. Click **OK** (see Figure 22-25 for completed assembly)

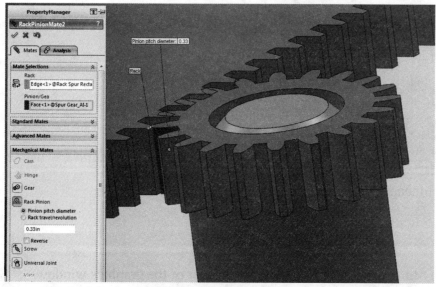

Figure 22-24 Mechanical mate condition

Figure 22-25 Completed rack-pinion assembly

The FeatureManager is shown in Figure 22-26. At this stage, it would be necessary to save the document under a preferred file name.

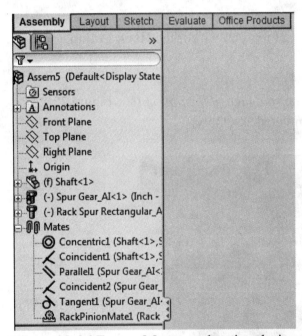

Figure 22-26 FeatureManager showing design tree

Animation

24. Click **Motion Study1** icon at the bottom right corner of the graphics window.
25. Click the **Motor** icon (see Figure 22-27)
26. Click the pinion as the **Component** (see Figure 22-27)
27. Set the **Motion Speed** as required (**100 rpm**) [see Figure 22-27]
28. Click **OK** (see Figure 22-28 for the position of the pinion at the end of simulation)

Figure 22-27 Motion of gear system

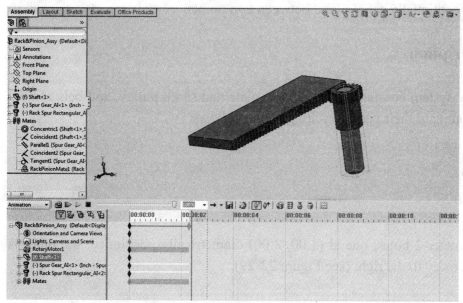

Figure 22-28 Position of the pinion at the end of simulation

Belts and Pulleys

Belts are the cheapest utility for power transmission between shafts that may not be axially aligned. Power transmission is achieved by specially designed belts and pulleys. The demands on a belt drive transmission system are large and this has led to many variations on the theme. They run smoothly and with little noise, and cushion motor and bearings against load changes, albeit with less strength than gears or chains. However, improvements in belt engineering allow use of belts in systems that only formerly allowed chains or gears.

A **belt** is a loop of flexible material used to link two or more rotating shafts mechanically. Belts may be used as a source of motion, to transmit power efficiently, or to track relative movement. Belts are looped over pulleys. In a two pulley system, the belt can either drive the pulleys in the same direction, or the belt may be crossed, so that the direction of the shafts is opposite. As a source of motion, a conveyor belt is one application where the belt is adapted to continually carry a load between two points.

Problem Description

A belt-and-pulley system consists of the support plate and shaft, pulley, and belt and the specifications relating to their geometry are given as follows:

Support Plate
Length = 6.00
Width = 4.00
Thickness = 0.5
Holes: 0.375 diameter-2 holes, one at (1.00, 2.00) diametrically positioned; the other is located 3.00 inch away to the right (see Figure 22-29).

Shaft
Length = 1.75
Diameter: 0.375

Pulley
Belt pitch = (0.200)—XL
Belt Width = 0.38
Pulley Style: Flanged
Number of Grooves = 20
Hub Diameter = 0.375

Overall Length = 0.5
Nominal Shaft Diameter = 3/8
Keyway: None

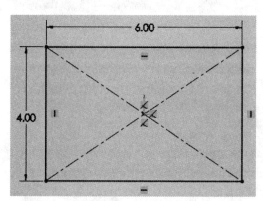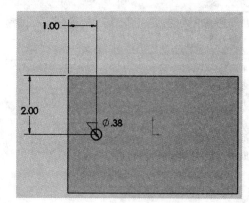

Figure 22-29 Support plate dimensions

Using SolidWorks, create an assembly model consisting of the support plate and shaft, pulley, and belt, and animate the movement of the belt and pulley.

Belt and Pulley Assembly Modeling Using SolidWorks

The belt and pulley assembly modelling consists of three main steps: inserting the sub-assembly of the support plate and shaft, inserting pulley, and inserting the belt.

Sub-assembly of Support Plate and Pin

The support plane and shaft are similar to the one used for the spur gear except for the specifications, so modelling details will not be given in this section.
1. Create a **New Assembly** document
2. Create an assembly of the support plate and two shafts (see Figure 22-6)

Inserting Timing Belt Pulley
3. Click **Design Library Toolbox > ANSI Inch > Power Transmission > Timing Belt Pulley** (see Figure 22-30)
4. Right-click the **Rack (Spur Timing Belt Pulley Rectangular)** tool and select **Create Part** (the Timing Belt Pulley PropertyManager is automatically displayed as shown in Figure 22-30)
5. Enter the data for Timing Belt Pulley as shown in Figure 22-31.
6. Click **OK** (If a warning box shown in Figure 22-32 appears, accept the error and click the **Close** box)

7. Click any point on the graphics drawing area (a duplicate of the timing belt pulley appears; see Figure 22-33)

8. Click **Cancel** in the **Insert Components PropertyManager**

Figure 22-30 Toolbox access for Timing Belt Pulley in the SolidWorks Design Library

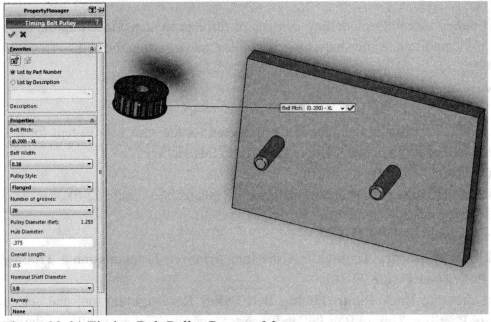

Figure 22-31 Timing Belt Pulley PropertyManager

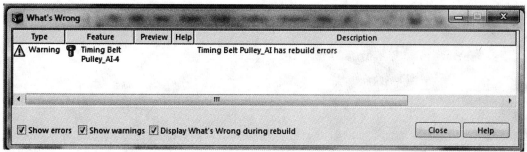

Figure 22-32 Warning box

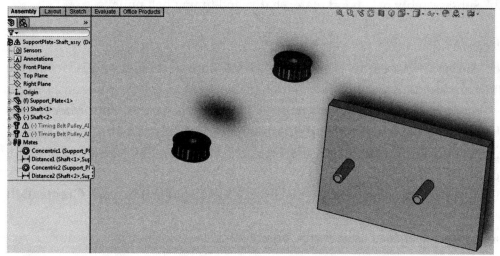

Figure 22-33 Duplicate of the timing belt pulley created

Mating

9. **Rotate** the individual timing belt pulley

10. Click **Mate**

11. Select the hole in the timing belt pulley and the outer surface of the shaft and apply **Concentric** mate

12. Select the top of the timing belt pulley and the top surface of the shaft and apply **Coincident**

    Repeat for the second timing belt pulley/shaft pair (see Figure 22-34 for sub-assembly)

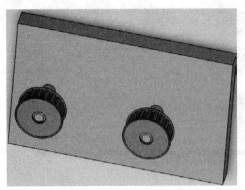

Figure 22-34 Sub-assembly of support plate, shafts, and timing belt pulleys

Inserting the Belt

13. Click **Insert > Assembly Feature > Belt/Chain** (see Figure 22-35 for the Belt/Chain insertion tool)

14. Click *one top surface on the left pulley's tooth* and *a second top surface on the right pulley's tooth* to define the **Belt Members** (see Figure 22-36)

15. In the **Properties** rollout, check the **Field** for **Use Belt Thickness** and assign a value of **0.14** (see Figure 22-36)

16. In the **Properties** rollout, check the **Fields** for **Engage Belt**, and **Create Belt Part**

    A belt feature is created as shown in Figure 22-37.

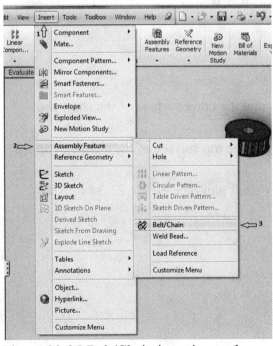

Figure 22-35 Belt/Chain insertion tool

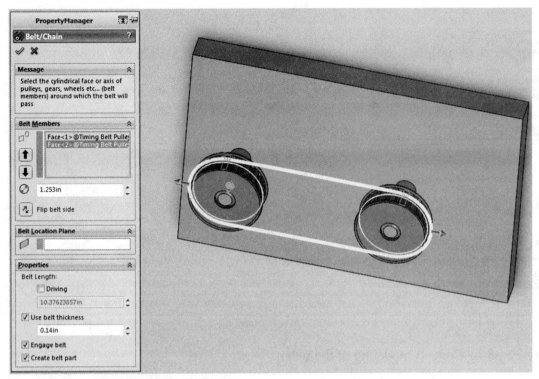

Figure 22-36 Belt Members defined

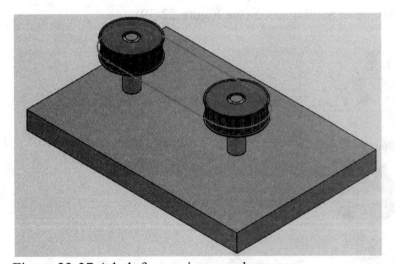

Figure 22-37 A belt feature is created

17. Expand **Belt1** in the FeatureManager
18. Right-click **[Belt1^...]<1>->?** and select **Edit Part** option (see Figure 22-38)

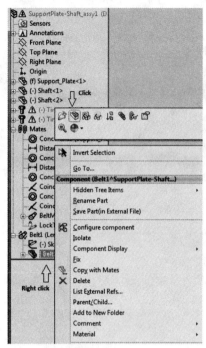

Figure 22-38 In-Context modeling of the belt

19. Click *any segment of the belt feature* (see Figure 22-39)
20. Click the **Sketch** icon to be in Sketch mode (see Figure 22-39)

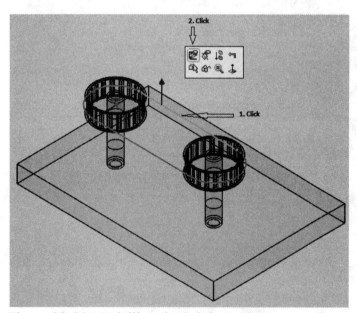

Figure 22-39 Modelling the belt in In-Context mode

21. Click **Features > Extrude Boss/Base** (the **Extrude PropertyManager** is
    displayed as shown in Figure 22-40)
22. In **Direction1** rollout, select **Mid-Plane**

23. Set the extrusion **Distance** to be **0.42**
24. Check the box for **Thin Feature** and set the **Thickness** to **0.14**
25. Click **OK**
26. Click **Edit Component** to exit editing the assembly

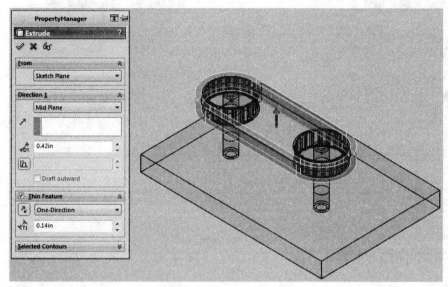

Figure 22-40 Extrude PropertyManager

Animation

27. Click **Motion Study1** icon at the bottom right corner of the graphics window.
28. Click the **Motor** icon (see Figure 22-41)
29. Click one of the pulleys as the **Component** (see Figure 22-41)
30. Set the **Motion Speed** as required (**100 rpm**) [see Figure 22-41]
31. Click **OK** (see Figure 22-28 for the position of the pinion at the end of simulation)

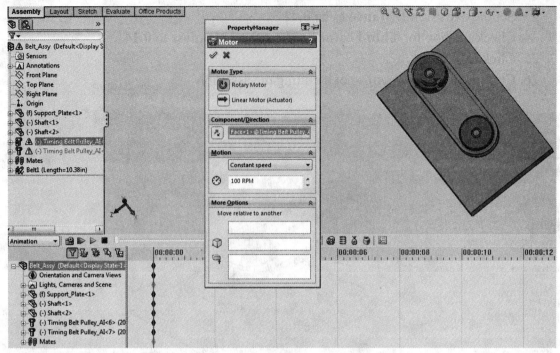

Figure 22-41 Motion PropertyManager

Chain Drive: Chains and Sprockets

Chain drive is a way of transmitting mechanical power from one place to another. It is often used to convey power to the wheels of a vehicle, particularly bicycles and motorcycles. It is also used in a wide variety of machines besides vehicles. Most often, the power is conveyed by a roller chain, known as the **drive chain** or **transmission chain**, passing over a sprocket gear, with the teeth of the gear meshing with the holes in the links of the chain. The gear is turned, and this pulls the chain putting mechanical force into the system.

SolidWorks creates chains and sprockets in a manner similar to that used for creating belts and pulleys.

Problem Description

A chain-and-sprocket system consists of the support plate and shaft, sprocket, and chain and the specifications relating to their geometry are given as follows:

Support Plate
Length = 20.00
Width = 10.00
Thickness = 1.00

Holes: 1.00 diameter-2 holes, one at (4.00, 5.00) diametrically positioned; the other is located 3.00 inch away to the right (see Figure 22-42).

Shaft
Length = 4.00
Diameter: 1.00

Sprocket
Chain Number = SC610
Number of Teeth = 24
Belt Width = 0.38
Pulley Style: None
Nominal Shaft Diameter = 1
Keyway: None

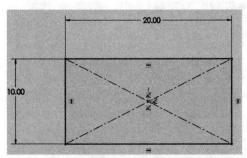 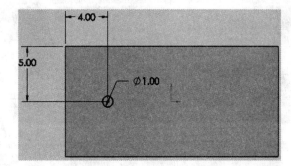

Figure 22-42 Support plate dimensions

Using SolidWorks, create an assembly model consisting of the support plate and shaft, sprocket, and chain, and animate the movement of the chain and sprocket.

Chain and Sprocket Assembly Modeling Using SolidWorks

The chain and sprocket assembly modelling consists of three main steps: inserting the sub-assembly of the support plate and shaft, inserting sprocket, and inserting the chain.

Sub-assembly of Support Plate and Pin

The support plane and shaft are similar to the one used for the spur gear except for the specifications, so modelling details will not be given in this section.
   1.   Start a **New Assembly** document

2. Open **SupportPlate-Shaft_assy** which is a 20x10x1 plate with 1 inch-dia-2 holes and a shaft, 1inch -dia-4 inch long [an assembly of the support plate and two shafts (see Figure 22-6]).

Inserting Timing Belt Pulley

3. Click **Design Library Toolbox > ANSI Inch > Power Transmission > Chain Sprockets** (see Figure 22-43a)
4. Right-click the **Silent Larger Sprocket** tool and select **Create Part** (the **Belt1 PropertyManager** is automatically displayed as shown in Figure 22-43b)
5. Enter the data for Timing Belt Pulley as shown in Figure 22-43b.
6. Click any point on the graphics drawing area (a duplicate of the timing belt pulley appears; see Figure 22-44)
7. Click **Cancel** in the **Insert Components PropertyManager**

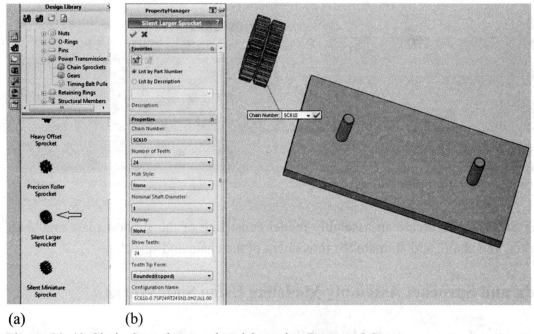

  (a)   (b)

Figure 22-43 Chain Sprockets tool and Sprocket PropertyManager

8. Click any point on the graphics drawing area (a duplicate of the sprocket appears; see Figure 22-44)
9. Click **Cancel** in the **Insert Components PropertyManager**

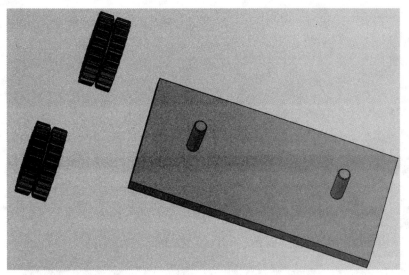

Figure 22-44 Duplicate of the timing belt pulley created

Mating

10. **Rotate** the individual sprocket
11. Click **Mate**
12. Select the hole in the sprocket and the outer surface of the shaft and apply **Concentric** mate
13. Select the top of the sprocket and the top surface of the shaft and apply **Coincident** (see Figure 22-45)

    Repeat for the second sprocket /shaft pair (see Figure 22-46 for sub-assembly)

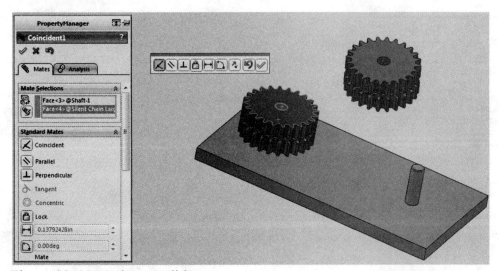

Figure 22-45 Mating conditions

Figure 22-46 Sub-assembly of support plate, shafts, and sprockets

Inserting the Chain

14. Click **Insert > Assembly Feature > Belt/Chain** (see Figure 22-47 for the Belt/Chain insertion tool)

15. Click *one top surface on the left sprocket's tooth* and *a second top surface on the right sprocket's tooth* to define the **Belt Members** (see Figure 22-48)

16. In the **Properties** rollout, check the **Field** for **Use Belt Thickness** and assign a value of **0.5** (see Figure 22-48)

17. In the **Properties** rollout, check the **Fields** for **Engage Belt**, and **Create Belt Part**

    A belt feature is created as shown in Figure 22-48.

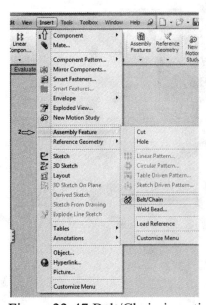

Figure 22-47 Belt/Chain insertion tool

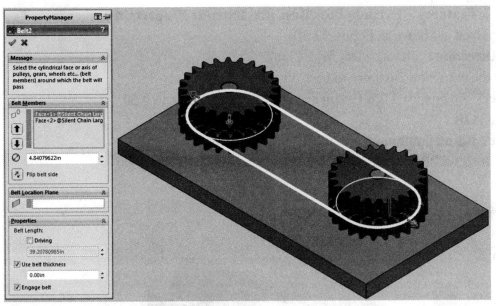

Figure 22-48 Belt Members defined

18. Expand **Belt1** in the FeatureManager
19. Right-click **[Belt1^...]<1>->?** and select **Edit Part** option (see Figure 22-49)

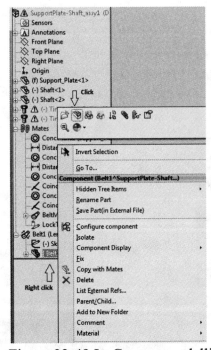

Figure 22-49 In-Context modelling of the belt

20. Click *any segment of the belt feature* (see Figure 22-50)
21. Click the **Sketch** icon to be in Sketch mode (see Figure 22-50)

22. Click **Features > Extrude Boss/Base** (the **Extrude PropertyManager** is displayed as shown in Figure 22-50)
23. In **Direction1** rollout, select **Mid-Plane**
24. Set the extrusion **Distance** to be **1.00**
25. Check the box for **Thin Feature** and set the **Thickness** to **0.50**
26. Click **OK**
27. Click **Edit Component** to exit editing the assembly
    Figure 22-51 shows the chain and sprocket assembly model

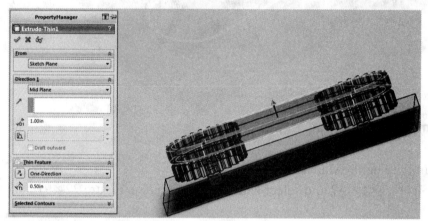

Figure 22-50 Extrude PropertyManager

Figure 22-51 Chain and sprocket assembly model

Figure 22-52 shows the FeatureManager for the chain and sprocket assembly model.

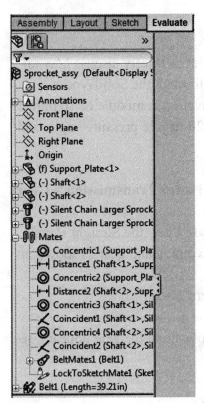

Figure 22-52 FeatureManager for the chain and sprocket assembly model

Animation

28. Click **Motion Study1** icon at the bottom right corner of the graphics window.
29. Click the **Motor** icon
30. Click one of the sprockets as the **Component**
31. Set the **Motion Speed** as required (**100 rpm**)
32. Click **OK**

BEVEL GEAR BOX DESIGN

Before discussing the gear box design for the bevel gears, let us briefly discuss how to use the Design Library Toolbox (which must be available through the SolidWorks Options). The first illustration is the creation of straight bevel gear: module of 10 mm, 25 teeth to mesh with another straight bevel gear of 63 teeth, 20-degree pressure angle, and face width of 51 mm (see Figure 22-53 and Figure 22-54).

1. Click **Design Library Toolbox > ANSI Metric > Power Transmission > Gears** (see Figure 22-7)
2. Right-click the **Straight Bevel** tool and select **Create Part** (the Straight Bevel PropertyManager is automatically displayed for the pinion and gear as shown in Figure 22-53)
3. Enter the data for pinion and gear as shown in Figure 22-53.
4. Click **OK**
5. Click any point on the graphics drawing area (a duplicate of the gear appears; see Figure 22-54)

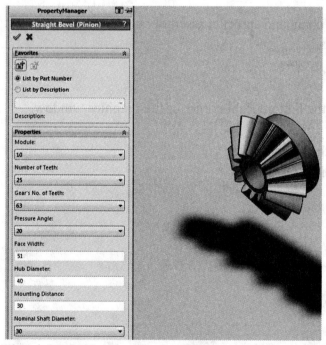

Figure 22-53 Preview in Straight Bevel PropertyManager

Figure 22-54 Straight Bevel created from specifications

The second illustration is the creation of straight bevel gear: module of 10 mm, 63 teeth to mesh with another straight bevel gear of 25 teeth, 20-degree pressure angle, and face width of 51 mm (see Figure 22-55 and Figure 22-56).

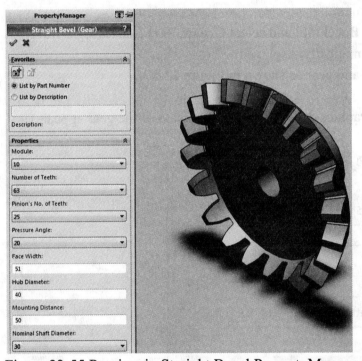

Figure 22-55 Preview in Straight Bevel PropertyManager

Figure 22-56 Straight Bevel created from specifications

Let us now design the gear box in the sub-subsequent sections.

Problem Description

Design a gear box consisting of an input straight bevel gear having 20 teeth, and an input straight bevel gear having 50 teeth. The diametral pitch is 2, 20-degree pressure angle, and face width of 2. Nominal shaft diameter is 1-3/8. [Note: Imperial Units are used]

Input

Pinion

1. Click **Design Library Toolbox > ANSI Metric > Power Transmission > Gears** (see Figure 22-7)
2. Right-click the **Straight Bevel** tool and select **Create Part** (the Straight Bevel PropertyManager is automatically displayed)
3. Enter the data for pinion and gear as shown in Figure 22-57.
4. Click **OK**
5. Click any point on the graphics drawing area (a duplicate of the gear appears)

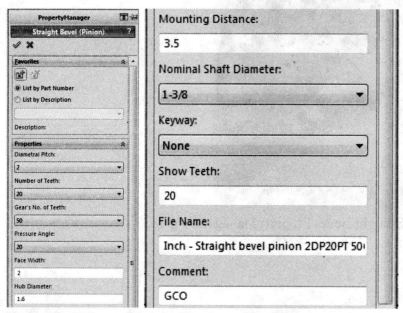

Figure 22-57 Input Straight Bevel specifications

Output

Gear

1. Click **Design Library Toolbox > ANSI Metric > Power Transmission > Gears** (see Figure 22-7)
2. Right-click the **Straight Bevel** tool and select **Create Part** (the Straight Bevel PropertyManager is automatically displayed)
3. Enter the data for pinion and gear as shown in Figure 22-58.
4. Click **OK**
5. Click any point on the graphics drawing area (a duplicate of the gear appears)

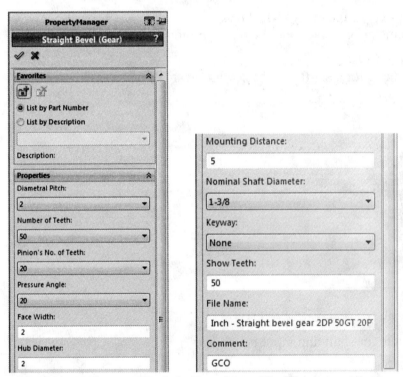

Figure 22-58 Output Straight Bevel specifications

Assembly Modeling

1. Open a **New Assembly SolidWorks** document
2. **Import** the input (pinion) and output (gear) bevel gears, and shafts into the graphics area for assembly (see Figure 22-59).

Figure 22-59 Input and output bevel gears, and shafts in graphics area for assembly

3. Create **Concentric** mate for a shaft and the *input* (pinion) bevel gear (Figure 22-60)

4. Create **Concentric** mate for a shaft and the *output* (gear) bevel gear (Figure 22-61)

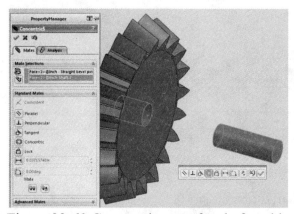

Figure 22-60 Concentric mate for shaft and input bevel gear

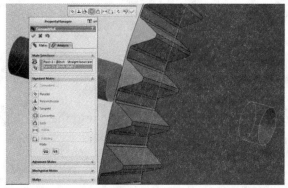

Figure 22-61 Concentric mate for shaft and output bevel gear

5. Apply **Concentric** mates between the shafts of the bevel gears (see Figure 22-62)

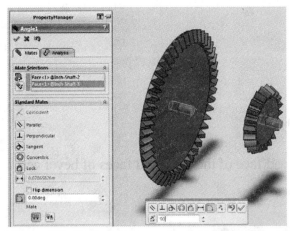

Figure 22-62 Bevel gear-shaft for input and output pairs

6. Click the **Mate > Mechanical Mates > Gear** and select the *inside faces hubs of both bevel gears* (The GearMate PropertyManager automatically displayed; see Figure 22-63)
7. Enter **1.38** as the gear **Ratio** (see Figure 22-63)
8. Ensure that gear teeth are manually aligned to enhance meshing (See Figure 22-64)

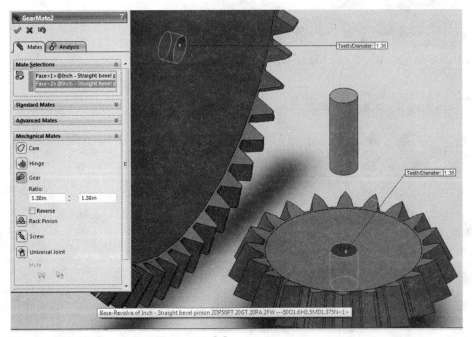

Figure 22-63 GearMate PropertyManager

Figure 22-64 Manual alignment of gear teeth

9. Apply **Coincident** mate between the end face of the shaft and faces of bevel gears (see Figure 22-65 and Figure 22-66)

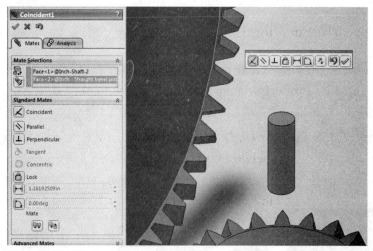

Figure 22-65 End face of shaft is coincident with face of bevel gear

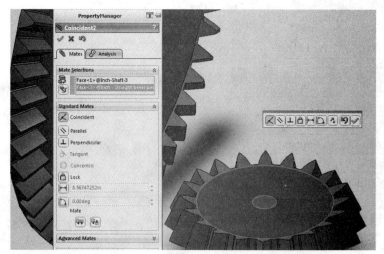

Figure 22-66 End face of shaft is coincident with face of bevel gear

Figure 22-67 shows the gear box complete without housing.

Figure 22-67 Gear box complete (without housing)

Summary

This chapter discusses in detail the design procedures for pinion and gear (spur-type), rack and pinion, belt and pulley, chain and sprocket, bevel gear transmission systems. Several examples are given to make the procedures clear. The power transmission systems are common in mechanical drive applications. It is important that students attempt the questions given at the end of this chapter in order to consolidate their understand of the materials presented.

Exercises

1. A gear system consists of the pinion (Gear 1) and gear (Gear 2) and the specifications relating to their geometry are given as follows:

Gear 1: Pinion	Gear 2: Gear
Diametral pitch = 24	Diametral pitch = 24
Number of teeth = 24	Number of teeth = 48
Face thickness = 0.5	Face thickness = 0.5
Bore = 0.5 diameter	Bore = 0.5 diameter
Hub = 1.0 diameter	Hub = 1.0 diameter
Pressure angle = 20 deg.	Pressure angle = 20 deg.

Using SolidWorks, create an assembly model consisting of the two spur gears, two pins and a support plate, and animate the movement of the gears.

2. A gear system consists of the pinion (Gear 1) and gear (Gear 2) and the specifications relating to their geometry are given as follows:

Gear 1: Pinion	Gear 2: Gear
Diametral pitch = 30	Diametral pitch = 30
Number of teeth = 36	Number of teeth = 72
Face thickness = 0.5	Face thickness = 0.5
Bore = 0.5 diameter	Bore = 0.5 diameter
Hub = 1.0 diameter	Hub = 1.0 diameter
Pressure angle = 20 deg.	Pressure angle = 20 deg.

Using SolidWorks, create an assembly model consisting of the two spur gears, two pins and a support plate, and animate the movement of the gears.

3. Design a gear system consisting of an input straight bevel gear having 25 teeth, and an input straight bevel gear having 63 teeth. The module is 10 mm, 20-degree pressure angle, and face width of 51 mm. Nominal shaft diameter is 30 mm (see Figure 22-53 to Figure 22-56).

Chapter 23
Cam Design

Objectives:

In this chapter you will learn:

- How to design cams
- About the relationship between cams and followers

Introduction

A *cam* is a mechanical device having a profile or groove machined on it, which gives an irregular or special motion to a *follower*. The type of follower and its motion depend on the shape of the profile or groove.

Types of Cams

Cams fall into two main classes, *radial (edge* or *plate) cams* and *cylindrical cams*. The follower of a radial cam reciprocates or oscillates in a plane perpendicular to the cam axis, whilst with a cylindrical cam the follower moves parallel to the cam axis.

Types of Followers

The *knife edge* or *point follower* is the simplest type of follower. It is not often used as it wears rapidly but it has the advantage that the cam profile can have any shape.

With the *roller follower* the rate of wear is reduced, but the profile of the cam must not have any concave portions with a radius smaller than the roller radius.

The *flat follower* is sometimes used but the cam profile must have no concave portions.

Creating Cams Using the Traditional Method

The traditional method of creating cam profiles is to define a displacement diagram and then transfer the displacement diagram to a *base circle*.

What is a base circle? A base circle is a circle passing through the nearest approach of the follower to the cam center.

Creating Cams in SolidWorks

SolidWorks creates cams by utilizing existing cam templates. There are templates for *circular* and *linear* cams and *internal* and *external* cams. The templates allow the designer to work directly on the cam profile and eliminate the need for a displacement diagram. The SolidWorks Toolbox must be available before we can access the Cams Tool. Therefore, the first step is to Add-In the Toolbox.

Problem Definition

Let us illustrate how to create a cam in SolidWorks with a circular cam having a 4.00-in base circle and a profile that rises 0.5 in over 90° using harmonic motion, dwells for 180°, falls 0.50 in over 45° using harmonic motions, and dwells for 45°.

SolidWorks Toolbox Add-ins

1. Open SolidWorks.
2. Open the model file.
3. Click the Add-Ins tool (see Figure 23-1).
4. Check SolidWorks Toolbox and SolidWorks Toolbox Browser (see Figure 23-2).
5. Click OK (Toolbox tool is added).

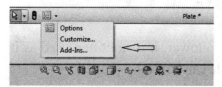

Figure 23-1 Add-Ins tool

Figure 23-2 SolidWorks Add-Ins PropertyManager

To Access the SolidWorks Cams Tool

To access the Cams tool:
1. Create a new part document.
2. Select the front plane.
3. Click the toolbox icon from the top of the CommandManager.
4. Click the Cams tool from the menu (see Figure 23-3). The Cam-Circular toolbox will be automatically displayed (see Figure 23-4).

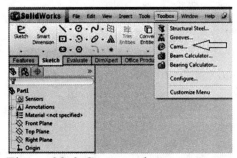

Figure 23-3 Cams tool

The Cam-Circular toolbox has three tabs: Setup, Motion, and Creation.

Cam-circular setup

1. Click the List button on the Setup tab of the Cam-Circular toolbox (see left side of Figure 23-4). The Favorites dialog will be displayed (see right side of Figure 23-4). This dialog lists the cam templates that can be used to create different cams.
2. Select Sample 2 - Inch Circular.
3. Click Load.

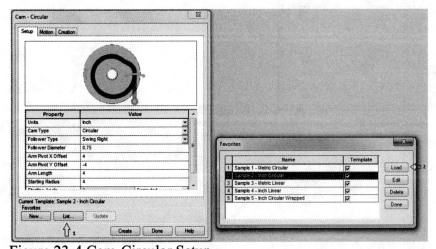

Figure 23-4 Cam-Circular Setup

4. Expand the Follower Type from the pull-down menu and set the type as Translating. The PropertyManager for the Circular-Cam, Translating-Follower appears (see Figure 23-5).
5. Define the Properties required for the Setup of the cam.

The base circle of the cam has a diameter of 4.00 in (radius of 2.00 in) and the follower has a diameter of 0.50 in (radius of 0.25 in). This means that the Starting Radius is 2.25 in (2.00 + 0.25). Therefore, in the Property rollout on the Setup tab enter the following:

      Units: Inch
      Cam Type: Circular
      Follower Type: Translating
      Follower Diameter: 0.50
      Starting Radius: 2.25
      Starting Angle: 0
      Rotation Direction: Clockwise

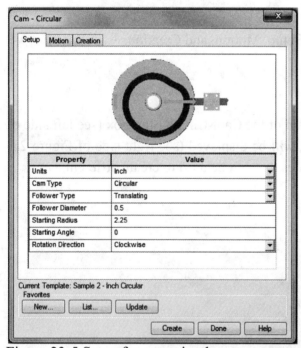

Figure 23-5 Setup for cam-circular

Cam-circular motion

From the problem definition, the motion of the circular cam has four sectors. It rises 0.5 in over 90° using harmonic motion, dwells for 180°, falls 0.50 in over 45° using harmonic motions, and dwells for 45°. This information is utilized to define the motion.

6. Select the Motion tab in the Cam-Circular toolbox.
7. Click Add to display the Motion Creation Details dialog (see Figure 23-6).
8. In the Motion Creation Details dialog, enter the first sector by setting the Motion Type to Harmonic, the Ending Radius to 2.75 in (2.25 + 0.5), and Degrees Motion to 90°.
9. Click OK.
10. Click Add.
11. For the second sector, set the Motion Type to Dwell and Degrees Motion to 180° (see the upper dialog in Figure 23-7).
12. Click OK.
13. Click Add.
14. For the third sector, set the Motion Type to Harmonic, the Ending Radius to 2.25 in, and Degrees Motion to 45° (see the middle dialog in Figure 23-7).
15. Click OK.
16. Click Add.
17. For the final sector, set the Motion Type to Dwell, and Degrees Motion to 45° (see the lower dialog in Figure 23-7).
18. Click OK.

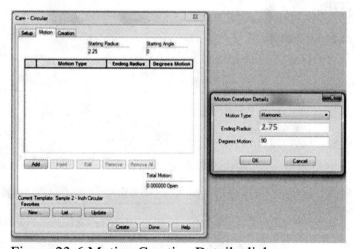

Figure 23-6 Motion Creation Details dialog

Figure 23-7 Motion Creation Details

Figure 23-8 shows the motion for the different sectors of the cam.

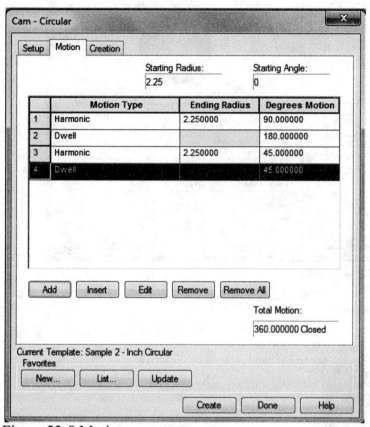

Figure 23-8 Motion summary

Cam-circular creation

19. Select the Creation tab.
20. Modify the default settings (see upper dialog in Figure 23-9) as follows (see lower dialog in Figure 23-9). Set the Blank Outside Diameter to 6.00 in, Thickness to 0.5 in; and Thru Hole Diameter to 1.5 in.
21. Set Track Type & Depth to Thru (the Blind condition requires a value).
22. Set Track Surfaces to Inner.
23. Click Create.
24. Click Done.

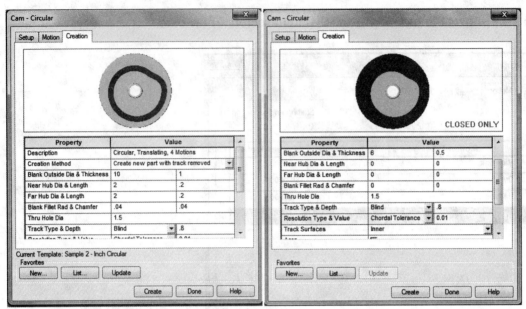

Figure 23-9 Creation tab for cam-circular

The final cam model is displayed in Figure 23-10.

Figure 23-10 Final cam model

Cam Model Modification

The cam model in Figure 23-10 fails to mate with the cam follower because of discontinuities of the face. This is what SolidWorks generates. Therefore, some modifications have been made to make assembly of the parts feasible. The steps given here are required to be followed by users to obtained feasible cam profiles other than the solutions that SolidWorks provide:

1. Design cam model based on given specifications.
2. Use **Convert Entities** tool, while in *Sketch mode* on one of the faces of the cam to extract the edges.

3. Use **Spline** tool to create a spline through the edges converted into entities; add short intervals where the shape of the spline deviates from the cam profile. You may explore other approaches.

4. Add **Construction line(s)** <at least one> from the cam center to one point on the profile (this is necessary for copying).

5. Click **Spline>Construction-line** and *Copy* <alternatively, use CTLR>c>.

6. Open a **New Part** document.

7. Select **Top** view and be *Sketch mode*.

8. Paste the copied **Spline** and center-line from previous document.

9. Move both the **Spline** and *Construction line* until origin matches the end of the construction line.

10. **Extrude** cam profile through *0.5-inch* (or as originally specified). See Figure 23-11 for the modified cam profile; it is smooth compared to that of Figure 23-10.

11. **Sketch** a 0.5-inch circle and **Extrude-Cut** to form hole in cam (or as originally specified).

12. Add two **Circles**, 0.5-inch and 1-inch diameter respectively, centers at the origin, and **Extrude** through 0.5-inch to create the hub (or as originally specified).

Figure 23-11 Modified cam profile

Creating a Hub

There are two ways to create a hub: manually and by using the Cam-Circular dialog.

In the manual method, the cam model is first obtained as shown in Figure 23-10. Then using the Sketch tool, a circle concentric with the circle that defines the shaft is sketched, and extruded, as shown in Figure 23-12. This is not an efficient method compared to the second method, using Cam-Circular dialog.

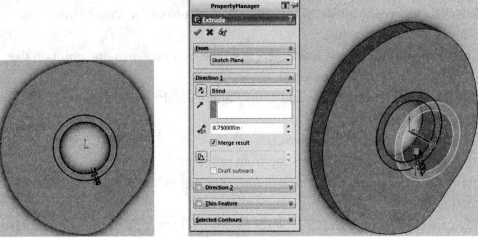

Figure 23-12 Manual method of creating a hub

Creating a Hub Using the Cam-Circular Dialog

This is easily achieved by defining the following fields in Figure 23-13:

    Near Hub Diameter = 1.5 in
    Near Hub Length = 0.75 in

The hub is created as shown in Figure 23-14.

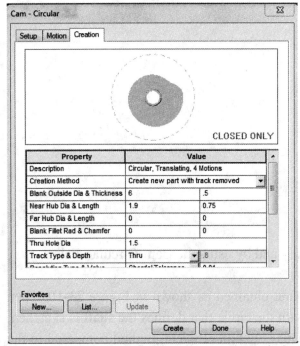

Figure 23-13 Hub definition in Creation tab for cam-circular

Creating a Hole for a Key Using the Hole Wizard

The Hole Wizard can be used to create a hole for a key (see Figure 23-14).

Type
1. Click the Type tab.
2. Click the Hole Wizard.
3. Select ANSI Inch Standard.
4. For Type, select the Tapered Hole.
5. For Size, select ¼-20.

Position
6. Click the Position tab.
7. Use the Smart Dimension tool to dimension the position of the center of the hole (see Figure 23-15).

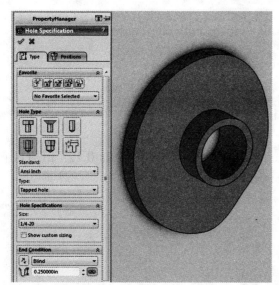

Figure 23-14 Creating a hole for a key using the Hole Wizard

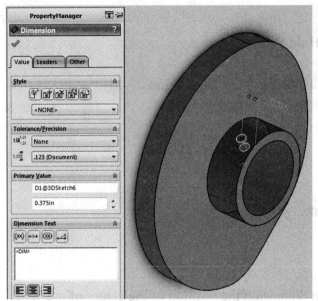

Figure 23-15 Hole location defined using the Smart Dimension tool

Cam Shaft Assembly

The following sections design the other components of the cam shaft assembly.

Spring

Section 6.2.1.1 of this textbook gives the steps involved in spring design.

The helix path diameter is 0.5 in and the diameter of the circular profile is 0.125 in. The other specifications for the helix are shown in Figure 23-16.

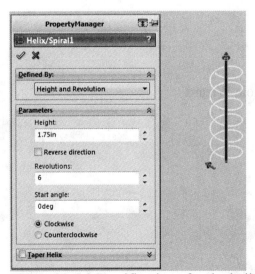

Figure 23-16 Specifications for the helix

Cam Follower Bracket

The cam follower bracket is modeled by creating a U-profile 1.00 in by 0.875 in by 1.00 in (see Figure 23-17). The thickness is 0.13 in and it is extruded in the Mid Plane direction by 0.5 in (see Figure 23-18).

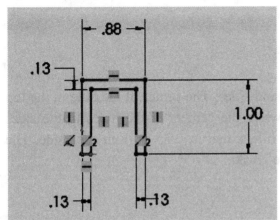

Figure 23-17 Profile for cam follower bracket

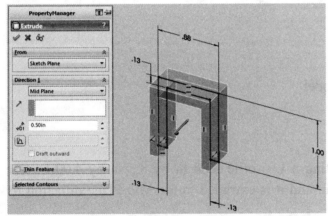

Figure 23-18 Extruding the profile

Face Filleting

The two arms of the U, Face<1> and Face<2>, are filleting using the Tangent Propagation option (see Figure 23-19).

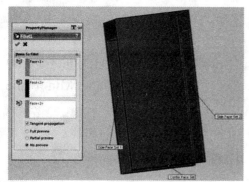

Figure 23-19 Face filleting the model

Holes of diameter 0.25 in are cut into the top and sides. The center of the hole in the top face coincides with the center of that face, while the centers of the holes in the sides coincide with the center used to generate the fillets, that is, 0.25 in from each side. The cam follower bracket model is shown in Figure 23-20.

Figure 23-20 Cam follower bracket model

Cam Bracket

The cam bracket is modeled by creating a U-profile 3.00 in by 8.5 in by 4.00 in (see Figure 23-21). The thickness is 0.25 in and it is extruded in the Mid Plane direction by 6.00 in (see Figure 23-22).

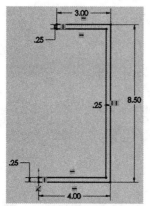

Figure 23-21 Profile for cam bracket

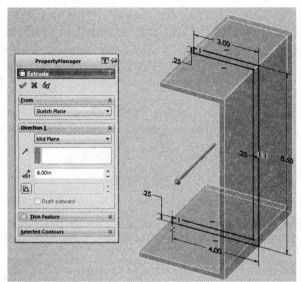

Figure 23-22 Extrusion of profile for cam bracket

Roller

The roller is modeled by creating a circle of diameter 0.50 in, and the hole is a concentric circle of diameter 0.25 in. Both circles are extruded through 0.5-in (see Figure 23-23).

Figure 23-23 Roller model

Cam Shaft

The cam shaft is modeled by creating a circle of diameter 1.5 in and extruded in the Mid Plane direction by 2.5 in (see Figure 23-24).

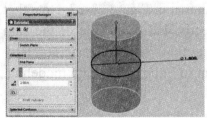

Figure 23-24 Cam shaft model

Handle

The handle is modeled by creating a circle of diameter 0.25 in and extruded in the Mid Plane direction by 2.75 in (see Figure 23-25).

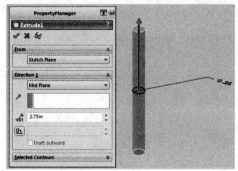

Figure 23-25 Handle model

Pin

The pin is modeled by creating a circle of diameter 0.25 in and extruded in the Mid Plane direction by 0.875 in (see Figure 23-26).

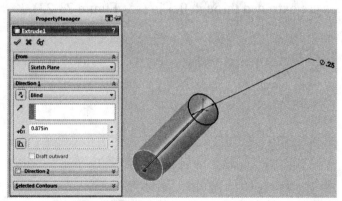

Figure 23-26 Pin model

Assembly of Cam Shaft Components

The assembly of all the parts designed in this chapter is shown in Figure 23-27. Note that the cam follower in Figure 23-27(i) will not mate correctly due to the file of the cam surface (patches) but the modified cam follower in Figure 23-27(ii) will mate correctly due to its smooth profile. This is the author's contribution to SolidWorks cam modeling. Try it out and you will have the experience for yourself.

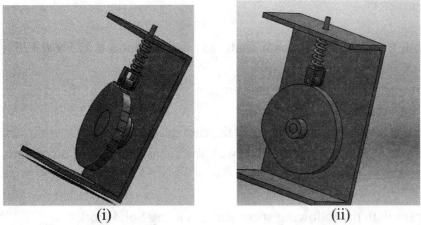

(i)   (ii)

Figure 23-27 Assembly of cam and follower

Exercises

1. Assemble the follower bracket, roller, handle, and pin. Name this the cam sub-assembly.
2. Assemble the cam sub-assembly, cam, cam shaft, and spring. Name this the cam assembly.

All files for this assembly are available in the textbook's resources database.

Project 1: Model the cam with the following specifications using SolidWorks:

Units: Inches
Cam Type: Circular
Follower Type: Translating
Follower Diameter = 0.5
Starting Radius = 2.00 [= (Base Circle Diameter + Follower Diameter)/2]
Starting Angle = 0°
Rotation Direction = Clockwise

Cam Motion:
Dwell 45°
Rise 0.375, Modified Trapezoidal Motion, 90°
Dwell 90°
Fall 0.375, Modified Trapezoidal Motion, 90°
Dwell 45°

Others:
Blank Outside Dia. = 5.00
Thickness = 0.50
The hub has an outer diameter of 1.00 in., and extends 0.50 in. from the surface of the cam.

The cam bore is 0.50-diameter

Create a keyway in both the cam and the cam shaft that will accept a 0.375 x 0.375 x 0.500-in square key. Is this keyway sizing feasible?

Make any modifications/adjustments to the cam-bracket and the length of the spring in order to accommodate the cam.

You are supplied parts and subassembly to complete the cam design.

Assemble the cam that you have modeled together with the subassembly and other parts given to you to complete a cam system.

Project 2: Model the cam with the following specifications using SolidWorks:

Units: Inches

Cam Type: Circular

Follower Type: Translating

Follower Diameter = 0.375

Starting Radius =1.4375 [= (Base Circle Diameter + Follower Diameter)/2]

Starting Angle = 0°

Rotation Direction = Clockwise

Cam Motion:

Dwell 45°

Rise 0.375, Harmonic Motion, 135°

Dwell 90°

Fall 0.375, Harmonic Motion, 90°

Others:

Blank Outside Dia. = 4.00

Thickness = 0.375

The hub has an outer diameter of 1.00 in., and extends 0.50 in. from the surface of the cam.

The cam bore is 0.50-diameter

Create a keyway in both the cam and the cam shaft that will accept a 0.375 x 0.375 x 0.500-in square key. Is this keyway sizing feasible?

Make any modifications/adjustments to the cam-bracket and the length of the spring in order to accommodate the cam.

You are supplied parts and subassembly to complete the cam design.

Assemble the cam that you have modeled together with the subassembly and other parts given to you to complete a cam system.

Chapter 24
Mechanism Design Using Blocks

Objectives:

In this chapter you will learn:
- How to create sketches of a mechanism
- How to save the sketches created as block files
- How to insert a block into the layout environment
- How to apply relations to the blocks
- How to convert blocks into parts

Introduction

A block is a set of entities grouped together as a single entity. Blocks are used to create complex mechanisms as sketches and to check their functionality before being developed into complex 3D models.

Blocks Toolbar

The Blocks toolbar, shown in Figure 24-1, is used to control the sketched entities of the blocks.

Figure 24-1 The Blocks toolbar

Problem Description

The different views of the parts of a reciprocating mechanism with required dimensions are shown in Figures 24-2, 24-3, and 24-4. We will create the sketches and save them as SolidWorks blocks. We will convert the blocks to parts and assemble the reciprocating mechanism.

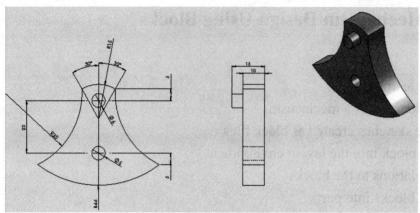

Figure 24-2 Crank front view, right view, and part

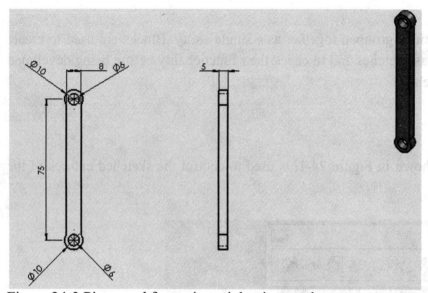

Figure 24-3 Piston rod front view, right view, and part

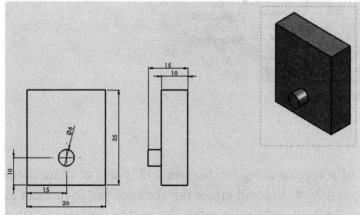

Figure 24-4 Piston tank front view, right view, and part

Creating Sketches of a Mechanism

Crank

1. Start a new SolidWorks part document.
2. Select the front plane.
3. Sketch the crank profile shown in Figure 24-5.

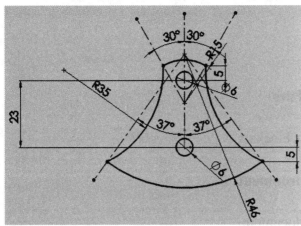

Figure 24-5 Sketch of crank

Piston rod

4. Start a new SolidWorks part document.
5. Select the front plane.
6. Sketch the piston rod profile shown in Figure 24-6.

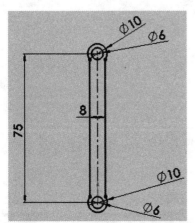

Figure 24-6 Sketch of piston rod

Piston tank

7. Start a new SolidWorks part document.
8. Select the front plane.

9. Sketch the piston tank profile shown in Figure 24-7.

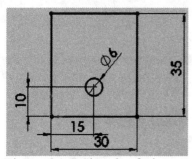

Figure 24-7 Sketch of piston tank

Saving the Sketches as Different Block Files

1. Save the sketch files as SolidWorks blocks.

Inserting the Block into the Layout Environment

1. Start a new SolidWorks assembly document.
2. Click the Create Layout button from the Begin Assembly PropertyManager (see Figure 24-8). The Layout CommandManager is displayed, as shown in Figure 24-9.
3. Click Insert Block from the Layout CommandManager (see Figure 24-9).

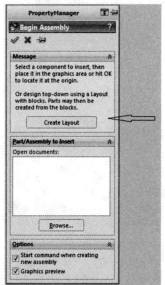

Figure 24-8 Begin Assembly PropertyManager

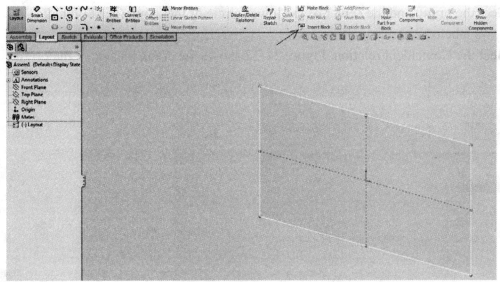

Figure 24-9 Layout CommandManager

4. Click the Browse button from the Insert Block PropertyManager (see Figure 24-10).

5. Select the crank, piston rod, and piston tank blocks from the file (see Figure 24-10).

6. Click OK.

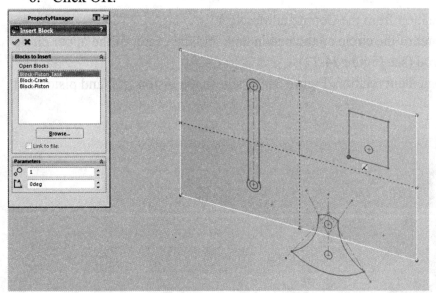

Figure 24-10 Opening the blocks for the crank, piston rod, and piston tank

Applying Relations to the Blocks

1. Click Add Relation from the CommandManager (see Figure 24-11, arrow labeled 1). The Add Relations PropertyManager appears.

2. Select the origin and the center of the lower circle of the crank (see Figure 24-11, arrows labeled 2 and 3).

3. Select the Coincident relation. Figure 24-12 shows the crank located at the origin.

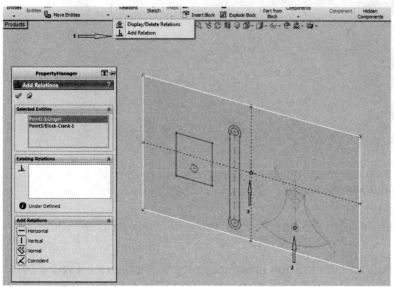

Figure 24-11 Add Relations PropertyManager for the crank

4. Click Add Relation from the CommandManager.

5. Select the center of the circle on the piston tank and the center of the upper circle of the piston rod (see Figure 24-12).

6. Select the Coincident relation. Figure 24-13 shows the piston tank and piston rod attached.

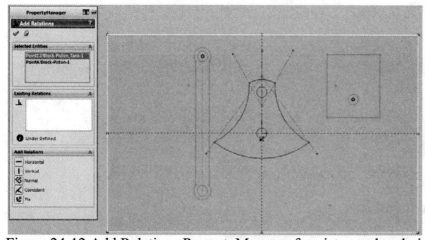

Figure 24-12 Add Relations PropertyManager for piston rod and piston tank

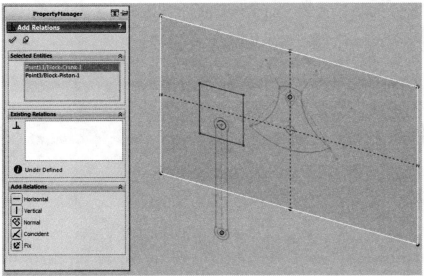

Figure 24-13 Piston tank and piston rod attached by a coincident relation

7. Click Add Relation from the CommandManager.
8. Select the center of the upper circle of the crank and the center of the lower circle of the piston rod (see Figure 24-14).
9. Select the Vertical relation. Figure 24-15 shows the crank vertically attached to the piston rod/piston tank (in a reciprocating relation).

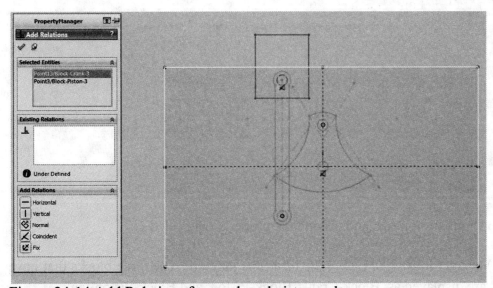

Figure 24-14 Add Relations for crank and piston rod

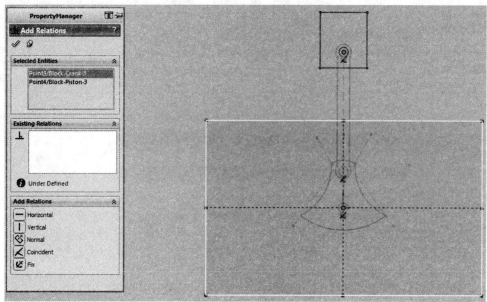

Figure 24-15 Crank vertically attached to piston rod/piston tank

Now, when the crank is rotated, the piston tank will reciprocate vertically due to the relations defined (see Figure 24-16).

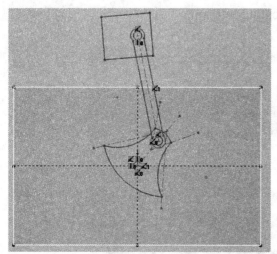

Figure 24-16 Crank, piston rod, and piston tank properly connected

The FeatureManager looks like Figure 24-17 at this juncture. The three blocks that have been created are displayed as: Block-Crank, Block-Piston, and Block-Piston-tank.

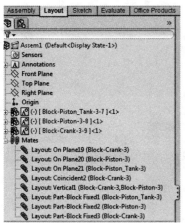

Figure 24-17 FeatureManager

Converting Blocks into Parts

1. From the Layout CommandManager, choose the Make Part From Block option (see Figure 24-18). The Make Part From Block PropertyManager appears, as shown in Figure 24-19.
2. In the Selected Blocks rollout, select the crank, piston rod, and piston tank (see Figure 24-19).
3. In the Selected Blocks rollout, select On Block.

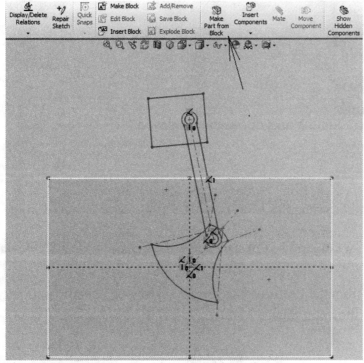

Figure 24-18 Make Part from Block option

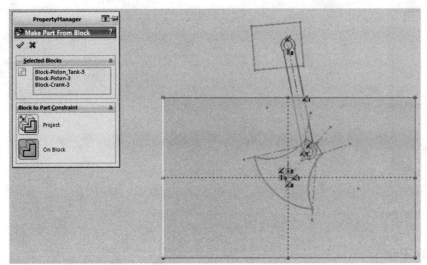

Figure 24-19 Make Part from Block PropertyManager

4. Click OK three times, each time the new SolidWorks document dialog is displayed and Part is selected by default (see Figure 24-20).

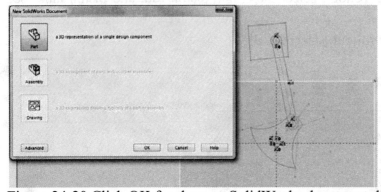

Figure 24-20 Click OK for the new SolidWorks document displayed

Extruding the Parts

Designing with blocks shares similar principles to in-context editing, which is used in the top-down approach.

Crank
1. Click on the crank block from the FeatureManager design tree. A window with in-context icons appears, as shown in Figure 24-21.
2. Click the edit part icon.

3. Expand the crank block tree and select Sketch1. If a sketch is not selected, there will be a message on the PropertyManager prompting the designer to select one (see Figure 24-22).

4. Click Extrude Base/Boss from the CommandManager. The Extrude PropertyManager appears, as shown in Figure 24-23.

5. Set the extrusion depth to 10 mm.

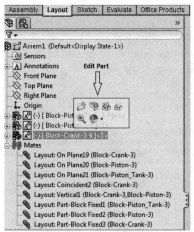

Figure 24-21 In-context editing

Figure 24-22 Extrude PropertyManager prompting user to select a sketch

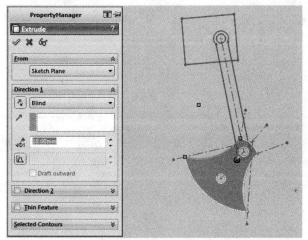

Figure 24-23 Extrude PropertyManager for the crank

Creating a boss to coincide with the upper circle on the crank

6. Click the right-hand side of the crank (see Figure 24-24) and start sketch mode.
7. Click the circle.
8. Click Convert Entities to extract this circle.
9. Click the Extrude Base/Bose tool.
10. Set the extrusion depth to 15 mm.

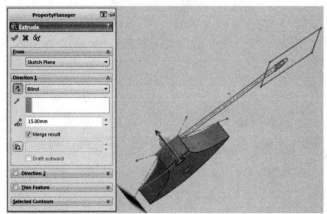

Figure 24-24 Extrude PropertyManager to create a boss

Piston rod

11. Click on the piston rod block from the FeatureManager design tree.
12. Click the edit part icon.
13. Expand the piston block tree and select Sketch1.
14. Click the Extrude Base/Boss tool from the CommandManager. The Extrude PropertyManager appears, as shown in Figure 24-25.
15. Set the extrusion depth to 5 mm. Reverse Direction 1 if it is in the wrong direction.

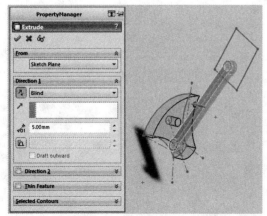

Figure 24-25 Extrude PropertyManager for the piston rod

Piston tank

16. Click on the piston block from the FeatureManager design tree.
17. Click the edit part icon.
18. Expand the piston tank block tree and select Sketch1.
19. Click the Extrude Base/Boss tool from the CommandManager. The Extrude PropertyManager appears, as shown in Figure 24-26.
20. Set the extrusion depth to 5 mm. Reverse Direction 1 if it is in the wrong direction.

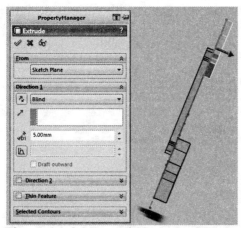

Figure 24-26 Extrude PropertyManager for the piston tank

The final reciprocating mechanism model is shown in Figure 24-27. As the crank is rotated, the piston rod and the piston tank will reciprocate along the vertical axis due to the relations defined at the block level (not at the assembly level).

Figure 24-27 Final reciprocating mechanism model

Summary

The block design is now complete. We note that the mating conditions were imposed on the blocks rather than on the assembly of parts. This is the advantage of using blocks because we can sketch in 2D and add relations to 2D sketches, which are synonymous with mates in assembly mode. When blocks are used, the Layout tool is used instead of the Assembly tool. Designing with blocks is similar to in-context editing used in the top-down approach, as we have already observed. Block design creates an assembly of blocks (instead of parts) and a sketch that defines a block is accessed in-context and extruded to convert it to a part.

Industrial and engineering designers often use blocks to experiment with various designs in 2D before committing resources to 3D design.

Chapter 25
Die Design

Objectives:

In this chapter you will learn:
- The scope of Die Design
- The components of a Die Set
- How to design a Die Holder of a Die Set
- How to design a Punch Holder of a Die Set
- How to design a Die Block
- How to design a Blanking Punch
- How to design a Punch Plate
- How to design a Pilot
- How to design a Stripper
- How to design a Back Gauge
- How to design a Front Spacer
- How to design an Automatic Stop
- How to assemble a Design Set

Scope of Die Design

Die design in a general sense involves either designing an entire press tool with all components taken together, or in a limited way involves designing that particular component which is machined to receive the blank.

Components of a Die Set

Die sets are made by several manufacturers and they may be purchased in a great variety of shapes and sizes. The major components of a die set are the die holder (the lower part of the die) and the punch holder (the upper part of the die) [see Figure 25-1]. The *punch shank* **A** is clamped in the ram of the press which is reciprocated up and down by a crank. In operation, the *punch holder* **B** moves up and down with the ram. *Bushings* **C**, pressed into the punch holder, slide on *guide posts* **D** to maintain precise alignment of cutting members of the die. The *die holder* **E** is clamped to the bolster plate (a thick steel plate fastened to the press frame) of the press by bolts passing through **slots F**.

The other components of a dies set include *die block*, *blanking punch*, *punch plate*, *pilot*, *stripper*, *back gauge*, *front spacer*, and *automatic stop*. Each of these has to be designed and all components have to be assembled to cut a particular *scrap strip*.

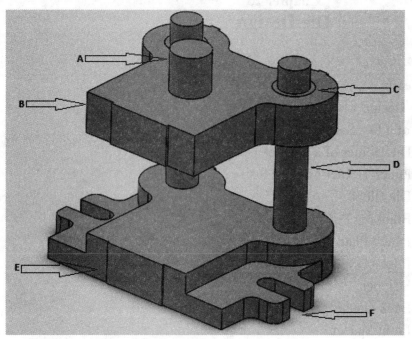

Figure 25-1 A typical die set

Pierce and Blank Die

The Pierce and Blank Die is one of the most basic to be studied. The steps involved include the following:

1. Carefully study the part print since the information given on it provides many clues for solving the design problem.
2. Design a scrap strip as a guide for laying out the view of the actual dies.
3. Design the parts of the die set and assemble them to have complete die set for producing the part.

In Pierce and Blank Die operation, the die pierces two holes at the first station, and then the pat is blanked out at the second station. The material from which the blanks are removed is cold-rolled steel strip.

Part Design

In manual method, the part drawing is the starting point for die design. Using CAD such as SolidWorks, the Part Design as well as the Part Drawing, are fairly easy and straightforward.

1. Start a **New SolidWorks Part** document.
2. Click the **Front Plane**.
3. Figure 25-2 shows the basic profile for the part.
4. Using the **Straight Slot tool**, a slot is sketched with centre-centre being **1.5-in** while the arc **Radius** is **9/16-in** (0.563-in).
5. **Extrude** the basic profile **0.0625-in** as shown in Figure 25-3. This is the blanked feature.

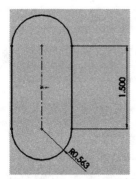

Figure 25-2 Basic profile for the part

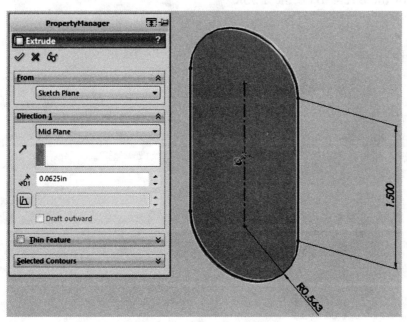

Figure 25-3 Basic profile extruded 0.0625-in

6. Sketch a **Circle** with its centre coinciding with the end arcs, **0.563-in** diameter (see Figure 25-4).

7. **Extrude-cut** the **Circle** in order to define a hole (see Figure 25-4).

8. **Mirror** the hole so as to have the pierced holes (see Figure 25-5); the blanked strip is shown in Figure 25-6.

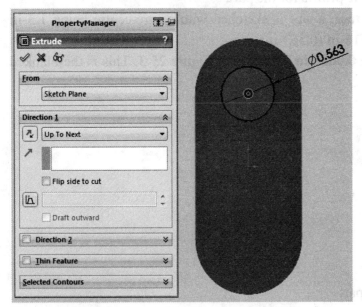

Figure 25-4 Extrude-cut for the circle to define a hole

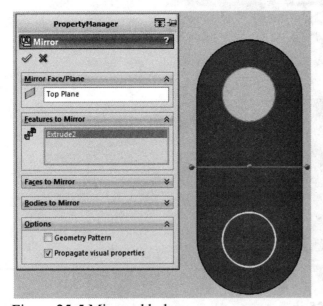

Figure 25-5 Mirrored hole

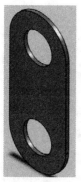

Figure 25-6 Pierced holes and blanked strip

Scrap Strip

A scrap strip is normally designed to guide the laying out of the views of the actual die. Manually this is sketched using pencil and paper. Using SolidWorks CAD software, the scrap strip is produced as shown in Figure 25-7, but we have only included dimensions to fully define the scrap strip layout.

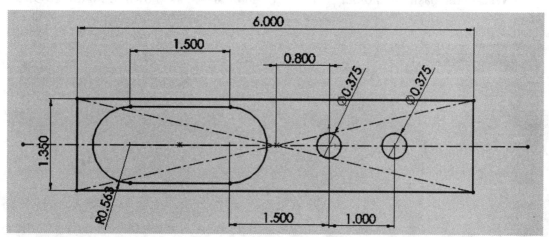

Figure 25-7 Scrap strip layout using SolidWorks CAD software

Design of a Die Holder of a Die Set

Designing the Die Holder of a Die Set is one of the major tasks in die design. Standard dimensions are available from manufacturers' websites.

1. Create the *basic profile* of a Die Set Die Holder on the **Top Plane** as shown in Figure 25-8.

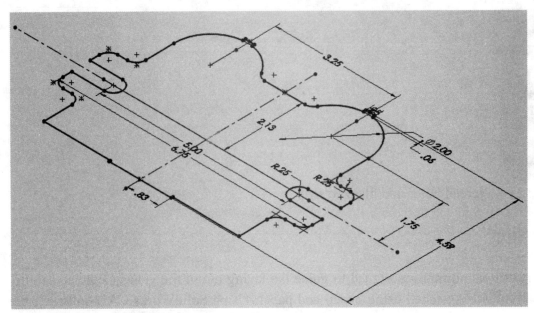

Figure 25-8 Sketch for die holder of a die set

2. **Extrude** the basic die holder sketch through **0.502-in** as shown in Figure 25-9.

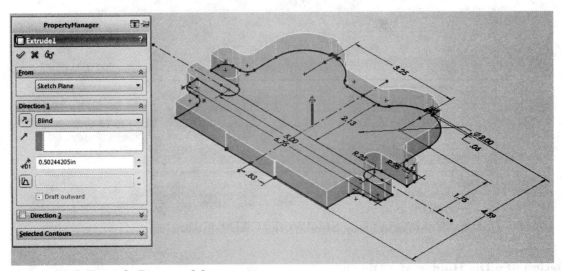

Figure 25-9 Extrude PropertyManager

3. **Extrude** an additional portion through a value **0.5-in** as shown in Figure 25-10.
4. **Create** one hole, **0.75-in** in diameter
5. **Mirror** the hole about the **Right Plane** as shown in Figure 25-11.

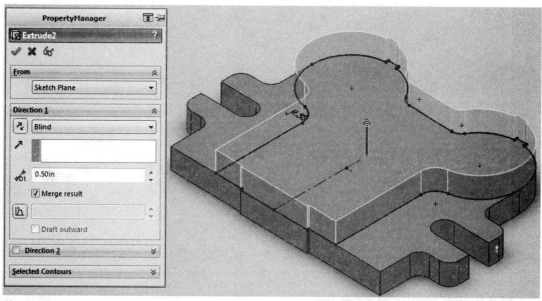

Figure 25-10 Extrusion of portion of upper surface

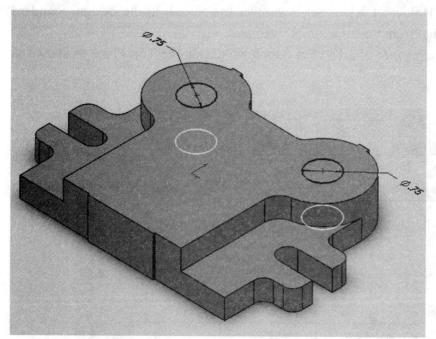

Figure 25-11 A hole created and mirrored about the Right Plane

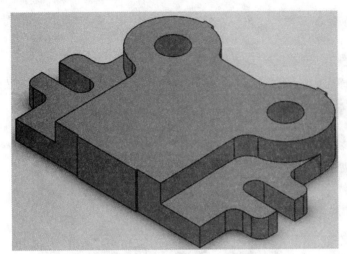

Figure 25-12 Die holder model

Design of a Punch Holder of a Die Set

Designing the Punch Holder of a Die Set is another major task in die design. Standard dimensions are available from manufacturers' websites.

1. Create the *basic profile* of a Die Set Punch Holder on the Top Plane as shown in Figure 25-13.

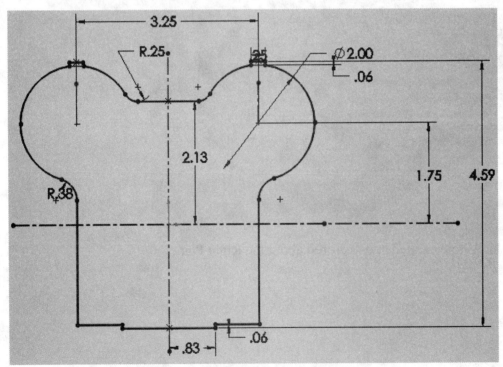

Figure 25-13 Basic profile of a Die Set Punch Holder

2. **Extrude** the basic punch holder sketch through **1.00-in** as shown in Figure 25-14.
3. Create one **Hole**, **1.00-in** in diameter as shown in Figure 25-15.
4. **Mirror** the hole about the **Right Plane** as shown in Figure 25-15.
5. Add the Punch Shank as shown in Figure 25-16.

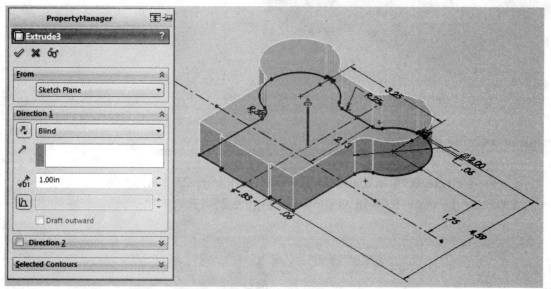

Figure 25-14 Basic punch holder sketch

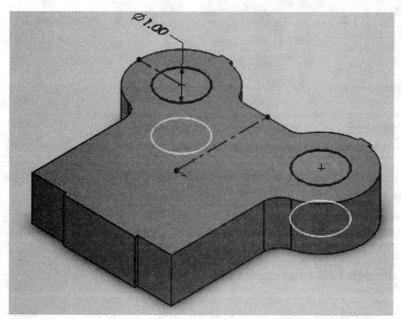

Figure 25-15 Create one hole and mirror about Right Plane

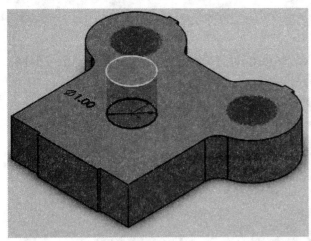

Figure 25-16 Add the Punch Shank

Design of a Guide Post

1. Create a **circle, 0.75-in** diameter as shown in Figure 25-17a.
2. **Extrude** the circle **5.00-in** as shown in Figure 25-17b.

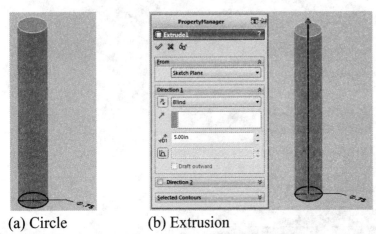

(a) Circle   (b) Extrusion

Figure 25-17 Extrude PropertyManager for guide post

Design of Bushing

1. Create two concentric **Circles, 0.75-in** and **1.00-in** in diameter respectively as shown in Figure 25-18.
2. Extrude the **Circles** through **1.00-in** as shown in Figure 25-18.

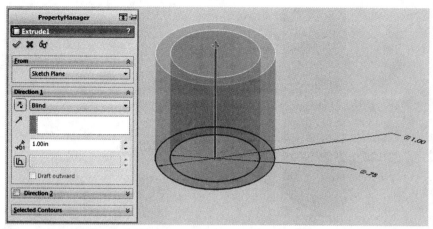

Figure 25-18 Extrude PropertyManager for bushing

Design of a Die Block

1. Create a **Rectangle**, **3.5-in** by **3.0-in** as shown in Figure 25-19.
2. Extrude the **Rectangle** through **0.9375-in** as shown in Figure 25-19.

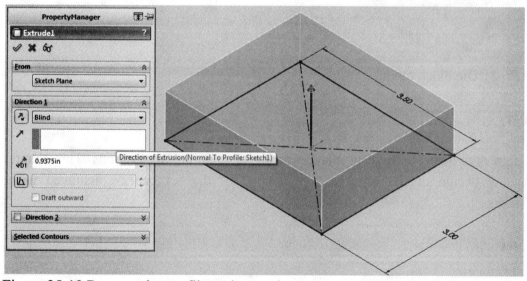

Figure 25-19 Rectangular profile and extrusion

3. Create **hole** using Hole Wizard with centre **0.63-in** from each edge near the corner of the feature; choose **Hole Size = "I"** and **All Drill Sizes** for the Tool (see Figure 25-20).
4. **Linear Pattern/Mirror** the hole to obtain the part (see Figure 25-20). The die block model is shown in Figure 25-21.

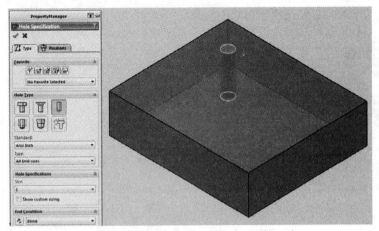

Figure 25-20 Create a hole using Hole Wizard

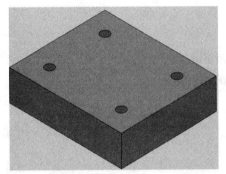

Figure 25-21 Die block model

Summary

Die design is extremely useful in manufacturing engineering applications. This chapter shows how design of the different components of die set can be achieved using SolidWorks.

Exercises

1. Design the Blanking Punch
2. Design the Punch Plate
3. Design the Pilot
4. Design the Stripper
5. Design the Back Gauge
6. Design the Front Spacer
7. Design the Automatic Stop
8. Assemble the components above with the partial die set complete Die Set
9. Produce the drawings of the parts and assembly drawing of the die set

Chapter 26
Aluminium Extrusion from Manufacturers' Internet Websites

Objectives:

In this chapter you will learn:

- How to access manufacturers' Internet websites for AutoCAD 2D aluminium section profiles
- How to convert the AutoCAD 2D aluminium section profiles into SolidWorks 3D extrusions
- Understood how to use the SolidWorks 3D Aluminium Extrusions to realize structural assemblies

ACCESSING MANUFACTURERS' AUTOCAD 2D ALUMINIUM SECTION PROFILES

Assuming some engineers belonging to a CAD company in Toronto, Canada are working with local customers, and delivering structural machine frames having particular configurations of aluminium sectional profiles. The Canadian CAD company partners with Bosch Rexroth in USA and needs to download profiles of interest for designing machine frames required by local customers. In today's business environment, manufacturers have several pieces of information relating to their products on their websites. It is no longer necessary to order hardcopy catalogue. The starting point would be for the engineers to access the Internet website of Bosch Rexroth for their products.

To download the cross-section of a Bosch Rexroth Extrusion, follow the following steps:
1. Google: "aluminum structural framing bosch rexroth download CAD"

To speed up getting to the correct homepage, look for the link having the sentence, "Download Bosch Rexroth CAD Files" as shown here:

Aluminum Framing - Bosch Rexroth
www13.**boschrexroth**-us.com/.../Load_Category.aspx?... - United States
Download **Bosch Rexroth** CAD Files · **Aluminum Framing** · Profiles · Connectors · Fasteners · Door Components · Ecosafe Guarding · Floor To **Frame** Elements **...**

2. Click the link to give the following URL:
http://www13.boschrexroth-us.com/partstream/Load_Category.aspx?category=Aluminum%20Framing&menu=1,0,0

The link accesses the homepage of Bosch Rexroth shown in Figure 26-1.

1. **Click Profiles**.
2. **Select 40 series** (see Figure 26-2).

Figure 26-1 Downloadable Bosch Rexroth CAD files (profiles, connectors, etc.)

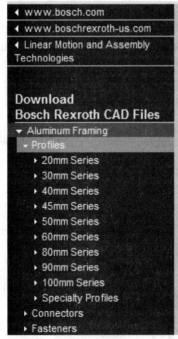

Figure 26-2 Series selection

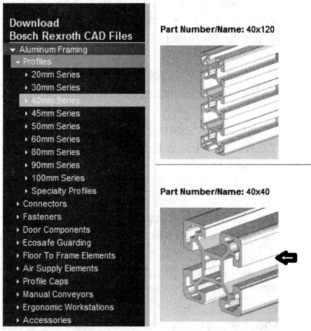

Figure 26-3 Part-number 40x40 selection

3. Click **Part Number/Name:** 40x40 (see Figure 26-3)

Clicking Part-number 40x40 brings up another page shown in Figure 26-4.

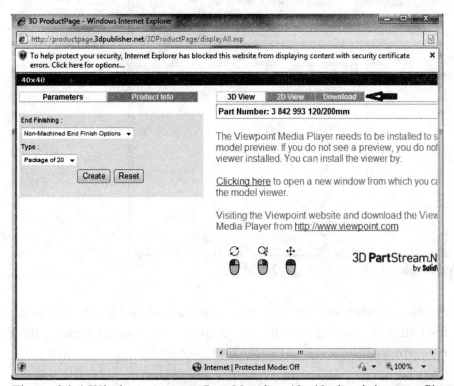

Figure 26-4 Window to create Part Number 40x40 aluminium profile

4. **Click Download** (top-right of Figure 26-4).
5. **Select DWG** file(s) (see Figure 26-5).
6. **Click Download** (bottom-right of Figure 26-6).

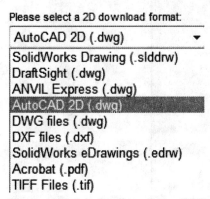

Figure 26-5 Selecting AutoCAD 2D (dwg) files from pull-down menu

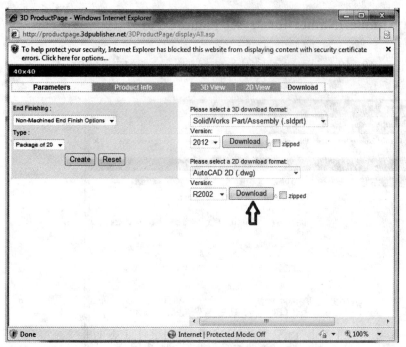

Figure 26-6 Downloading AutoCAD 2D (dwg) file

When the *Download* button is clicked, a new page shown in Figure 26-7 is displayed. This is the final step of downloading the CAD file(s). An icon in yellow, showing the Part Number is displayed as shown in Figure 26-7.

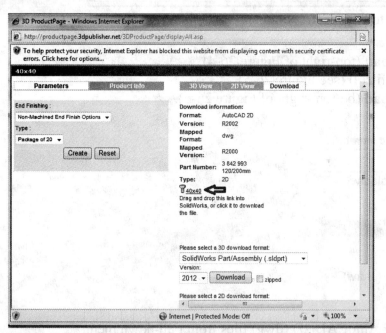

Figure 26-7 Final step in downloading AutoCAD 2D (dwg) file

7. **Drag** and **drop** this link ▆40x40 into SolidWorks, or click it to download the file.

8. **Save** the downloaded file (see Figure 26-8) in a folder of interest.

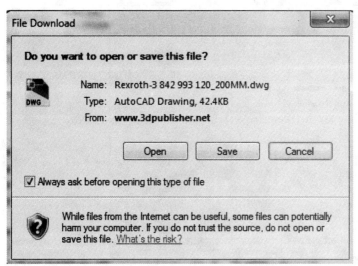

Figure 26-8 Save AutoCAD 2D (dwg) file

CREATING A SOLIDWORKS SKETCH FROM AUTOCAD 2D SECTION PROFILE

In this section, we will show how to create a SolidWorks Sketch from the AutoCAD 2D Section Profile that is imported. The following steps should be followed.

1. **Open** a **New SolidWorks Part Document**.
2. Select **Front Plane** (marked "1" in Figure 26-9).
3. Click **Insert > DXF/DWG** (marked "2" in Figure 26-9).
4. Filter **DWG files** (see Figure 26-10).
5. Select the document marked, **Rexroth-3842 993 120_200MM** (see Figure 26-10).
6. Click **Open** to open the aluminium profile.

Figure 26-9 Importing DWG file (AutoCAD) to SolidWorks

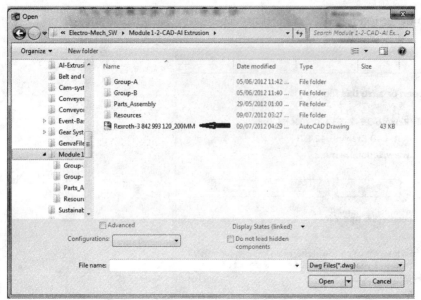

Figure 26-10 Locating the Rexroth file that is already saved

The DXF/DWG Import page automatically shows up on the screen as shown in Figure 26-11.

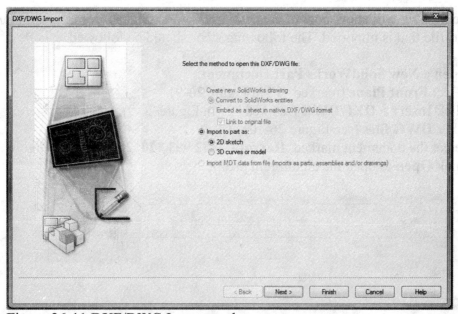

Figure 26-11 DXF/DWG Import tool

7. Click **Next> Millimeters > Next > Finish**.

[See Figure 26-12 for choosing Units ("Inches" chosen) of imported data and preview]

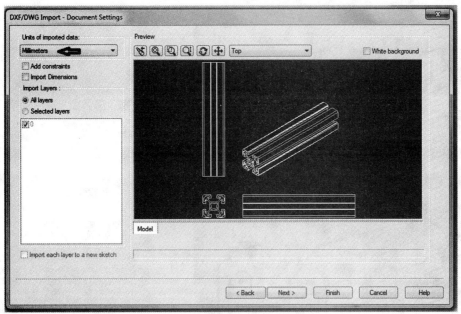

Figure 26-12 Units of imported data and preview

When the Finish option is clicked, the views for the aluminium section are automatically displayed. If you do not see the view, hit the "F" button on the keyboard to display the views. Figure 26-13 shows the views.

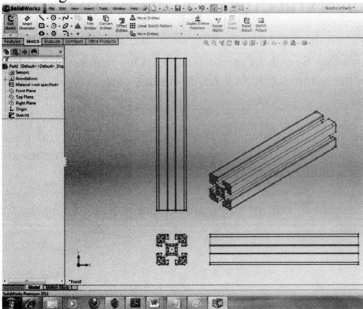

Figure 26-13 Views for the aluminium section

8. Delete the **Top**, **Side**, and **Isometric** views.

We can confirm using the Measure tool that the width and length of the **Rexroth-3842 993 120_200MM** profile imported is 40 mm x 40 mm (see Figure 26-14).

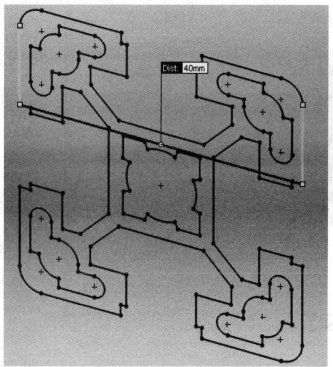

Figure 26-14 Profile of the **Rexroth-3842 993 120_200MM** imported

CREATING SOLIDWORKS STRUCTURAL ELEMENTS USING AUTOCAD 2D SECTION PROFILE

Begin your design by extruding Sketch to create features. Our features are extrusions of the profile imported from the manufacturer's website (in this case, having a dimension of 40 mm by 40 mm).

You can now build your structural frame by creating different structural elements of different lengths obtained from the initial profile and saving them using names associated with their lengths for ease of future usage.

We will now create four lengths of our imported aluminium profile having the following dimensions:
1) 1200 mm
2) 900 mm
3) 800 mm
4) 300 mm with 45° cuts at each end

Let us create an aluminium feature that is 800 mm long from the 40 mm x 40 mm section. The step involved is to extrude the profile of the **Rexroth-3842 993 120_200MM** in Figure 26-14 through a distance of 800 mm. The preview is shown in Figure 26-15 while the feature is shown in Figure 26-16.

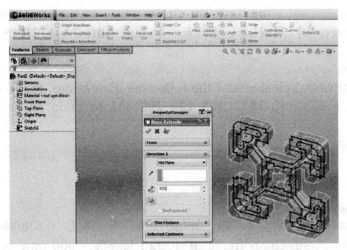

Figure 26-15 3D preview of the aluminium extrusion

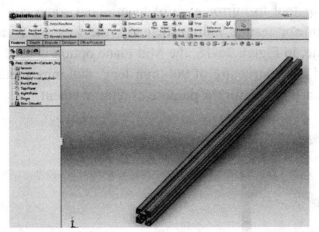

Figure 26-16 3D An aluminium extrusion realized in SolidWorks environment

Save this feature as aluminium_800_40x40 so that we can easily associate the name with the part.

We simply repeat the process for other features named:
aluminium_300_40x40
aluminium_900_40x40
aluminium_1200_40x40

An easy way of creating subsequent features from the first one (aluminium_800_40x40) is to Save As and then change the name to aluminium_300_40x40 for example. Then edit the feature and change the length to 300. The procedure can then be repeated for lengths 900 and 1200 respectively. This approach is very efficient since the cross-sectional dimensions are the same for all the features. At the end of the exercise, the 300 mm long feature is given cut 45° at each end.

Creating SolidWorks Structural Machine Frame Using AutoCAD 2D Section Profile

The task is to use the four structural elements of the following dimensions, that we have modelled using the imported **Rexroth-3842 993 120_200MM** to build an assembly shown in Figure 26-17:

1) 1200 mm
2) 900 mm
3) 800 mm
4) 300 mm with 45° cuts at each end

The remaining task reduces to starting a *New SolidWorks Assembly* document and creating an assembly of parts. A structural frame of overall length = 900 mm, width = 800 mm, and height = 1200 mm is obtained simply by Inserting each of these in the assembly and then we use Mirror tool to mirror each of them about some convenient Planes. In order to be able to mirror feature more efficiently, the way we create the features is important. For example, in Figure 26-15, the Mid Plane option is used which facilitates Mirroring. Figure 26-17 is a structure of 900 mm long, 800 mm wide, 1200 mm high, having three braces at each corner for the purpose of reinforcement.

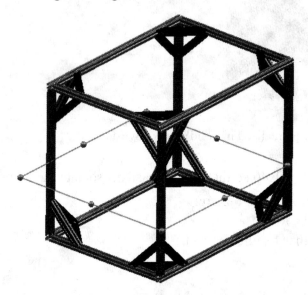

Figure 26-17 Frame structure

Different configurations can easily be obtained using the procedure presented in this chapter.

References

http://www13.boschrexroth-us.com/

Exercises

Question 1: Assuming you are an engineer employed in a company that utilizes aluminum extrusions produced by another company, which has AutoCAD drawings of different cross-sectional profiles on their website. Import a profile (20mmx20mm cross-section) from Bosch Rexroth website and use it to model a frame-structure (see Figure P1), using SolidWorks CAD software for your company; maintain the orientation shown. There are three configurations to create: 700 mm, 800 mm (for the base), and 1250 mm (the other dimension). Dimension your 3D structure.

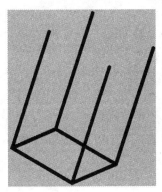

Figure P1

Question 2: Assuming you are an engineer employed in a company that utilizes aluminum extrusions produced by another company, which has AutoCAD drawings of different cross-sectional profiles on their website. Import a profile (30mmx30mm cross-section) from Bosch Rexroth website and use it to design a frame-structure (see Figure P2) using SolidWorks CAD software for your company; maintain the orientation shown. There are three configurations to create: 500 mm, 600 mm (for the base), and 1000 mm (the other dimension). Dimension your 3D structure.

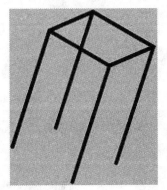

Figure P2

Chapter 27
Geneva Wheel Mechanism

Objectives:
In this chapter you will learn:
- How to determine the basic design parameters of the Geneva wheel mechanism
- How to use the SolidWorks to model and simulate Geneva wheel mechanism

Historical Background

The name derives from the earliest application of the device in *mechanical watches*, especially in Switzerland and Geneva. Geneva mechanism was originally invented by a watch maker. The watch maker only put a limited number of slots in one of the rotating disks so that the system could only go through so many rotations. This prevented the spring on the watch from being wound too tight, thus giving the mechanism its other name, the Geneva Stop Clock mechanism in 18th century pocket watch application. Other applications of the Geneva drive include the pen change mechanism in *plotters*, automated sampling devices, *indexing* tables in assembly lines.

Introduction

Geneva wheel mechanism translates a continuous rotation into an intermittent rotary motion, using an intermittent gear where the drive wheel has a pin that reaches into a slot of the driven wheel and thereby advances it by one step, and having a raised circular blocking disc that locks the driven wheel in position between steps.

The Geneva wheel mechanism is a timing device used in many counting instruments and in other applications where an intermittent rotary motion is required. Essentially, the Geneva mechanism consists of a rotating disk with a pin and another rotating disk with slots (usually four) into which the pin slides. Once the number of slots and crank diameter are known, the layout can be constructed with the basic knowledge of geometry.

There are three types of Geneva wheels:
1. External, which is the most popular, and which is covered in this chapter.
2. Internal, which is also very common.
3. Spherical, which is extremely rare.

The Geneva wheel mechanism discussed in this chapter has many applications for the product designer, tool engineer, and others involved in the design and manufacture of machinery, tooling, and mechanical devices and assemblies used in the industrial context.

Principles of Operation of the Geneva Drive

Geneva mechanism is a simple mechanism which does not require any complicated design parts. However, the mechanism requires correct dimension and close tolerance for the correct engagements and disengagements. Parts of Geneva mechanism are: crank and Geneva wheel.

Crank

Crank is the driving member. Main parts of crank are pin (roller) and a circular segment. Roller which rolls or slides in the slots and the circular segment guide effectively locks the wheel against rotation when the roller is not in engagement and also positions the wheel for correct engagement of the roller with the next slot.

Geneva Wheel

Geneva wheel is a driven member, which contains a number of radial cuts called slots. Slots are the radial path for rolling the rollers. Number of slots are depends on the type of drive. Slot surface should be perfectly smooth. If the slot surface is not smooth, this may cause a wear on slot or roller. This will change the timing between driver and driven

In the most common arrangement, the driven wheel has four slots and thus advances for each rotation of the drive wheel by one step of 90°. If the driven wheel has n slots, it advances by $360°/n$ per full rotation of the driver.

Geneva mechanism can theoretically have from 3 to any number of slots. In practice from 4 to 12 is enough to cover most requirements. From a practical standpoint, the follower can have a minimum of three slots and a maximum of 18. Most followers are made with four, five, six or eight slots, which correspond to index lengths of 90, 72, 60 and 45 degrees, respectively because the mechanism needs to be well lubricated, it is often enclosed in an oil capsule.

Advantages and Disadvantages

Geneva wheels may be the simplest and least expensive of all intermittent motion mechanism. As mentioned before, they come in a wide variety of sizes, ranging from those used in instruments, to those used in machines tools to index spindle carriers weighing several tons. They have good motion-curve characteristics compared to ratchets, but exhibit more "jerk," or instantaneous change in acceleration, than do better cam systems (the Geneva, you will remember, is a special type of cam system).

The Geneva maintains good control of its load at all times, since it is provided with locking ring surfaces, as shown in fig, to hold the output during dwell periods. In addition, if properly sized to the load, the Geneva generally exhibits very long life (about 20 years).

The Geneva is not a versatile mechanism. It can be used to produce no less than three, and usually no more than 18 dwells per revolution of the output shaft. Furthermore, once the number of dwells has been selected, the designer is well locked into a given set of motion curves. The ratio of dwell period is also established once the number of dwells per revolution has been selected. Also, all Geneva acceleration curves start and end with finite acceleration and deceleration. This means they produce jerk.

The geometry and kinematics of the external Geneva drive mechanism summarized in the subsequent sections are from Walsh (2000) [1] where they are described in detail.

Geometry of the External Geneva Mechanism

The crank and wheel schematic is shown in Figure 27-1 while the geometry is shown in Figure 27-2.

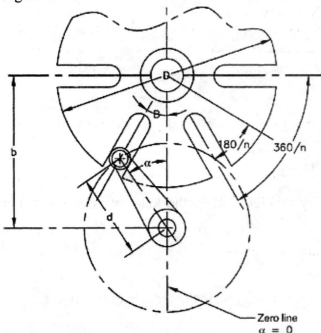

Figure 27-1 External Geneva mechanism

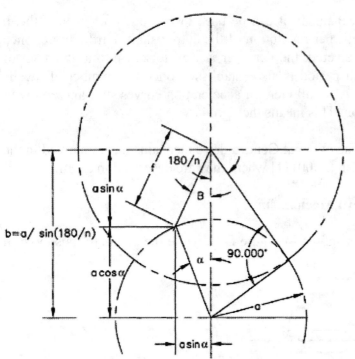

Figure 27-2 External Geneva geometry

Kinematics of the External Geneva Drive

Based on the external Geneva geometry of Figure 27-2, the kinematics can be better understood.

Assumed or given: a, n, d, and p.

Let $m = 1/\sin(180/n)$

a = crank radius of driving member (this is normally on the inner side of the roller)

n = number of slots in drive

d_r = roller diameter

p = constant velocity of driving crank

b = center distance = $a \times m$

D = diameter of driven Geneva wheel = $2\sqrt{d_r^2/4 + a^2 \cot^2(180/n)}$

ω = constant angular velocity of driving crank = $p\pi/30$ rad/s

β = angular displacement of driven member corresponding to crank angle α

$$\beta = \frac{m - \cos\alpha}{\sqrt{1 + m^2 - 2m\cos\alpha}}$$

The slot width, stop arc radius, stop disc radius, and clearance arc need to be defined. To do this, we present other formulas from [3] based on Figure 27-3 and Figure 27-4:

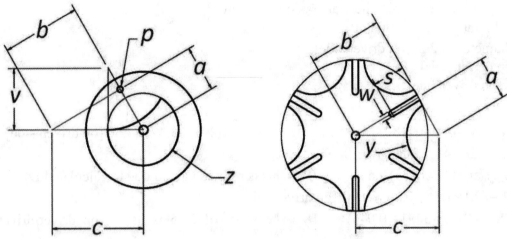

Figure 27-3 Geneva Drive   Figure 27-4 Geneva Driven

Where,
a = drive crank radius
n = driven slot quantity
p = drive pin diameter
t = allowed clearance

$c = center\ dist. = a / \sin(180/n)$ [Note: in the previous presentation, this is b]

$b = Geneva\ wheel\ radius = \sqrt{c^2 - a^2}$ (Note: in the previous presentation, this is $D/2$)

$s = slot\ center\ length = (a+b) - c$

$w = slot\ width = p + t$

$y = stop\ arc\ radius = a - (p \times 1.5)$

$z = stop\ disc\ radius = y - t$

$v = clearance\ arc = bz / a$

The value of the clearance arc, v using the above relation is often low; therefore, we present another formula that the author derived, which seems to be more consistent:

$$v = clearance\ arc = (r_1 + r_2)\cos(180/n) - \varepsilon; \qquad \varepsilon = 4.6\% v$$

where the radii are b and y respectively.

SolidWorks Modeling and Simulation of Geneva Wheel Mechanism

This section puts together the geometry and kinematics covered so far in modeling Geneva wheel mechanism similar to methods presented in [4, 5]. For our configuration, the author used the dimensions in Enzo to model the Geneva wheel mechanism and simulated it. The geometric definitions are first discussed to ensure that user understand how the geometric relations required in defining the mechanism for it to properly function.

For our illustrative example, there are 6 slots. Therefore,

Let $m = 1/\sin(180/6) = 1/\sin(30)$

$a = 1$ (diameter of 2/2) [on driver side]

$n = 6$ [on driven side]

$d_r = 0.2$ [on driver side]

$b = 1/\sin(30) = 2$

$D = 2\sqrt{d_r^2/4 + a^2 \cot^2(180/n)} = 2\sqrt{(0.1)^2 + (1)^2 \cot^2(30)} = 3.47 \approx 3.50$ [on driven side]

$p = d_r/2 = 0.2/2 = 0.1$ [on driver side]

$a = (D/2)\tan 30^o = (1.75)\tan 30^o = 1.01$ (This is refined valued due to calculated D)

$y = 1.01 - (0.1 \times 1.5) = 0.86 \approx 0.90$ [on driver side]

$v = (1.75 + 0.9)\cos(30)[1 - 0.046] = 2.18$ (The value of 2.15 is used) [on driver/driven sides]

Using these design parameters, the driver (wheel) and driven wheel (Geneva gear) are modeled using the detailed parts descriptions given. This is a design phase, and consequently, the estimations should be carefully done to ensure that the assembled parts function correctly.

The step-by-step procedure for using SolidWorks to model the Geneva wheel mechanism is now given. We assume that each part has now been modeled as discussed. The parts are assembled and then at the motion simulation stage, two contact properties must be defined for the Geneva wheel mechanism to properly function. The definition of the contacts is the key to the successful implementation of the motion simulation. If the pin is not separated from the wheel, there could be problem to get the assembly to function correctly. Users must define the following contacts:

1. Between the Geneva gear and the Wheel
2. Between the Geneva gear and the Pin

1. Open the "**Assem1Enz**"assembly from the downloaded files (see Figure 27-5).

Figure 27-5 Assembly of Geneva mechanism parts or the

2. Switch to **Motion study** and set the model orientation as required (see Figure 27-6).

Figure 27-6 Switch to Motion study

3. Change the Motion study type to "**Basic Animation**"(see Figure 27-7).

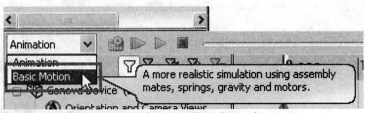

Figure 27-7 Basic Motion mode selected

4. Click on "**Contact**"(see Figure 27-8).

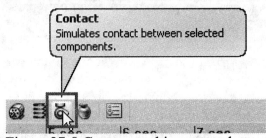

Figure 27-8 Contact tool is accessed

5. Now in the **Contact property manager** click on the pin to keep it visible as we need to use it twice (see Figure 27-9).

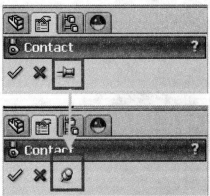

Figure 27-9 Pin the Contact PropertyManager

6. Now under components selection box, select "**GenevaGear_Enz-1**" and "**GenevaPin_Enz-1**" parts (see Figure 27-10).

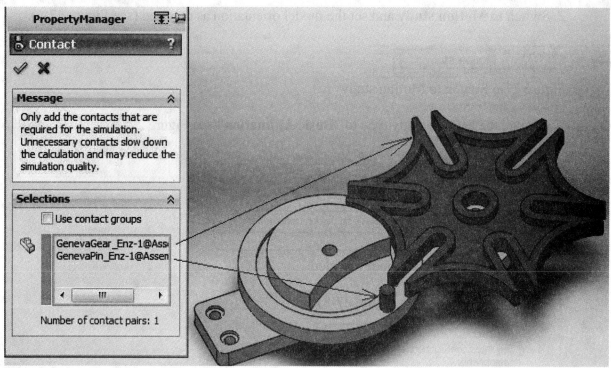

Figure 27-10 First set of Contacts is defined

7. Click **OK** to apply the contact.

8. With Contact property manager visible, select "**GenevaGear_Enz-1**" and "**GenevaWheel_Enz-2**" parts and click **OK** to apply the contact. You can now close the Contact property manager (see Figure 27-11).

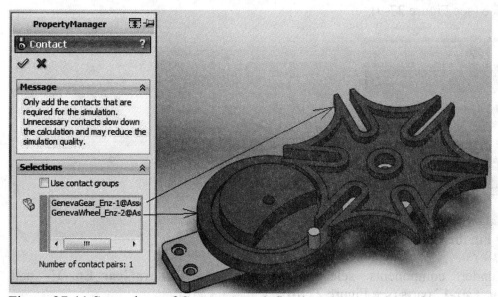

Figure 27-11 Second set of Contacts are defined

10. Click on "**Motor**"(see Figure 27-12).

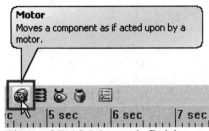

Figure 27-12 Motor definition tool accessed

11. Set the motor type to "**Rotary motor**". Select the cylindrical face or circular edge of "Geneva Wheel" part to define the direction of motion. Set the motion function to "**Constant Speed**" and RPM to 30 (see Figure 27-13).

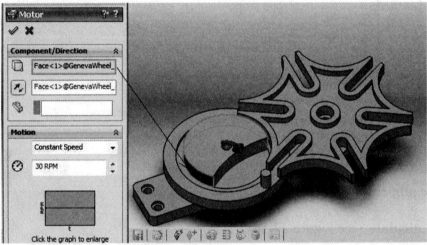

Figure 27-13 Engaging face on the wheel is selected

12. Click **OK** and apply the motor.

13. Now click on "**Motion Study Properties**" (see Figure 27-14).

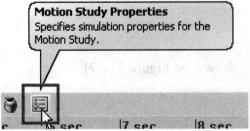

Figure 27-14 Accessing motion study properties

14. In the Motion Study Properties property manager under basic motion, set the **frames per second to 30** (the larger the number, the smoother the motion) and set the **Geometry Accuracy** and **3D Contact Resolution** settings to **high side** (move the sliders to right).

This will make collision simulation more accurate and smoother motion, but requires more time to compute (see Figure 27-15).

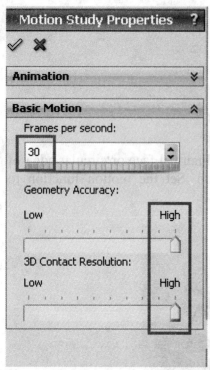

Figure 27-15 Adjusting the motion study properties

15. Click OK to set the properties.

16. Finally click on "**Calculate**"(see Figure 27-16).

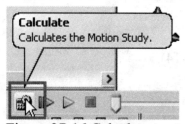

Figure 27-16 Calculate to start simulation

17. And now is the show time. Hit **play** to enjoy the show (see Figure 27-17).

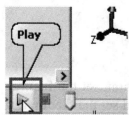

Figure 27-17 Play

You can change and experiments with the settings to get a better animation. Click on **save** if you want to export the animation as **AVI or series of pictures** (see Figure 27-18). You can change other settings in the save window.

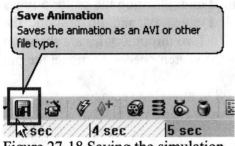

Figure 27-18 Saving the simulation

Summary

This chapter has presented design issues related to Geneva wheel mechanism as well as the modeling and simulation procedure for the mechanism.

References

[1] Ronald A. Walsh, Chapter 11: Mechanisms, Linkage Geometry, and Calculations, From *Handbook of Machining and Metalworking Calculations*, McGraw-Hill, 2000

[2]http://www.scribd.com/doc/83874208/Mechanisms-Linkage-Geometry-And-Calculations

[3] http://newgottland.com/2012/01/08/make-geneva-wheels-of-any-size/#

[4] http://morldtechgossips.blogspot.ca/2012/06/geneva-mechanism.html

[5]http://gupta9665.wordpress.com/2011/04/22/animating-geneva-mechanism-in-solidworks/

Projects

Figures P1 and P3 describe the sketches needed to model a sector of the Geneva gear (Figure P3). The full model of the Geneva gear obtained by replicating the sector 5 times (using circular pattern tool) is shown in Figure P4. Figures P5 and P6 describe the sketches needed to model the Geneva wheel (Figure P7). Two through-holes are shown in Figure P7; they are 21.796 apart. Figure P8 describes the sketch needed to model the pin (Figure P9).

1. Use the information provided in Figures P1—P8 to model the components.
2. Model a base on your own to support the Geneva gear and wheel.
3. Assemble all components using SolidWorks.
4. Simulate the Geneva mechanism (your final model should look like Figure P10).

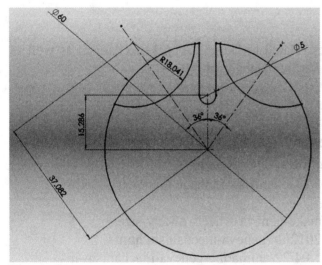

Figure P1

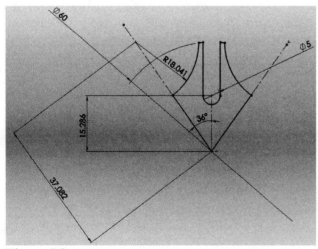

Figure P2

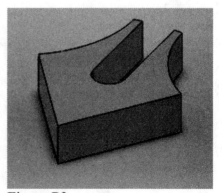

Figure P3

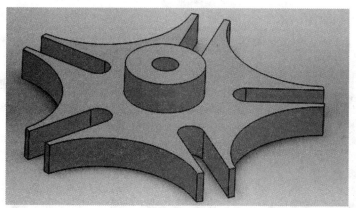

Figure P4

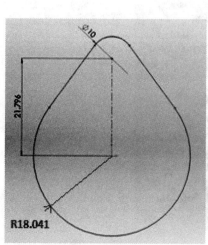

Figure P5

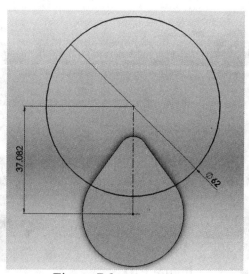

Figure P6

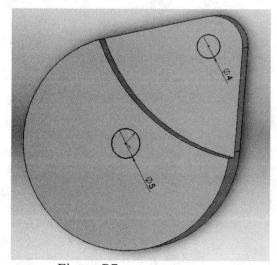

Figure P7

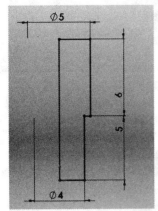

Figure P8

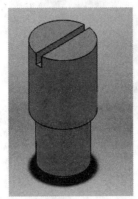

Figure P9

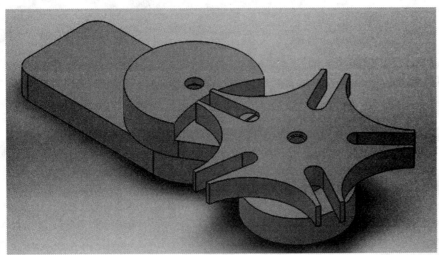

Figure P10

Event-based Motion Analysis

Objectives:

In this chapter you will learn:
- How Event-based Motion Analysis works
- About the role of Event-based Motion Analysis in the new design paradigm
- About how to simulate Event-based Motion Analysis SolidWorks routing

Introduction

SolidWorks Event-based Motion Analysis is the state-of-the-art motion analysis launched in 2010 (SolidWorks Corp., Chapter 15—Motion Studies, Reference 1) for handling real-life applications, such as are applicable in the beverage industry, assembly lines, and in generally in environments where motions are encountered. Machine designers typically follow the meta-process shown in Figure 28-1 while the new machining design process afforded by event-based simulation is shown in Figure 28-2.

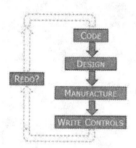

Figure 28-1 Meta-process

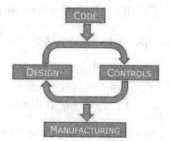

Figure 28-2 New machining design process

Event-based Motion View

With SolidWorks Simulation® Professional added in, one can use a Motion Analysis study to calculate the motion of an assembly that incorporates event-based motion control. To display the event-based view, from a motion study, select Motion Analysis from the Motion Study Type list (MotionManager toolbar) and click Event-based Motion View ▦ (right end of the MotionManager toolbar).

Tasks

Event-based motion requires a set of tasks. The tasks can be sequential or can overlap in time. Each task is defined by a triggering event and its associated task action. Task actions control or define motion during the task. The result of an event-based motion task is an action. Tasks are named and described as shown in Table 28-1.

Table 28-1

Name	📝	Displays task names. Click a cell to modify the name.
Description		Displays task descriptions. Click a cell to modify the description.

Triggers

A task trigger (Table 28-2) is the event that drives the motion control action for a task. One can define task triggers based on time, previous tasks, or sensed values, such as component position.

Table 28-2

Trigger		One can create triggers from: Sensors: Interference detection Detects collisions. Proximity Detects motion of a body crossing a line. Dimension Detects the relative position of components from dimensions. Previous tasks in the event schedule Start and finish times for task actions Double-click a cell to modify the trigger.
		Specifies triggering task.
		Specifies triggering sensor. You can include sensors to trigger actions only when you set the Alert condition in the Sensor PropertyManager.
		Specifies a time-based trigger.
Condition		Alert On. Triggers action when sensor is triggered. Alert Off. Triggers action when sensor is off. Task Start. Triggers action at start of a triggering task. Task End. Triggers action at end of a triggering task.
Time/Delay		For triggering tasks or sensors, displays time delay for starting the task action. Click a cell to modify the delay. For time-based triggers, displays start time of the task action. Click a cell to modify the time.

Actions

A task action defines or constrains the motion of one or more components in the assembly. One can define actions to suppress or activate mates, stop motion, or to change values for motors, forces, or torques. One can define a task action to: (1) Start, stop, or change the value of a constant speed motor, constant force, constant torque, or a servo motor; (2) Stop the motion; (3) Suppress a selected mate. Actions are defined by feature, action, value, duration, and profile (Table 28-3), while time is defined by start/finish (Table 28-4).

Table 28-3 Actions in EBMA

Feature		
Feature	⚏	Indicates linear motor action.
	⚙	Indicates rotary motor action.
	⚙ (2)	Indicates multiple motor action.
	⬀ (3)	Indicates action by a mixed selection of features.
	⬉	Indicates force action.
	↻	Indicates torque action.
	▯▯	Indicates suppressed or included mate action.
	🛑	Indicates stop motion.
		Double-click a cell to select one or more features. Select only features to which you can apply the same action.
Action		On. Turns on motors, forces, or torques, and includes selected mates for duration of action. Off. Turns off motors, forces, or torques, and excludes selected mates for duration of action. Change. Changes value of constant speed motors, servo motors, or constant forces or torques. Stop. Stops constant speed or servo motors. Click a cell to change the action.
Value		Specifies changed constant for changed constant speed motors, or constant forces or torques.
Duration		Specifies action duration for changed constant speed motors, or constant forces or torques.
Profile		Specifies shape of constant speed motor profile, or constant force or torque profile. The profile is calculated from the value and duration. Click a cell to change the profile.
	∠	Linear
	⊨	Constant Acceleration
	⊭	Cycloidal
	⊬	Harmonic
	⋈	Cubic

Time: Table 4

Start	Displays start time for task action.
End	Displays end time for task action.

Example 1

To understand how SolidWorks Event-based Motion Analysis (EBMA) works, we will consider the motion of a block through a maze shown in Figure 28-3. Simulate the EBMA.

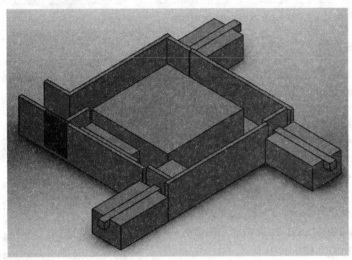

Figure 28-3 Maze configuration

SolidWorks Event-based Motion Analysis (EBMA) Simulation Solution

The parts and assembly are first created by the user; then *Motion Analysis* is *Added-In* before the simulation can proceed. The simulation starts with a *time trigger*, which can be equal to or greater than zero seconds. The subsequent tasks (or actions) are triggered to occur after the previous one finishes. We will now work through how to define the *Tasks*, *Triggers*, and *Actions* before carrying out the required simulation.

Preambles
1. Open the assembly document, **Assem_Maze**.
2. Click **Add-Ins** (see Figure 28-4).
3. Select Motion Study 2 (you could start with Study 1 or any other).
4. Expand the drop-down menu for motion-type at the bottom-left corner of the Graphics Window.
5. Select **SolidWorks Motion Analysis** (see Figure 28-5).
6. Click **OK**.

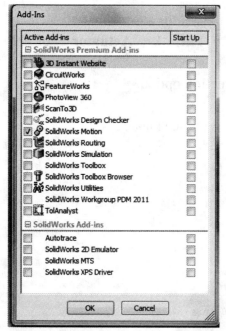

Figure 28-4 Add-Ins

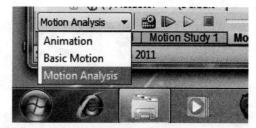

Figure 28-5 Motion Analysis option

Define Linear Actuators (Motors)

1. Click the **Motor** icon at the bottom of the *Motion Analysis* window
   For **Motor Type**, select **Linear Motor (Actuator)** (see Figure 28-6).
2. The **Motor PropertyManager** is automatically displayed.

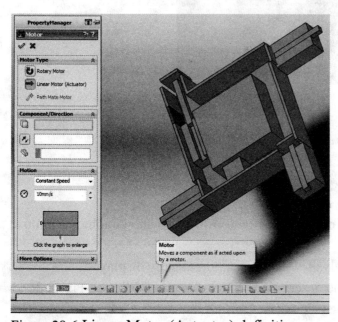

Figure 28-6 Linear Motor (Actuator) definition

3. Select **Face<1>@Actuator-1** of the actuator as the **Motor Location**.
4. **Motor Direction** is automatically assigned to **Face<1>@Actuator-1** of the actuator.
5. Reverse if required by clicking the **Reverse Direction** option.
6. For Motion, select **Servo Motor**.
7. For second Motion description, select **Displacement** (see Figure 28-7).

Note that:

Motor 5 = Motor 1

Motor 6 = Motor 2

Motor 7 = Motor 3

Motor 8 = Motor 4

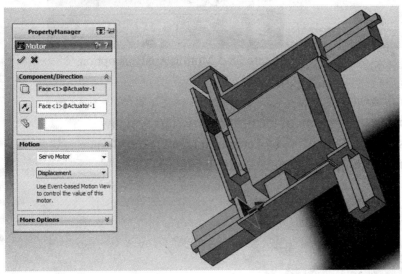

Figure 28-7 Motor PropertyManager

The procedure for defining motors is repeated for the other three motors.

Event-Based Motion Analysis Definitions

1. Click the **Expand MotionManager** at the bottom-right of the Graphics Window (see Figure 28-8).
   [The Event-Based Motion Analysis window is automatically displayed]
2. **Click** the + (**plus**) sign with the description "**Click here to add**" (see Figure 28-9) to add Tasks to the **Task Name** (see Figure 28-10).

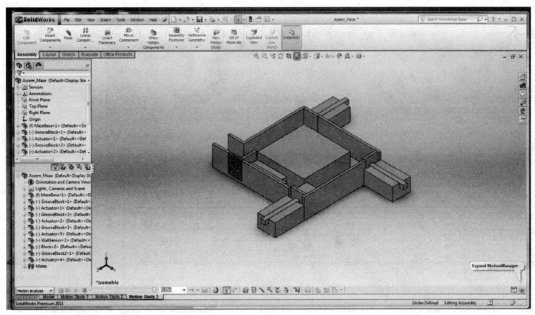

Figure 28-8 Expand MotionManager gateway to Event-based Motion Analysis

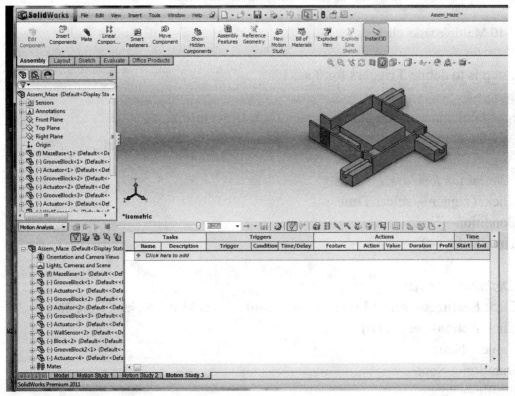

Figure 28-9 Adding Tasks

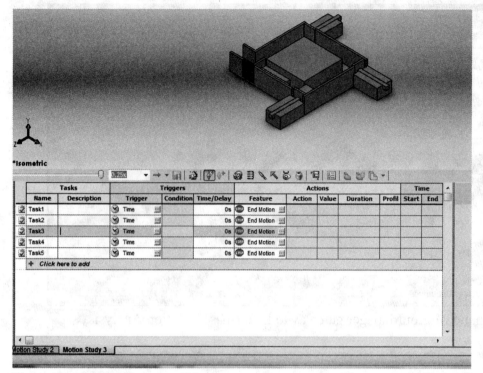

Figure 28-10 Multiple tasks clicked

Our first step is to define **Triggers for Task1**.

In the second column add descriptions under **Task Description**

3. Add the description: *2 last actuators off*.

Triggers Definition for Task 1:

4. Click **Trigger**— select **Time**
5. Condition—None
6. Time/Delay—0

Actions Definition for Task 1

7. Click **Features**—select **LinearMotor7 and LinearMotor8** (see Figure 28-11)
8. Click **Action**—select **Off**
9. Value—None
10. Duration—None
11. Profile—None

Figure 28-11 Actions definitions using linear motors

Our second step is to define **Triggers for Task2**.

In the second column add descriptions under **Task Description**
    12. Add the description: *Extend actuator 1*.

Triggers Definition for Task 2:
    13. Click **Trigger**— select **Task1** (see Figure 28-12).
    14. Condition— select **Task End**.
    15. Time/Delay—<None>.

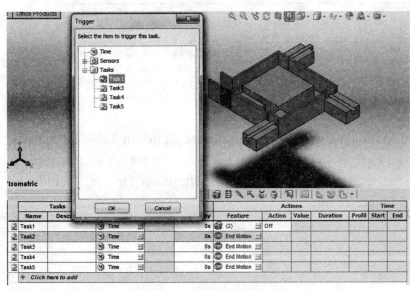

Figure 28-12 Trigger definition using Task 1

Actions Definition for Task 2

1. Click **Features**—select **LinearMotor5** (see Figure 28-13).
2. Click **Action**—select **Change** (see Figure 28-14).
3. Value—enter **155 mm**.
4. Duration—enter **1 s**.
5. Profile—select **Cycloidal**.
6. Start—enter **0**.
7. Finish—enter **1 s**.

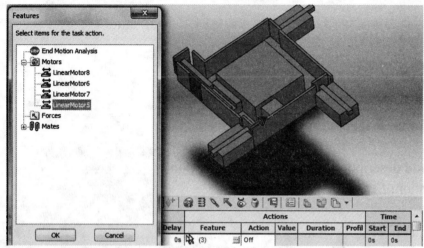

Figure 28-13 Actions-feature definition for Task 2 using first linear motor

Tasks		Triggers			Actions					Time	
Name	**Description**	**Trigger**	**Condition**	**Time/Delay**	**Feature**	**Action**	**Value**	**Duration**	**Profil**	**Start**	**End**
Task1		Time		0s	(2)	Off					
Task2		Task1	Task En	\<None\>	LinearMotor	Change ▼	0mm	0s	╱		
Task3		Time		0s	End Motion	On					
Task4		Time		0s	End Motion	Off					
Task5		Time		0s	End Motion	Change					
✚ **Click here to add**											

Figure 28-14 Actions-action definition for Task 2 with Change selected

Details of the Event-based Motion View for this example are shown in Table 28-5, based on actual simulation. As an exercise, readers should follow the entries in this table to complete the definitions for each task. The complete definitions for the Event-based Motion View are shown in Figure 28-15.

Table 28-5 Complete definitions for the Event-based Motion View

Tasks		Triggers			Actions				
Name	Descriptions	Trigger	Condition	Time/Delay	Feature	Action	Value	Dur	Profile
Task 1	2 last actuators off	Time	-	0 s	LMotor 7,8	Off	-	-	-
Task 2	Extend actuator 1	Task 1	Task End	<None>	LMotor 5	Change	155	1 s	Cyc
Task 3	Extend actuator 2	Task 2	Task End	<None>	LMotor 6	Change	155	1 s	Cyc
Task 4	Retract actuator 1	Task 3	Task End	<None>	LMotor 5	Change	-155	.5 s	Linear
Task 5	Actuator 3 on	Task 4	Task End	<None>	LMotor 7	On	-	-	-
Task 6	Extend actuator 3	Task 5	Task End	<None>	LMotor 7	Change	155	1 s	Cyc
Task 7	Retract actuator 3	Task 6	Task End	<None>	LMotor 7	Change	-155	.5 s	Linear
Task 8	Retract actuator 2	Task 6	Task End	<None>	LMotor 6	Change	-155	.5 s	Linear
Task 9	Actuator 4 on	Task 8	Task End	<None>	LMotor 8	On	-	-	-
Task 10	Extend actuator 4	Task 9	Task End	<None>	LMotor 8	Change	155	1 s	Cyc
Task 11		Time	-	5 s					

Key: LMotor = Linear Motor; Cyc = Cycloidal motion; Dur = Duration

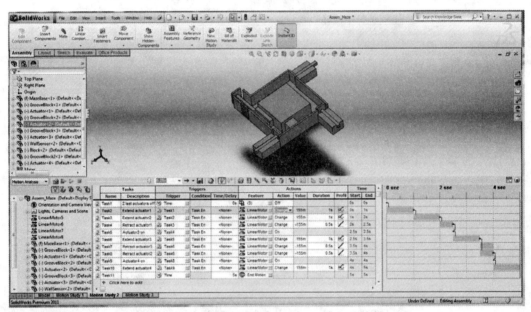

Figure 28-15 Event-based Motion View for the maze problem

Summary

To date, there is hardly any comprehensive step-by-step documentation on Event-based Motion Analysis that users can follow to understand how motion simulations can be realized. There are however, dozens of YouTube documentations on the subject, which are extremely challenging to follow in order to understand the detailed steps involved in Event-based Motion Analysis. This chapter fills the gap.

Reference

1. SolidWorks Corp. What's New in SolidWorks version 2010?
http://www.scribd.com/doc/87413953/167/Servo-Motors-for-Event-based-Motion-Analysis#outer_page_107

Chapter 29
Electrical Routing

Objectives:

In this chapter you will learn:

- How to **Add Routing** to SolidWorks and set routing options
- How to Manually create a route by **dragging** connectors from the electrical routing Design Library to create a harness

INTRODUCTION

When designing wiring systems, the preferred approach is to model the wiring as a wiring harness. A cable harness, also known as a wire harness, cable assembly, wiring assembly or wiring loom, is a string of cables and/or wires which are used to design wiring systems. This method has many advantages over modeling wires and cables individually. It allows SolidWorks to make many calculations for the user, and greatly reduces errors. There are two ways to model a wiring harness.

Electrical Routing with Clips

The easiest way to model a harness is to use clips. You can place clips as required in the assembly. The harness is then routed through the clips.

Using a From-To List

A *From-To List* automates much of the wiring process. It contains each of the wires and cables in the design, and identifies the wire type to use and the required connectivity. Using a *From-To List* eliminates the need to enter wiring data manually, makes the design process easier, and improves the accuracy of electrical routes.

CREATING THE HOUSING

The illustration in this chapter starts with creating a housing (an open container with a number of holes) through which electrical plugs will be positioned. The plugs are connected or wired using routing cables.

1. Open a **New SolidWorks Part** document.
2. Select the **Top Plane** and be **Sketch Mode**.
3. Select the **Centre Rectangle** and dimension it, length = 30 inches and width = 24 inches.
4. **Extrude Mid Plane** through a distance (height) = 6 inches.
   Figure 29-1 shows the solid obtained.
5. Click the **Shell** option.
6. Select *top of the object* and apply **Thickness** = 0.12 inches.

A shelled model is obtained as shown in Figure 29-1.

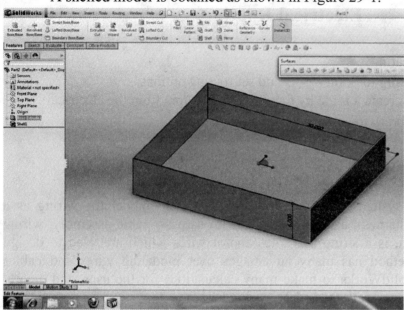

Figure 29-1 Shelled object to create the hollow circuit base

7. Select the right face and be Normal To (Perpendicular) mode to bring this face perpendicular to your view.

8. Be in Sketch Mode.

9. Sketch a circle and dimension it to be 5-inch diameter, position its centre 4-inches from the right edge and 1.75-inches from the top edge (see Figure 29-2).

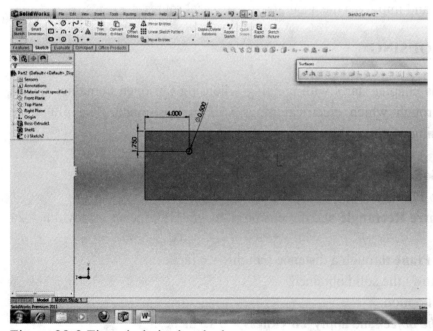

Figure 29-2 First circle is sketched

10. **Extrude Cut** the circle through the right face of the hollow housing (see Figure 29-3).

11. **Linear Pattern** 3 replications (see Figure 29-4).

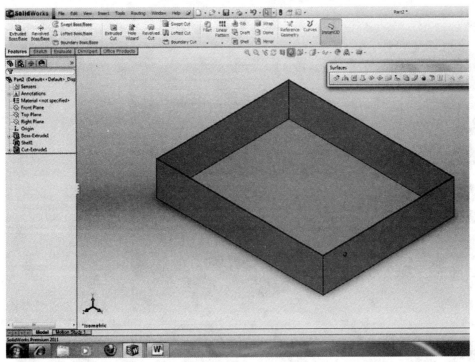

Figure 29-3 Extrude cut for first hole

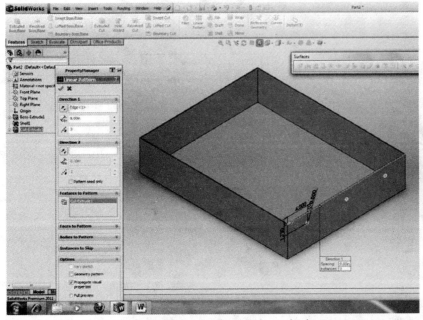

Figure 29-4 Linear patterning to obtain three holes

12. **Mirror** the 3 patterns about the Right Plane (see Figure 29-5).
13. **Linear Pattern** the 3 replications on the Right Plane downward at a distance of 2.5-inches (see Figure 29-6).
14. **Save** the 3D model as Circuit_Base (name).

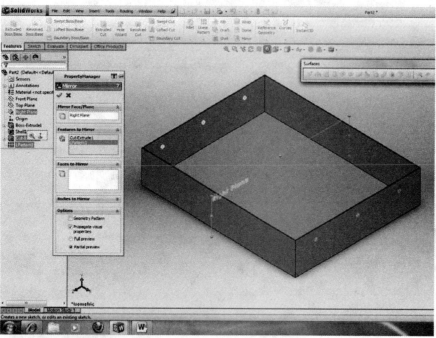

Figure 29-5 Mirrored holes about the Right Plane

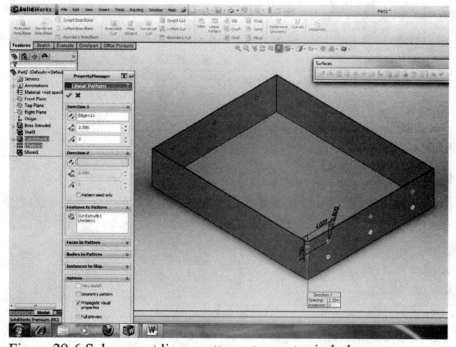

Figure 29-6 Subsequent linear patterns to create six holes

CREATING THE ELECTRICAL HARNESS

So far we have model the housing as a part. We need to open a New SolidWorks Assembly document and insert the housing as the first part in the assembly.

1. Open New SolidWorks Assembly.
2. Insert the first part as Circuit_Base (already modelled).

Before creating the electrical harness, first add in SolidWorks Routing.

3. Click **Tools > Add-Ins** (see Figure 29-7).
4. Select **SolidWorks Routing**.
   Select SolidWorks Routing in the Start Up column to activate Routing every time you start the SolidWorks application.
5. Click **OK**.

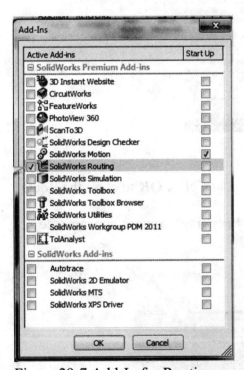

Figure 29-7 Add-In for Routing

Start the route by inserting route components, which vary by route type, into the assembly. These components define the start and end connection points of the path.

Next, you insert plug connectors from the Design Library into the assembly. When you drag a component from the Routing Library into the assembly, the Route Properties PropertyManager appears. When you close it, a new subassembly for the route harness opens in 3D sketch mode. Assembly colors appear gray in 3D sketch mode. In addition, the Auto Route PropertyManager appears.

6. Rotate the assembly to view the holes in the inside wall (see Figure 29-8).
7. From the electrical folder in the Routing Library, select **plug-5pindin.sldprt**.
8. **Drag** the plug into the assembly and mate it with the *middle hole* on the left side.

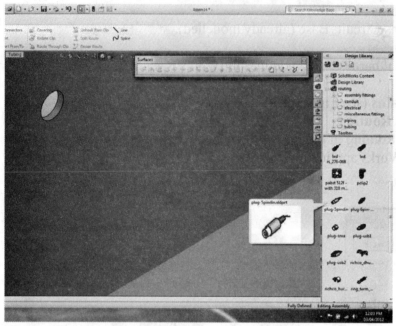

Figure 29-8 Drag a plug from Design Library

9. Click **Yes** if prompted to set options for routing, and click **OK** to close the Route Properties PropertyManager if it appears.
   The assembly turns gray and the **Auto Route PropertyManager** appears (see Figure 29-9).

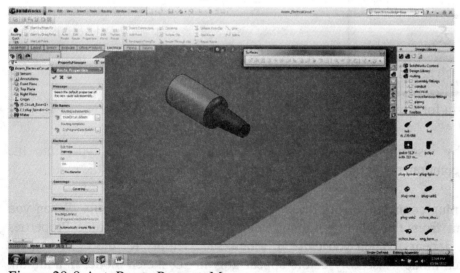

Figure 29-9 AutoRoute PropertyManager

10. Click **OK** to complete the insertion of the first plug (see Figure 29-10)

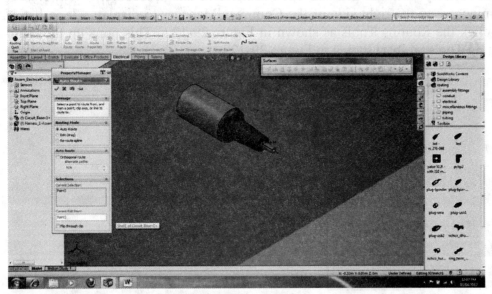

Figure 29-10 First plug is completely inserted

11. Rotate the assembly to view the six holes opposite the plug.
12. Drag another **plug-5pindin.sldprt** into the assembly and mate it with the lower middle hole on the side opposite the first plug (see Figure 29-11).

Figure 29-11 Second plug is completely inserted

CREATING THE ROUTE USING THE AUTOROUTE

Each route component has a CPoint. CPoints are the connection points from which you connect electrical route segments. When you drag routing components into the assembly, a small length of cable extends a stub from the CPoint. Most electrical routing options are available only when you edit a route. If you exit this mode, select **Edit Route** (**Electrical Routing toolbar**) to continue.

Next, you use **Auto Route** to route cables between the stub ends of two components. The **Auto Route PropertyManager** must be open to perform this procedure. If it is closed, right-click anywhere to the right side of the CommandManager to display a long list of tools. Then click the Routing Tools as shown in Figure 29-12.a. This pops up the **Auto Route** (Routing Tools toolbar) shown in Figure 29-12.b.

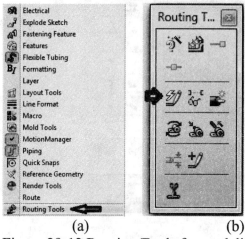

(a)   (b)

Figure 29-12 Routing Tools for modeling

1. Zoom in on one of the plugs in the assembly and select the stub at the end of its CPoint.
   The Auto Route PropertyManager displays the selected point in Current Selection.
2. Zoom to the other plug and select its end stub.
   The route connecting the two points appears (see Figure 29-13).
3. Click **OK**. Routing is complete (see Figure 29-14).

Figure 29-13 AutoRoute PropertyManager for routing the two plugs

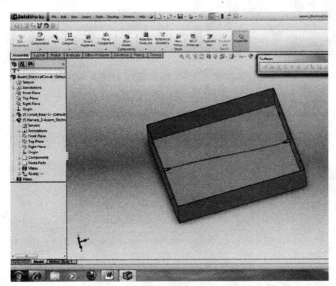

Figure 29-14 Routing of the two plugs

Next, specify the details of the wires running through the harness.

4. Click **Routing > Edit Wires** (Electrical Routing toolbar).
5. Click **Add Wire** in the PropertyManager (see Figure 29-15). The **Electrical Library** is automatically displayed (see Figure 29-16).
6. Select 20g blue.
   Selecting 20g blue assigns the 20-gauge blue wire part to the internal cable wire when you complete this procedure.
   20g blue appears in **Selected Wires**.
7. Click **OK** in the Electrical Library.

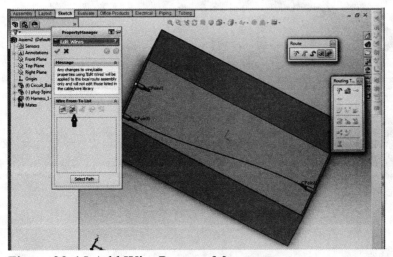

Figure 29-15 Add Wire PropertyManager

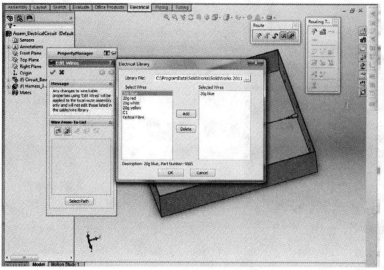

Figure 29-16 Electrical Library

8. Click **Select Path** in the **Edit Wires PropertyManager**.
9. Select the cable (see Figure 29-17).
10. Click **OK**.
11. Under **From - To Parameters**, select **1** for Pin for each plug.
12. Click **OK**.
    The harness contains a single 20-gauge blue wire connected to Pin 1 on each plug (see Figure 29-18).
13. Click **Exit 3D Sketch** and click **Edit Component** to exit assembly mode.

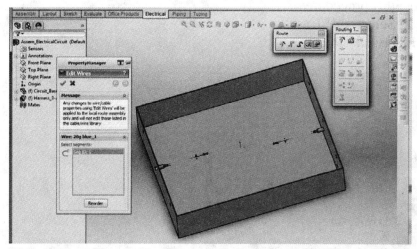

Figure 29-17 Select the cable

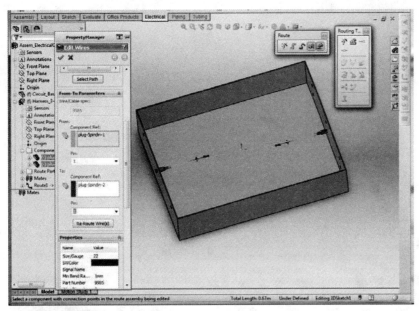

Figure 29-18 Pin assignment

Reference

http://help.solidworks.com/2012/English/SolidWorks/sldpiping/c_modeling_electrical_ro utes.htm

Chapter 30
Customized Internal and External Threads

Objectives:
In this chapter you will learn:
- How to model **customized internal threads**
- How to model **customized external threads**
- How to model **internal threads** to become **external threads**

The Hole Wizard tool is preferred for creating standard internal threads (nuts, drilled holes, etc.) while Toolbox is preferred for creating standard external threads (bolts, screws, etc.). However, when non-standard threads (internal/external) are required, it is still recommended to use the Hole Wizard tool for creating internal threads (select the nearest standard thread) while manual methods have to be used to create customized external threads.

Customized Internal Threads

As discussed, it is recommended to use the **Hole Wizard** tool for creating internal threads (select the nearest standard thread). For a 2-inch diameter, 5-inch long tube, a *1-12-tapped hole* is created using the **Hole Wizard** tool (see Figure 30-1).

Note that when you first click a surface before invoking the **Hole Wizard** tool, you will be in 2D Sketching mode, whereas when you do not first click a surface before invoking the **Hole Wizard** tool, you will be in 3D Sketching mode. This distinction is important because if affects how to go about dimensioning the position of the hole created.

The other point worth noting is that the threads created using the **Hole Wizard** tool could be designated as cosmetic threads and displayed accordingly.

Cosmetic Threads
For shaded display of cosmetic threads, click **Options**. On the **Document Properties** tab, select **Detailing**. Under **Display filter**, select or check the box for **Shaded cosmetic threads**.

Figure 30-1 Internal Threading using Hole Wizard

Customized External Threads

As discussed, manual methods have to be used to create customized external threads.

Problem Description

Let us consider a lens cap with base circle diameter of 4.9 inch, depth of 1.725 inch and 5-degree draft angle. External threads are to be created, 0.45 inch from the top of the larger diameter with a pitch of 0.25 inch and 2.5 revolutions while still maintaining 5-degree draft angle.

SolidWorks Solution

As could be observed from the problem description, this part cannot be automatically created using the **SolidWorks Toolbox** nor the **Design Library** because the part is not a standard one. To create the threads, we need to follow the principles based on **Swept Parts**, already covered.

1. Click **New** from the Menu bar, accepting imperial units.
2. Right-click **Front Plane** form the **FeatureManager**.
3. Click **Sketch** from the **CommandManager** or from the **Context tool bar**.
4. Click the **Circle** Sketch tool and sketch a circle centred at the origin.
5. Click **Smart Dimension** and dimension the diameter as **4.9**. (see Figure 30-2)

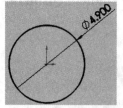

Figure 30-2 Sketch1

Insert and Extruded Base Feature

6. Click **Extruded Boss/Base** feature tool. (the Extrude PropertyManager appears as in Figure 30-3)
7. Accept the default Blind condition and set the Distance as 1.725. (see Figure 30-3)
8. Click the **Draft On/Off** button to activate it. (this makes it possible to model a drafted feature) [see Figure 30-3]
9. Click the **Draft Outward** box. (this make the draft to be outward) [see Figure 30-3]
10. Enter **5 deg** for Angle.
11. Click **OK** to complete the extrusion.

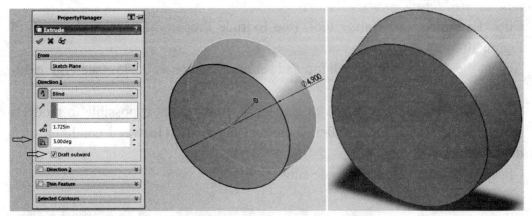

Figure 30-3 Extrusion of Sketch1 to create a draft

Creating a Sketch for Extruded Cut Feature

12. Click the *front face* of the smaller diameter.
13. Click **Sketch** from the **CommandManager** or from the **Context tool bar**.
14. Click the **Circle** Sketch tool and sketch a circle centred at the origin.
15. Click **Smart Dimension** and dimension the diameter as **3.875**. (see Figure 30-4)

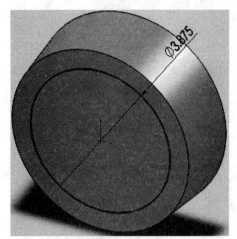

Figure 30-4 Sketch2 for Extrude Cut Feature

Insert and Extruded Base Feature

16. Click **Extruded Cut** feature tool. (the Extrude PropertyManager appears as in Figure 30-5)

17. Accept the default **Blind** condition and set the Distance as 0.275. (see Figure 30-5)

18. Click the **Draft On/Off** button to activate it. (this makes it possible to model a drafted feature) [see Figure 30-5; Note that the **Draft Outward** condition of **5 deg** is still active]

19. Click **OK** to complete the extrude cut.

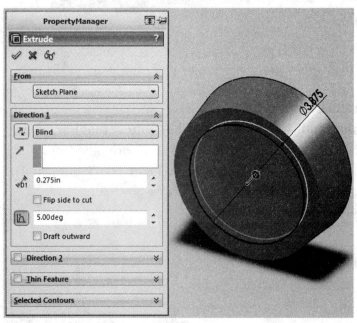

Figure 30-5 Extrude Cut Feature

Inserting the Shell Feature

20. Click the **Shell** Feature tool from the CommandManager (the Shell PropertyManager appears as shown in Figure 30-6).

21. Click *both the inner smaller and larger circular faces* (Face<1> and Face<2>] (see Figure 30-6).

22. Set shelling **Thickness** as **0.15**.

23. Click **OK** to complete shelling.

Figure 30-6 Shell1 PropertyManager

Creating a Part-Revolved Thin Cut Feature

24. Click the **Right-Plane**.

25. Click **Hidden Lines Visible** from the **Heads-Up View** toolbar. (see Figure 30-7)

26. Click **Sketch** from the **CommandManager** or from the **Context tool bar**.

27. Sketch *a horizontal dimension line*.

28. Click the *top slanted edge*.

29. Click **Convert Entities** to extract the edge.

30. Click the **left vertex** and drag it towards the right vertex.

31. Click **Smart Dimension** and dimension the slanting edge as **0.25**. (see Figure 30-8)

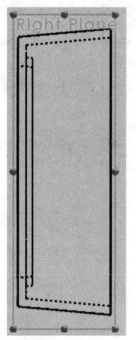
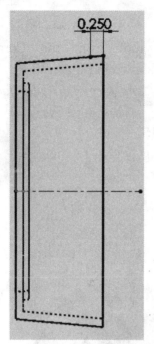

Figure 30-7   Figure 30-8

32. Click **Revolved Cut** from the **CommandManager** (a warning message appears as shown in Figure 30-9).

33. Accept the warning by clicking **Yes** (see Figure 30-10 for the revolved cut FeatureManager).

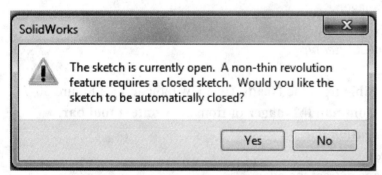

Figure 30-9 Open sketch warning

34. Expand the Thin Feature rollout and set the Thickness as 0.05. (see Figure 30-10)

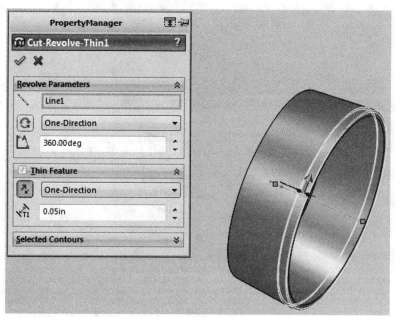

Figure 30-10 Revolved Cut FeatureManager

Creating Path for External Threads

35. Click **Top View** from the **View Orientation** tool.

36. Click *the top narrow strip face of the model*. (at the larger diameter) [see Figure 30-11]

37. Click **Features > Plane** and create a plane **Plane1**, **0.45** from the **Top**. (see Figure 30-12)

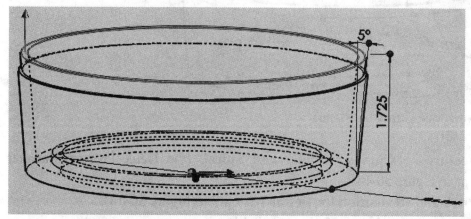

Figure 30-11 Selecting strip of the top face of the model

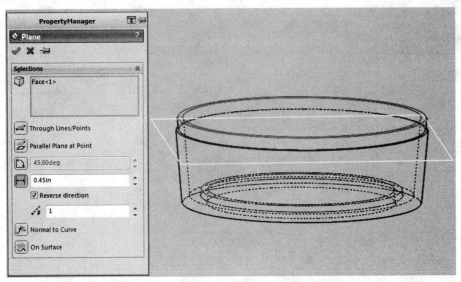

Figure 30-12 Plane1

38. Right-click **Plane1**.
39. Click **Sketch** from the **CommandManager** or from the **Context tool bar**.
40. Click the *inner circle of the narrow strip of the top face of the model*.
41. Click **Convert Entities** to extract the circle unto Plane1. (see Figure 30-13)

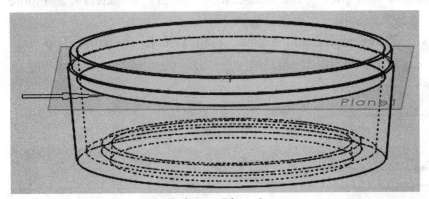

Figure 30-13 Converted Entity on Plane1

42. Click **Features > Curves > Helix and Spiral**. (the Helix PropertyManager appears as in Figure 30-14)
43. Select **Pitch and Revolution** for **Define By**: option (Figure 30-14).
44. Enter the value of **Pitch** as **0.25** (Figure 30-14).
45. Enter the **Number of Revolution** as **2.5** (Figure 30-14).
46. Click **OK** the complete the Path definition.
47. **Exit Sketch** (this is a very important step).

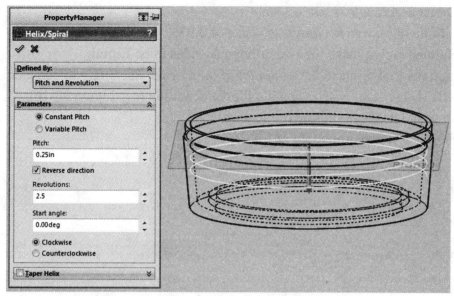

Figure 30-14 Helix definition to complete Path

Creating Profile for External Threads

48. Click **Features > Plane** (see Plane PropertyManager in Figure 30-15).
49. Click the **Normal to Curve** option (see Figure 30-15).
50. Click *one end point of the Helix* (see Figure 30-15).
51. Click the **Helix** from the graphics window (see Figure 30-15).
52. Click **OK** to define Plane2 which is orthogonal to the helix at any point.

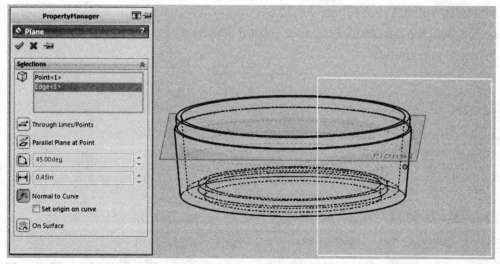

Figure 30-15 Plane2

53. Right-click **Plane2**.
54. Click **Sketch** from the **CommandManager** or from the **Context tool bar**.

55. Sketch a **Corner Rectangle**.

56. Dimension *a side of Corner Rectangle* to a size of **0.075**.

57. Use the **Relations** tool to make the two orthogonal sides to be **Equal**.

58. Use the **Relations** tool to make the *Midpoint of the Corner Rectangle* to coincide with the **Helix (Edge<1>)** by selecting the **Pierce** condition (see Figure 30-16).

59. Click **OK** to complete the definition of the profile.

60. **Exit Sketch** (this is a very important step).

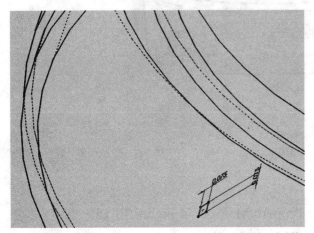

Figure 30-16 Hexagonal centre pierces the helix

Creating External Threads

Click Swept Boss/Base (the Sweep PropertyManager appears as in Figure 30-17).

Click **Profile** as **Sketch5 (Corner Rectangle)**.

Click **Path** as **Helix/Spiral1** (see Figure 30-17).

Click **OK** to complete the part modelling (see Figure 30-18).

Save the completed part model.

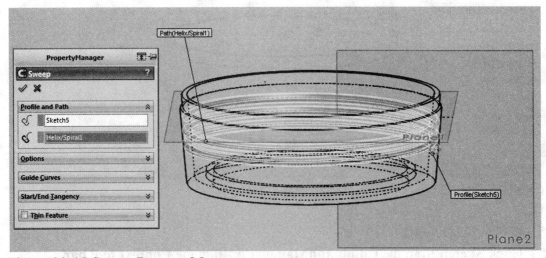

Figure 30-17 Sweep PropertyManager

Figure 30-18 Completed part model

Editing Features

Editing Features or Modification of Part Model involves a proper understanding of the FeatureManager (see Figure 30-19a). Our goal is to change the internal threads to external threads.

61. Suppress the Cut-Revolve-Thin feature (see Figure 30-19b).

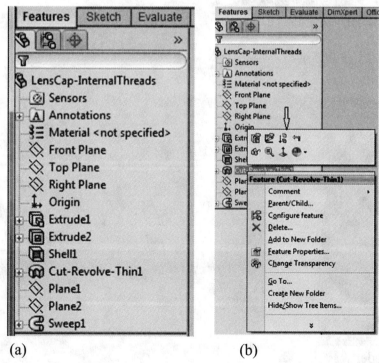

(a)   (b)

Figure 30-19 FeatureManager of the completed part model

62. Expand the **Sweep1** tree.

63. Right-click the *base sketch*, **Sketch4**.

64. Click **Edit Sketch** to be in Sketch mode.

65. Delete the *base sketch*, **Sketch4**.

66. Click the *outer circle of the narrow strip of the top face of the model*.

67. Click **Convert Entities** to extract the circle unto Plane1 (see Figure 30-20).

68. Exit Sketch (see Figure 30-21 for the modified part model).

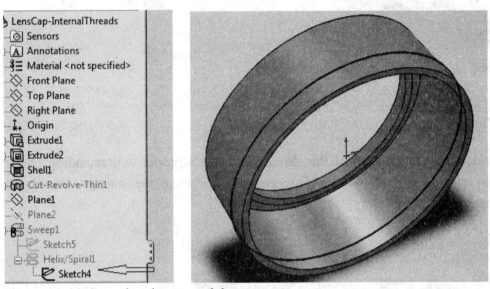

Figure 30-20 Completed part model

Figure 30-21 Modified part model

UNIFIED THREAD STANDARD

The **Unified Thread Standard** (UTS) defines a standard thread form and series—along with allowances, tolerances, and designations—for screw threads commonly used in the United States and Canada. It has the same 60° profile as the ISO metric screw thread used in the rest of the world, but the characteristic dimensions of each UTS thread (outer diameter and pitch) were chosen as an inch fraction rather than a round millimeter value. The UTS is currently controlled by ASME/ANSI in the United States.

Basic Profile

Each thread in the series is characterized by its major diameter D_{maj} and its pitch, P. UTS threads consist of a symmetric V-shaped thread (see Figure 30-22). In the plane of the thread axis, the flanks of the V have an angle of 60° to each other. The outermost 0.125 and the innermost 0.25 of the height H of the V-shape are cut off from the profile.

The pitch P is the distance between thread peaks. For UTS threads, which are single-start threads, it is equal to the lead, the axial distance that the screw advances during a 360° rotation. UTS threads do not usually use the pitch parameter; instead a parameter known as threads per inch (TPI) is used, which is the reciprocal of the pitch.

The basic profile of all UTS threads is the same as that of all ISO metric screw threads. Only the commonly used values for D_{maj} and P differ between the two standards.

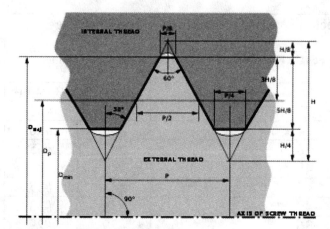

Figure 30-22 Basic profile

The relationship between the height H and the pitch P is found using the following equation:

$$H = \cos(30^o) \times P = \frac{\sqrt{3}}{2} \times P \approx 0.866 \times P$$

In an external (male) thread (e.g., on a bolt), the major diameter D_{maj} and the minor diameter D_{min} define *maximum* dimensions of the thread. This means that the external thread must end flat at D_{maj}, but can be rounded out below the minor diameter D_{min}. Conversely, in an internal (female) thread (e.g., in a nut), the major and minor diameters are *minimum* dimensions, therefore the thread profile must end flat at D_{min} but may be rounded out beyond D_{maj}.

The minor diameter D_{min} and effective pitch diameter D_p are derived from the major diameter and pitch as

$$D_{min} = D_{maj} - 2 \times \frac{5}{8} \times H = D_{maj} - \frac{5\sqrt{3}}{8} \times P = D_{maj} - 1.082532 \times P$$

$$D_p = D_{maj} - 2 \times \frac{3}{8} \times H = D_{maj} - \frac{3\sqrt{3}}{8} \times P = D_{maj} - 0.649519 \times P$$

Designation

The standard designation for a UTS thread is a number indicating the nominal (major) diameter of the thread, followed by the pitch measured in threads per inch. For diameters smaller than ¼ inch, the diameter is indicated by an integer number defined in the standard, for all other diameters, the value in inch is given. This number pair is optionally followed by the letters UNC, UNF or UNEF if the diameter-pitch combination is from the "coarse", "fine" or "extra fine" series, and may also be followed by a tolerance class.

Major diameter [in (mm)]	Threads per inch			Tap drill size	
	Coarse (UNC)	Fine (UNF)	Extra fine (UNEF)	Coarse	Fine
#0 = 0.0600 (1.5240)	–	80			3/64 in
#1 = 0.0730 (1.8542)	64	72		#53	#53
#2 = 0.0860 (2.1844)	56	64		#50	#50
#3 = 0.0990 (2.5146)	48	56		#47	#45
#4 = 0.1120 (2.8448)	40	48		#43	#42
#5 = 0.1250 (3.1750)	40	44		#38	#37
#6 = 0.1380 (3.5052)	32	40		#36	#33
#8 = 0.1640 (4.1656)	32	36		#29	#29
#10 = 0.1900 (4.8260)	24	32		#25	#21
#12 = 0.2160 (5.4864)	24	28	32	#16	#14
¼ (6.3500)	20	28	32	#7	#3
5/16 (7.9375)	18	24	32	F	I
3/8 (9.5250)	16	24	32	5/16 in	Q

7/16 (11.1125)	14	20	28	U	25/64 in
1/2 (12.7000)	13	20	28	27/64 in	29/64 in
9/16 (14.2875)	12	18	24	31/64 in	33/64 in
5/8 (15.8750)	11	18	24	17/32 in	37/64 in
3/4 (19.0500)	10	16	20	21/32 in	11/16 in
7/8 (22.2250)	9	14	20	49/64 in	13/16 in
1 (25.4000)	8	14*	20	7/8 in	59/64 in

*1-12 was formerly a widespread standard, but 1-14 is current UNF

Calculating the Major Diameter of a Numbered Screw Greater Than or Equal to 0

The following formula is used to calculate the major diameter of a numbered screw greater than or equal to 0:

Major diameter = Screw # × 0.013" + 0.060".

Example 1: A number 10 calculates as: #10 × 0.013" + 0.060" = 0.190" major diameter.

Example 2: #6-32 UNC 2B (major diameter: #6 × 0.013" + 0.060" = 0.1380 inch, pitch: 32 tpi)

Unified Miniature Screw Thread Series

A Unified Miniature screw thread series is defined in ANSI standard B1.10, for fasteners of 0.3 to 1.4 millimeters (0.0118 to 0.0551 inch) diameter. These sizes are intended for watches, instruments, and miniature mechanisms and are interchangeable with threads made to ISO Standard 68. These screw sizes are denoted by multiple zeroes, *i.e.* #000.

Calculating the Major Diameter of a Numbered Screw Greater Than or Equal to 0

The formula for number sizes smaller than size #0 is given by:

Major diameter = 0.060" - Zero size × 0.013"

Where with the zero size being the number of zeroes after the first

Example 3: A #00 screw is 0.047" diameter (0.060" – (2-1) × 0.013")

Example 4: A #000 screw is 0.034" diameter (0.060" – (3-1) × 0.013")

UNIFIED THREAD STANDARD

The **Unified Thread Standard (UTS)** defines a standard thread form and series—along with allowances, tolerances, and designations—for screw threads commonly used in the United States and Canada. UTS threads consist of a symmetric V-shaped thread. In the plane of the thread axis, the flanks of the V have an angle of 60° to each other. The outermost 0.125 and the innermost 0.25 of the height *H* of the V-shape are cut off from the profile.

Each thread in the series is characterized by its major diameter D_{maj} and its pitch, P. The geometry of the threads is fully defined based on dimensions that are based on the height and minor diameter.

The relationship between the height H and the pitch P is found using the following equation:

$$H = \cos(30^o) \times P = \frac{\sqrt{3}}{2} \times P \approx 0.866 \times P$$

(1)

The minor diameter D_{min} is derived from the major diameter and pitch as

$$D_{min} = D_{maj} - 2 \times \frac{5}{8} \times H = D_{maj} - \frac{5\sqrt{3}}{8} \times P = D_{maj} - 1.082532 \times P$$

(2)

EXTERNAL THREADS

The basic profile of an external thread is shown in Figure 30-23. An isosceles triangle is constructed such its height y is equal to $6H/8$. A horizontal line is drawn at a distance of H/8 from the vertical vertex of the triangle to produce a landing of P/8 in dimension. Hence, the actual height of the thread is $5H/8$. This height is obtained from subtracting H/8 from the height of the isosceles triangle $(6H/8 - H/8)$. There are three dimensions that are of interest to us for constructing the profile of external threads: base-dimension, top-dimension, and height.

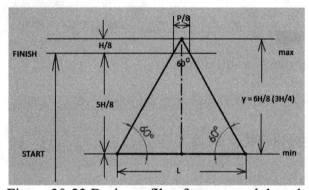

Figure 30-23 Basic profile of an external thread

$$\tan 60^o = \frac{(H/8)}{(P/8)} = \frac{(6H/8)}{L}$$

[Note: we have omitted dividing 'fall' (P/8 and L respectively) by 2 for both numerator and denominator, since this will cancel out]

$$L = \frac{6P}{8} = 0.75 \times P$$

Alternatively, we can obtain the length from the following:

$$\sin 60^o = \frac{(6H/8)}{L}$$

$$L = \frac{6H}{8\sin 60^o} = \frac{6 \times 0.866P}{8\sin 60^o} = 0.75 \times P$$

$$h = \frac{5H}{8} = \frac{5 \times 0.866P}{8} = 0.54125 \times P$$

INTERNAL THREADS

The basic profile of an internal thread is shown in Figure 30-24. An isosceles triangle is constructed such its height y is equal to $7H/8$. A horizontal line is drawn at a distance of H/4 or 2H/8 from the vertical vertex of the triangle to produce a landing of P/4 in dimension. Hence, the actual height of the thread is $5H/8$. This height is obtained from subtracting 2H/8 from the height of the isosceles triangle $(7H/8 - 2H/8)$. There are three dimensions that are of interest to us for constructing the profile of external threads: base-dimension, top-dimension, and height.

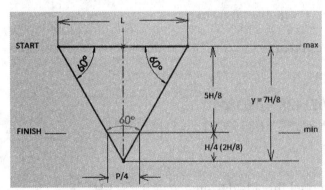

Figure 30-24 Basic profile of an internal thread

$$\tan 60^o = \frac{(H/4)}{(P/4)} = \frac{(7H/8)}{L}$$

[Note: we have omitted dividing 'fall' (P/4 and L respectively) by 2 for both numerator and denominator, since this will cancel out]

$$L = \frac{7P}{8} = 0.875 \times P$$

Alternatively, we can obtain the length from the following:

$$\sin 60^o = \frac{(7H/8)}{L}$$

$$L = \frac{7H}{8\sin 60^o} = \frac{7 \times 0.866P}{8\sin 60^o} = 0.875 \times P$$

$$h = \frac{5H}{8} = \frac{5 \times 0.866P}{8} = 0.54125 \times P$$

We now summarize the quantities needed for defining external and internal threads in Table 1.

Table 1 Parameters for external and internal threads

	External Thread	**Internal Thread**
$L_{bottom} = L$	$0.75 \times P$	$0.875 \times P$
L_{top}	$P/8$	$P/4$
h	$0.54125 \times P$	$0.54125 \times P$
D_{helix}	$D_{min} = D_{maj} - 1.082532 \times P$	D_{max}

Example 5

Determine the dimensions required to model threads designated as $1\frac{1}{2} - 14UNF - 3A$

Solution

The threads are external since the last letter is A.

The maximum diameter is $D_{max} = 1.5''$.

Teeth per inch is 14, therefore the pitch, $P = 1/14 = 0.071428$

$L_{bottom} = \quad 0.75 \times P = 0.75 \times 0.071428 = 0.05357''$

$L_{top} \quad\quad P/8 = 0.071428/8 = 0.0089''$

$h \quad\quad 0.54125 \times P = 0.54125 \times 0.071428 = 0.03866''$

$D_{helix} \quad D_{min} = D_{maj} - 1.082532 \times P = 1.5 - 1.082532/14 = 1.422676''$

Example 6

Determine the dimensions required to model threads designated as $1\frac{1}{2} - 14UNF - 3B$

Solution

The threads are external since the last letter is B.

The maximum diameter is $D_{max} = 1.5''$.

Teeth per inch is 14, therefore the pitch, $P = 1/14 = 0.071428''$

$L_{bottom} = \quad 0.875 \times P = 0.875 \times 0.071428 = 0.0625''$

$L_{top} \quad\quad P/4 = 0.071428/8 = 0.017857''$

$h \quad\quad 0.54125 \times P = 0.54125 \times 0.071428 = 0.03866''$

$D_{helix} \quad D_{maj} = 1.5''$

References
http://www.nollinc.com/index.php/contents/Products/Leadscrews/UNV.html
http://en.wikipedia.org/wiki/Unified_Thread_Standard

Exercises
1. Use the **Unified Thread Standard (UTS)** theory presented in this chapter to model *external* threads for the problem definition of the completed part model of Figure 30-18.

2. Use the **Unified Thread Standard (UTS)** theory presented in this chapter to model *external* threads for the problem definition of the completed part model of Figure 30-21.

Chapter 31
Sustainability Design for Parts

Objectives:

In this chapter you will learn:

- About SolidWorks Sustainability
- How to use the SolidWorks Sustainability tools to analyze the environmental impact of a design throughout the life cycle of a product

Introduction

SolidWorks Sustainability evaluates the environmental impact of a design throughout the life cycle of a product. The engineer or designer can compare results from different designs to ensure a sustainable solution for the product and the environment. Sustainability measures the following areas of environmental impact: carbon footprint, energy consumption, air acidification, and water eutrophication. These are briefly defined.

Carbon Footprint - This is a measure of carbon dioxide and equivalents, such as carbon monoxide and methane that are released into the atmosphere primarily by burning fossil fuels.

Energy Consumption - All forms of nonrenewable energy consumed over the entire life cycle of the product.

Air Acidification - Acidic emissions occur, such as sulfur dioxide and nitrous oxides, which eventually lead to acid rain.

Water Eutrophication - Contamination of water ecosystems is due to waste water and fertilizers, resulting in algae blooms and the eventual death of plant and animal life.

SolidWorks measures the environmental impact based on the following parameters:
- Materials used
- Manufacturing process and region
- Transportation and use region
- End of life disposal

SolidWorks Solution Procedure

SolidWorks follows five steps in environmental impact assessment on a part:
1. Activating the Sustainability Application
2. Selecting a Material
3. Setting the Manufacturing and Use Options
4. Setting the Transportation and Use Options
5. Comparing Similar Materials

Problem Description

This example uses Sustainability to perform an environmental impact analysis of a part. We analyze a common part used in holding dish in the kitchen shown in Figure 31-1.

Figure 31-1 Model for study

Activate the Sustainability Application

1. Start a New SolidWorks document.
2. Open the part for sustainability study, **dish_container.sldprt**.
3. Click **Sustainability (Tools toolbar)** or **Tools > Sustainability**. (see Figure 31-2).
   The application opens in the **Task Pane** (see Figure 31-3).

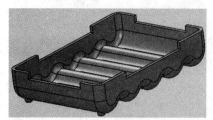
Figure 31-2 Sustainability study gateway

4. Click 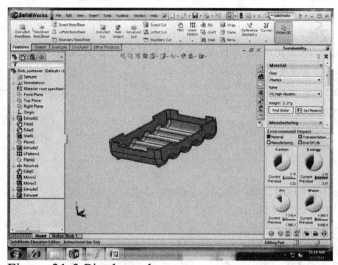to keep the **Task Pane** open (see Figure 31-3).

Figure 31-3 Pin the task pane

Selecting a Material

Select the material used for the part.
1. Under **Material** (see Figure 31-4):
    a. In **Class**, select **Plastic**s.
    b. In **Name**, select **PC High Viscosity**.
    SolidWorks displays the part's weight. The **Environmental Impact** dashboard at the bottom of the **Task Pane** provides real-time feedback about the environmental impact of the engineer's or designer's design.

Figure 31-4 Material selection

Setting the Manufacturing and Use Options

Select the manufacturing process and the regions where the part is manufactured and used.
1. Under **Manufacturing**, in **Process**, select **Injection Molded** (see Figure 31-5).
2. For **Region**, click **North America** on the map (see Figure 31-5).

    On each Sustainability map, Japan has its own region.

Figure 31-5 Manufacturing process and regions related to part

3. Under **Transportation and Use**, for **Use Region**, click **North America** (see Figure 31-6).

    Data is not available for all regions. Regions that contain data are highlighted when the engineer or designer hovers over them.

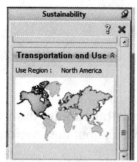

Figure 31-6 Regional identification

Comparing Similar Materials

Now the engineer or designer sets the baseline material and compare it with other materials, in order to minimize the environmental impact, using the **Environmental Impact** dashboard.

1. At the bottom of the **Task Pane**, click **Set Baseline** (see Figure 31-7).
   The **Baseline** bar for each environmental impact adjusts to show the values for the selected material, **PC High Viscosity** (see Figure 31-8).

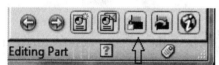

Figure 31-7 Baseline selection

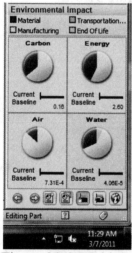

Figure 31-8 PC high viscosity

Next the engineer or designer tries to find a similar material that is a better environmental choice.

2. Under **Material**, click **Find Similar** (see Figure 31-9).

The dialog box displays the current material with values for multiple parameters.

Figure 31-9 Material selection continues

3. Set these values (see Figure 31-10):

Property	Condition
Density	~ (Approximately)
Tensile Strength	> (Greater than)

4. Click **Find Similar** next to the list in the dialog box (see Figure 31-10).
A list of similar materials appears. The engineer or designer selects materials from this list to compare them to the original material. The **Environmental Impact** dashboard at the bottom of the dialog box gives the engineer or designer an intermediate feedback on the selections made.
To filter the list, select the checkbox next to the materials to list and click **Show** selected only.

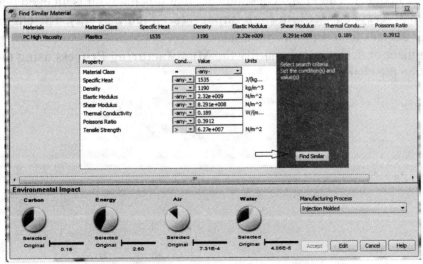

Figure 31-10 Set values

5. Under the **Materials** column, select **Acrylic (Medium-high impact)**.
   Click the *name of the material, not the checkbox*. Click **Accept** (see Figure 31-11).
   In the dialog box's Environmental Impact dashboard, a green bar for Selected appears above the black bar for Original for all four impact areas. The pie charts are updated.

   The bar's green color and shorter length indicate that the selected material, Acrylic (Medium-high impact), is a better environmental choice than the original material, PC High Viscosity, represented by the black baseline (see Figure 31-11).

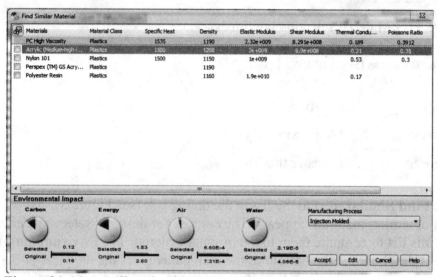

Figure 31-11 Acrylic selection

6. Select **Nylon 101** to see how it compares to the original material. The bars and pie charts are updated. The visual cues indicate that this material is an even better choice than **Acrylic (Medium-high impact)** (see Figure 31-12). The engineer or designer decides to accept this material.
   The engineer or designer can modify the **Manufacturing Process** using the menu next to the pie charts.

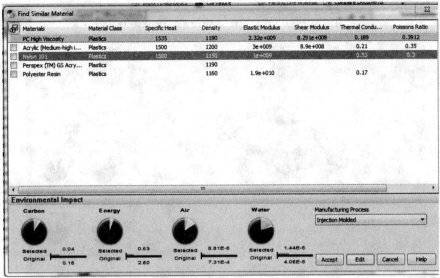

Figure 31-12 Nylon as an option

7. Click **Accept** (see Figure 31-13).
   The dialog box closes.

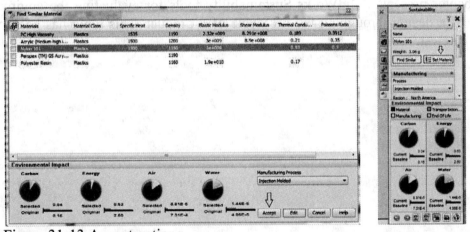

Figure 31-13 Accept options

In the **Task Pane,** under **Material, Plastics Nylon 101** is the current material.
The Environmental Impact dashboard is updated.

8. In the **Task Pane,** under **Material,** click **Set Materials** (see Figure 31-14).
   The material for the part is updated as **Plastics Nylon 101** in the
   FeatureManager (see Figure 31-14)

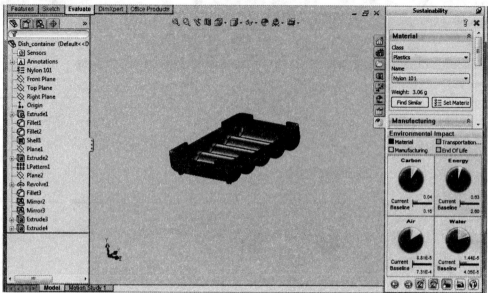

Figure 31-14 Optimal solution

Summary

This chapter presents SolidWorks Sustainability tools for evaluating the environmental impact of a design throughout the life cycle of a product. This topic has become a hot area of interest.

Exercises

Evaluate the environmental impact using SolidWorks Sustainability tools on the parts shown in Figure 31-P-1 to P-4; files are available in the resources archive for this book.

1. Pulley

Figure 31-P-1 Part for which the mold is being designed: pulley

2. Bowl

Figure 31-P-2 Part for which the mold is being designed: bowl

3. Plastic cover

Figure 31-P-3 Part for which the mold is being designed: plastic cover

4. Sump

Figure 31-P-4 Part for which the mold is being designed: sump

Chapter 32
Geometric Dimensioning & Tolerancing

Objectives:
In this chapter you will learn:

- How to interpret diagram applications specifying maximum material condition (MMC) and least material condition (LMC)
- How to determine geometric tolerances for produced sizes at MMC and LMC
- How to insert tolerances to drawings
- How to insert half-, offset-, and aligned-section views to drawings

INTRODUCTION

Conventional tolerancing refers to tolerances related to dimensioning practices without regard to geometric tolerancing. On the other hand, geometric tolerancing is the dimensioning and tolerancing of individual features of parts in which the permissible variations relate to characteristic form, profile, orientation, run out, or the relationship between features. In this chapter, we will consider conventional tolerancing then move on to geometric tolerancing.

There are three systems for applying dimensions and tolerances to a drawing: baseline, chain and direct. Let us illustrate the concept of dimensional tolerance built-up by using unspecified tolerance value of **±0.2** for the following examples (Figures 32-1 to 32-3).

Baseline Dimensioning is a common method of dimensioning machines parts whereby each feature dimension originates from a common surface, axis, or center plane. Tolerance build up is less likely to occur than when using chain dimensioning (see Figure 32-1). There are two dimensions between X and Y (16 and 26); hence the tolerance accumulation is 2(±2) = ±4.

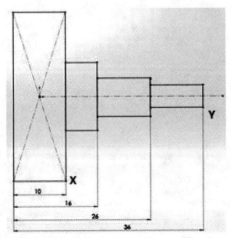

Figure 32-1 Baseline dimensioning

Chain Dimensioning also known as point-to-point dimensioning is a method of dimensioning form one feature to the next. Tolerance build up is more likely to occur than when using baseline dimensioning (see Figure 32-2). Each dimension is dependent on the previous dimension or dimensions. There are three dimensions between X and Y (6, 10 and 10); hence the tolerance accumulation is $3(\pm2) = \pm6$.

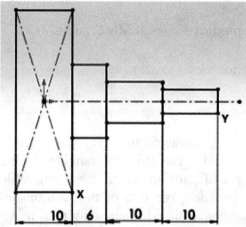

Figure 32-2 Chain dimensioning

Direct Dimensioning is applied to control the size or location of one or more specific features. Tolerance build up is least likely to occur than when using the other types of dimensioning (see Figure 32-3). There is one dimension between X and Y (26); hence the tolerance accumulation is ±2.

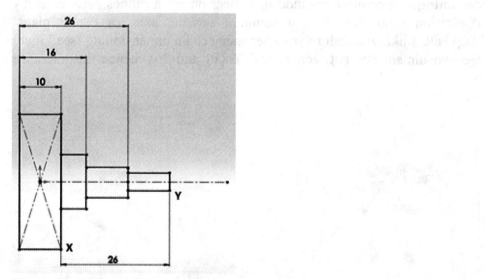

Figure 32-3 Direct dimensioning

Tolerance Study Using SolidWorks

When a feature is sketched and any one side is dimensioned and the value accepted by clicking the OK sign, the Dimension PropertyManager automatically appears as shown in Figure 32-4.

Figure 32-4 Dimensions PropertyManager

Select the Limit option to display the **Upper (+)** and **Lower (-)** level options. In this illustration we dimension the bottom horizontal edge as 75 and accept this value.

1. Click the **Tolerance/Precision** toolbar
2. Select **Limit** option
3. Fill the **Upper Limit** as **1** and **Lower Limit** as **1** (see Figure 32-5a)
   Maximum dimension becomes 76 and Minimum dimension becomes 74; (see Figure 32-5b)
4. Click **OK**

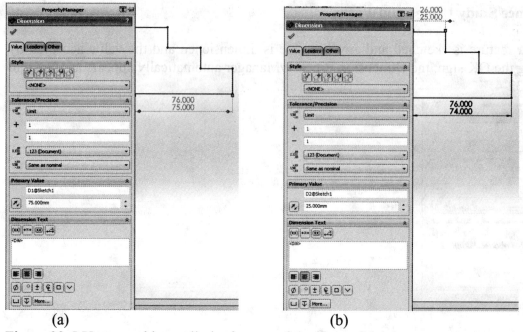

(a)   (b)

Figure 32-5 Upper and lower limits for one of the lines of the feature

Chain Dimensioning Tolerance Calculation

Repeat for the two top (leftmost) lines starting with the length of 25 and using upper limit =1 and lower limit = -1 as shown in Figure 32-6a. The horizontal length A is not dimensioned. Its length is dependent of the tolerances of the two top leftmost horizontal lengths.

We will now determine the tolerance of length A. The principle used is to determine the maximum length of A and the minimum length of A. The difference will give us the indication of tolerance accumulation for the dimensions used in the computation.

Maximum Length of A:
Length A will be maximum when the overall length is at its longest value and the other distances are at their shortest values.

Minimum Length of A:
Length A will be minimum when the overall length is at its shortest value and the other distances are at their longest values.

A Max	A Min
76	74
-24	-26
-24	-26
28	22

The difference between A (Max and Min) is 28 – 22 = 6. This illustration describes the chain dimensioning concept.

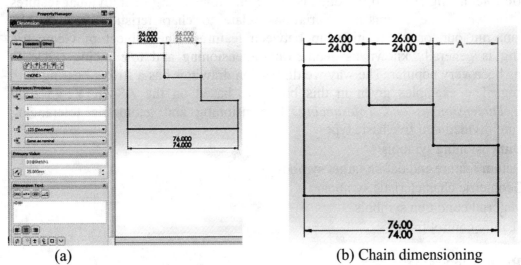

(a)   (b) Chain dimensioning

Figure 32-6 Upper and lower limits for one of the lines of the feature

Baseline Dimensioning *Tolerance Calculation*

Figure 32-7a shows the SolidWorks Dimensioning tool for tolerancing. We will now determine the tolerance of length A.

A Max	A Min
76	74
-49	-51
27	23

The difference between A (Max and Min) is 27 – 23 = 4.

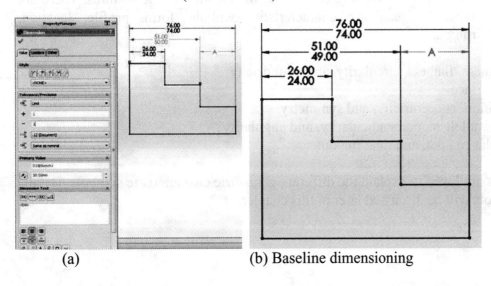

(a)   (b) Baseline dimensioning

Figure 32-7 Upper and lower limits for one of the lines of the feature

GEOMETRIC DIMENSIONING AND TOLERANCING (GD&T)

Geometric tolerancing refers to the dimensioning and tolerancing of individual features of parts in which the permissible variations relate to characteristic form, profile, orientation, run out, or the relationship between features. The subject of Geometric tolerancing is generally known as geometric dimensioning and tolerancing (GD&T) which has been very popular. The way we dimension drawings has a strong bearing with tolerancing. The examples given in this book are based on the ASME Y14.5-2009 standard, *Dimensioning and Tolerancing*. Dimensioning and geometric tolerancing symbols are divided into five basic types:
- Dimensioning symbols
- Datum feature and datum target symbols
- Geometric characteristic symbols
- Material condition symbols
- Feature control frame.

Datum Reference Frame

Datum features are selected based on the importance to the design of the part. In general there are three orthogonal datum features to be selected: the datum reference frame (DRF). These three datum features are referred to as the *primary datum*, *secondary datum*, and *tertiary datum*. The primary datum is the most important, followed by the two others according to their placement in the *GD&T Note*.

Geometric Characteristic Symbols

Geometric Characteristic Symbols are symbols used in GD&T to provide specific controls related to the form of an object, the orientation of the features, the outline of features, the relationship of features to an axis, or the location of the features. There are normally five types of geometric characteristic symbols: form, profile, location, orientation, and run out.

Form: straightness, flatness, circularity, and cylindricity
Profile: line, surface
Location: position, concentricity, and symmetry
Orientation: parallelism, perpendicularity, and angularity
Run out: circular run out, and total run out

Two examples are given to explain the different geometric characteristic symbols. Details of these symbols will be discussed later in this chapter.

Example 1: A block is shown in Figure 32-8 for which we want to define the datum reference frame (DFR).

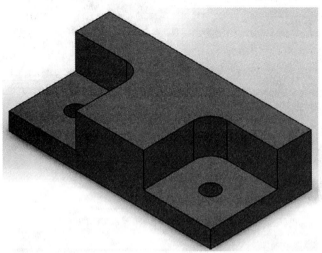

Figure 32-8 A block

1. Click the **DimXpertManager**. (see Figure 32-9)
2. Click the **Auto Dimension Scheme** option. (see Figure 32-9)

   The **Auto Dimension Scheme** Manager is automatically displayed. (see Figure 32-10)

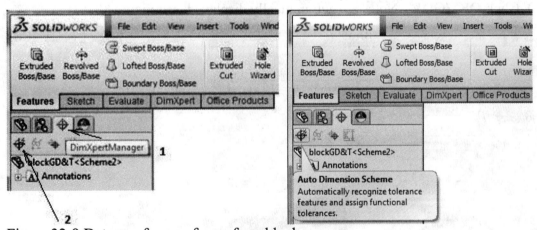

Figure 32-9 Datum reference frame for a block

3. Under **Settings > Part Type**, click the **Prismatic** radio button. (see Figure 32-10)
4. Under **Settings > Tolerance Type**, click the **Geometric** radio button. (see Figure 32-10)
5. Under **Datum Selection**, click the *back face* of the block as **Primary datum (A)**.
6. Under **Datum Selection**, click the *rightmost face* of the block as **Secondary datum (B)**.
7. Under **Datum Selection**, click the *bottom face* of the block as **Tertiary datum (C)**.

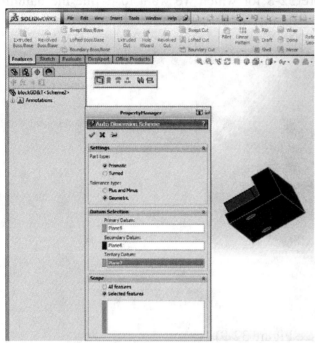

Figure 32-10 The *Auto Dimension Scheme* Manager is automatically displayed

8. Under **Scope**, click the **Selected features** radio button. (see Figure 32-11)
9. Select the two holes. (see Figure 32-11)
10. Click **OK**. (GD&T Notes are automatically displayed; see Figure 32-12)

Figure 32-11 The two holes are chosen as the Selected features

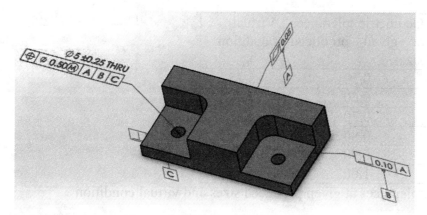

Figure 32-12 GD&T Notes for the block model

Referring to Figure 32-12, we find that:
- The back face of the block is designated A; it has a *Form* of *Flatness*
- The right face of the block is designated B; it has an *Orientation* of *Perpendicularity* with respect to A
- The bottom face of the block is designated C; it has an *Orientation* of *Perpendicularity* with respect to A

Applying Maximum Material Condition

Maximum material condition (MMC) is the condition in which a feature contains the maximum amount of material within the stated limits of size. When MMC is used in the feature control frame, the given geometric tolerance is maintained when the feature is produced.

External Feature:
MMC – Produced size + Given geometric tolerance = Applied geometric tolerance

Internal Feature:
Produced size - MMC + Given geometric tolerance = Applied geometric tolerance

In Figure 32-12, there are two types of tolerances: feature tolerance and positional tolerance. The feature tolerance is for the hole while positional tolerance is for locating the centre of the hole. Let us distinguish these tolerances.

MMC hole = 5 - 0.25 = 4.75
LMC hole = 5 + 0.25 = 5.25
Given geometric tolerance = 0.50

Geometric tolerance at given produced sized of 4.85 = 4.85 – 4.75 + 0.50 = 0.60.
Virtual condition = 4.85 + 0.60 = 5.45.
The calculations for geometric tolerances at given produced sizes and virtual condition are listed in Figure 32-13.

	Possible produced size	Geometric tolerances at given produced sizes	Virtual condition
MMC →	4.75	0.50	5.25
	4.85	0.60	5.45
	4.95	0.70	5.65
	5.05	0.80	5.85
	5.15	0.90	6.05
LMC →	5.25	1.00	6.25

Figure 32-13 Geometric tolerances at given produced sizes and virtual condition

Expanding the **DimXpertManager** reveals the datum reference frame made up of planes A (Flatness2), B (Perpendicularity1 with respect to A), and C (Perpendicularity1 with respect to A), as well as the two hole features (Simple Hole3 and Simple Hole4) (see Figure 32-14).

Save the object together with the GD&T features (see Figure 32-14).

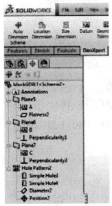

Figure 32-14 GD&T features for the block model

Example 2: Another example involves a revolved shape about an axis in which four holes are drilled through the top portion. Figures 32-15 and 32-16 show pertinent dimensions with tolerances, while Figure 32-17 shows the object.

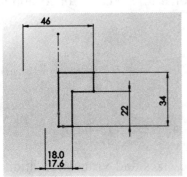
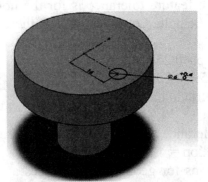

Figure 32-15 Sketch for creating the model   Figure 32-16 Sketch for creating a hole

The following steps show the SolidWorks GD&T tools required:

1. Click the **DimXpertManager**.
2. Click the **Auto Dimension Scheme** option.
   The **Auto Dimension Scheme** Manager is automatically displayed.
3. Under **Settings > Part Type**, click the **Prismatic** radio button.
4. Under **Settings > Tolerance Type**, click the **Geometric** radio button.
5. Under **Datum Selection**, click the *bottom face* of the upper boss as **Primary datum (A)**.
6. Under **Datum Selection**, click the *outer face* of the lower boss as **Secondary datum (B)**.
   [See Figure 32-17 for the model and GD&T features and descriptions]

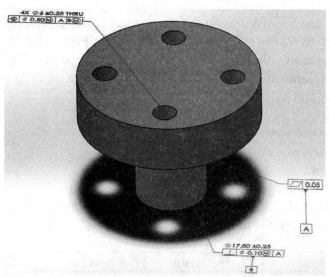

Figure 32-17 GD&T features and descriptions for the model

As could be observed, the datum A is a flat surface with tolerance of 0.05 while datum B is perpendicular to A with a tolerance of 0.10 with maximum material condition related. There are four holes with limits shown. With respect to datum A and datum B (only two in this case), the holes have:

MMC hole = 6 - 0.25 = 5.75
LMC hole = 6 + 0.25 = 6.25
Given geometric tolerance = 0.50 (M)

Geometric tolerance at given produced sized of 5.85 = 5.85 – 5.75 + 0.50 = 0.60.
Virtual condition = 5.85 + 0.60 = 6.45.
The calculations for geometric tolerances at given produced sizes and virtual condition are listed in Figure 32-18.

	Possible produced size	Geometric tolerances at given produced sizes	Virtual condition
MMC →	5.75	0.50	6.25
	5.85	0.60	6.45
	5.95	0.70	6.65
	6.05	0.80	6.85
	6.15	0.90	7.05
LMC →	6.25	1.00	7.25

Figure 32-18 Geometric tolerances at given produced sizes and virtual condition

Geometric Dimensioning and Tolerancing with SolidWorks

We will now discuss in details how to use SolidWorks to define geometric dimensioning & tolerancing and apply the concepts to views of orthogonal drawings. Figure 32-19 shows the list of geometric tolerance symbols that are commonly used in drawings. The list summarizes the following types of tolerance:

Form: straightness, flatness, circularity, and cylindricity
Profile: line, surface
Location: position, concentricity, and symmetry
Orientation: parallelism, perpendicularity, and angularity
Run out: circular run out, and total run out

Form tolerances are applicable to single (individual) features or elements of single features; therefore, form tolerances are not related to datums.

	Type of Tolerance	Characteristic	Symbol
For individual features	Form	Straightness	—
		Flatness	⬭
		Circularity	○
		Cylindricity	⌭
Individual or related features	Profile	Profile of a plane	⌒
		Profile of a surface	⌓
Related features	Orientation	Angularity	∠
		Perpendicularity	⊥
		Parallelism	//
	Location	Position	⌖
		Concentricity	◎
		Symmetry	≡
	Runout	Circular runout	↗
		Total runout	↗↗

Figure 32-19 List of geometric tolerance symbols

The following subsections discuss the particulars of the form tolerances - straightness, flatness, circularity, and cylindricity.

Straightness

Straightness is a condition where an element of a surface, or an axis, is a straight line. A straightness tolerance specifies a tolerance zone within which the considered element or derived median line must lie. A straightness tolerance is applied in the view where the elements to be controlled are represented by a straight line. Straightness tolerances are most often applied to circular or matching objects to help ensure that the parts are not barrelled or warped within the given feature tolerance range, and therefore, do not fit together well. Figure 32-20 shows a cylindrical object dimensioned and toleranced using an MMC condition applied to the tolerance. The surface of the cylinder may vary within the specified range: that is from 21 to 19.

The Allowable Tolerance Zone (ATZ) is defined as the Feature Size + Flatness Size. Figure 32-21 shows how to define ATZ and the Virtual Condition.

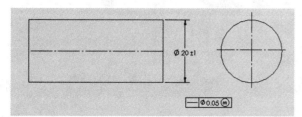

Figure 32-20 Cylindrical object dimensioned and toleranced using an MMC condition

	Measured size	Allowable Tolerance Zone (ATZ)	Virtual condition
MMC →	21.0	0.0 + 0.05 = 0.05	21.0 + 0.05 = 21.05
	20.9	0.1 + 0.05 = 0.15	21.0 + 0.15 = 21.15
	20.8	0.2 + 0.05 = 0.25	21.0 + 0.25 = 21.25
	20.7	0.3 + 0.05 = 0.35	21.0 + 0.35 = 21.35
	20.6		
	.		
	.		
	19.7	1.3 + 0.05 = 1.35	21.0 + 1.35 = 22.35
	19.6	1.4 + 0.05 = 1.45	21.0 + 1.45 = 22.45
	19.5	1.5 + 0.05 = 1.55	21.0 + 1.55 = 22.55
	.		
	.		
	19.2	1.8 + 0.05 = 1.85	21.0 + 1.85 = 22.85
	19.1	1.9 + 0.05 = 1.95	21.0 + 1.95 = 22.95
LMC →	19.0	2.0 + 0.05 = 2.05	21.0 + 2.05 = 23.05

Figure 32-21 Allowable Tolerance Zone at given measured sizes and virtual condition

Flatness

Flatness is the condition of a surface having all elements in one plane. Flatness tolerances are used to define the amount of variation permitted in an individual surfaced. A flatness tolerance specifies a tolerance zone defined by two parallel planes within which the surface must lie. Figure 32-22 shows a rectangular object which varies in height from 25.5 to 24.5. How flat is the top surface? This question can be better answered if an additional flatness tolerance value is added (0.3 in this case). Although the feature can vary based on the tolerance of ±0.5 specified, but the surface could not vary by more than 0.3. When a flatness tolerance is specified, the feature control frame is attached to a leader directed to the surface or to an extension line of the surface. It is placed in a view where the surface elements to be controlled are represented by a line. Where the considered surface is associated with a size dimension, the flatness tolerance must be less than the size tolerance. Notice that the value of the flatness tolerance is normally less than the feature tolerance (0.3 < 0.5).

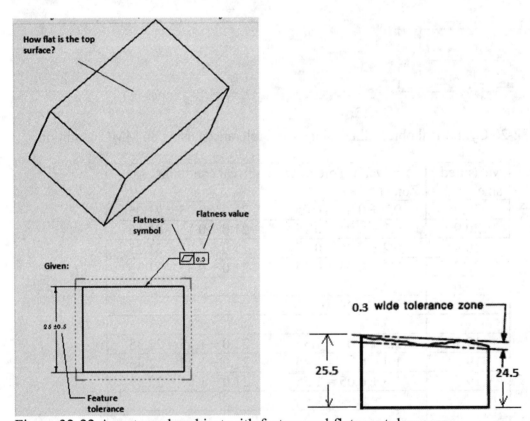

Figure 32-22 A rectangular object with feature and flatness tolerances

Circularity

A circularity tolerance is used to limit the amount of variation in the roundness of a surface of revolution. It is measured at individual cross sections along the length of the object. Circularity tolerance specifies a tolerance zone bounded by two concentric circles within which each circular element of the surface must lie. It is a condition of a surface of revolution where:

1. With respect to a cylinder or cone, all points of the surface intersected by any plane perpendicular to a common axis are equidistant from that axis.
2. With respect to a sphere, all points of the surface intersected by any plane passing through a common center are equidistant from that center.

Figure 32-23 shows a cylindrical object with feature and circularity tolerance specified. In this case, we note that although the cylinder can vary in length from 19 to 21, but the circularity tolerance is only applied to any cross section and never violate the circularity requirement. This means that MMC cannot be applied. The section A-A for which the circularity tolerance is applied is specified as shown.

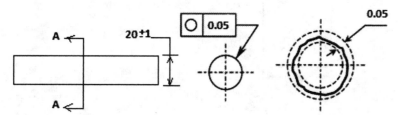

Figure 32-23 A cylindrical object with feature and circularity tolerance

Cylindricity

Cylindricity tolerances are used to define a tolerance zone both around individual circular cross sections of an object and also along its length. The resulting tolerance zone looks like two concentric cylinders. Figure 32-24 shows a shaft that includes a cylindricity tolerance that establishes a tolerance zone of 0.2. This means that since the maximum measured diameter is 15.3, the minimum diameter cannot be less than 15.1 (15.3 − 0.2) anywhere on the cylindrical surface.

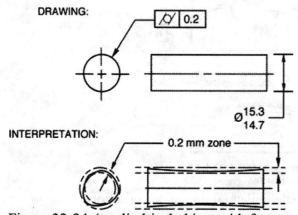

Figure 32-24 A cylindrical object with feature and cylindricity tolerance

Line Profile

Profiles of line tolerances are specified to irregular surfaces (see Figure 32-25). Profiles of line tolerances are particularly helpful when tolerancing an irregular surface that is consistently changing, such as an airplane wing.

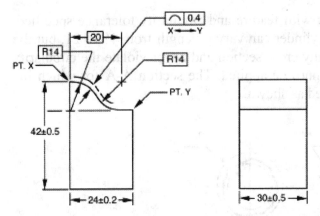

Figure 32-25 Line profile

Surface Profile

Profiles of surface tolerances are specified to irregular surfaces (see Figure 32-26). Four cases are identified. In case A, Figure 32-26, a 0.02 bilateral tolerance is specified with no further information. Therefore, the outside tolerance is 0.01 and the inside tolerance is 0.01. In case B, Figure 32-26, an unequal distributed bilateral tolerance is specified in which the outside has a tolerance of 0.02 and the inside has a tolerance of 0.005.

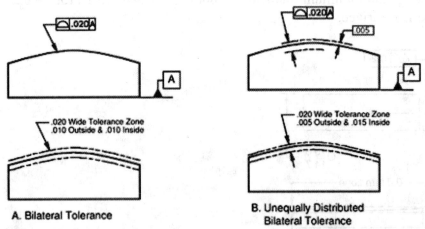

Figure 32-26 Bilateral and unequally distributed bilateral tolerance definitions

In case C, Figure 32-27, a 0.02 unilateral tolerance is specified for the outside tolerance, while in case D, a 0.02 unilateral tolerance is specified for the inside tolerance.

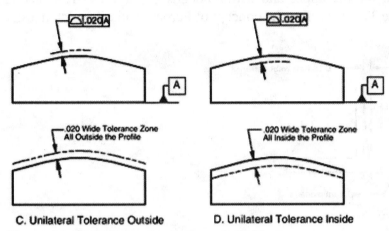

C. Unilateral Tolerance Outside   D. Unilateral Tolerance Inside

Figure 32-27 Unilateral tolerance definitions

Parallelism

Parallelism tolerances are used to ensure that all points are within two parallel planes that are parallel to a referenced datum plane (see Figure 32-28).

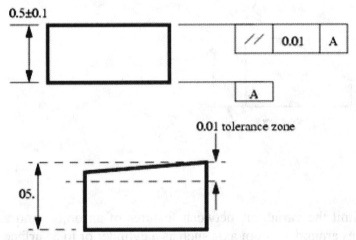

Figure 32-28 Parallelism

Perpendicularity

Perpendicularity tolerances are used to limit the amount of variation for a surface or feature within two planes parallel to a specified datum. Figure 32-29 shows an L-shape in which the bottom surface is assigned as datum G and the left side is toleranced so that it must be perpendicular within a limit of 0.15 to datum G. The object also has a horizontal dimension and tolerance of plus/minus 1, which is the location tolerance. The 10±1 controls the location of the horizontal bottom edge, but does not necessarily control the shape. For example the bottom edge can take the extreme values of 11 or 9. However, applying the perpendicularity tolerances means that the bottom edge is limited to perpendicularity 0.15 within for the upper and lower bounds of 11 or 9. The second diagram to the right in Figure 32-29 clarifies the concept of Perpendicularity tolerances.

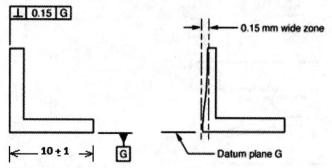

Figure 32-29 Perpendicularity

Angularity

Angularity tolerances are used to limit the variance of surfaces and axes that are at an angle relative to the datum (see Figure 32-30).

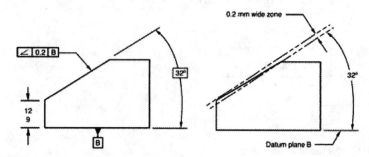

Figure 32-30 Angularity

Circular Runout

Run out tolerances are used to limit the variations between features of an object and a datum. They are applied to surfaces around a datum axis such as a cylinder or to a surface constructed perpendicular to a datum axis. There are two types: circular and total. Figure 32-31 show a circular run out tolerance.

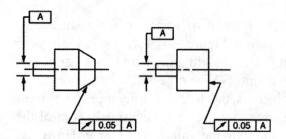

Figure 32-31 Circular run out

Using SolidWorks to Define Tolerances in Drawings

To use SolidWorks to define tolerances in drawings requires that the Drawing Document should be active. Figure 32-32 shows the tools for defining tolerances in SolidWorks. The steps are fairly straightforward:

1. Click **Annotation** (1) to show the ConfigurationManager required.
2. Click **Datum Feature** (2) to define datums.
3. Click **Geometric Tolerance** (3) to define tolerances.
4. Click **Surface Finish** (4) if needed for surface finish definition.

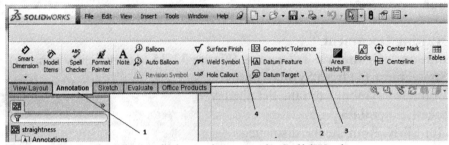

Figure 32-32 Tool for defining tolerances in SolidWorks

When **Geometric Tolerance** (3) is clicked, the Geometric Tolerance PropertiesManager is automatically displayed as shown in Figure 32-33. All the tolerance symbols are accessed by clicking the Symbol pull-down button. The box Tolerance 1 is used to show the tolerance value. Then select Primary as A, or Secondary as B, or Tertiary as C as the case may be; these are the datum surfaces.

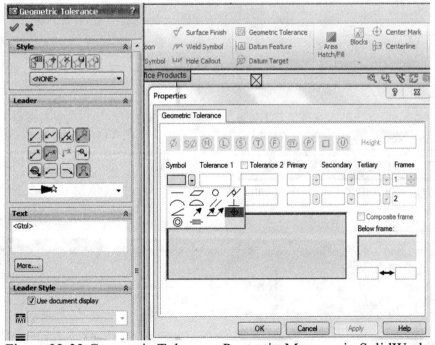

Figure 32-33 Geometric Tolerance PropertiesManager in SolidWorks

Example 3: Figure 32-34 shows a cylindrical object with diameteral dimension given. Add a straightness tolerance with an MMC condition of 0.05 across the diameter.

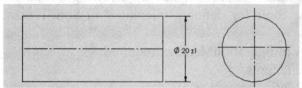

Figure 32-34 A cylindrical object with diameteral dimension

SolidWorks Solution

1. Open the **Drawing Document**.
2. Click **Annotation** > **Geometric Tolerance**. (Figure 32-35 automatically appears)
3. Select the Straightness (–) from **Symbol** option.
4. Select the **Diameter** symbol from the list displayed.
5. For **Tolerance 1** Enter **0.05**.
6. Select **(M)** for MMC from the list displayed.
7. Click **OK**. (tolerance automatically displayed on drawing; see Figure 32-36)

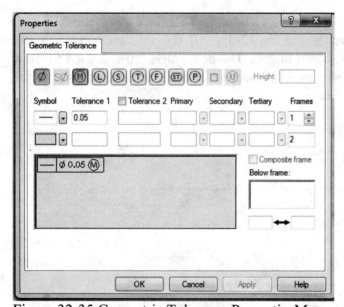

Figure 32-35 Geometric Tolerance PropertiesManager

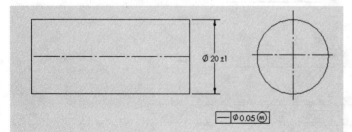

Figure 32-36 Cylindrical object dimensioned and toleranced using an MMC condition

Example 4: Define the lower edge of the part in Figure 32-37 as datum A, and the right vertical edge of the part as datum B and perpendicular to datum A within a tolerance of 0.001.

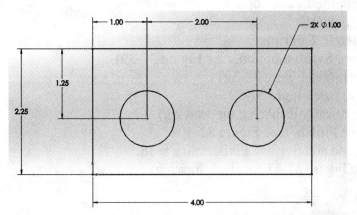

Figure 32-37 Part for tolerance definition using SolidWorks

SolidWorks Solution

1. Open the **Drawing Document**.
2. Click **Annotation** > **Datum Feature**. (Figure 32-38 automatically appears)
3. Select 'A' from the **Label Settings** option.
4. Select the filled triangle from the **Leader** option.
5. Locate the datum symbol on the drawing.
6. Click **OK**.

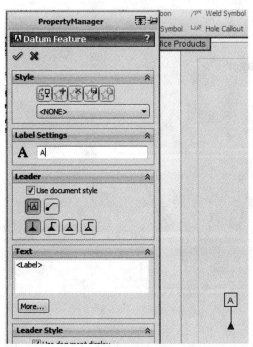

Figure 32-38 Datum Feature PropertyManager

7. Click **Annotation** > **Datum Feature**.
8. Select 'B' from the **Label Settings** option.
9. Select the filled triangle from the **Leader** option.
10. Click on the 'B' label and click **OK**.
11. Click **Annotation** > **Geometric Tolerance**.
12. Select the Perpendicular from **Symbol** option. (see Figure 32-39)
13. For **Tolerance 1** Enter **0.001**. (see Figure 32-39)
14. Select **A** for Primary Datum. (see Figure 32-39)
15. Click **OK**. (tolerance automatically displayed on drawing)
16. Click **Annotation** > **Surface Finish**. (see Figure 32-40)
17. Select appropriate Symbol and add Surface Finish value = 16.
18. Click **OK** to complete. (see Figure 32-41 for final drawing)

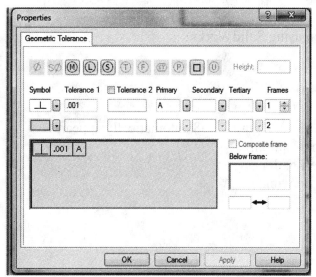

Figure 32-39 Geometric Tolerance PropertiesManager

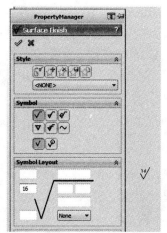

Figure 32-40 Surface Finish PropertiesManager

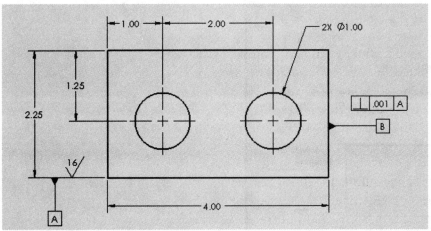

Figure 32-41 Drawing with dimensions surface finishing, datums and tolerances

Example 5: Define a feature tolerance of 0.001 for the hole and apply a .001 positional tolerance about the hole's center point at the maximum material condition for the drawing shown in Figure 32-42.

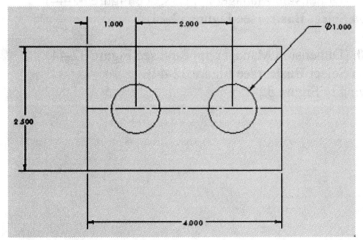

Figure 32-42 Basic drawing

SolidWorks Solution

1. Open the **Drawing Document**.
2. Click **Annotation** > **Geometric Tolerance**.
3. Select **Position** from **Symbol** option. (see Figure 32-43)
4. Select **Diameter** from **Symbol** option. (see Figure 32-43)
5. For **Tolerance 1** Enter **0.001**. (see Figure 32-43)
6. Select **(M)** for from **Symbol** option. (see Figure 32-43)
7. Click **OK**. (tolerance automatically displayed on drawing)

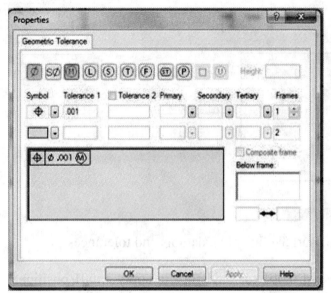

Figure 32-43 Geometric Tolerance PropertiesManager

8. Click the dimension **2.000**. (Dimension Manager appears; see Figure 32-44)
9. From **Tolerance/Precision** Select **Basic**. (see Figure 32-44)
10. Click **OK**.
11. Click the dimension **2.500**. (Dimension Manager appears; see Figure 32-44)
12. From **Tolerance/Precision** Select **Basic**. (see Figure 32-44)
13. Click **OK**. (see final drawing in Figure 32-45)

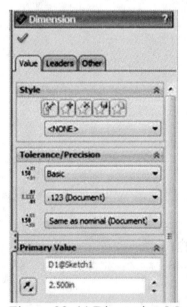

Figure 32-44 Dimension Manager

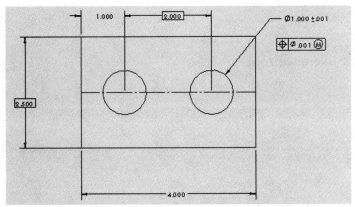

Figure 32-45 Complete annotations on drawing

Hole Locations and Joining a Shaft to a Toleranced Hole

When rectangular dimensions are used, the location of the center of a hole is defined by two linear dimensions. The result is a rectangular tolerance zone whole size is based on the linear dimension's tolerances. Figure 32-46 shows the location and size dimensions for a hole, together with the resulting tolerance zone. The dimensions of the tolerance zone are each twice the size of the linear dimension tolerances (2 x 0.2 = 0.4; 2 x 0.3 = 0.6).

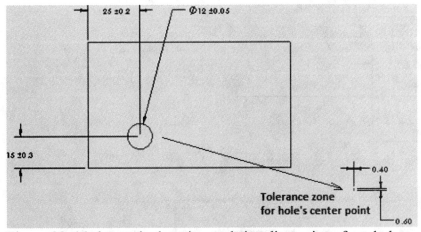

Figure 32-46 shows the location and size dimensions for a hole

Example 6: What is the largest diameter shaft that will always fit into the hole shown in Figure 32.46?

Solution

For line dimensions and tolerances,

$$S_{max} = H_{min} - DTZ$$

Where

S_{max} = maximum shaft diameter

H_{min} = minimum hole diameter

DTZ = diagonal distance across the tolerance zone

$$DTZ = \sqrt{(0.4)^2 + (0.6)^2} = 0.72$$

$$H_{min} = 12 - 0.05 = 11.95$$

$$S_{max} = 11.95 - 0.72 = 11.23$$

Example 7: Parts A and B in Figure 32-47 are to be joined by a common shaft. The total tolerance for the shaft is to be 0.05. What are the minimum and maximum shaft diameters?

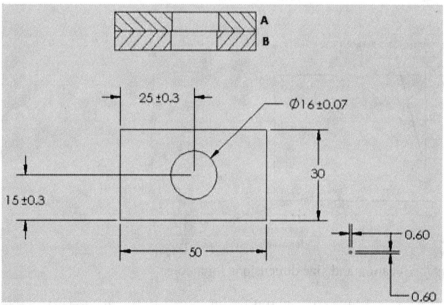

Figure 32-47 Parts A and B to be joined by a common shaft

Solution

Since both objects A and B have the same dimensions and tolerances and are floating relative to each other,

$$S_{max} = H_{min} - DTZ$$

$$DTZ = \sqrt{(0.6)^2 + (0.6)^2} = 0.85$$

$$H_{min} = 16 - 0.07 = 15.93$$

$$S_{max} = 15.93 - 0.85 = 15.08$$

$$S_{min} = S_{max} - 0.05 = 15.08 - 0.05 = 15.03$$

$$\therefore S_{max} = 15.08$$
$$S_{min} = 15.03$$

Example 8: Parts A and B in Figure 32-48 are to be joined by a common shaft whose maximum diameter is .248. What is the minimum hole-size for the parts that will always accept the shaft? What is the maximum hole-size if the total tolerance for the hole is 0.005?

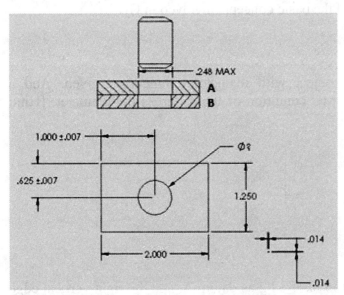

Figure 32-48 Parts A and B to be joined by a common shaft

Solution

Since both objects A and B have the same dimensions and tolerances and are floating relative to each other,

$$S_{max} = H_{min} - DTZ$$

$$DTZ = \sqrt{(.014)^2 + (.014)^2} = .02$$

$$H_{min} = S_{max} + DTZ$$

$$H_{min} = .248 + .02 = .268$$

$$H_{max} = .268 + .005 = .273$$

$$\therefore H_{max} = .273$$
$$H_{min} = .268$$

Summary

This chapter deals with geometric dimensioning and tolerancing (GD&T) which is very important in the manufacturing industry since production on the shop floor is significantly affected by the proper dimensioning and tolerancing of the machined parts. The discussions and examples given in this chapter are based on the ASME Y14.5-2009 standard, *Dimensioning and Tolerancing*. The materials provided in this chapter are sufficient for beginners to understand the basic concepts involved in GD&T.

Exercises

1: Figure P1 shows a cylindrical object with diameteral dimension given. Add a straightness tolerance with an MMC condition of 0.025 across the diameter. [Hint: See Example 3]

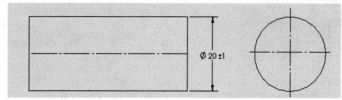

Figure P1

2: Define the lower edge of the part in Figure P2 as datum A, and the right vertical edge of the part as datum B and perpendicular to datum A within a tolerance of 0.001. Include a surface finish value of 32 to datum A. [Hint: See Example 4]

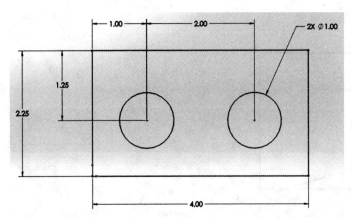

Figure P2

3: Define a feature tolerance of 0.002 for the hole and apply a .002 positional tolerance about the hole's center point at the maximum material condition for the drawing shown in Figure P3. [Hint: See Example 5]

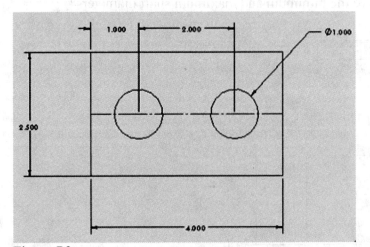

Figure P3

4: What is the largest diameter shaft that will always fit into the hole shown in Figure P4? [Hint: See Example 6]

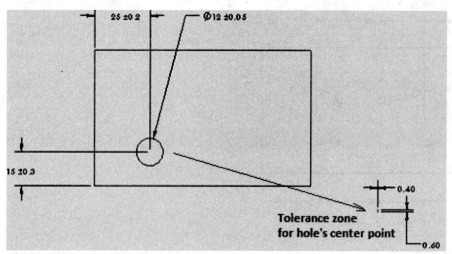

Figure P4

5: Parts A and B in Figure P5 are to be joined by a common shaft. The total tolerance for the shaft is to be 0.05. What are the minimum and maximum shaft diameters?
[Hint: See Example 7]

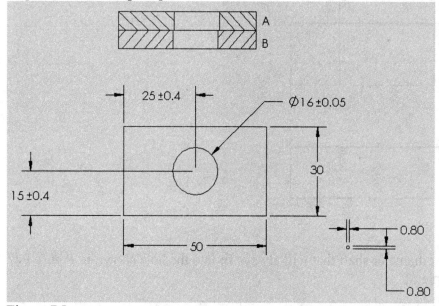

Figure P5

6: Parts A and B in Figure P6 are to be joined by a common shaft whose maximum diameter is .248. What is the minimum hole-size for the parts that will always accept the shaft? What is the maximum hole-size if the total tolerance for the hole is 0.005?
[Hint: See Example 8]

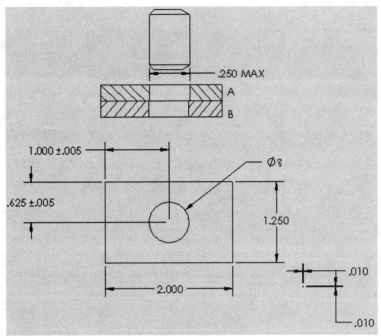

Figure P6

Chapter 33

Evaluating the Cost of Machined Parts

Objectives:

In this chapter you will learn:

- How to change Model Geometry and know it affects cost
- How to add Material to the Stock Body and know it affects cost
- How to examine the CostingManager: Setup Folder
- How to examine the CostingManager: Mill Operations
- How to change Material Costs
- How to change the Stock Body
- How to change the Quantity of Parts to Manufacture and know it affects cost
- How to include a Discount
- How to apply Custom Operations and know it affects cost
- How to compare Material Costs
- How to carryout automatic manufacturing cost estimation for machined parts

INTRODUCTION

Manufacturing cost is one of the main factors in a machine design process in order to choose the most suitable solution; therefore, accurate estimation in the early design phases is fundamental. Design to cost implies to manage a vast amount of manufacturing knowledge that has to be linked to the design parameters.

Cost management or costing is a process for planning, managing, and controlling the costs of doing business. Ideally, product design projects should have customized costing plans and companies as a whole should integrate costing into their business models. When properly implemented, costing translates into reduced costs for products and services, as well as increased value being delivered to the customer.

Taking this approach to costing helps a company determine whether they accurately estimated expenses initially, and will help to more closely predict expenses in the future. However, costing cannot be used in isolation–projects must be organized and conducted with costing as a vital part of an overall business strategy.

A project that is defined through costing will facilitate effective management of the costs it incurs. Effective costing strategies will help deliver a high quality product within a predetermined budget, as well as making it more valuable to the customer.

Feature based 3D CAD models contain data useful for cost estimation but, despite the numerous work on features recognition and extraction, no cost estimation software system yet assures reliable results. SolidWorks 3D CAD software now has a tool for rapid manufacturing cost estimation where design features are automatically linked to manufacturing operations. Engineers and designers can now optimize designs, make informed decisions, and save time and development costs using SolidWorks 3D CAD software to automatically generate real-time manufacturing cost estimates for sheet metal and machined parts. The most current SolidWorks Costing functionality has been enhanced to make it more comprehensive than the previous version. Automatic cost estimation estimates part manufacturing costs using built-in cost templates. These manufacturing templates are customizable, allowing entry of specific manufacturing costs and data, such as material, labor, machine speed and feeds, and setup costs. For the first time, designers can get automatic, real-time estimates of part manufacturing costs for sheet metal and machined parts with SolidWorks Costing, using built-in cost templates that can be customized for your specific operation. Design and manufacturing groups can share knowledge directly through the templates, enabling designers to make more informed product design decisions based on automatic cost estimation.

SolidWorks Costing functionality includes the ability to:
- Design to a cost target using fast, repeatable data analysis
- Automatically track costs for both native SolidWorks or non-native imported models as the design develops
- Automate the quoting process for manufacturing
- Customize standard cost templates as needed to mirror in-house or outsourced manufacturing environments
- Update costs automatically with every design change—no extra work required
- Share manufacturing knowledge directly between design and manufacturing through costing templates

Using SolidWorks Costing, designers can automatically calculate manufacturing cost estimates to ensure they are within design cost goals, and manufacturers can instantly create detailed quotes that are accurate to their specific manufacturing costs and processes. SolidWorks Costing works directly from 3D models–no pre-processing of the models is required. As a design is created, manufacturing costs are automatically calculated allowing designers to always have a current and accurate cost estimate.

SolidWorks Costing lets more people in your organization become engaged in reducing product cost while maintaining product quality. It provides a method for establishing and monitoring cost priorities. It improves both bottom line (cost reduction) and top line (increasing sales through higher quality products). Costing is part of an overall business solution that maximizes profits and product quality.

SolidWorks Costing is a tool for getting more people to think about both material and process costs from different perspectives. Engineering personnel can leverage costing/cost reduction knowledge and pass it along to others within an organization, so costing is repeatable and becomes a vital aspect of overall corporate culture.

The SolidWorks Costing template contains the procedures a user or the user's manufacturing supplier would use for manufacturing the part. The user can specify information such as material costs and sizes, costs of manufacturing operations, and manufacturing setup costs in the template.

This chapter briefly presents the geometric modeling of the parts for which manufacturing cost estimates is to be carried out, and then the SolidWorks automatic manufacturing Cost Estimation tool is discussed so that users can use it for carrying out costing task for their product during the design stage. This way, the overall costs from design to manufacturing can be minimized because changes can to be made to the model before deciding on the optimal solution.

Model for Automatic Manufacturing Cost Estimation

1. Open a SolidWorks Part Document.
2. Choose Front Plane.
3. Create the Sketch shown in Figure 33-1.
4. Revolve about the vertical centerline (see Figure 33-2 and Figure 33-3 for part).

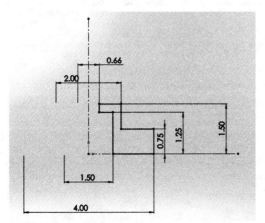

Figure 33-1 Sketch for creating part

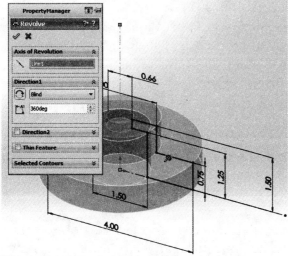

Figure 33-2 Revolve PropertyManager

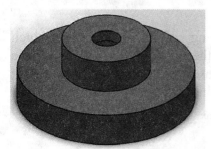

Figure 33-3 Revolved part

5. Create construction-circle for inserting three holes (see Figure 33-4).
6. Create a circle for inserting radial hole (see Figure 33-5).
7. Create multiple holes using Circular Pattern to realize final model (see Figure 33-6).

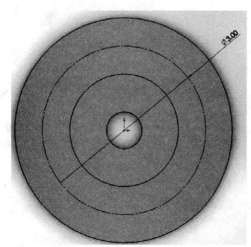

Figure 33-4 Construction-circle for creating three holes

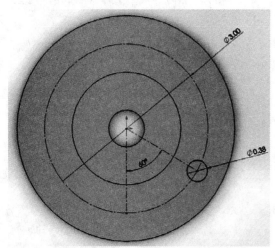

Figure 33-5 Circle for radial hole

Figure 33-6 Final model

Now that the model is ready, we will now learn how to use SolidWorks automatic manufacturing cost estimation tool for this product.

Automatic Manufacturing Cost Estimation

1. Open the **Part Document** for the part to be examined for costing (Figure 33-6).
2. Click **Tools > Costing** or **Evaluate > Costing** [see Figure 33-7(a) or (b)].
3. In the **Costing Task Pane**, under Material:
   a. Set **Class** to **Steel**. (see Figure 33-8)
   b. Set **Name** to **AISI 4340 Steel, annealed**. (see Figure 33-9)

The Costing tool estimates the manufacturing cost using the material information in the part.
The **Costing Task Pane** displays the Estimated Cost Per Part. (see Figure 33-10)

Costing Task Pane Item	Description
Comparison	Based on the data in the template and the part in the graphics area, the Costing tool calculates the cost of the part.
Breakdown	A breakdown of the cost calculation indicates that the material and manufacturing (labor, machine time, and overhead) account for certain percentages of the total cost.

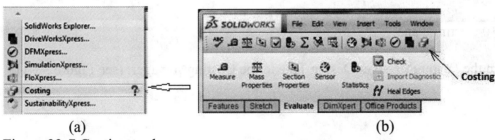

(a)   (b)

Figure 33-7 Costing tool

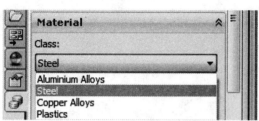

Figure 33-8 Class option in Costing Pane

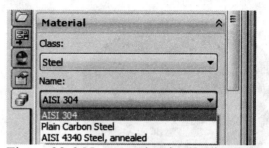

Figure 33-9 Name option in Costing Pane

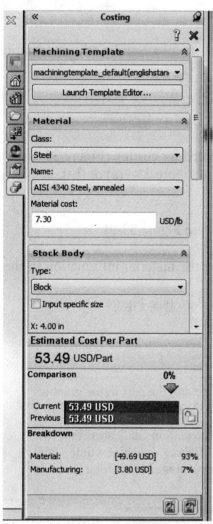

Figure 33-10 Costing Pane

Switch from the FeatureManager Design Tree to the CostingManager. (see Figure 33-11)

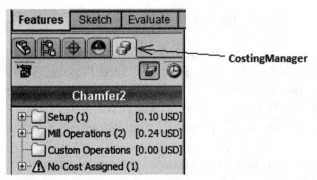

Figure 33-11 CostingManager

Notice that the color of the model changes and is automatically encased within a box (see Figure 33-12).

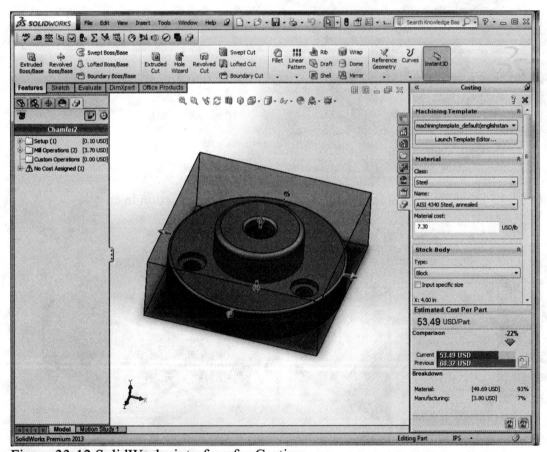

Figure 33-12 SolidWorks interface for Costing

Changing Model Geometry

Next, you change the model geometry to see how it affects manufacturing costs.
1. In the Costing Task Pane, click Auto Show.
2. In the graphics area, double-click the part.

3. Change the dimension from **.75** to **.5** and click **Click to Update** to Rebuild. (see Figure 33-13)
   The Estimated Cost per Part decreases because you added material to the part.
4. In the graphics area, right-click the hole and click Suppress. (see Figure 33-14) [Note that you cannot suppress the slot in the CostingManager because the CostingManager shows manufacturing features, not SolidWorks features.]
5. In the Costing Task Pane, under Estimated Cost per Part, click where it reads Click to Update.
   You manually update the cost estimate because you changed the model geometry. The Estimated Cost per Part decreases because you simplified the part.

Figure 33-13 Dimension reduced from .75 to .5 resulting in reduction in cost

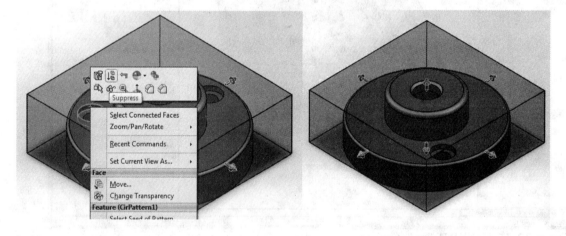

Figure 33-14 Suppression of holes resulting in reduction in cost

Adding Material to the Stock Body

Surfaces on the part sometimes require high tolerance or specific surface finishes. Next, you add more material on the stock body so the part can be precisely machined to meet specific tolerances and surface finishes.

1. In the Costing Task Pane, under Stock Body, for +Y, type **0.5** and press Enter. (see Figure 33-15) You must type **0.5**, not **.5**.
2. Click to Update.
3. Change +Y back to 0.
4. Clear Preview stock.
5. Click to Update.

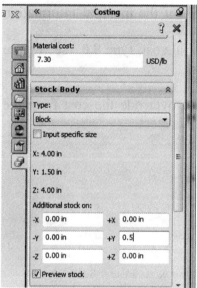

Figure 33-15 Adding material to the stock body

Examining the CostingManager: Setup Folder

The CostingManager on the left side of the SolidWorks software window shows how the Costing tool categorizes each operation required for manufacturing the part. Next, you examine the Setup folder to see the operations included in each setup cost.

The Setup folder contains the costs associated with manufacturing setups such as setting up machines to run a batch (lot) of parts. Each operation to manufacture the part requires a setup cost.

1. In the CostingManager, expand Setup.
   There is one Setup Operation in the Setup folder.

Examining the CostingManager: Mill Operations

The Mill Operations folder contains information on all of the features to be milled in the part. Next, you examine the Mill Operations folder to see the operations included in each setup cost.

1. Expand Mill Operations.
   There are three features to be milled.
2. Expand Mill 1.

This is a chamfer.

Changing Material Costs

The Costing Task Pane on the right side of the SolidWorks software window displays the input values that determine the cost of manufacturing the part. Next, you change the material cost to see how it affects the manufacturing cost.

The Costing Task Pane contains a section for Material. All of the material information comes from the Costing template.

1. In the Costing Task Pane, under Material, for Material cost, type **8.0**. (see Figure 33-16)
2. Press Enter.
   The text box appears in yellow to indicate that you overrode the cost from the template. Additionally, the Estimated Cost per Part increases.

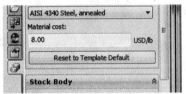

Figure 33-16 Change material cost

Changing the Stock Body

Stock body is the raw material from which the part is manufactured. Next, you change the stock body to see how it affects the manufacturing cost.

1. Under **Stock Body**, in **Type**, select **Plate**.
   There are three types of stock bodies in machining Costing: block, plate, and cylinder. [Note: when you select Plate, the software uses cutting operations such as waterjet and laser to create the through-cuts on the part, rather than milling and drilling. When you select the stock body, you not only control the stock but also the operations that remove material from the part. Choosing Plate costs less than choosing Block]
   The software selects the plate thickness that is closest to the part thickness. The thickest plate available in the template is 1.0 inch, but the part thickness is 1.5 inch. The warning icon indicates that the plate stock is not thick enough. Because the part is much thicker than the plate thicknesses available in the template, you need to use block stock. (see Figure 33-18)
2. Under **Stock Body**, in **Type**, select **Block**.
   Block generally fits all geometries. The software selects the smallest rectangular cuboid to fit the part.
3. Click **to Update** to update.

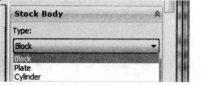

Figure 33-17 Change the stock body

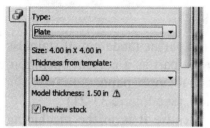

Figure 33-18 Warning icon appears

Changing the Quantity of Parts to Manufacture

Next, you change the quantity of parts to manufacture to see how it affects the manufacturing cost.

1. Under Quantity, set Total number of parts to **1** and press Enter.

   The Lot size also changes to **1**. The Estimated Cost per Part increases because the machine setup costs are distributed over the lot. Each part carries more of the setup cost when there are fewer parts in the lot.

   The Lot size is the number of parts run in one machine setup. For example, if you run 200 parts and run 100 parts per lot, you need two machine setups. (see Figure 33-19)

2. Under Quantity, set Total number of parts to **100** and press Enter.

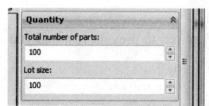

Figure 33-19 Quantity of part to manufacture

Including a Discount

Next, you add a discount to the part to see how it affects the manufacturing cost.

1. Under Markup/Discount, select Markup/Discount.

   Under Markup/Discount, you can apply markups or discounts to the part. If you want to add a profit margin, type a positive value. If you get a discount from a vendor, type a negative value.

   Type **-10** for % of Total Cost and press Enter. (see Figure 33-20)

   The Estimated Cost per Part decreases by the **10%** discount.

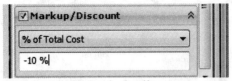

Figure 33-20 Include discount

Applying Custom Operations

Next, you apply a custom operation to the part. Because the part is made out of stainless steel and will not rust, you do not need to apply paint to the part as a custom operation. But we will merely show the steps required in case you need to apply paint.

1. In the CostingManager, click Add Custom Operation. (see Figure 33-21)
   Painting is already listed as a custom operation because it is in the machining template. The PropertyManager displays all of the cost information associated with the painting operation.
2. Click OK.
   The Estimated Cost per Part increases.

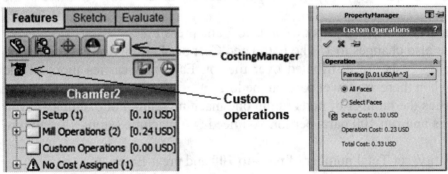

Figure 33-21 Add Custom Operation

Note that because AISI is stainless steel, painting is not required to prevent rust and you can remove the painting operation.

Comparing Material Costs

Next, you set a baseline price to compare alternative materials for the part.

1. In the Costing Task Pane, under Estimated Cost per Part, click Set Baseline.
2. Under Material, in Name, select Plain Carbon Steel.
   The Estimated Cost per Part decreases.
3. Next, you apply a custom operation to the part because the part is made out of Plain Carbon steel and will rust.
4. In the CostingManager, expand Custom Operations.
5. Right-click Painting <1> - Face and click Remove Custom Operation.
   The Estimated Cost per Part decreases, but the stainless steel part is still significantly more expensive than the plain carbon steel part.

6. In the Costing Task Pane, under Estimated Cost per Part, click Set Baseline to remove the baseline price.

Adding Library Features

Next, you add a library feature to the part to see how it affects the cost; otherwise skip.
1. In the FeatureManager design tree, right-click any library feature that was suppressed.
   The library feature appears in the part.
2. In the Costing Task Pane, Click to Update.
   The Estimated Cost per Part increases.
3. In the CostingManager, expand Library Features.
   The library feature appears. Library features are included in the cost estimate only if the template has information for the feature. You can edit templates to include any library feature.

Creating a Report

Next, you create a report of the Costing results.
1. At the bottom of the Costing Task Pane, click Generate Report. (see Figure 33-22)
   The report opens in Microsoft Word.
2. Close the report.

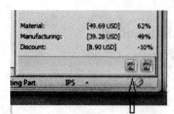

Figure 33-22 Generate Report

Summary

We have completed the discussion on costing, which is a new feature in SolidWorks. In this chapter we have learnt how to specify: information such as material costs and sizes in the template; costs of manufacturing operations in the template; and manufacturing setup costs in the template.

Also we examined the impact of the following on cost: changing model geometry; adding material to the stock body; changing material costs; changing the stock body; changing the quantity of parts to manufacture; including a discount; and applying custom operations.

Not only that, we also covered the following: examining the CostingManager: Setup Folder; examining the CostingManager: Mill Operations; and comparing Material Costs.

Exercises

P1: Create the part in Figure P1 and evauate the cost of the machined part.
Part Name: V-block
Material: A-steel

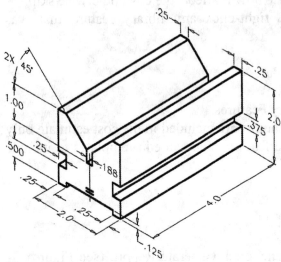

Figure P1

P2: Create the part in Figure P2 and evauate the cost of the machined part.
Part Name: Angle Bracket
Material: Mild steel
Specific Instruction: Center $2X \phi 15$ holes and provide location dimensions

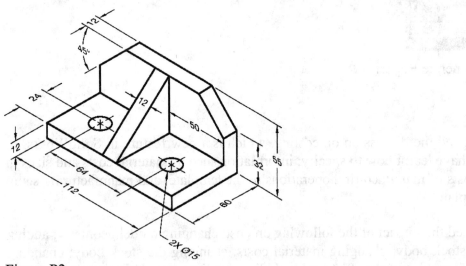

Figure P2

P3: Create the part in Figure P3 and evauate the cost of the machined part.
Part Name: Support
Material: Mild steel

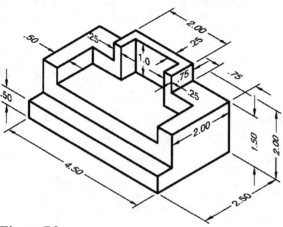

Figure P3

References

Germani, Michele; Cicconi, Paolo; Mandolini, Marco, Manufacturing Cost Estimation During Early Phases of Machine Design, Proceedings of the 18th International Conference on Engineering Design (ICED 11), Impacting Society through Engineering Design, Vol. 5: Design for X / Design to X, Lyngby/Copenhagen, Denmark, 15.-19.08., 2011, pp. 198-209

http://www.solidworks.com/sw/products/3d-cad/manufacturing-cost-estimation.htm

http://www10.mcadcafe.com/blogs/jeffrowe/2013/02/07/cost-management-moves-up-front-in-design-process-with-solidworks-2013/

Chapter 34

Finite Element Analysis Using SolidWorks

Objectives:

In this chapter you will learn:

- What COSMOS is used for
- The historical trend leading to SolidWorks Simulation
- The SolidWorks Simulation interface
- The fundamental steps involved in finite element analysis (FEA)
- Static analysis with solid elements
- The effect of mesh variations on analysis outputs
- How to use SolidWorks Simulation to solve stress analysis problems

Introduction to COSMOS/SolidWorks Simulation

What is SolidWorks Simulation?

The Structural Research & Analysis Corporation (SRAC) developed an engineering analysis software product called COSMOS, based on finite element analysis (FEA). SRAC was established in 1982 and it made significant contributions toward FEA for engineering analysis.

In 1995 SRAC partnered with the SolidWorks Corporation and developed COSMOS Works, which became the top-selling analysis solution. The commercial success of COSMOS Works integrated with SolidWorks CAD software resulted in Dassault Systemes, parent of SolidWorks Corporation, acquiring SRAC in 2001. In 2003, SRAC operations merged with SolidWorks Corporation. In the 2009 revision, COSMOS Works was renamed SolidWorks Simulation. This historical perspective is important. SolidWorks Simulation is fully integrated into the SolidWorks Simulation CAD software. SolidWorks Simulation can be used to create and edit model geometry. SolidWorks Simulation is solid-driven, parametric, and feature-driven and runs on Windows.

There are a number of well-known commercially available FEA packages:

Software	Owner
ANSYS	ANSYS, Inc.
ABACUS SolidWorks Simulation/ COSMOS Works	Dassault Systemes
I-DEAS	UGS
Pro/MECHANICA	PTC

The functionalities, historical trends, and scope of the SolidWorks family of products are summarized in Table 34-1. A conceptual model of SolidWorks Simulation is shown in Figure 34-1.

Table 34-1 The SolidWorks family

Functionality	Until 2008	From 2009	Scope
	COSMOS Works[*]	SolidWorks Simulation[+]	Static, frequency, buckling, fatigue, drop test analyses, linear dynamic, nonlinear thermal analysis: temperature, temperature gradient, heat flow
Stress Analysis: FEA-based	COSMOS FloWorks	SolidWorks Flow Simulation	Fluid flow, heat transfer, forces
Motion Analysis	COSMOS Motion	SolidWorks Motion	Kinematic modeling/analysis of mechanisms
Animation	COSMOS Animation	SolidWorks Animation	Animation of modeled systems

[*]Designer and Professional versions

[+]SolidWorks SimulationXpress is an introductory version of SolidWorks Simulation

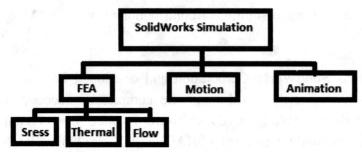

Figure 34-1 SolidWorks Simulation

Product Development Cycle (PDC)

In the industry, the product development cycle has the following steps:
1. Build model in a CAD system (Inventor, CATIA, Pro/E, SolidWorks, etc.).
2. Prototype the design.
3. Test the prototype in the field.
4. Evaluate the results of the field tests.
5. Modify the design based on the field test results.

The process continues until a satisfactory solution is reached.

FEA could be used to replace field tests in the PDC.

Advantages of Analysis
- Reduced cost by simulation instead of tests
- Reduced development time
- Improved products

What is finite element analysis?

Finite Element Analysis (FEA) is a numerical method, usually modeled on a computer, which analyzes the stresses in a part. The results would otherwise be difficult to obtain. It can be used to predict the failure of a part or structure, due to unknown stresses, by showing problem areas and allowing designers to see all of the theoretical internal stresses. This method of product design and testing is far cheaper than the manufacturing costs of building and testing each sample. For fracture analysis, FEA calculates the stress intensity factors.

FEA, however, has many applications such as for fluid flow and heat transfer. While this range is growing, one thing will remain the same: the theory of how the method works.

FEA is used in new product design, and existing product refinement. A company is able to verify that a proposed design will perform to the client's specifications prior to manufacturing or construction. It is used to ensure that a modified product or structure will meet its new specifications. In the case of structural failure, FEA may be used to help determine the design modifications necessary to overcome the problem.

There are generally two types of analysis that are used in industry: 2D modeling and 3D modeling. While 2D modeling is simple and only requires a relatively normal computer, it tends to yield less accurate results. 3D modeling, however, produces more accurate results while sacrificing the ability to run on all but the fastest computers. For each of these modeling schemes, the programmer can insert numerous algorithms (functions) to make the system behave linearly or non-linearly. Linear systems are far less complex and generally do not take into account plastic deformation. Non-linear systems do account for plastic deformation, and many also are capable of testing a material all the way to fracture.

The stiffness of a member can be used to provide a simplified overview of the mathematical basis of finite element analysis. We begin by considering a simple member of original length L subject to an external axial deformation, ΔL. Force and deformation are related by

$$\Delta L = \frac{F.L}{A.E}$$

where E is the modulus of elasticity, F is the force, L is the length of the member, and the cross-sectional area is A.

The strain, which is the change in length divided by the original length, is defined as

$$\varepsilon = \frac{\Delta L}{L}$$

From the classical stress–strain relation, the stress can be determined as

$$\sigma = E\varepsilon$$

In other words, finite element analysis starts from a simple mathematical description of the deformation in a part due to some loading, then progresses to determine the strain, and finally finds the stress in the part. However, it should be noted that this stress formulation is only valid within the elastic region where stress is proportional to strain.

How does finite element analysis work?

In FEA, a part is divided into a number of simple elements:
- Rod
- Beam
- Plate/shell/composite
- Shear panel
- Solid
- Spring
- Mass
- Rigid element
- Viscous damping element

The most commonly used elements are solid, shell, and beam.

Solid elements

The majority of parts analyzed with FEA utilize 3D models, based on solid geometry, to define the boundaries of the part or assembly. The solid element is either a first-order tetrahedron (see Figure 34-2), which has four flat faces and four vertices or a second-order tetrahedron (see Figure 34-3), which has four flat faces and ten nodes that are the four vertices and the mid-points of its edges. Solid elements have three degrees of freedom per node consisting of three deformations.

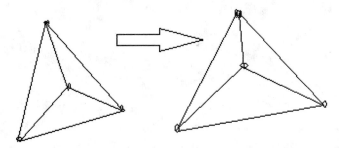

Before deformation   **After deformation**

Figure 34-2 First-order tetrahedral element before and after deformation

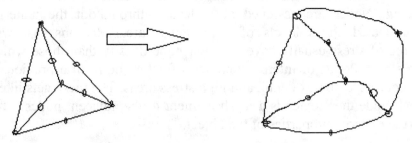

Before deformation   **After deformation**

Figure 34-3 Second-order tetrahedral element before and after deformation

Shell elements

Thin-walled parts, such as sheet metal parts, are analyzed using shell elements (see Figure 34-4). Thin-walled parts are commonly found in tanks, beverage containers, plastic parts, thin-walled pressure vessels, etc. Shell elements have six degrees of freedom per node consisting of three deformations and three rotations.

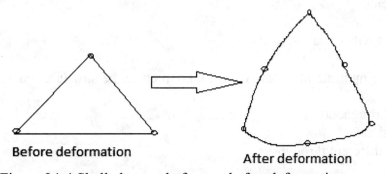

Before deformation

After deformation

Figure 34-4 Shell element before and after deformation

Beam elements

Beam or truss elements are commonly used in structural members since the number of nodes and elements is greatly reduced (see Figure 34-5). A beam element should be used when the length-to-height ratio (l/h) is greater than or equal to 20:1.

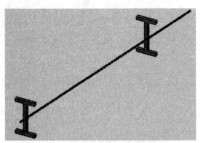
Figure 34-5 Beam element

FEA uses a complex system of points or nodes to make a grid called a mesh. This mesh is programmed to contain the material and structural properties that define how the structure will react under loading. Nodes are assigned at a density throughout the material depending on the anticipated stress levels of a particular area. Regions that will experience a high degree of stress usually have a higher node density than those which experience little or no stress. Points of interest include: a fracture point of a previously tested material, fillets, corners, complex detail, and high stress areas. The mesh acts like a spider's web; from each node there extends a mesh element to the adjacent nodes. This web of vectors carries the material properties of the object.

A wide range of objective functions (variables within the system) are available for minimization or maximization:
- Mass, volume, temperature
- Strain energy, stress, strain
- Force, displacement, velocity, acceleration

Different loading conditions may be applied to a system:
- Point, pressure, thermal, gravity, and centrifugal static loads
- Thermal loads derived from heat transfer analysis
- Enforced displacements
- Heat flux and convection
- Point, pressure and gravity dynamic loads

Many FEA programs can use multiple materials within the structure. he structure would be classified as:
- Isotropic, identical throughout
- Orthotropic, identical at 90°
- General anisotropic, different throughout

Types of Engineering Analysis

Structural analysis uses linear and non-linear models. Linear models use simple parameters and assume that the material is not plastically deformed. Non-linear models stress the material past its elastic capabilities. The stress in the material varies with the amount of deformation.

Vibration analysis is used to test a material against random vibrations, shock, and impact. Each of these may act on the natural vibration frequency of the material, which, in turn, may cause resonance and subsequent failure.

Fatigue analysis helps designers to predict the life of a material or structure by showing the effects of cyclic loading on a specimen. Such analysis can show the areas where crack propagation is most likely to occur. Failure due to fatigue may also show the damage tolerance of the material.

Heat Transfer analysis models the conductivity or thermal fluid dynamics of the material or structure. The heat transfer may be steady-state or transient. Steady-state transfer refers to constant thermo-properties in the material and yields linear heat diffusion.

Principles of Finite Element Analysis

The methodology for FEA can be summarized as follows:
- Build the mathematical model using the CAD geometry (simplified if required), material properties, loads, restraints, types of analysis, etc. Different types of loads and connectors are shown in Tables 20-2 and 20-3.
- Build the finite element model by discretizing the mathematical model into solid elements, shell elements, beam elements, etc.
- Solve the finite element model (use the solver provided in SolidWorks Simulation).
- Analyze the results.

Table 34-3 Types of Connectors

Rigid connectors
Spring connectors
Pin connectors
Elastic support connectors

Table 34-2 Types of Loads

Structural Loads	Thermal Loads
Remote loads	Convection
Bearing loads	Radiation
Centrifugal loads	Conduction
Force	Temperature
Gravity	Heat flux
Pressure	Heat power
Shrink fit	

Build the mathematical model

The starting point for FEA using SolidWorks Simulation is the availability of a CAD model. If the part is complex, the model may need to be simplified (for example by removing fillets). Material properties are then assigned. The type of analysis is specified. Define the restraints and loads. This completes the mathematical model, as illustrated in Figure 34-6.

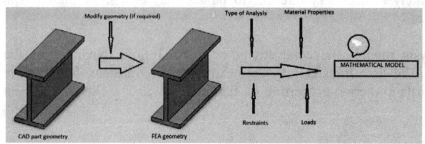

Figure 34-6 Mathematical model for FEA

Build the finite element model

Discretize the mathematical model using any of the following: solid elements, shell elements, or beam elements (see Figure 34-7). This is also known as meshing the model. The geometry, loads, and restraints are all discretized and applied to the nodes of the elements. The elements are appropriately renumbered.

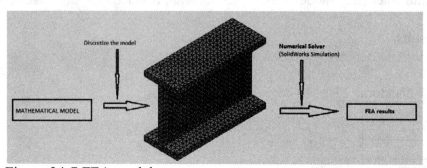

Figure 34-7 FEA model

Solve the finite element model

The finite element model is solved using a solver provided in SolidWorks Simulation (see Figure 34-7). Solving FEA problems can take seconds for a simple model or hours for a complex model. Even for small problems, the number of nodes can run into thousands. Coarse elements yield inferior solutions compared to fine elements. The costs, in terms of computation time, are inversely proportional to the quality of the solution.

Analyze the results

It is not enough to simply accept any results from FEA. The results have to be analyzed to ensure that they are correctly interpreted. There are a number of sources of errors, which users of FEA software should understand. Modifying the geometry of a part can be a major source of error if the modification is made without thinking how the solution would be affected. For example, not all fillets should be removed from a part. Some fillets are necessary to reduce corner stresses. Discretizing the model is another area where errors could arise. The mesh size has a significant impact on the quality of the solution as previously discussed.

SolidWorks Simulation Add-ins

SolidWorks Simulation is an add-in, which must be enabled:
1. Open SolidWorks.
2. Open a model file.
3. Click Add-Ins (see Figure 34-8).
4. Check SolidWorks Simulation (see Figure 34-9).
5. Click OK (Simulation tool is added).

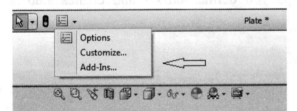

Figure 34-8 Add-Ins option

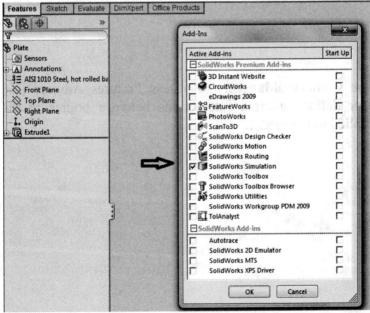

Figure 34-9 SolidWorks add-ins

SolidWorks Simulation CommandManager

The SolidWorks Simulation CommandManager has a number of advisors. These are found in the menus for Study, Fixtures, External Loads, Connections, Run, and Results, as shown in Figure 34-10. A simulation advisor is a set of tools that guides you through the analysis process. The simulation advisor works with the SolidWorks Simulation interface by starting the appropriate PropertyManager and linking to online help topics for additional information.

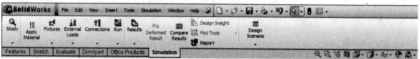

Figure 34-10 SolidWorks Simulation CommandManager

Study Advisor

Click Study (from Simulation CommandManager) to access Study Advisor (see Figure 34-11). The simulation advisor tab appears in the task pane. It recommends study types and outputs to expect. Study Advisor helps you define sensors and creates studies automatically.

Figure 34-11 Study Advisor

Fixtures Advisor

Click Fixtures (from Simulation CommandManager) to access Fixtures Advisor (see Figure 34-12). Fixtures Advisor defines internal interactions between bodies in the model. Fixtures are restraints applied to the model.

Figure 34-12 Fixtures Advisor

External Loads Advisor

Click External Loads (from Simulation CommandManager) to access External Loads Advisor (see Figure 34-13). External Loads Advisor defines external interactions between the model and the environment. There are several types of external loads: force/torque, pressure, gravity, centrifugal force, bearing load, remote load/mass, distributed load, temperature, flow effects, thermal effects, etc.

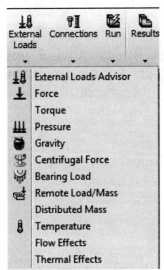

Figure 34-13 External Loads Advisor

Connections Advisor

Click Connections (from Simulation CommandManager) to access Connections Advisor (see Figure 34-14). Connections Advisor suggests techniques for connecting components within an assembly model.

Figure 34-14 Connections Advisor

Run Advisor

Click Run (from Simulation CommandManager) to access Run Advisor (see Figure 34-15). Run Advisor solves the simulation problem.

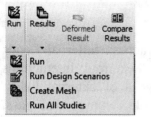

Figure 34-15 Run Advisor

Results Advisor

Click Results (from Simulation CommandManager) to access Results Advisor (see Figure 34-16). It provides tips for interpreting and viewing the output of the simulation. Also, it helps to determine if frequency or buckling might be areas of concern.

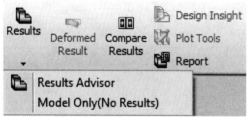

Figure 34-16 Results Advisor

Design Scenario

Click Design Scenario (from Simulation CommandManager) to access Design Scenario (see Figure 34-17).

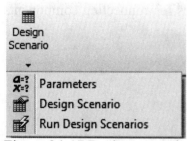

Figure 34-17 Design scenario

SolidWorks Simulation Toolbars

Another way to access the functions for creating, solving, and analyzing a model is through the SolidWorks Simulation toolbars (see Figure 34-18).

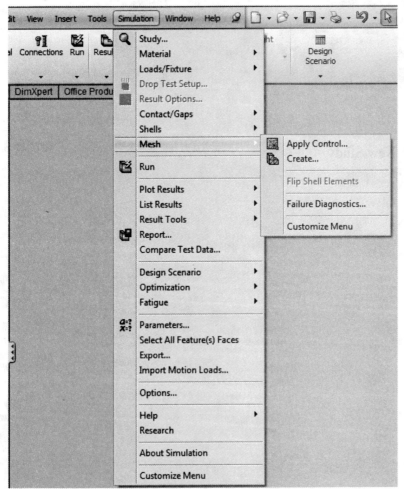

Figure 34-18 SolidWorks Simulation toolbars

Starting a New Study in SolidWorks Simulation

1. Open a model file.
2. Click Simulation > New Study (see Figure 34-19).

The Study PropertyManager has the following options, as shown in Figure 34-20:
*   Static (the default)
*   Frequency
*   Buckling
*   Thermal
*   Drop Test
*   Fatigue
*   Optimization
*   Nonlinear
*   Linear Dynamic
*   Pressure Vessel Design

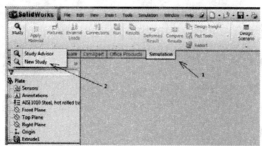

Figure 34-19 Simulation > New Study

Figure 34-20 Study PropertyManager

When any of the study options (Static, Frequency, Buckling, Thermal, etc.) is selected in the PropertyManager and OK is clicked, the SolidWorks SimulationManager appears below the FeatureManager. The following options are roots of the SimulationManager:
- Connections
- Fixtures
- External Loads
- Mesh

Basic SolidWorks Simulation Steps

The steps involved in SolidWorks Simulation for solving FEA problems (any of the study options) are summarized as follows:
1. Geometric preparation (if required)
2. Apply material to the model

3. Define connections
4. Define fixtures
5. Define external loads
6. Create the model mesh
7. Run the model solution

Analyze the results

Finite Element Analysis of a Sheet Metal Part

The problem that we solve is one of the sheet metal parts that we designed in chapter 19.

Start a new study in SolidWorks Simulation:
1. Select Simulation > New Study.
2. Click OK (to use the default study option, Static).

We are now ready to define the analysis model. The user has to define the connections, fixtures, external loads, and mesh (see Figure 34-21). If material has already been assigned to the part, then Material is not listed as one of the options. Applying materials during part design is the preferred approach, especially in cases where several parts make up an assembly.

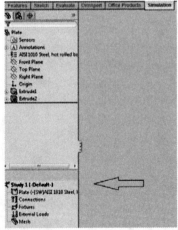

Figure 34-21 Study folders in SimulationManager

Defining Connections

3. Right-click the Connections folder and select the appropriate connections (see Figure 21-22).

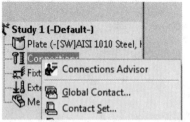

Figure 34-22 Assigning connections

Defining Fixtures

4. Right-click the Fixtures folder and select the appropriate fixtures (see Figure 34-23).
5. Click Fixed Geometry and select the faces to fix (the preview of Figure 34-24 appears).

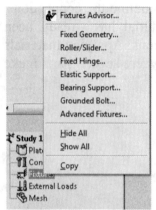

Figure 34-23 Assigning fixtures

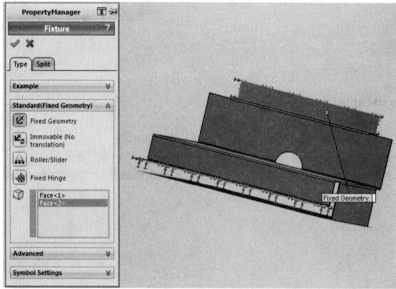

Figure 34-24 Fixtures preview for fixed geometry

Defining External Loads

6. Right-click the External Loads folder and select the appropriate external loads (see Figure 34-25).
7. Click Force, a preview appears (see Figure 34-26).
8. For the force, check Normal.
9. Select the face to apply the pressure, and enter a value of 1.5 kPa (for reverse pressures, check Reverse direction).

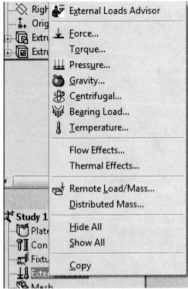

Figure 34-25 Assigning external loads

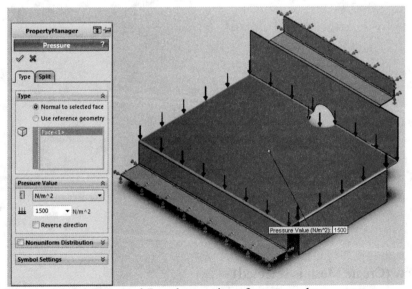

Figure 34-26 External Loads preview for normal pressure

Defining the mesh

10. Right-click the Mesh folder and select the appropriate mesh (see Figure 34-27).
11. Click Create Mesh (the preview of Figure 34-28 appears). Note that we can control the mesh density by moving the slider from Coarse to Fine. The element size (4.786 mm) and the element size tolerance (0.239 mm) are automatically established based on the geometric features of the SolidWorks model. The meshed model is shown in Figure 34-29.

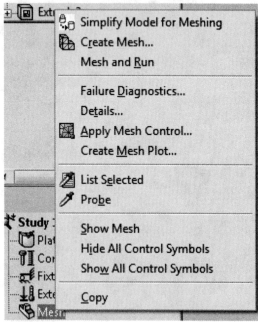

Figure 34-27 Assigning the mesh

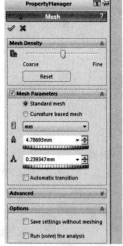

Figure 34-28 Mesh preview (Create Mesh is selected)

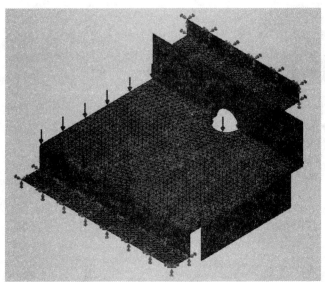

Figure 34-29 Meshed model

Running the model solution

12. Click Run Advisor in the Simulation CommandManager.

The results are shown (see Figure 34-30) and three plots are automatically created in the Results folder:
- Stress1: von Mises stresses
- Displacement1: resultant stresses
- Strain1: equivalent strain

Figure 34-30 Model solution based on von Mises criterion

The pressure is increased to 3.5 kPa (see Figure 34-31) leading to the stress distribution shown in Figure 34-32.

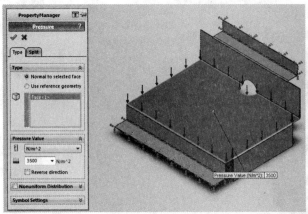

Figure 34-31 Model at 3500 Pa (3.5 kPa) loading

Figure 34-32 Model solution based on von Mises criterion

The pressure is increased to 20 kPa, see Figure 34-33 leading to the stress distribution shown in Figure 34-34. Note the high stress level around the sharp edges, which is consistent with what we expect in practice.

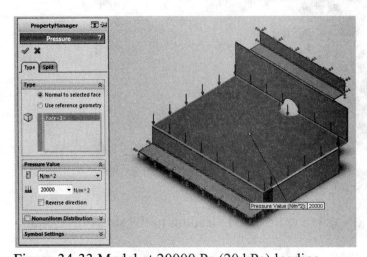

Figure 34-33 Model at 20000 Pa (20 kPa) loading

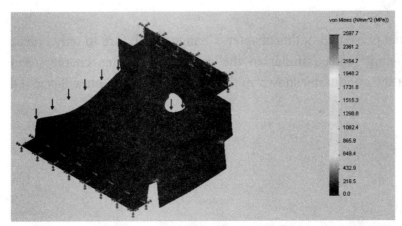

Figure 34-34 Model solution based on von Mises criterion

Reverse 20 kPa loading results is shown in Figure 23-35. Beyond 20 kPa loading, the model begins to experience large deflection and becomes unstable.

Figure 34-35 Model solution based on von Mises criterion

Summary

When we run FEA software we must understand the results. For simple parts with classical solutions, it is good engineering practice to compare the FEA solution with a manual calculation. Once we have mastered FEA, then we can be more confident of our results when we solve complex, unfamiliar problems. In this chapter, we have applied FEA to analyse the loading of sheet metal part that we had earlier designed. By increasing the pressure loading, we are able to track the limit beyond which large deflection occurs. This kind of analysis is important in the design stage in order to anticipate how a model designed should be loaded in practical usage. Design Scenario tool can be used to realize multiple design solution from which the optimum is chosen.

Exercises

1. Figure P1 shows the model presented in this chapter. Change the fixture to only one as shown. Apply the following loads (similar to the ones used in this chapter) and compare results between the conditions shown in this problem and the ones discussed earlier in the chapter:
    (a) 1.5 kPa loading;
    (b) 3.5 kPa loading; and
    (c) 20 kPa loading.

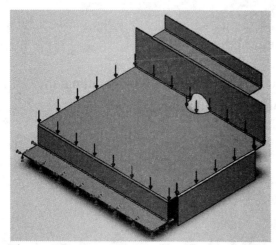

Figure P1

2. In Figure P2, the fixtures are labeled *Fixture 1* and *Fixture 2*. Apply the three different loading conditions of problem 1 to this model on the face marked, *Face to load*.

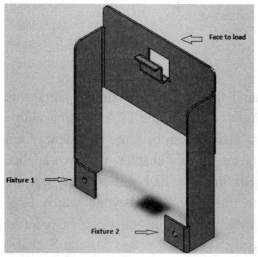

Figure P2